Skip·Beat!

Skip·Beat!

11
Story & Art by Yoshiki Nakamura

Skip·Beat!

Volume 11

CONTENTS

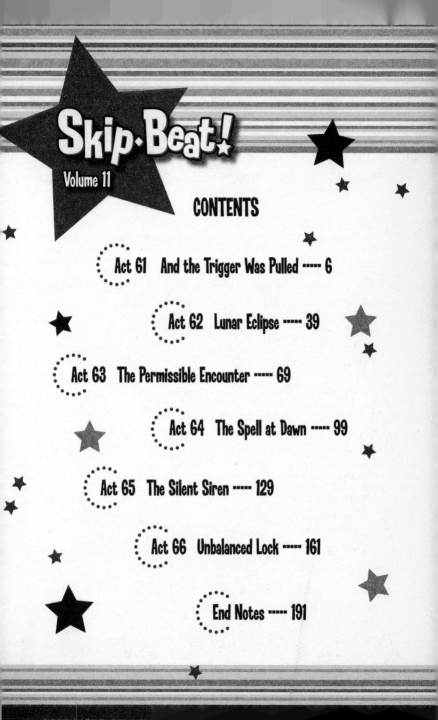

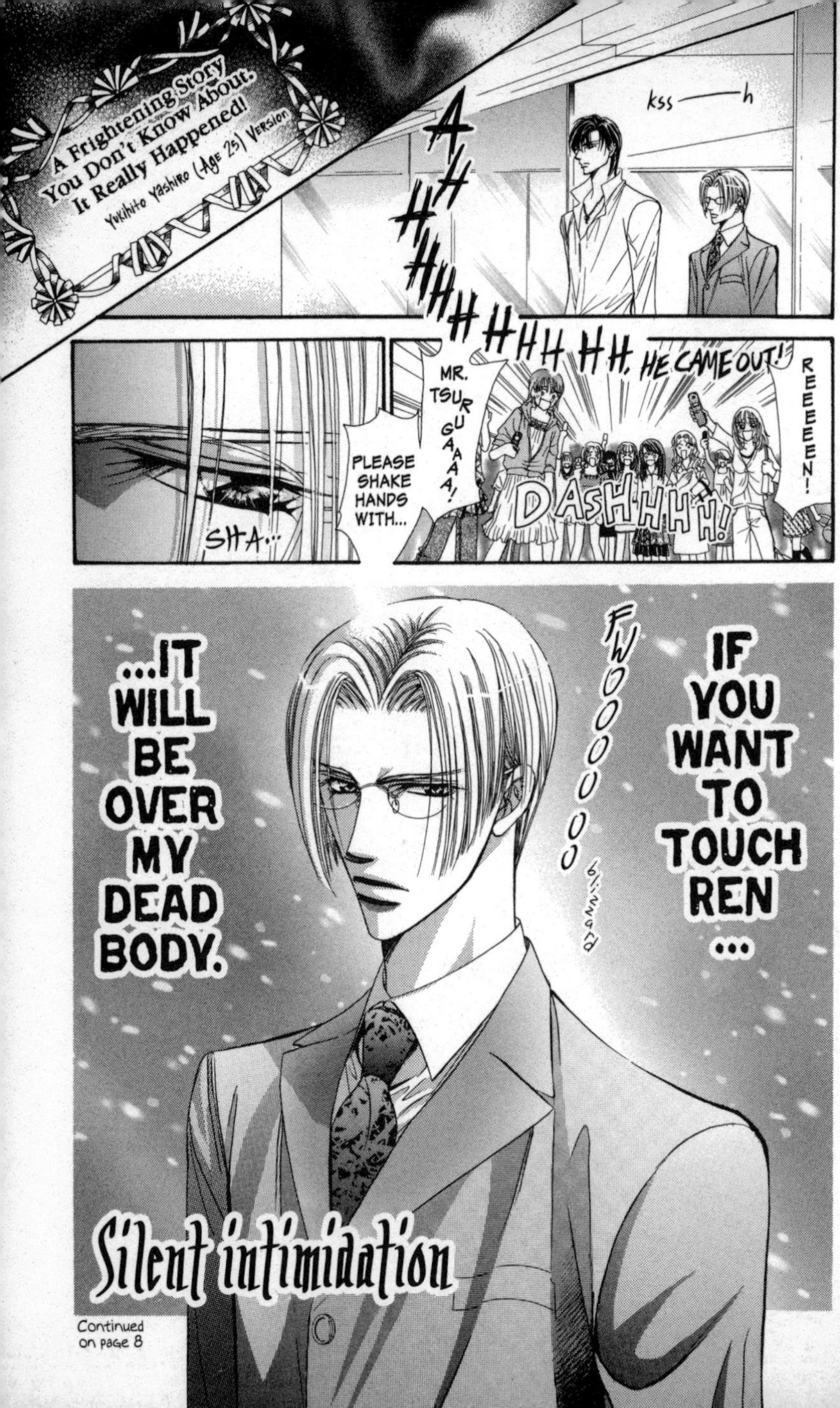
A Frightening Story You Don't Know About. It Really Happened!
Yukihito Yashiro (Age 25) Version
kss——h
AHHHHHHHHHHHHH, HE CAME OUT!
REEEEEN!
MR. TSURUGAAAA!
DASHHHHH!
PLEASE SHAKE HANDS WITH...
SHA...
IF YOU WANT TO TOUCH REN...
FWOOOOOOO
blizzard
...IT WILL BE OVER MY DEAD BODY.
Silent intimidation
Continued on page 8

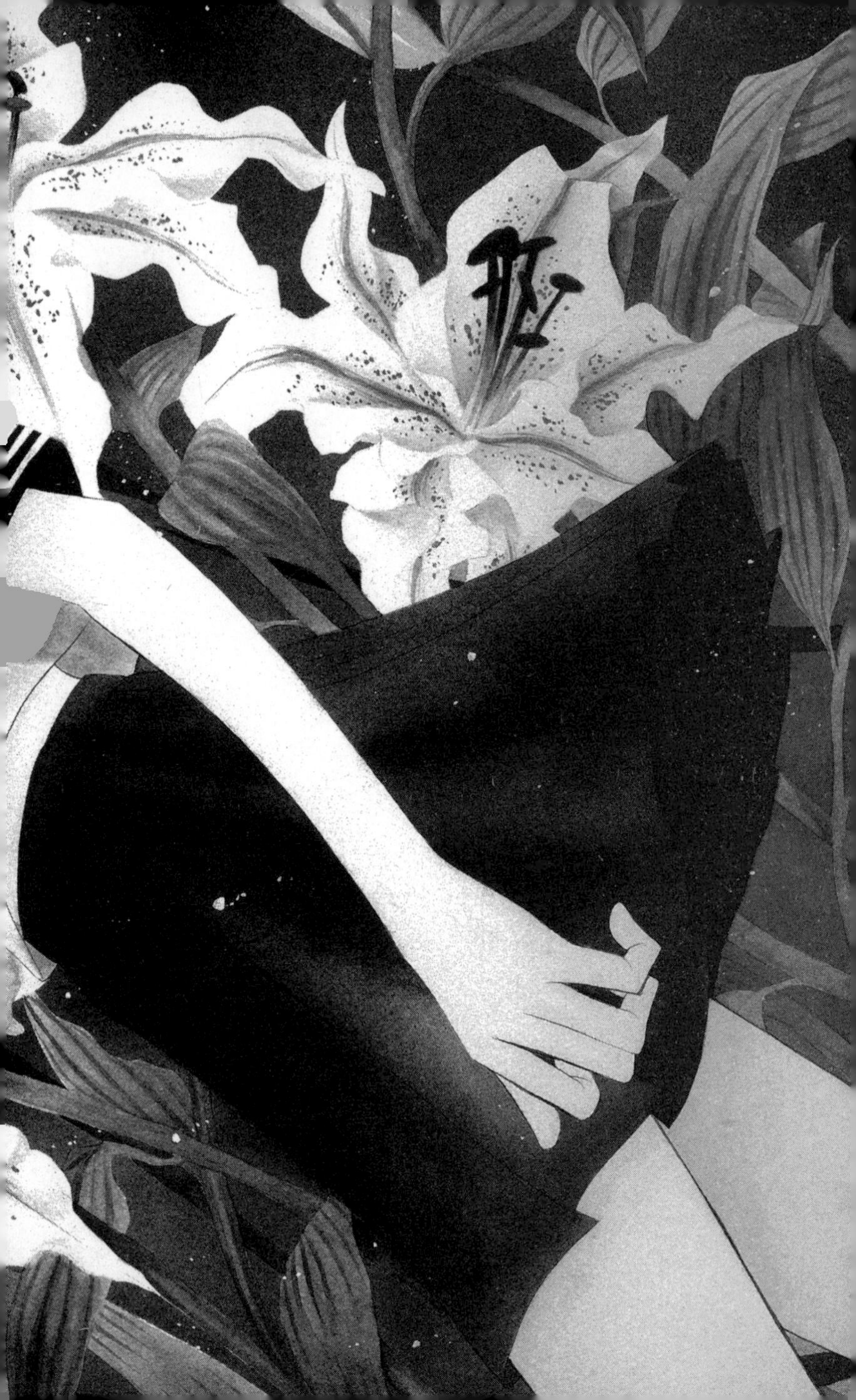

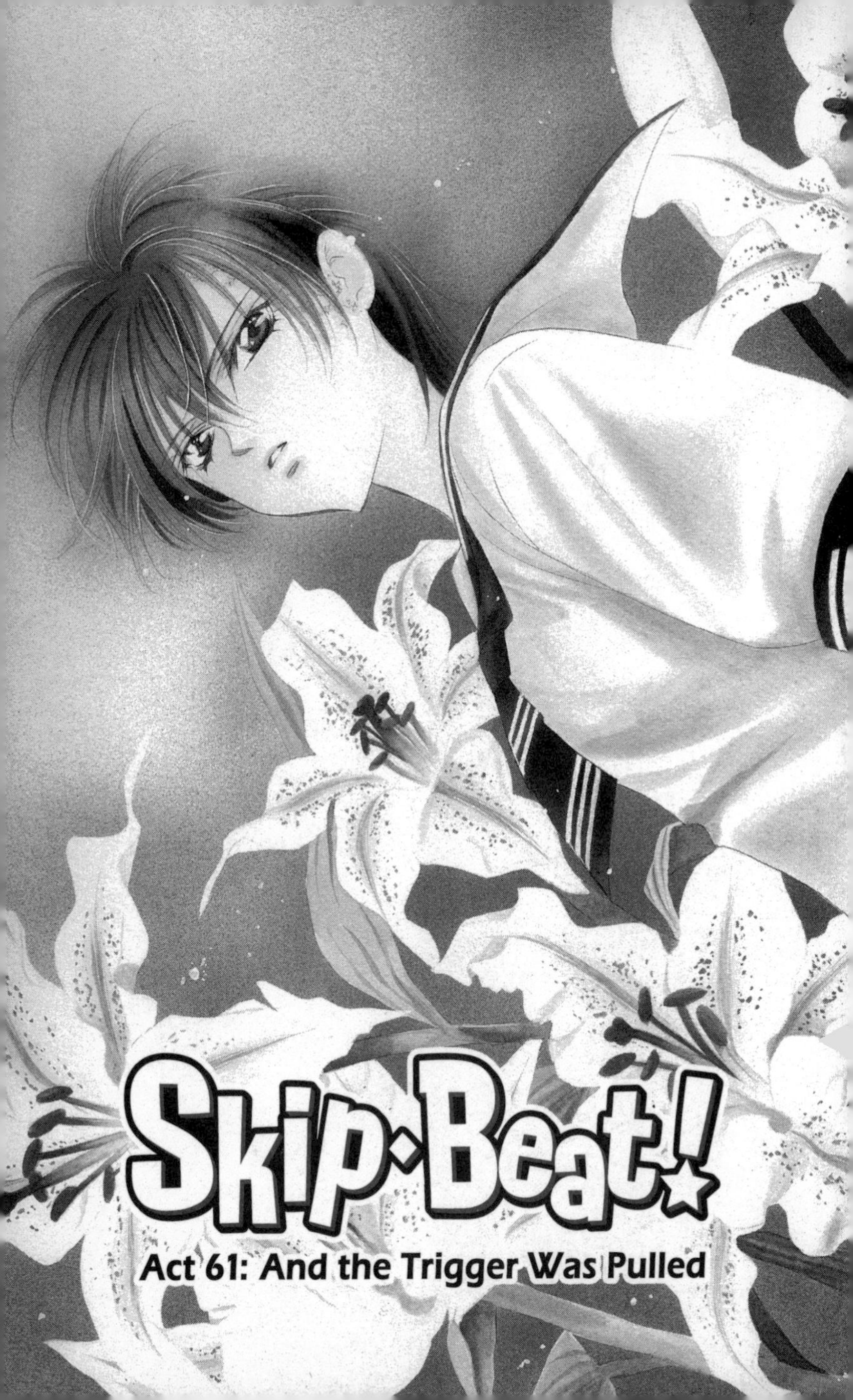
Skip·Beat!
Act 61: And the Trigger Was Pulled

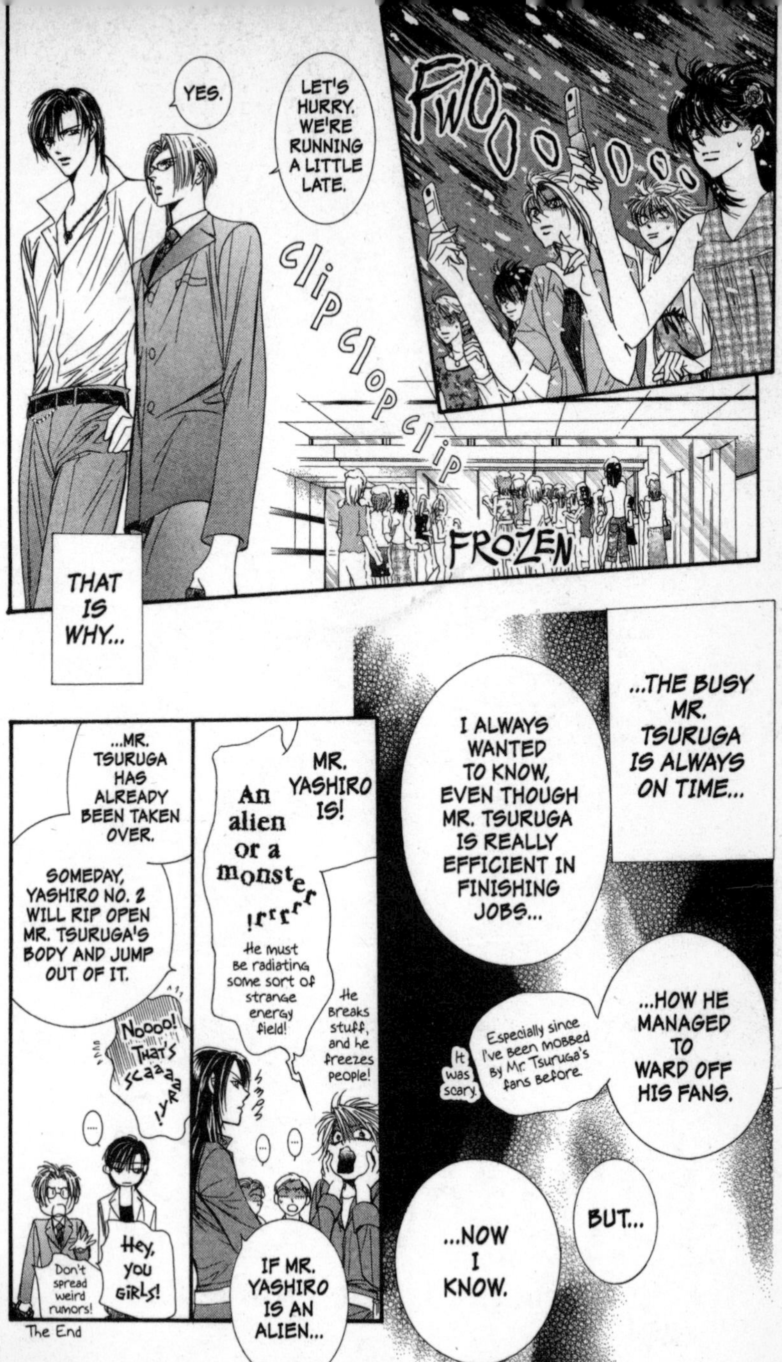
FWOOOOOOO
CLIP CLOP CLIP CLOP CLIP
FROZEN
LET'S HURRY. WE'RE RUNNING A LITTLE LATE.
YES.
THAT IS WHY...
...THE BUSY MR. TSURUGA IS ALWAYS ON TIME...
I ALWAYS WANTED TO KNOW, EVEN THOUGH MR. TSURUGA IS REALLY EFFICIENT IN FINISHING JOBS...
...HOW HE MANAGED TO WARD OFF HIS FANS.
Especially since I've been mobbed by Mr. Tsuruga's fans before.
It was scary.
BUT...
...NOW I KNOW.
MR. YASHIRO IS!
An alien or a monsterrrr!rrrrr
He must be radiating some sort of strange energy field!
He breaks stuff, and he freezes people!
...
...
IF MR. YASHIRO IS AN ALIEN...
...MR. TSURUGA HAS ALREADY BEEN TAKEN OVER.
SOMEDAY, YASHIRO NO. 2 WILL RIP OPEN MR. TSURUGA'S BODY AND JUMP OUT OF IT.
Noooo! That's scaaaary!
....
Hey, you girls!
Don't spread weird rumors!
The End

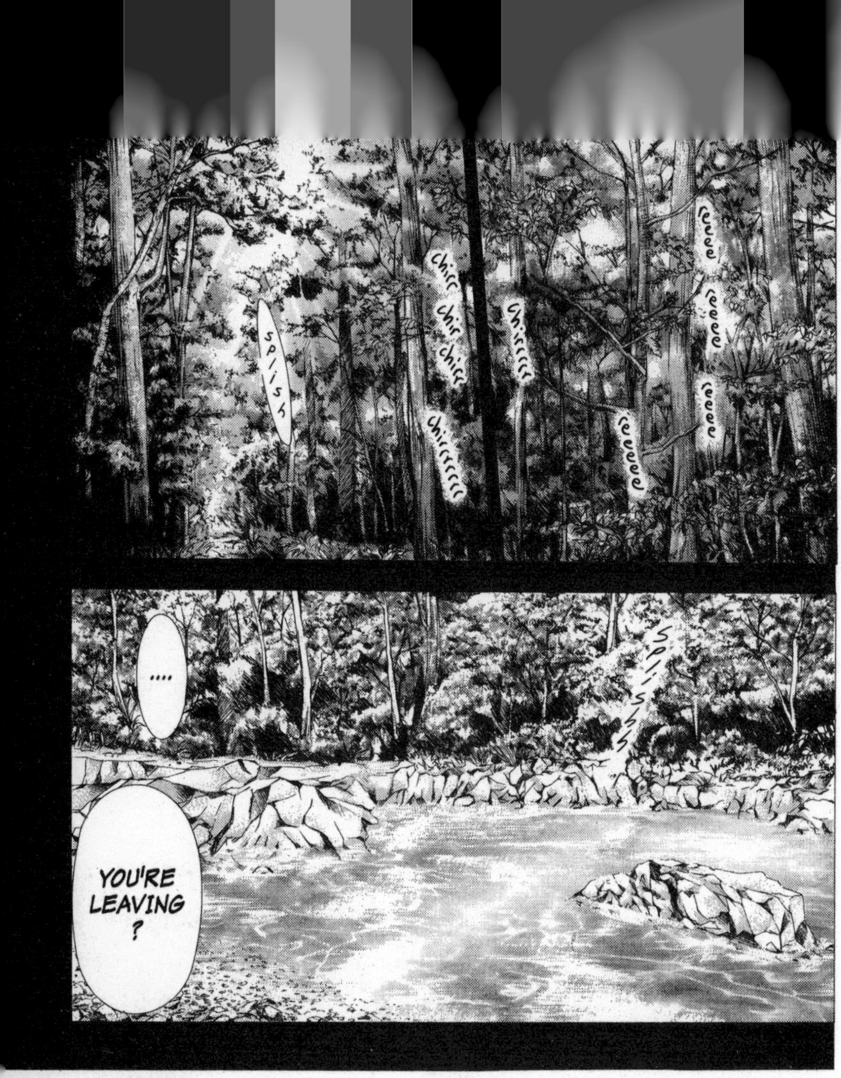
reeee
reeee
reeee
reeeee
chirrrrrr
chirr chirr chirr
chirrrrrrrr
splish
splishhh
....
YOU'RE LEAVING?

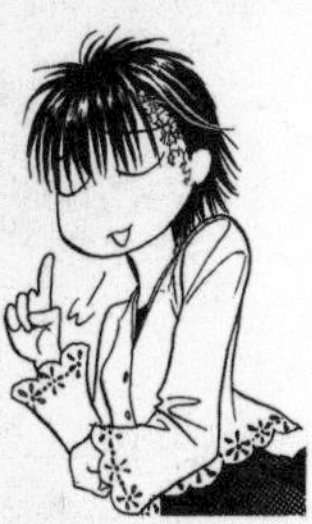

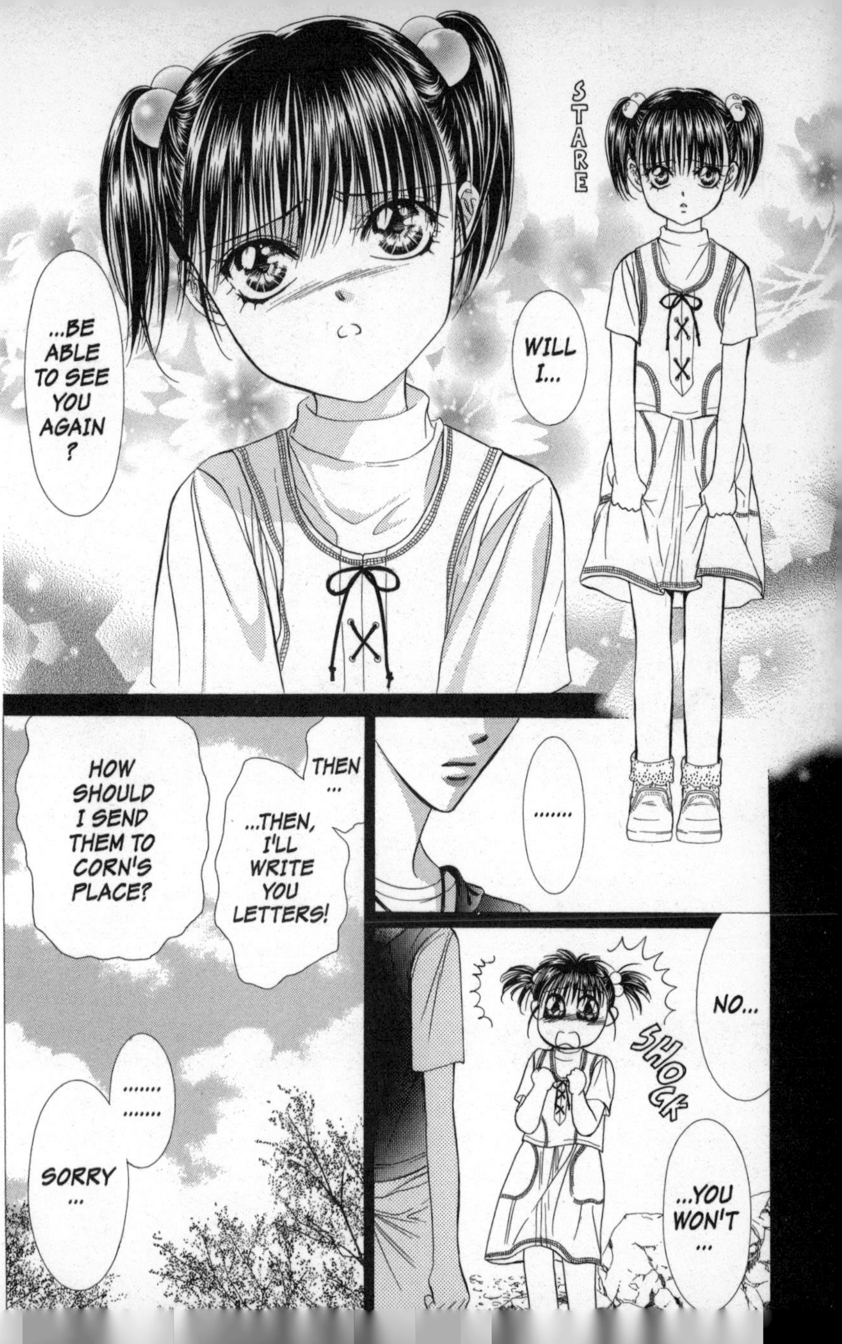
STARE
WILL I...
...BE ABLE TO SEE YOU AGAIN?
......
NO...
SHOCK
...YOU WON'T...
THEN...
...THEN, I'LL WRITE YOU LETTERS!
HOW SHOULD I SEND THEM TO CORN'S PLACE?
....
SORRY...

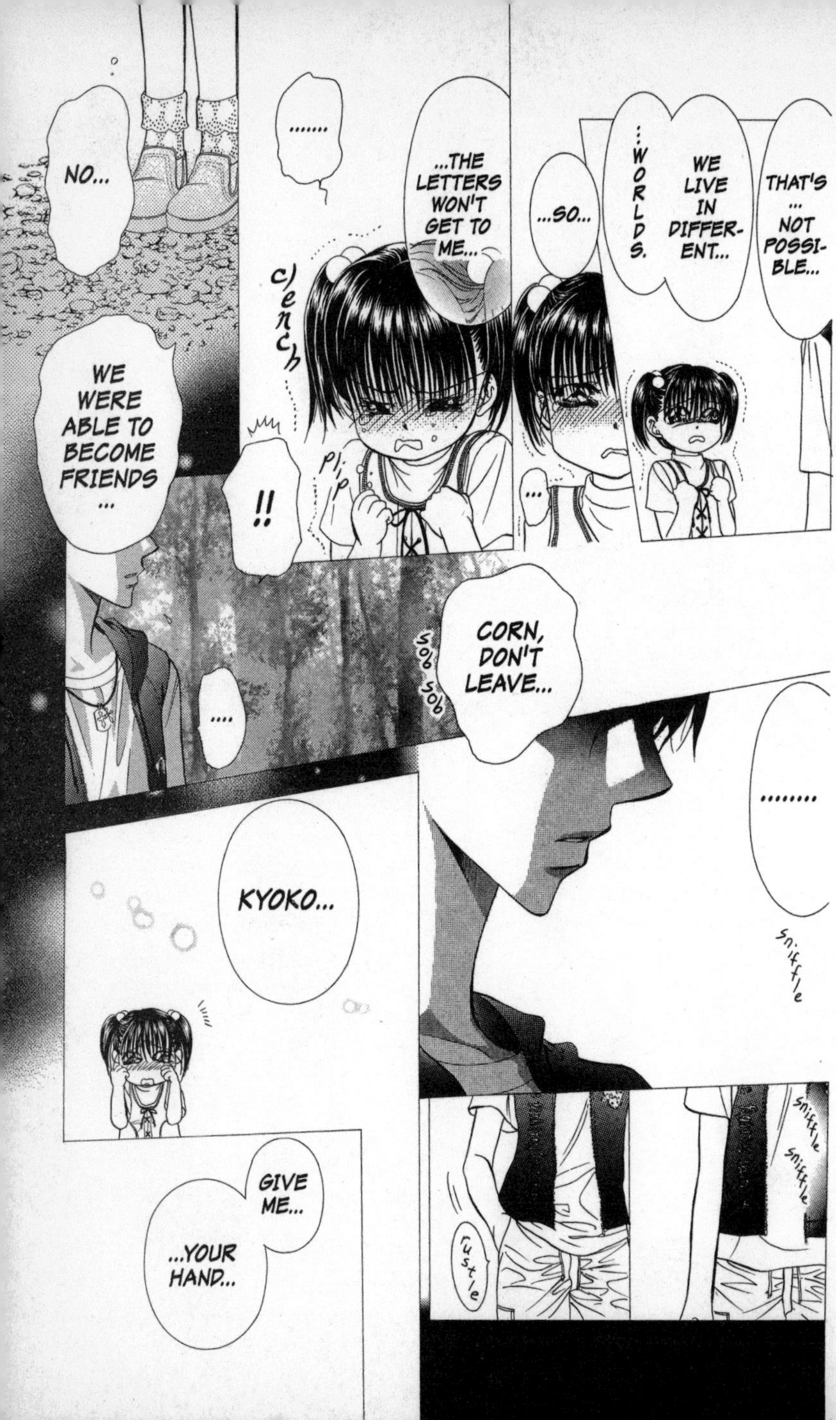
THAT'S... NOT POSSIBLE...
WE LIVE IN DIFFERENT...
...WORLDS.
...SO...
...
...THE LETTERS WON'T GET TO ME...
....
clench
plip
!!
NO...
WE WERE ABLE TO BECOME FRIENDS...
....
CORN, DON'T LEAVE...
sob sob
....
sniffle
KYOKO...
sniffle
sniffle
rustle
GIVE ME...
...YOUR HAND...

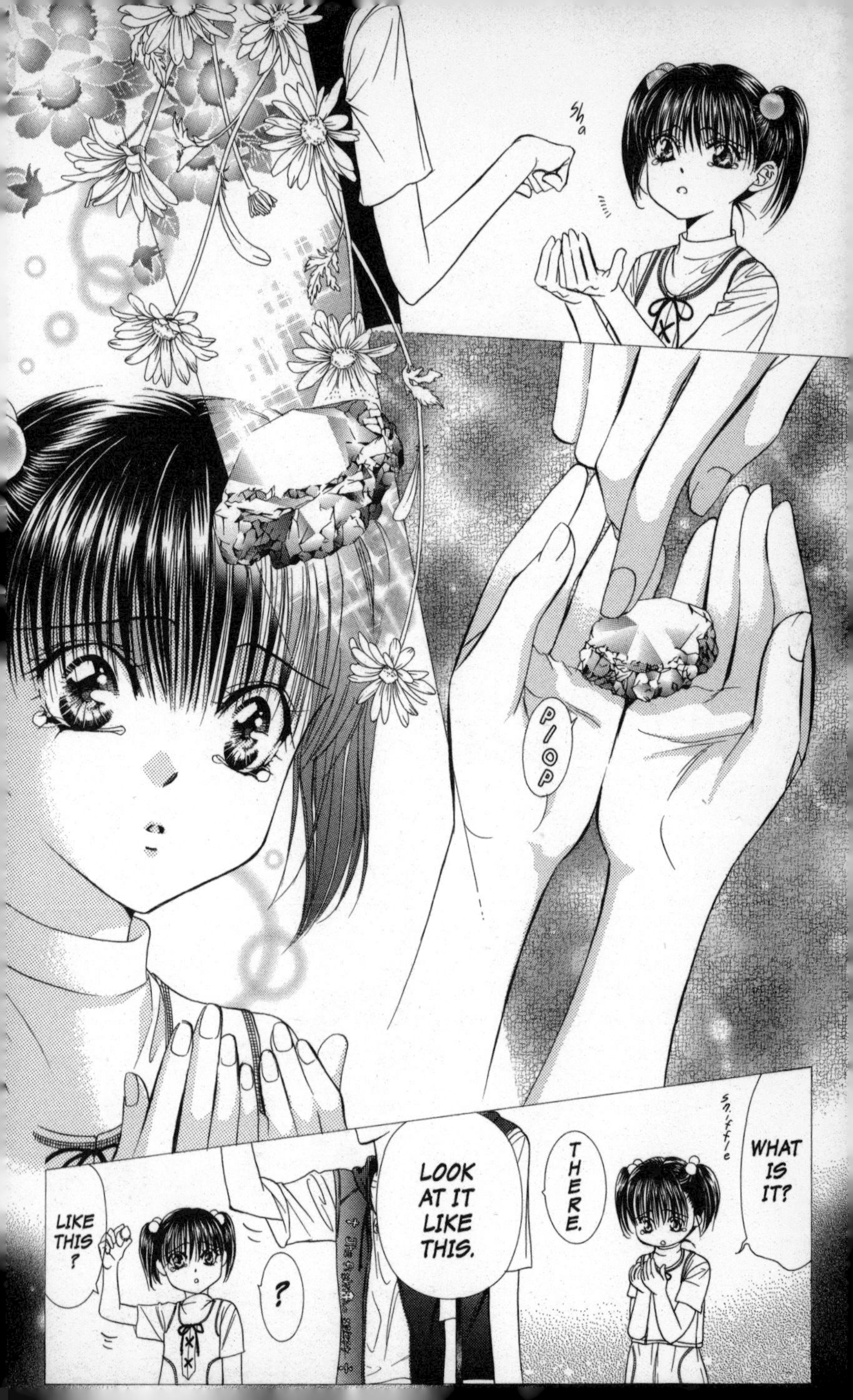
sha
PIOP
WHAT IS IT?
sniffle
THERE.
LOOK AT IT LIKE THIS.
?
LIKE THIS?

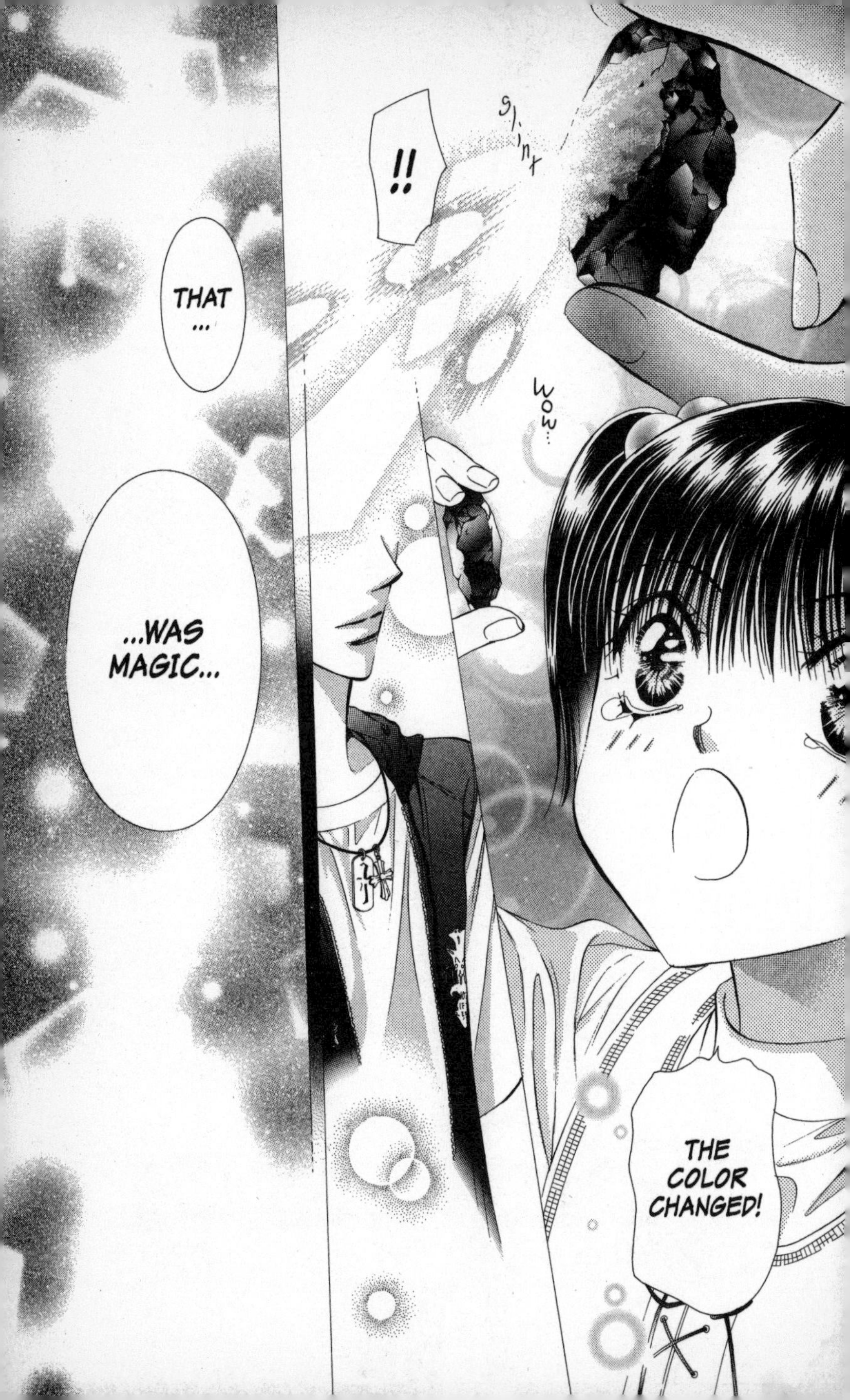
glint
!!
WOW...
THE COLOR CHANGED!
THAT ...
...WAS MAGIC...

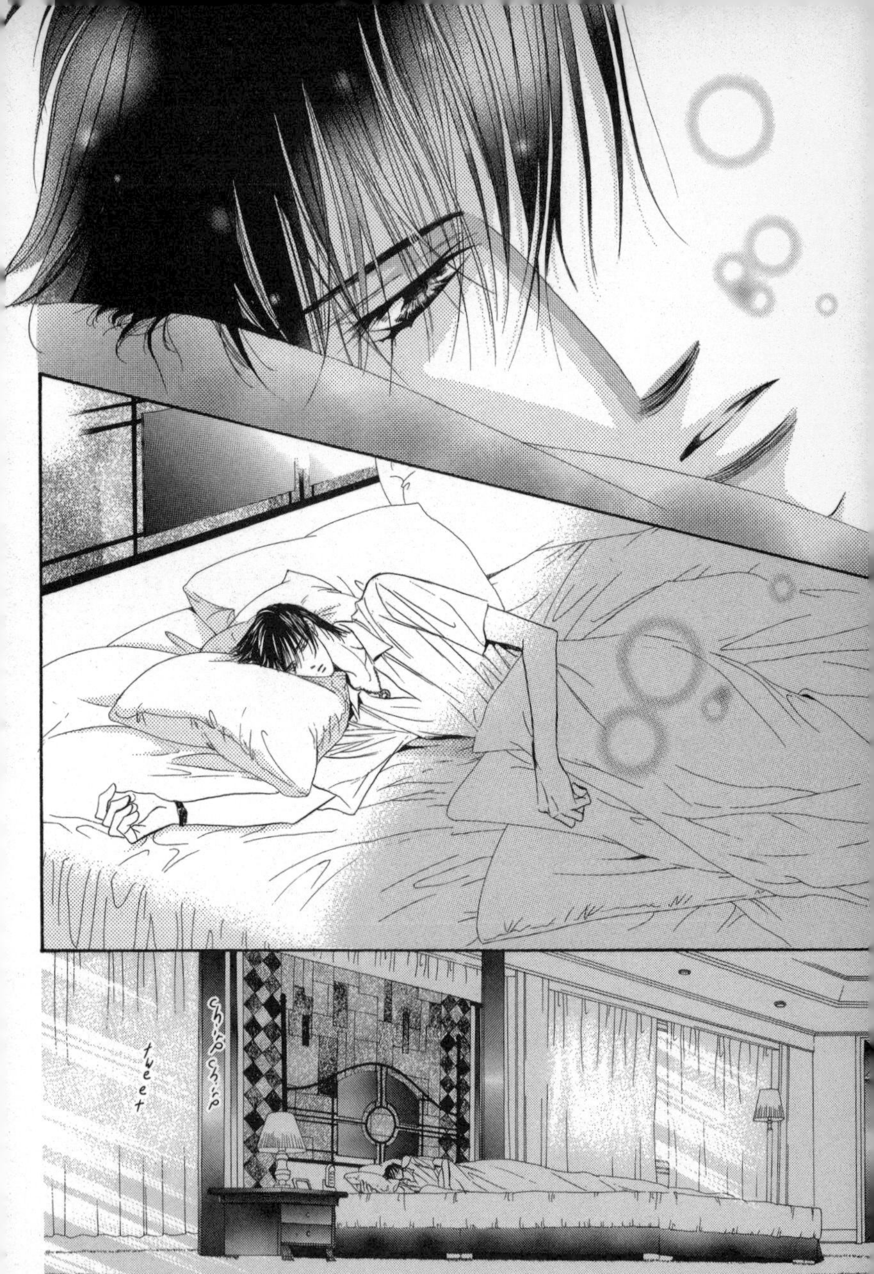
chirp chirp
tweet

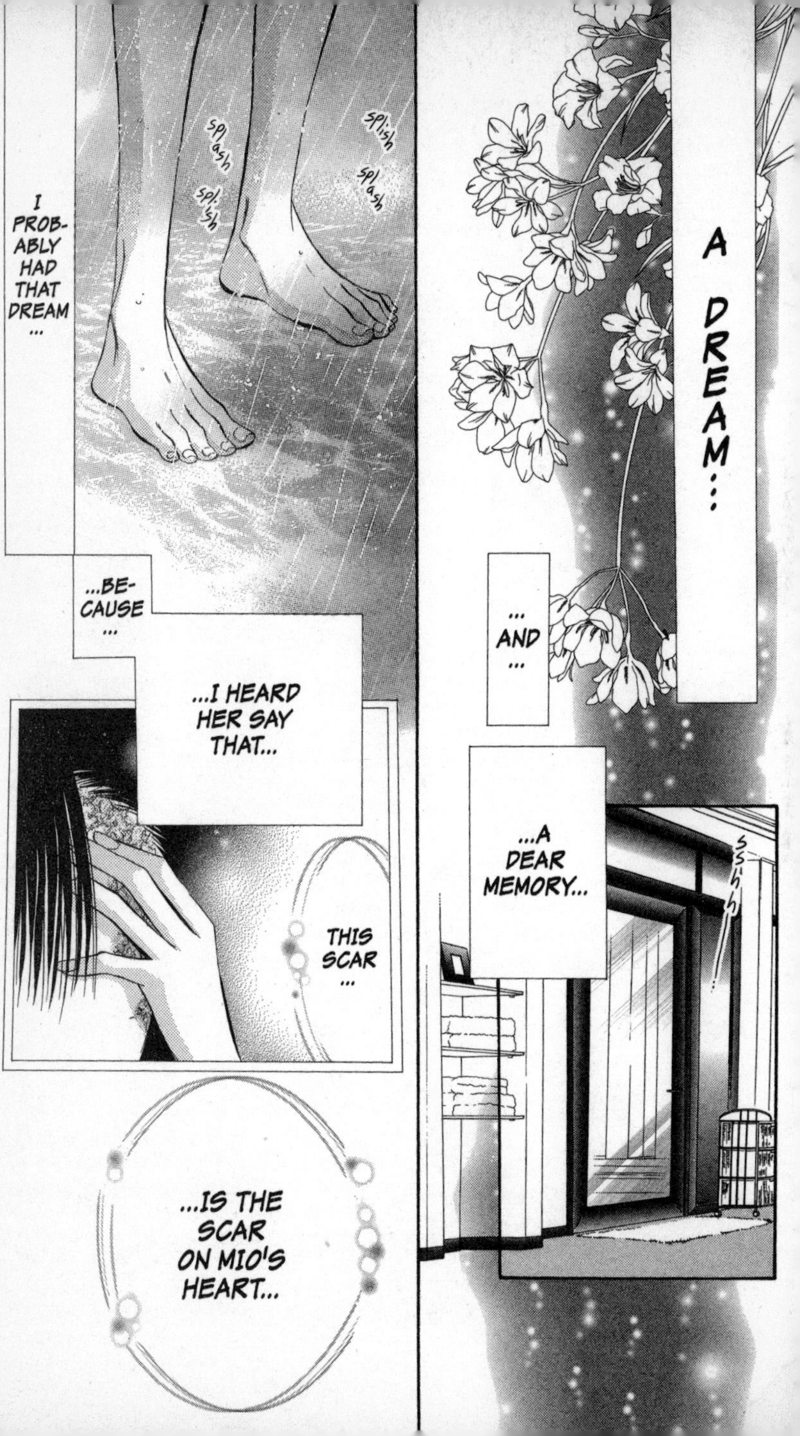
A DREAM...
...AND...
...A DEAR MEMORY...
sshhh...
splish
splash
splash
splish
I PROBABLY HAD THAT DREAM...
...BE-CAUSE...
...I HEARD HER SAY THAT...
THIS SCAR...
...IS THE SCAR ON MIO'S HEART...

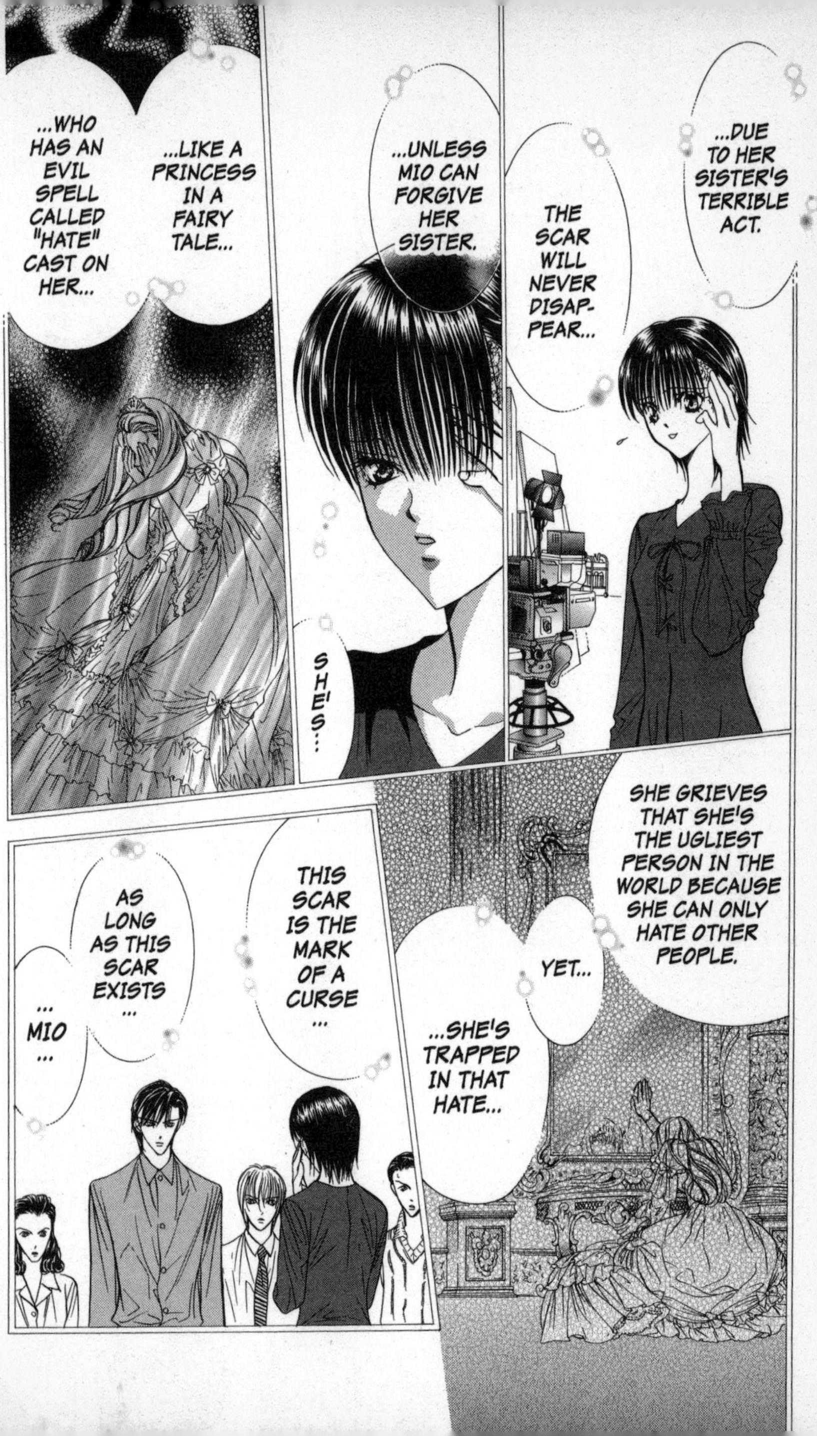
...DUE TO HER SISTER'S TERRIBLE ACT.
THE SCAR WILL NEVER DISAPPEAR...
...UNLESS MIO CAN FORGIVE HER SISTER.
SHE'S...
...LIKE A PRINCESS IN A FAIRY TALE...
...WHO HAS AN EVIL SPELL CALLED "HATE" CAST ON HER...
SHE GRIEVES THAT SHE'S THE UGLIEST PERSON IN THE WORLD BECAUSE SHE CAN ONLY HATE OTHER PEOPLE.
YET...
...SHE'S TRAPPED IN THAT HATE...
THIS SCAR IS THE MARK OF A CURSE...
AS LONG AS THIS SCAR EXISTS...
...MIO...

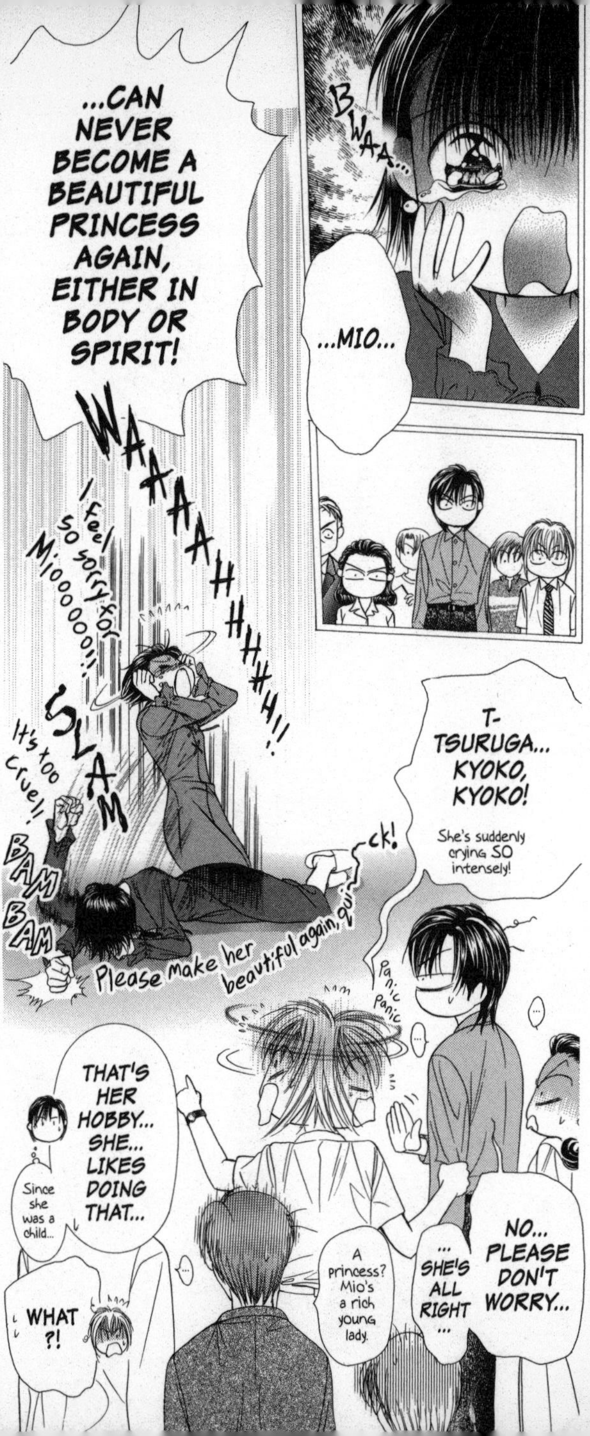
BWAA...
...MIO...
...CAN NEVER BECOME A BEAUTIFUL PRINCESS AGAIN, EITHER IN BODY OR SPIRIT!
WAAAAAHHHHH!!
I feel so sorry for Mioooooo!!
SLAM
It's too cruel!!
BAM BAM
Please make her beautiful again qui-ck!
T-TSURUGA... KYOKO, KYOKO!
She's suddenly crying SO intensely!
Panic Panic
...
...
NO... PLEASE DON'T WORRY...
...SHE'S ALL RIGHT...
A princess? Mio's a rich young lady.
THAT'S HER HOBBY... SHE... LIKES DOING THAT...
Since she was a child...
...
WHAT?!

The Story of... A Frightening Story You Don't Know About. It Really Happened!

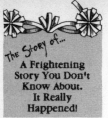

Thank you for reading *Skip•Beat!* this time around, too. Finally... (an even more far-away look compared to the previous volume), finally, we enter the Ren chapter (I just named it now) in the Tsukigomori arc...the previous volume was Kyoko and Ogata's chapter...

Now's the beginning of the main part of the Tsukigomori arc. Everybody, please don't get discouraged, but come with meeeeeee!! All riiiiiight?! Do your beeeeeest?! (You do your best.) ← The readers' reply...

By the way, about the extra manga I drew for the beginning of this volume...I drew it because I wanted the readers to see how Yashiro actually does his work, because recently, he's been too round, uncool and merry...

...I mean, that was Yashiro's image that I had when *Skip•Beat!* initially started... (tears)...he was a cool guy...he was a cool guy......so I hope in the battlefield, he's exhibiting that coolness... tears...

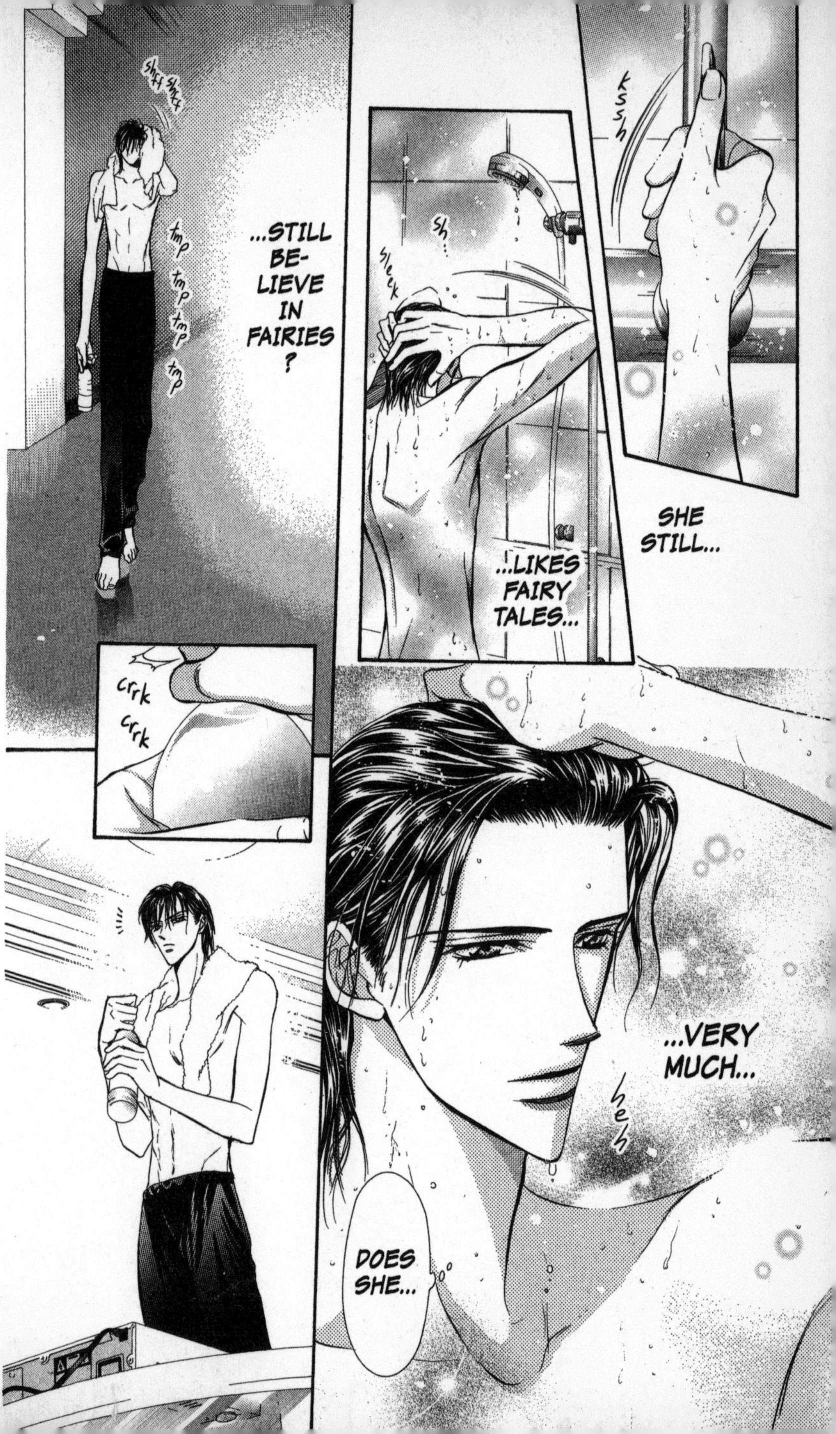
kssh
SHE STILL...
sh...
sleek
...LIKES FAIRY TALES...
...VERY MUCH...
heh
DOES SHE...
shff shff
tmp tmp tmp tmp
...STILL BE-LIEVE IN FAIRIES?
crrk crrk

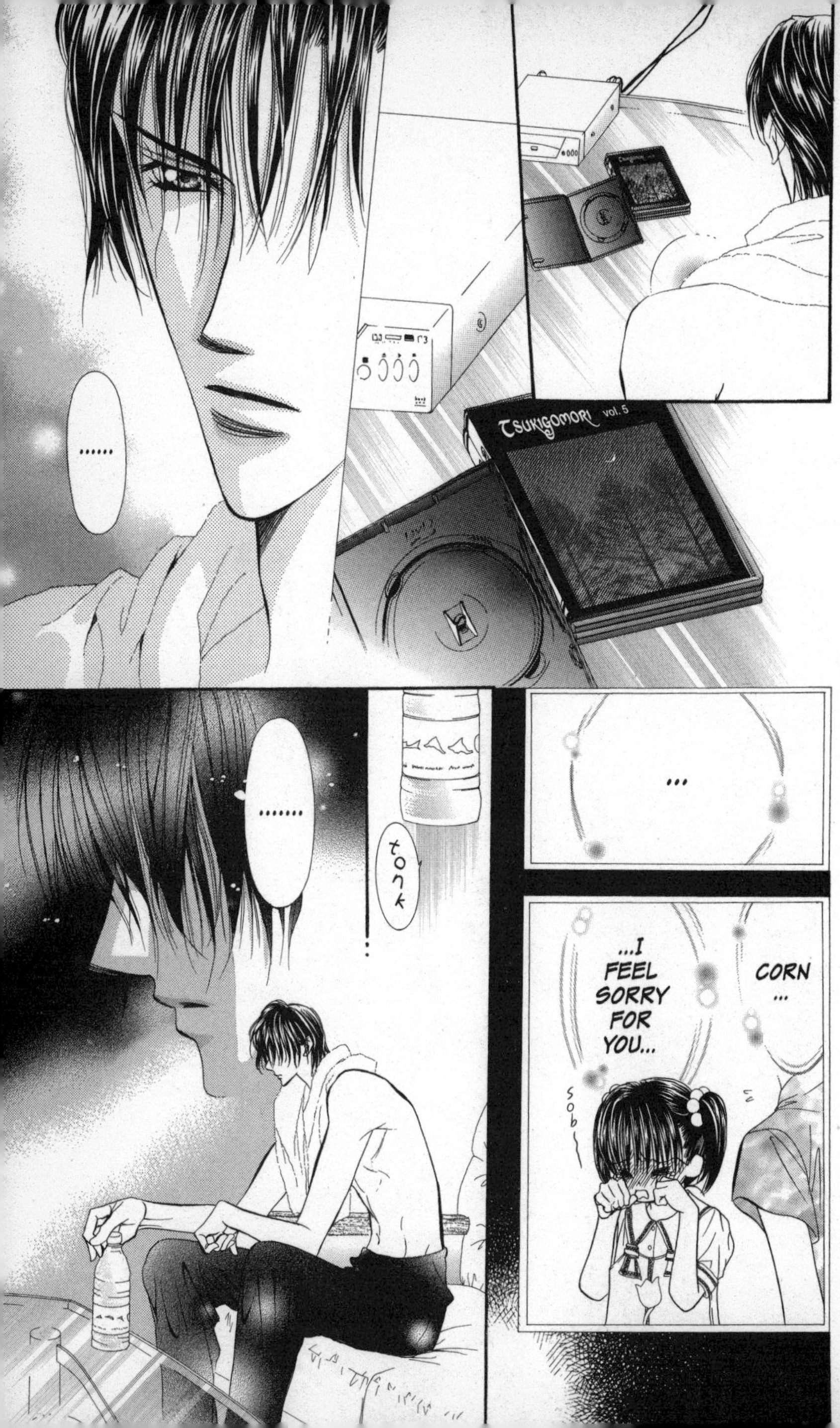
TSUKIGOMORI vol. 5
......
...
CORN ...
...I FEEL SORRY FOR YOU...
sob
....
tonk

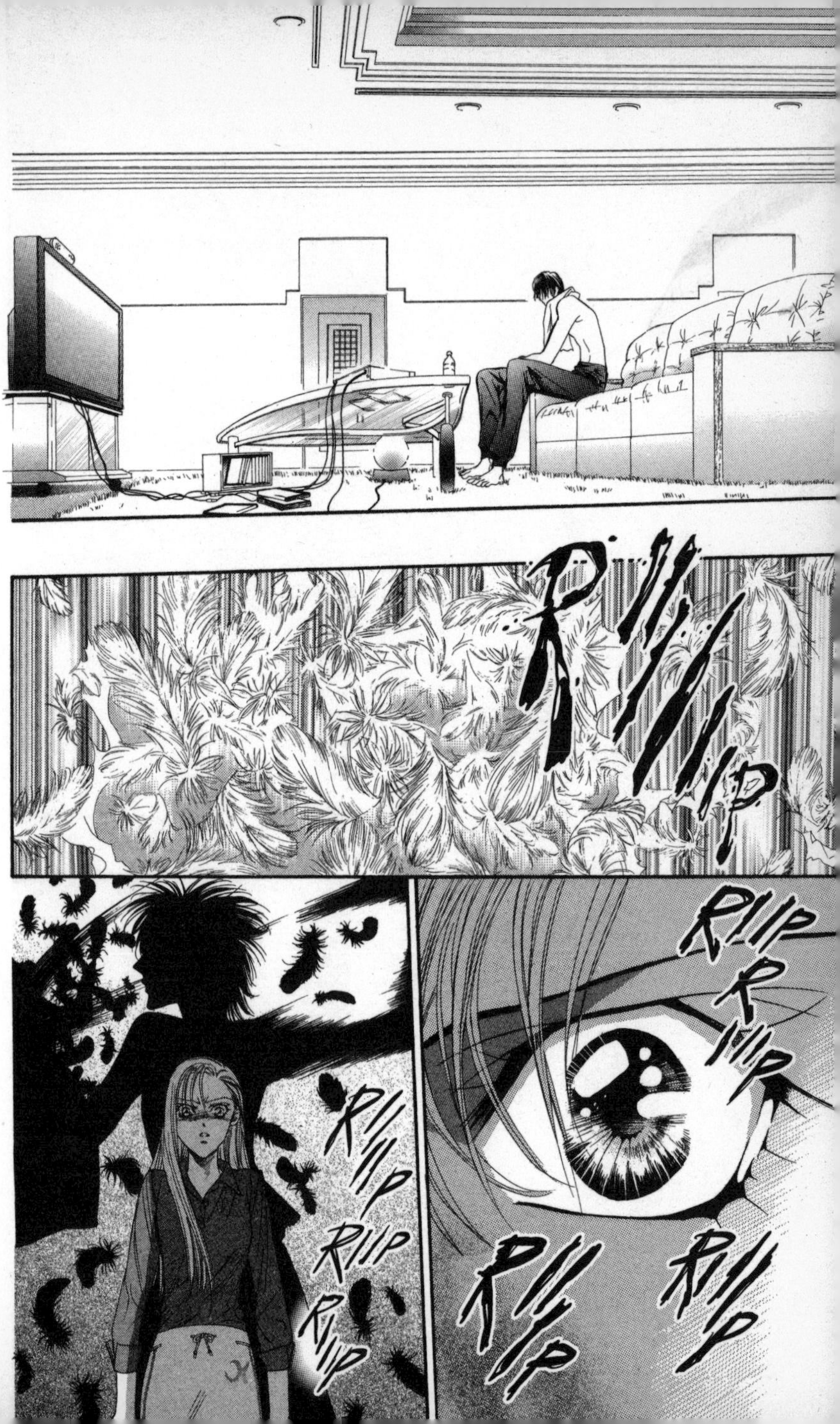
RIIIIIP
RIIP
RIIP
RIIP
RIIP
RIIP
RIIIP
RIIP
RIIP

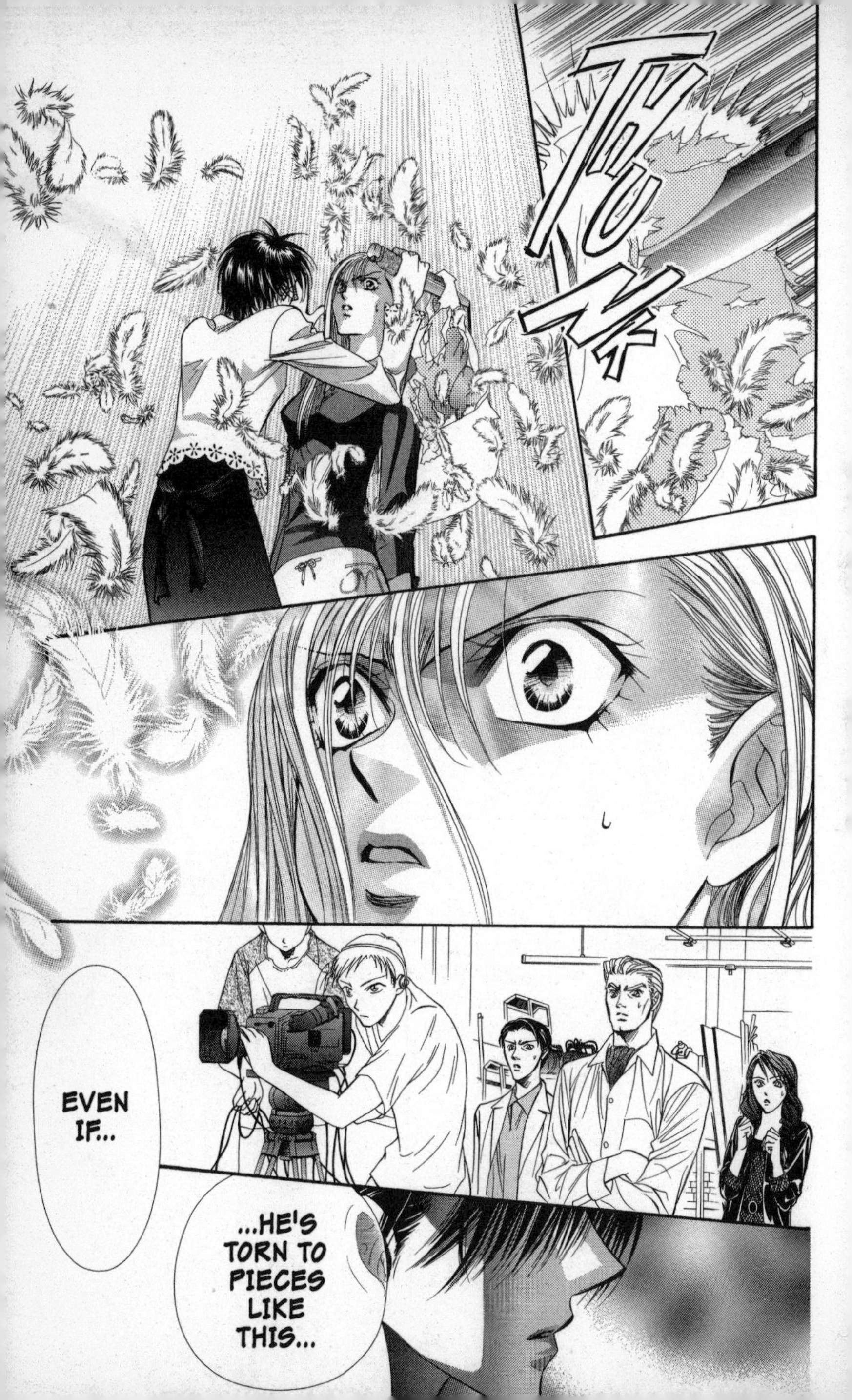
THUNK
EVEN IF...
...HE'S TORN TO PIECES LIKE THIS...

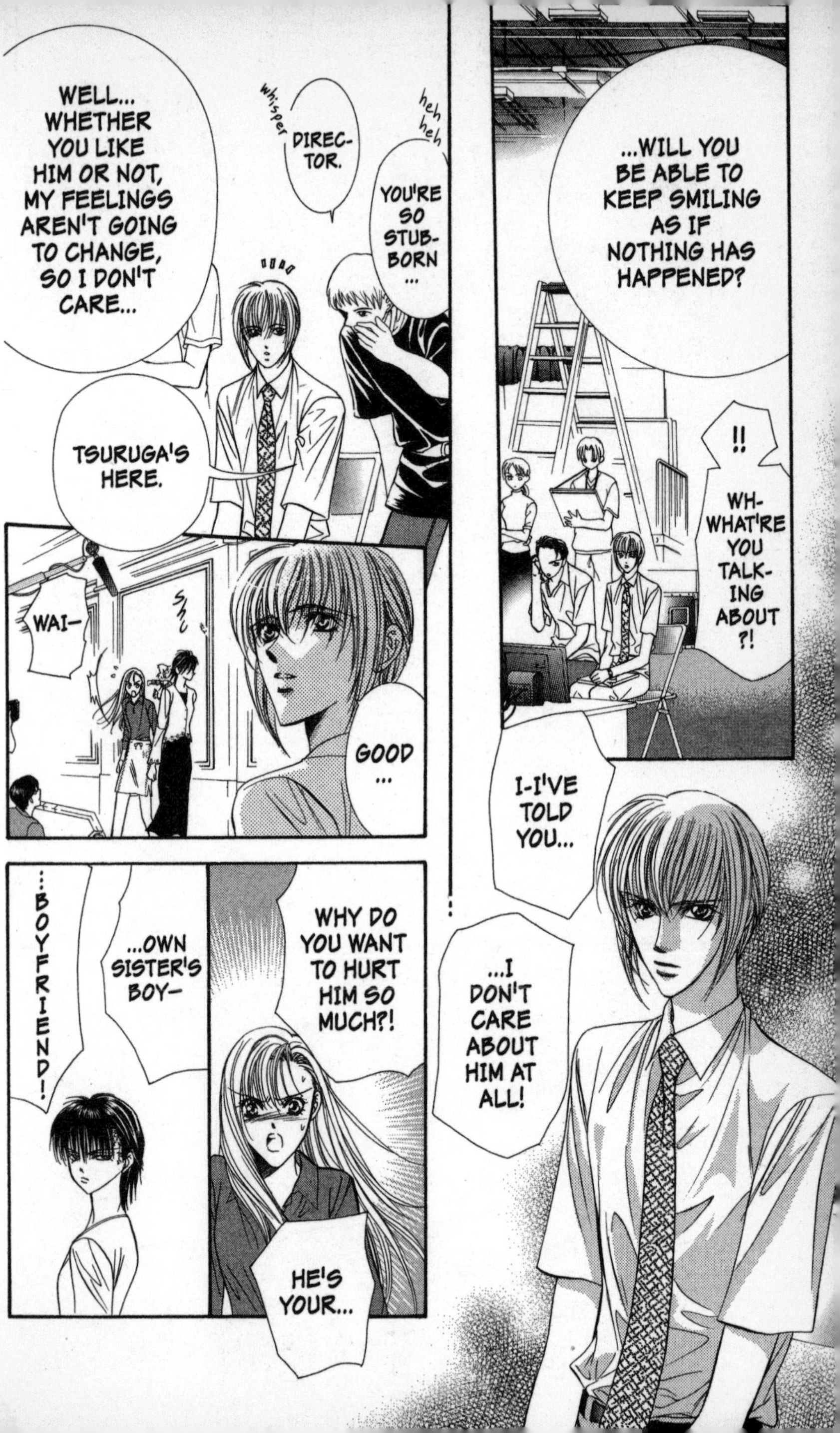
...WILL YOU BE ABLE TO KEEP SMILING AS IF NOTHING HAS HAPPENED?
!!
WH-WHAT'RE YOU TALKING ABOUT?!
I-I'VE TOLD YOU...
...I DON'T CARE ABOUT HIM AT ALL!
heh heh
YOU'RE SO STUBBORN...
whisper
DIRECTOR.
WELL... WHETHER YOU LIKE HIM OR NOT, MY FEELINGS AREN'T GOING TO CHANGE, SO I DON'T CARE...
TSURUGA'S HERE.
GOOD...
WAI-
WHY DO YOU WANT TO HURT HIM SO MUCH?!
HE'S YOUR...
...OWN SISTER'S BOY-
...BOYFRIEND!

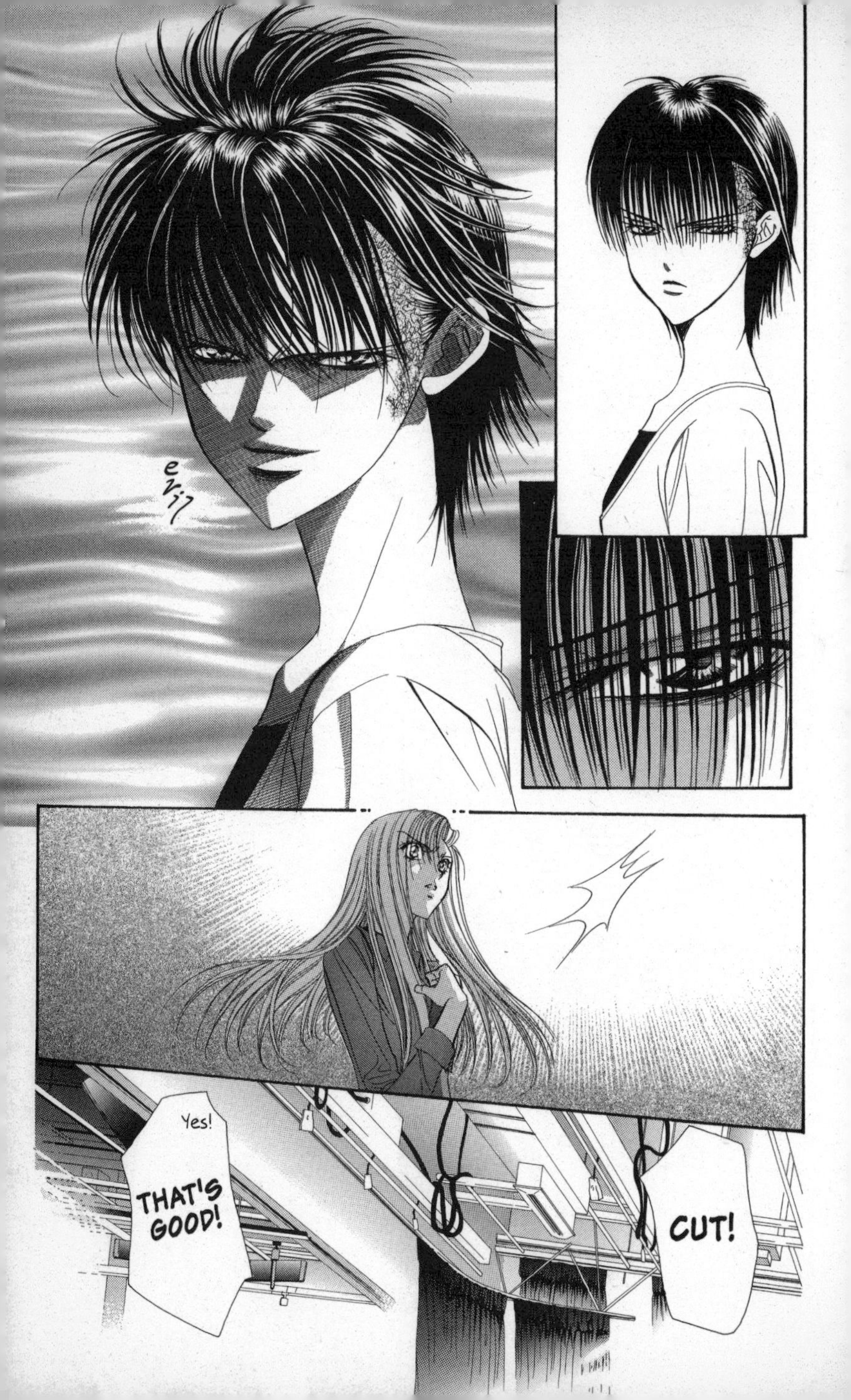
CUT!
Yes!
THAT'S GOOD!

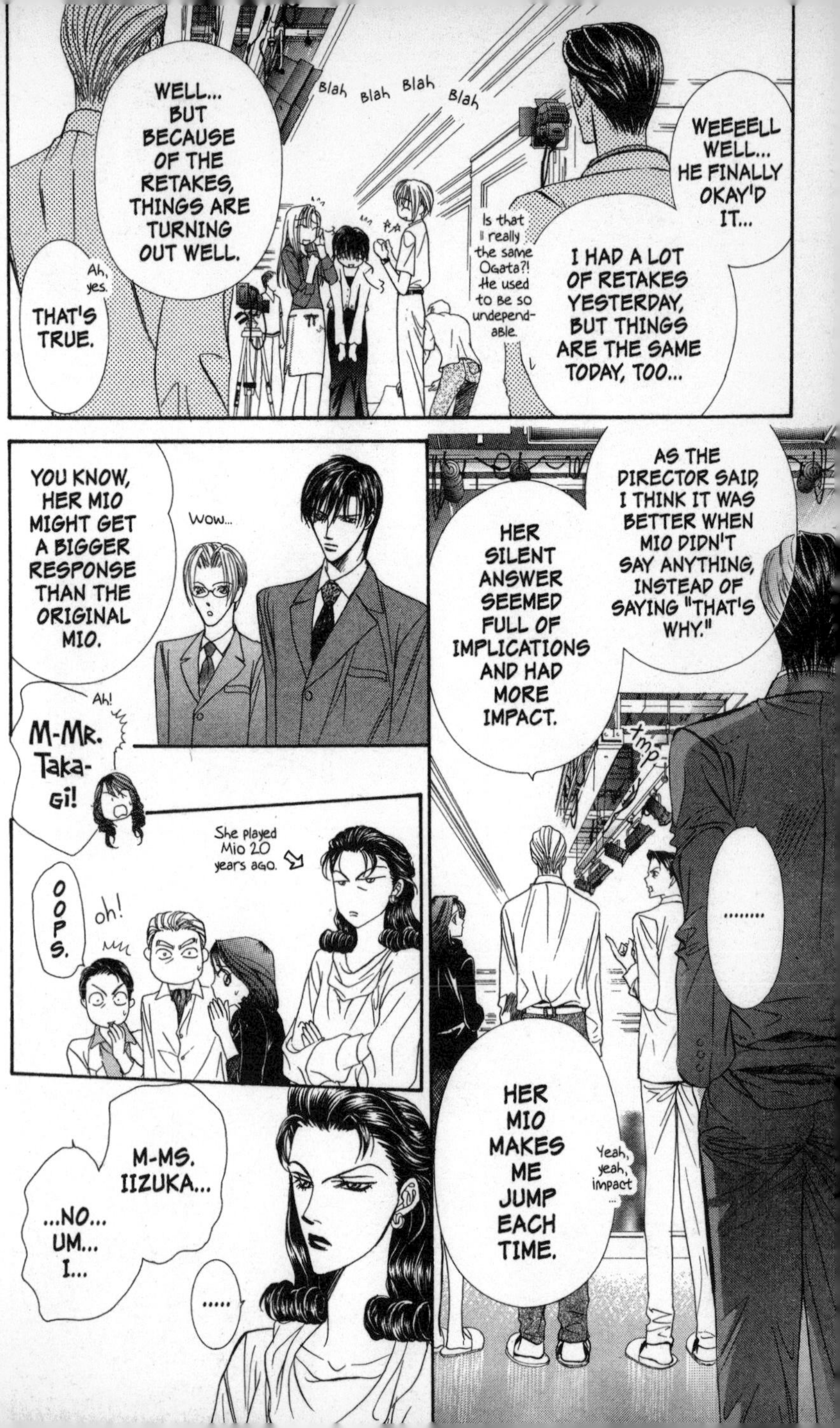
WEEEELL WELL... HE FINALLY OKAY'D IT...
I HAD A LOT OF RETAKES YESTERDAY, BUT THINGS ARE THE SAME TODAY, TOO...
Is that really the same Ogata?! He used to be so undependable.
Blah Blah Blah Blah
WELL... BUT BECAUSE OF THE RETAKES, THINGS ARE TURNING OUT WELL.
Ah, yes.
THAT'S TRUE.
AS THE DIRECTOR SAID, I THINK IT WAS BETTER WHEN MIO DIDN'T SAY ANYTHING, INSTEAD OF SAYING "THAT'S WHY."
HER SILENT ANSWER SEEMED FULL OF IMPLICATIONS AND HAD MORE IMPACT.
tmp
....
HER MIO MAKES ME JUMP EACH TIME.
Yeah, yeah, impact ...
YOU KNOW, HER MIO MIGHT GET A BIGGER RESPONSE THAN THE ORIGINAL MIO.
Wow...
Ah!
M-Mr. Taka-gi!
She played Mio 20 years ago.
oh!
OOPS.
M-MS. IIZUKA...
...NO... UM... I...
.....

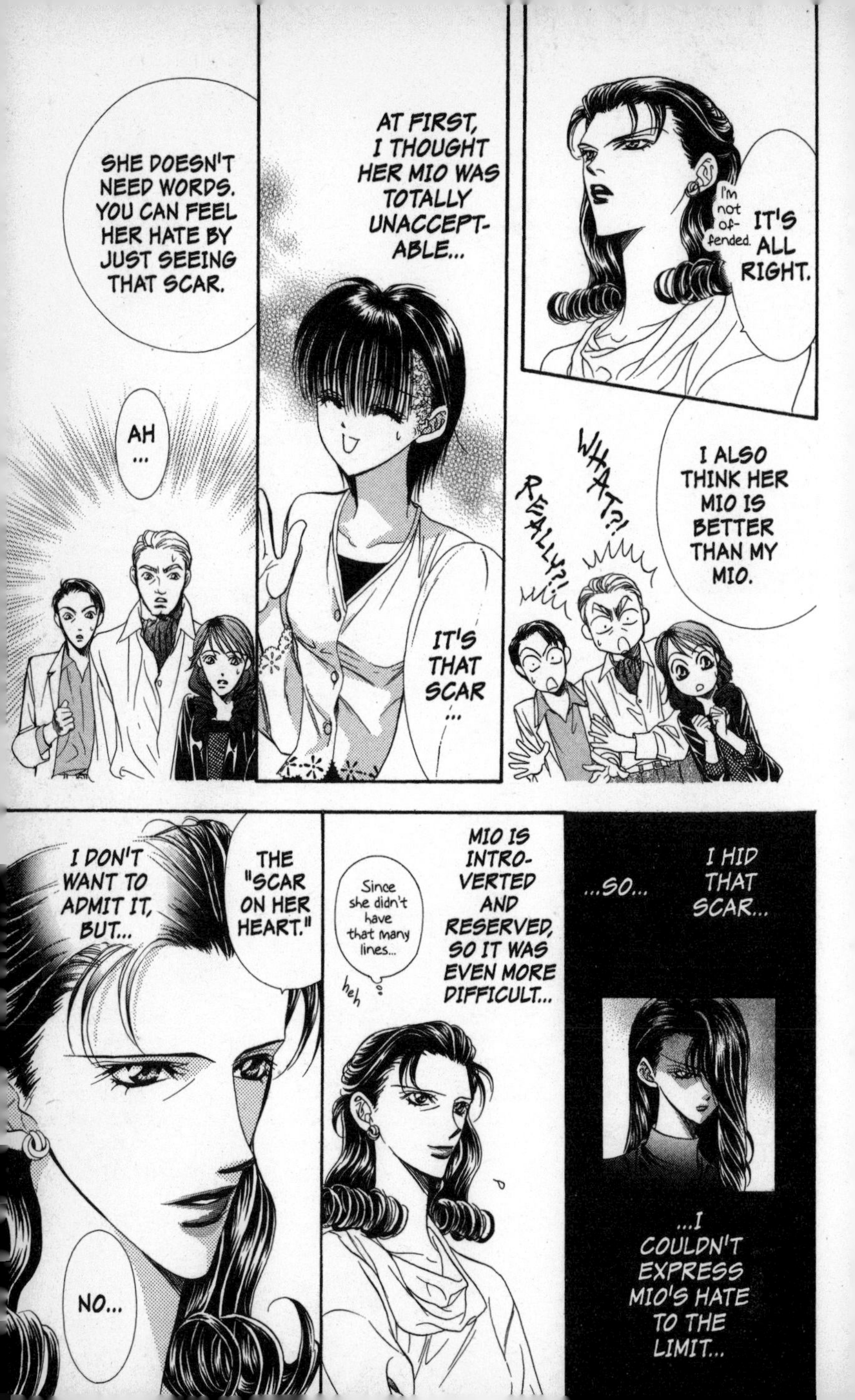
I'm not offended.
IT'S ALL RIGHT.
I ALSO THINK HER MIO IS BETTER THAN MY MIO.
WHAT?!
REALLY?!
AT FIRST, I THOUGHT HER MIO WAS TOTALLY UNACCEPTABLE...
IT'S THAT SCAR...
SHE DOESN'T NEED WORDS. YOU CAN FEEL HER HATE BY JUST SEEING THAT SCAR.
AH...
I HID THAT SCAR...
...SO...
...I COULDN'T EXPRESS MIO'S HATE TO THE LIMIT...
MIO IS INTROVERTED AND RESERVED, SO IT WAS EVEN MORE DIFFICULT...
Since she didn't have that many lines...
heh
THE "SCAR ON HER HEART."
I DON'T WANT TO ADMIT IT, BUT...
NO...

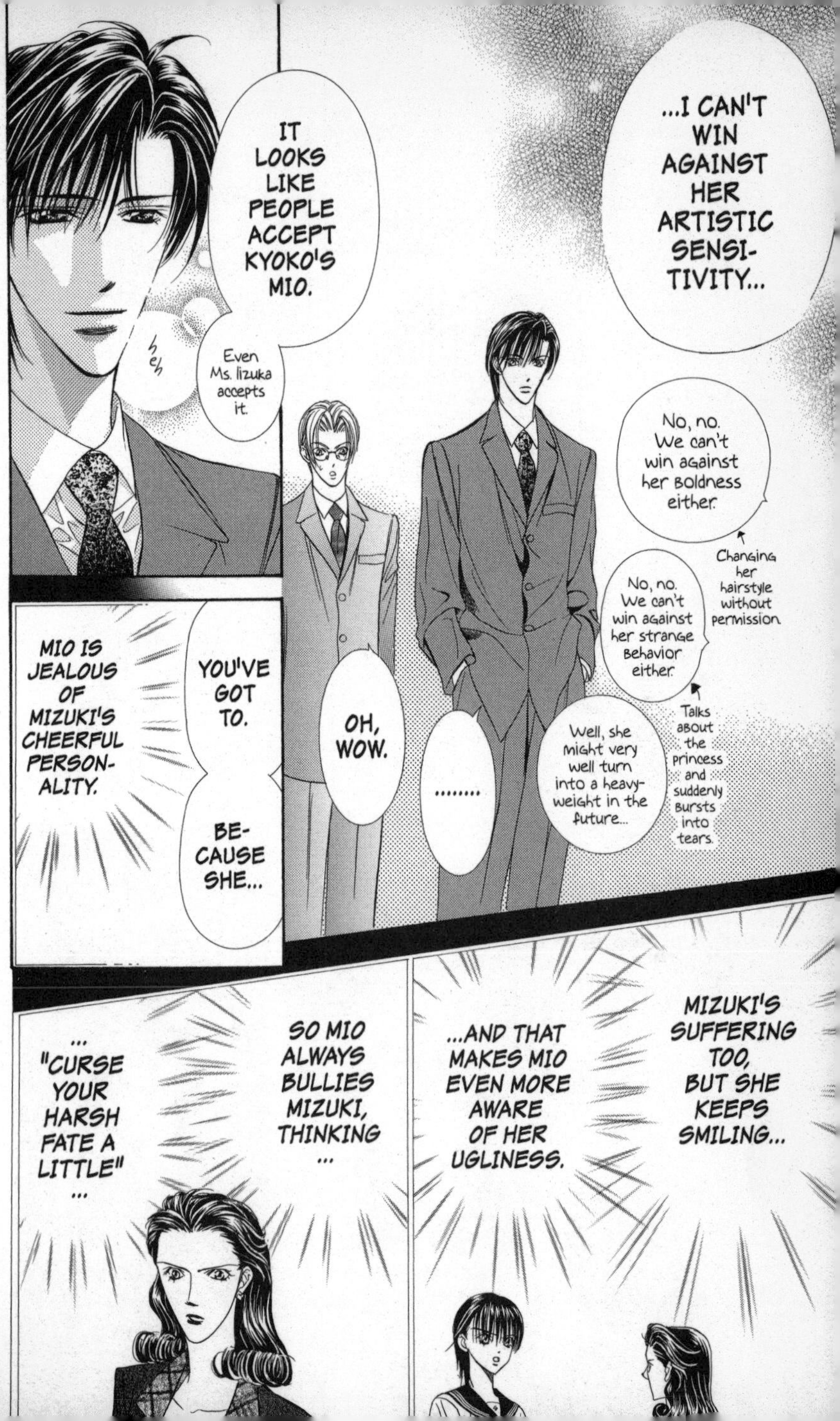
...I CAN'T WIN AGAINST HER ARTISTIC SENSI-TIVITY...
No, no. We can't win against her boldness either.
Changing her hairstyle without permission.
No, no. We can't win against her strange behavior either.
Talks about the princess and suddenly bursts into tears.
Well, she might very well turn into a heavy-weight in the future...
....
OH, WOW.
IT LOOKS LIKE PEOPLE ACCEPT KYOKO'S MIO.
heh
Even Ms. Iizuka accepts it.
YOU'VE GOT TO.
BE-CAUSE SHE...
MIO IS JEALOUS OF MIZUKI'S CHEERFUL PERSON-ALITY.
MIZUKI'S SUFFERING TOO, BUT SHE KEEPS SMILING...
...AND THAT MAKES MIO EVEN MORE AWARE OF HER UGLINESS.
SO MIO ALWAYS BULLIES MIZUKI, THINKING ...
... "CURSE YOUR HARSH FATE A LITTLE" ...

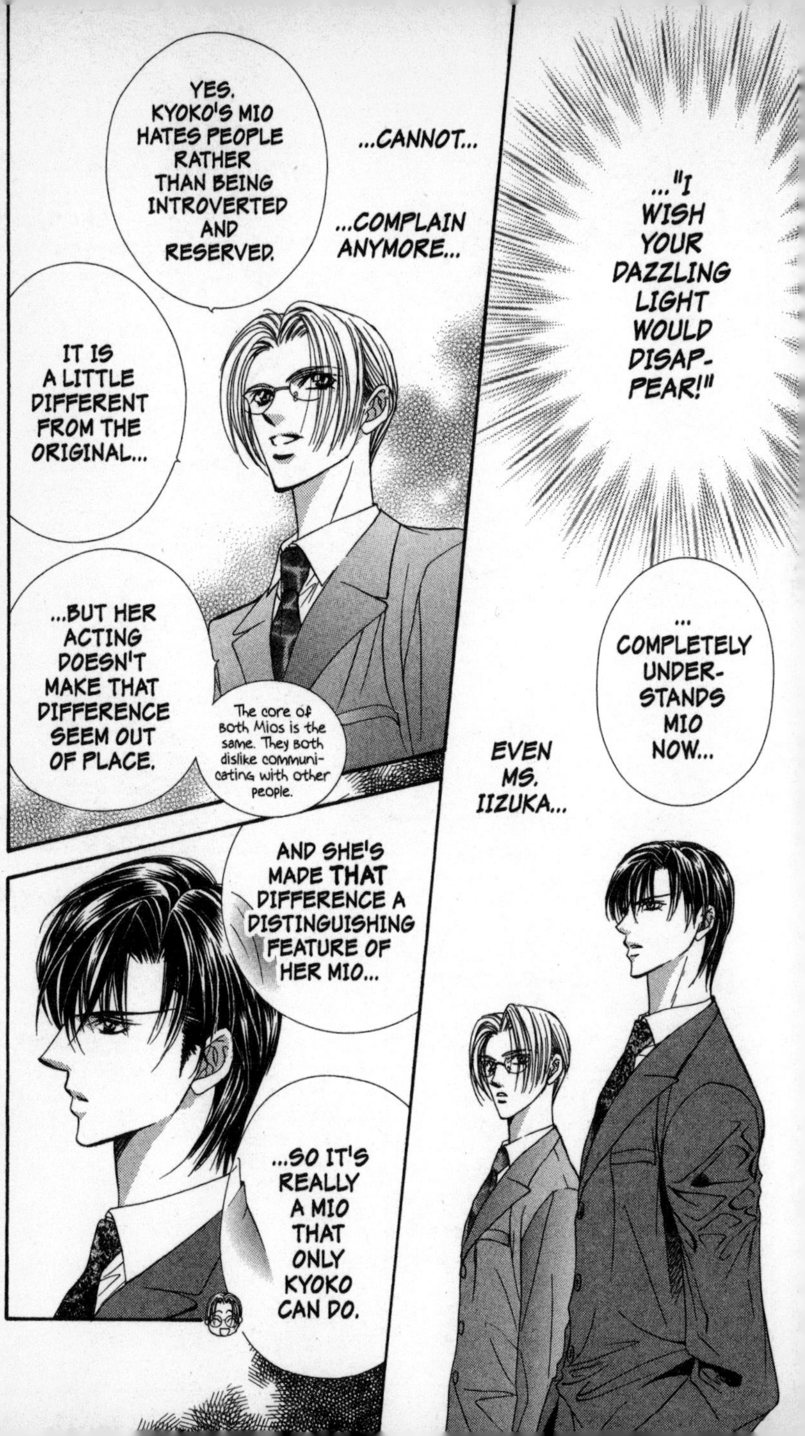
..."I WISH YOUR DAZZLING LIGHT WOULD DISAP-PEAR!"
... COMPLETELY UNDER-STANDS MIO NOW...
EVEN MS. IIZUKA...
...CANNOT...
...COMPLAIN ANYMORE...
YES. KYOKO'S MIO HATES PEOPLE RATHER THAN BEING INTROVERTED AND RESERVED.
IT IS A LITTLE DIFFERENT FROM THE ORIGINAL...
...BUT HER ACTING DOESN'T MAKE THAT DIFFERENCE SEEM OUT OF PLACE.
The core of both Mios is the same. They both dislike communi-cating with other people.
AND SHE'S MADE THAT DIFFERENCE A DISTINGUISHING FEATURE OF HER MIO...
...SO IT'S REALLY A MIO THAT ONLY KYOKO CAN DO.

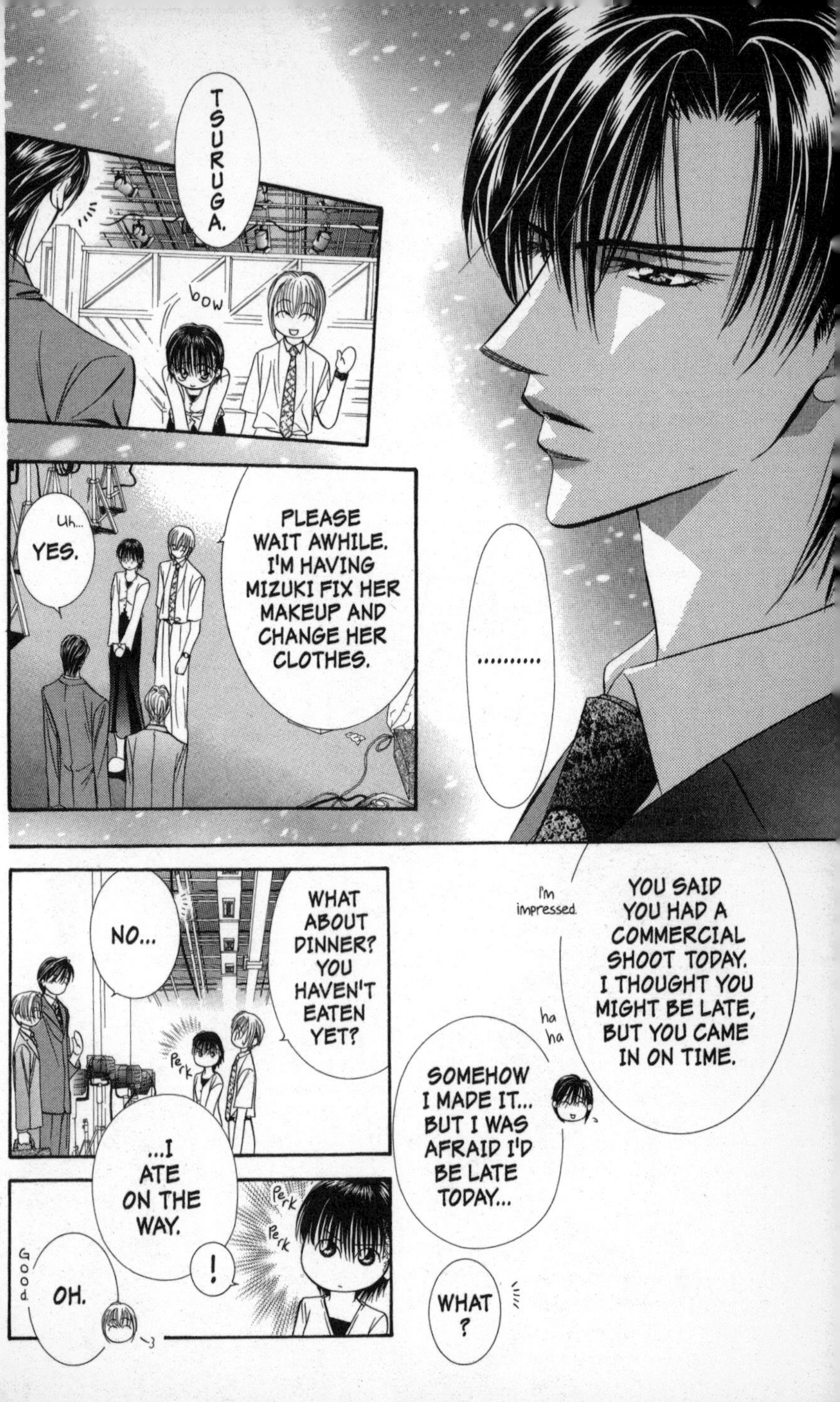
....
TSURUGA.
bow
PLEASE WAIT AWHILE. I'M HAVING MIZUKI FIX HER MAKEUP AND CHANGE HER CLOTHES.
Uh... YES.
YOU SAID YOU HAD A COMMERCIAL SHOOT TODAY. I THOUGHT YOU MIGHT BE LATE, BUT YOU CAME IN ON TIME.
I'm impressed.
ha ha
SOMEHOW I MADE IT... BUT I WAS AFRAID I'D BE LATE TODAY...
WHAT ?
WHAT ABOUT DINNER? YOU HAVEN'T EATEN YET?
NO...
Perk
...I ATE ON THE WAY.
Perk
Perk
!
OH.
Good

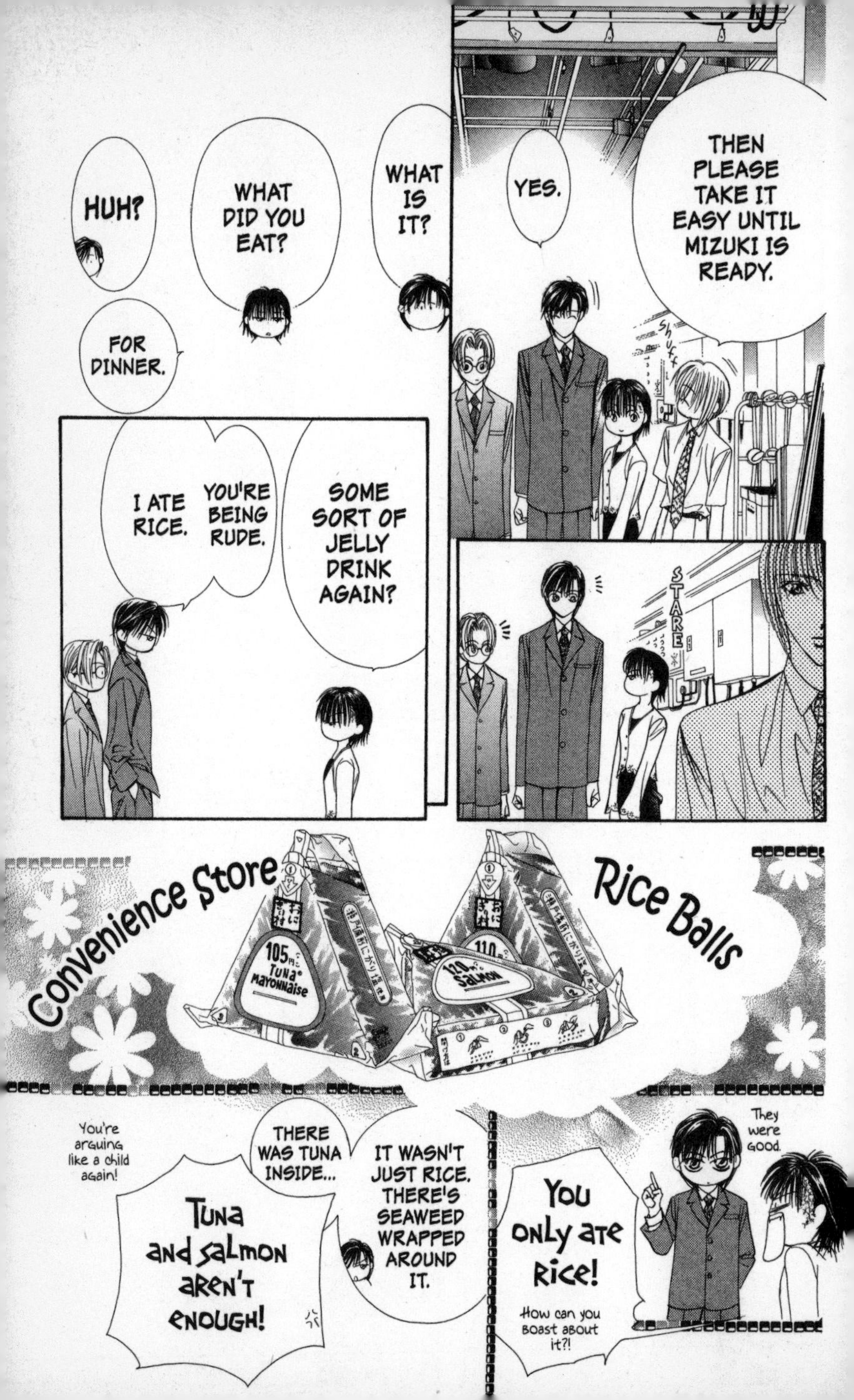
THEN PLEASE TAKE IT EASY UNTIL MIZUKI IS READY.
YES.
SHUXX
STARE
WHAT IS IT?
WHAT DID YOU EAT?
HUH?
FOR DINNER.
SOME SORT OF JELLY DRINK AGAIN?
YOU'RE BEING RUDE.
I ATE RICE.
Convenience Store
Rice Balls
105円 Tuna Mayonnaise
120円 Salmon
They were good.
You only ate rice!
How can you boast about it?!
IT WASN'T JUST RICE. THERE'S SEAWEED WRAPPED AROUND IT.
THERE WAS TUNA INSIDE...
Tuna and salmon aren't enough!
You're arguing like a child again!

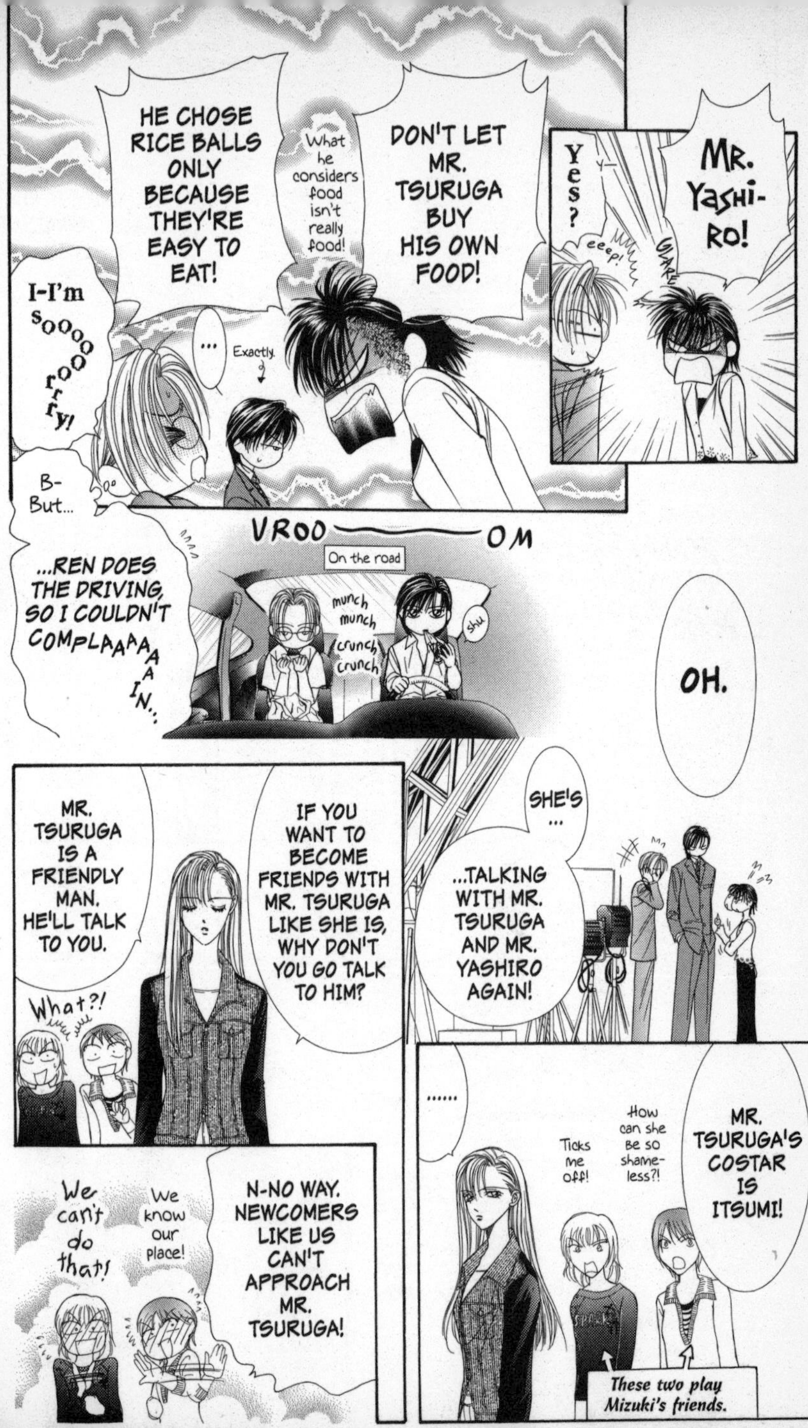
MR. YASHIRO!
Yes?
Y—
eeep!
GLARE
DON'T LET MR. TSURUGA BUY HIS OWN FOOD!
What he considers food isn't really food!
HE CHOSE RICE BALLS ONLY BECAUSE THEY'RE EASY TO EAT!
I-I'm sooooorrrry!
...
Exactly.
B-But...
OH.
VROO——OM
On the road
...REN DOES THE DRIVING, SO I COULDN'T COMPLAAAAAAIN...
munch munch
crunch crunch
shu
SHE'S...
...TALKING WITH MR. TSURUGA AND MR. YASHIRO AGAIN!
IF YOU WANT TO BECOME FRIENDS WITH MR. TSURUGA LIKE SHE IS, WHY DON'T YOU GO TALK TO HIM?
MR. TSURUGA IS A FRIENDLY MAN. HE'LL TALK TO YOU.
What?!
MR. TSURUGA'S COSTAR IS ITSUMI!
How can she be so shameless?!
Ticks me off!
......
These two play Mizuki's friends.
N-NO WAY. NEWCOMERS LIKE US CAN'T APPROACH MR. TSURUGA!
We know our place!
We can't do that!

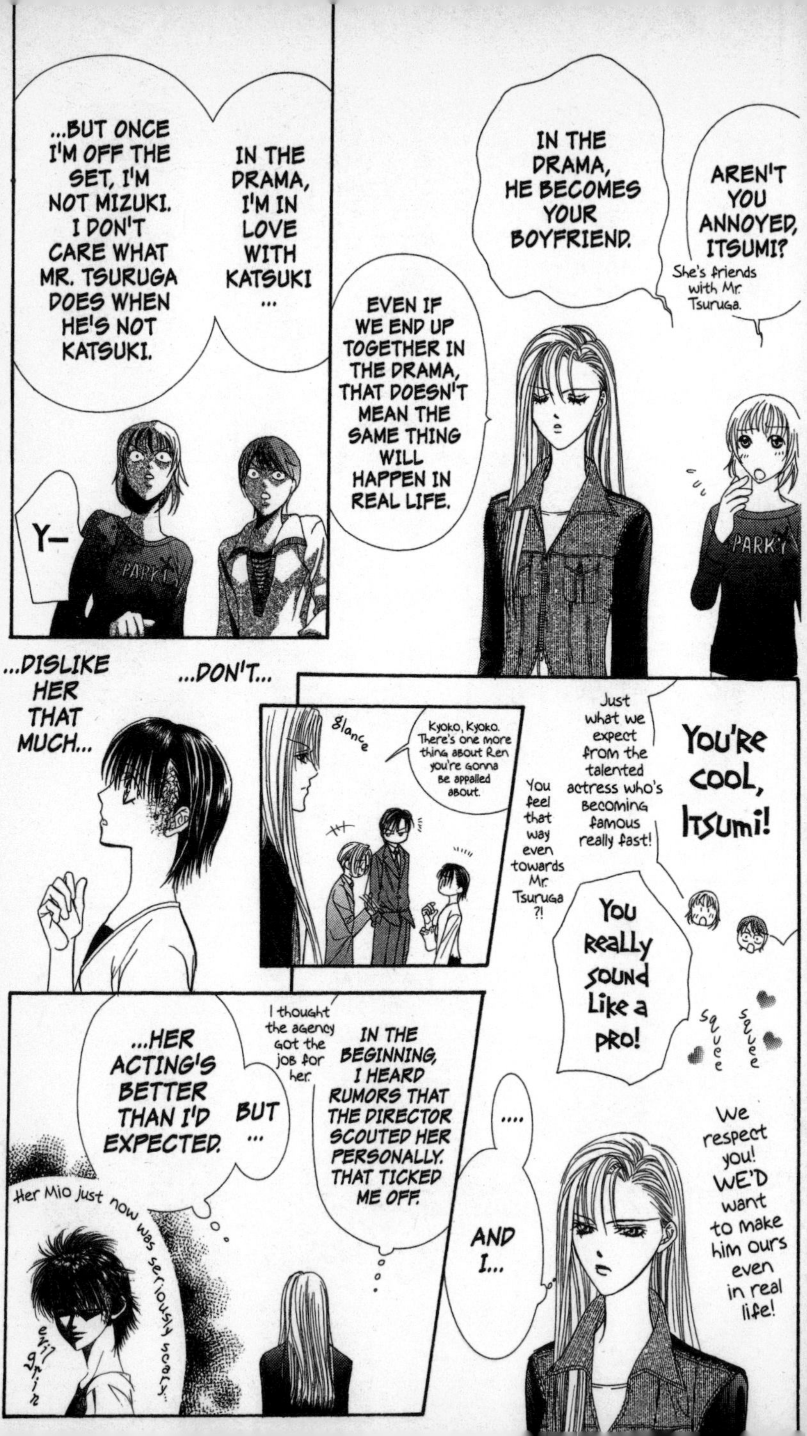
AREN'T YOU ANNOYED, ITSUMI?
She's friends with Mr. Tsuruga.
IN THE DRAMA, HE BECOMES YOUR BOYFRIEND.
EVEN IF WE END UP TOGETHER IN THE DRAMA, THAT DOESN'T MEAN THE SAME THING WILL HAPPEN IN REAL LIFE.
IN THE DRAMA, I'M IN LOVE WITH KATSUKI...
...BUT ONCE I'M OFF THE SET, I'M NOT MIZUKI. I DON'T CARE WHAT MR. TSURUGA DOES WHEN HE'S NOT KATSUKI.
Y—
You're cool, Itsumi!
Just what we expect from the talented actress who's becoming famous really fast!
You feel that way even towards Mr. Tsuruga?!
You really sound like a pro!
squee
squee
glance
Kyoko, Kyoko. There's one more thing about Ren you're gonna be appalled about.
...DON'T...
...DISLIKE HER THAT MUCH...
We respect you! WE'D want to make him ours even in real life!
....
AND I...
IN THE BEGINNING, I HEARD RUMORS THAT THE DIRECTOR SCOUTED HER PERSONALLY. THAT TICKED ME OFF.
I thought the agency got the job for her.
BUT...
...HER ACTING'S BETTER THAN I'D EXPECTED.
Her Mio just now was seriously scary...
evil grin

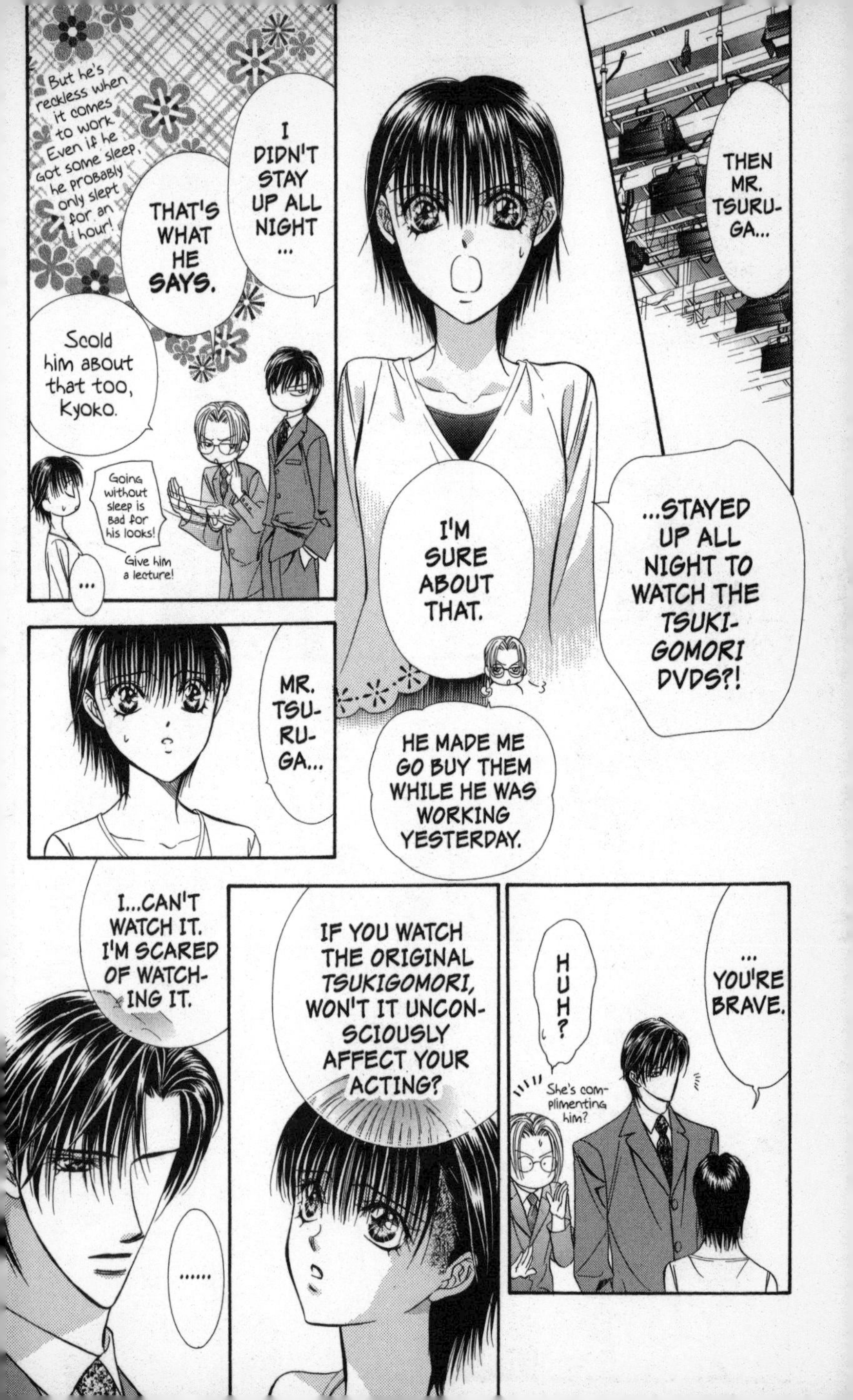
THEN MR. TSURU-GA...
...STAYED UP ALL NIGHT TO WATCH THE TSUKI-GOMORI DVDS?!
I'M SURE ABOUT THAT.
HE MADE ME GO BUY THEM WHILE HE WAS WORKING YESTERDAY.
I DIDN'T STAY UP ALL NIGHT ...
THAT'S WHAT HE SAYS.
But he's reckless when it comes to work. Even if he got some sleep, he probably only slept for an hour!
Scold him about that too, Kyoko.
Going without sleep is bad for his looks!
Give him a lecture!
...
MR. TSU-RU-GA...
... YOU'RE BRAVE.
HUH?
She's com-plimenting him?
IF YOU WATCH THE ORIGINAL TSUKIGOMORI, WON'T IT UNCON-SCIOUSLY AFFECT YOUR ACTING?
I...CAN'T WATCH IT. I'M SCARED OF WATCH-ING IT.
......

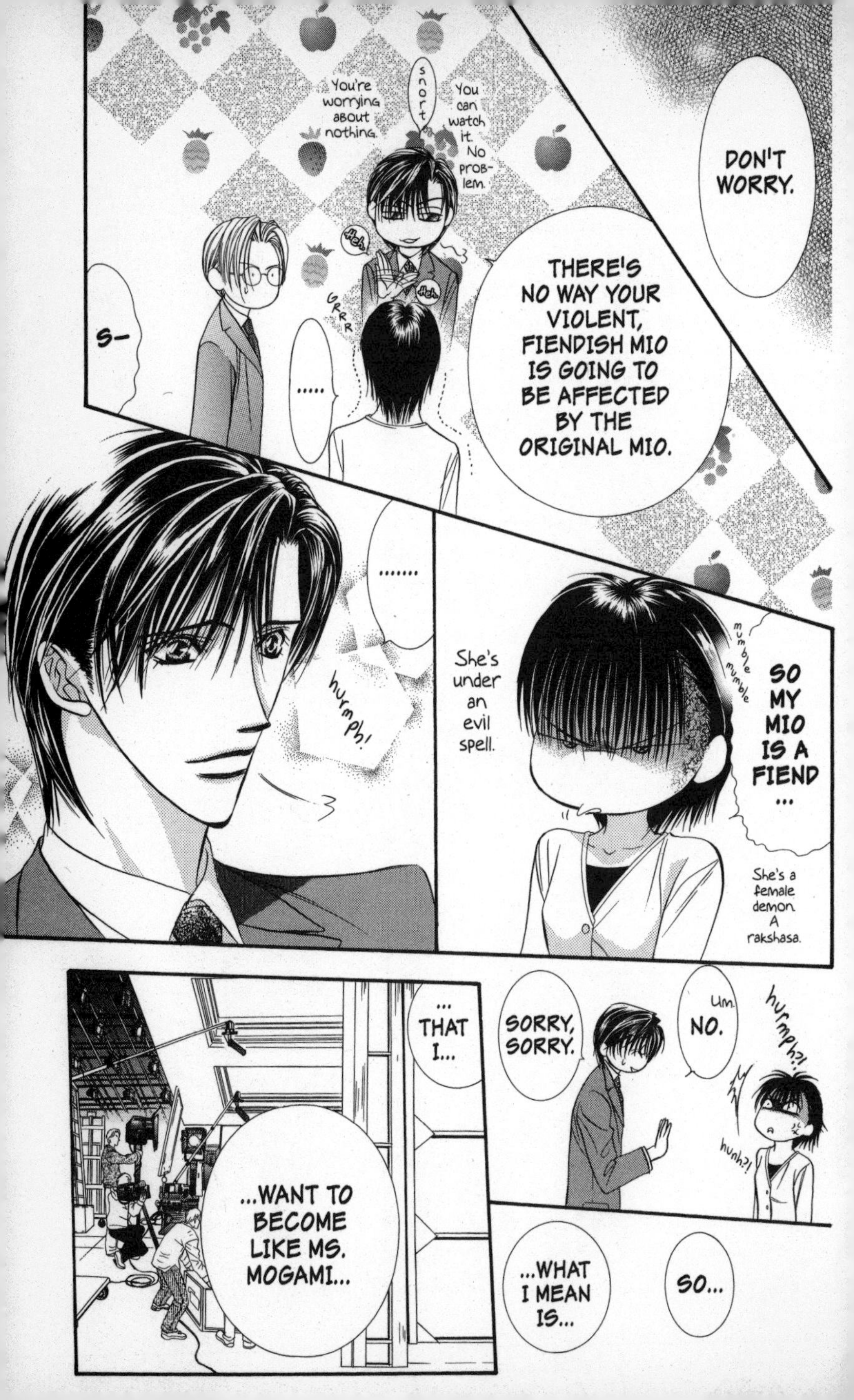
DON'T WORRY.
THERE'S NO WAY YOUR VIOLENT, FIENDISH MIO IS GOING TO BE AFFECTED BY THE ORIGINAL MIO.
You can watch it. No prob- lem.
snort
You're worrying about nothing.
Heh
Heh
GRRR
......
S-
SO MY MIO IS A FIEND...
mumble mumble
She's under an evil spell.
She's a female demon. A rakshasa.
....
hurmph!
Um.
NO.
hurmph?!
hunh?!
SORRY, SORRY.
... THAT I...
SO...
...WHAT I MEAN IS...
...WANT TO BECOME LIKE MS. MOGAMI...

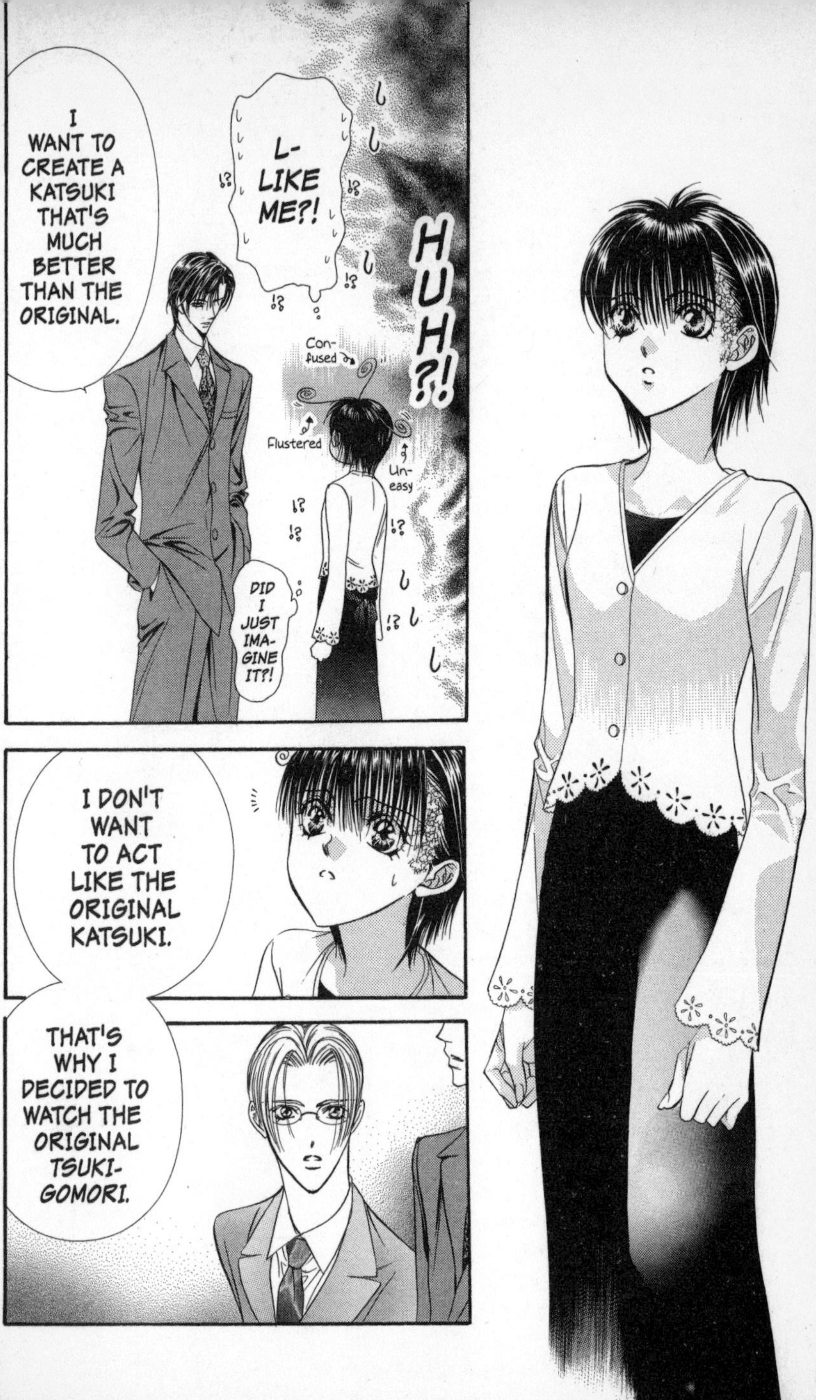
I WANT TO CREATE A KATSUKI THAT'S MUCH BETTER THAN THE ORIGINAL.
L-LIKE ME?!
HUH?!
Con-fused
Flustered
Un-easy
DID I JUST IMA-GINE IT?!
I DON'T WANT TO ACT LIKE THE ORIGINAL KATSUKI.
THAT'S WHY I DECIDED TO WATCH THE ORIGINAL TSUKI-GOMORI.

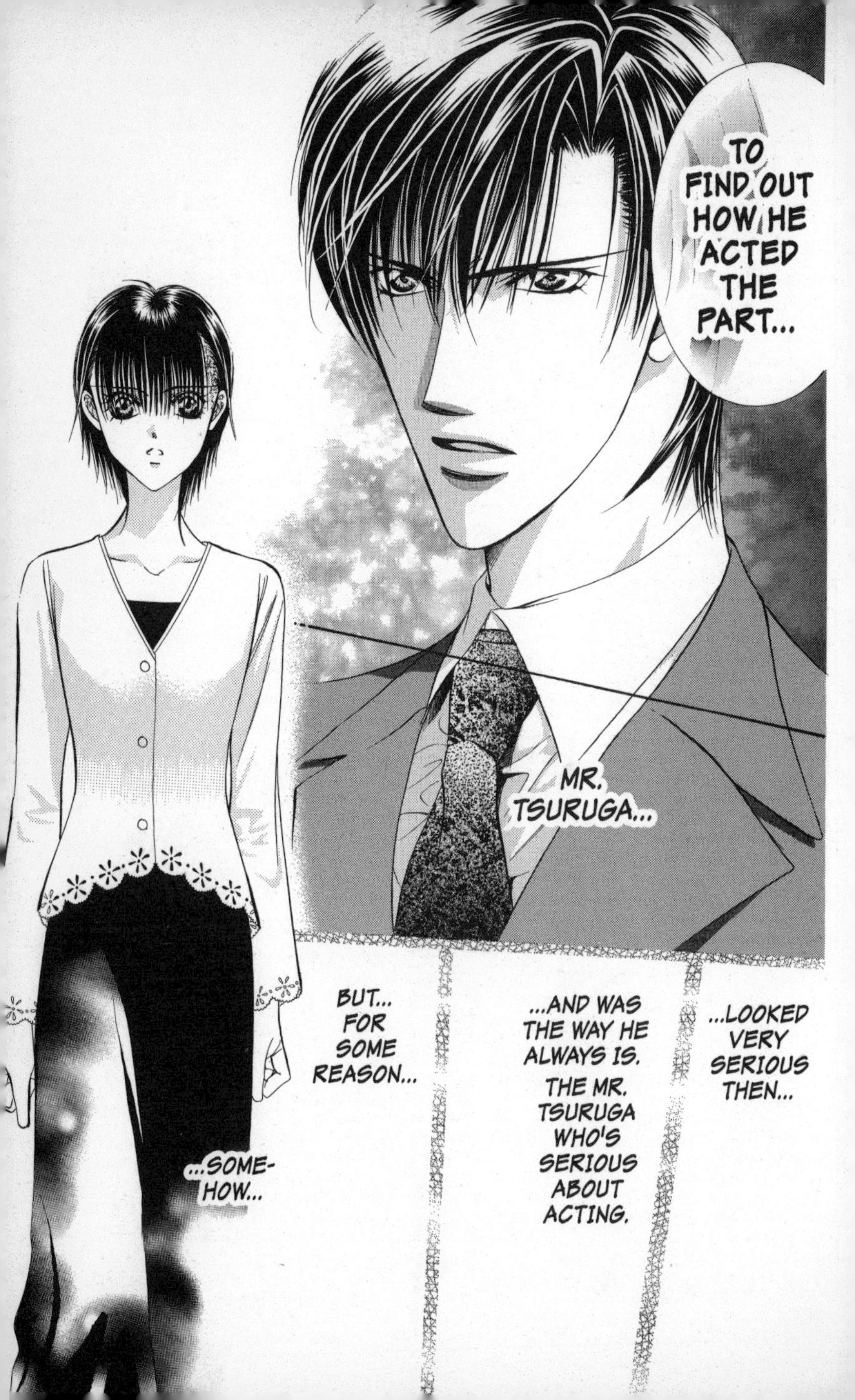
TO FIND OUT HOW HE ACTED THE PART...
MR. TSURUGA...
...LOOKED VERY SERIOUS THEN...
...AND WAS THE WAY HE ALWAYS IS.
THE MR. TSURUGA WHO'S SERIOUS ABOUT ACTING.
BUT... FOR SOME REASON...
...SOME-HOW...

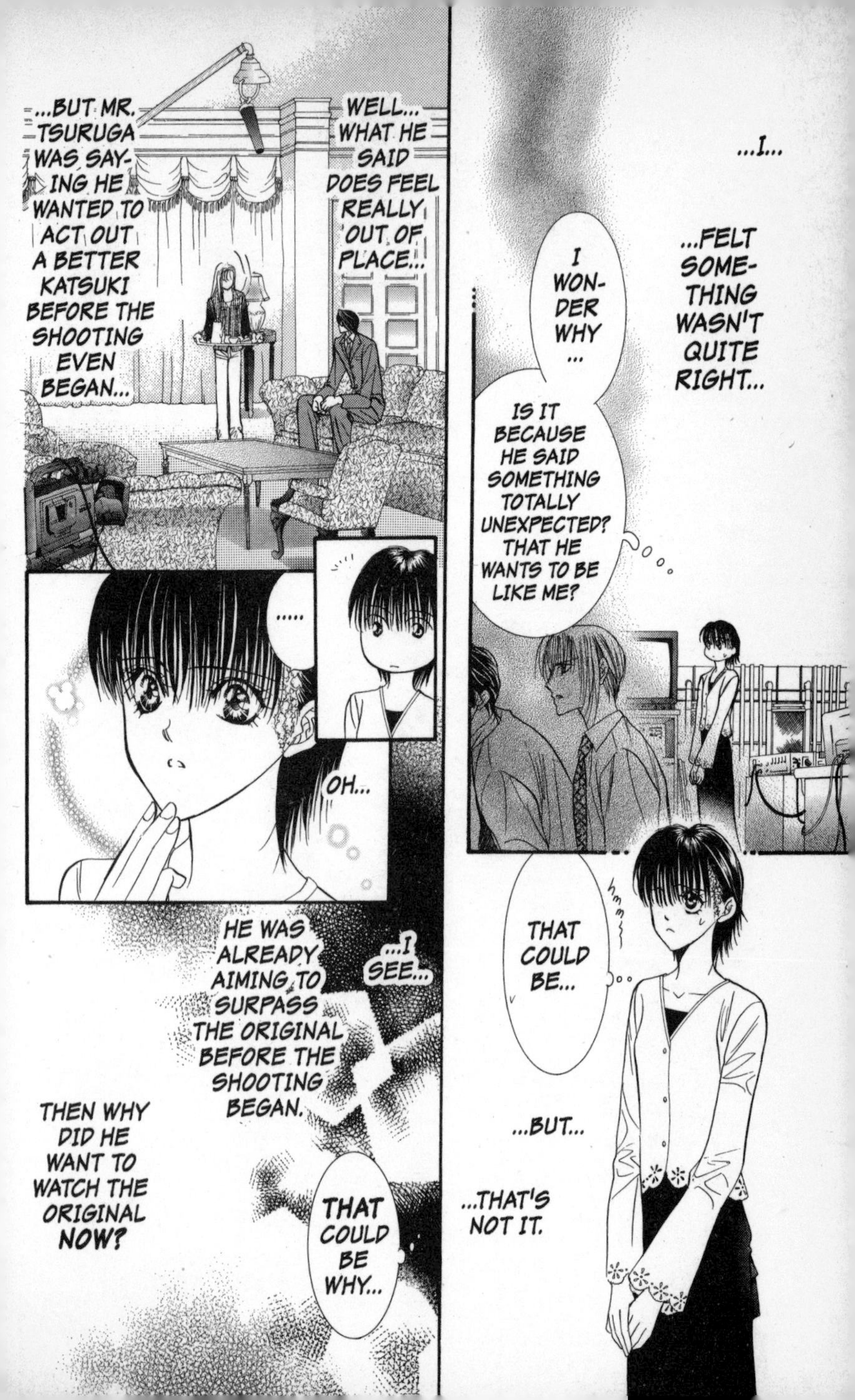
...I...
...FELT SOMETHING WASN'T QUITE RIGHT...
I WONDER WHY...
IS IT BECAUSE HE SAID SOMETHING TOTALLY UNEXPECTED? THAT HE WANTS TO BE LIKE ME?
THAT COULD BE...
...BUT...
...THAT'S NOT IT.
WELL... WHAT HE SAID DOES FEEL REALLY OUT OF PLACE...
...BUT MR. TSURUGA WAS SAYING HE WANTED TO ACT OUT A BETTER KATSUKI BEFORE THE SHOOTING EVEN BEGAN...
.....
OH...
...I SEE...
HE WAS ALREADY AIMING TO SURPASS THE ORIGINAL BEFORE THE SHOOTING BEGAN.
THAT COULD BE WHY...
THEN WHY DID HE WANT TO WATCH THE ORIGINAL NOW?

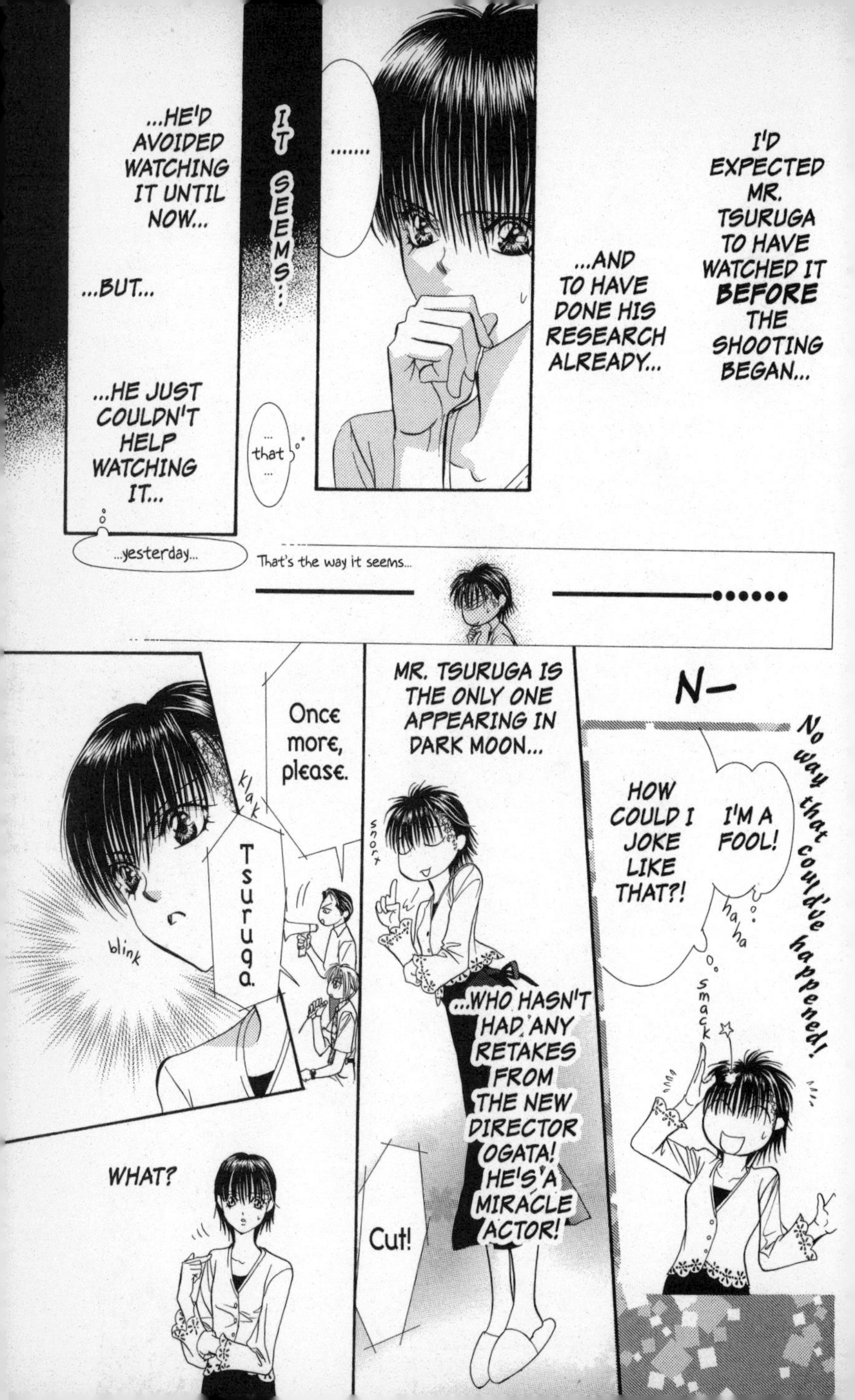
I'D EXPECTED MR. TSURUGA TO HAVE WATCHED IT BEFORE THE SHOOTING BEGAN...
...AND TO HAVE DONE HIS RESEARCH ALREADY...
......
IT SEEMS...
...HE'D AVOIDED WATCHING IT UNTIL NOW...
...BUT...
...that...
...HE JUST COULDN'T HELP WATCHING IT...
...yesterday...
That's the way it seems...
N—
No way that could've happened!
I'M A FOOL!
HOW COULD I JOKE LIKE THAT?!
haha
smack
MR. TSURUGA IS THE ONLY ONE APPEARING IN DARK MOON...
snort
...WHO HASN'T HAD ANY RETAKES FROM THE NEW DIRECTOR OGATA! HE'S A MIRACLE ACTOR!
Cut!
Once more, please.
klak
Tsuruga.
blink
WHAT?

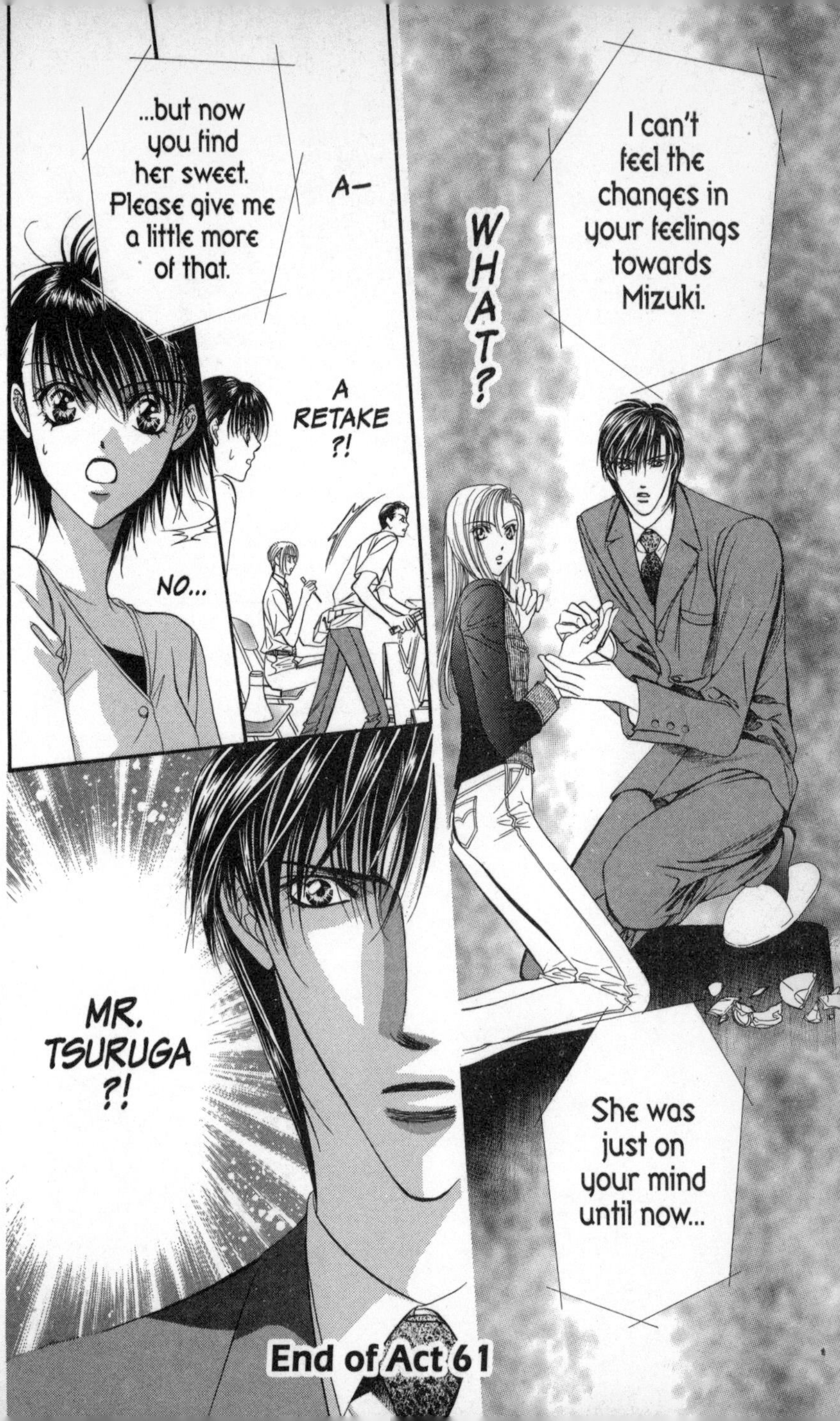
I can't feel the changes in your feelings towards Mizuki.
WHAT?
She was just on your mind until now...
...but now you find her sweet. Please give me a little more of that.
A—
A RETAKE ?!
NO...
MR. TSURUGA ?!
End of Act 61

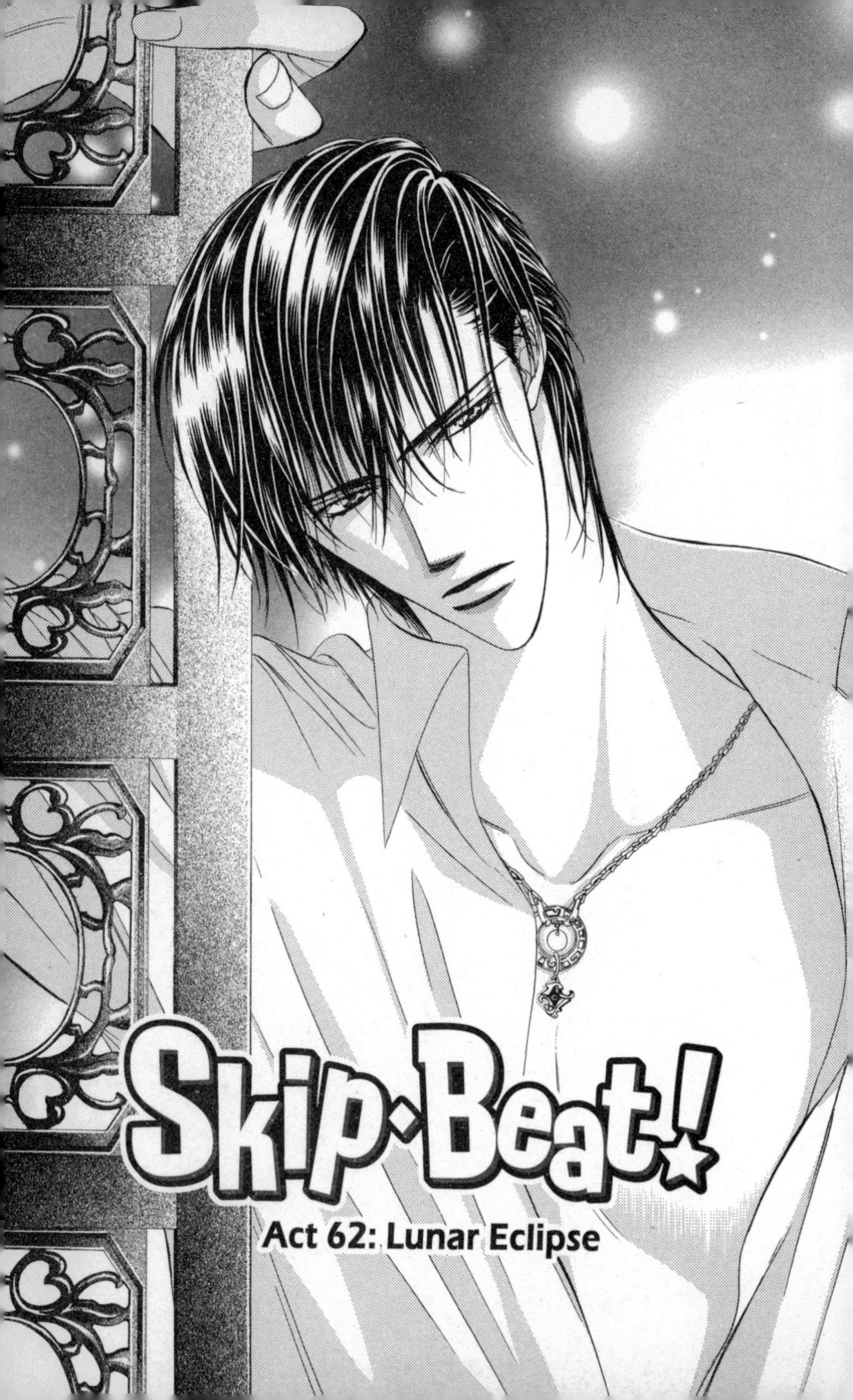
Skip·Beat!
Act 62: Lunar Eclipse

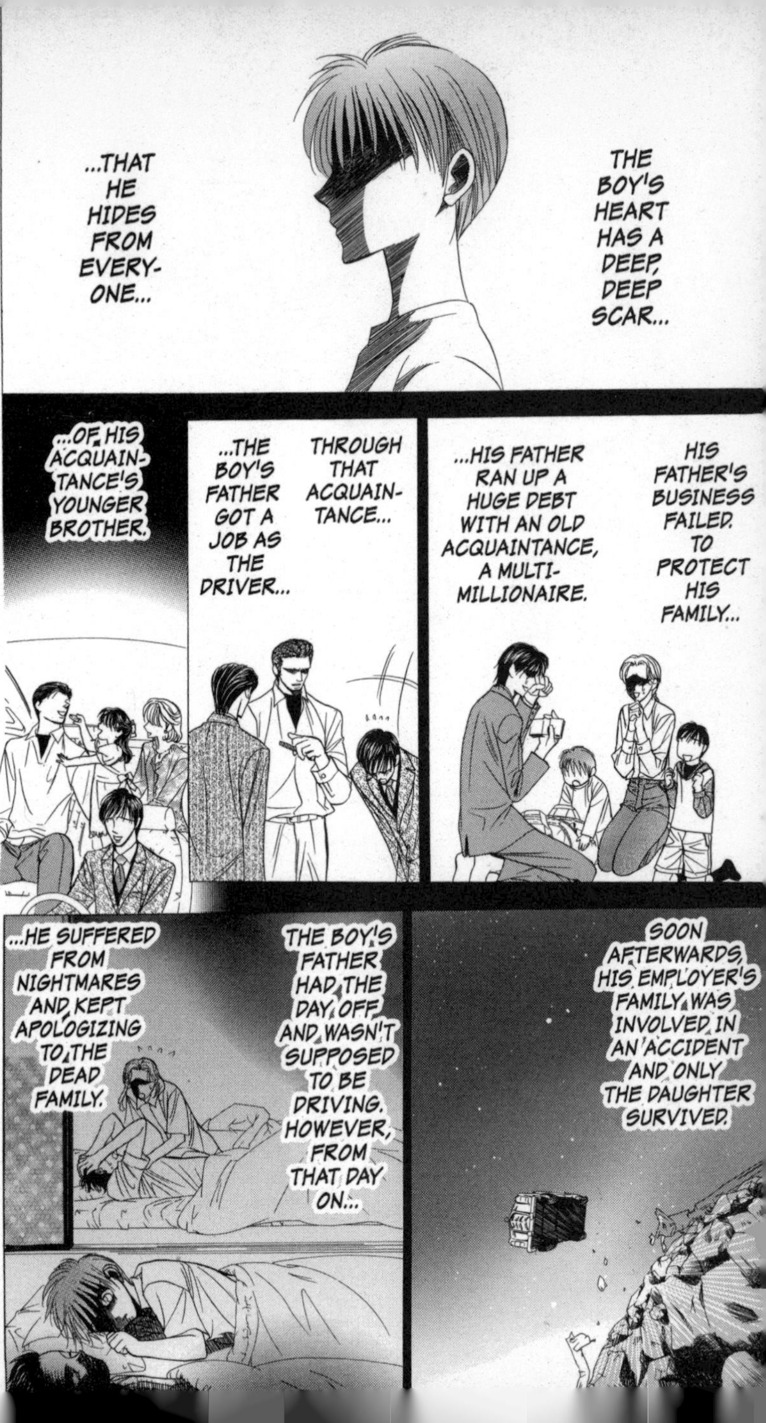
THE BOY'S HEART HAS A DEEP, DEEP SCAR...
...THAT HE HIDES FROM EVERY-ONE...
HIS FATHER'S BUSINESS FAILED. TO PROTECT HIS FAMILY...
...HIS FATHER RAN UP A HUGE DEBT WITH AN OLD ACQUAINTANCE, A MULTI-MILLIONAIRE.
THROUGH THAT ACQUAIN-TANCE...
...THE BOY'S FATHER GOT A JOB AS THE DRIVER...
...OF HIS ACQUAIN-TANCE'S YOUNGER BROTHER.
SOON AFTERWARDS, HIS EMPLOYER'S FAMILY WAS INVOLVED IN AN ACCIDENT AND ONLY THE DAUGHTER SURVIVED.
THE BOY'S FATHER HAD THE DAY OFF AND WASN'T SUPPOSED TO BE DRIVING. HOWEVER, FROM THAT DAY ON...
...HE SUFFERED FROM NIGHTMARES AND KEPT APOLOGIZING TO THE DEAD FAMILY.

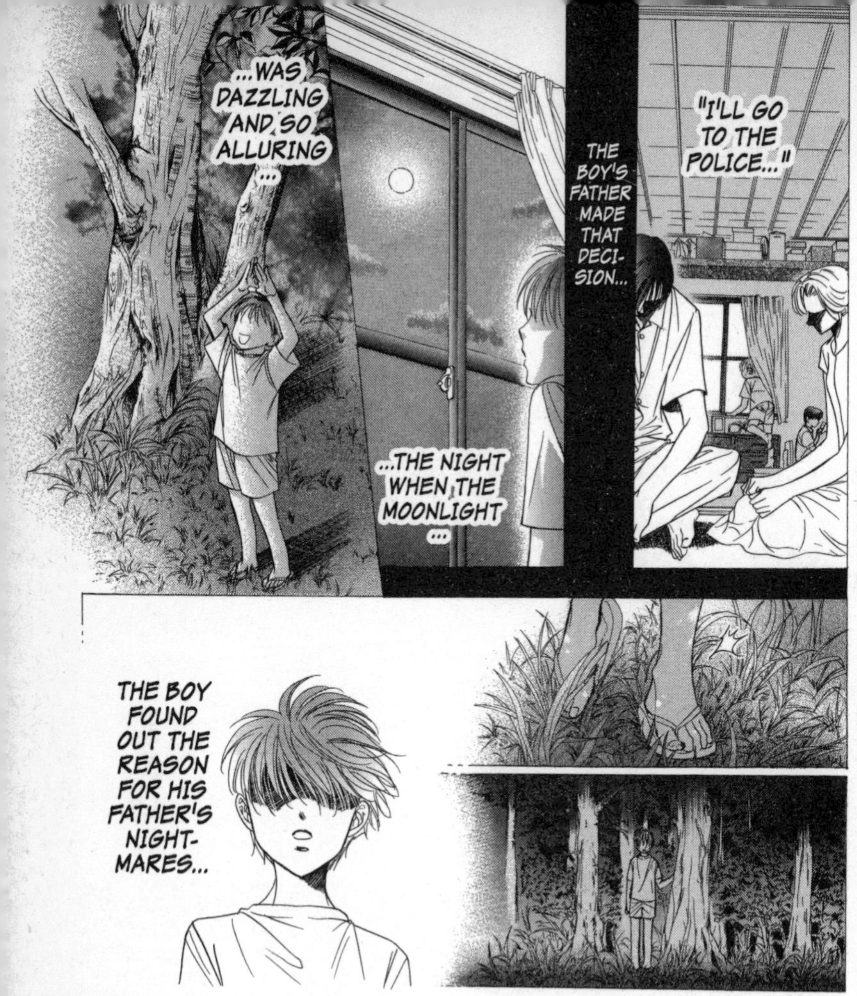
"I'LL GO TO THE POLICE..."
THE BOY'S FATHER MADE THAT DECISION...
...THE NIGHT WHEN THE MOONLIGHT...
...WAS DAZZLING AND SO ALLURING...
THE BOY FOUND OUT THE REASON FOR HIS FATHER'S NIGHTMARES...

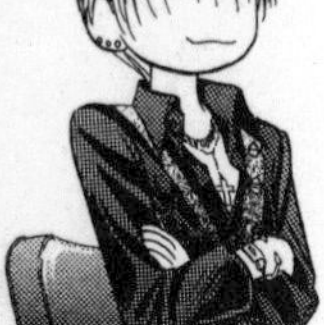

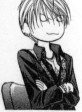

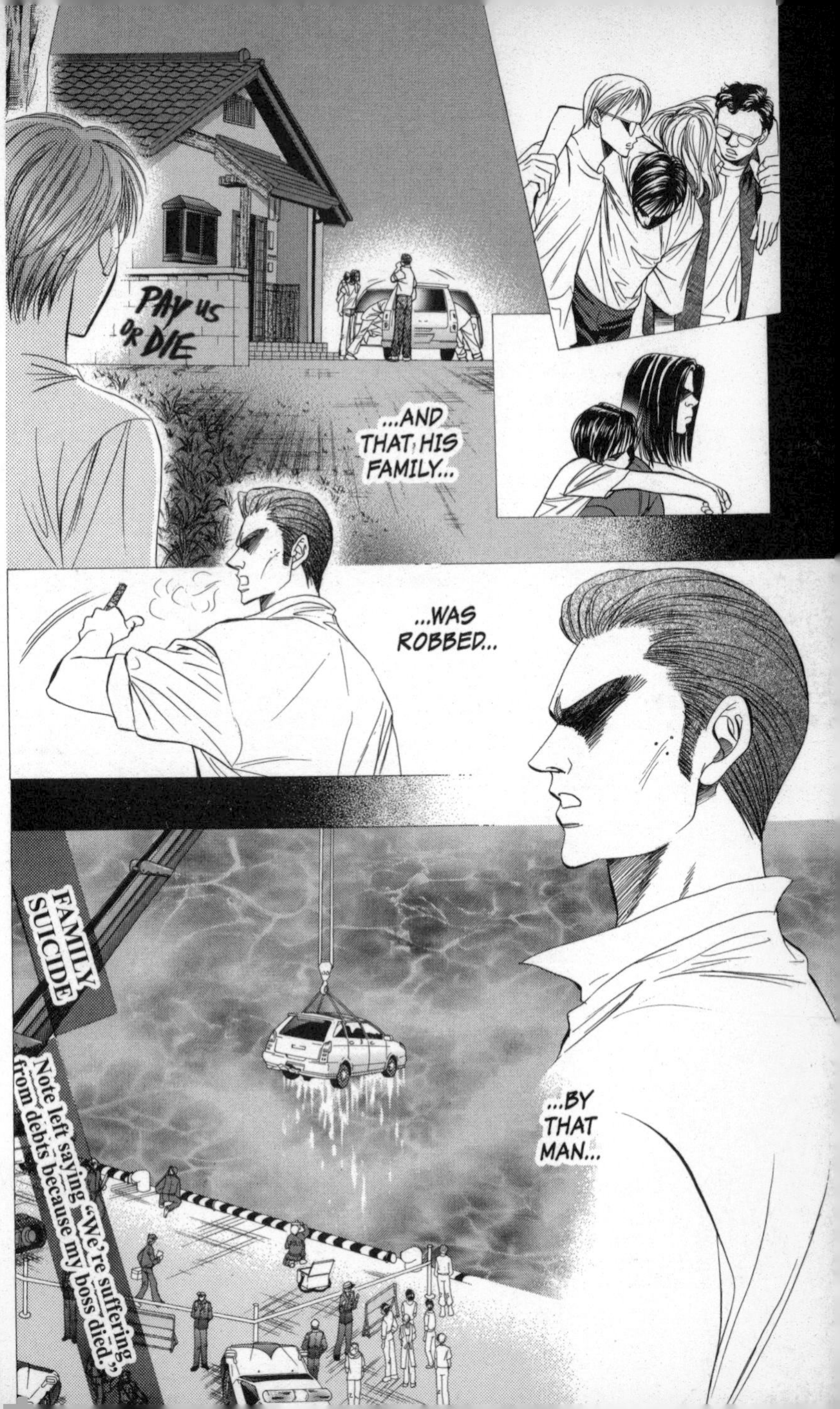
PAY US OR DIE
...AND THAT HIS FAMILY...
...WAS ROBBED...
...BY THAT MAN...
FAMILY SUICIDE
Note left saying "We're suffering from debts because my boss died."

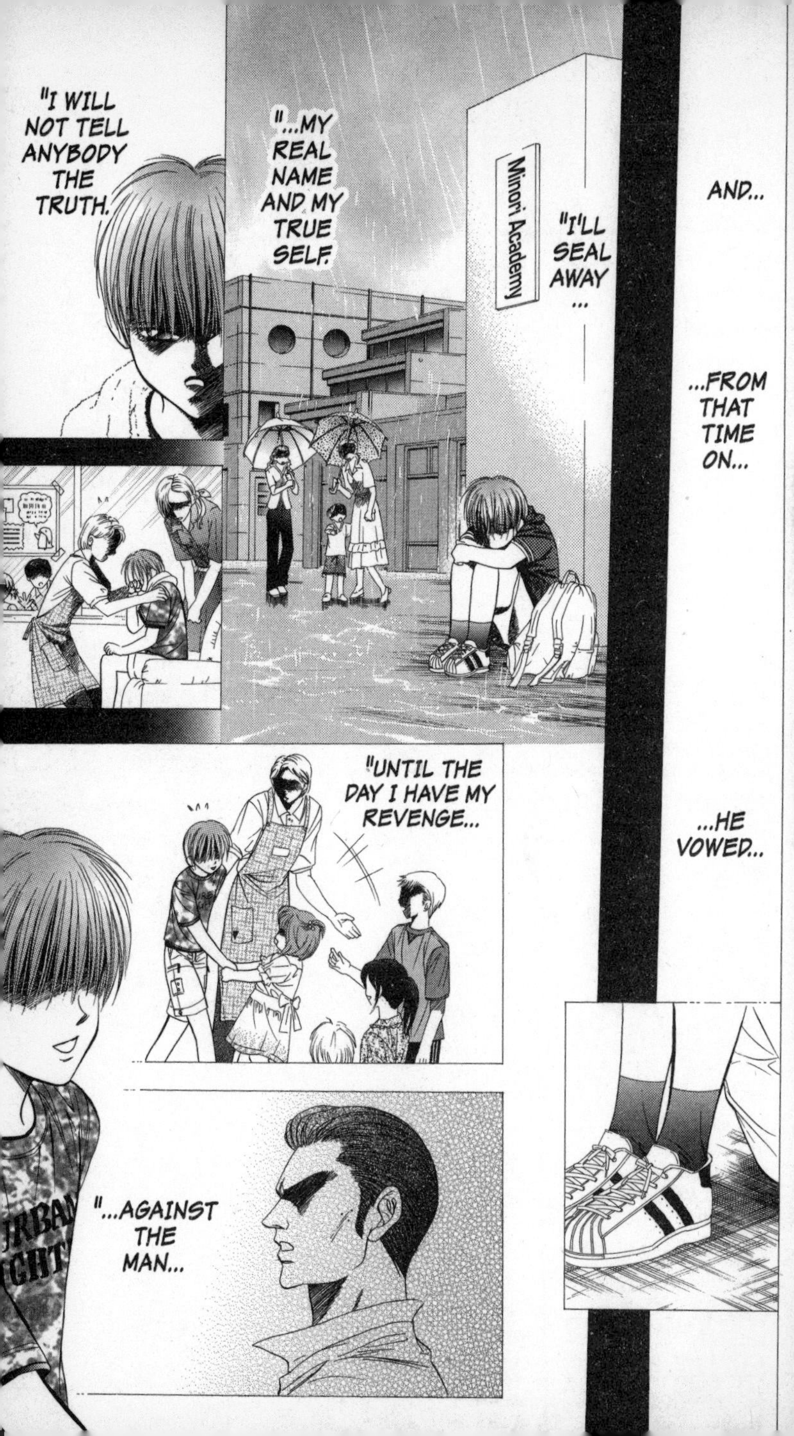

AND...
...FROM THAT TIME ON...
...HE VOWED...
Minori Academy
"I'LL SEAL AWAY...
"...MY REAL NAME AND MY TRUE SELF.
"I WILL NOT TELL ANYBODY THE TRUTH.
"UNTIL THE DAY I HAVE MY REVENGE...
"...AGAINST THE MAN...
URBAN
GHT

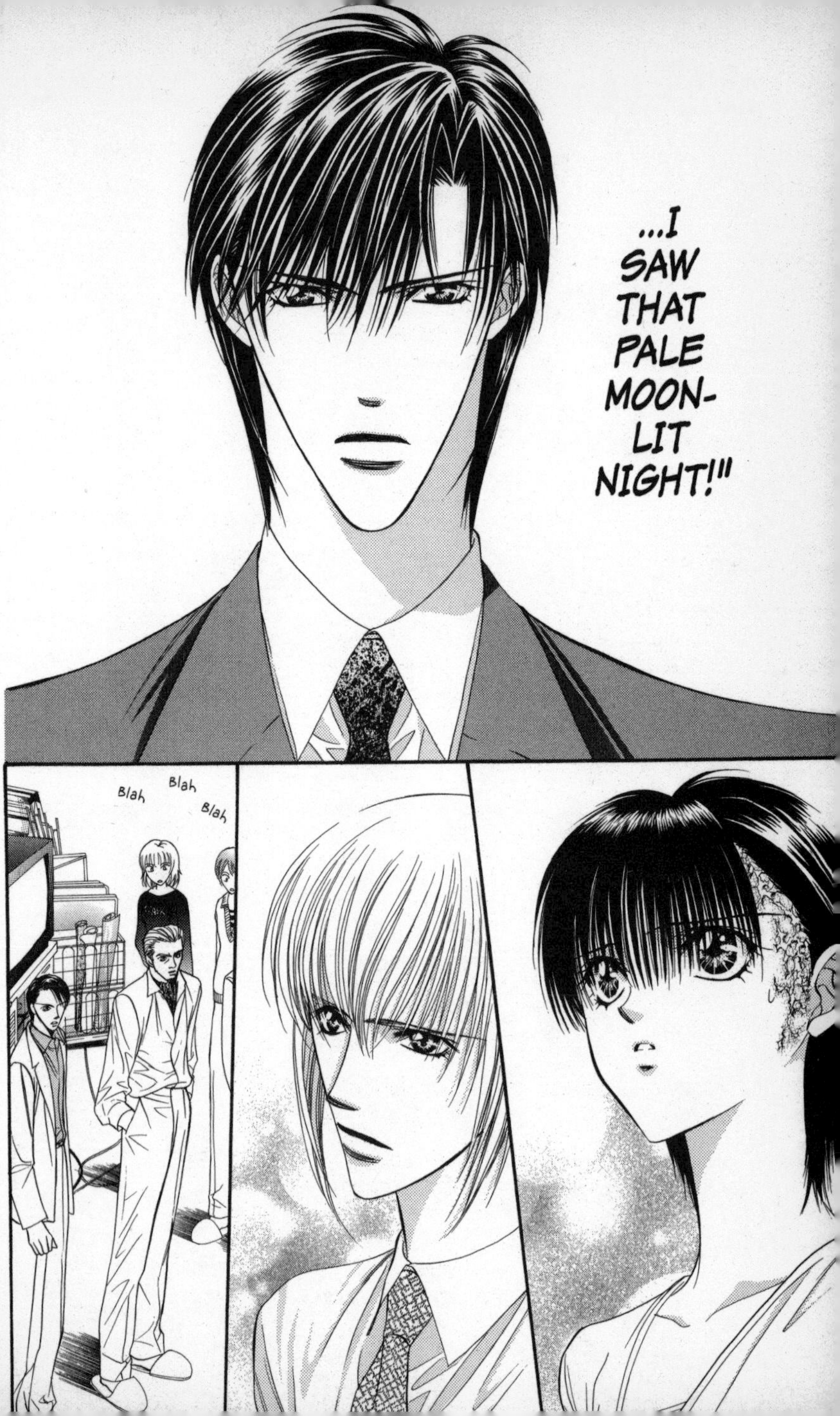
...I SAW THAT PALE MOON-LIT NIGHT!"
Blah
Blah
Blah

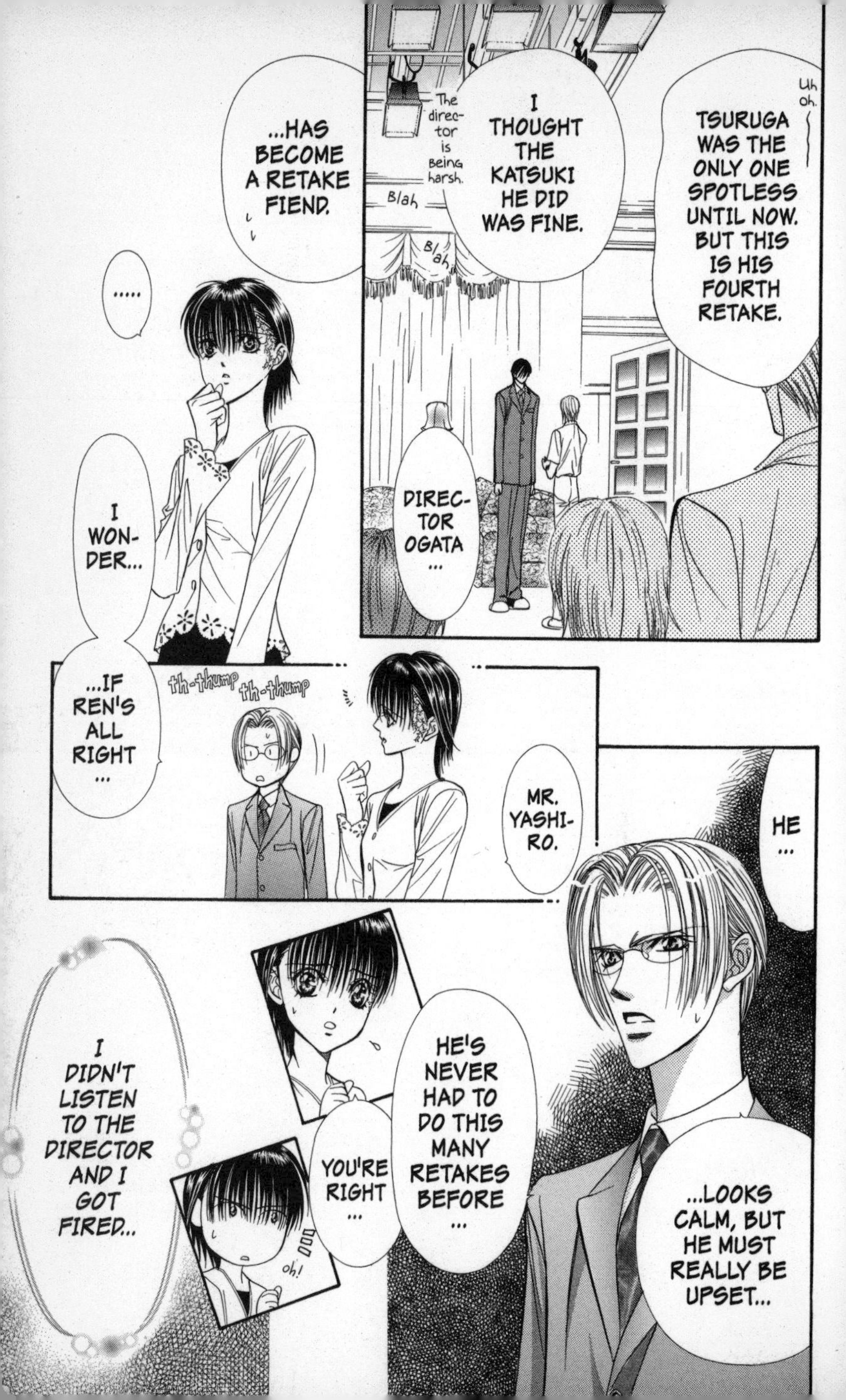
Uh oh.
TSURUGA WAS THE ONLY ONE SPOTLESS UNTIL NOW. BUT THIS IS HIS FOURTH RETAKE.
I THOUGHT THE KATSUKI HE DID WAS FINE.
The director is being harsh.
Blah
Blah
DIRECTOR OGATA...
...HAS BECOME A RETAKE FIEND.
.....
I WONDER...
...IF REN'S ALL RIGHT...
th-thump th-thump
MR. YASHIRO.
HE...
...LOOKS CALM, BUT HE MUST REALLY BE UPSET...
HE'S NEVER HAD TO DO THIS MANY RETAKES BEFORE...
YOU'RE RIGHT...
oh!
I DIDN'T LISTEN TO THE DIRECTOR AND I GOT FIRED...

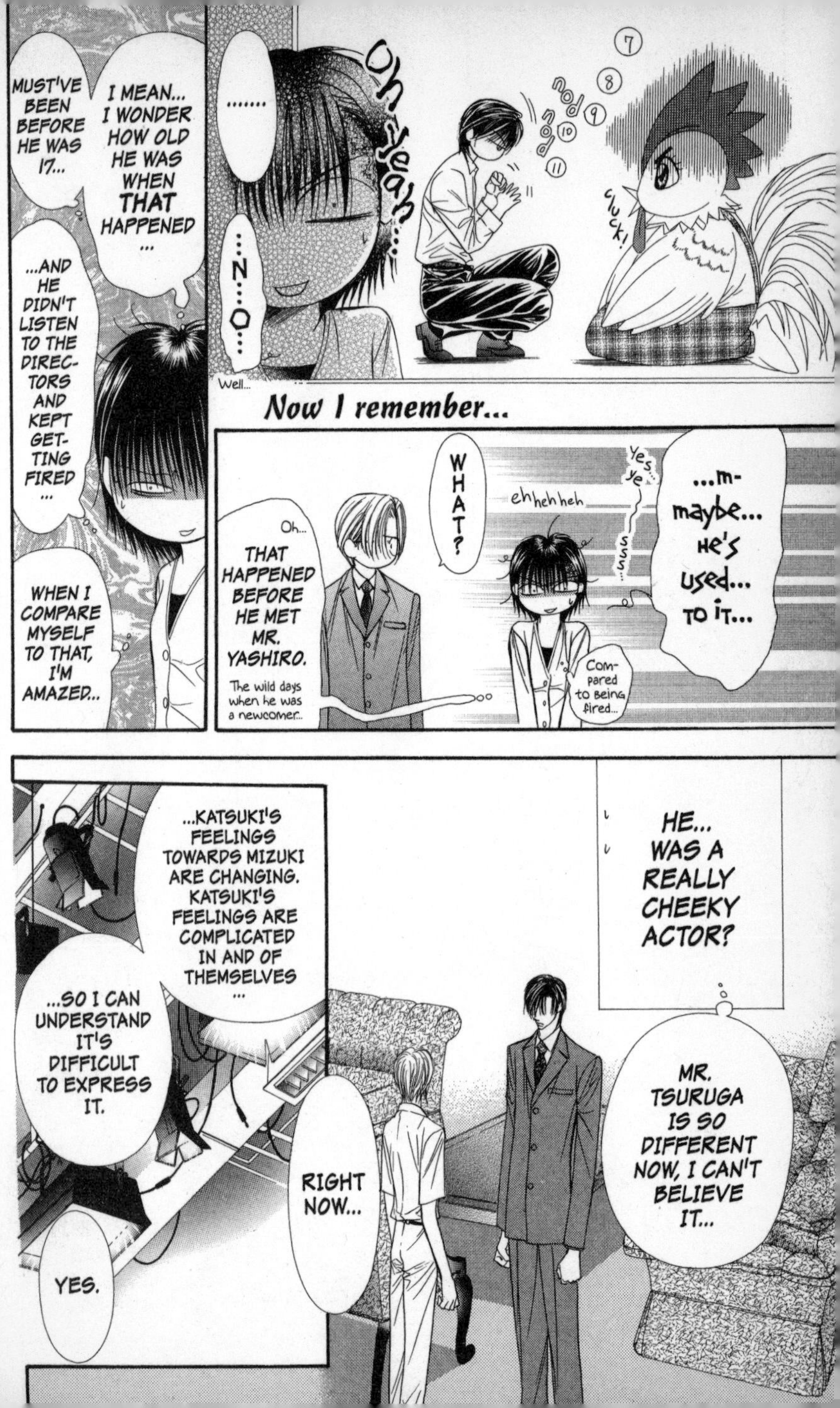
7
nod 8
nod 9
10
11
cluck!
Oh yeah...
....
...N...O...
Well...
Now I remember...
...m-maybe... he's used... to it...
Yes... ye sss...
ehhehheh
Compared to being fired...
WHAT?
Oh...
THAT HAPPENED BEFORE HE MET MR. YASHIRO.
The wild days when he was a newcomer...
I MEAN... I WONDER HOW OLD HE WAS WHEN THAT HAPPENED...
MUST'VE BEEN BEFORE HE WAS 17...
...AND HE DIDN'T LISTEN TO THE DIRECTORS AND KEPT GETTING FIRED...
WHEN I COMPARE MYSELF TO THAT, I'M AMAZED...
HE... WAS A REALLY CHEEKY ACTOR?
MR. TSURUGA IS SO DIFFERENT NOW, I CAN'T BELIEVE IT...
...KATSUKI'S FEELINGS TOWARDS MIZUKI ARE CHANGING. KATSUKI'S FEELINGS ARE COMPLICATED IN AND OF THEMSELVES...
...SO I CAN UNDERSTAND IT'S DIFFICULT TO EXPRESS IT.
RIGHT NOW...
YES.

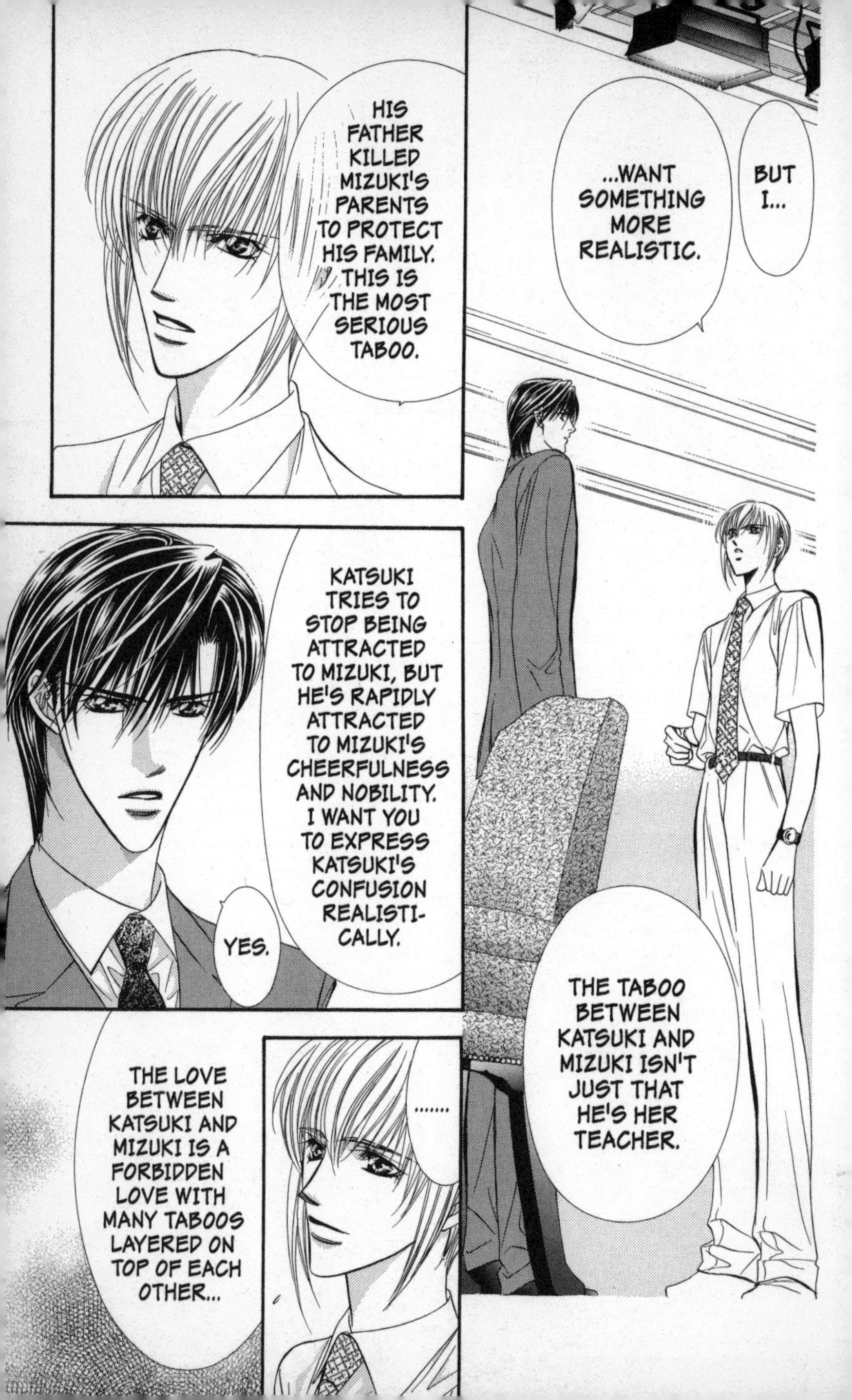

BUT I...
...WANT SOMETHING MORE REALISTIC.
THE TABOO BETWEEN KATSUKI AND MIZUKI ISN'T JUST THAT HE'S HER TEACHER.
HIS FATHER KILLED MIZUKI'S PARENTS TO PROTECT HIS FAMILY. THIS IS THE MOST SERIOUS TABOO.
KATSUKI TRIES TO STOP BEING ATTRACTED TO MIZUKI, BUT HE'S RAPIDLY ATTRACTED TO MIZUKI'S CHEERFULNESS AND NOBILITY. I WANT YOU TO EXPRESS KATSUKI'S CONFUSION REALISTI-CALLY.
YES.
....
THE LOVE BETWEEN KATSUKI AND MIZUKI IS A FORBIDDEN LOVE WITH MANY TABOOS LAYERED ON TOP OF EACH OTHER...

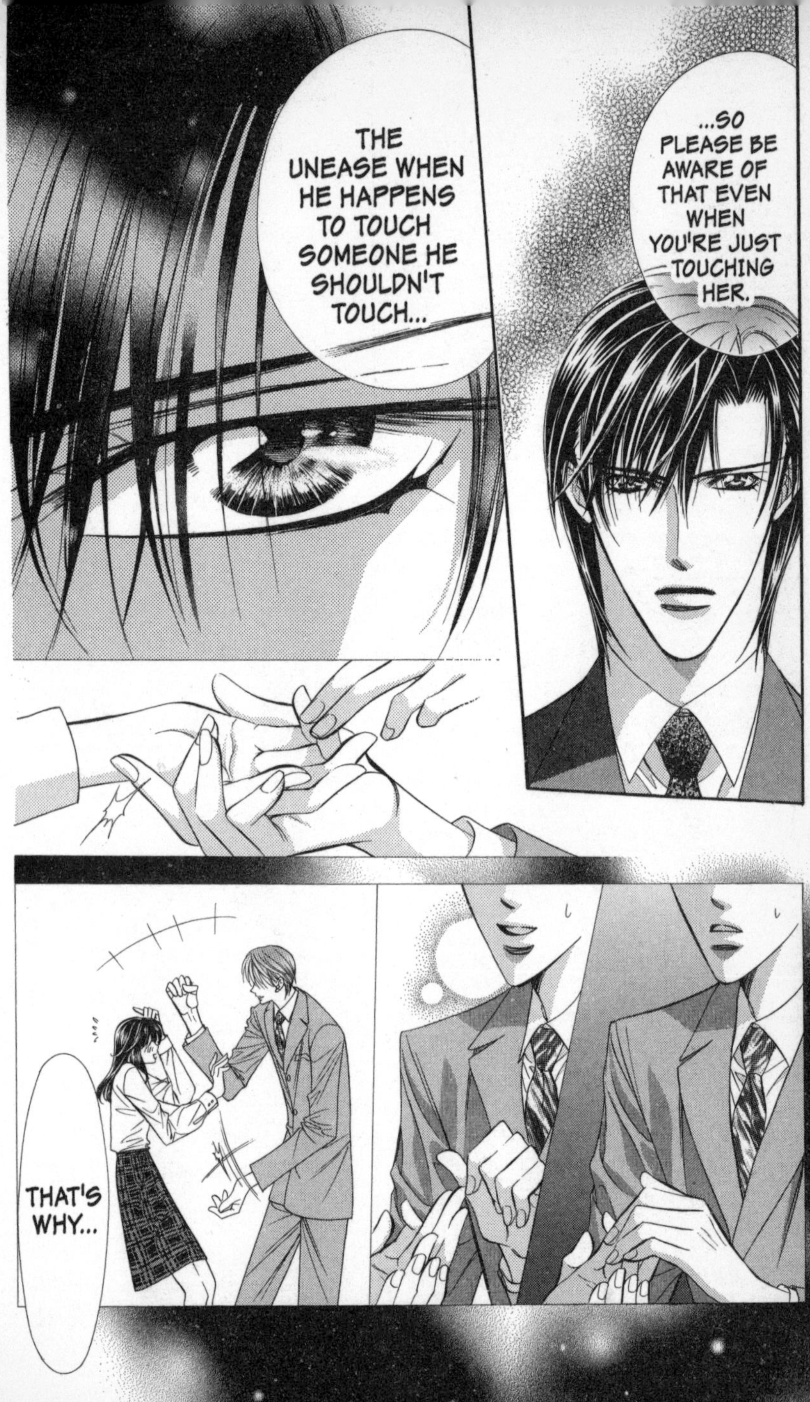
...SO PLEASE BE AWARE OF THAT EVEN WHEN YOU'RE JUST TOUCHING HER.
THE UNEASE WHEN HE HAPPENS TO TOUCH SOMEONE HE SHOULDN'T TOUCH...
THAT'S WHY...

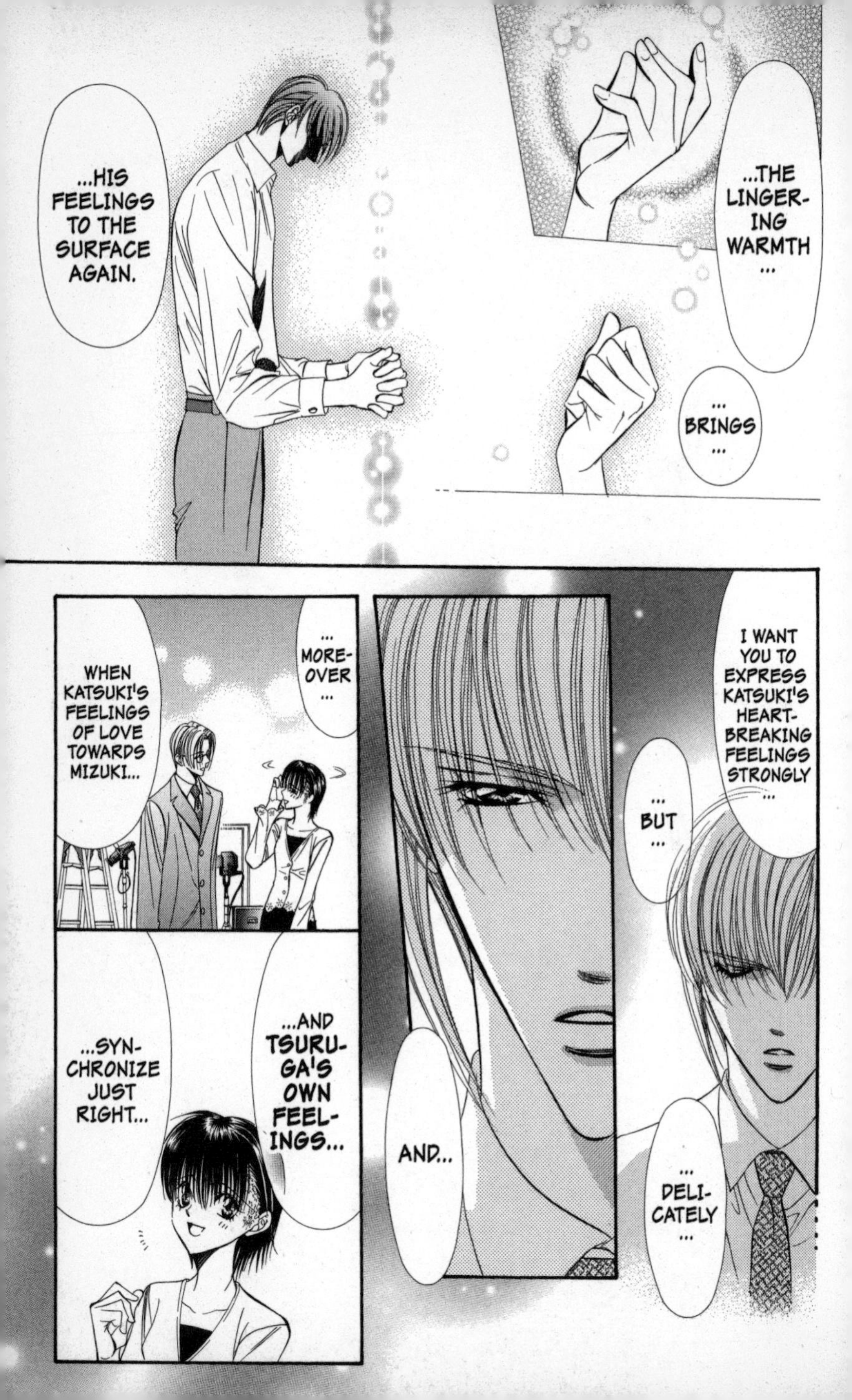
...THE LINGER-ING WARMTH...
...BRINGS...
...HIS FEELINGS TO THE SURFACE AGAIN.
I WANT YOU TO EXPRESS KATSUKI'S HEART-BREAKING FEELINGS STRONGLY...
...BUT...
...DELI-CATELY...
AND...
...MORE-OVER...
WHEN KATSUKI'S FEELINGS OF LOVE TOWARDS MIZUKI...
...AND TSURU-GA'S OWN FEEL-INGS...
...SYN-CHRONIZE JUST RIGHT...

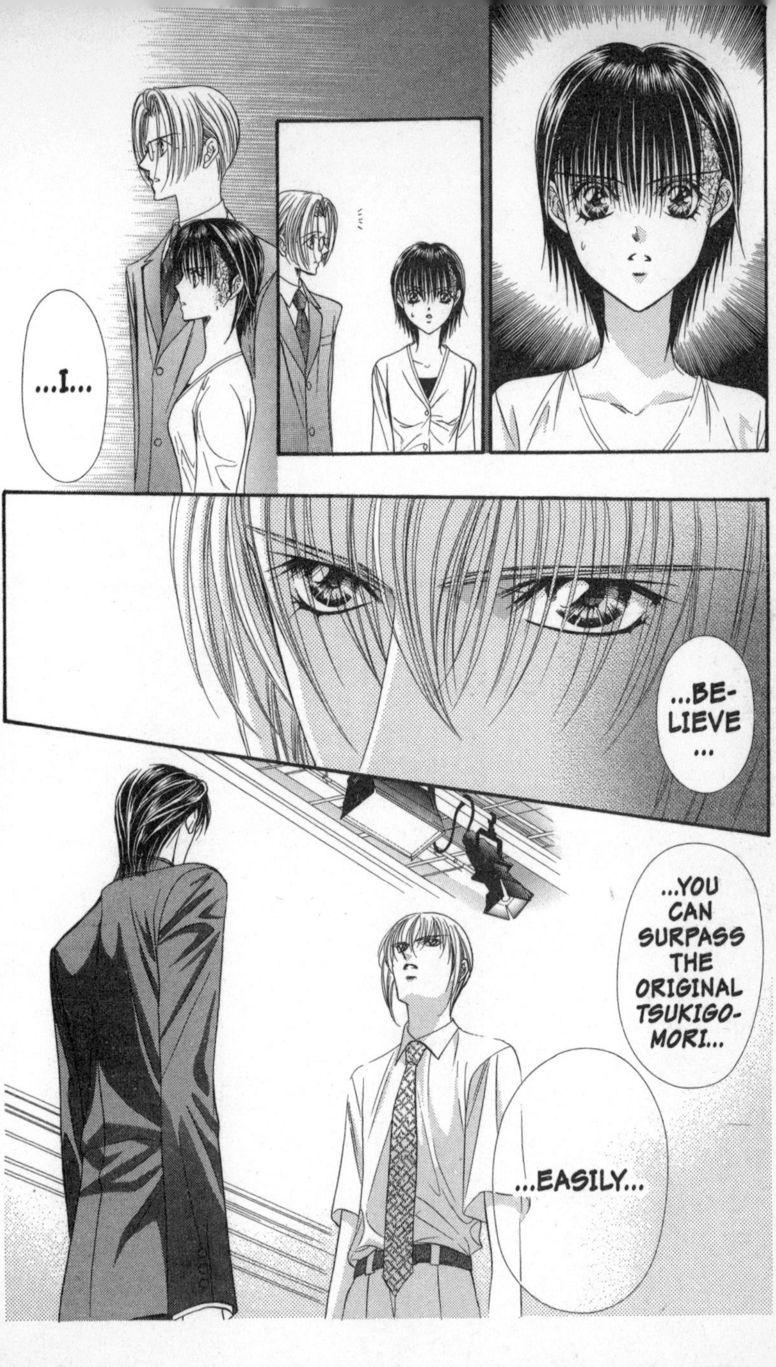
...I...
...BE-
LIEVE
...
...YOU
CAN
SURPASS
THE
ORIGINAL
TSUKIGO-
MORI...
...EASILY...

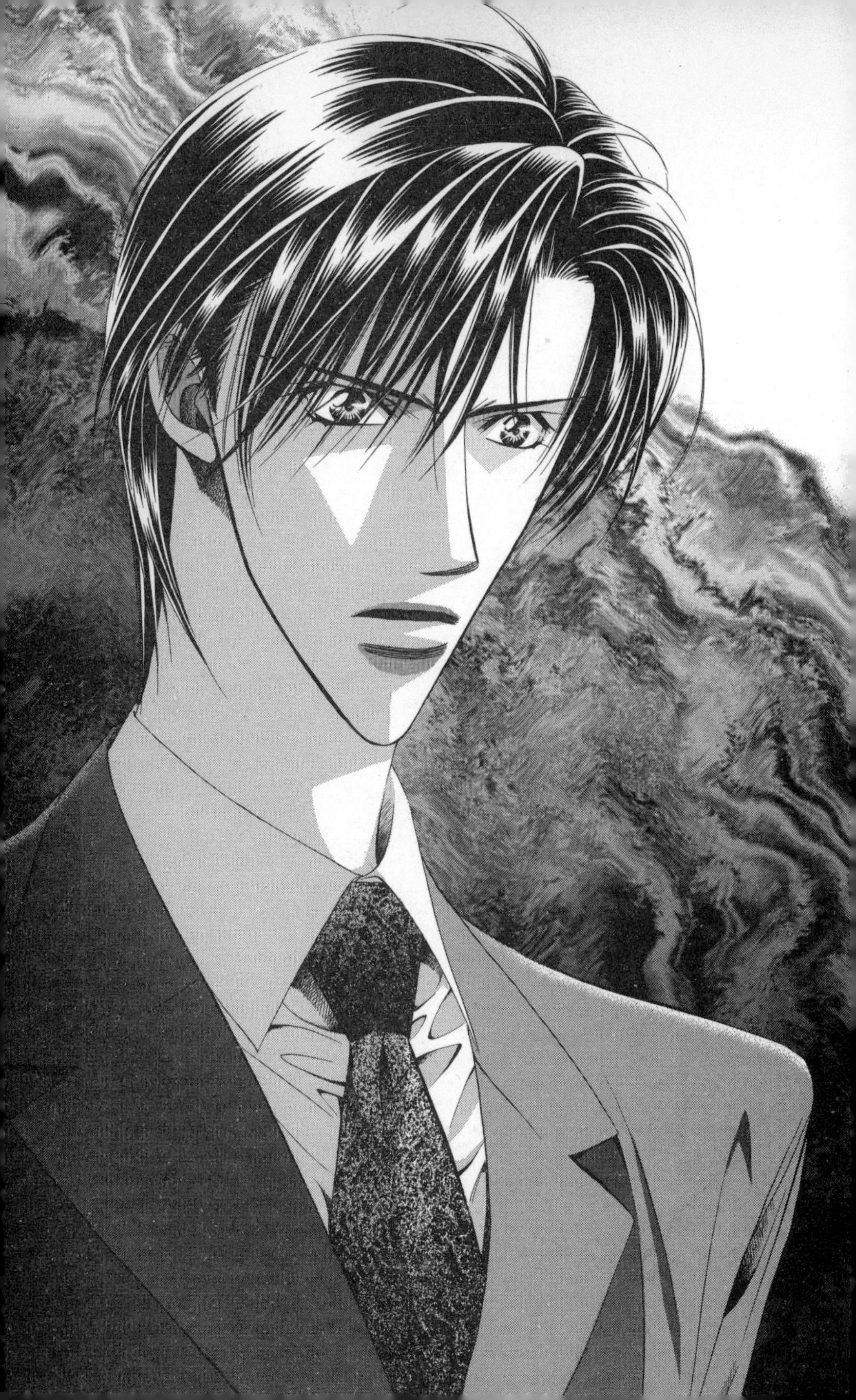

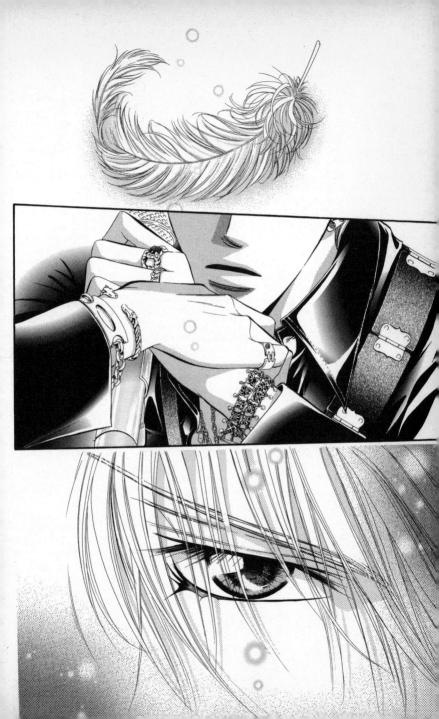

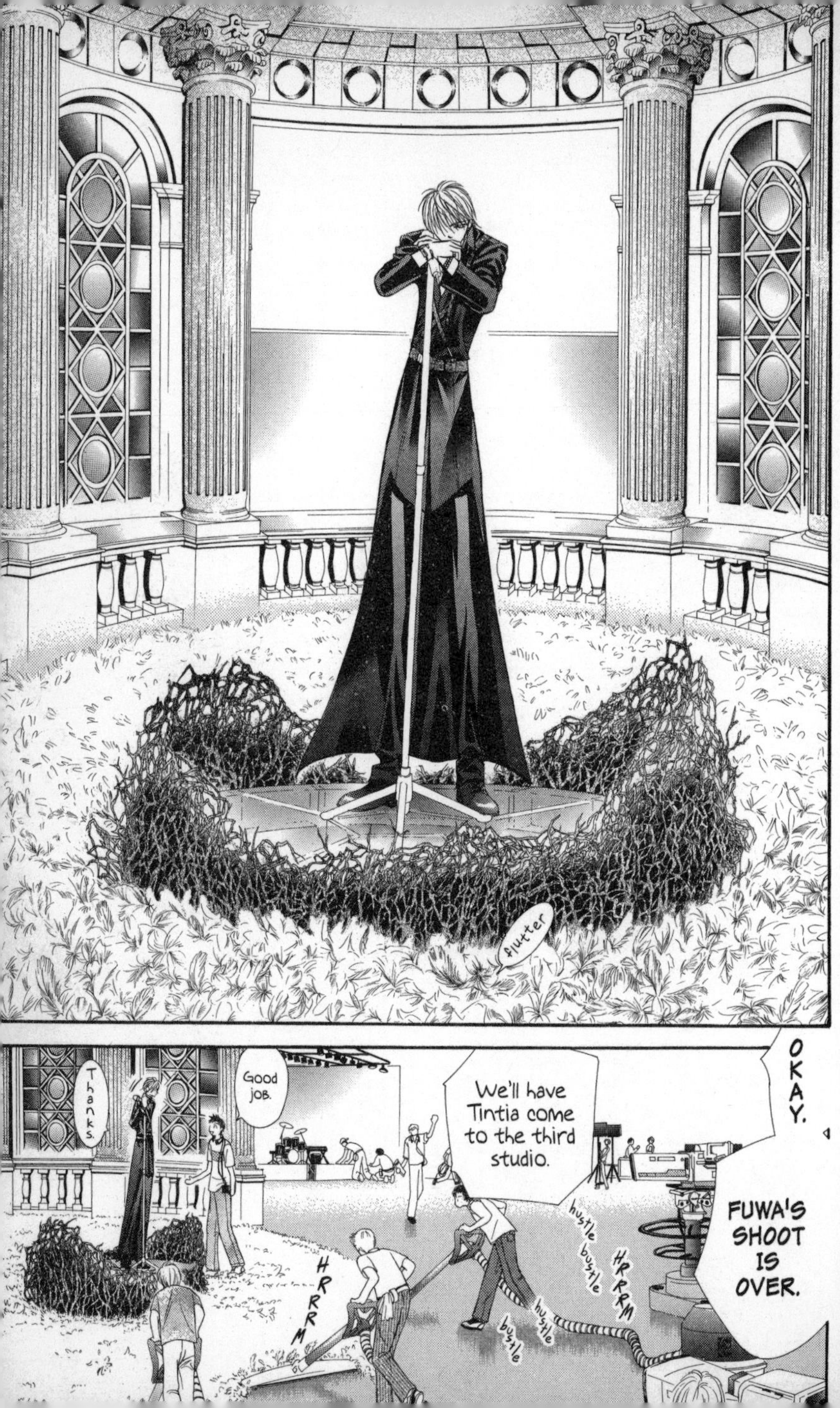
flutter
OKAY.
FUWA'S SHOOT IS OVER.
We'll have Tintia come to the third studio.
hustle bustle
HRRRM
hustle bustle
HRRRM
Good job.
Thanks.

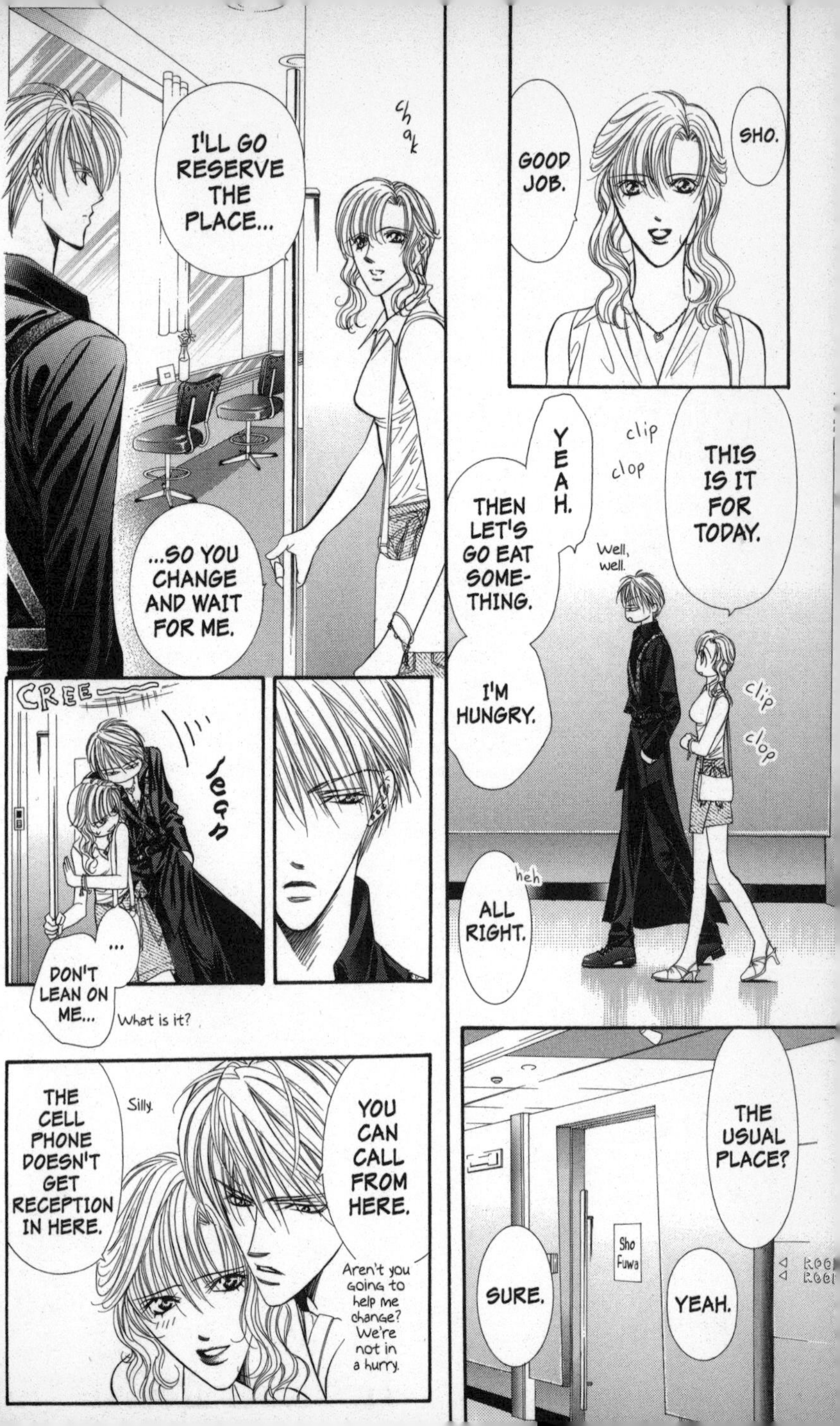

SHO.
GOOD JOB.
THIS IS IT FOR TODAY.
clip
clop
YEAH.
THEN LET'S GO EAT SOME-THING.
I'M HUNGRY.
Well, well.
clip
clop
heh
ALL RIGHT.
THE USUAL PLACE?
YEAH.
SURE.
Sho Fuwa
I'LL GO RESERVE THE PLACE...
chak
...SO YOU CHANGE AND WAIT FOR ME.
CREE
lean
...
DON'T LEAN ON ME...
What is it?
YOU CAN CALL FROM HERE.
THE CELL PHONE DOESN'T GET RECEPTION IN HERE.
Silly.
Aren't you going to help me change? We're not in a hurry.

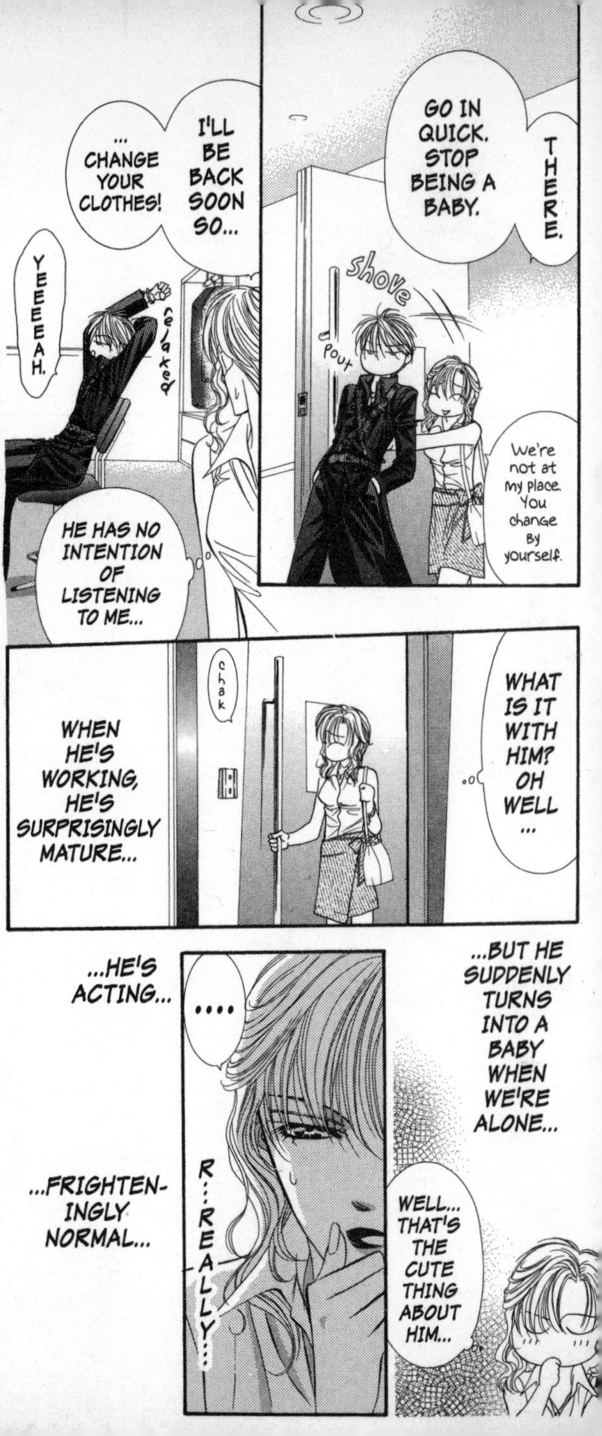
THERE.
GO IN QUICK. STOP BEING A BABY.
Shove
Pout
We're not at my place. You change by yourself.
I'LL BE BACK SOON SO...
...CHANGE YOUR CLOTHES!
YEEEEAH.
relaxed
HE HAS NO INTENTION OF LISTENING TO ME...
WHAT IS IT WITH HIM? OH WELL...
chak
WHEN HE'S WORKING, HE'S SURPRISINGLY MATURE...
...BUT HE SUDDENLY TURNS INTO A BABY WHEN WE'RE ALONE...
WELL... THAT'S THE CUTE THING ABOUT HIM...
....
R...REALLY...
...HE'S ACTING...
...FRIGHTENINGLY NORMAL...

Katsuki Tachibana

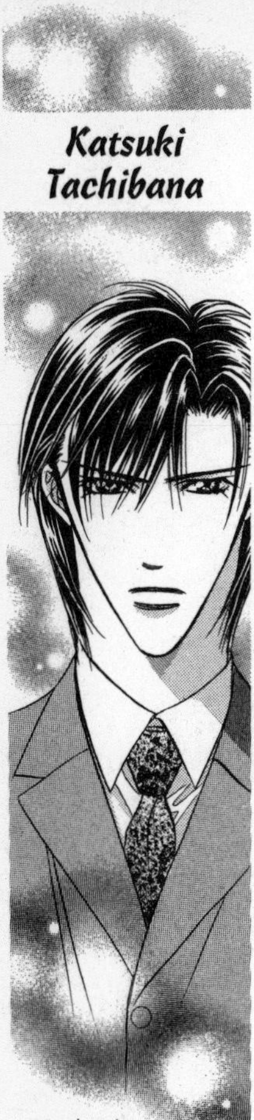

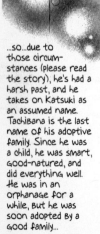

...so...due to those circumstances (please read the story), he's had a harsh past, and he takes on Katsuki as an assumed name. Tachibana is the last name of his adoptive family. Since he was a child, he was smart, good-natured, and did everything well. He was in an orphanage for a while, but he was soon adopted by a good family...

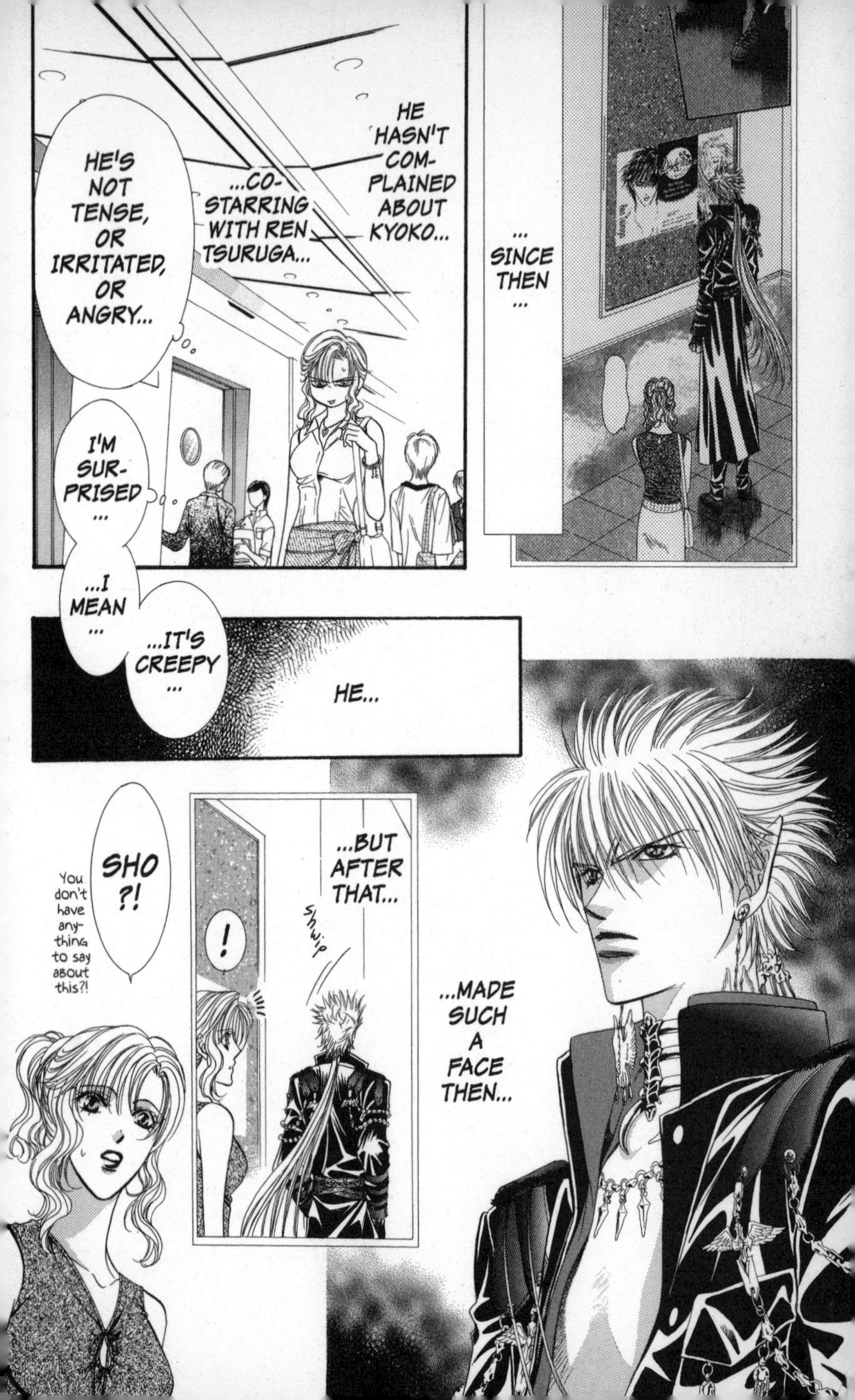
...SINCE THEN...
...
HE HASN'T COMPLAINED ABOUT KYOKO...
...CO-STARRING WITH REN TSURUGA...
HE'S NOT TENSE, OR IRRITATED, OR ANGRY...
I'M SURPRISED...
...I MEAN...
...IT'S CREEPY...
HE...
...BUT AFTER THAT...
!
shwip
...MADE SUCH A FACE THEN...
SHO?!
You don't have anything to say about this?!

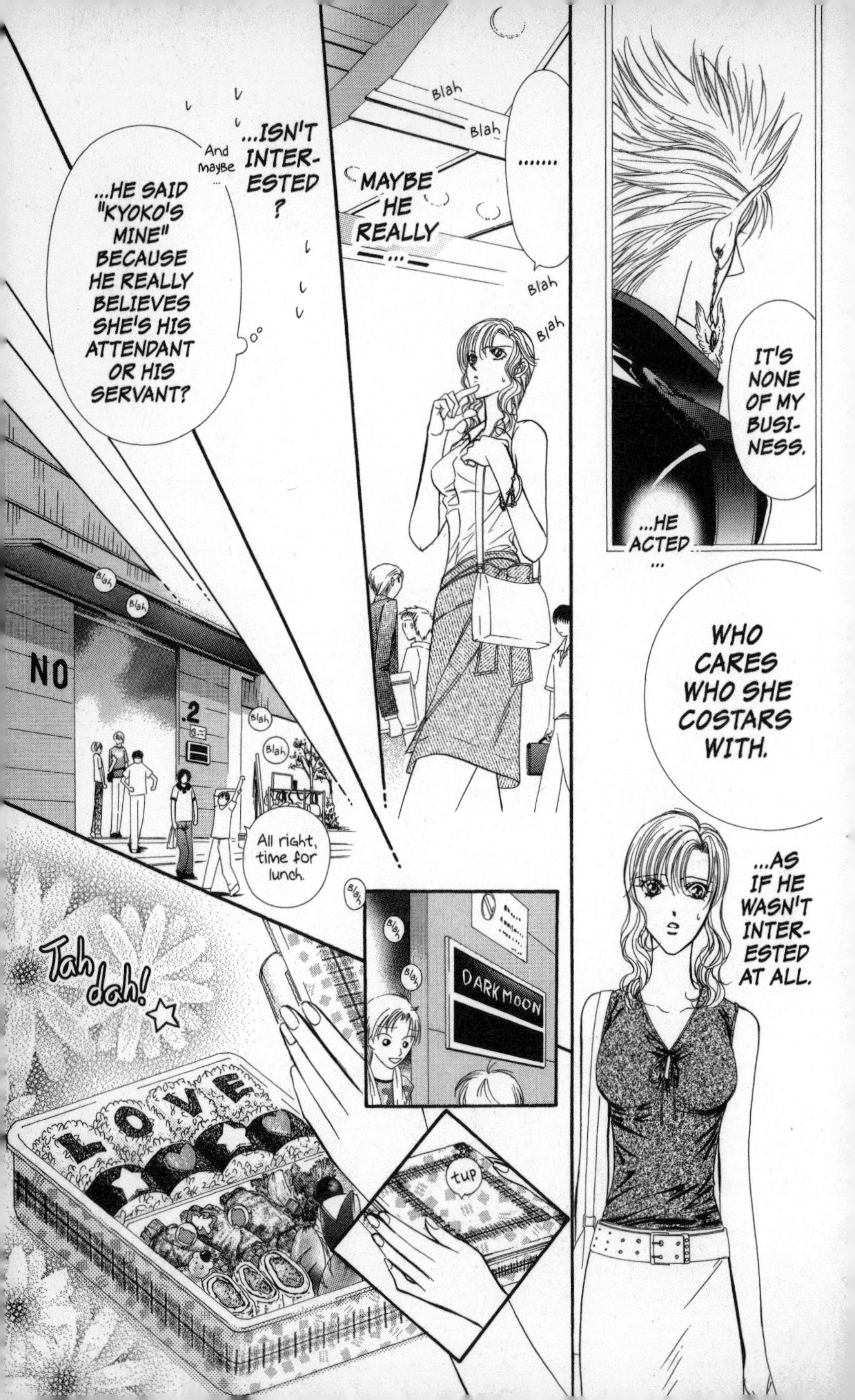
IT'S NONE OF MY BUSINESS.
...HE ACTED...
WHO CARES WHO SHE COSTARS WITH.
...AS IF HE WASN'T INTERESTED AT ALL.
Blah
Blah
......
Blah
Blah
MAYBE HE REALLY—...
...ISN'T INTERESTED?
And maybe...
...HE SAID "KYOKO'S MINE" BECAUSE HE REALLY BELIEVES SHE'S HIS ATTENDANT OR HIS SERVANT?
NO
Blah
Blah
Blah
Blah
All right, time for lunch.
Blah
Blah
Blah
DARK MOON
tup
Tah dah!
LOVE

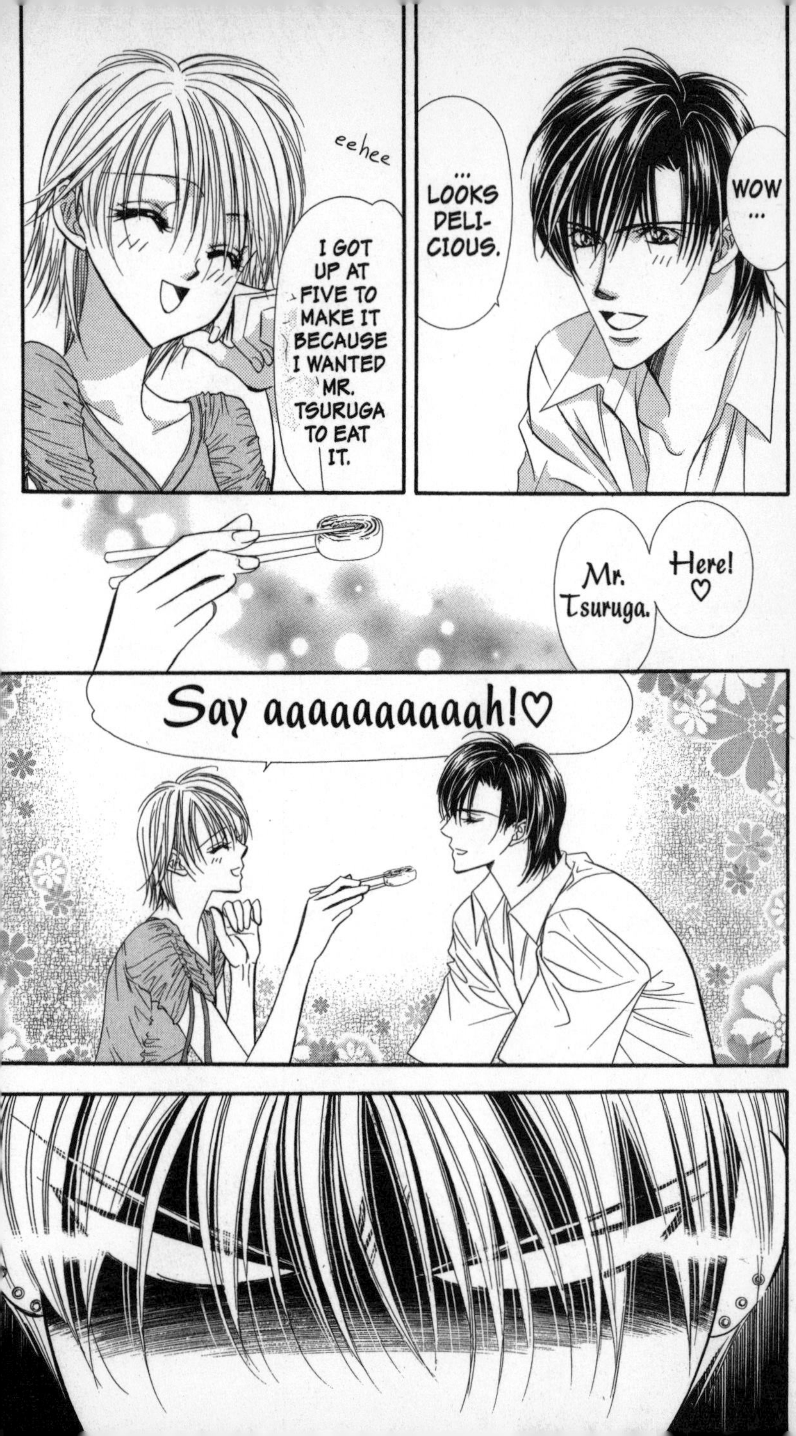
WOW ...
... LOOKS DELI- CIOUS.
eehee
I GOT UP AT FIVE TO MAKE IT BECAUSE I WANTED MR. TSURUGA TO EAT IT.
Here! ♡
Mr. Tsuruga.
Say aaaaaaaaaah!♡

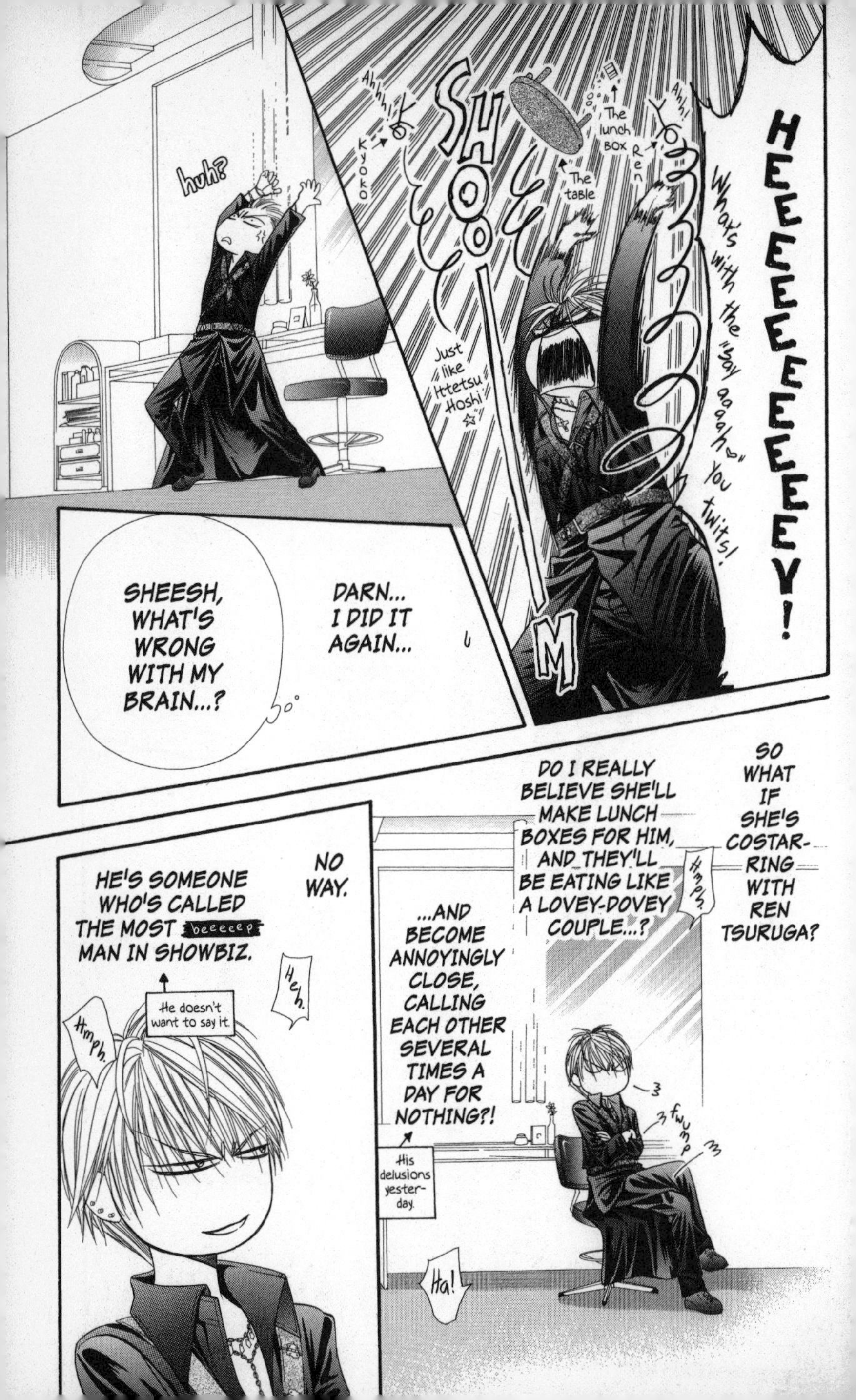
HEEEEEEEEEY!
What's with the "say aaaah♥" you twits!
Ahh! Ren
The lunch box
The table
Ahhh! Kyoko
SHOOOM
Just like Ittetsu Hoshi ☆
huh?
DARN... I DID IT AGAIN...
SHEESH, WHAT'S WRONG WITH MY BRAIN...?
SO WHAT IF SHE'S COSTARRING WITH REN TSURUGA?
Hmph.
DO I REALLY BELIEVE SHE'LL MAKE LUNCH BOXES FOR HIM, AND THEY'LL BE EATING LIKE A LOVEY-DOVEY COUPLE...?
...AND BECOME ANNOYINGLY CLOSE, CALLING EACH OTHER SEVERAL TIMES A DAY FOR NOTHING?!
His delusions yesterday.
fwump
Ha!
NO WAY.
HE'S SOMEONE WHO'S CALLED THE MOST beeeeep MAN IN SHOWBIZ.
Heh.
He doesn't want to say it.
Hmph.

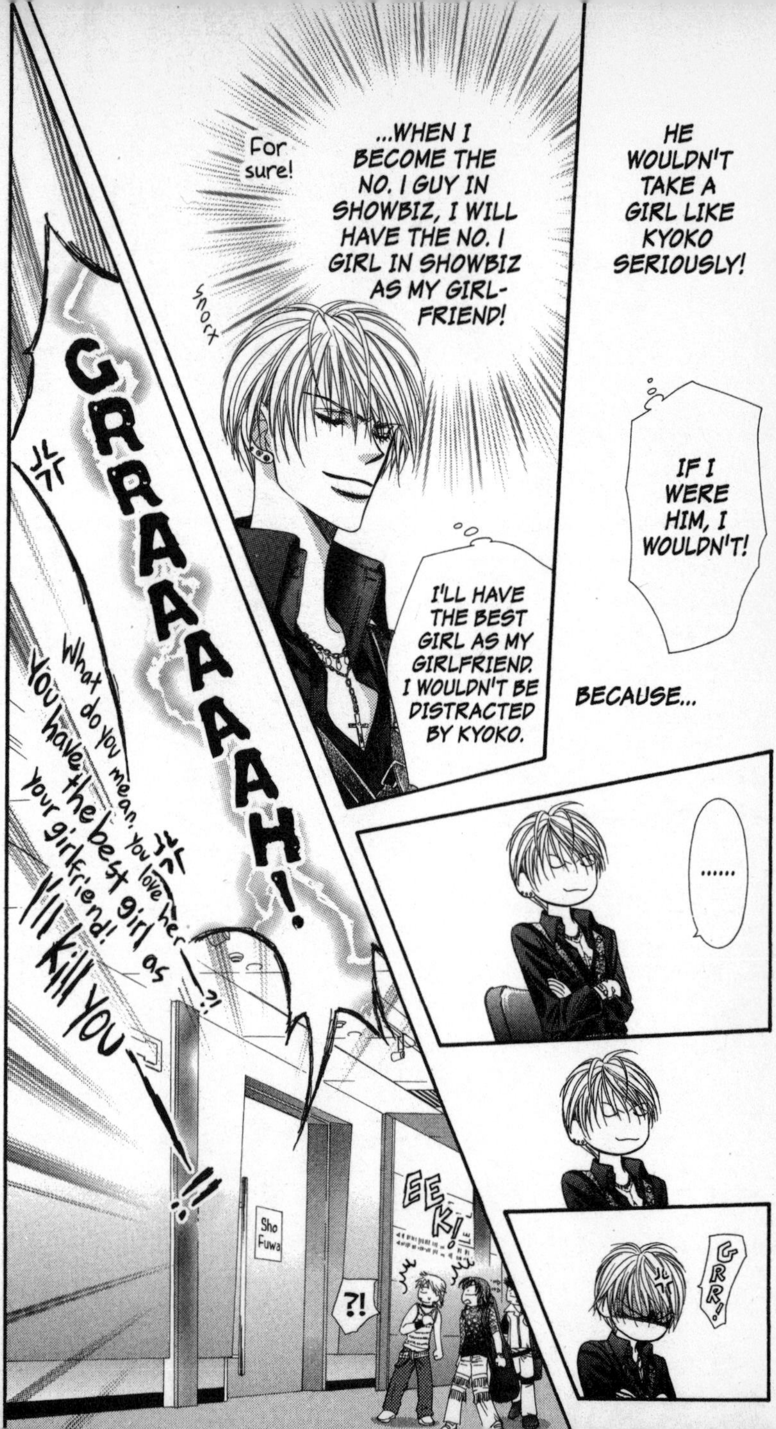

HE WOULDN'T TAKE A GIRL LIKE KYOKO SERIOUSLY!
IF I WERE HIM, I WOULDN'T!
BECAUSE...
...WHEN I BECOME THE NO. 1 GUY IN SHOWBIZ, I WILL HAVE THE NO. 1 GIRL IN SHOWBIZ AS MY GIRLFRIEND!
For sure!
snort
I'LL HAVE THE BEST GIRL AS MY GIRLFRIEND. I WOULDN'T BE DISTRACTED BY KYOKO.
......
GRR!
GRAAAAAH!
What do you mean, you love her...?!
You have the best girl as your girlfriend!
I'll kill you!!
EEK!
?!
Sho Fuwa

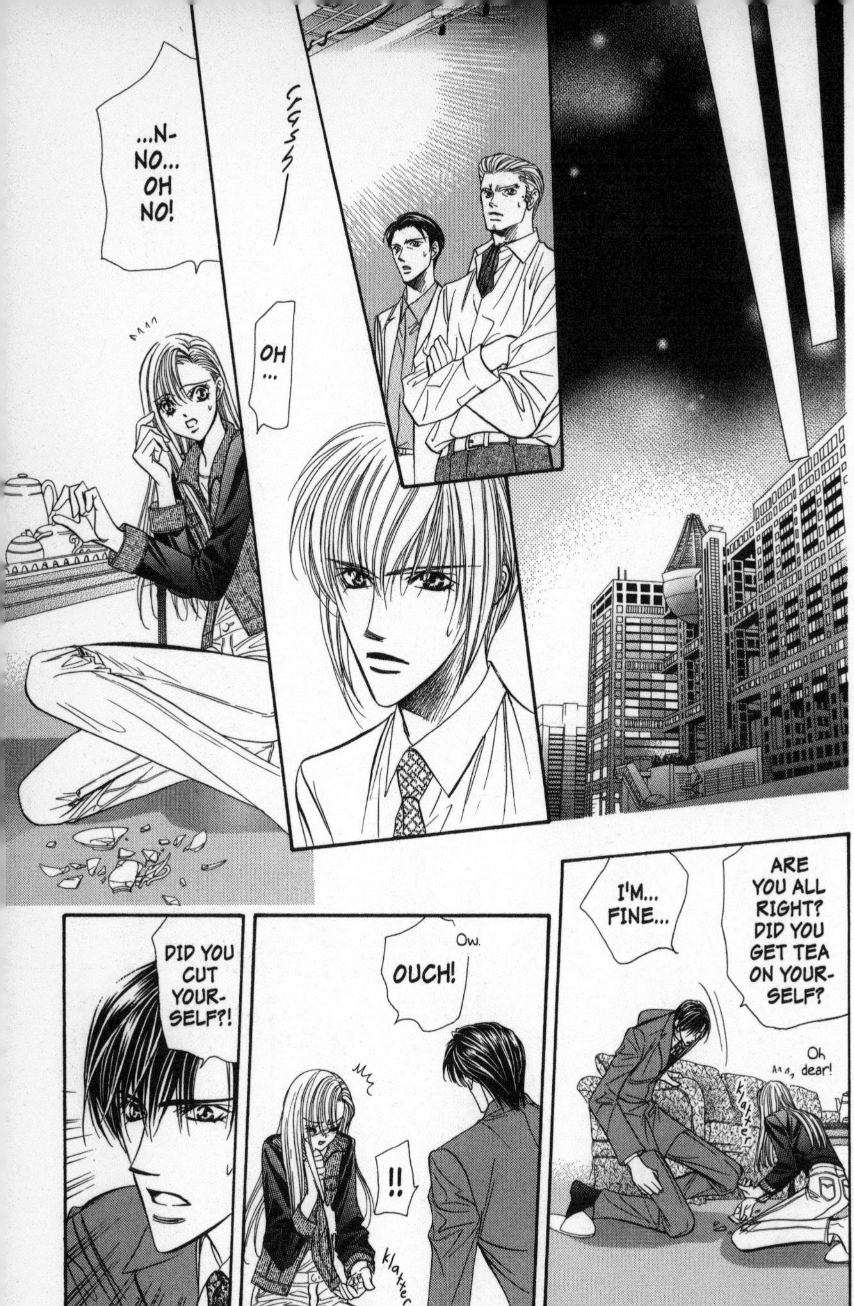
OH ...
...N- NO... OH NO!
ARE YOU ALL RIGHT? DID YOU GET TEA ON YOURSELF?
I'M... FINE...
Oh dear!
klatter
Ow.
OUCH!
!!
klatter
DID YOU CUT YOURSELF?!

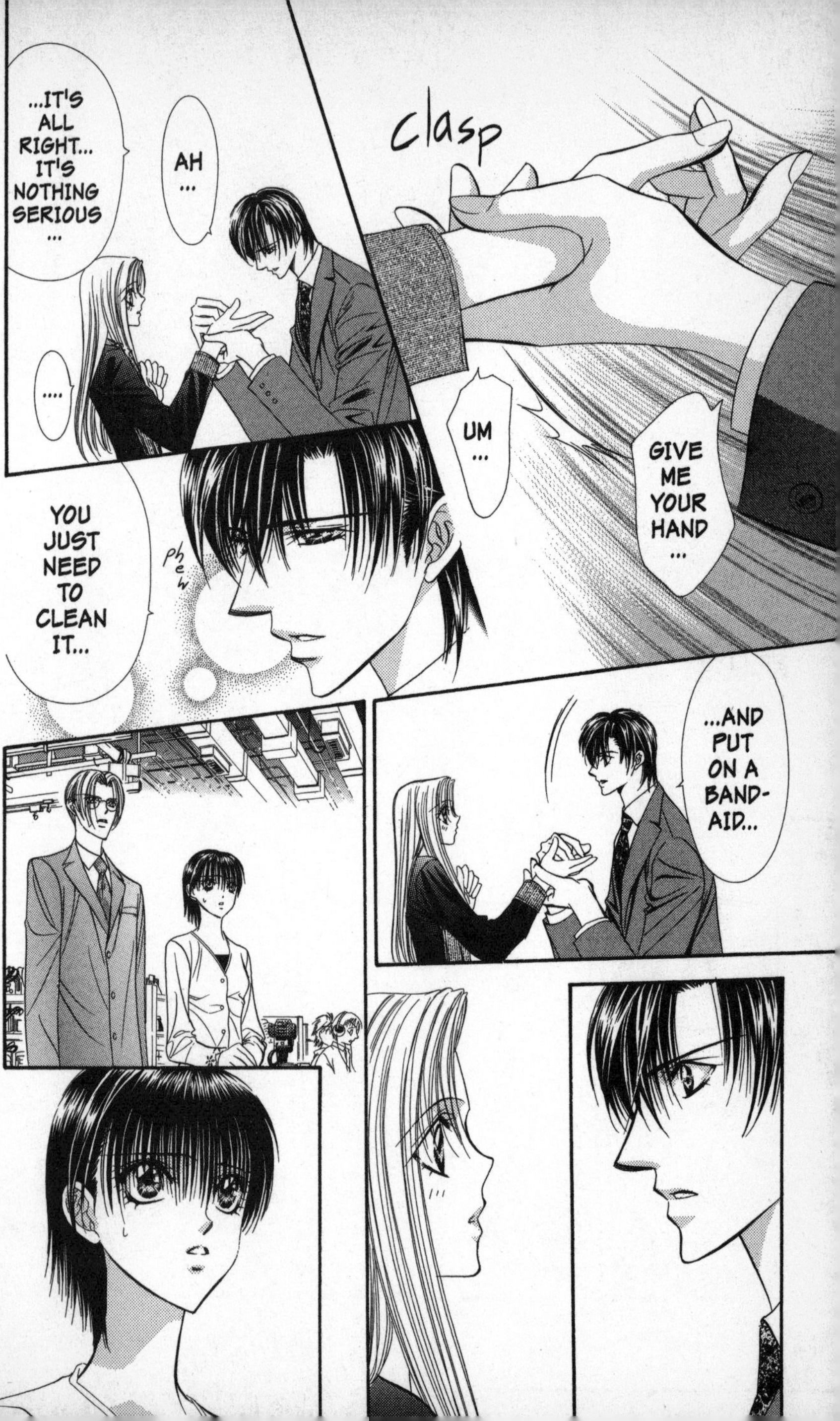
clasp
GIVE ME YOUR HAND ...
UM ...
AH ...
...IT'S ALL RIGHT... IT'S NOTHING SERIOUS ...
....
phew
YOU JUST NEED TO CLEAN IT...
...AND PUT ON A BAND-AID...

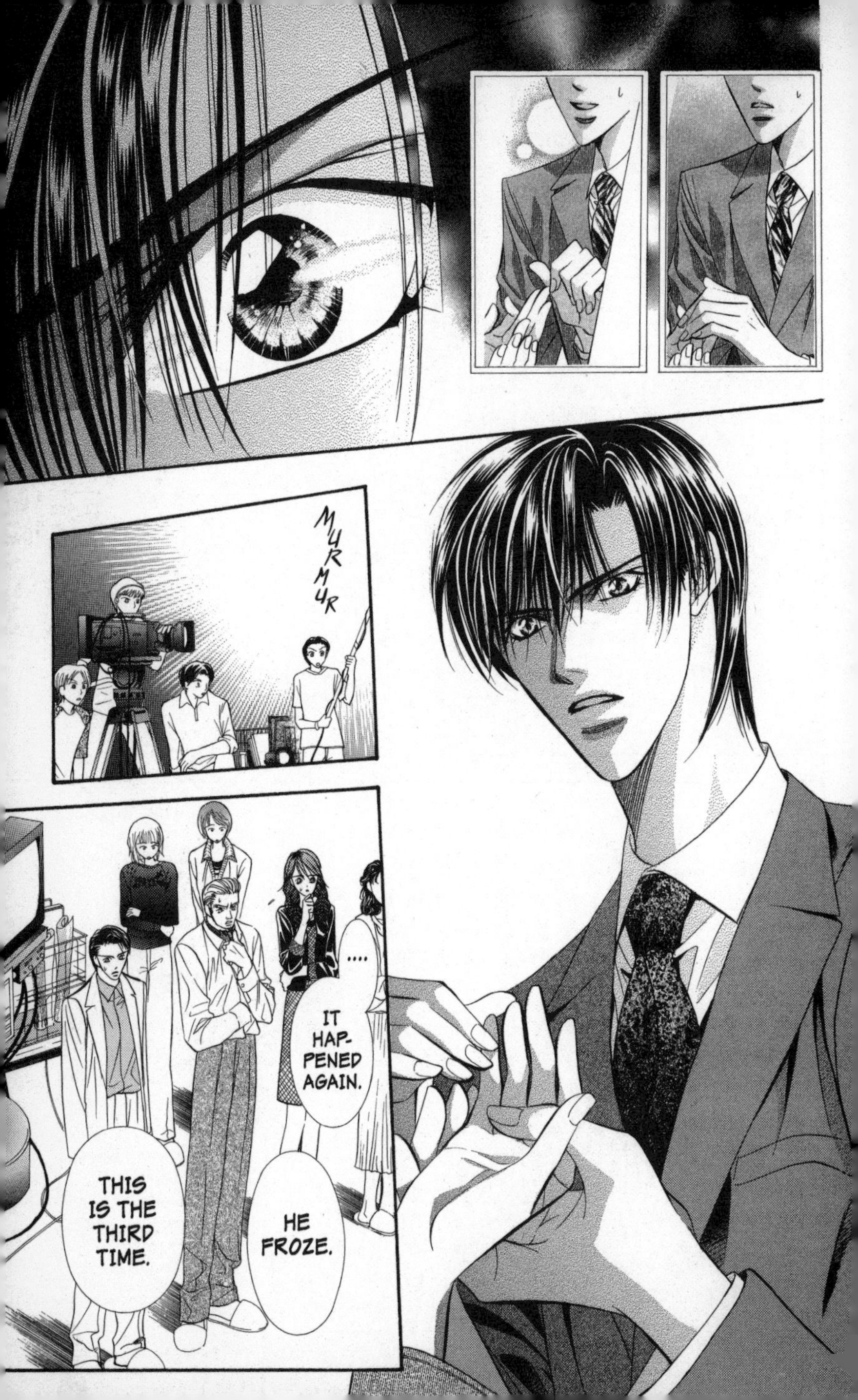
MURMUR
....
IT HAPPENED AGAIN.
HE FROZE.
THIS IS THE THIRD TIME.

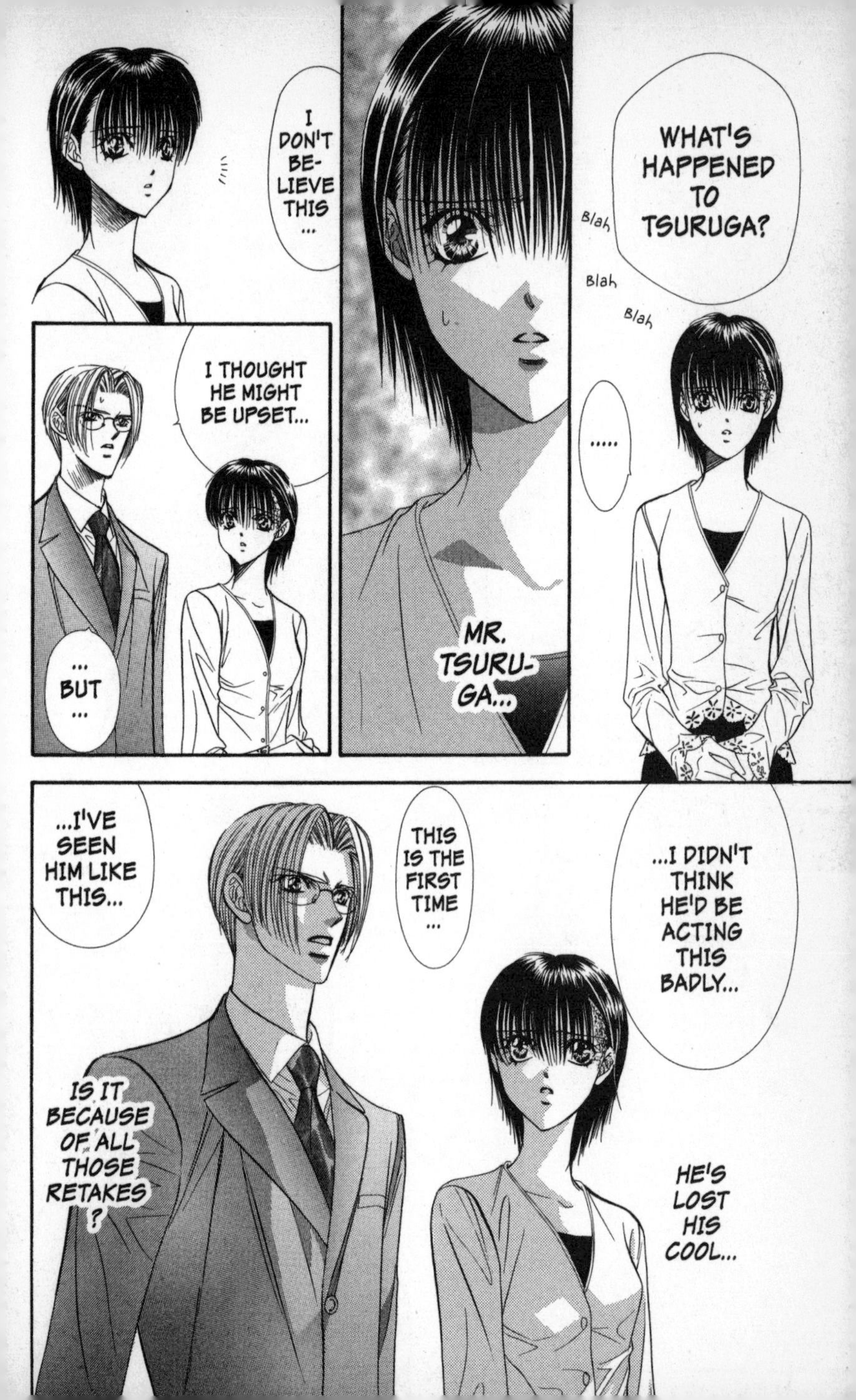

WHAT'S HAPPENED TO TSURUGA?
Blah
Blah
Blah
.....
MR. TSURUGA...
I DON'T BE-LIEVE THIS ...
I THOUGHT HE MIGHT BE UPSET...
... BUT ...
...I DIDN'T THINK HE'D BE ACTING THIS BADLY...
HE'S LOST HIS COOL...
THIS IS THE FIRST TIME ...
...I'VE SEEN HIM LIKE THIS...
IS IT BECAUSE OF ALL THOSE RETAKES?

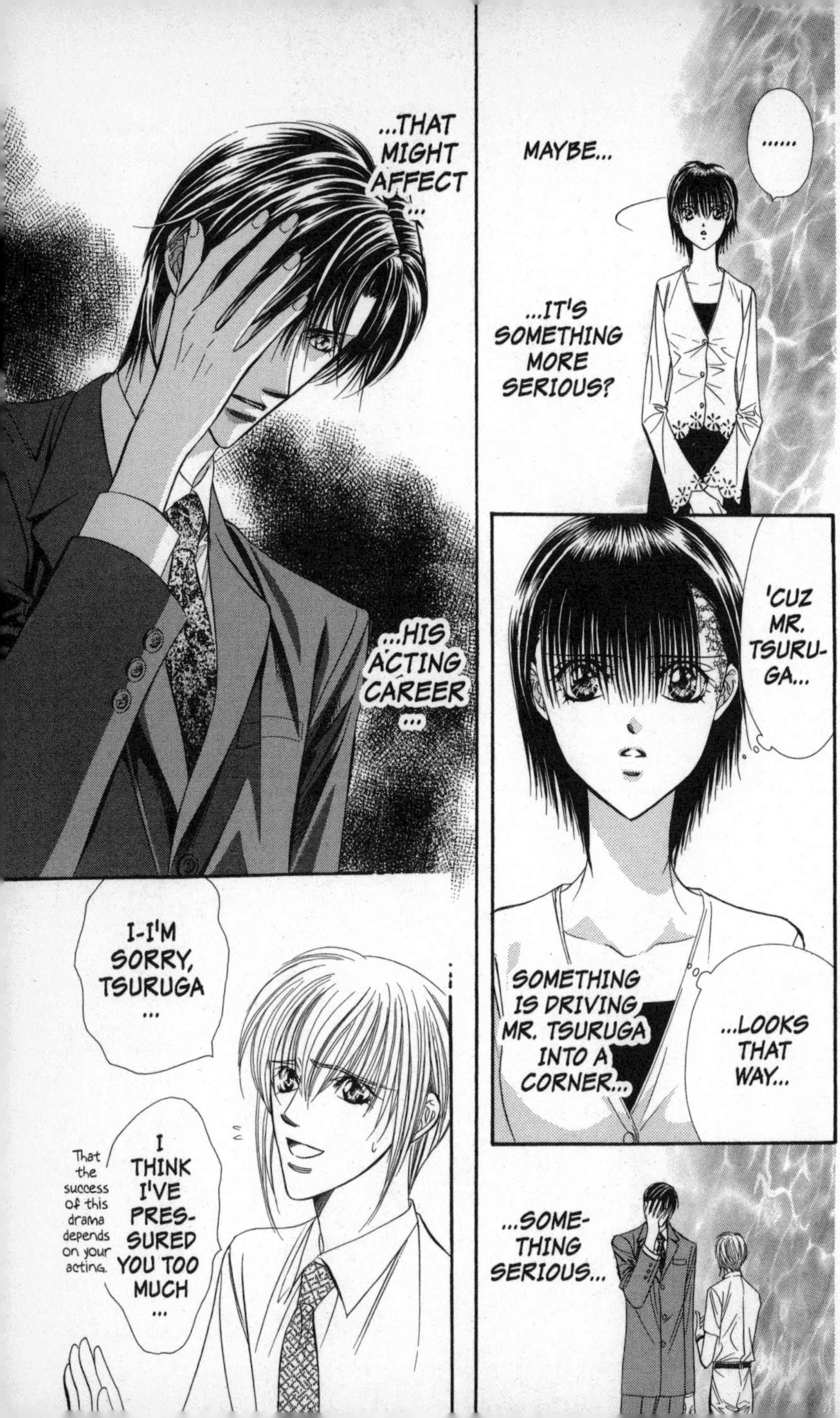
......
MAYBE...
...IT'S SOMETHING MORE SERIOUS?
'CUZ MR. TSURU-GA...
...LOOKS THAT WAY...
SOMETHING IS DRIVING MR. TSURUGA INTO A CORNER...
...SOME-THING SERIOUS...
...THAT MIGHT AFFECT...
...HIS ACTING CAREER...
I-I'M SORRY, TSURUGA...
I THINK I'VE PRES-SURED YOU TOO MUCH...
That the success of this drama depends on your acting.

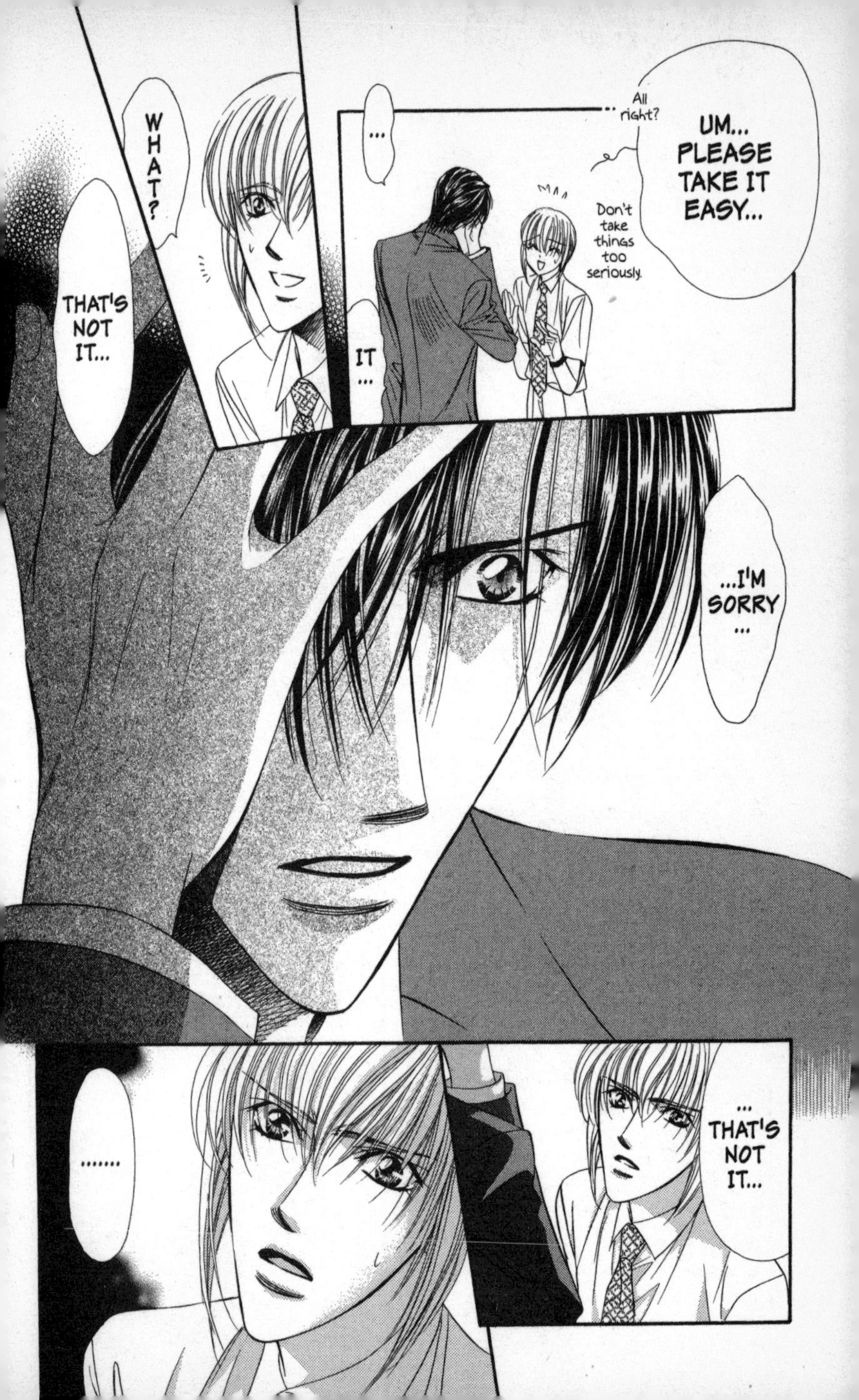
UM... PLEASE TAKE IT EASY...
All right?
Don't take things too seriously.
...
IT ...
WHAT?
THAT'S NOT IT...
...I'M SORRY ...
... THAT'S NOT IT...
....

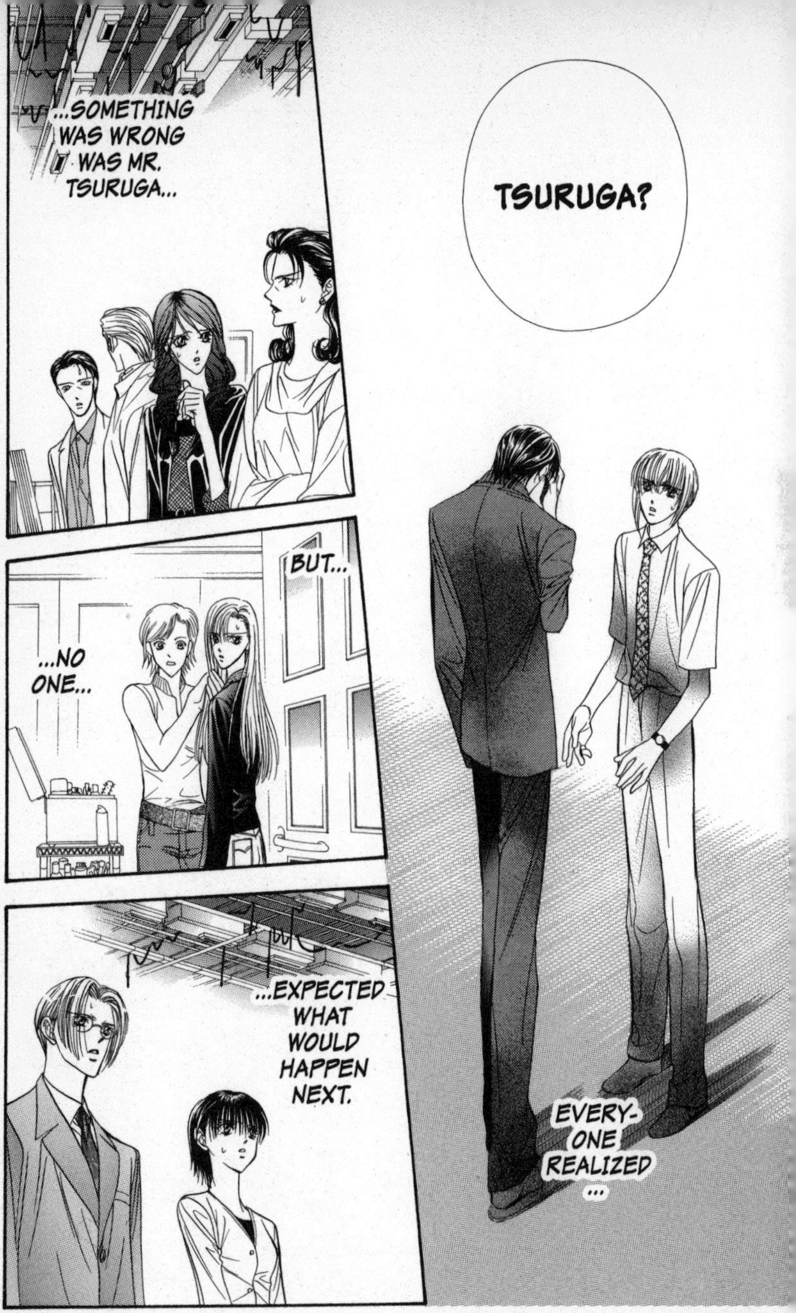
TSURUGA?
EVERY-ONE REALIZED...
...SOMETHING WAS WRONG WAS MR. TSURUGA...
BUT...
...NO ONE...
...EXPECTED WHAT WOULD HAPPEN NEXT.

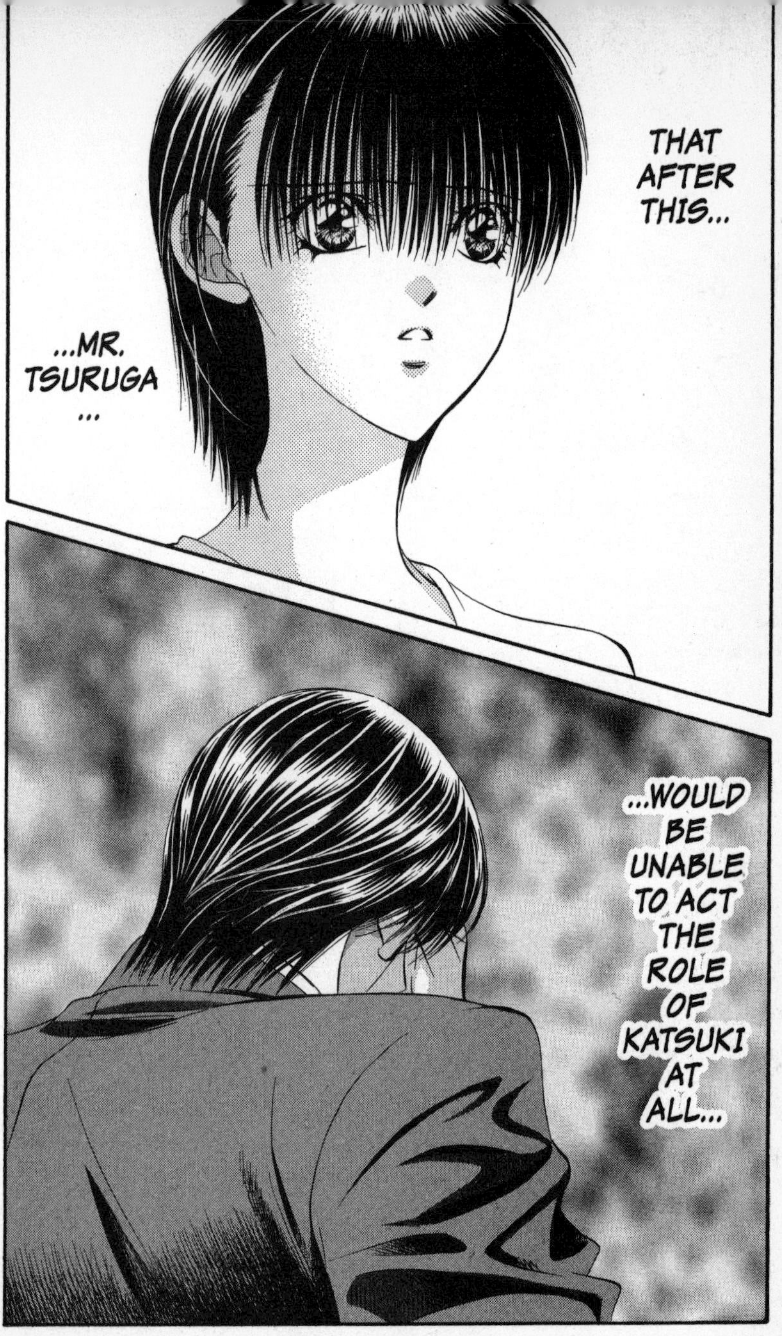
THAT AFTER THIS...
...MR. TSURUGA ...
...WOULD BE UNABLE TO ACT THE ROLE OF KATSUKI AT ALL...

End of Act 62

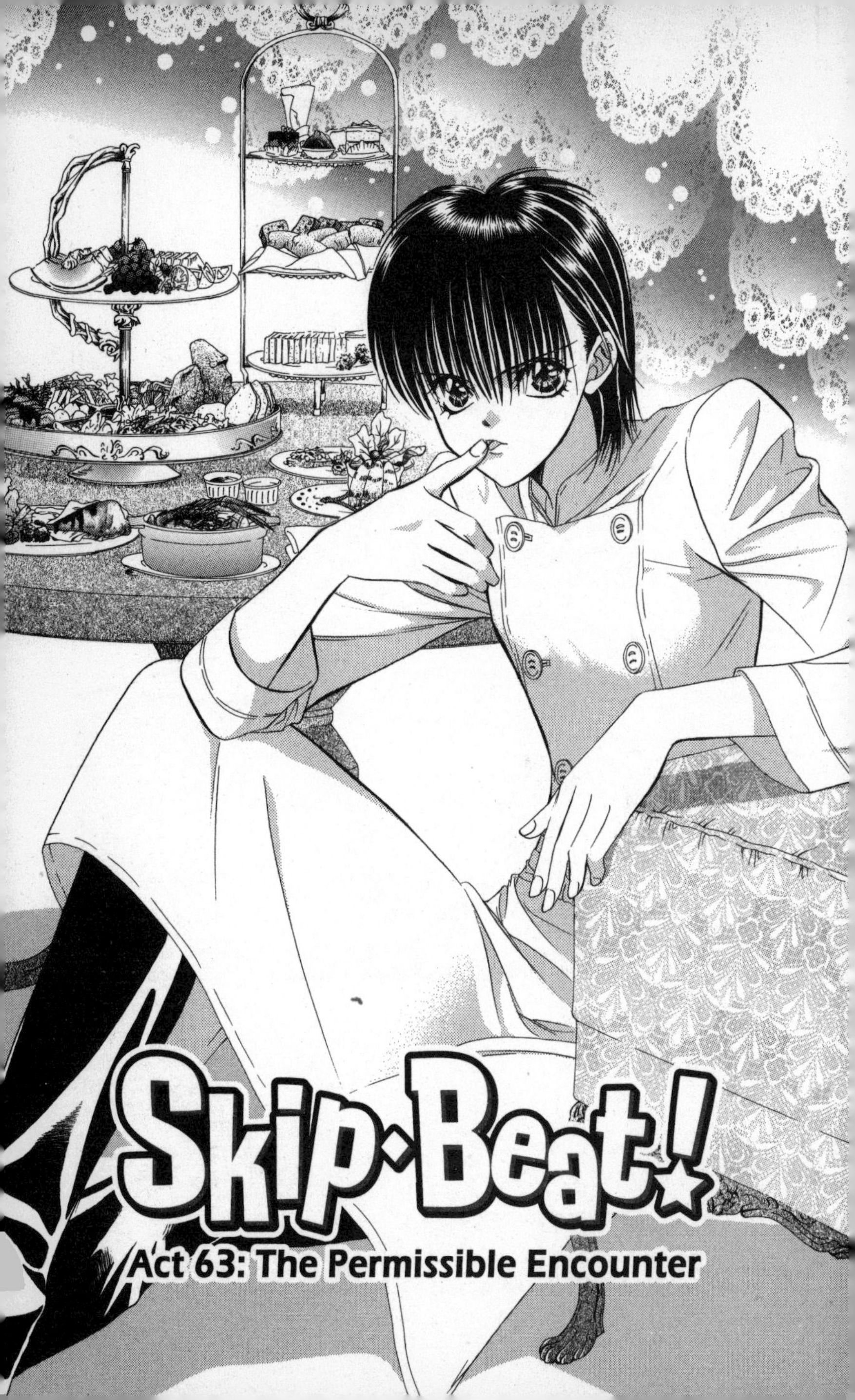
Skip·Beat!
Act 63: The Permissible Encounter

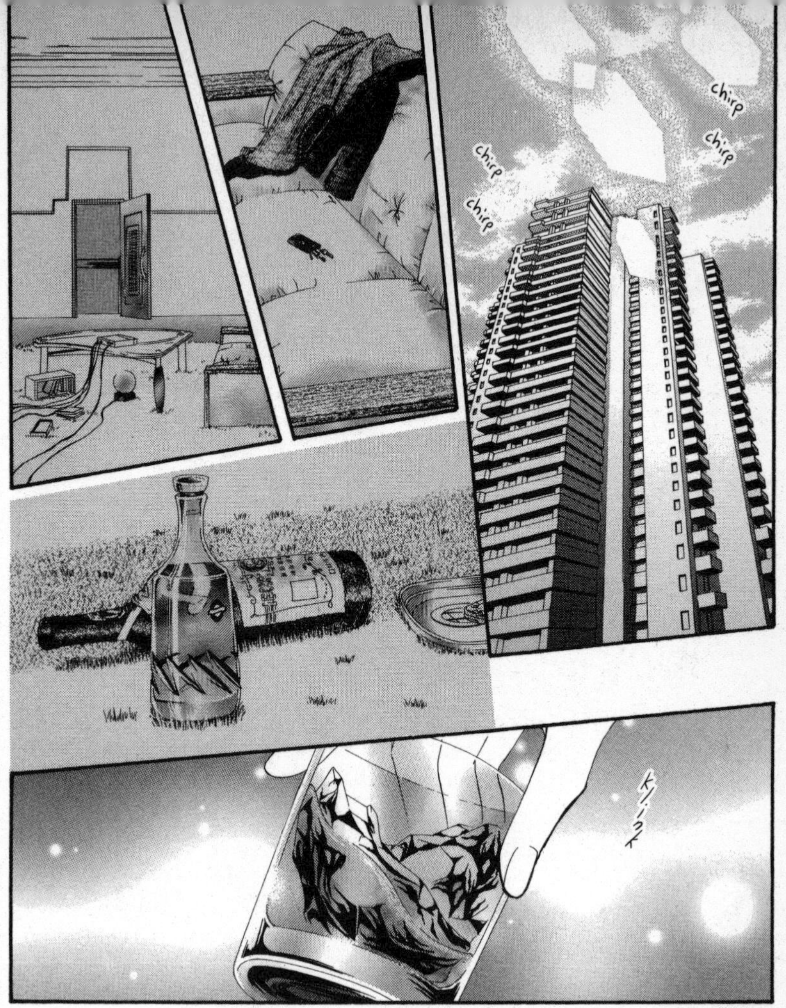
chirp
chirp
chirp
chirp
KLINK

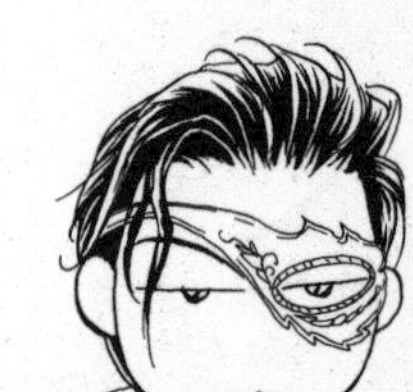

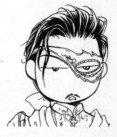

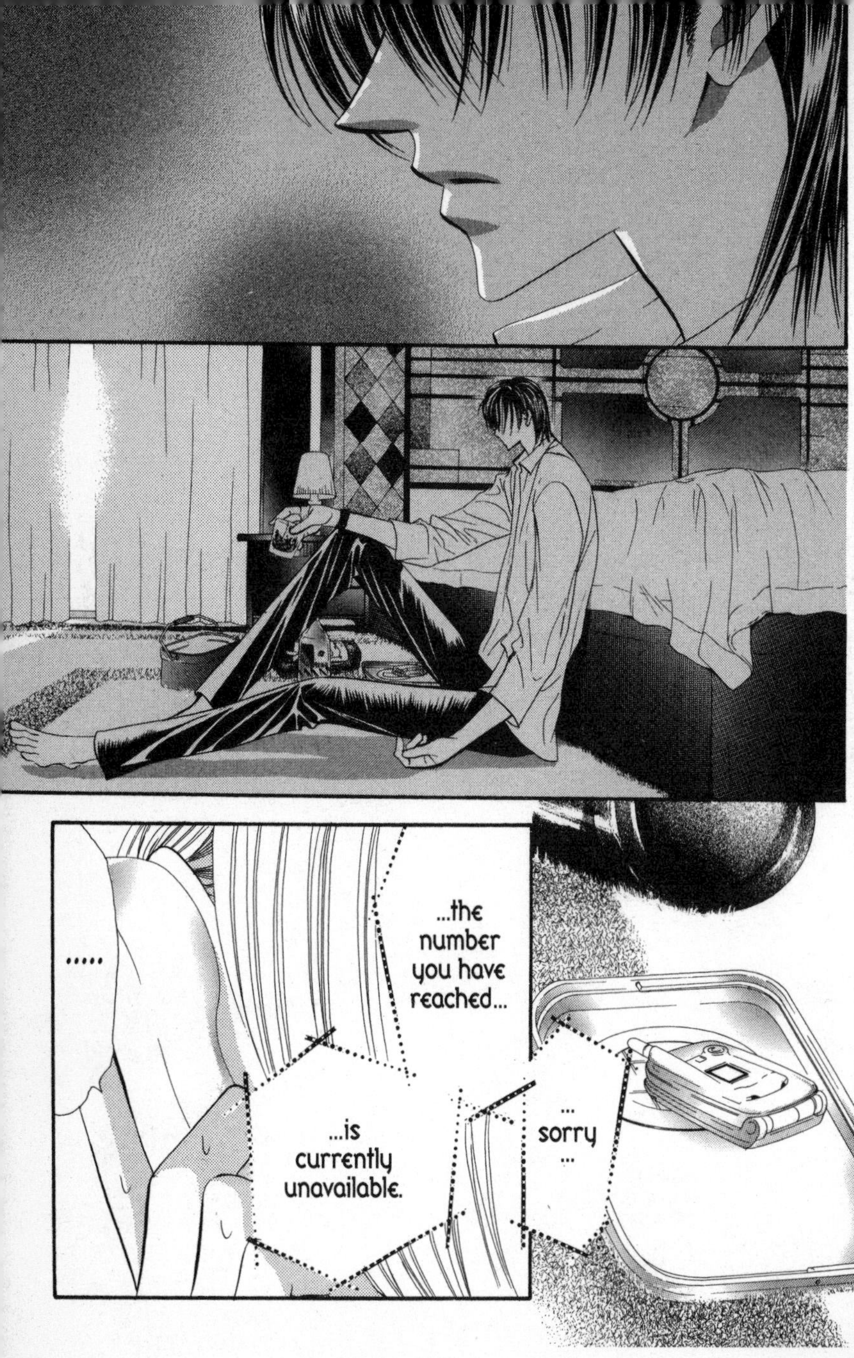
... sorry ...
...the number you have reached...
.....
...is currently unavailable.

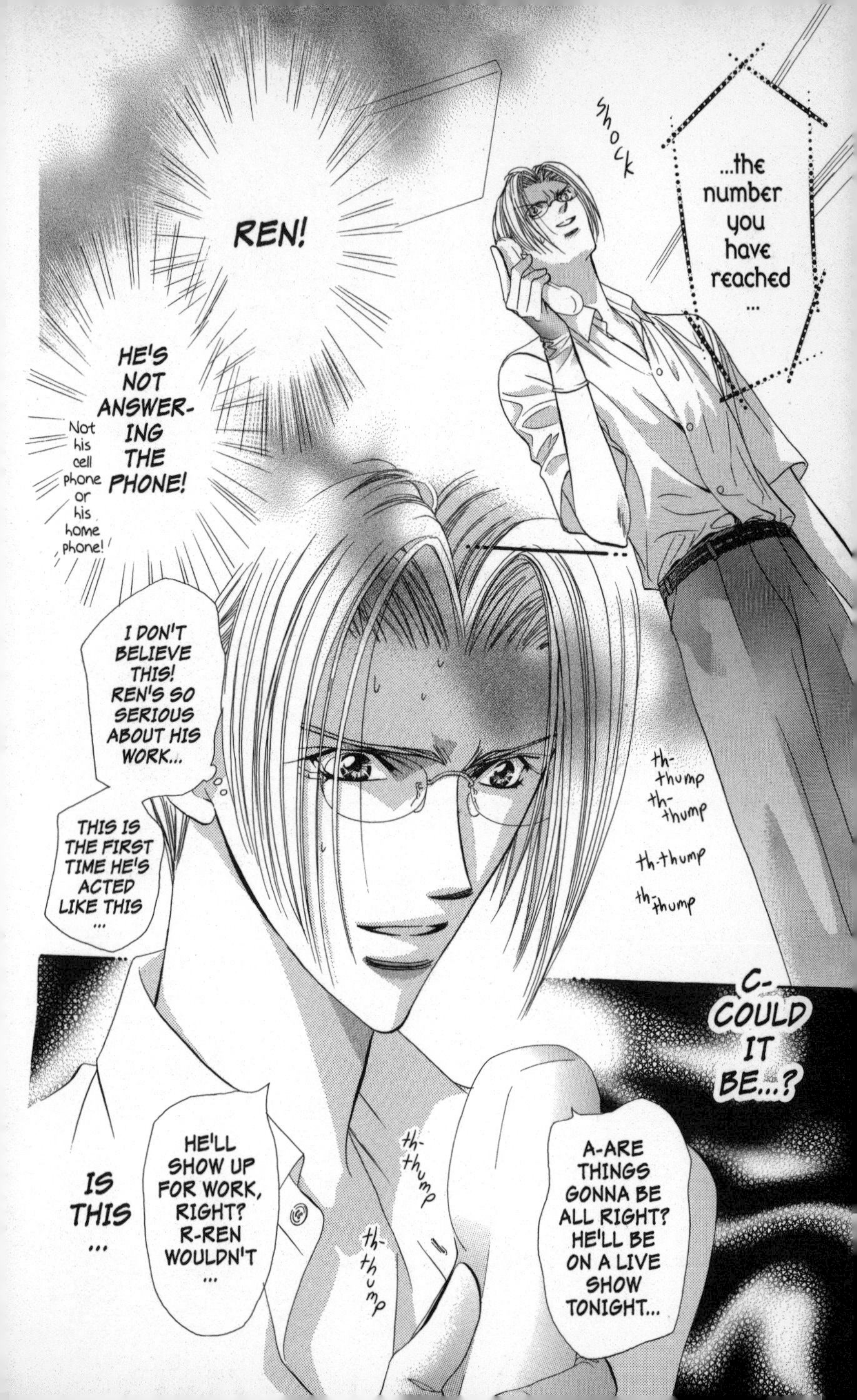
...the number you have reached ...
Shock
REN!
HE'S NOT ANSWERING THE PHONE!
Not his cell phone or his home phone!
I DON'T BELIEVE THIS! REN'S SO SERIOUS ABOUT HIS WORK...
THIS IS THE FIRST TIME HE'S ACTED LIKE THIS ...
th-thump th-thump
th-thump
th-thump
C-COULD IT BE...?
A-ARE THINGS GONNA BE ALL RIGHT? HE'LL BE ON A LIVE SHOW TONIGHT...
th-thump
th-thump
HE'LL SHOW UP FOR WORK, RIGHT? R-REN WOULDN'T ...
IS THIS ...

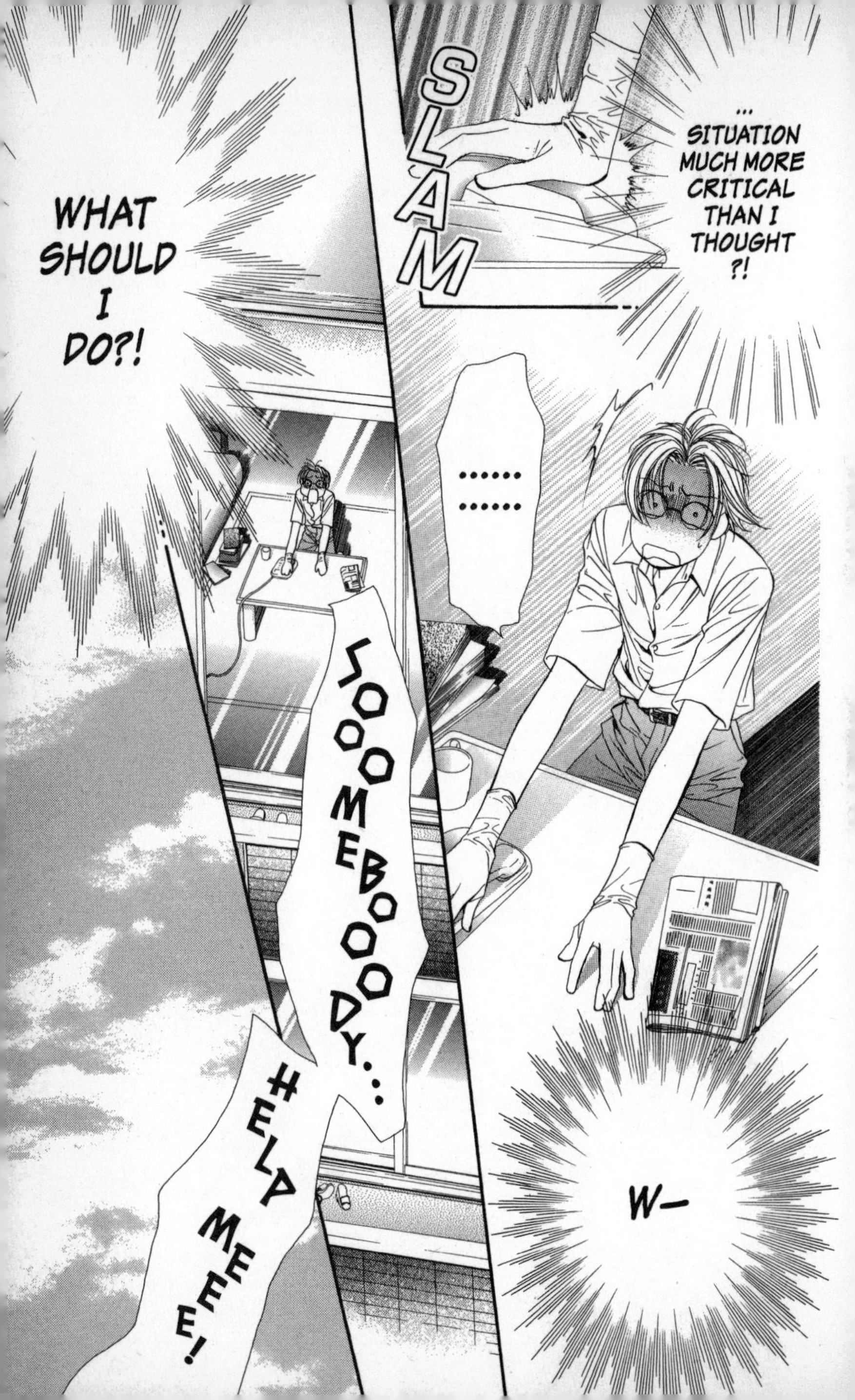
SLAM
...SITUATION MUCH MORE CRITICAL THAN I THOUGHT?!
......
......
W–
WHAT SHOULD I DO?!
SOOOMEBOOODY...
HELP MEEEE!

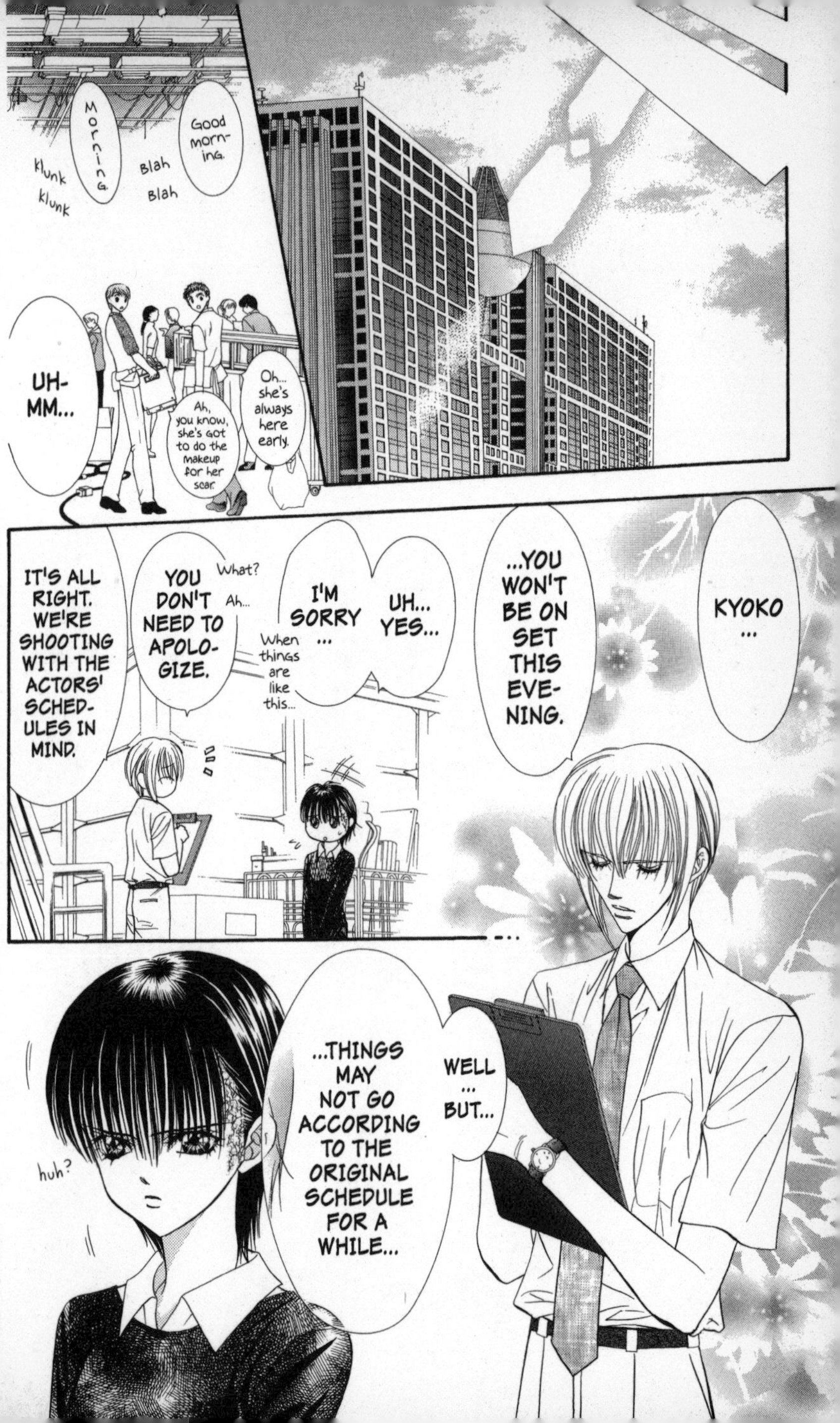
Good morning.
Morning.
Blah Blah
klunk klunk
Oh... she's always here early.
Ah, you know, she's got to do the makeup for her scar.
UH-MM...
KYOKO...
...YOU WON'T BE ON SET THIS EVENING.
UH... YES...
I'M SORRY...
When things are like this...
What?
Ah...
YOU DON'T NEED TO APOLOGIZE.
IT'S ALL RIGHT. WE'RE SHOOTING WITH THE ACTORS' SCHEDULES IN MIND.
...
WELL... BUT...
...THINGS MAY NOT GO ACCORDING TO THE ORIGINAL SCHEDULE FOR A WHILE...
huh?

Please read this sidebar like the narration for

"A Stormy Life Always" ☺

When he settles down as the son of the Tachibana family, Katsuki starts investigating the Hongo family. He then decides to target one person for his revenge. His target is the eldest daughter of the Hongo family, Misao, who's close to him in age. His plan is to use Misao to get into the Hongo family, and to destroy the family completely from the inside.

In order to make meeting her seem natural, he begins to study music. Music was supposed to help connect him with Misao.

And now...Katsuki's detailed plan, which was in the works for quite some time, is progressing smoothly, and everything is supposed to go according to Katsuki's scenario...yes, until he meets Mizuki...the sole survivor of the family that his own father killed for his family's happiness...he meets Mizuki, and is caught in a forbidden love that he can't control, which is so bitter and yet at the same time terribly sweet.

———...

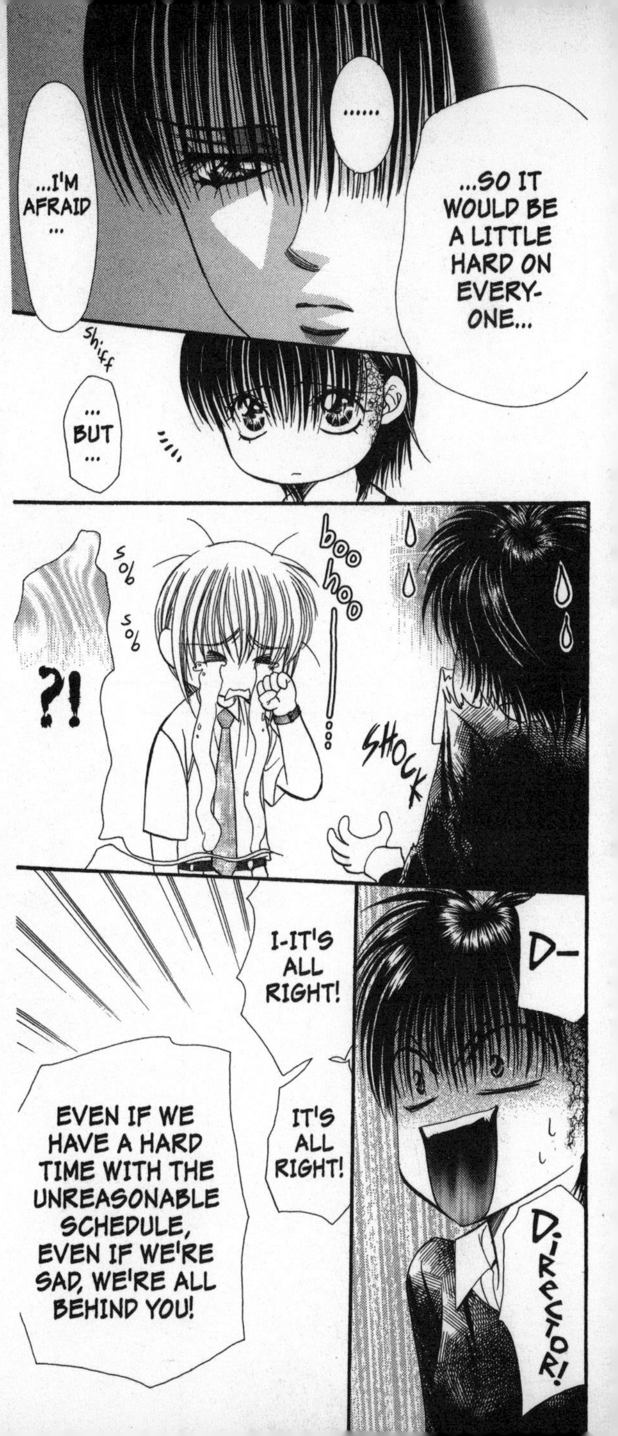
......
...SO IT WOULD BE A LITTLE HARD ON EVERY-ONE...
...I'M AFRAID...
shiff
...BUT...
boo hoo—!!!
SHOCK
sob sob
?!
D—
D-DIRECTOR!
I-IT'S ALL RIGHT!
IT'S ALL RIGHT!
EVEN IF WE HAVE A HARD TIME WITH THE UNREASONABLE SCHEDULE, EVEN IF WE'RE SAD, WE'RE ALL BEHIND YOU!

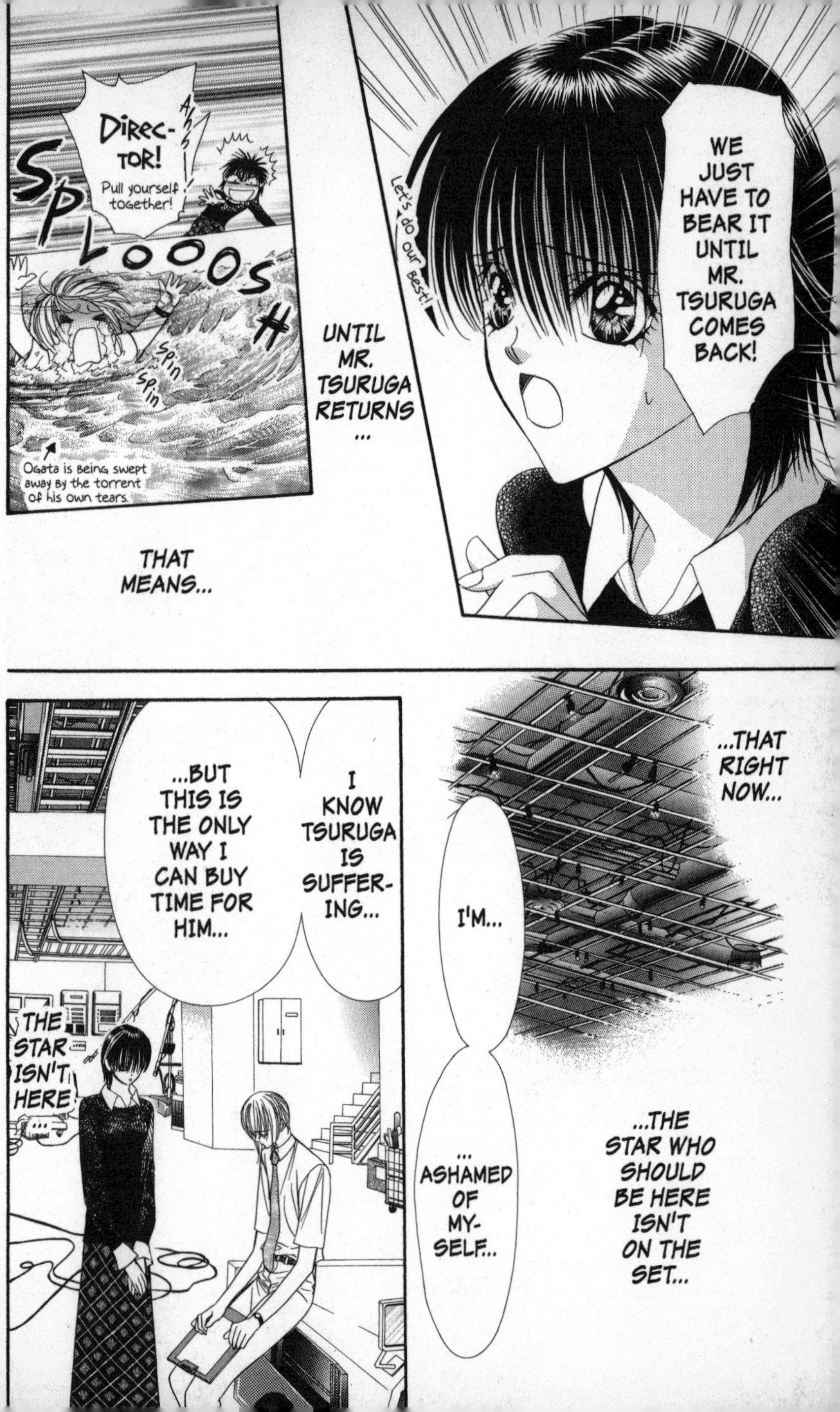
WE JUST HAVE TO BEAR IT UNTIL MR. TSURUGA COMES BACK!
Let's do our best!
UNTIL MR. TSURUGA RETURNS...
DIREC-TOR!
Ahh!
Pull yourself together!
SPLOOOSH
Spin
Spin
Ogata is being swept away by the torrent of his own tears.
THAT MEANS...
...THAT RIGHT NOW...
I'M...
...ASHAMED OF MY-SELF...
...THE STAR WHO SHOULD BE HERE ISN'T ON THE SET...
I KNOW TSURUGA IS SUFFER-ING...
...BUT THIS IS THE ONLY WAY I CAN BUY TIME FOR HIM...
THE STAR ISN'T HERE...

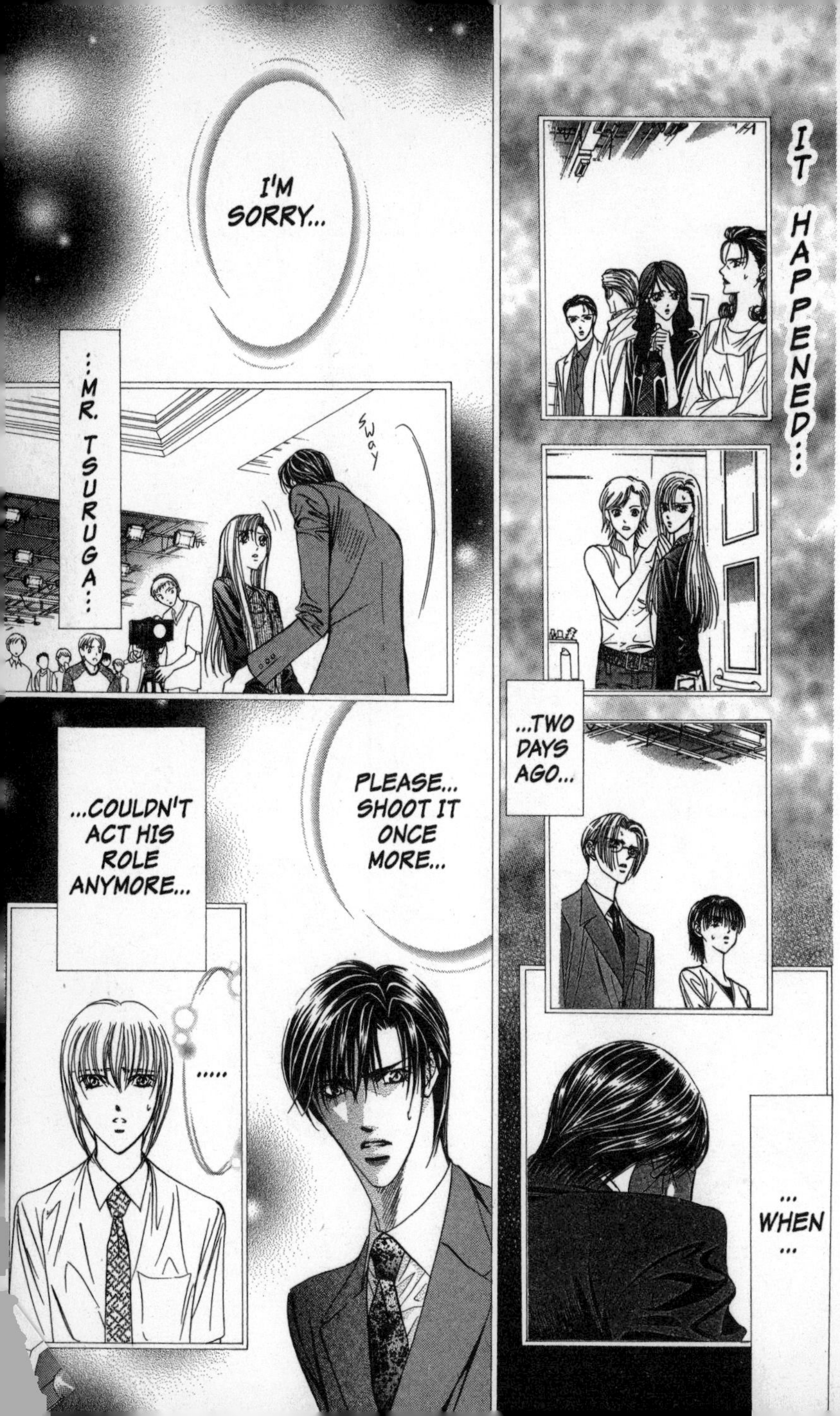

IT HAPPENED...
...TWO DAYS AGO...
...WHEN...
I'M SORRY...
...MR. TSURUGA...
sway
PLEASE... SHOOT IT ONCE MORE...
...COULDN'T ACT HIS ROLE ANYMORE...
.....

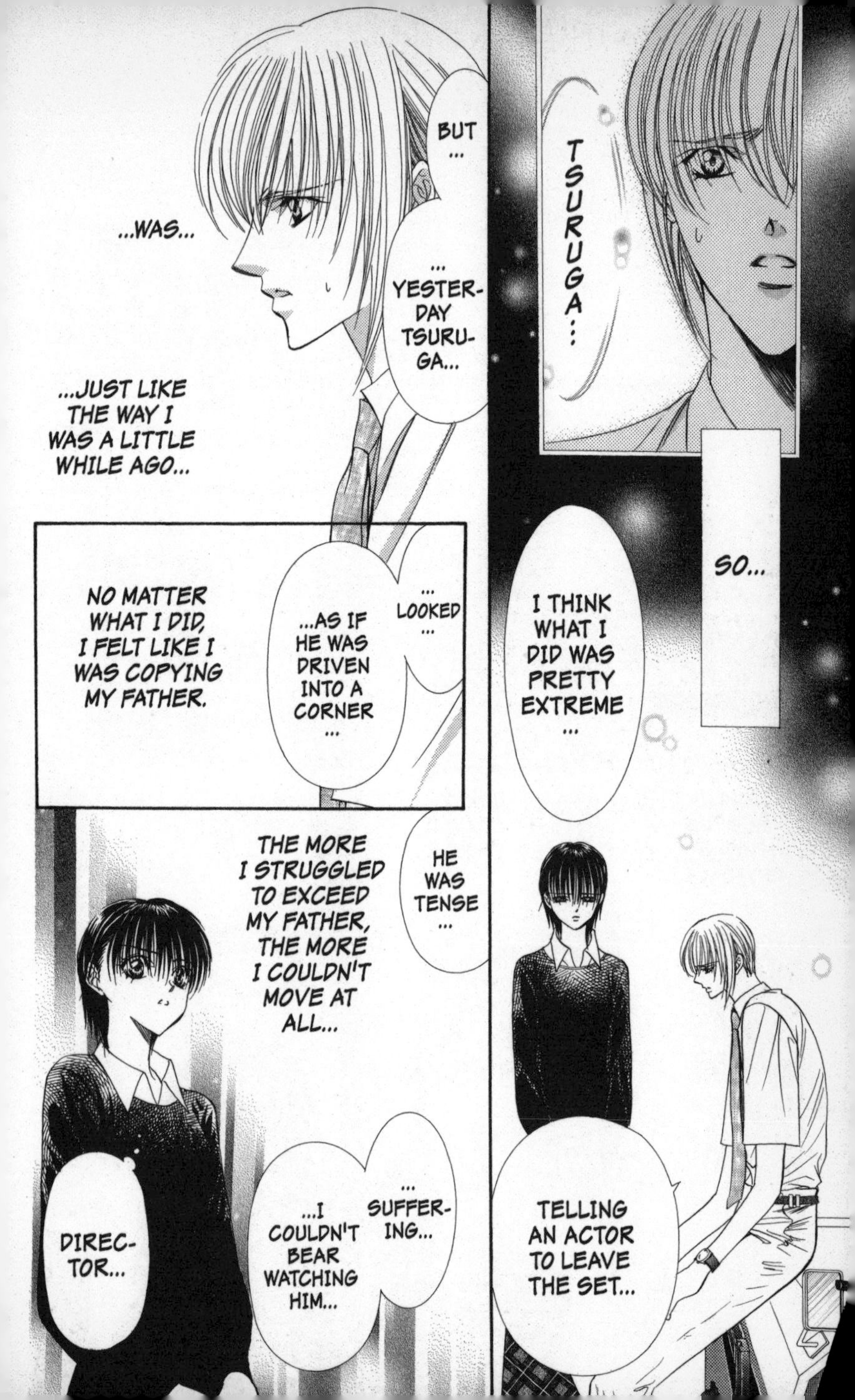
TSURUGA...
SO...
I THINK WHAT I DID WAS PRETTY EXTREME...
TELLING AN ACTOR TO LEAVE THE SET...
BUT...
...YESTERDAY TSURUGA...
...LOOKED...
...AS IF HE WAS DRIVEN INTO A CORNER...
...WAS...
...JUST LIKE THE WAY I WAS A LITTLE WHILE AGO...
NO MATTER WHAT I DID, I FELT LIKE I WAS COPYING MY FATHER.
HE WAS TENSE...
THE MORE I STRUGGLED TO EXCEED MY FATHER, THE MORE I COULDN'T MOVE AT ALL...
...SUFFERING...
...I COULDN'T BEAR WATCHING HIM...
DIRECTOR...

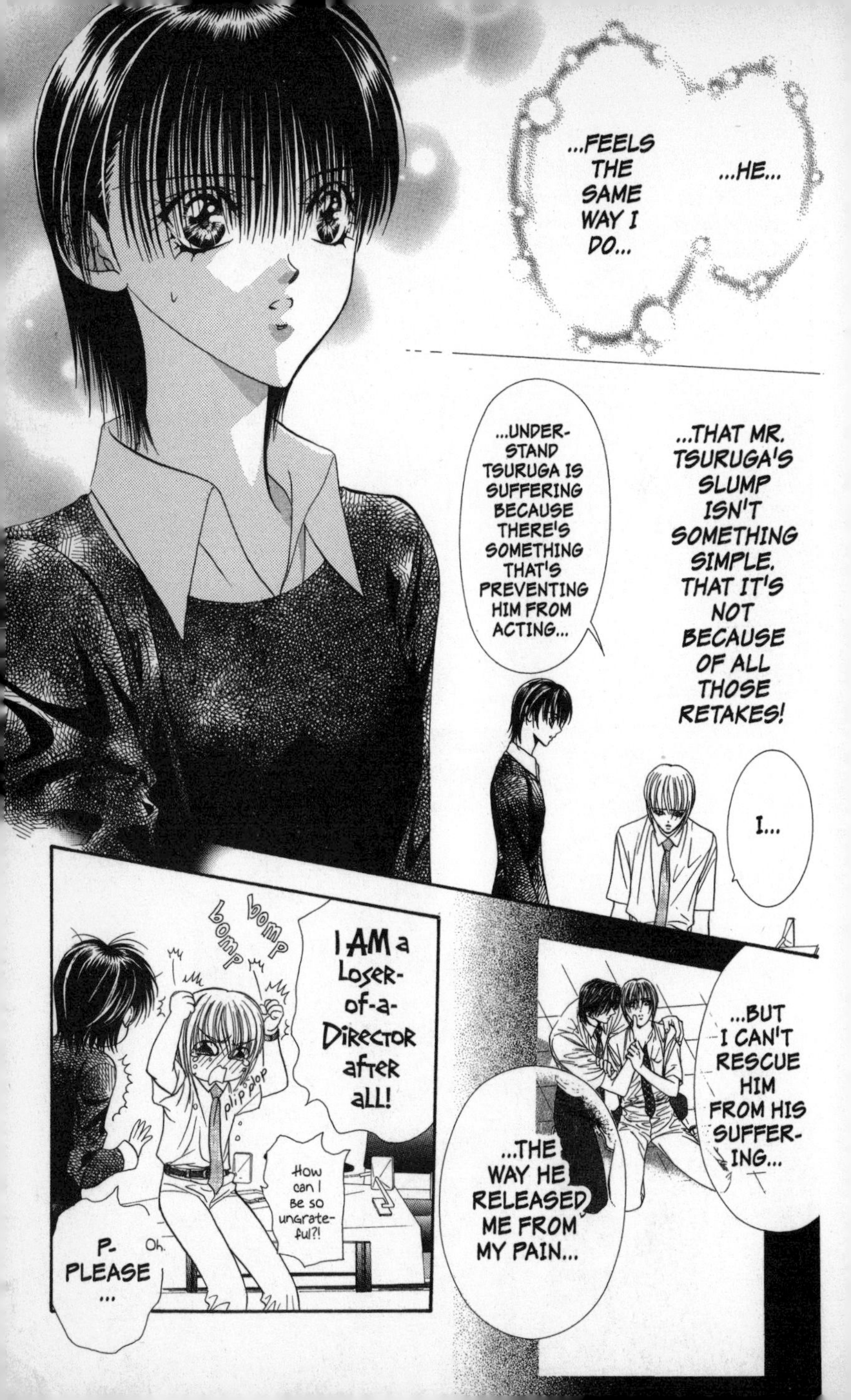
...HE...
...FEELS THE SAME WAY I DO...
...THAT MR. TSURUGA'S SLUMP ISN'T SOMETHING SIMPLE. THAT IT'S NOT BECAUSE OF ALL THOSE RETAKES!
...UNDER-STAND TSURUGA IS SUFFERING BECAUSE THERE'S SOMETHING THAT'S PREVENTING HIM FROM ACTING...
I...
...BUT I CAN'T RESCUE HIM FROM HIS SUFFER-ING...
...THE WAY HE RELEASED ME FROM MY PAIN...
bomp bomp
I AM a Loser-of-a-Director after all!
plip plop
How can I be so ungrate-ful?!
Oh.
P-PLEASE ...

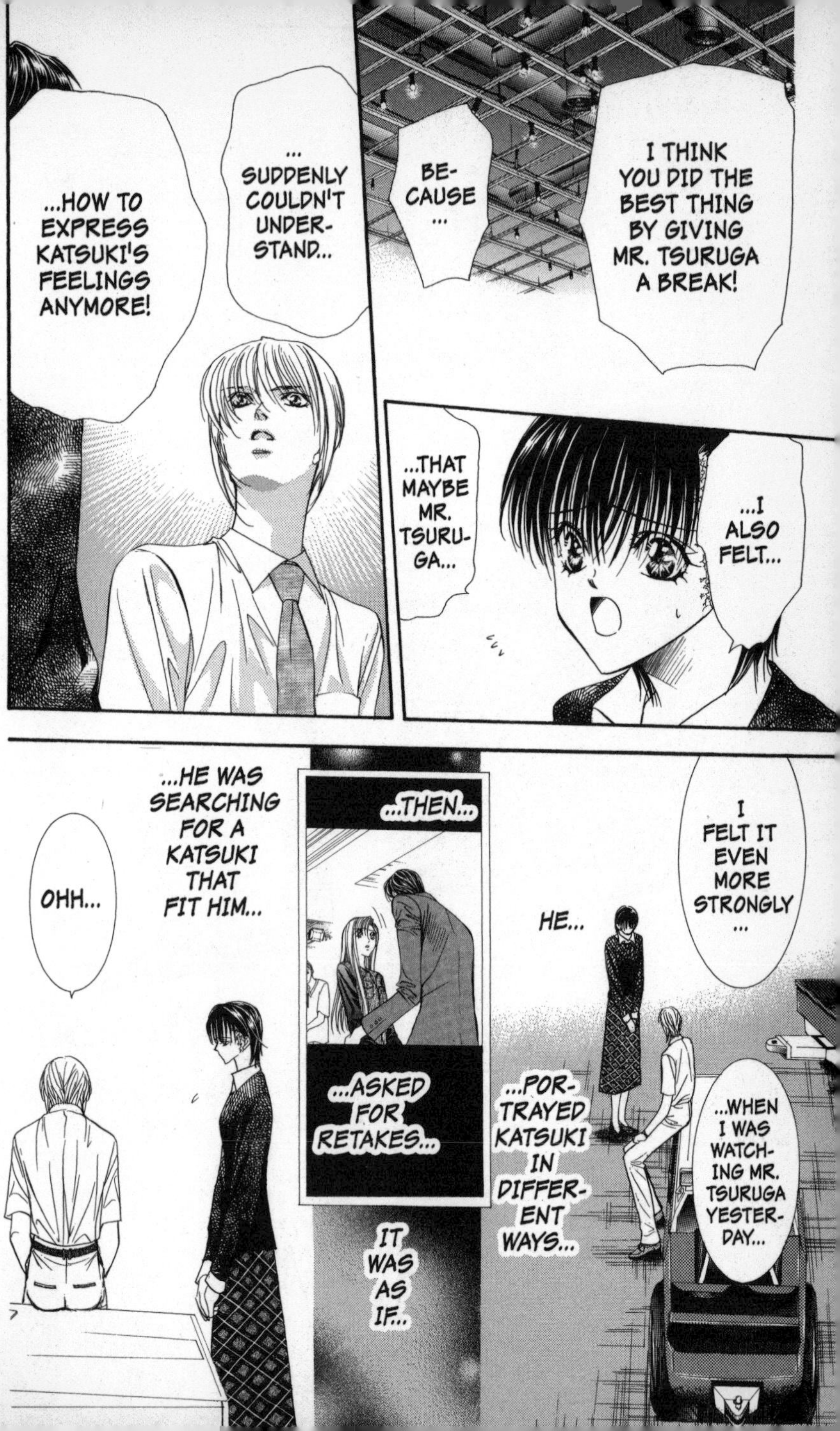
I THINK YOU DID THE BEST THING BY GIVING MR. TSURUGA A BREAK!
BE-CAUSE...
...I ALSO FELT...
...THAT MAYBE MR. TSURU-GA...
...SUDDENLY COULDN'T UNDER-STAND...
...HOW TO EXPRESS KATSUKI'S FEELINGS ANYMORE!
I FELT IT EVEN MORE STRONGLY...
...WHEN I WAS WATCH-ING MR. TSURUGA YESTER-DAY...
HE...
...POR-TRAYED KATSUKI IN DIFFER-ENT WAYS...
...THEN...
...ASKED FOR RETAKES...
IT WAS AS IF...
...HE WAS SEARCHING FOR A KATSUKI THAT FIT HIM...
OHH...

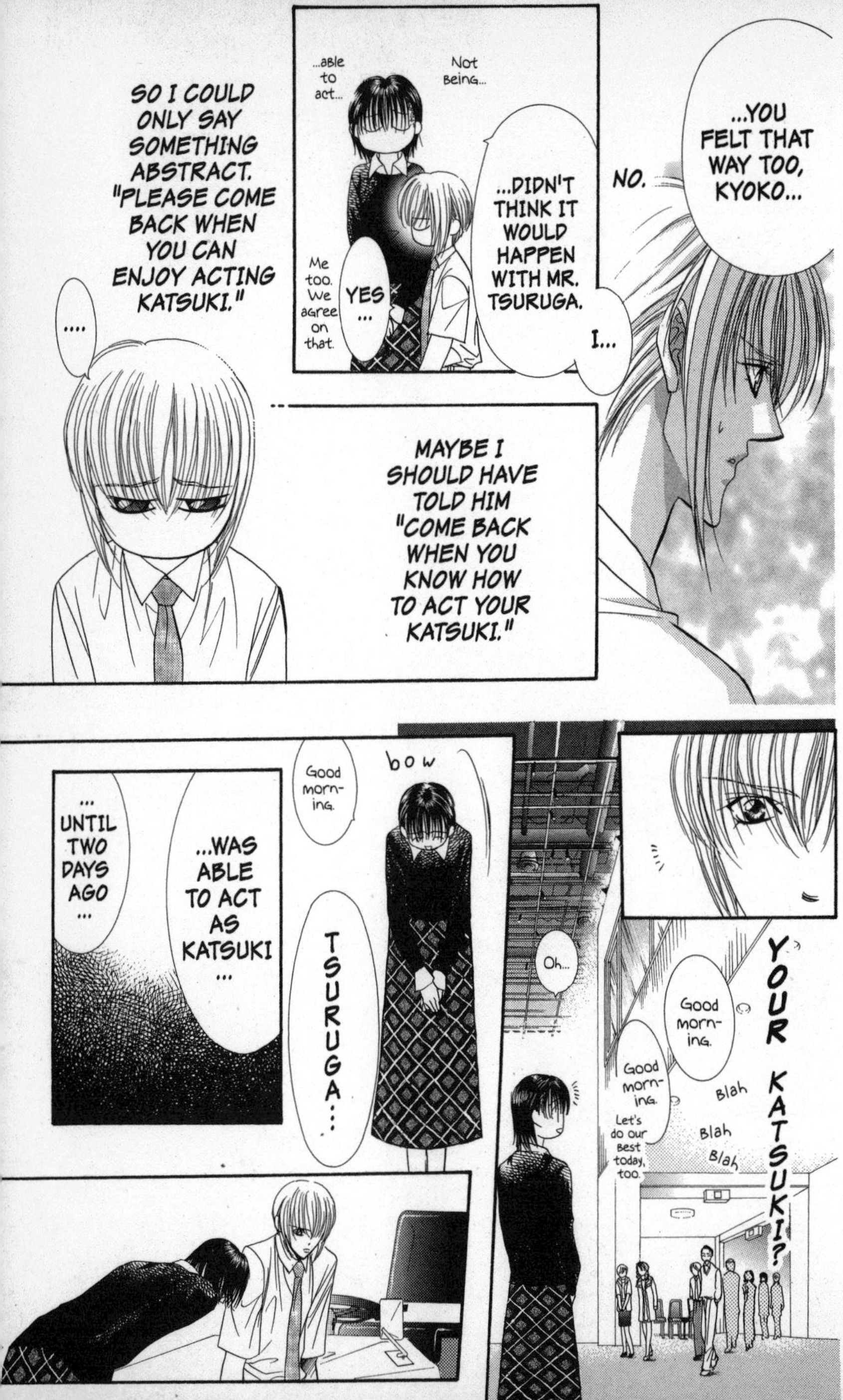
...YOU FELT THAT WAY TOO, KYOKO...
NO.
I...
...DIDN'T THINK IT WOULD HAPPEN WITH MR. TSURUGA.
Not being...
...able to act...
YES...
Me too. We agree on that.
SO I COULD ONLY SAY SOMETHING ABSTRACT. "PLEASE COME BACK WHEN YOU CAN ENJOY ACTING KATSUKI."
....
MAYBE I SHOULD HAVE TOLD HIM "COME BACK WHEN YOU KNOW HOW TO ACT YOUR KATSUKI."
YOUR KATSUKI?
Good morn-ing.
Good morn-ing.
Let's do our best today, too.
Blah
Blah
Blah
Oh...
bow
Good morn-ing.
TSURUGA...
...WAS ABLE TO ACT AS KATSUKI...
...UNTIL TWO DAYS AGO...

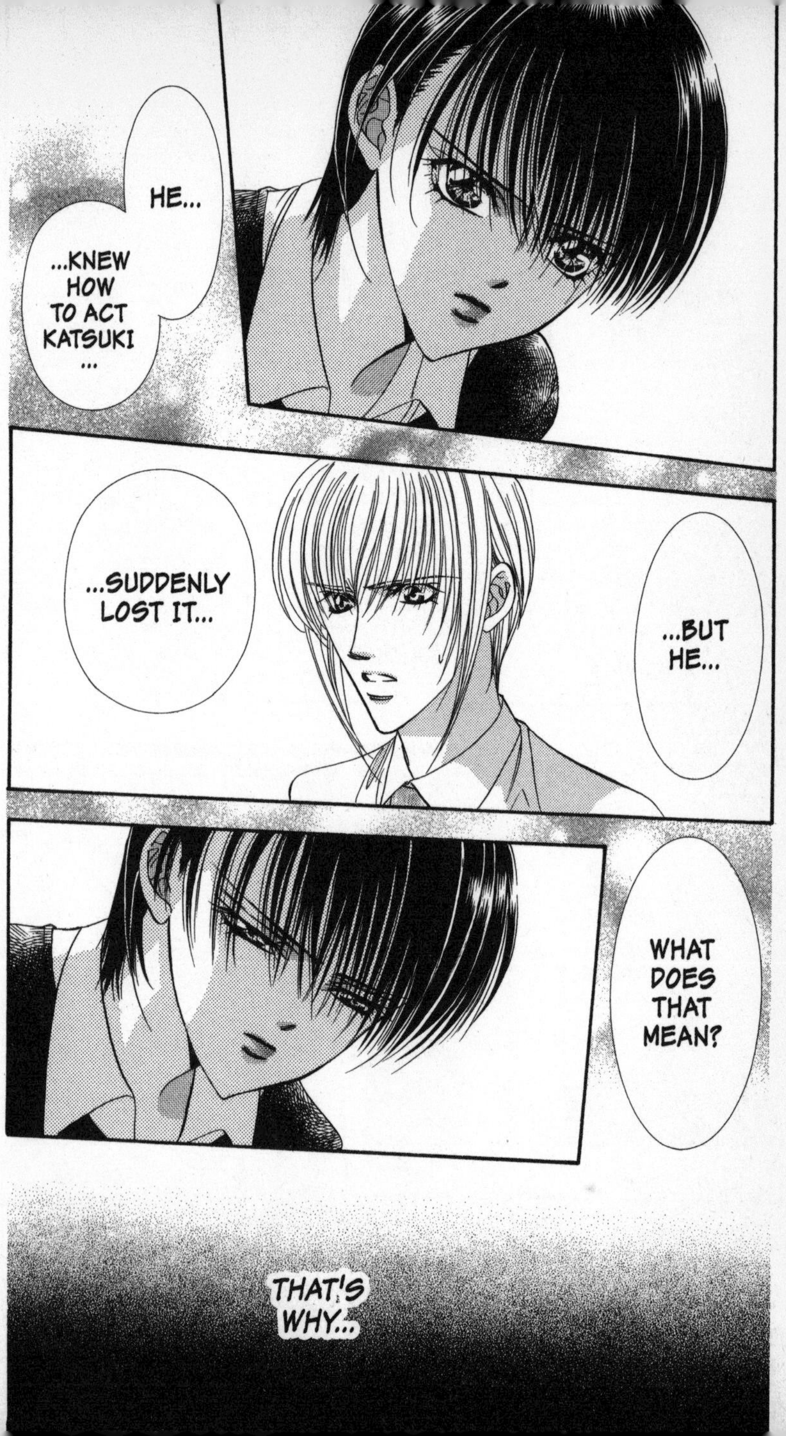
HE...
...KNEW HOW TO ACT KATSUKI ...
...BUT HE...
...SUDDENLY LOST IT...
WHAT DOES THAT MEAN?
THAT'S WHY...

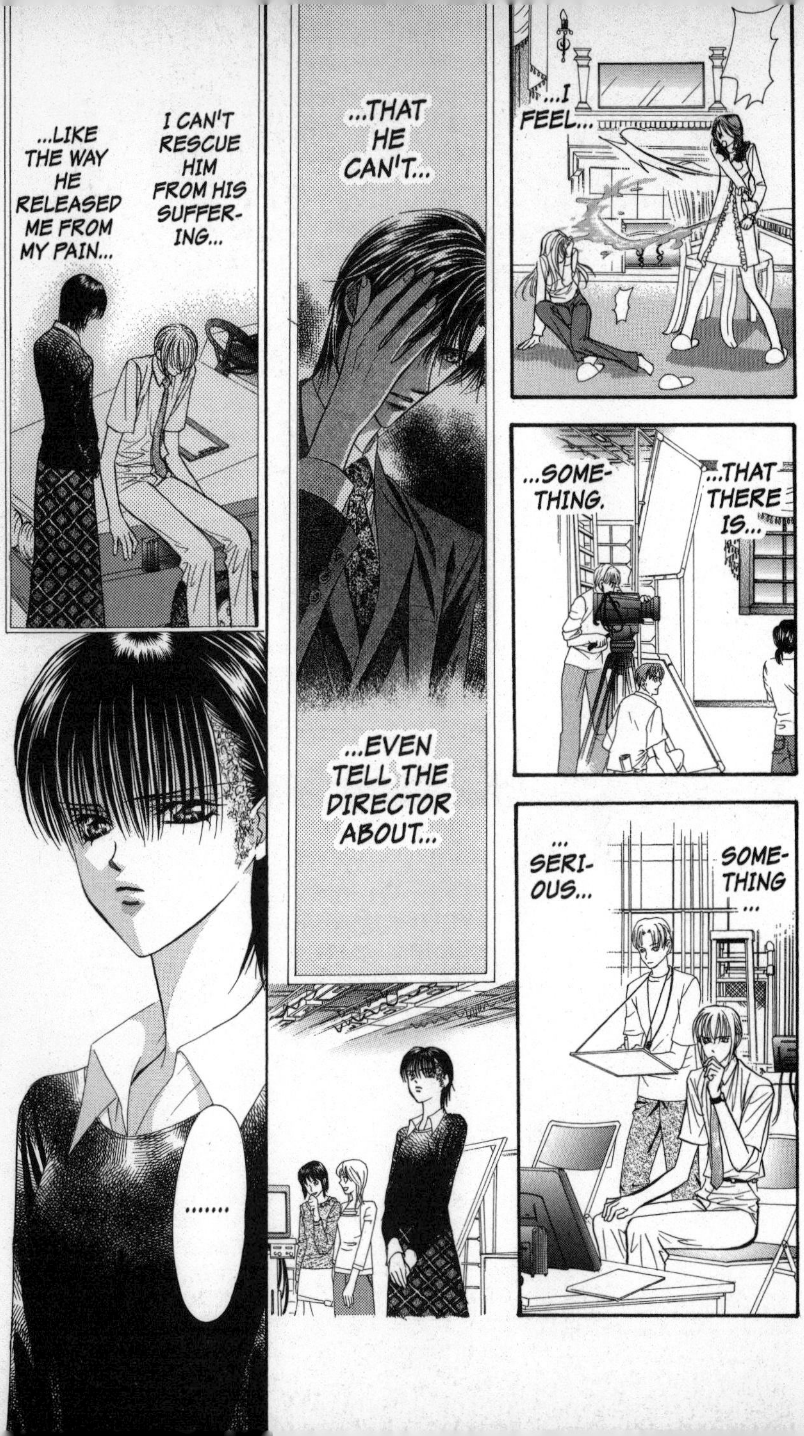
...I FEEL...
...THAT THERE IS...
...SOME-THING.
SOME-THING...
...SERI-OUS...
...THAT HE CAN'T...
...EVEN TELL THE DIRECTOR ABOUT...
I CAN'T RESCUE HIM FROM HIS SUFFER-ING...
...LIKE THE WAY HE RELEASED ME FROM MY PAIN...
....

...BECAUSE...

...I'M A NEWCOMER TALENTO...

...WHO'S JUST STARTED ACTING...

THAT MAY BE TRUE, BUT...

THIS GIRL WILL FIND A MAID YOU'LL BE SATISFIED WITH.

...PLEASE... GIVE THIS GIRL SOME TIME.

THINGS WILL BE ALL RIGHT.

MS. IIZUKA...

IT'S THE SAME...

I CAN'T HELP...

IF THINKING ABOUT ASPECTS OF THE CHARACTER'S BACKGROUND AND STATE OF MIND THAT AREN'T MENTIONED IN THE SCRIPT.

...FOR ME TOO....

...LIKE HE HELPED ME...

IF YOU'RE MIO...

WHAT'S HER PERSONALITY?

...HOW WOULD YOU SAY THAT LINE

HOW DOES SHE SPEAK

...MR. TSURUGA...

...ADVICE ABOUT ACTING...

I CAN'T GIVE HIM...

Menacing look

Why would I tell you about my problems?!

Hunh?!

GRR GRR

...OR...

Actually, if I were asked...

IF I WERE MR. TSURUGA, I WOULDN'T TELL A JUNIOR MY PROBLEMS, ESPECIALLY IF IT'S SOMETHING THAT AFFECTS MY ACTING CAREER...

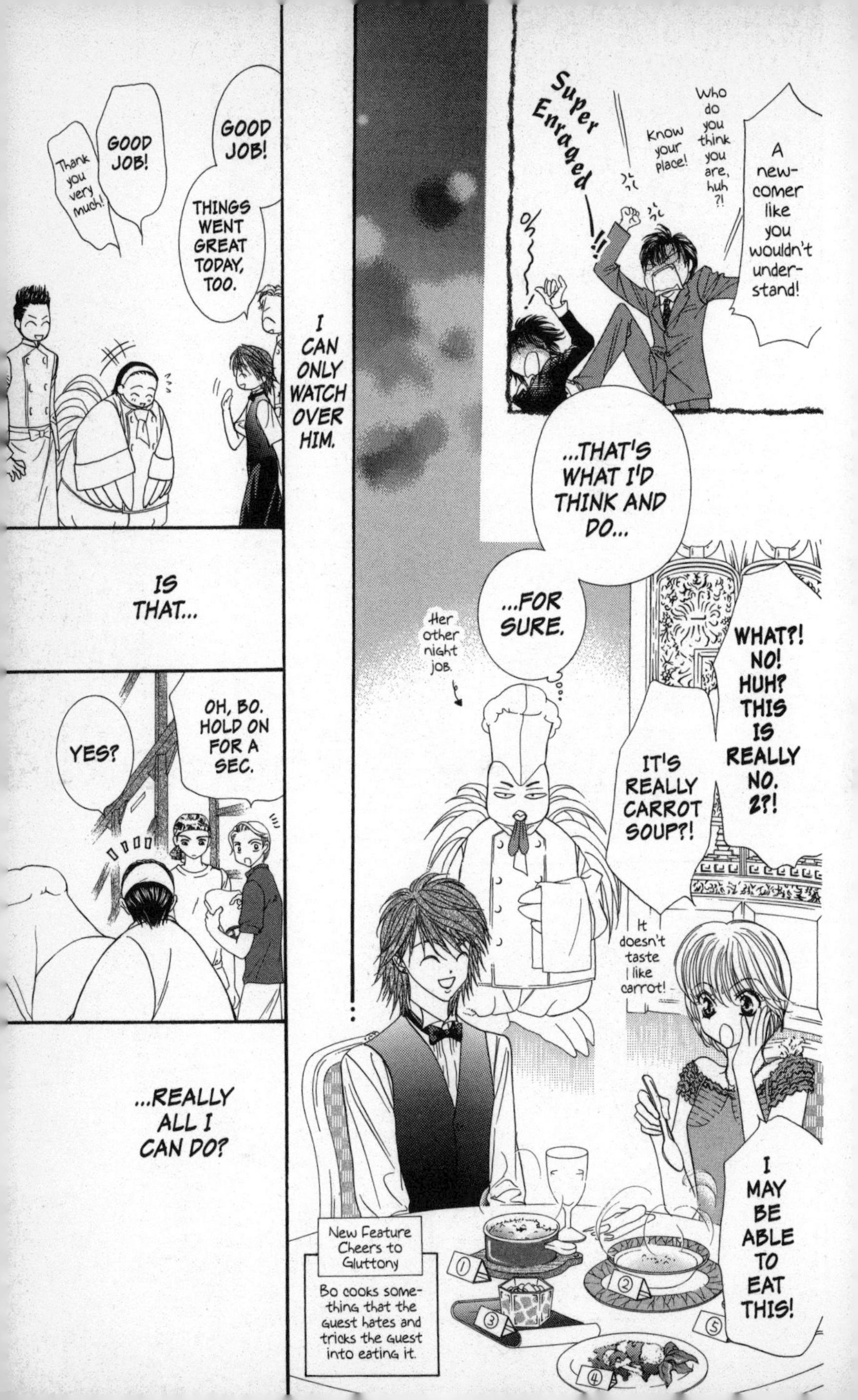
A newcomer like you wouldn't understand!
Who do you think you are, huh?!
Know your place!
Super Enraged!!
...THAT'S WHAT I'D THINK AND DO...
...FOR SURE.
I CAN ONLY WATCH OVER HIM.
WHAT?! NO! HUH? THIS IS REALLY NO. 2?!
IT'S REALLY CARROT SOUP?!
Her other night job.
It doesn't taste like carrot!
I MAY BE ABLE TO EAT THIS!
New Feature Cheers to Gluttony
Bo cooks something that the guest hates and tricks the guest into eating it.
GOOD JOB!
THINGS WENT GREAT TODAY, TOO.
GOOD JOB!
Thank you very much!
IS THAT...
OH, BO. HOLD ON FOR A SEC.
YES?
...REALLY ALL I CAN DO?

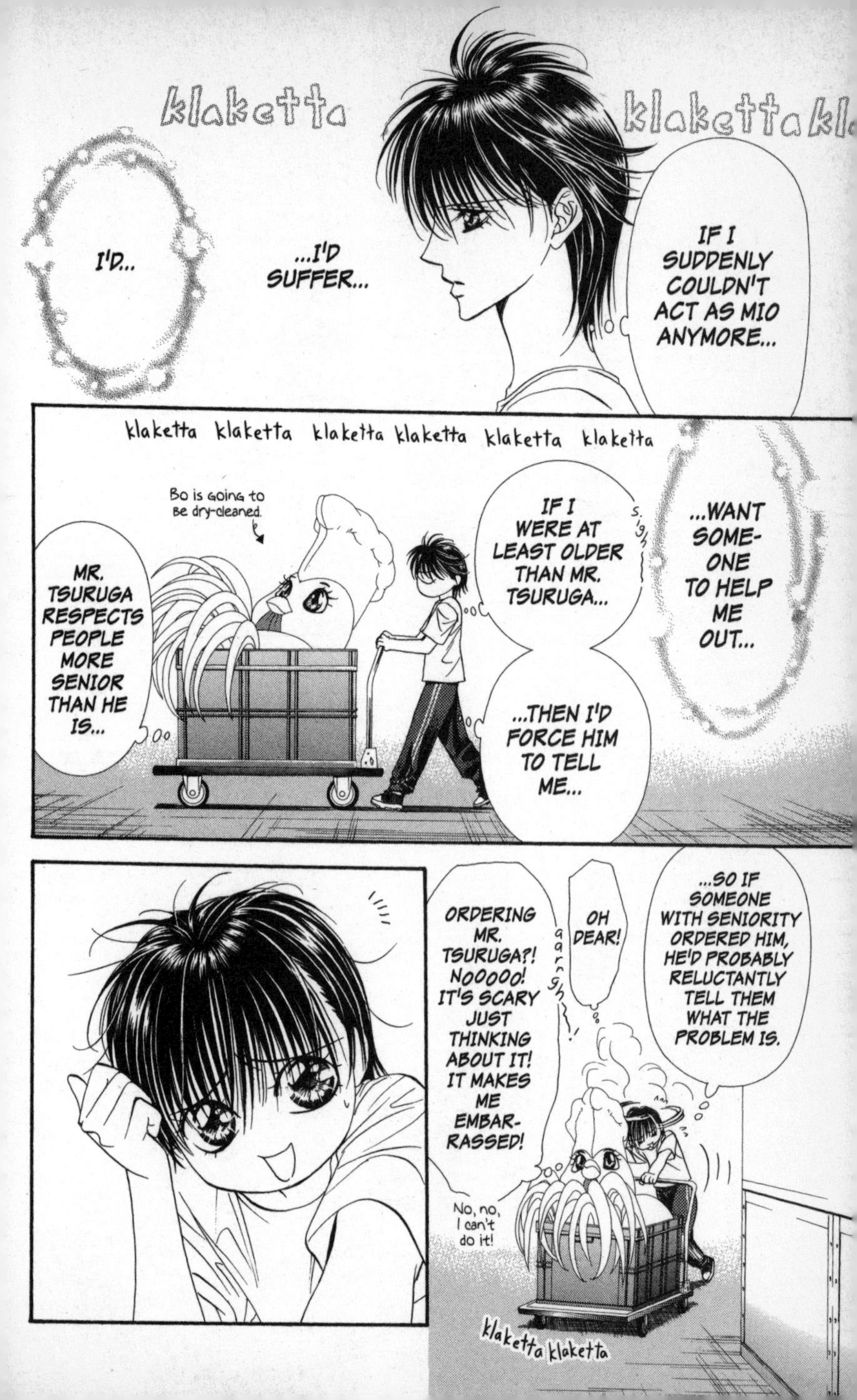
klakettaklakettakl
IF I SUDDENLY COULDN'T ACT AS MIO ANYMORE...
...I'D SUFFER...
I'D...
klaketta
klaketta klaketta klaketta klaketta klaketta klaketta
...WANT SOMEONE TO HELP ME OUT...
sigh
IF I WERE AT LEAST OLDER THAN MR. TSURUGA...
...THEN I'D FORCE HIM TO TELL ME...
Bo is going to be dry-cleaned.
MR. TSURUGA RESPECTS PEOPLE MORE SENIOR THAN HE IS...
...SO IF SOMEONE WITH SENIORITY ORDERED HIM, HE'D PROBABLY RELUCTANTLY TELL THEM WHAT THE PROBLEM IS.
OH DEAR!
aargh!
ORDERING MR. TSURUGA?! NOOOOO! IT'S SCARY JUST THINKING ABOUT IT! IT MAKES ME EMBARRASSED!
No, no, I can't do it!
klaketta klaketta

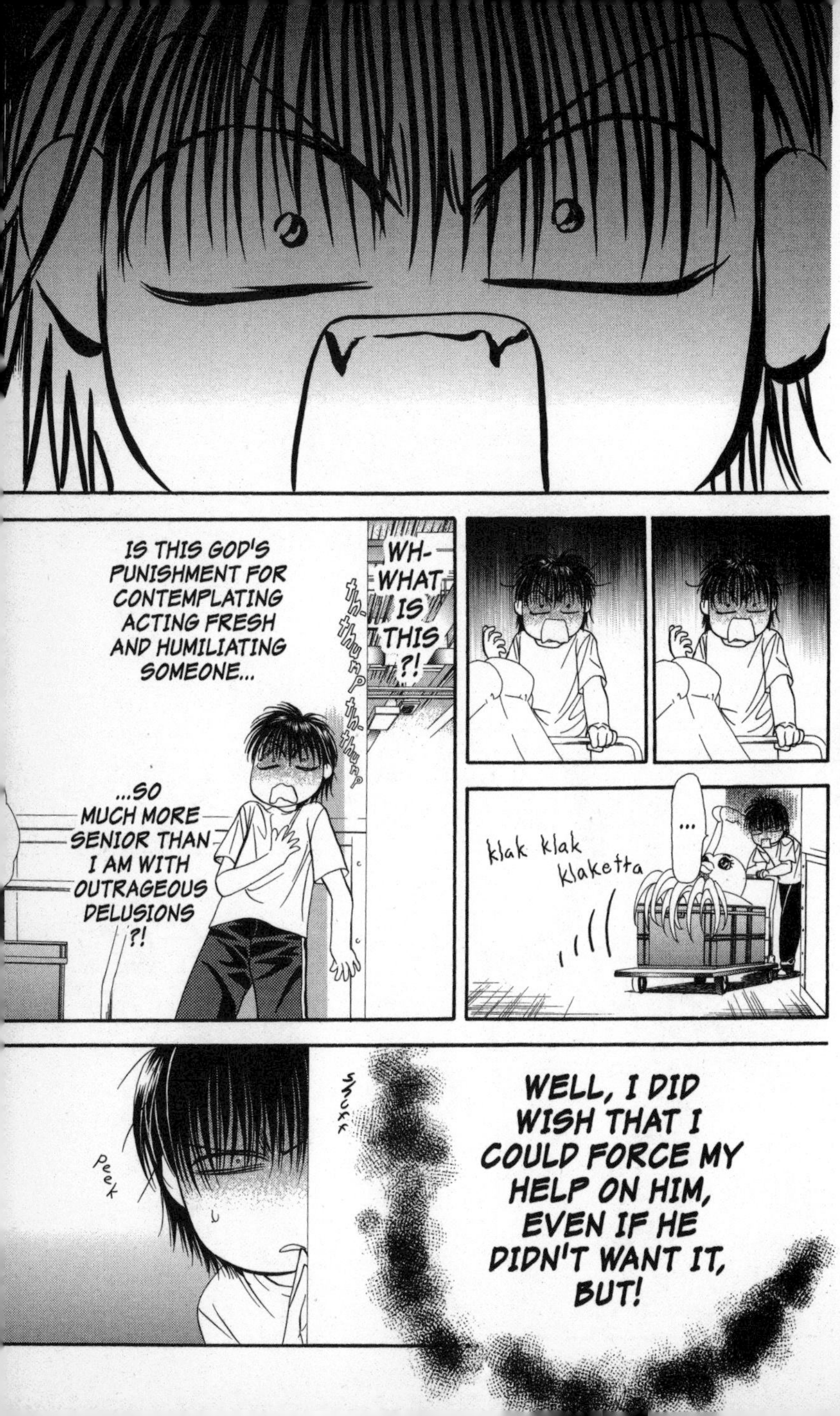
...
klak klak klaketta
WH-WHAT IS THIS?!
thu-thump thu-thump
IS THIS GOD'S PUNISHMENT FOR CONTEMPLATING ACTING FRESH AND HUMILIATING SOMEONE...
...SO MUCH MORE SENIOR THAN I AM WITH OUTRAGEOUS DELUSIONS?!
WELL, I DID WISH THAT I COULD FORCE MY HELP ON HIM, EVEN IF HE DIDN'T WANT IT, BUT!
snukk
Peek

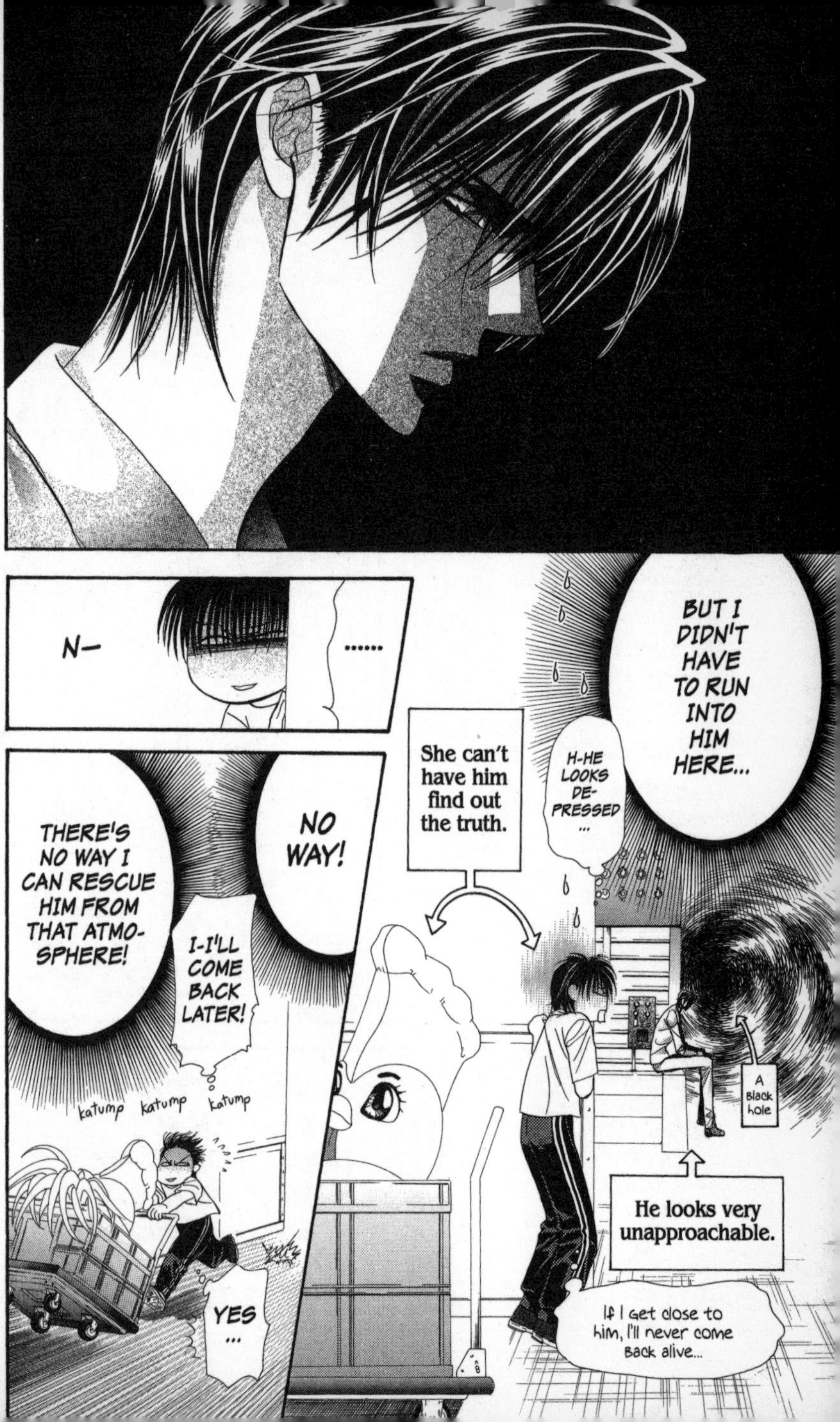
BUT I DIDN'T HAVE TO RUN INTO HIM HERE...
H-HE LOOKS DE-PRESSED...
She can't have him find out the truth.
A Black hole
He looks very unapproachable.
If I get close to him, I'll never come Back alive...
......
N—
NO WAY!
THERE'S NO WAY I CAN RESCUE HIM FROM THAT ATMO-SPHERE!
I-I'LL COME BACK LATER!
katump katump katump
YES ...

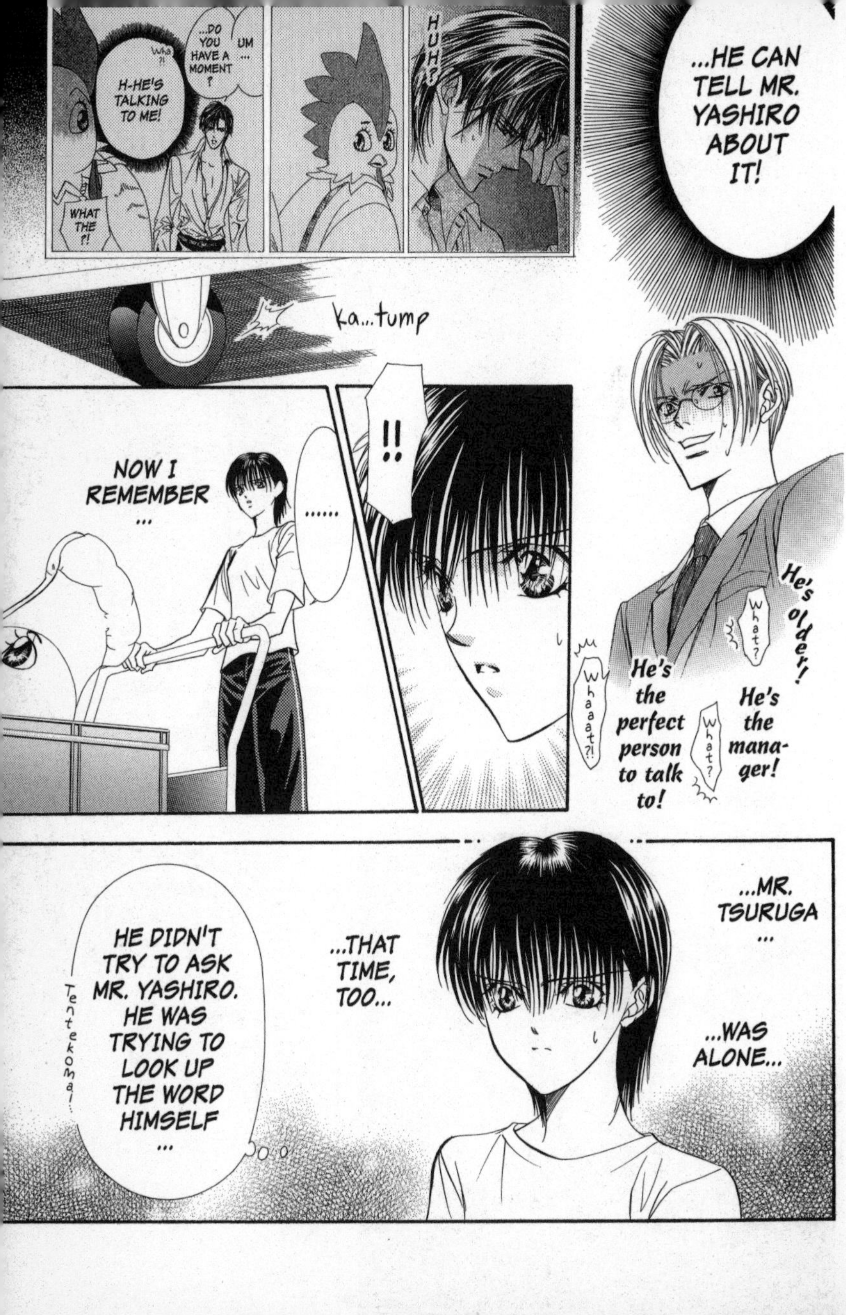
...HE CAN TELL MR. YASHIRO ABOUT IT!
HUH?
...DO YOU HAVE A MOMENT?
UM ...
Wha ?!
H-HE'S TALKING TO ME!
WHAT THE ?!
ka...tump
He's older!
What?
He's the manager!
What?
He's the perfect person to talk to!
Whaaat?!
!!
......
NOW I REMEMBER ...
...MR. TSURUGA ...
...WAS ALONE...
...THAT TIME, TOO...
HE DIDN'T TRY TO ASK MR. YASHIRO. HE WAS TRYING TO LOOK UP THE WORD HIMSELF ...
Tentekomai...

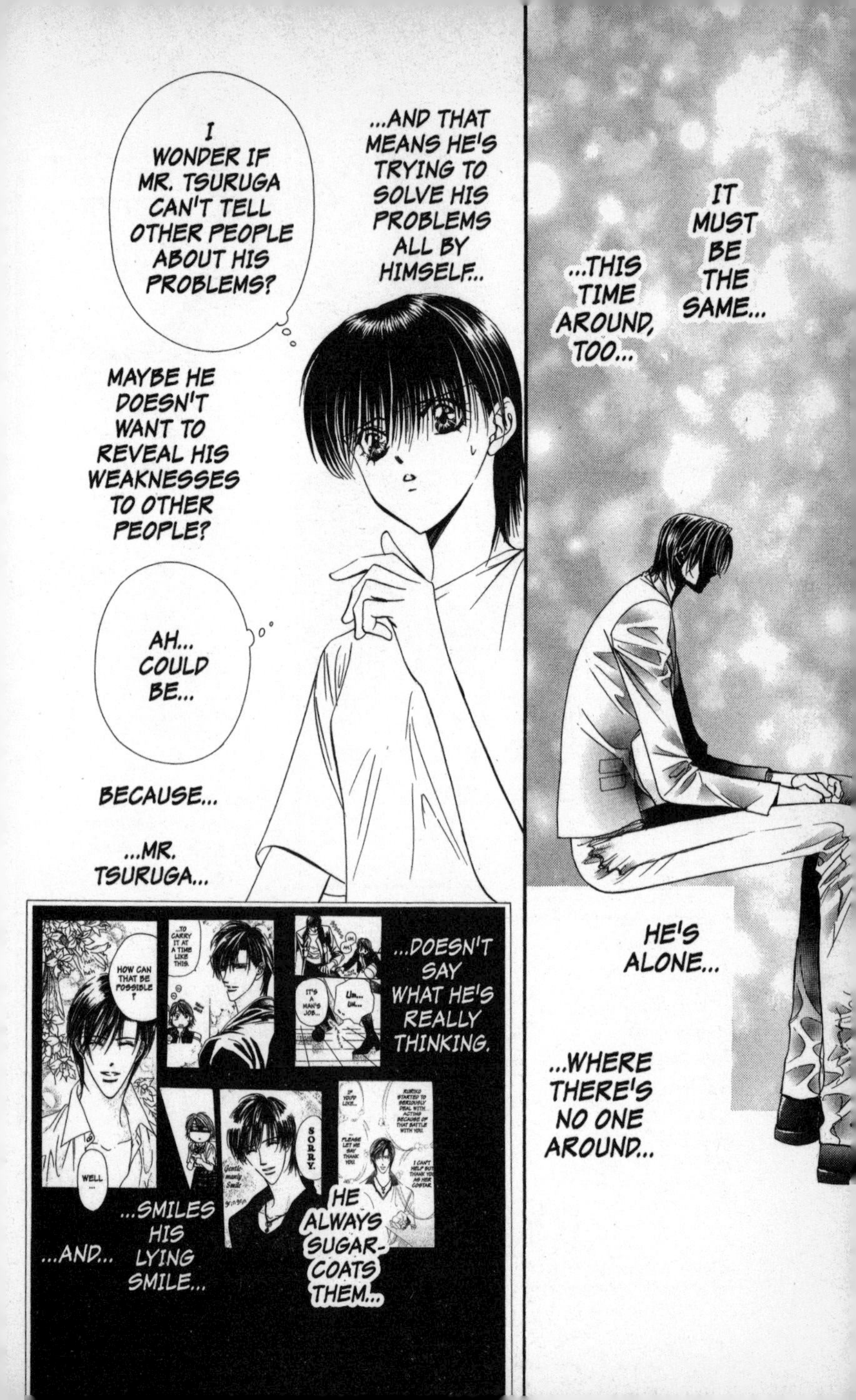
IT MUST BE THE SAME...
...THIS TIME AROUND, TOO...
HE'S ALONE...
...WHERE THERE'S NO ONE AROUND...
...AND THAT MEANS HE'S TRYING TO SOLVE HIS PROBLEMS ALL BY HIMSELF...
I WONDER IF MR. TSURUGA CAN'T TELL OTHER PEOPLE ABOUT HIS PROBLEMS?
MAYBE HE DOESN'T WANT TO REVEAL HIS WEAKNESSES TO OTHER PEOPLE?
AH... COULD BE...
BECAUSE...
...MR. TSURUGA...
...DOESN'T SAY WHAT HE'S REALLY THINKING.
IT'S A MAN'S JOB...
...TO CARRY IT AT A TIME LIKE THIS.
HOW CAN THAT BE POSSIBLE?
WELL...
SORRY.
HE ALWAYS SUGAR-COATS THEM...
...SMILES HIS LYING SMILE...
...AND...

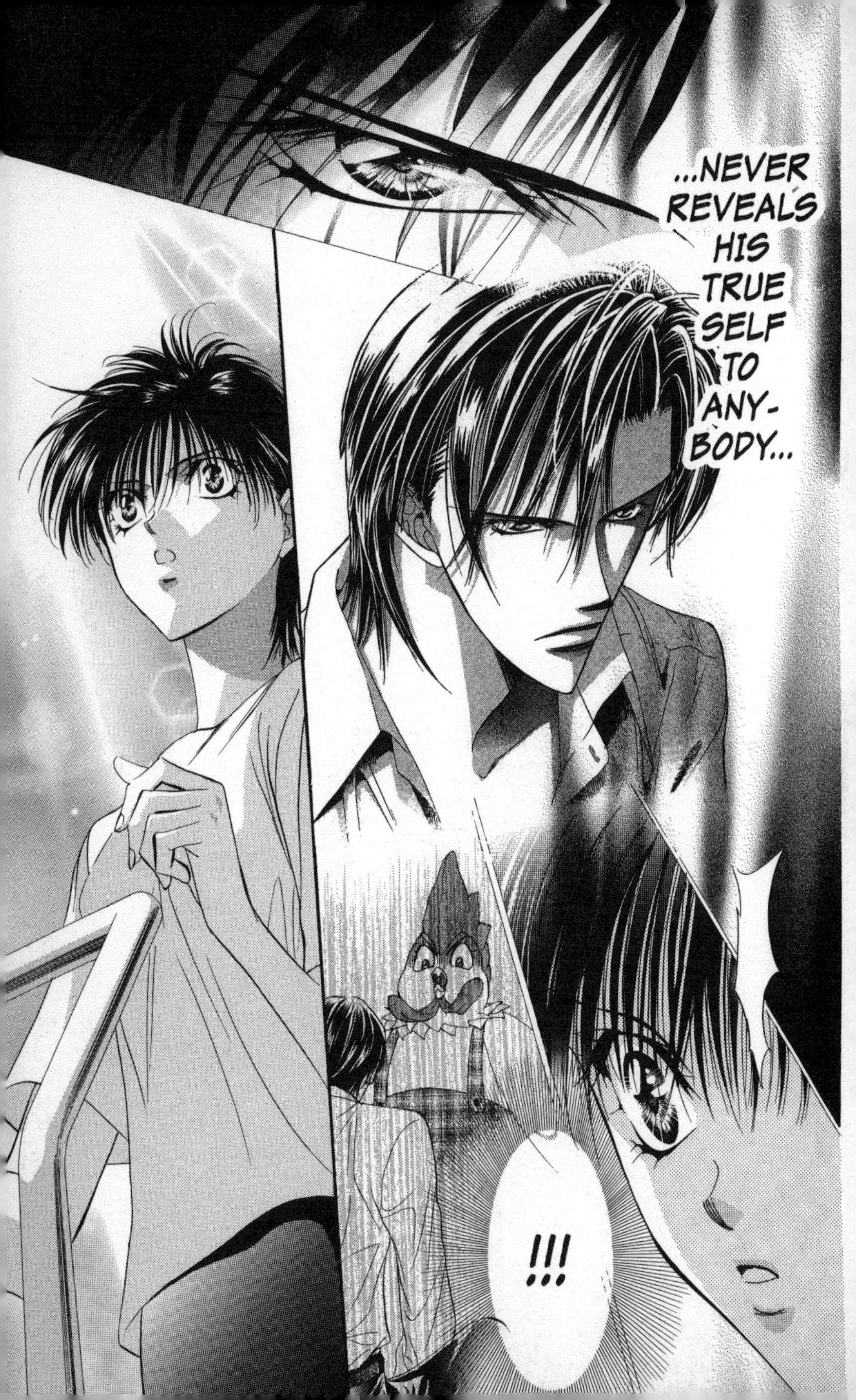
...NEVER REVEALS HIS TRUE SELF TO ANY-BODY...
!!!

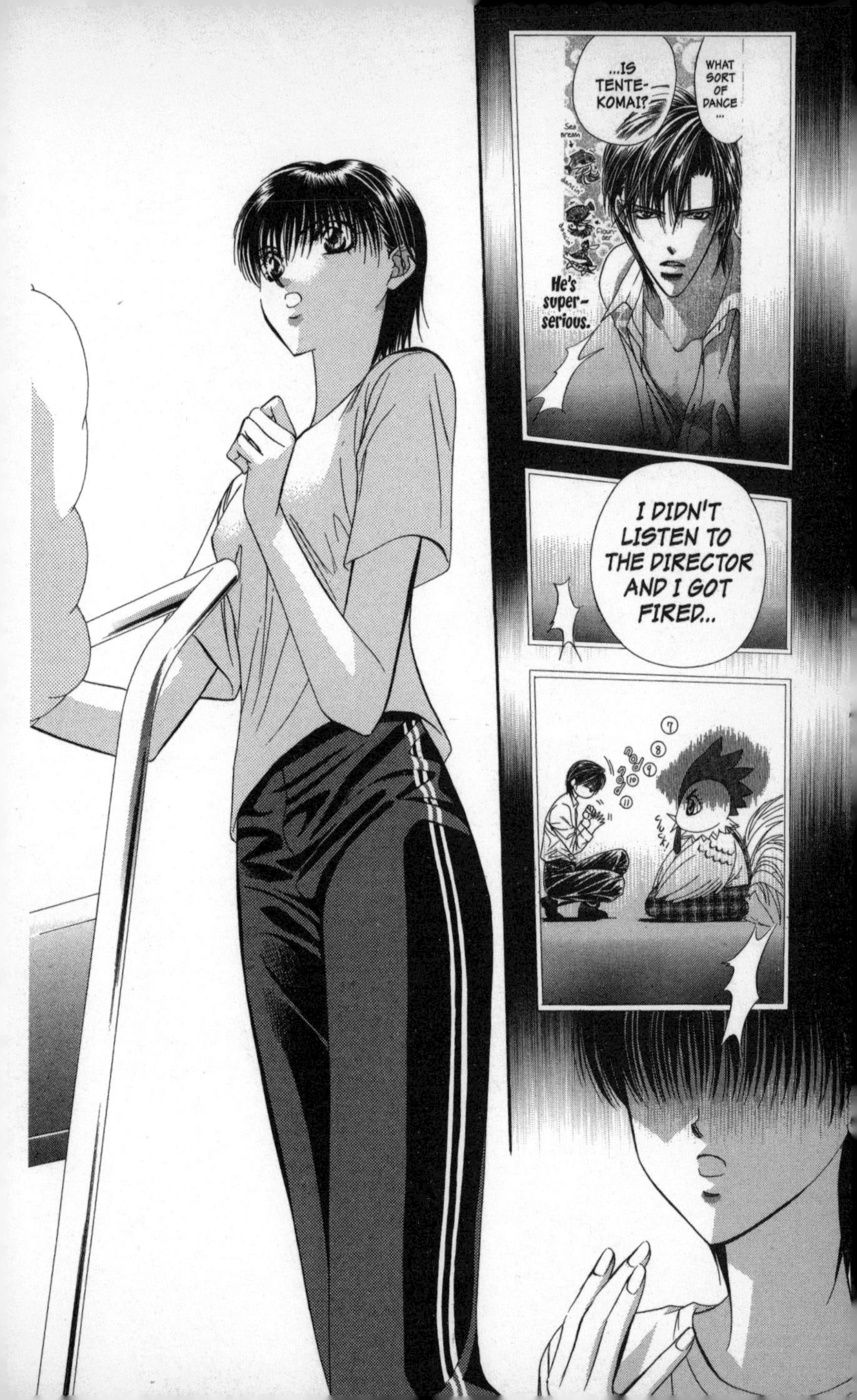
WHAT SORT OF DANCE ...
...IS TENTE-KOMAI?
He's super-serious.
I DIDN'T LISTEN TO THE DIRECTOR AND I GOT FIRED...
CLUCK!

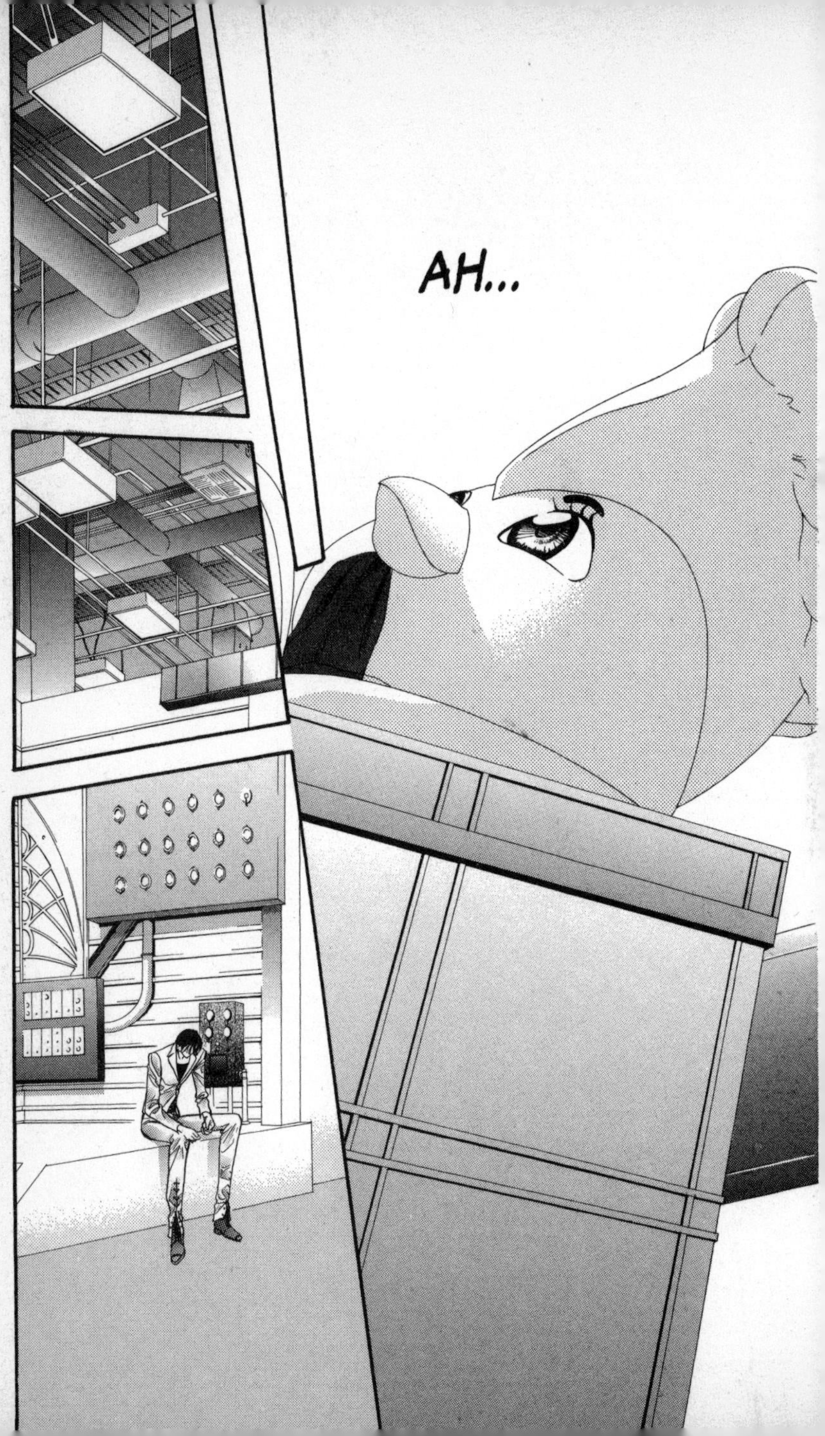
AH...

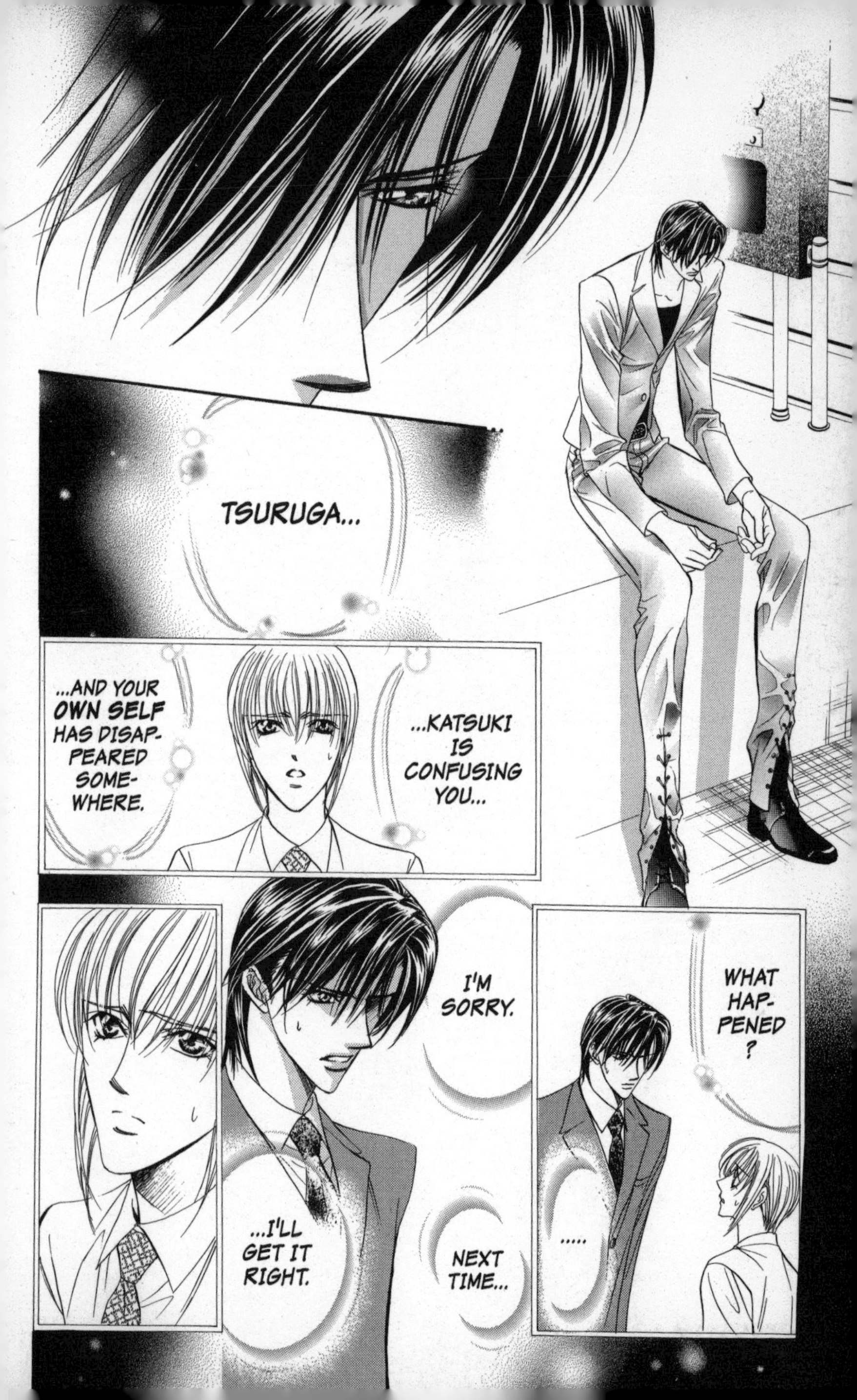
TSURUGA...
...KATSUKI IS CONFUSING YOU...
...AND YOUR OWN SELF HAS DISAPPEARED SOMEWHERE.
WHAT HAPPENED?
.....
I'M SORRY.
NEXT TIME...
...I'LL GET IT RIGHT.

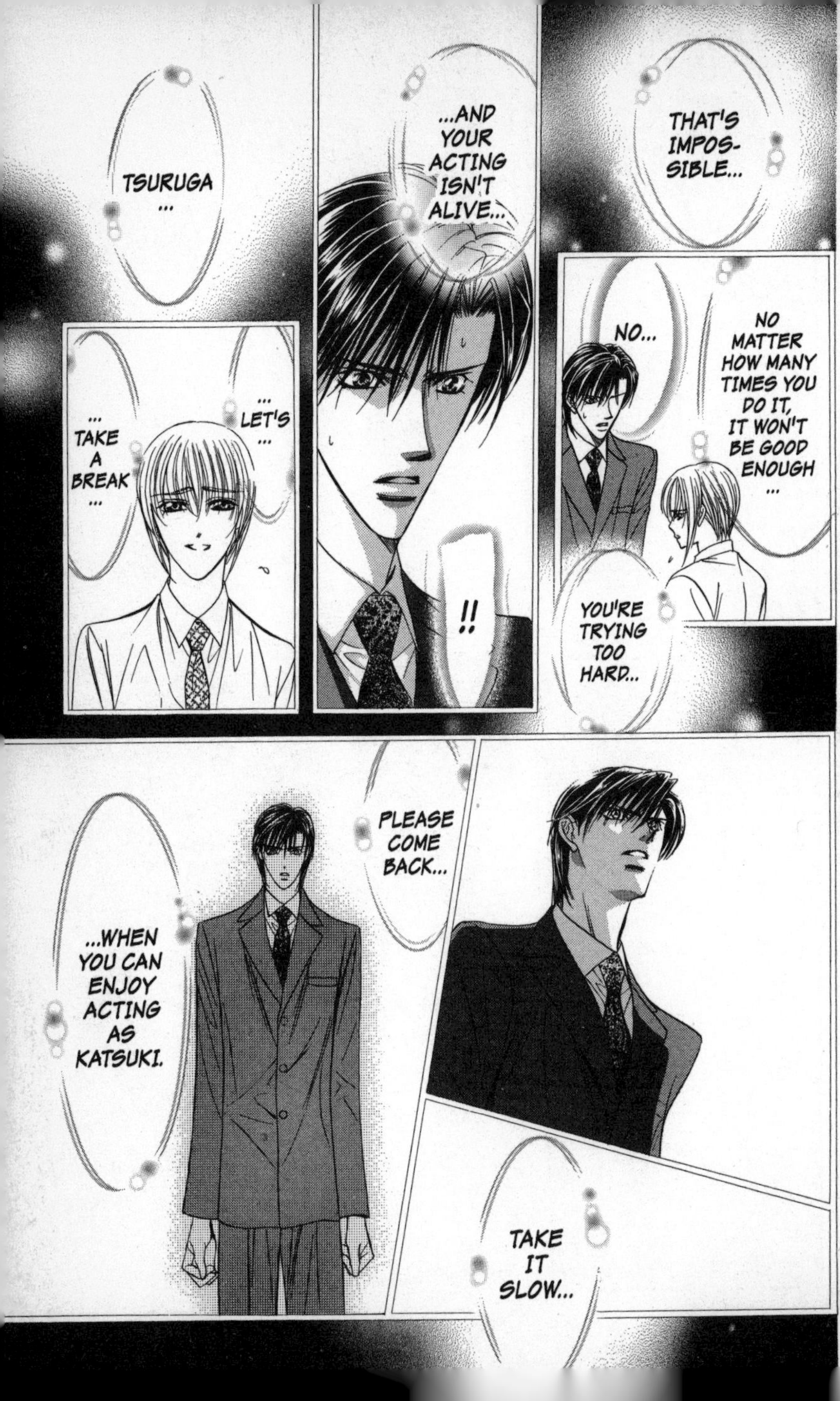
THAT'S IMPOS-SIBLE...
NO MATTER HOW MANY TIMES YOU DO IT, IT WON'T BE GOOD ENOUGH...
NO...
YOU'RE TRYING TOO HARD...
...AND YOUR ACTING ISN'T ALIVE...
!!
TSURUGA...
...LET'S...
...TAKE A BREAK...
TAKE IT SLOW...
PLEASE COME BACK...
...WHEN YOU CAN ENJOY ACTING AS KATSUKI.

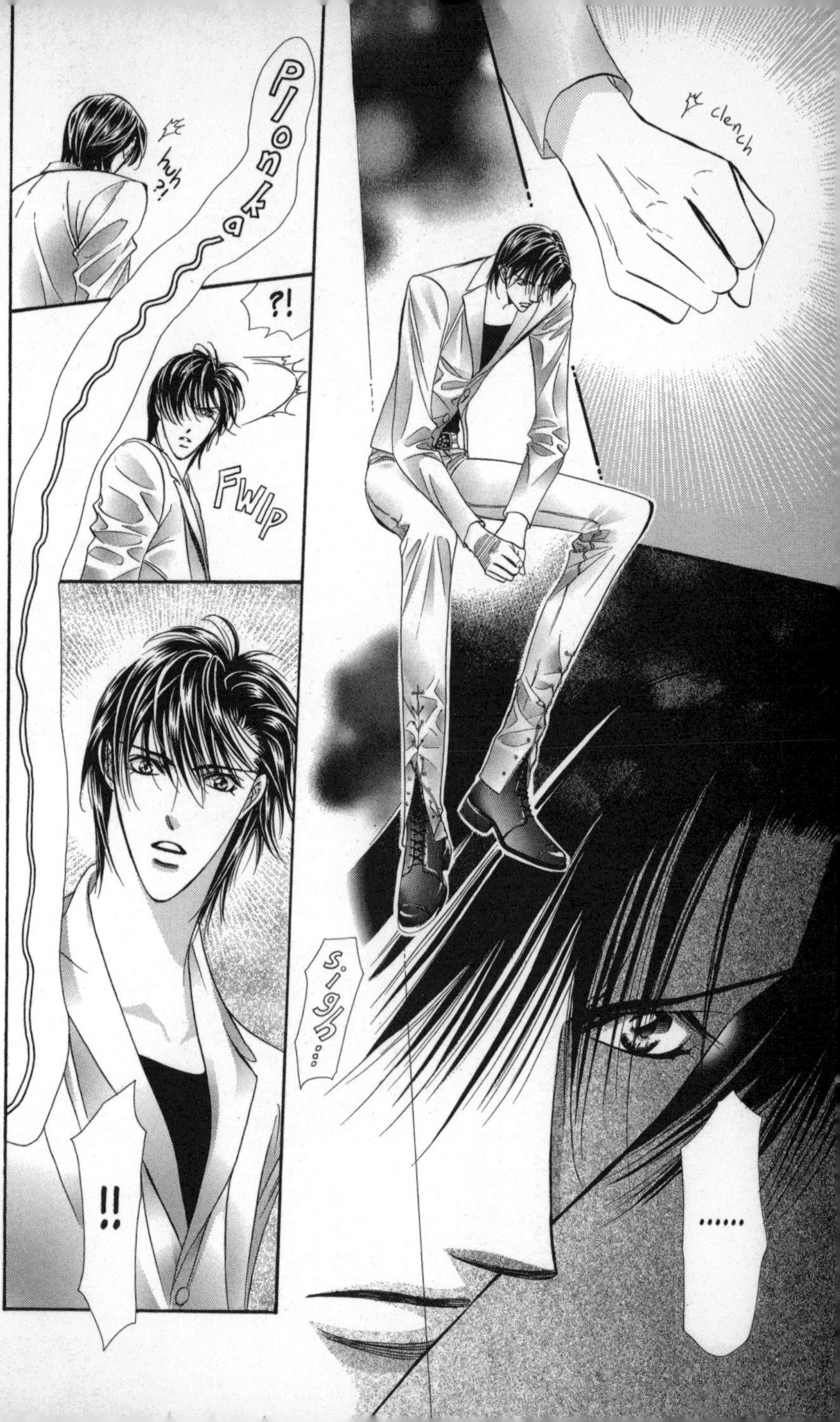
clench
sigh...
......
Plomka~
huh ?!
?!
FWIP
!!

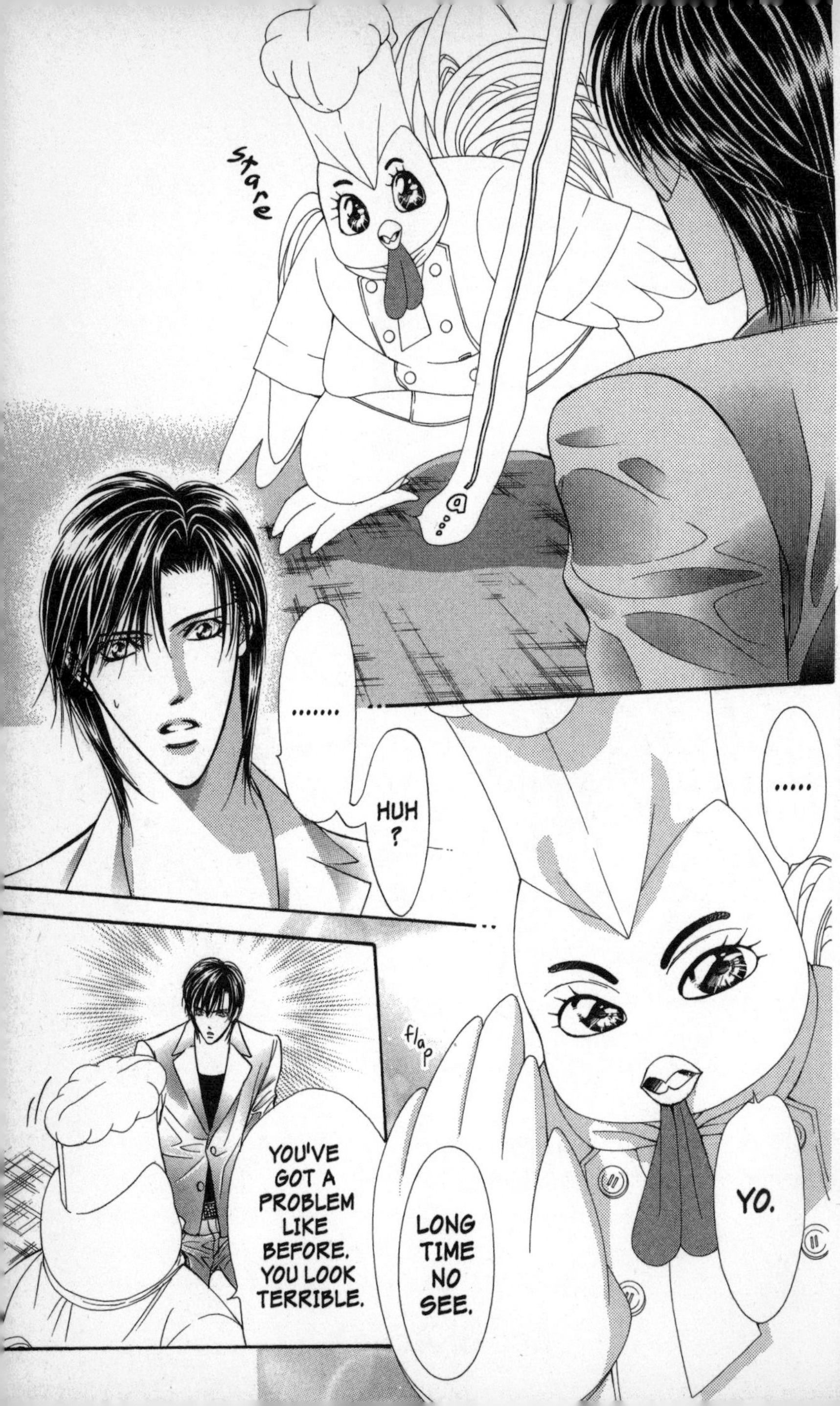
Stare
.....
flap
YO.
LONG TIME NO SEE.
....
HUH?
YOU'VE GOT A PROBLEM LIKE BEFORE. YOU LOOK TERRIBLE.

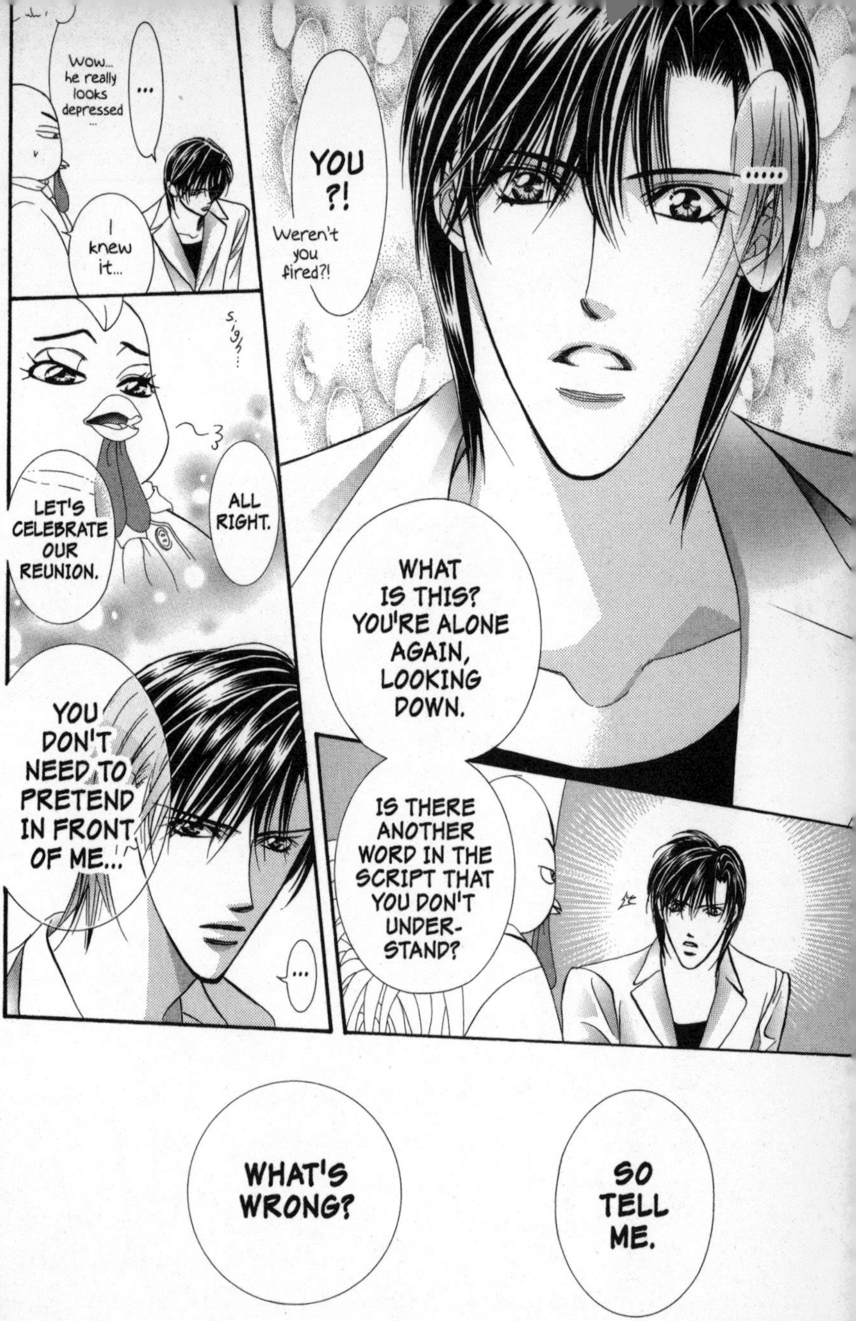
......
YOU ?!
Weren't you fired?!
WHAT IS THIS? YOU'RE ALONE AGAIN, LOOKING DOWN.
IS THERE ANOTHER WORD IN THE SCRIPT THAT YOU DON'T UNDER-STAND?
...
Wow... he really looks depressed ...
I knew it...
sigh...
ALL RIGHT.
LET'S CELEBRATE OUR REUNION.
YOU DON'T NEED TO PRETEND IN FRONT OF ME...!
...
SO TELL ME.
WHAT'S WRONG?

End of Act 63

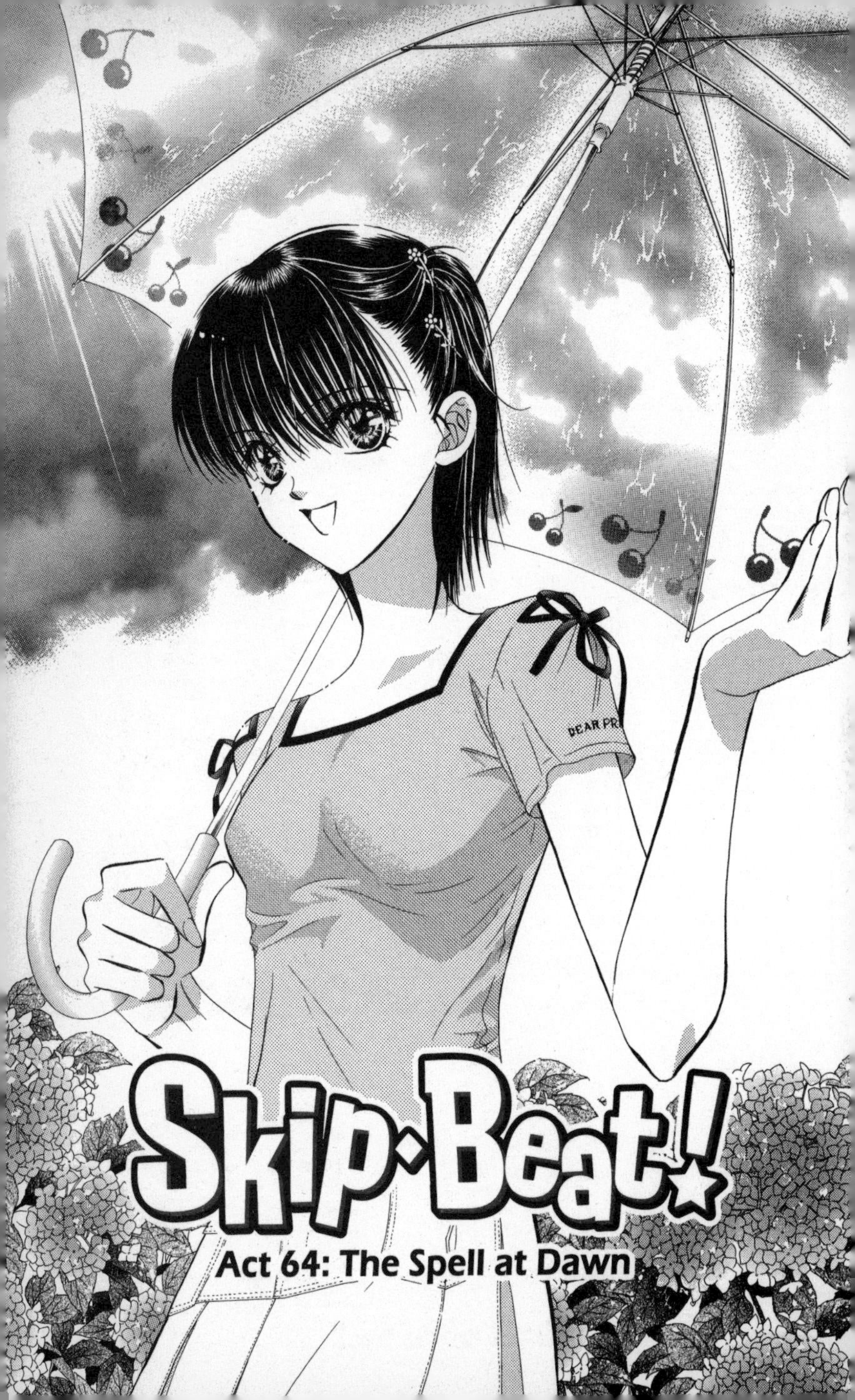
Skip·Beat!
Act 64: The Spell at Dawn

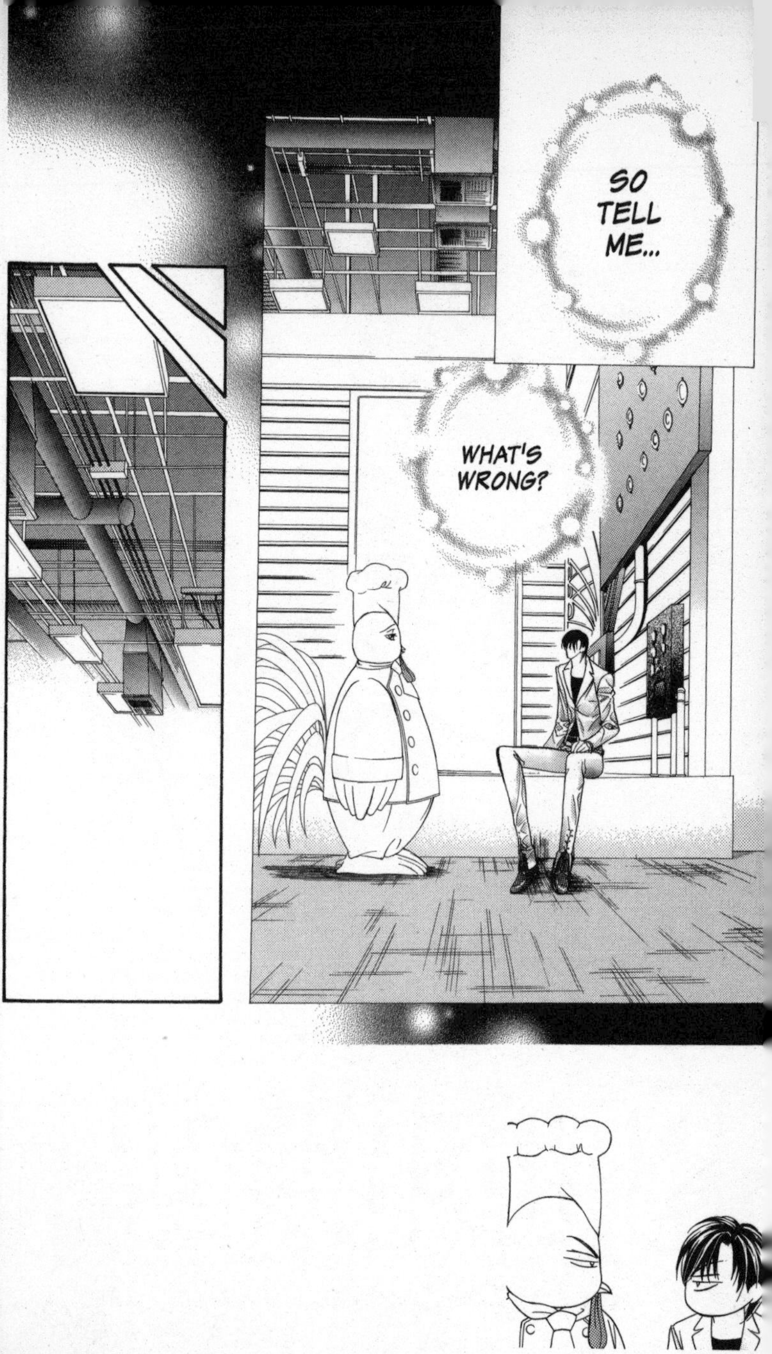
SO TELL ME...
WHAT'S WRONG?

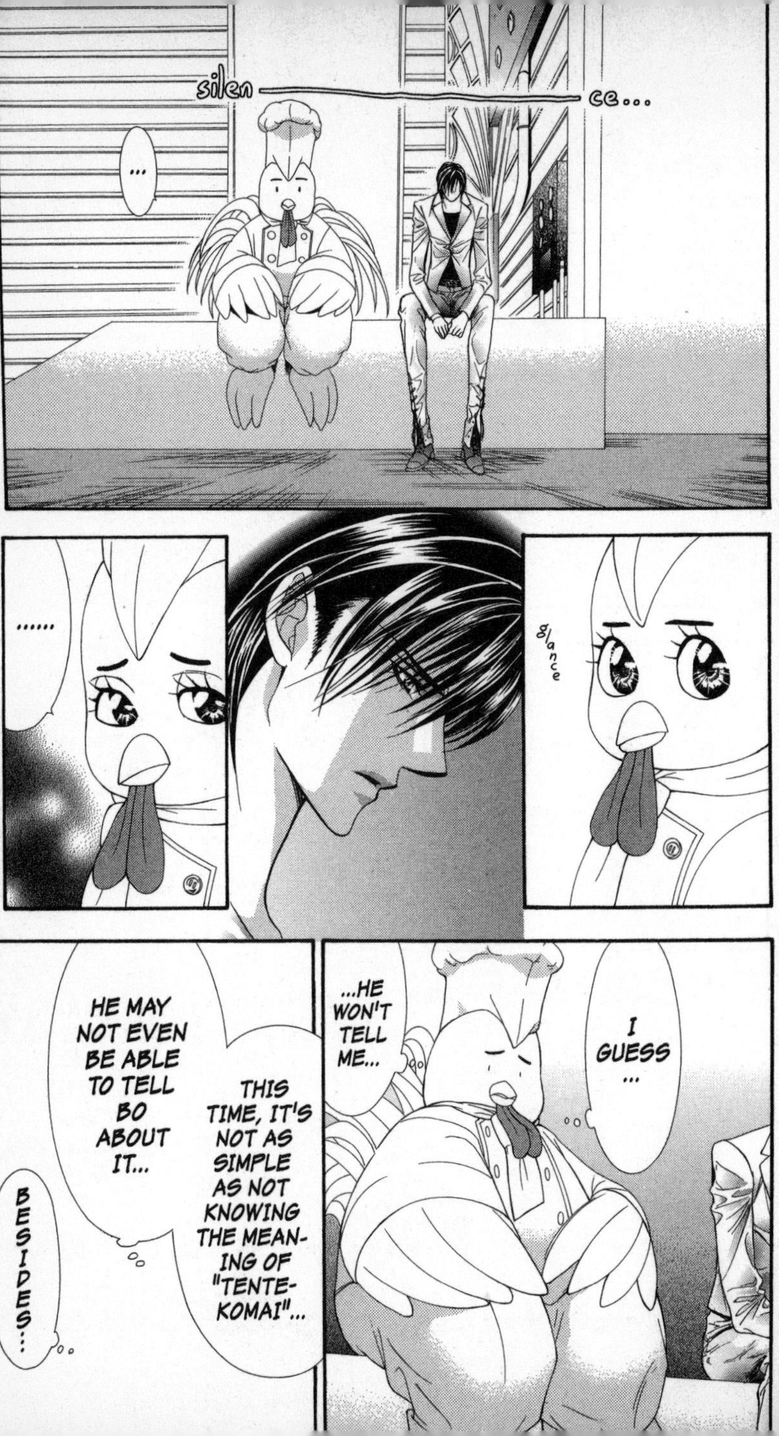
silen——ce...
...
glance
......
I GUESS...
...HE WON'T TELL ME...
THIS TIME, IT'S NOT AS SIMPLE AS NOT KNOWING THE MEANING OF "TENTE-KOMAI"...
HE MAY NOT EVEN BE ABLE TO TELL BO ABOUT IT...
BESIDES...

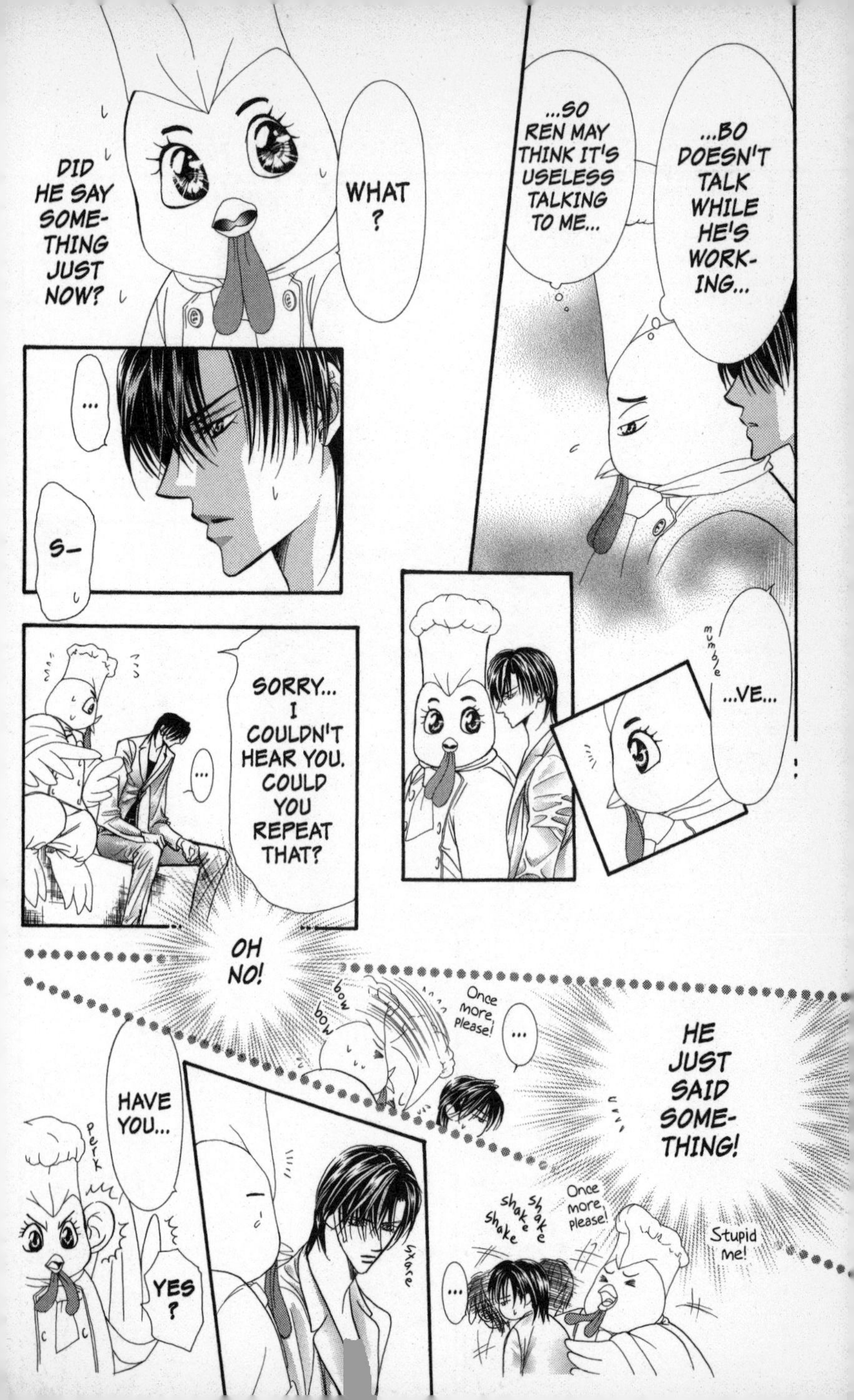

...BO DOESN'T TALK WHILE HE'S WORKING...
...SO REN MAY THINK IT'S USELESS TALKING TO ME...
mumble
...VE...
WHAT?
DID HE SAY SOMETHING JUST NOW?
...
S–
SORRY... I COULDN'T HEAR YOU. COULD YOU REPEAT THAT?
...
OH NO!
HE JUST SAID SOMETHING!
Once more, please!
...
bow bow
Once more, please!
shake shake shake
Stupid me!
...
HAVE YOU...
perk
YES?
stare

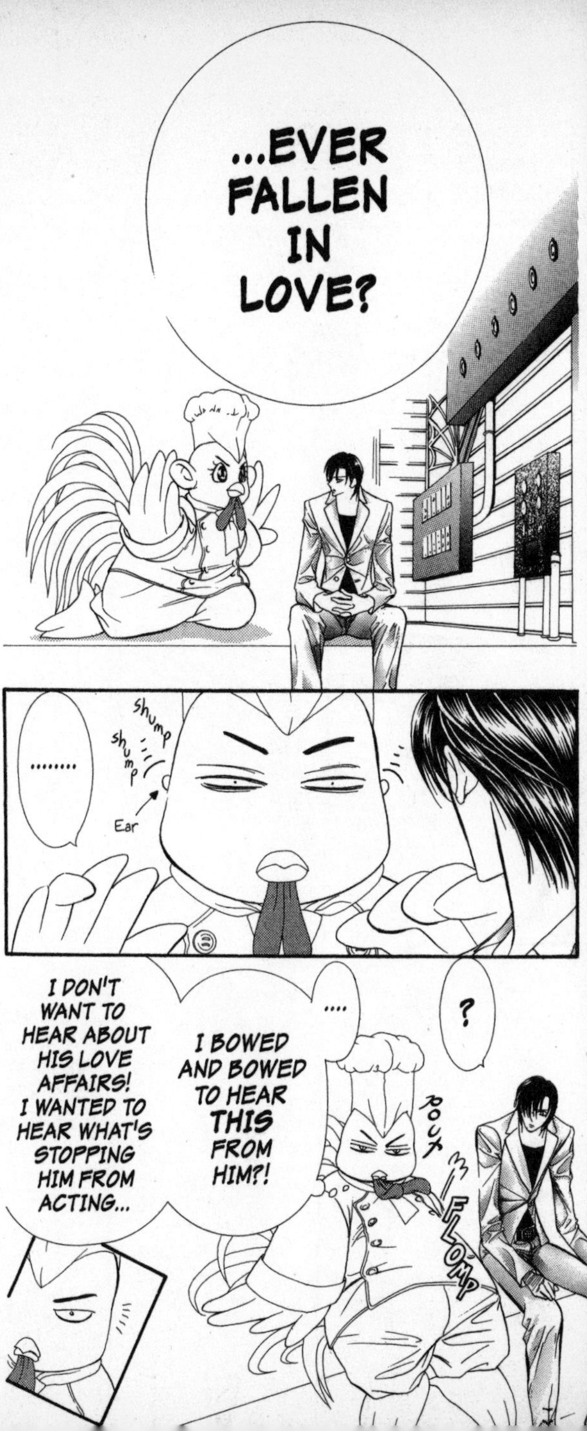
...EVER FALLEN IN LOVE?
....
shump shump
Ear
?
....
I BOWED AND BOWED TO HEAR THIS FROM HIM?!
I DON'T WANT TO HEAR ABOUT HIS LOVE AFFAIRS! I WANTED TO HEAR WHAT'S STOPPING HIM FROM ACTING...
POUT
FLOMP

About the Role

Readers' letters asked about Ren's role, about whether someone who's 20 can become a teacher...I don't think I really need to explain it here...but I will. Just because Ren is 20 doesn't mean that he can't play roles that are older than his real age. So it's all right. The important thing is whether he can play the role and look natural in it. The way Ren looks, he can probably play a 25-year-old... Because he looks older than he really is...yes...

By the way...

I wanted to put this in the story, but I haven't had a chance to do so, so I'll write it here. DARK MOON will be a 19-episode series. It is a little longer than current dramas...no...in the '80s, not all the dramas were as short as they are now... And...since this is a large-scale production... right?...

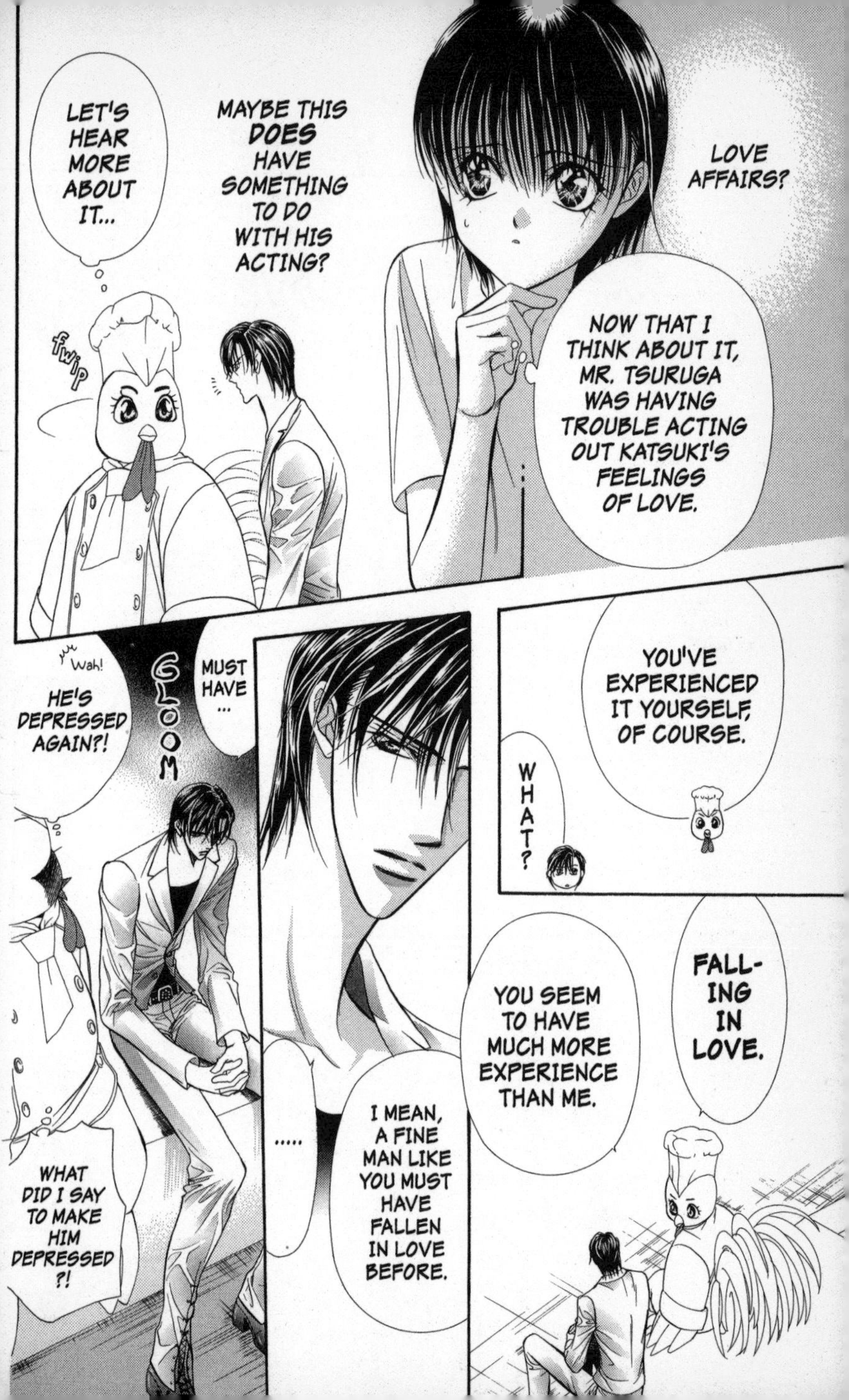
LOVE AFFAIRS?
NOW THAT I THINK ABOUT IT, MR. TSURUGA WAS HAVING TROUBLE ACTING OUT KATSUKI'S FEELINGS OF LOVE.
MAYBE THIS DOES HAVE SOMETHING TO DO WITH HIS ACTING?
LET'S HEAR MORE ABOUT IT...
fwip
YOU'VE EXPERIENCED IT YOURSELF, OF COURSE.
WHAT?
FALLING IN LOVE.
YOU SEEM TO HAVE MUCH MORE EXPERIENCE THAN ME.
I MEAN, A FINE MAN LIKE YOU MUST HAVE FALLEN IN LOVE BEFORE.
.....
MUST HAVE ...
GLOOM
Wah!
HE'S DEPRESSED AGAIN?!
WHAT DID I SAY TO MAKE HIM DEPRESSED ?!

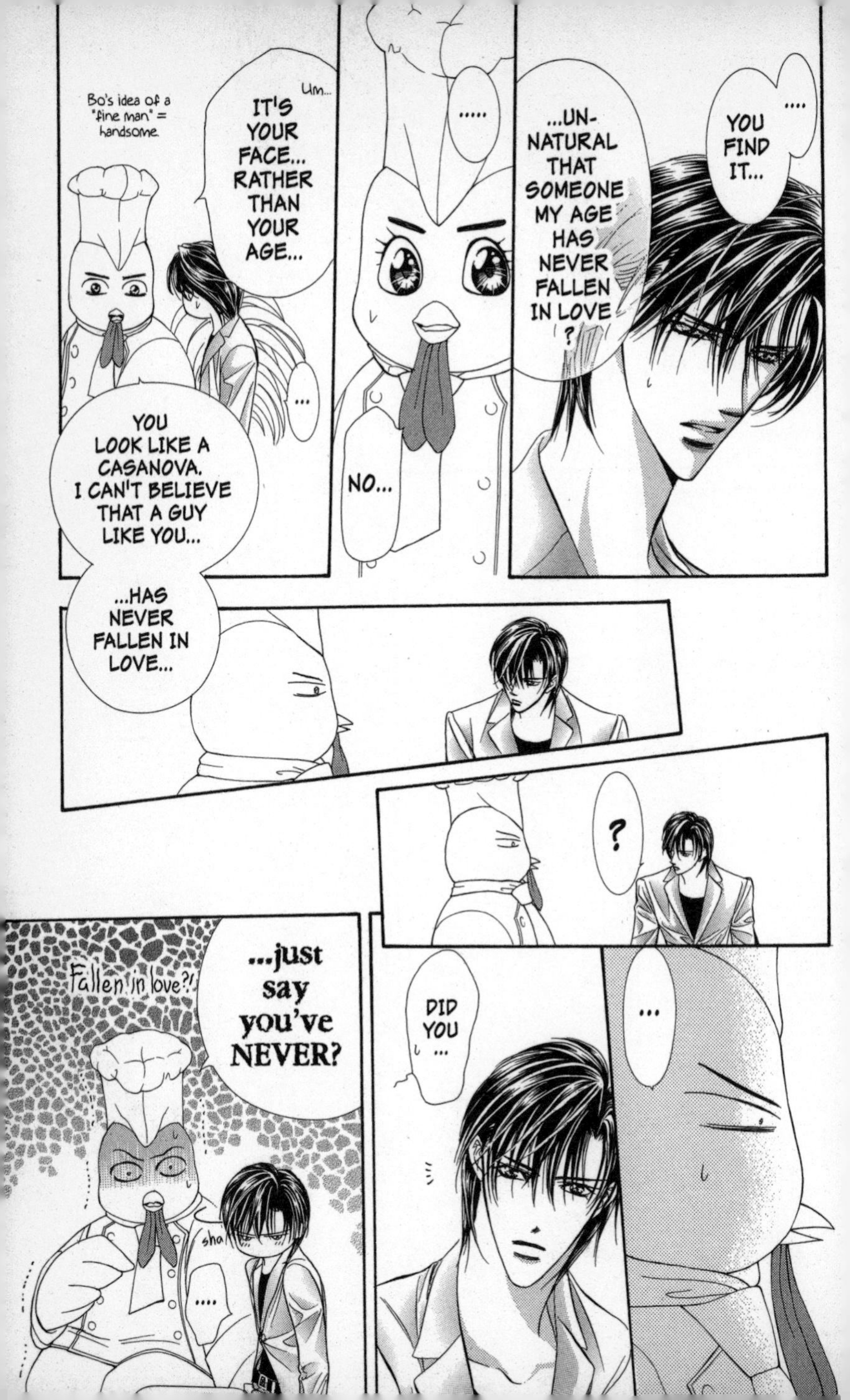
....
YOU FIND IT...
...UN-NATURAL THAT SOMEONE MY AGE HAS NEVER FALLEN IN LOVE?
.....
NO...
...
Um...
IT'S YOUR FACE... RATHER THAN YOUR AGE...
Bo's idea of a "fine man" = handsome.
YOU LOOK LIKE A CASANOVA. I CAN'T BELIEVE THAT A GUY LIKE YOU...
...HAS NEVER FALLEN IN LOVE...
?
...
DID YOU ...
...just say you've NEVER?
Fallen in love?!
sha
....

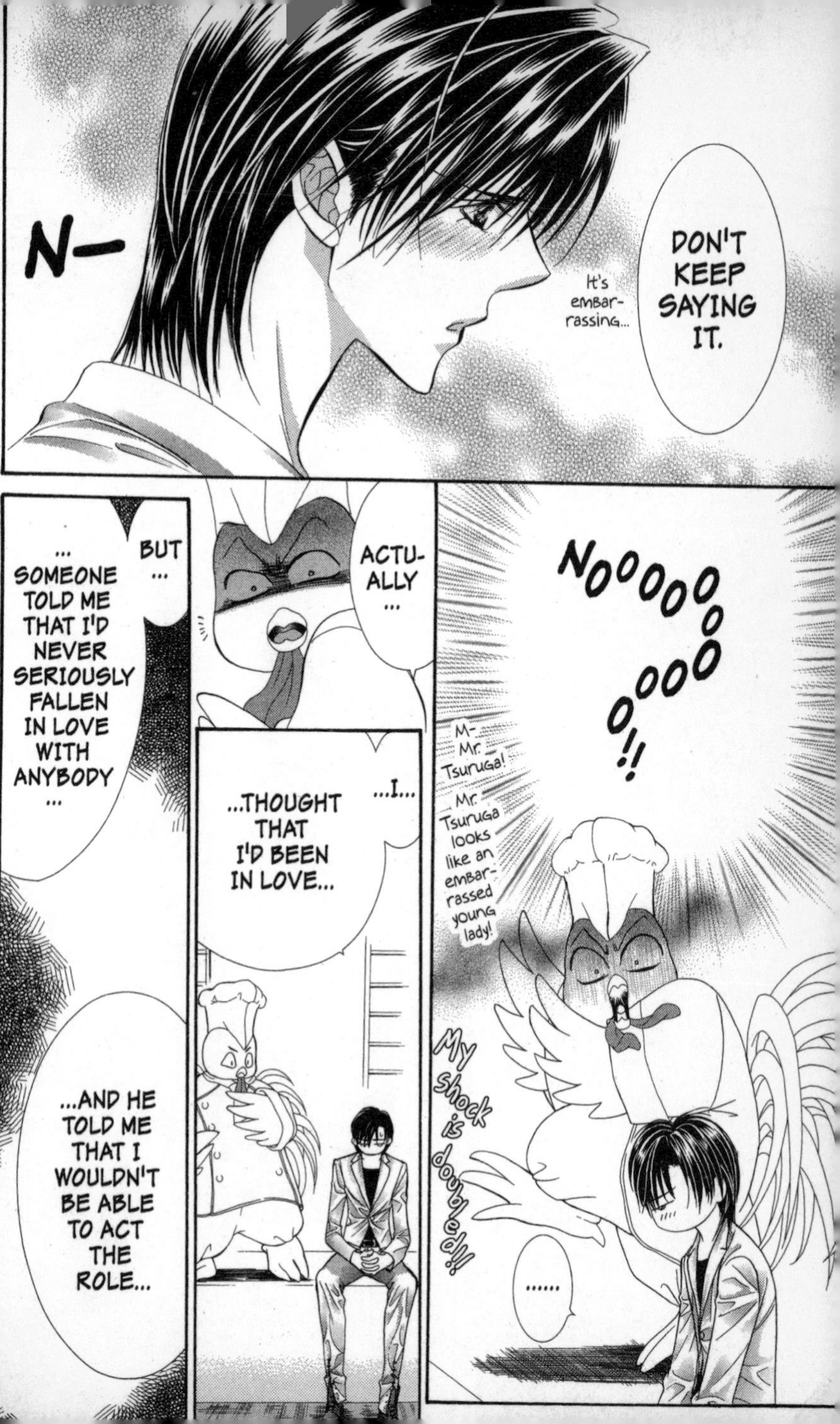

DON'T KEEP SAYING IT.
It's embarrassing...
N—
NOOOOOOOOOOOO!!
M-Mr. Tsuruga!
Mr. Tsuruga looks like an embarrassed young lady!
My shock is doubled!!
......
ACTUALLY...
...I...
...THOUGHT THAT I'D BEEN IN LOVE...
BUT...
...SOMEONE TOLD ME THAT I'D NEVER SERIOUSLY FALLEN IN LOVE WITH ANYBODY...
...AND HE TOLD ME THAT I WOULDN'T BE ABLE TO ACT THE ROLE...

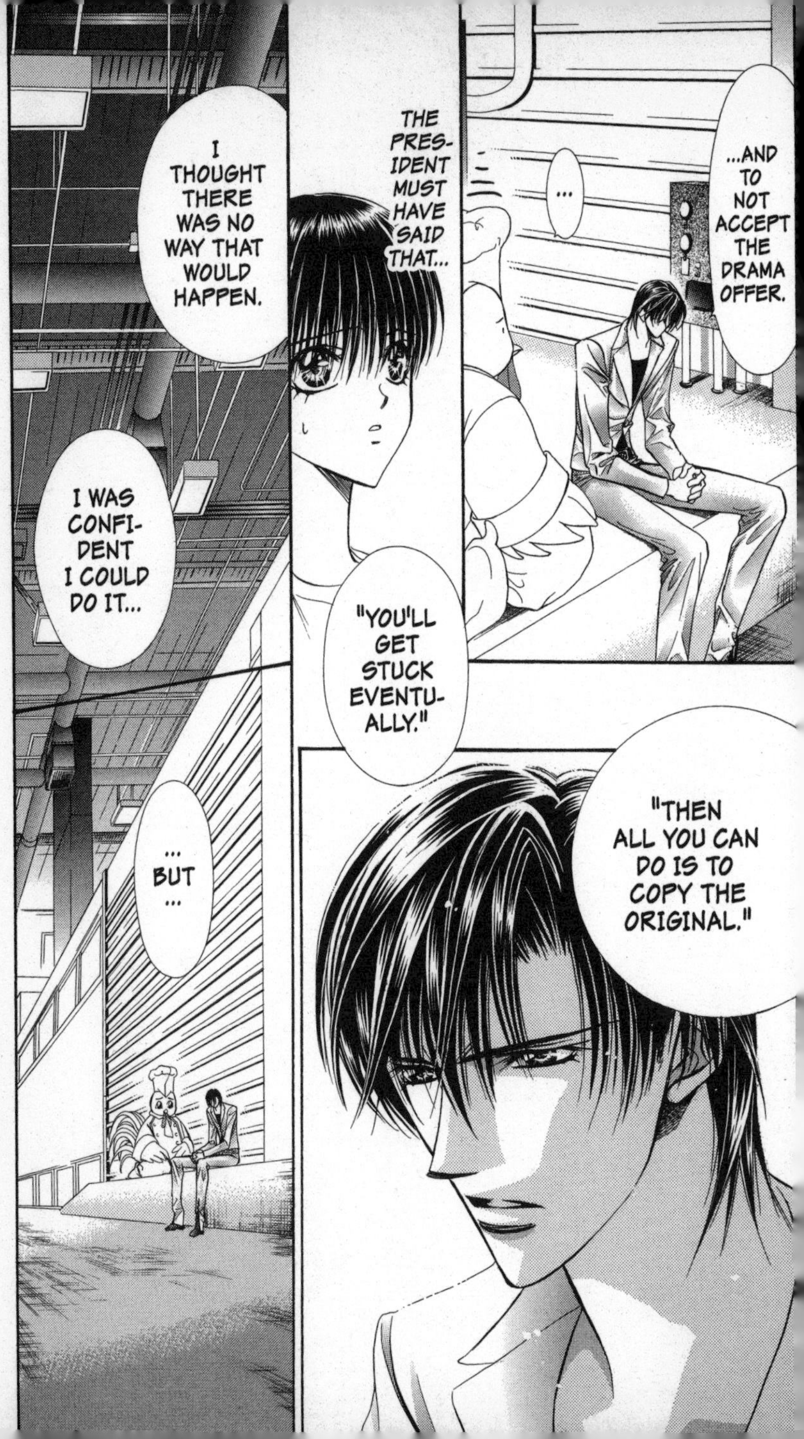
...AND TO NOT ACCEPT THE DRAMA OFFER.
...
THE PRESIDENT MUST HAVE SAID THAT...
"YOU'LL GET STUCK EVENTUALLY."
"THEN ALL YOU CAN DO IS TO COPY THE ORIGINAL."
I THOUGHT THERE WAS NO WAY THAT WOULD HAPPEN.
I WAS CONFIDENT I COULD DO IT...
... BUT ...

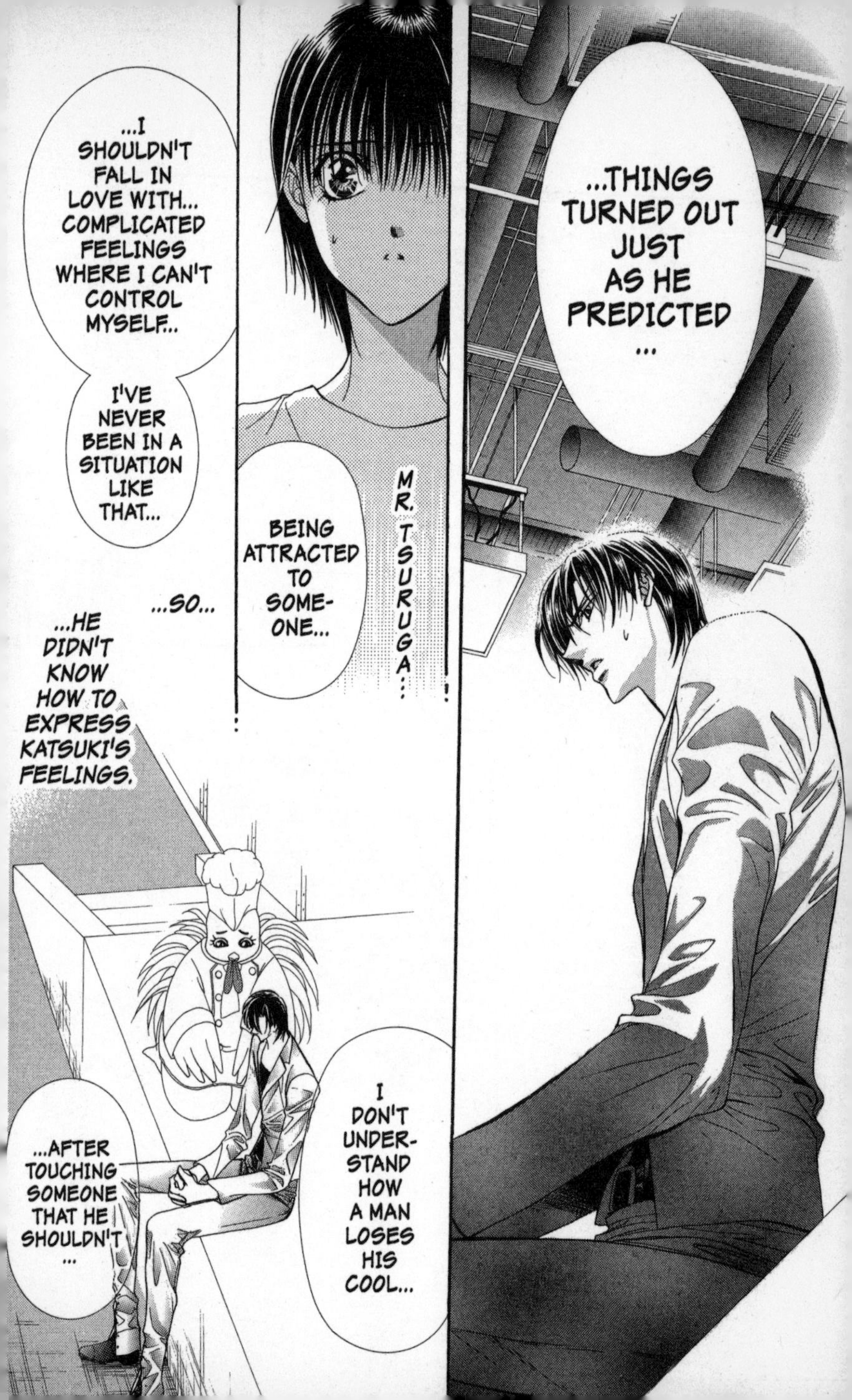
...THINGS TURNED OUT JUST AS HE PREDICTED...
MR. TSURUGA...!
BEING ATTRACTED TO SOME-ONE...
...I SHOULDN'T FALL IN LOVE WITH... COMPLICATED FEELINGS WHERE I CAN'T CONTROL MYSELF...
I'VE NEVER BEEN IN A SITUATION LIKE THAT...
...SO...
...HE DIDN'T KNOW HOW TO EXPRESS KATSUKI'S FEELINGS.
I DON'T UNDER-STAND HOW A MAN LOSES HIS COOL...
...AFTER TOUCHING SOMEONE THAT HE SHOULDN'T...

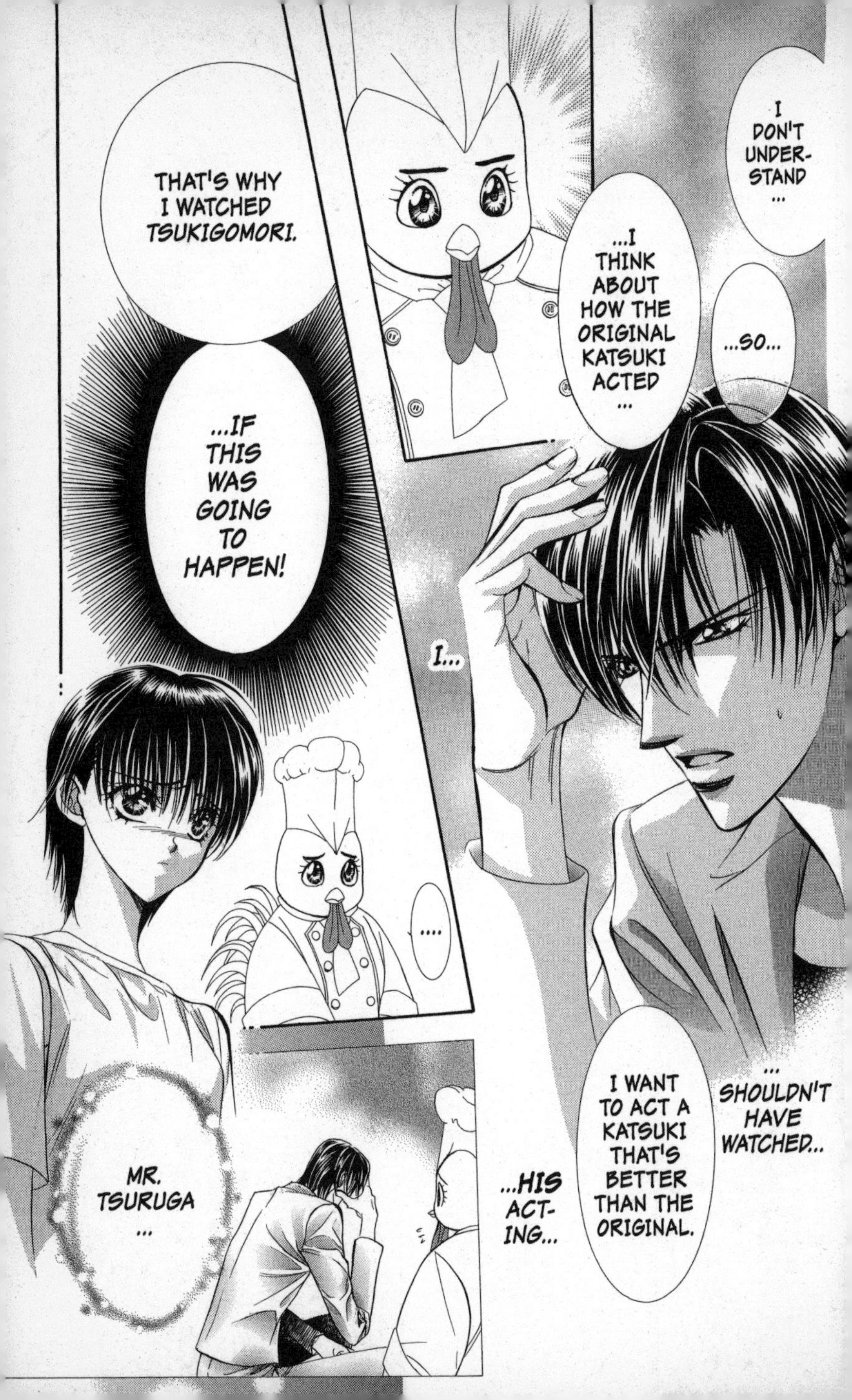
I DON'T UNDER-STAND...
...SO...
...I THINK ABOUT HOW THE ORIGINAL KATSUKI ACTED...
THAT'S WHY I WATCHED TSUKIGOMORI.
...IF THIS WAS GOING TO HAPPEN!
I...
...SHOULDN'T HAVE WATCHED...
...HIS ACT-ING...
I WANT TO ACT A KATSUKI THAT'S BETTER THAN THE ORIGINAL.
....
MR. TSURUGA...

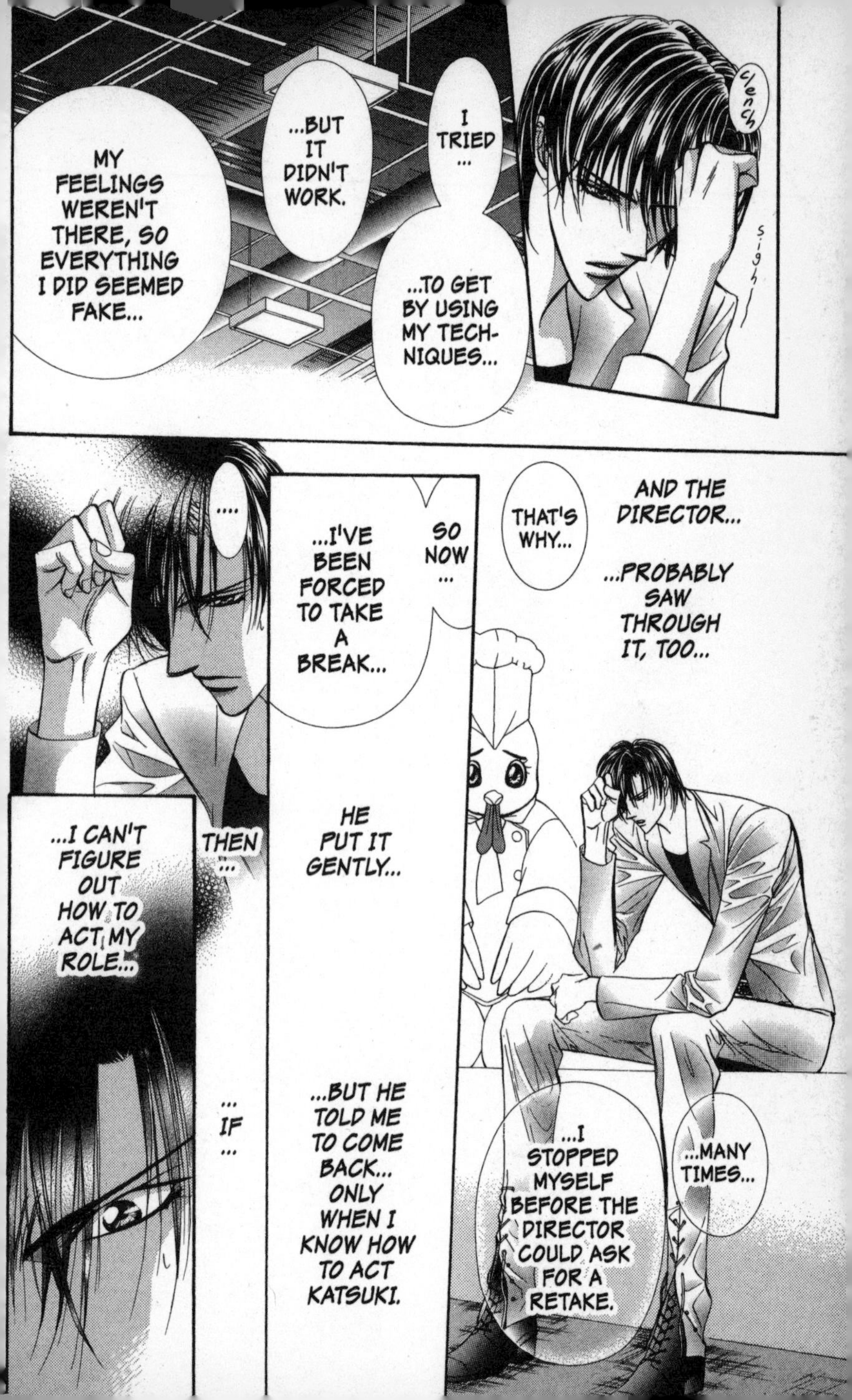
clench
sigh
I TRIED...
...TO GET BY USING MY TECHNIQUES...
...BUT IT DIDN'T WORK.
MY FEELINGS WEREN'T THERE, SO EVERYTHING I DID SEEMED FAKE...
AND THE DIRECTOR...
...PROBABLY SAW THROUGH IT, TOO...
THAT'S WHY...
...MANY TIMES...
...I STOPPED MYSELF BEFORE THE DIRECTOR COULD ASK FOR A RETAKE.
SO NOW...
...I'VE BEEN FORCED TO TAKE A BREAK...
HE PUT IT GENTLY...
...BUT HE TOLD ME TO COME BACK... ONLY WHEN I KNOW HOW TO ACT KATSUKI.
....
THEN...
...I CAN'T FIGURE OUT HOW TO ACT MY ROLE...
...IF...

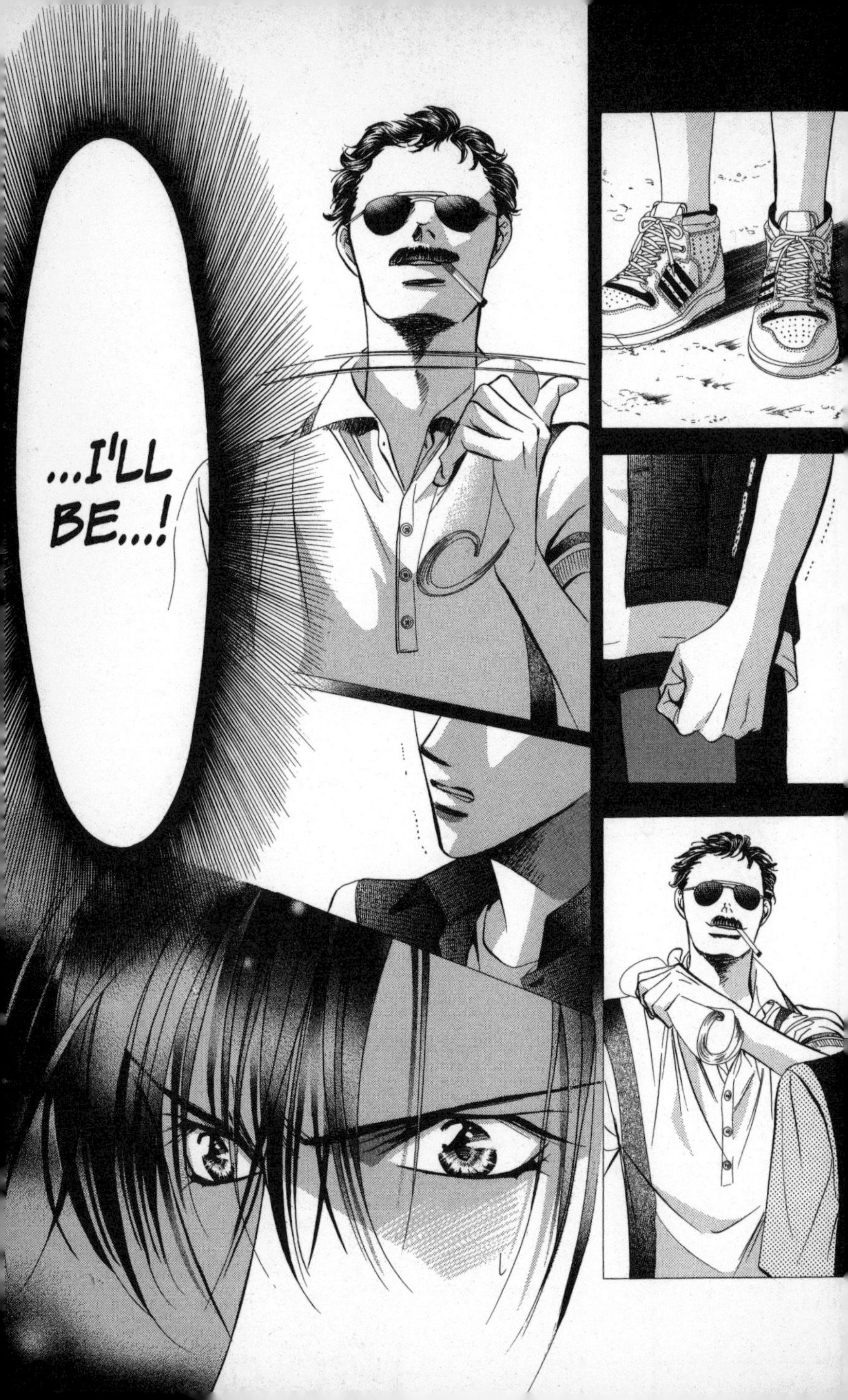
...I'LL BE...!

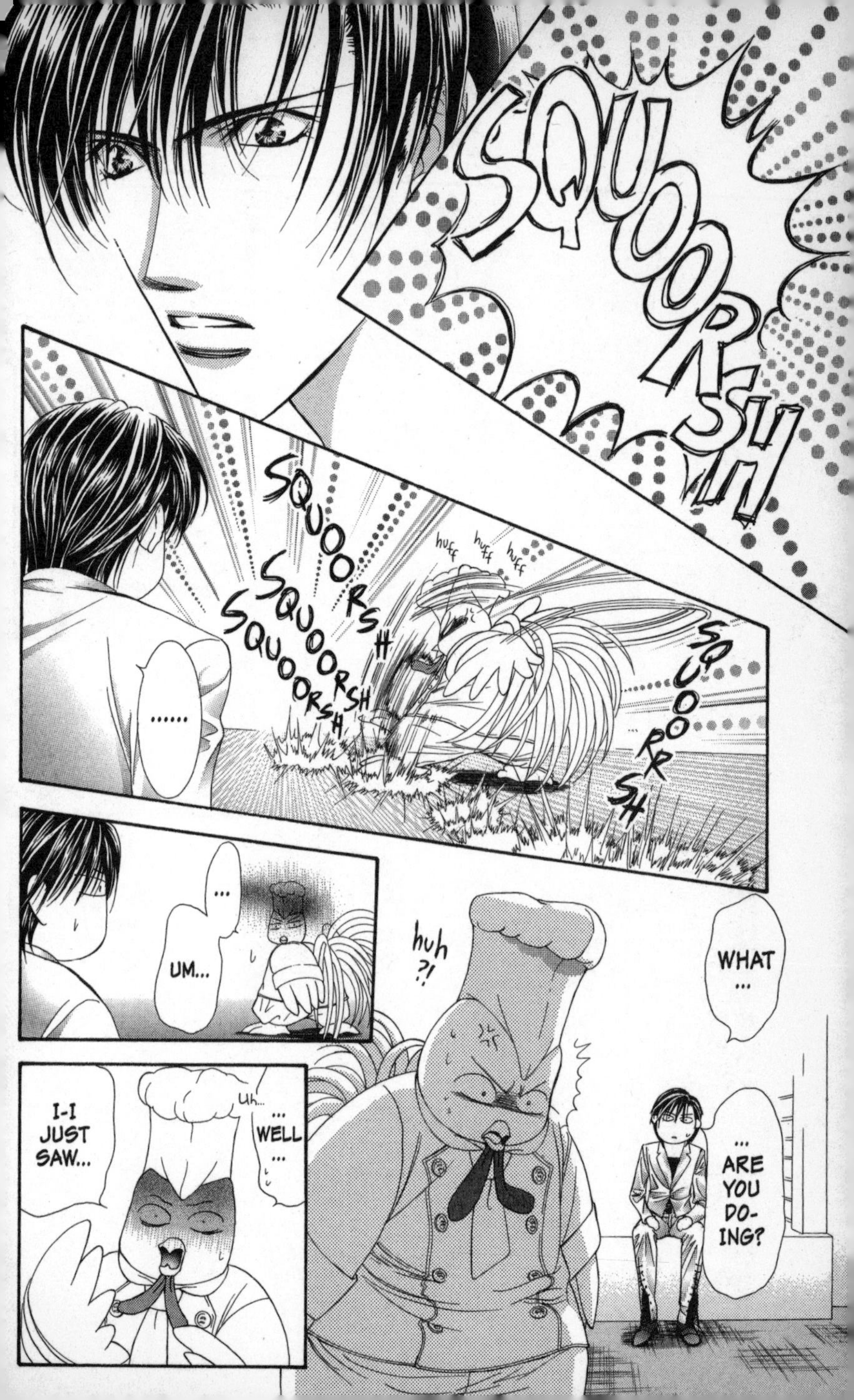
SQUOOORSH
SQUOOORRSH
huff huff huff
SQUOOORSH SQUOOORSH SQUOOORSH
......
WHAT ...
... ARE YOU DOING?
huh ?!
... UM...
Uh... ... WELL ...
I-I JUST SAW...

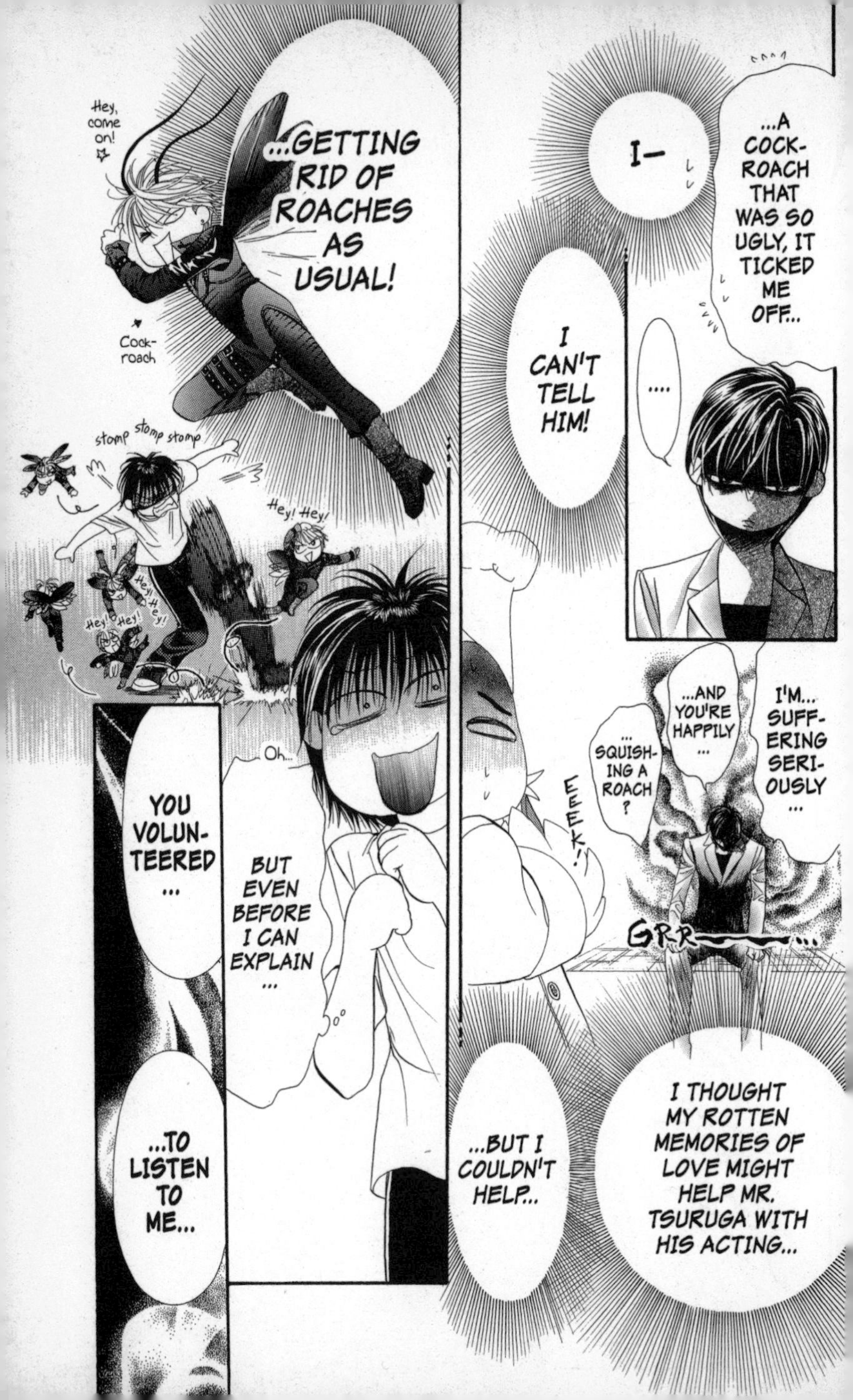

I—
...A COCKROACH THAT WAS SO UGLY, IT TICKED ME OFF...
....
I CAN'T TELL HIM!
I'M... SUFFERING SERIOUSLY...
...AND YOU'RE HAPPILY...
...SQUISHING A ROACH?
GRR—...
EEEK!
I THOUGHT MY ROTTEN MEMORIES OF LOVE MIGHT HELP MR. TSURUGA WITH HIS ACTING...
...BUT I COULDN'T HELP...
...GETTING RID OF ROACHES AS USUAL!
Hey, come on!
Cockroach
stomp stomp stomp
Hey! Hey!
Hey! Hey!
Hey! Hey!
Oh...
BUT EVEN BEFORE I CAN EXPLAIN...
YOU VOLUNTEERED...
...TO LISTEN TO ME...

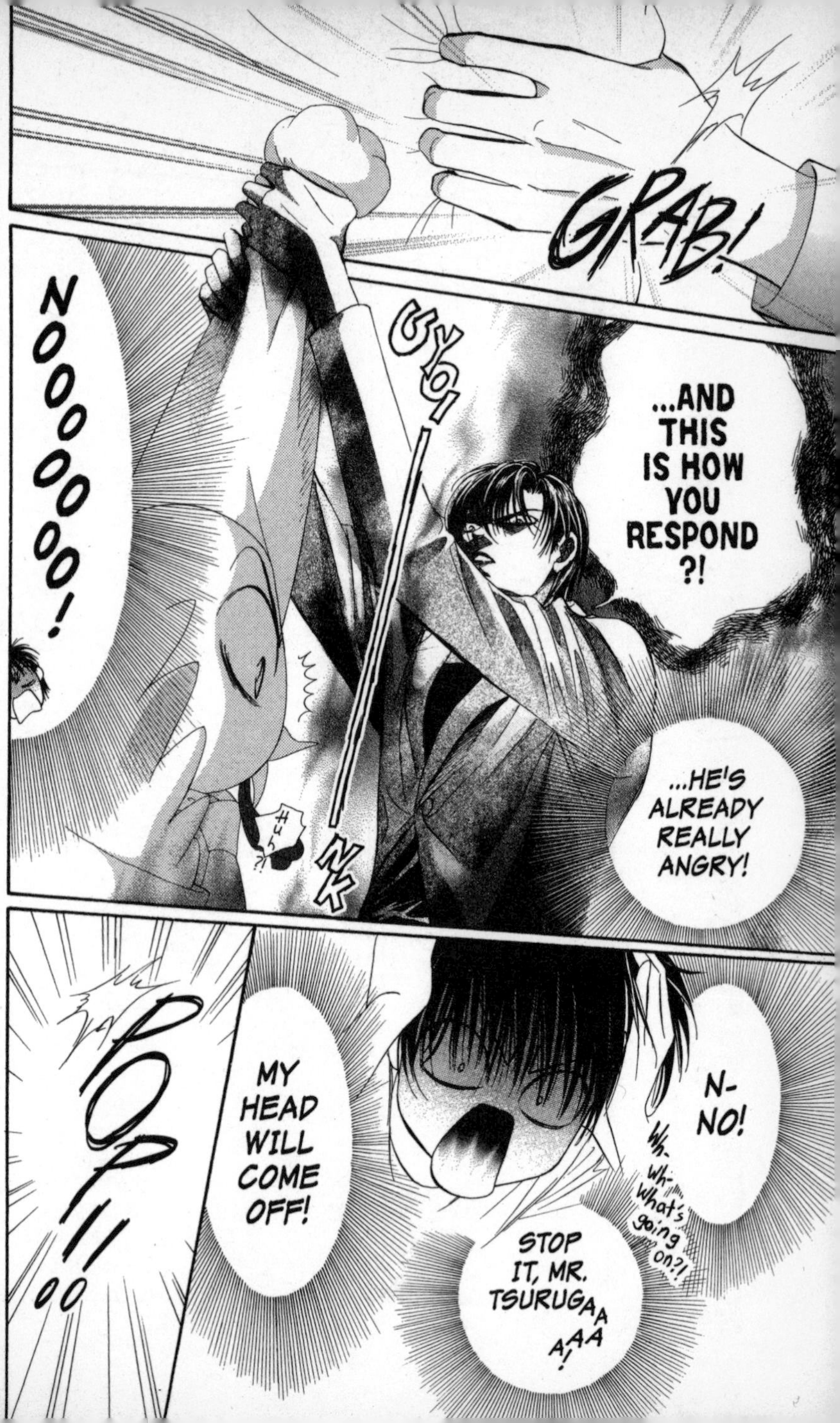
GRAB!
...AND THIS IS HOW YOU RESPOND?!
...HE'S ALREADY REALLY ANGRY!
UYOI—NK
NOOOOOOOOO!
Huh?!
N-NO!
Wh-Wh-What's going on?!
STOP IT, MR. TSURUGAAAAAA!
MY HEAD WILL COME OFF!
POP!!

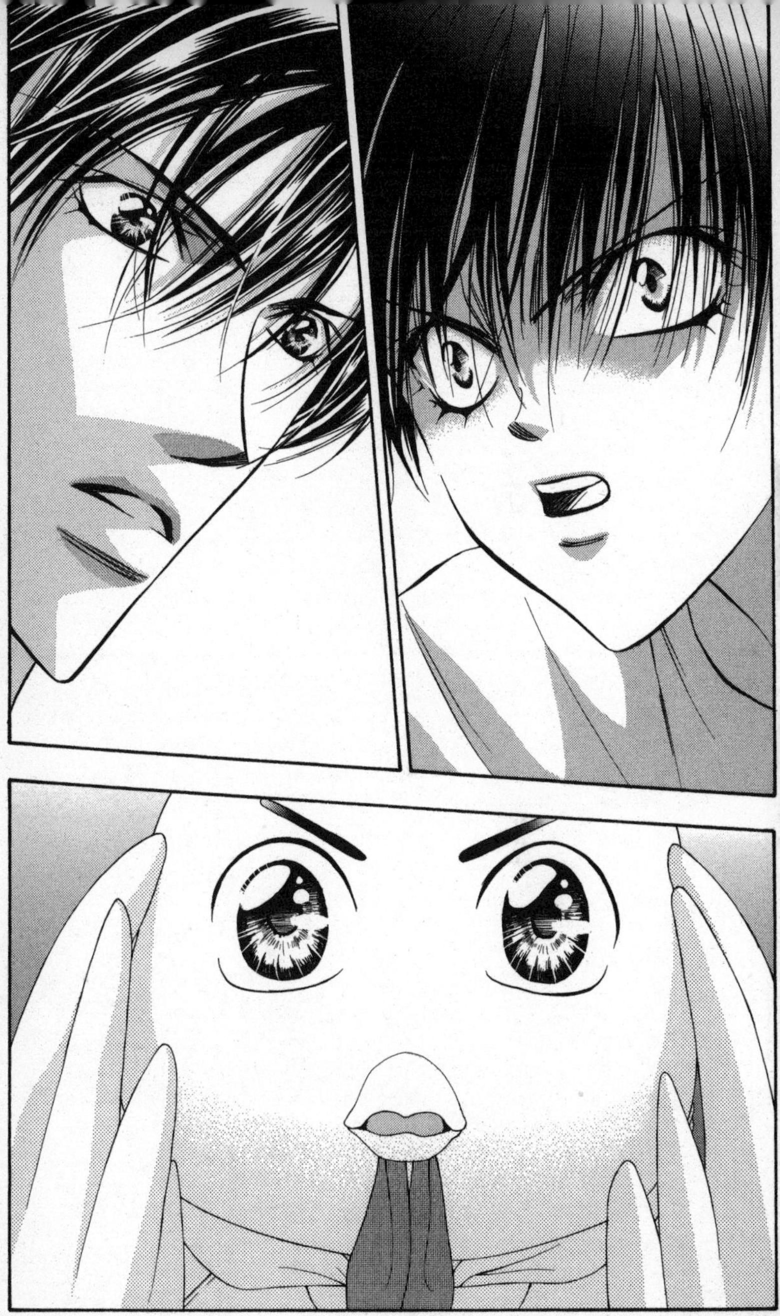

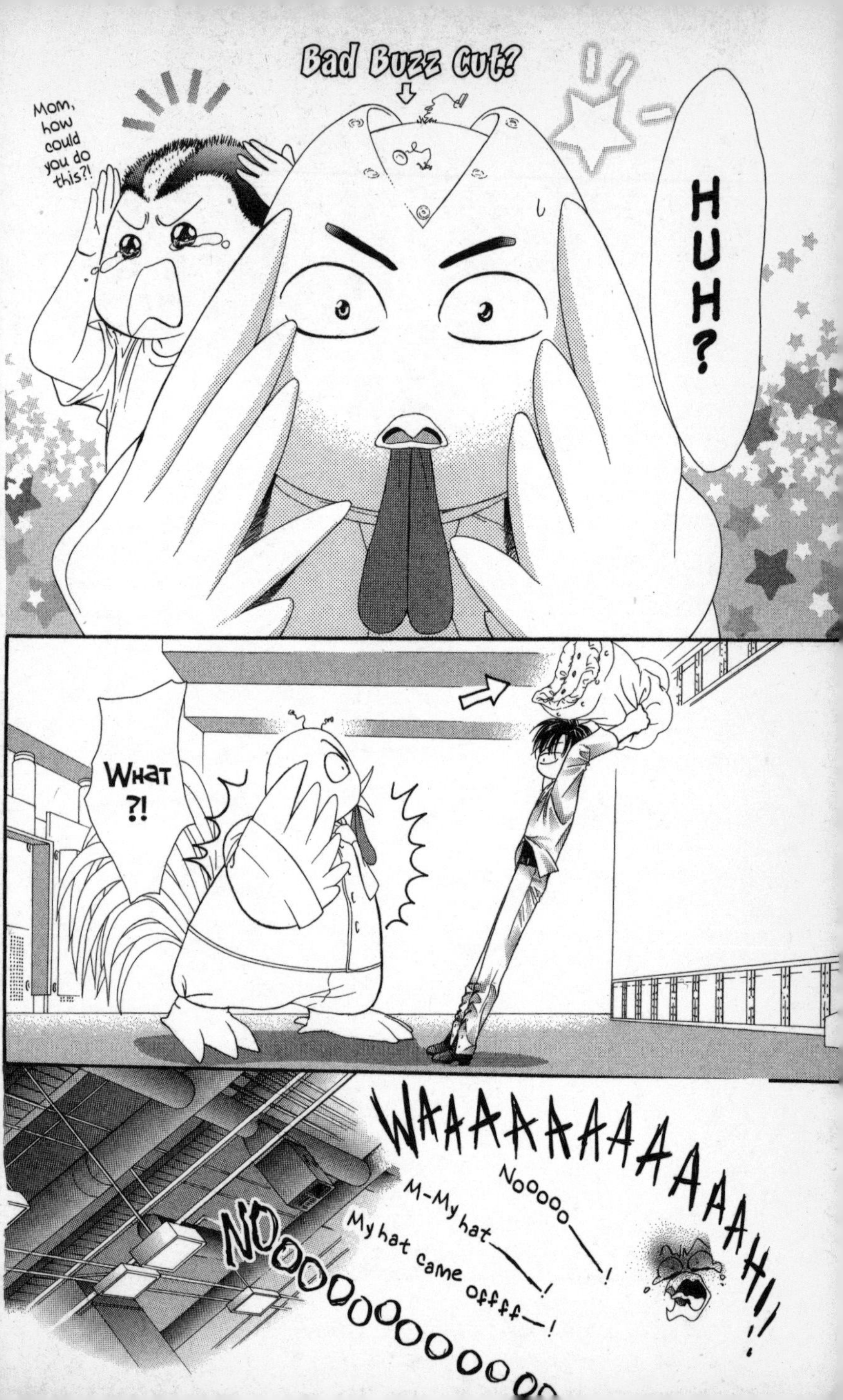
HUH?
Bad Buzz Cut?
Mom, how could you do this?!
What?!
WAAAAAAAAAAAAH!!
Nooooo—!
M-My hat—!
My hat came offff—!
NOOOOOOOOOOOOOO

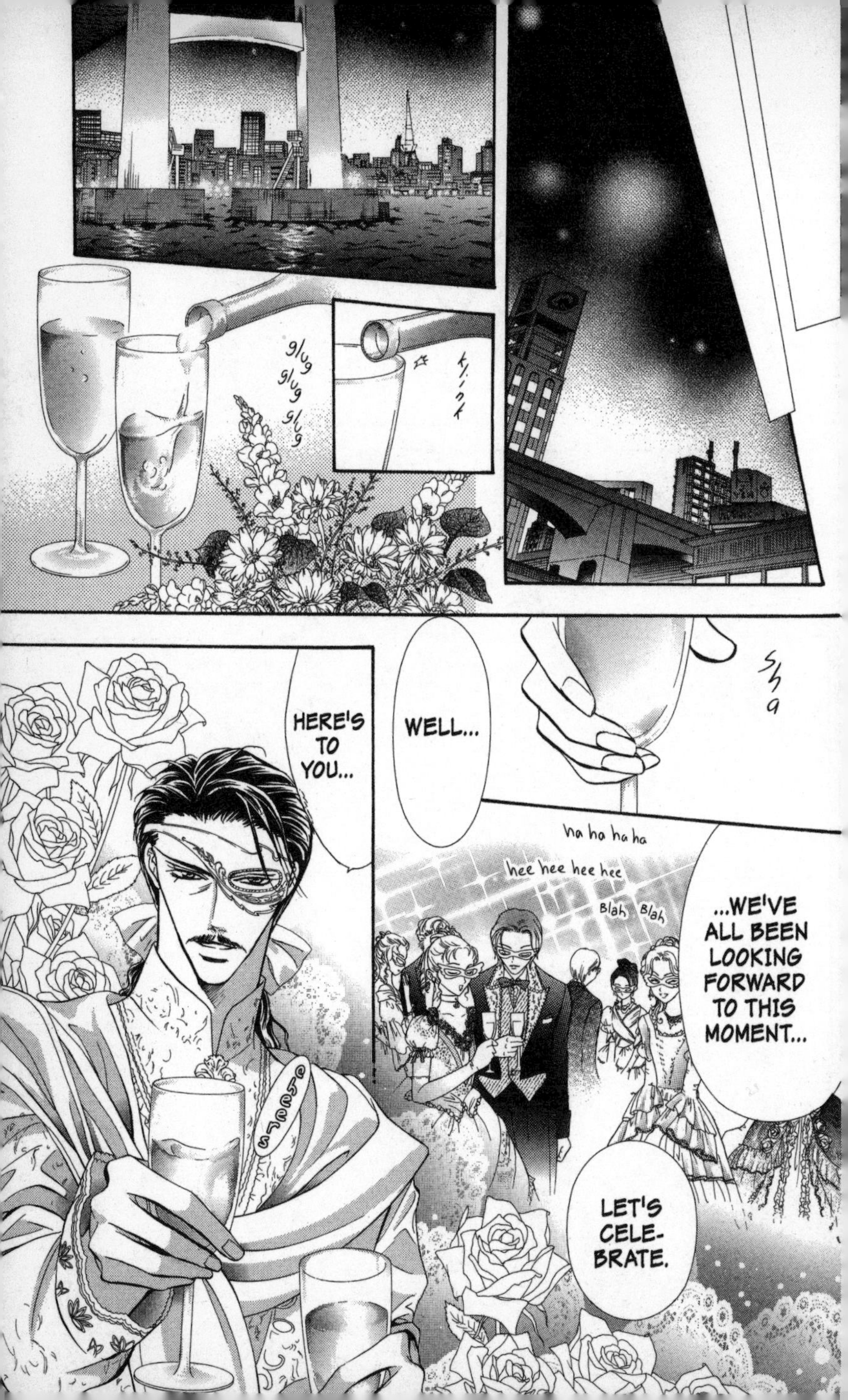

klink
glug glug glug
sha
WELL...
ha ha ha ha
hee hee hee hee
Blah Blah
...WE'VE ALL BEEN LOOKING FORWARD TO THIS MOMENT...
LET'S CELE-BRATE.
HERE'S TO YOU...

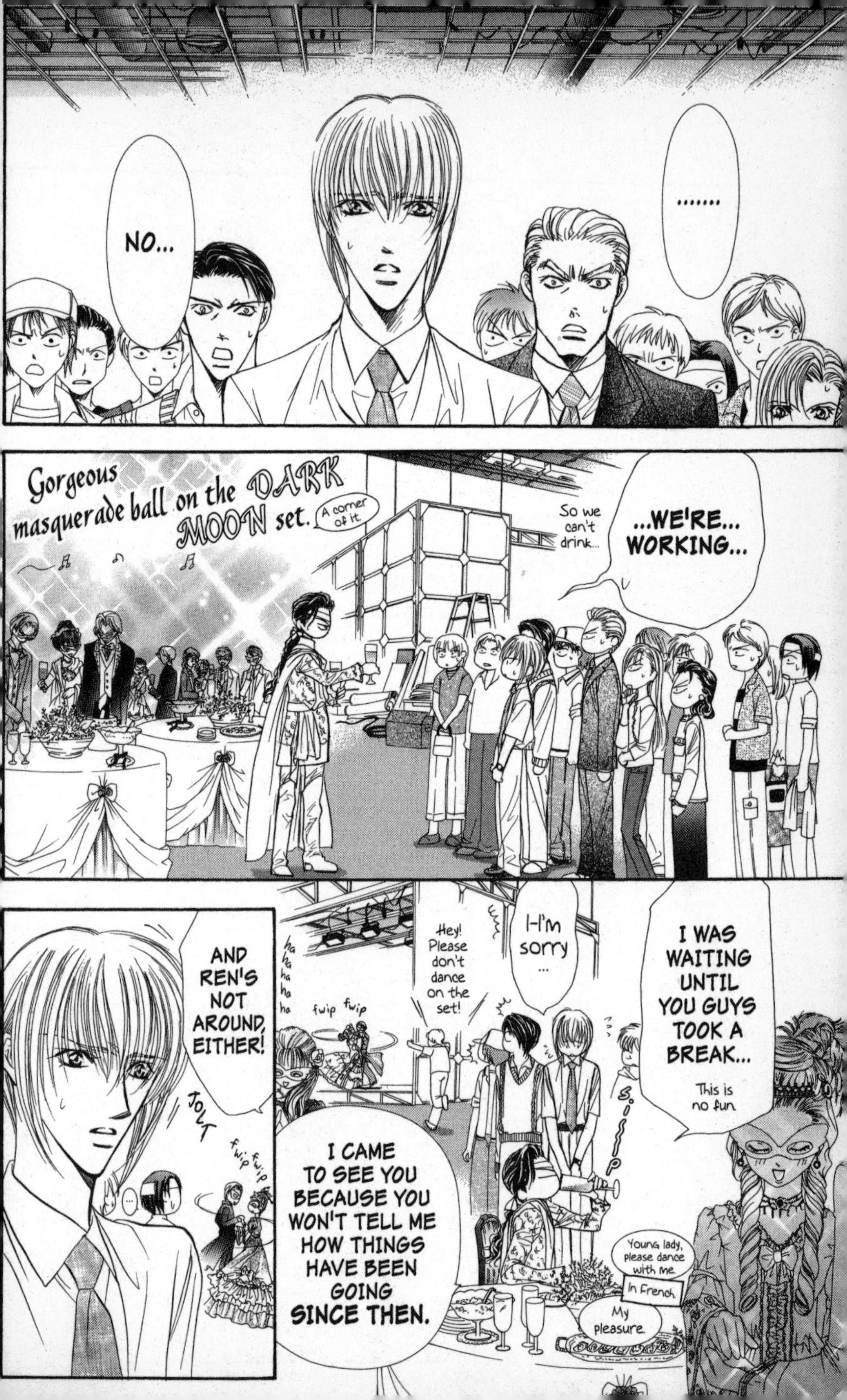
....
NO...
...WE'RE... WORKING...
So we can't drink...
Gorgeous masquerade ball on the DARK MOON set.
A corner of it.
I WAS WAITING UNTIL YOU GUYS TOOK A BREAK...
This is no fun.
I-I'm sorry...
Hey! Please don't dance on the set!
ha ha ha ha ha ha
fwip fwip
SIIIP
Young lady, please dance with me.
In French.
My pleasure.
I CAME TO SEE YOU BECAUSE YOU WON'T TELL ME HOW THINGS HAVE BEEN GOING SINCE THEN.
...
AND REN'S NOT AROUND, EITHER!
JOLT
fwip fwip

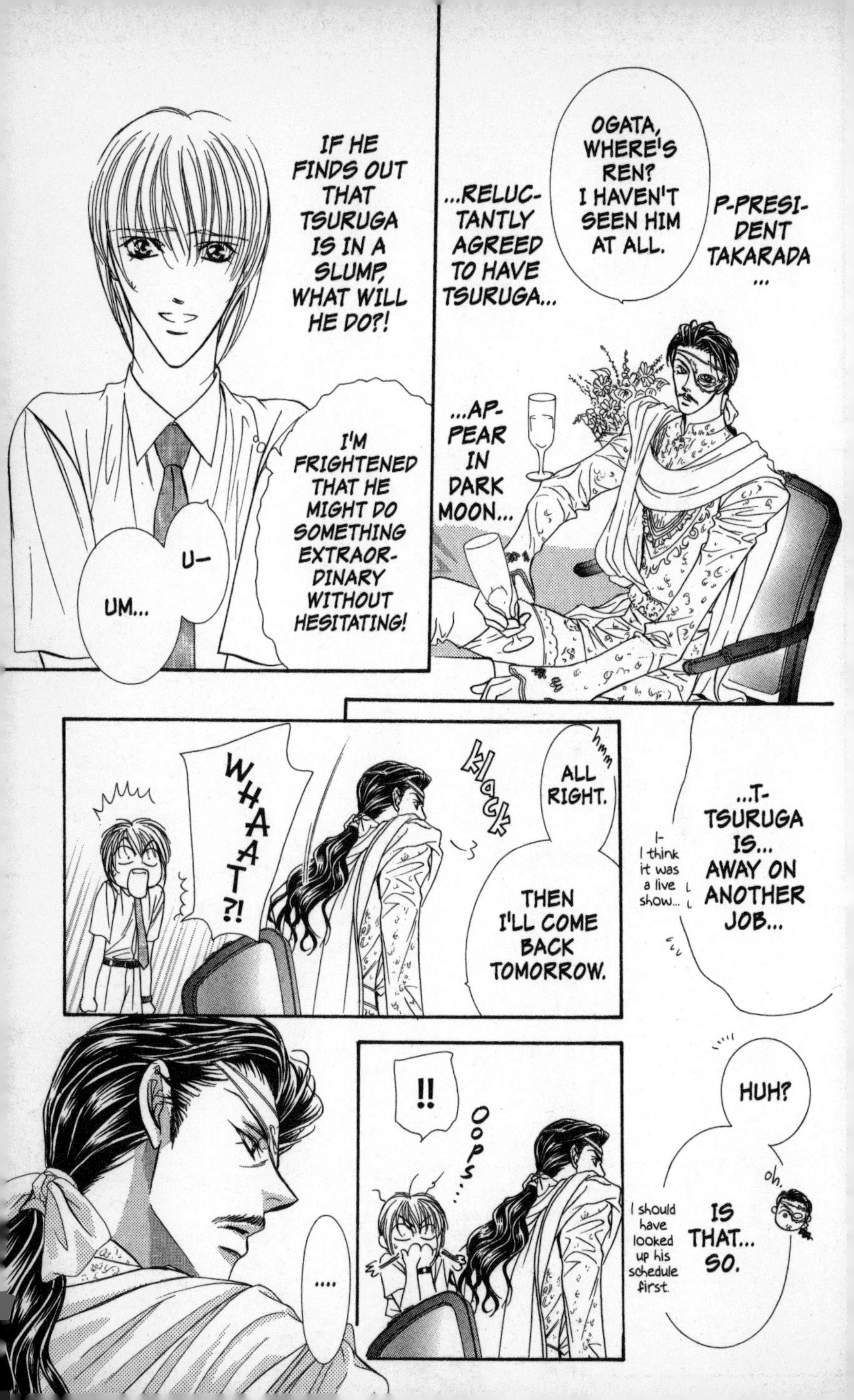
P-PRESIDENT TAKARADA...
OGATA, WHERE'S REN? I HAVEN'T SEEN HIM AT ALL.
...RELUCTANTLY AGREED TO HAVE TSURUGA...
...APPEAR IN DARK MOON...
IF HE FINDS OUT THAT TSURUGA IS IN A SLUMP, WHAT WILL HE DO?!
I'M FRIGHTENED THAT HE MIGHT DO SOMETHING EXTRAORDINARY WITHOUT HESITATING!
U- UM...
...T-TSURUGA IS... AWAY ON ANOTHER JOB...
I- I think it was a live show...
hmm
ALL RIGHT.
THEN I'LL COME BACK TOMORROW.
klack
WHAAAT?!
HUH?
oh.
IS THAT... SO.
I should have looked up his schedule first.
!!
Oops...
....

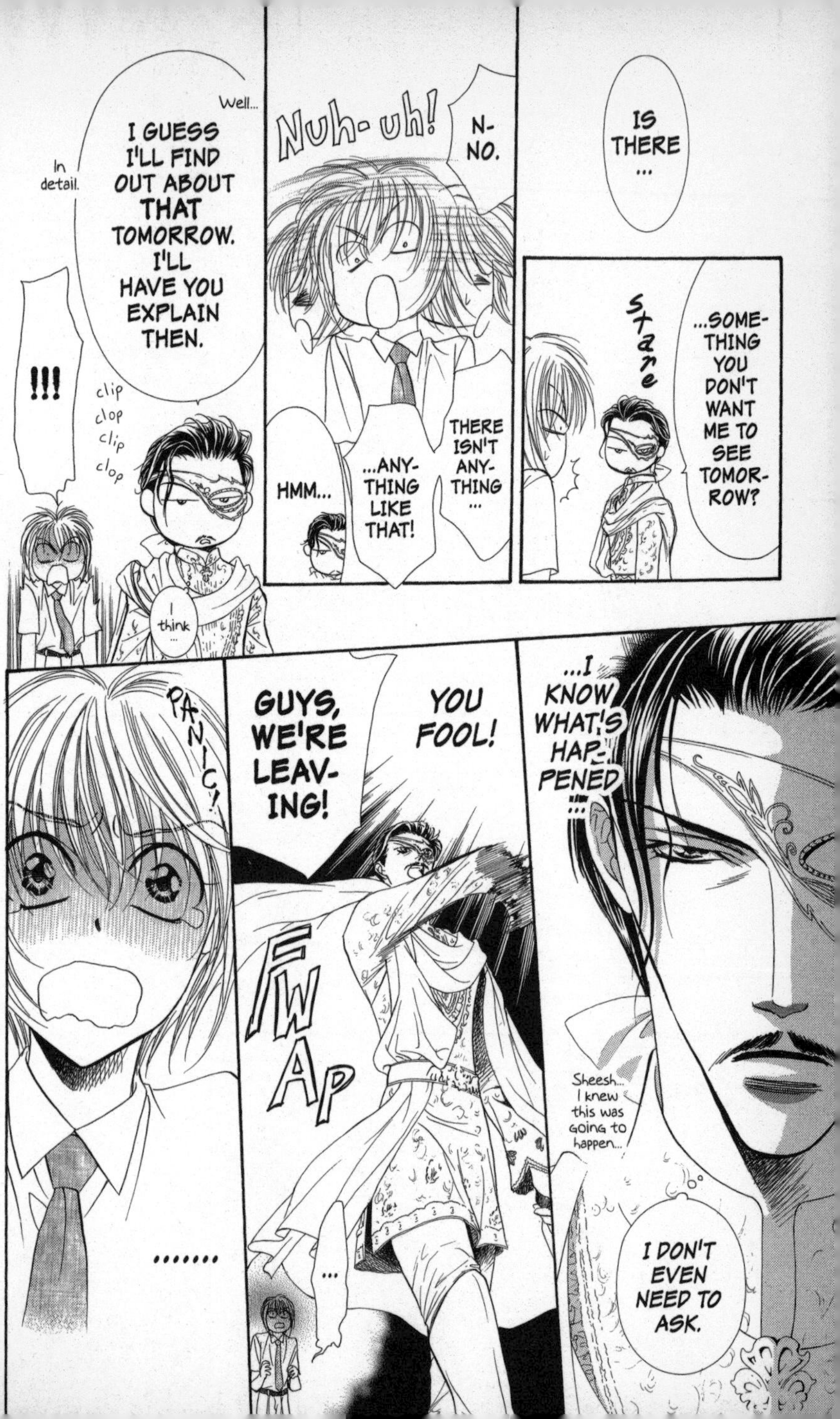
IS THERE ...
Stare
...SOMETHING YOU DON'T WANT ME TO SEE TOMORROW?
N-NO.
Nuh-uh!
THERE ISN'T ANYTHING ...
...ANYTHING LIKE THAT!
HMM...
Well...
I GUESS I'LL FIND OUT ABOUT THAT TOMORROW. I'LL HAVE YOU EXPLAIN THEN.
In detail.
!!!
clip clop clip clop
I think ...
...I KNOW WHAT'S HAPPENED ...
Sheesh... I knew this was going to happen...
I DON'T EVEN NEED TO ASK.
YOU FOOL!
GUYS, WE'RE LEAVING!
FWAP
...
PANIC!
....

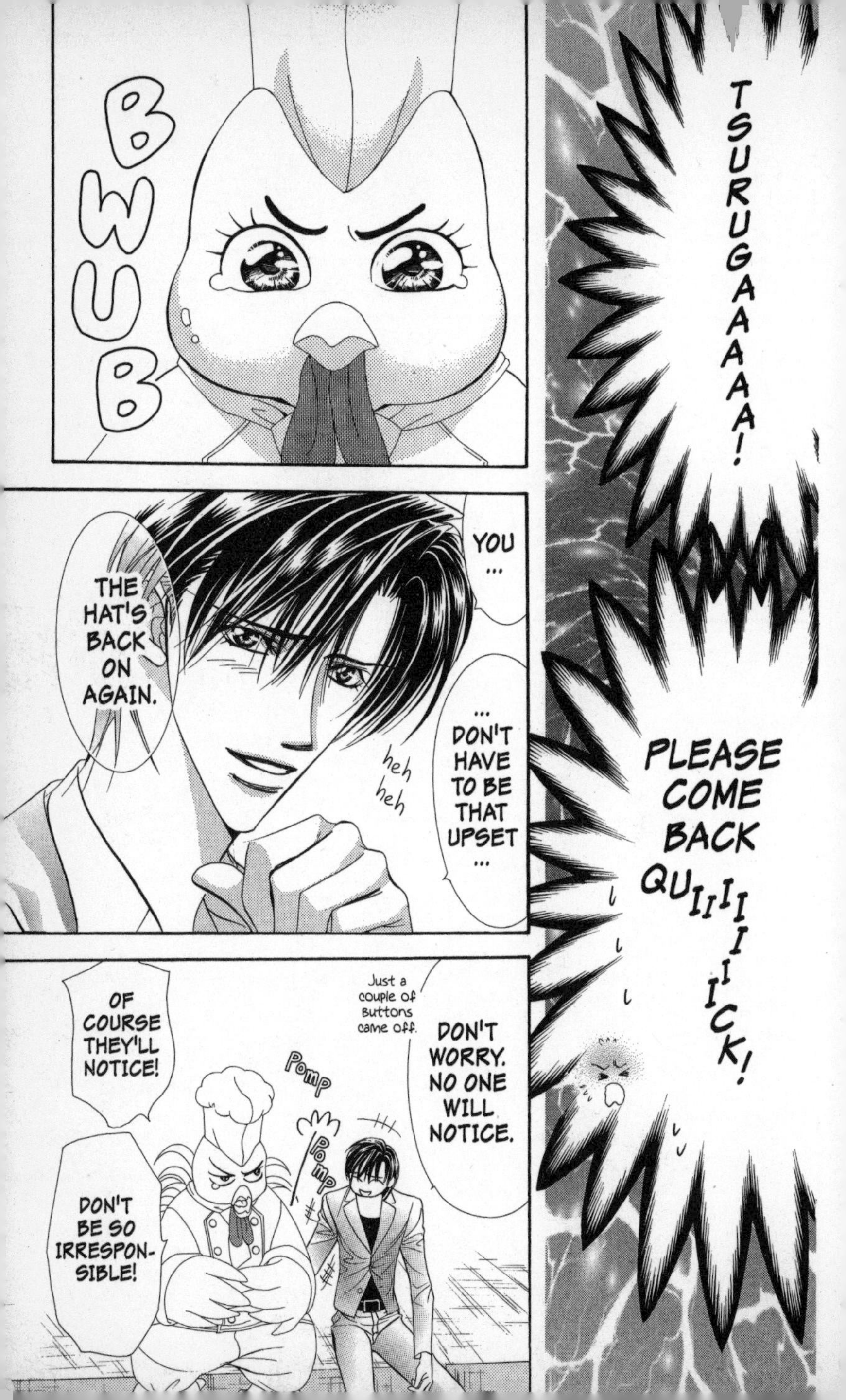
TSURUGAAAAAA!
PLEASE COME BACK QUIIIIIICK!
BWUB
YOU ...
... DON'T HAVE TO BE THAT UPSET ...
heh heh
THE HAT'S BACK ON AGAIN.
Just a couple of buttons came off.
DON'T WORRY. NO ONE WILL NOTICE.
Pomp
Pomp
OF COURSE THEY'LL NOTICE!
DON'T BE SO IRRESPON-SIBLE!

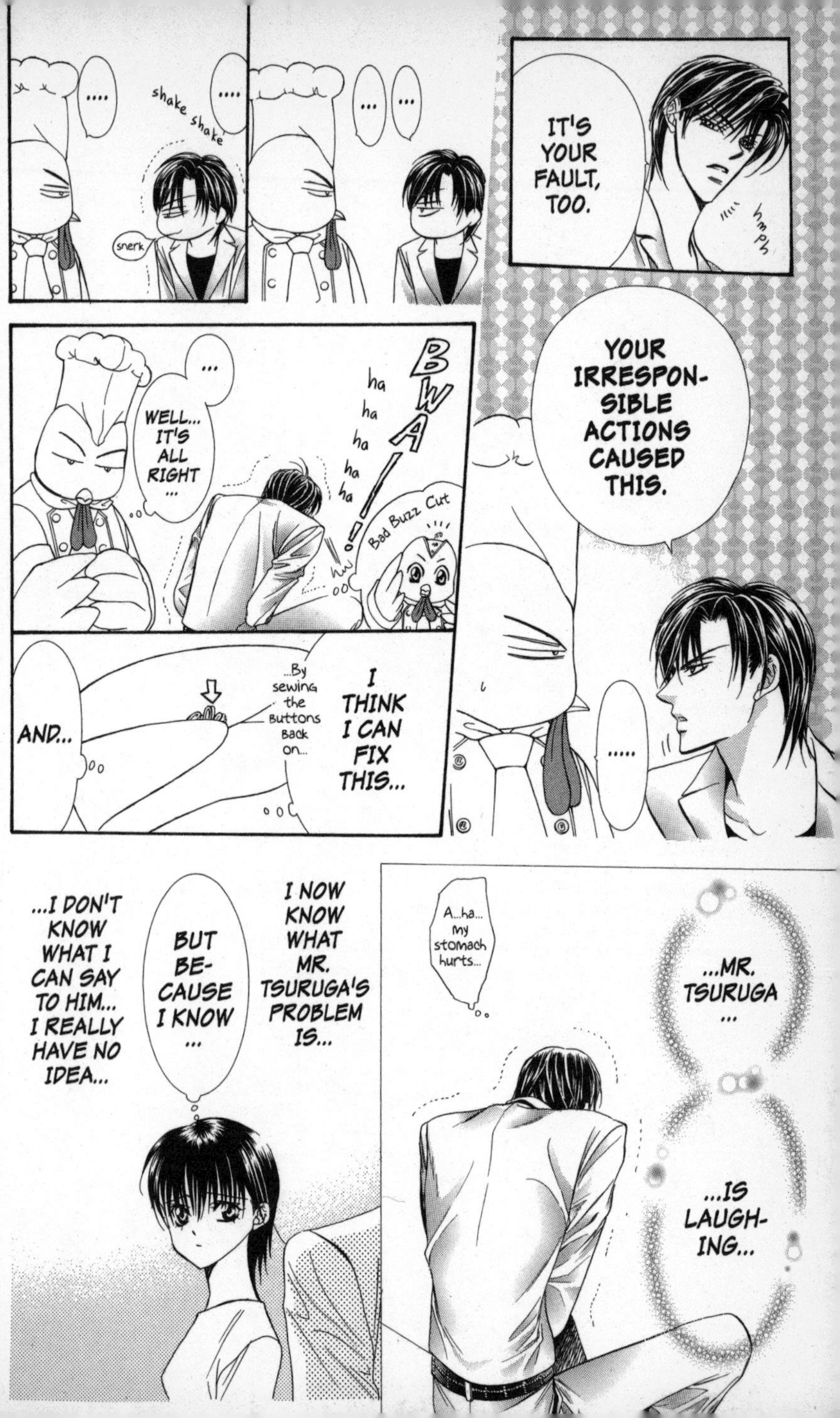
IT'S YOUR FAULT, TOO.
hmph
...
...
....
....
shake shake
snerk
YOUR IRRESPONSIBLE ACTIONS CAUSED THIS.
.....
BWA!
ha ha ha ha ha
...
WELL... IT'S ALL RIGHT ...
Bad Buzz Cut
I THINK I CAN FIX THIS...
...By sewing the Buttons Back on...
AND...
...MR. TSURUGA ...
...IS LAUGHING...
A...ha... my stomach hurts...
I NOW KNOW WHAT MR. TSURUGA'S PROBLEM IS...
BUT BECAUSE I KNOW ...
...I DON'T KNOW WHAT I CAN SAY TO HIM... I REALLY HAVE NO IDEA...

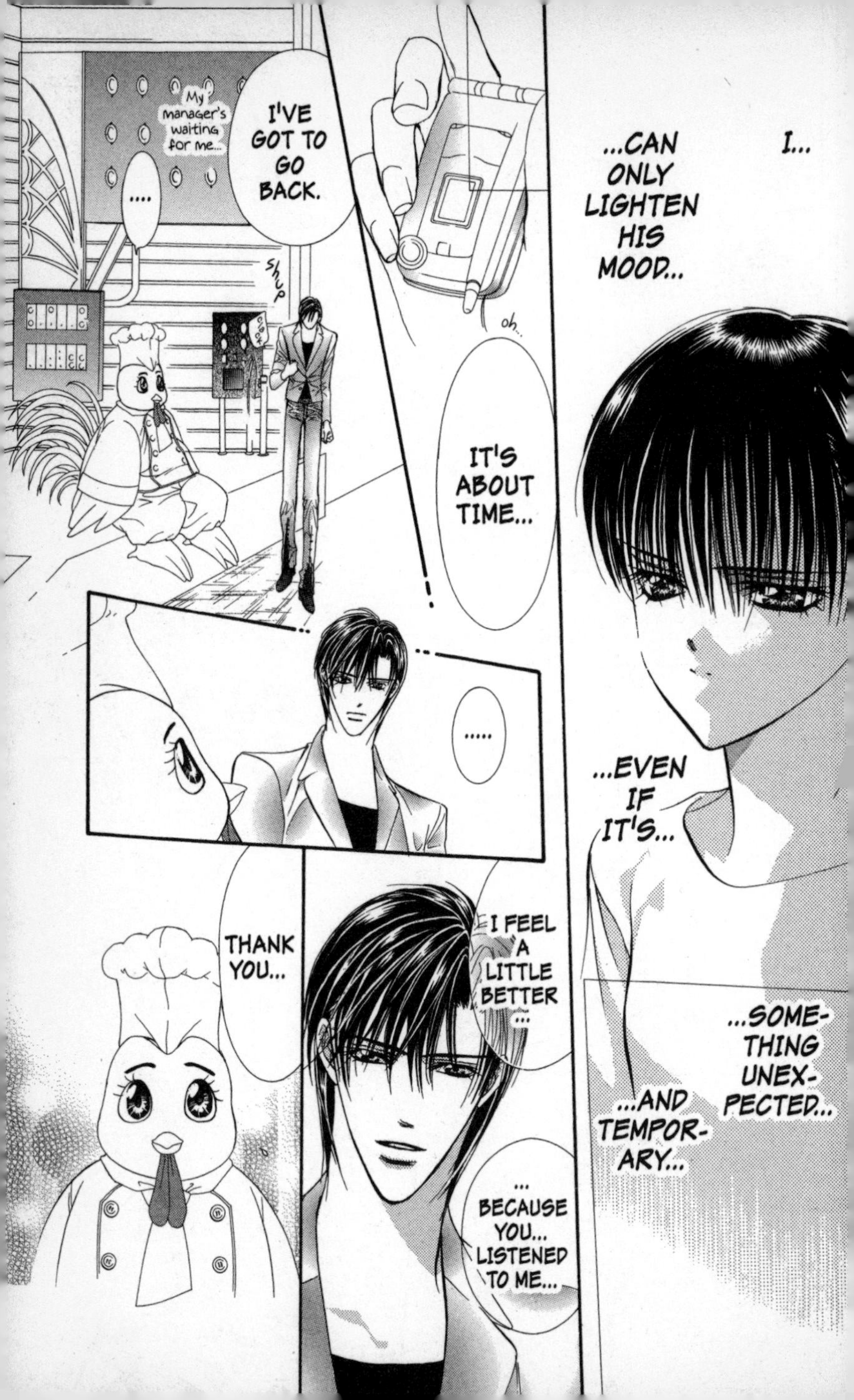
I...
...CAN ONLY LIGHTEN HIS MOOD...
...EVEN IF IT'S...
...SOME-THING UNEX-PECTED...
...AND TEMPOR-ARY...
oh...
IT'S ABOUT TIME...
I'VE GOT TO GO BACK.
My manager's waiting for me...
....
shup
click
.....
I FEEL A LITTLE BETTER...
...BECAUSE YOU... LISTENED TO ME...
THANK YOU...

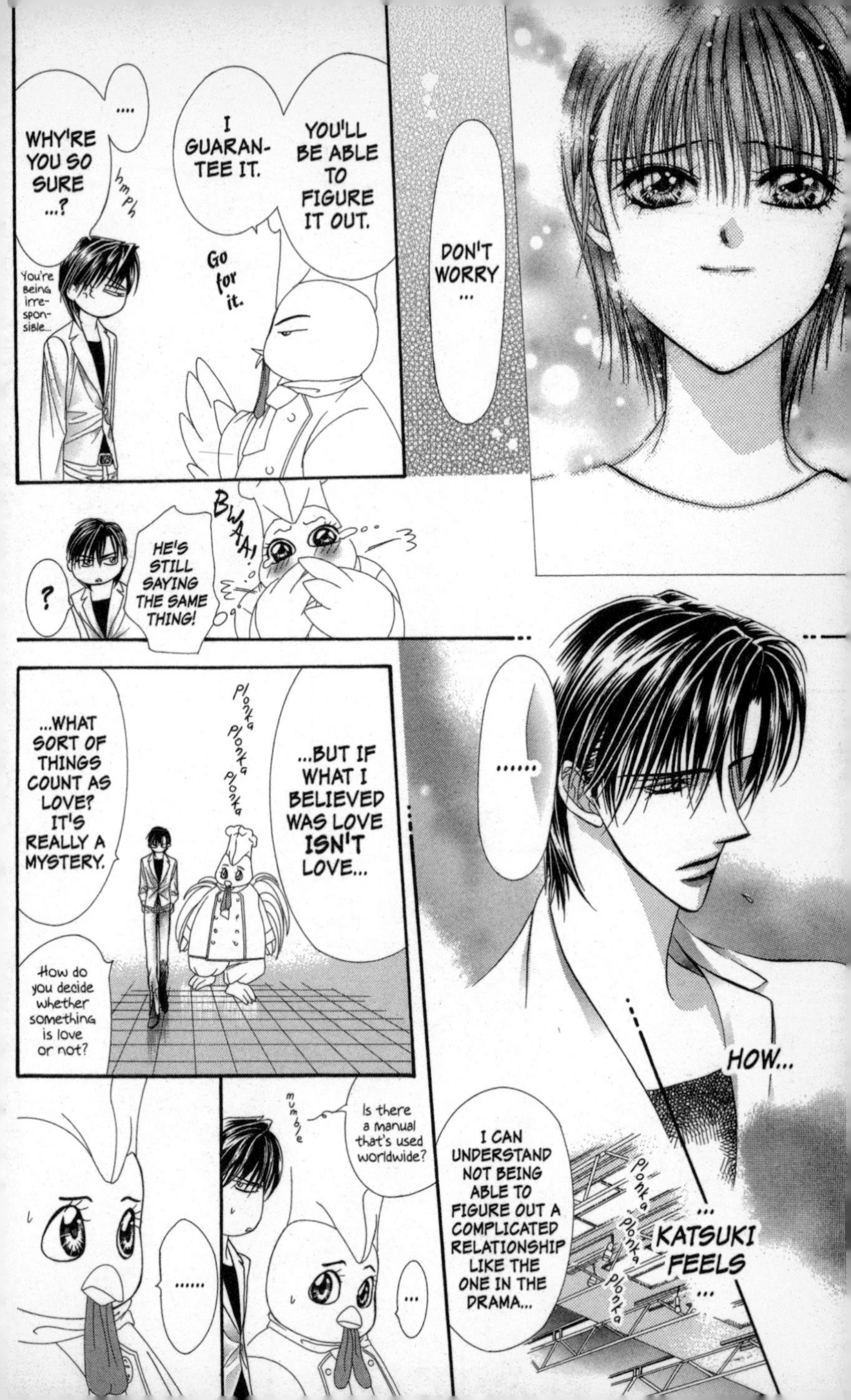
DON'T WORRY ...
YOU'LL BE ABLE TO FIGURE IT OUT.
I GUARAN-TEE IT.
Go for it.
....
WHY'RE YOU SO SURE ...?
hmph
You're being irre-spon-sible...
BWAAI!
HE'S STILL SAYING THE SAME THING!
?
......
HOW...
... KATSUKI FEELS ...
Plonka plonka plonka
I CAN UNDERSTAND NOT BEING ABLE TO FIGURE OUT A COMPLICATED RELATIONSHIP LIKE THE ONE IN THE DRAMA...
...BUT IF WHAT I BELIEVED WAS LOVE ISN'T LOVE...
Plonka plonka plonka plonka
...WHAT SORT OF THINGS COUNT AS LOVE? IT'S REALLY A MYSTERY.
How do you decide whether something is love or not?
Is there a manual that's used worldwide?
mumble
...
......

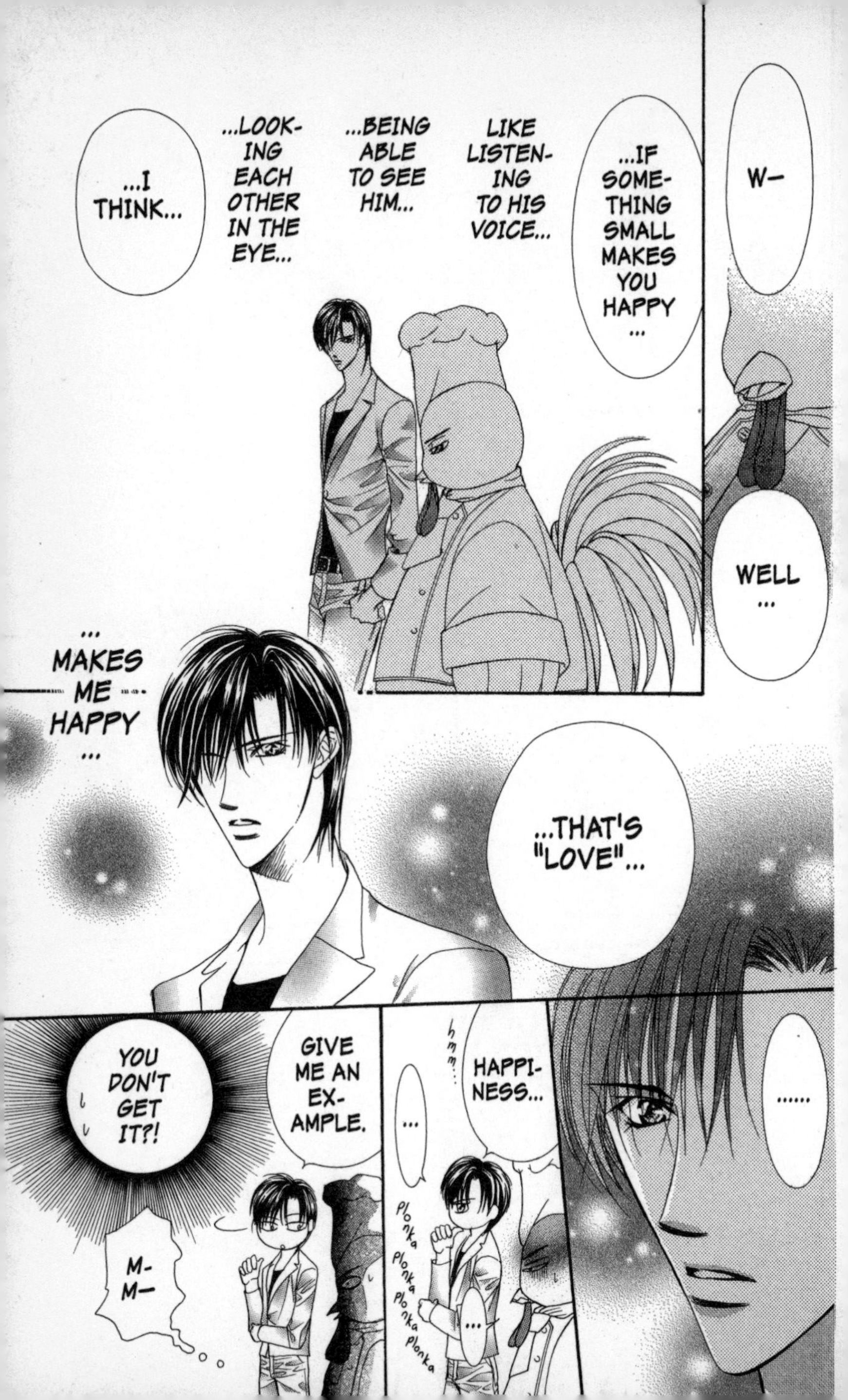
W—
WELL...
...IF SOMETHING SMALL MAKES YOU HAPPY...
LIKE LISTENING TO HIS VOICE...
...BEING ABLE TO SEE HIM...
...LOOKING EACH OTHER IN THE EYE...
...I THINK...
...MAKES ME HAPPY...
...THAT'S "LOVE"...
......
HAPPINESS...
hmm...
...
plonka plonka plonka plonka
...
GIVE ME AN EXAMPLE.
YOU DON'T GET IT?!
M-M—

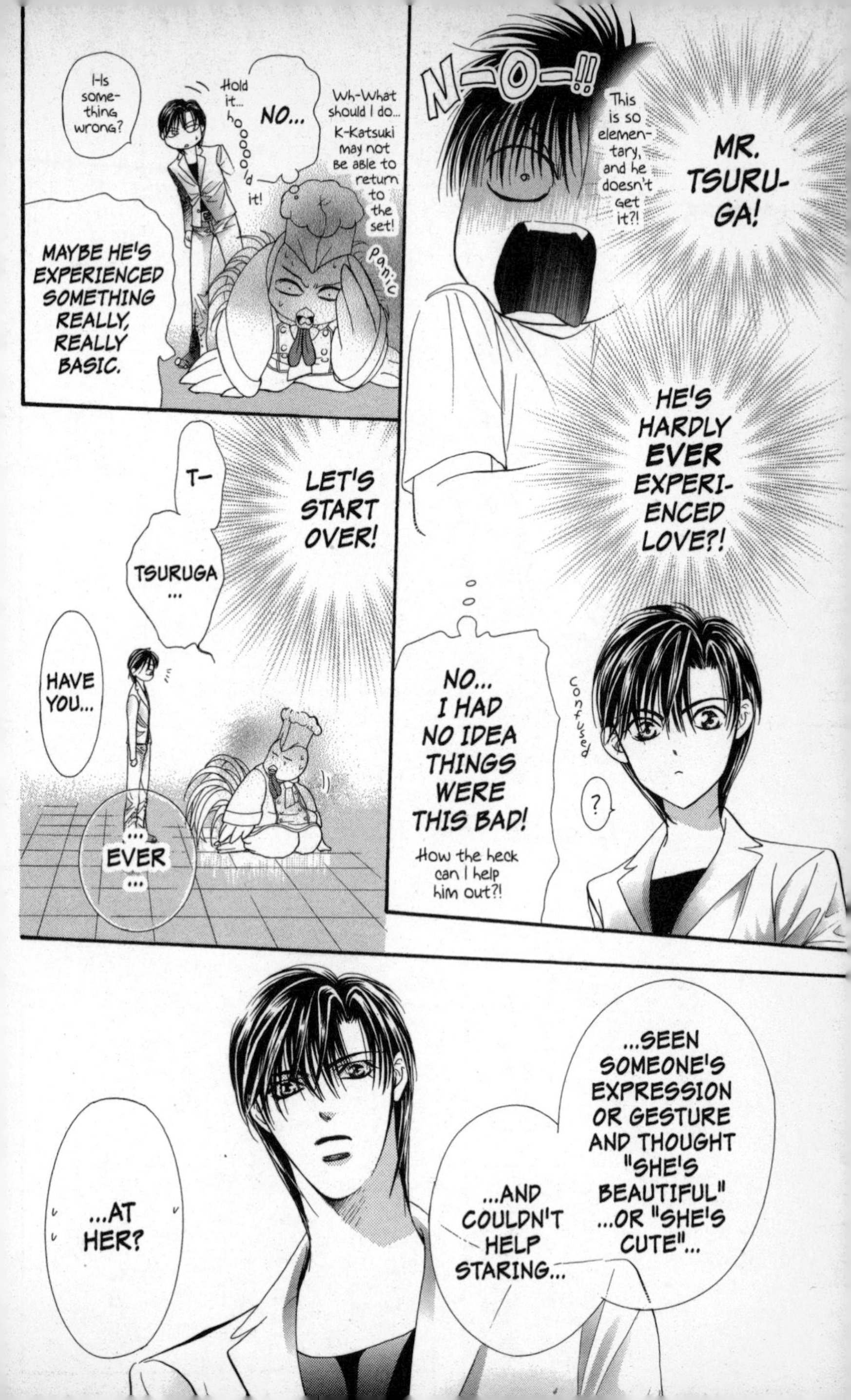
N-O-!!
This is so elementary, and he doesn't get it?!
MR. TSURUGA!
HE'S HARDLY EVER EXPERIENCED LOVE?!
Wh-What should I do... K-Katsuki may not be able to return to the set!
NO...
Hold it... hoooooold it!
I-Is something wrong?
Panic
MAYBE HE'S EXPERIENCED SOMETHING REALLY, REALLY BASIC.
NO... I HAD NO IDEA THINGS WERE THIS BAD!
How the heck can I help him out?!
Confused
?
LET'S START OVER!
T-
TSURUGA...
HAVE YOU...
...EVER...
...SEEN SOMEONE'S EXPRESSION OR GESTURE AND THOUGHT "SHE'S BEAUTIFUL" ...OR "SHE'S CUTE"...
...AND COULDN'T HELP STARING...
...AT HER?

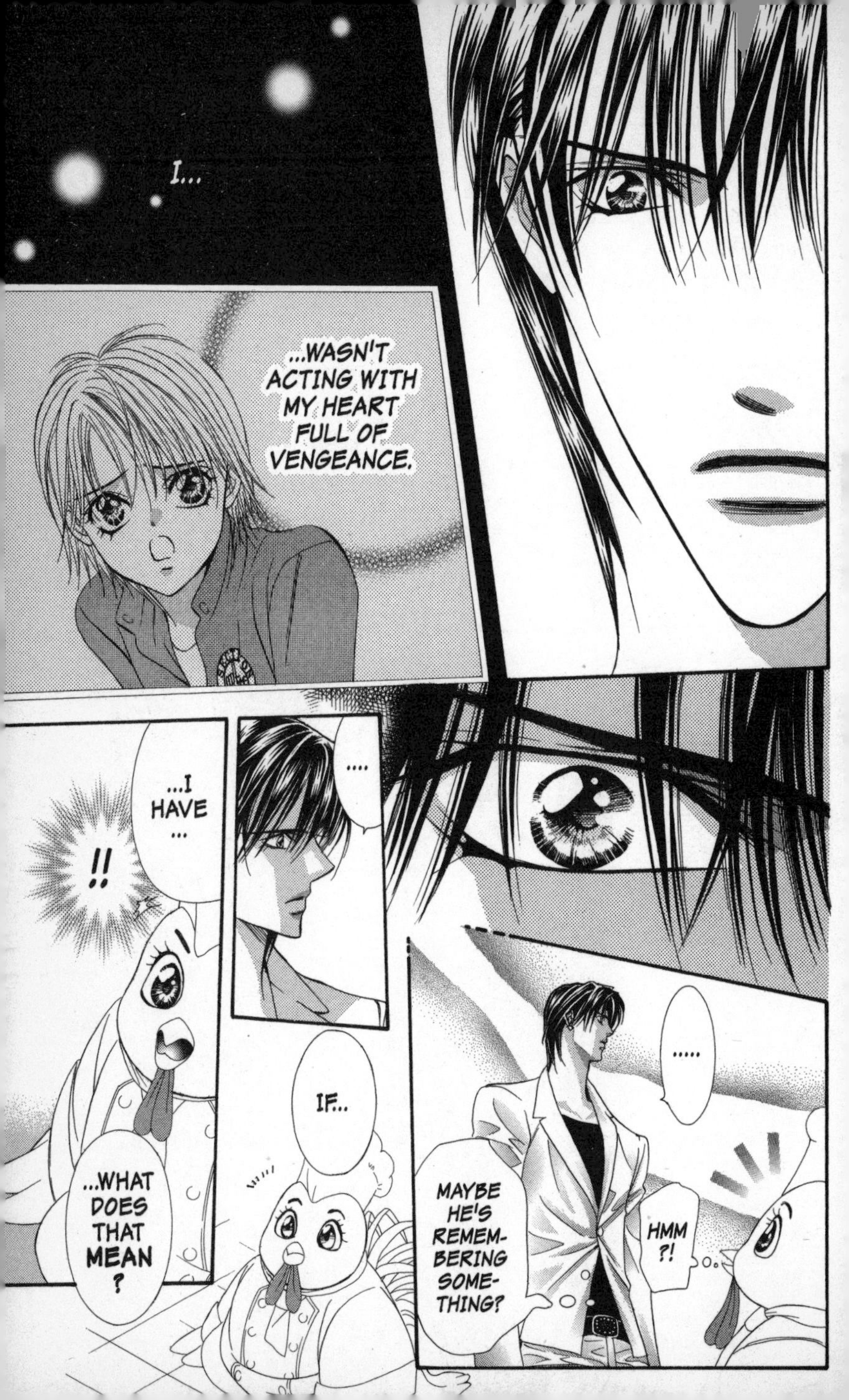
I...
...WASN'T ACTING WITH MY HEART FULL OF VENGEANCE.
....
.....
HMM ?!
MAYBE HE'S REMEM-BERING SOME-THING?
IF..
...I HAVE ...
!!
...WHAT DOES THAT MEAN ?

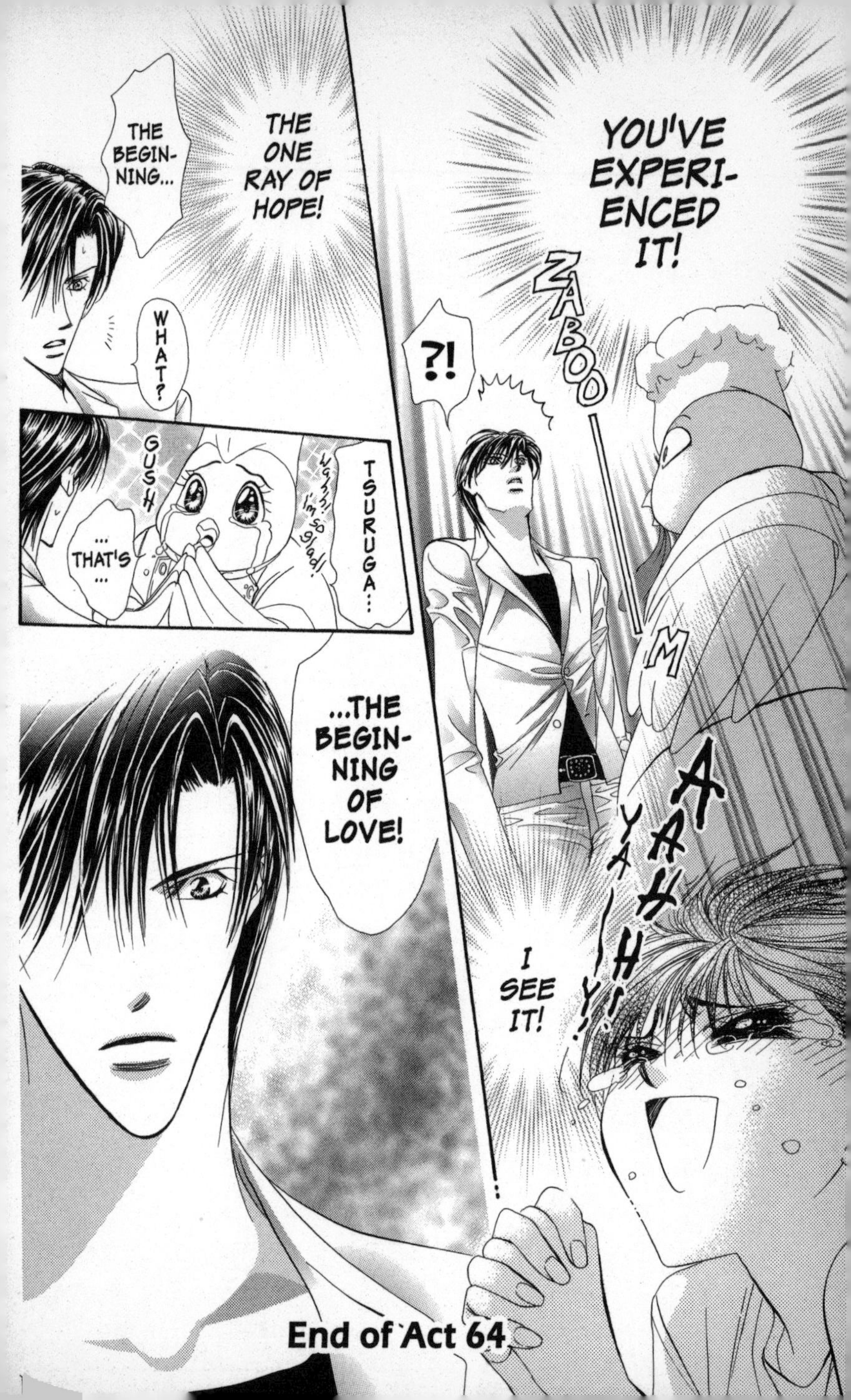
YOU'VE EXPERIENCED IT!
ZABOOM
?!
AAHH!!
YA—Y!!
I SEE IT!
...
THE ONE RAY OF HOPE!
THE BEGINNING...
WHAT?
TSURUGA...
Waahh! I'm so glad!
GUSH
...THAT'S...
...THE BEGINNING OF LOVE!

End of Act 64

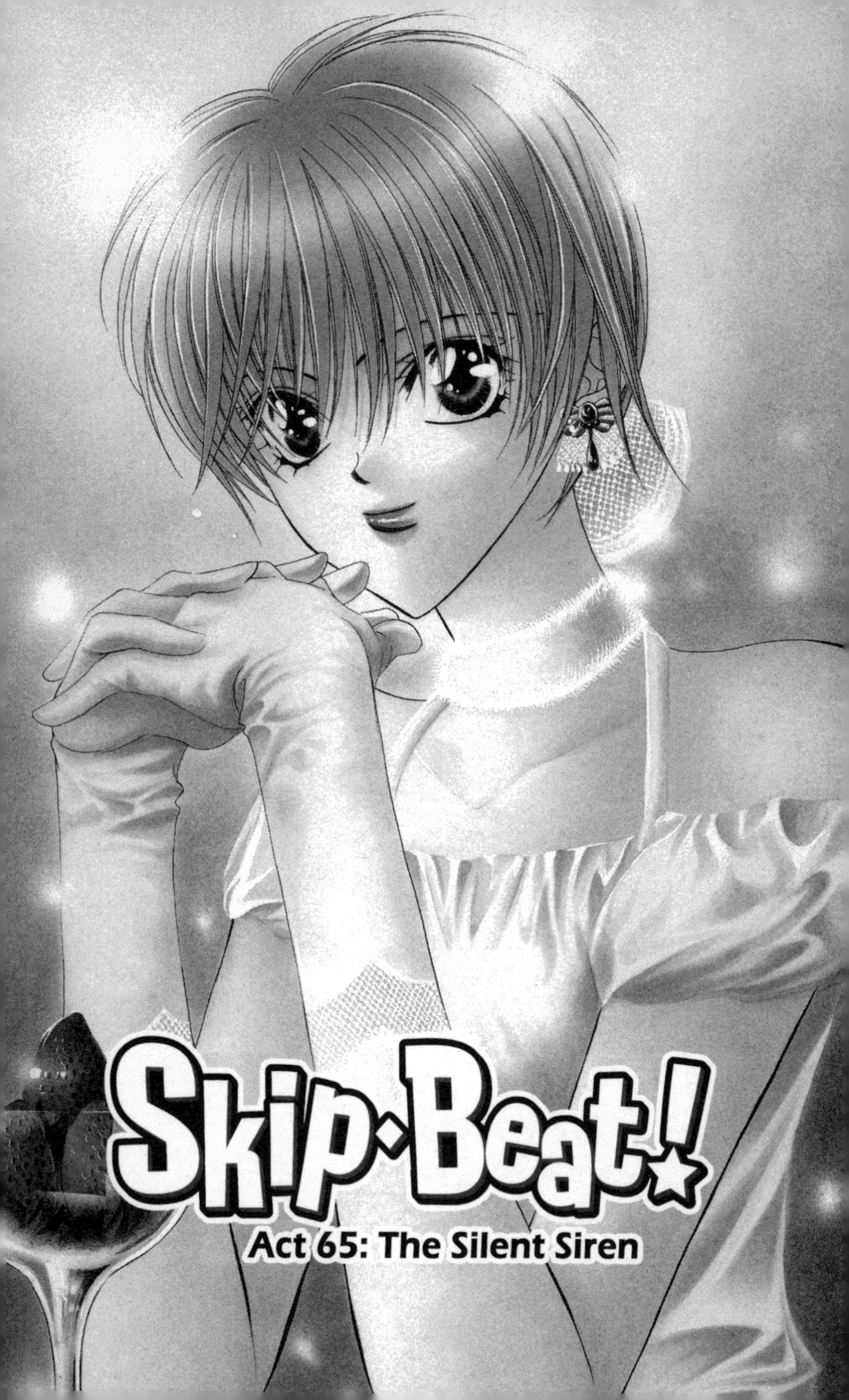
Skip·Beat!
Act 65: The Silent Siren

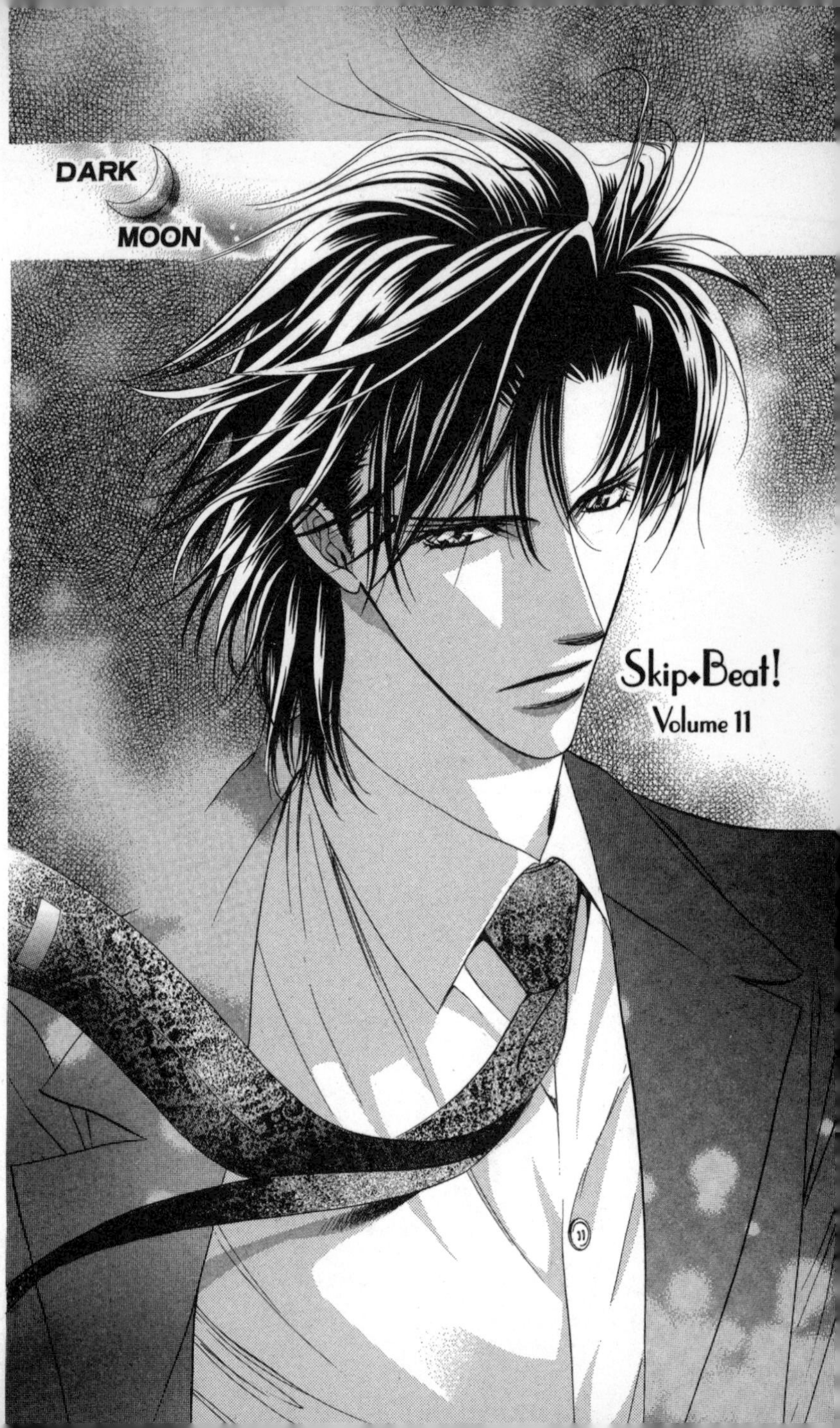
DARK
MOON
Skip•Beat!
Volume 11

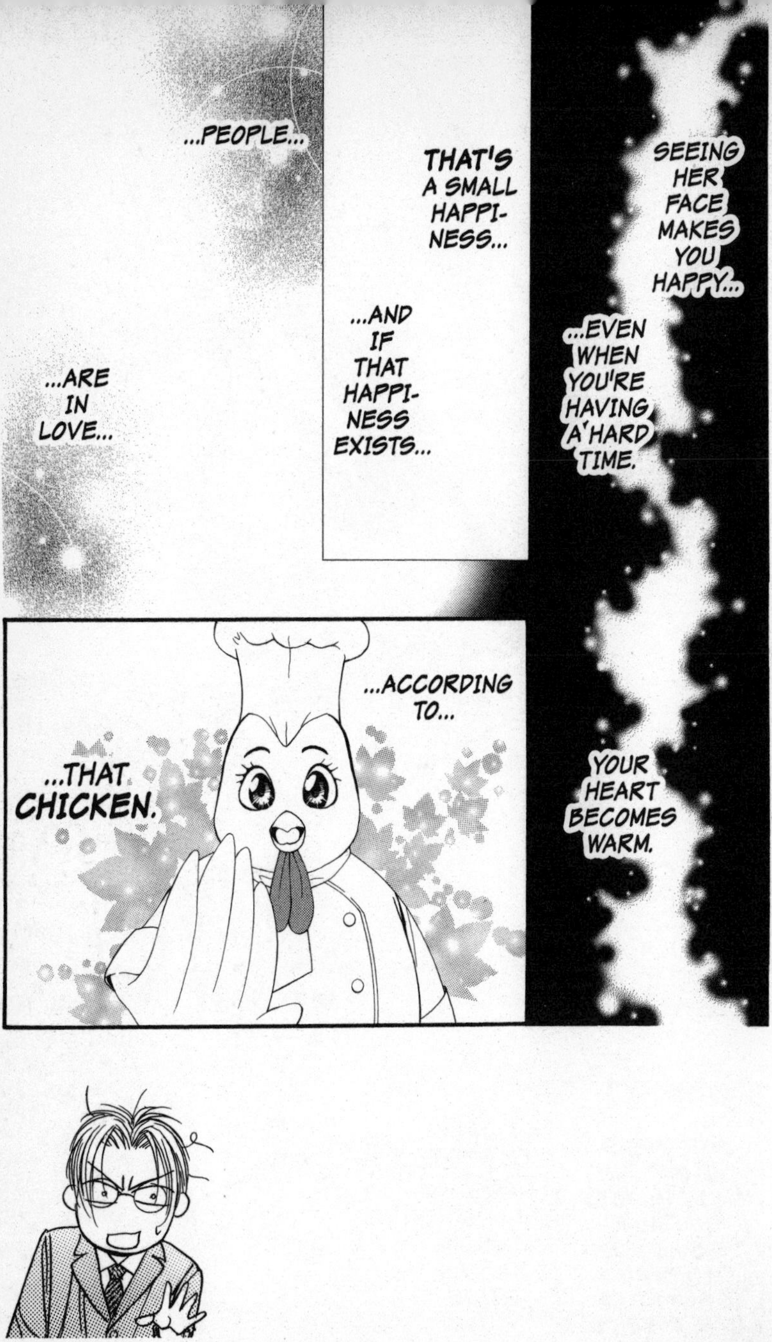
SEEING HER FACE MAKES YOU HAPPY...
...EVEN WHEN YOU'RE HAVING A HARD TIME.
YOUR HEART BECOMES WARM.
THAT'S A SMALL HAPPINESS...
...AND IF THAT HAPPINESS EXISTS...
...PEOPLE...
...ARE IN LOVE...
...ACCORDING TO...
...THAT CHICKEN.

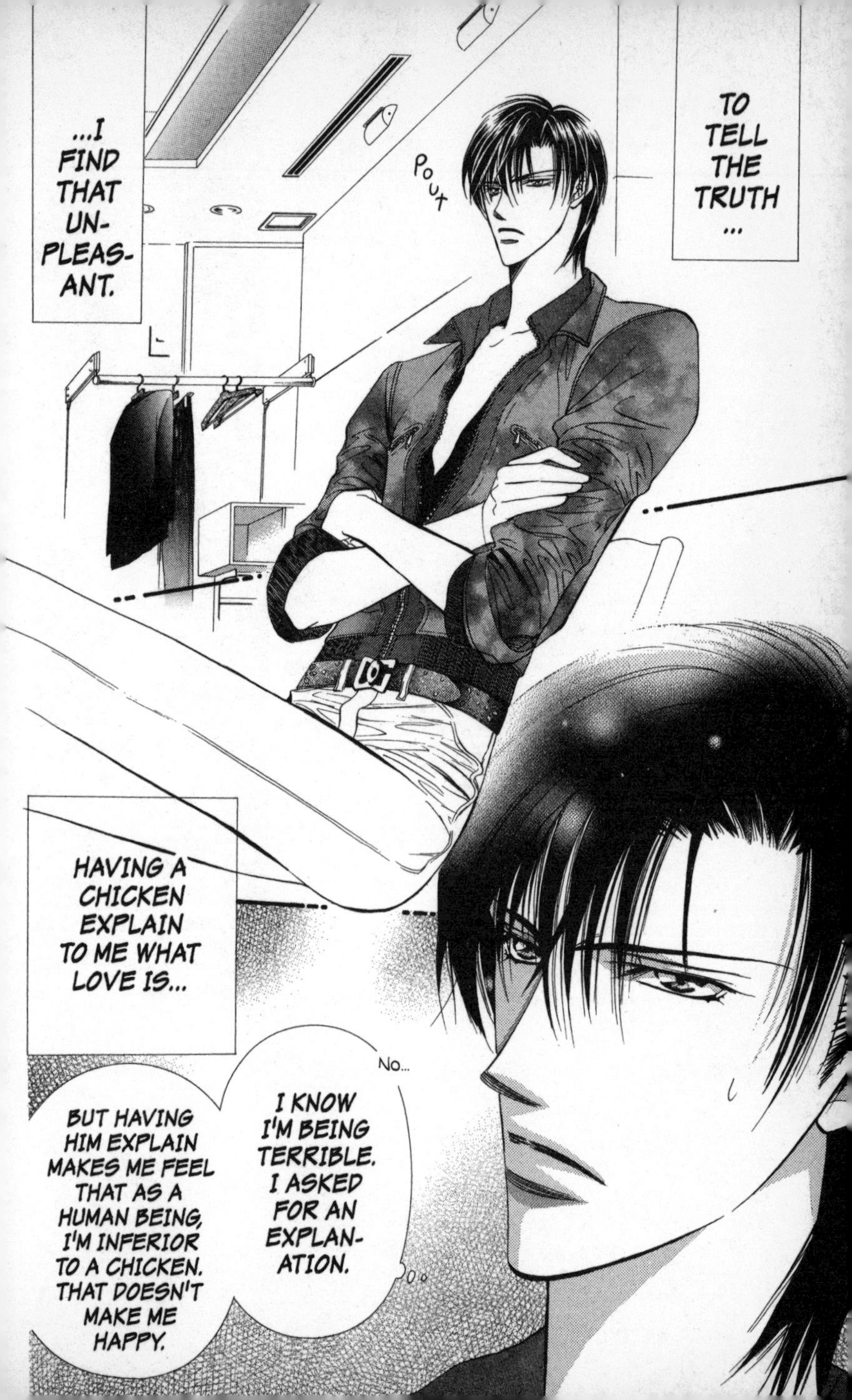
TO TELL THE TRUTH...
...I FIND THAT UNPLEASANT.
Pout
HAVING A CHICKEN EXPLAIN TO ME WHAT LOVE IS...
No...
I KNOW I'M BEING TERRIBLE. I ASKED FOR AN EXPLANATION.
BUT HAVING HIM EXPLAIN MAKES ME FEEL THAT AS A HUMAN BEING, I'M INFERIOR TO A CHICKEN. THAT DOESN'T MAKE ME HAPPY.

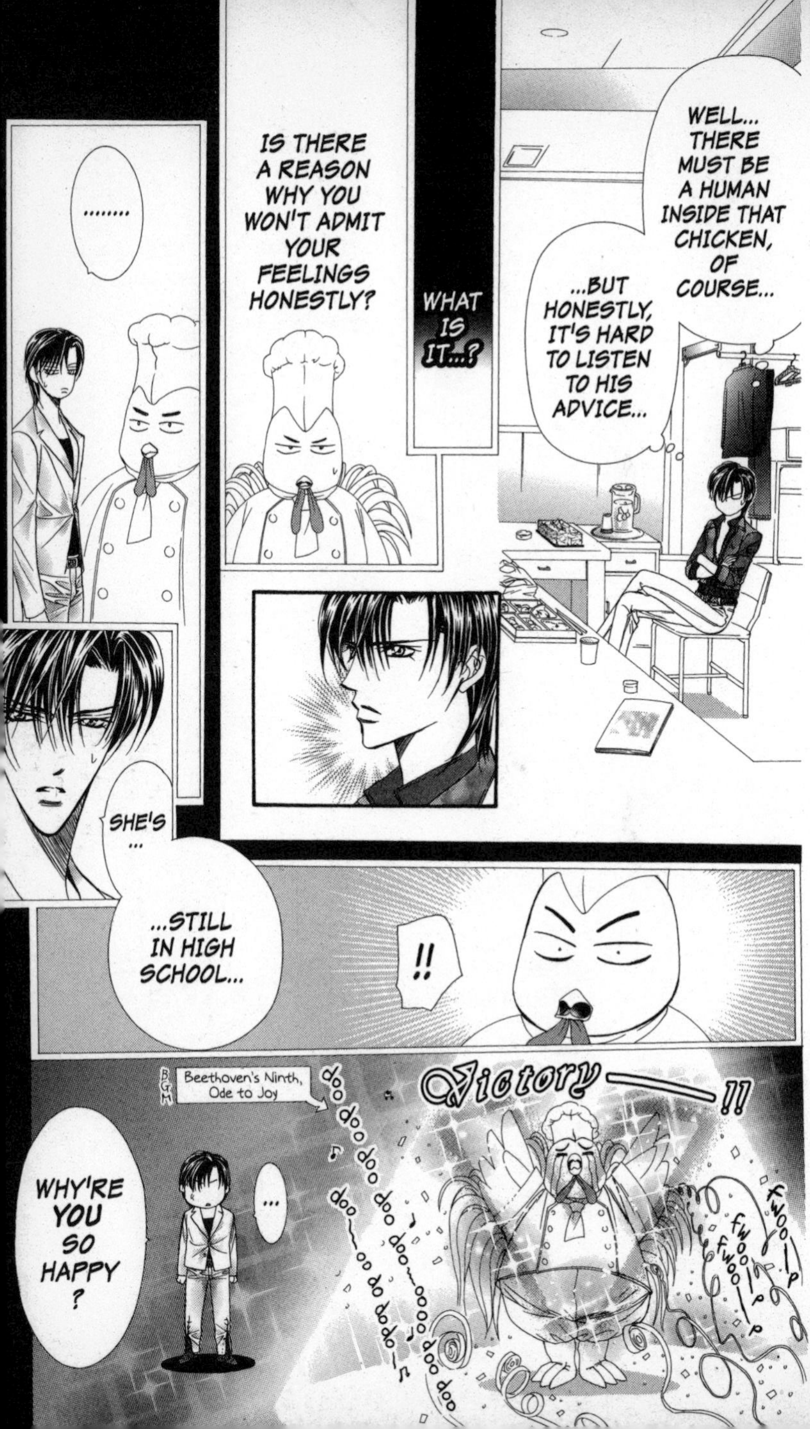
WELL... THERE MUST BE A HUMAN INSIDE THAT CHICKEN, OF COURSE...
...BUT HONESTLY, IT'S HARD TO LISTEN TO HIS ADVICE...
WHAT IS IT...?
IS THERE A REASON WHY YOU WON'T ADMIT YOUR FEELINGS HONESTLY?
....
SHE'S ...
...STILL IN HIGH SCHOOL...
!!
Victory—!!
FWOOOP FWOOOP FWOOOP
doo doo doo doo doo— oooo doo doo
doo— oo do dodo—
BGM Beethoven's Ninth, Ode to Joy
...
WHY'RE YOU SO HAPPY?

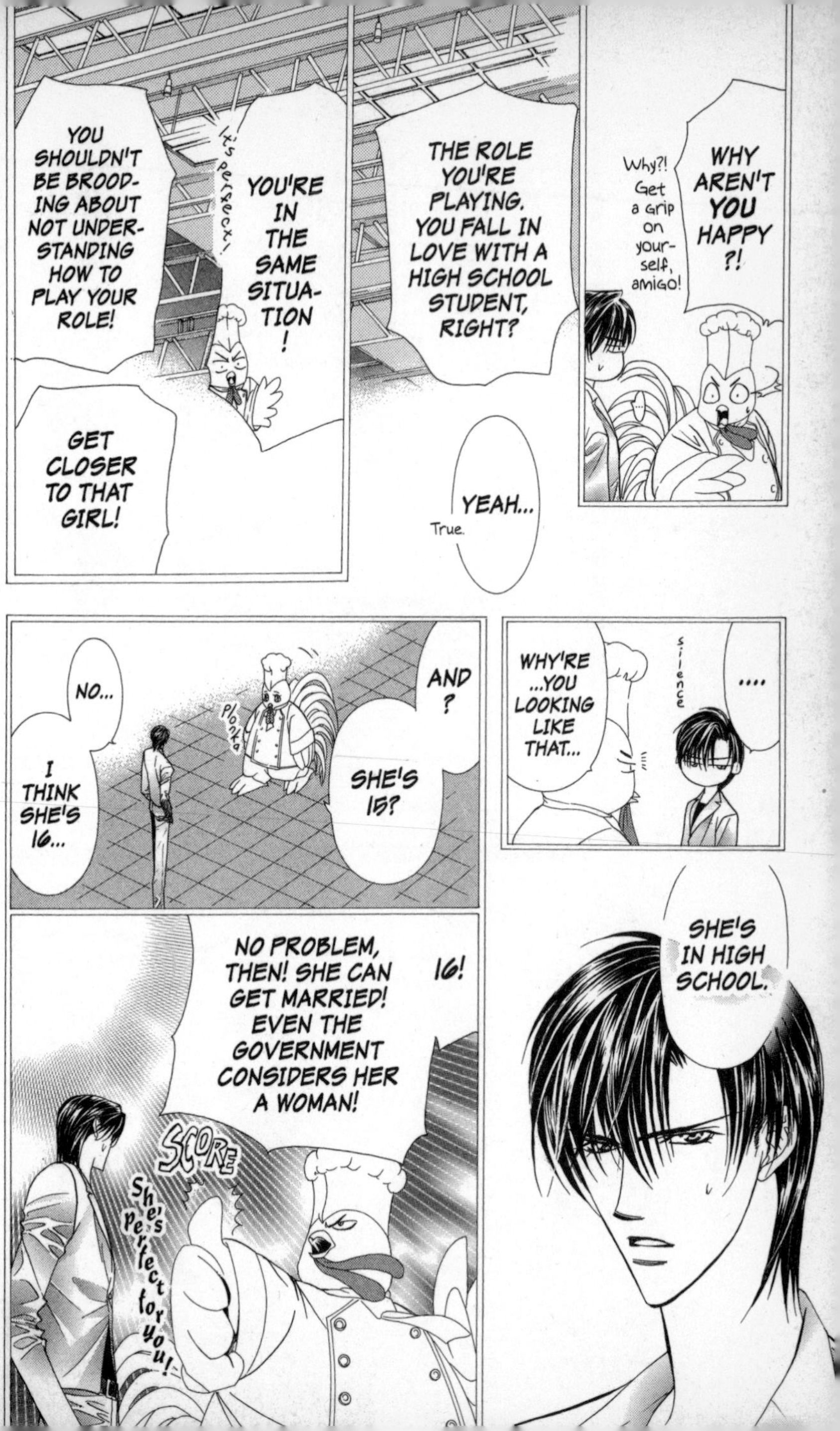
WHY AREN'T YOU HAPPY?!
Why?! Get a grip on yourself, amigo!
...
THE ROLE YOU'RE PLAYING. YOU FALL IN LOVE WITH A HIGH SCHOOL STUDENT, RIGHT?
YEAH...
True.
YOU'RE IN THE SAME SITUATION!
It's perfect!
YOU SHOULDN'T BE BROODING ABOUT NOT UNDERSTANDING HOW TO PLAY YOUR ROLE!
GET CLOSER TO THAT GIRL!
....
silence
WHY'RE ...YOU LOOKING LIKE THAT...
AND?
SHE'S 15?
Plonk
NO...
I THINK SHE'S 16...
SHE'S IN HIGH SCHOOL.
16!
NO PROBLEM, THEN! SHE CAN GET MARRIED! EVEN THE GOVERNMENT CONSIDERS HER A WOMAN!
SCORE
She's perfect for you!

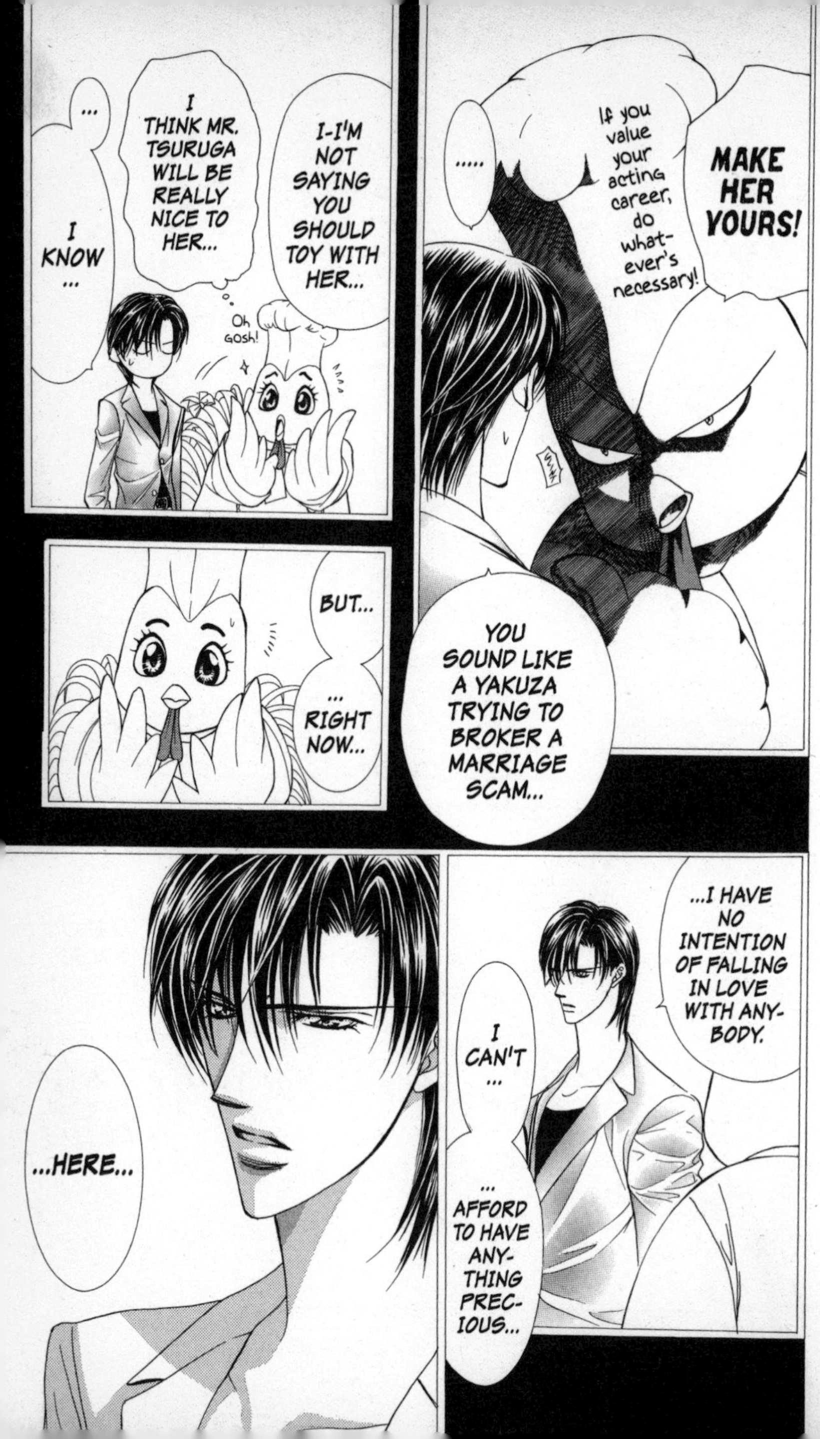
MAKE HER YOURS!
If you value your acting career, do whatever's necessary!
.....
YOU SOUND LIKE A YAKUZA TRYING TO BROKER A MARRIAGE SCAM...
I-I'M NOT SAYING YOU SHOULD TOY WITH HER...
I THINK MR. TSURUGA WILL BE REALLY NICE TO HER...
...
I KNOW ...
Oh Gosh!
BUT...
... RIGHT NOW...
...I HAVE NO INTENTION OF FALLING IN LOVE WITH ANYBODY.
I CAN'T ...
... AFFORD TO HAVE ANYTHING PRECIOUS...
...HERE...

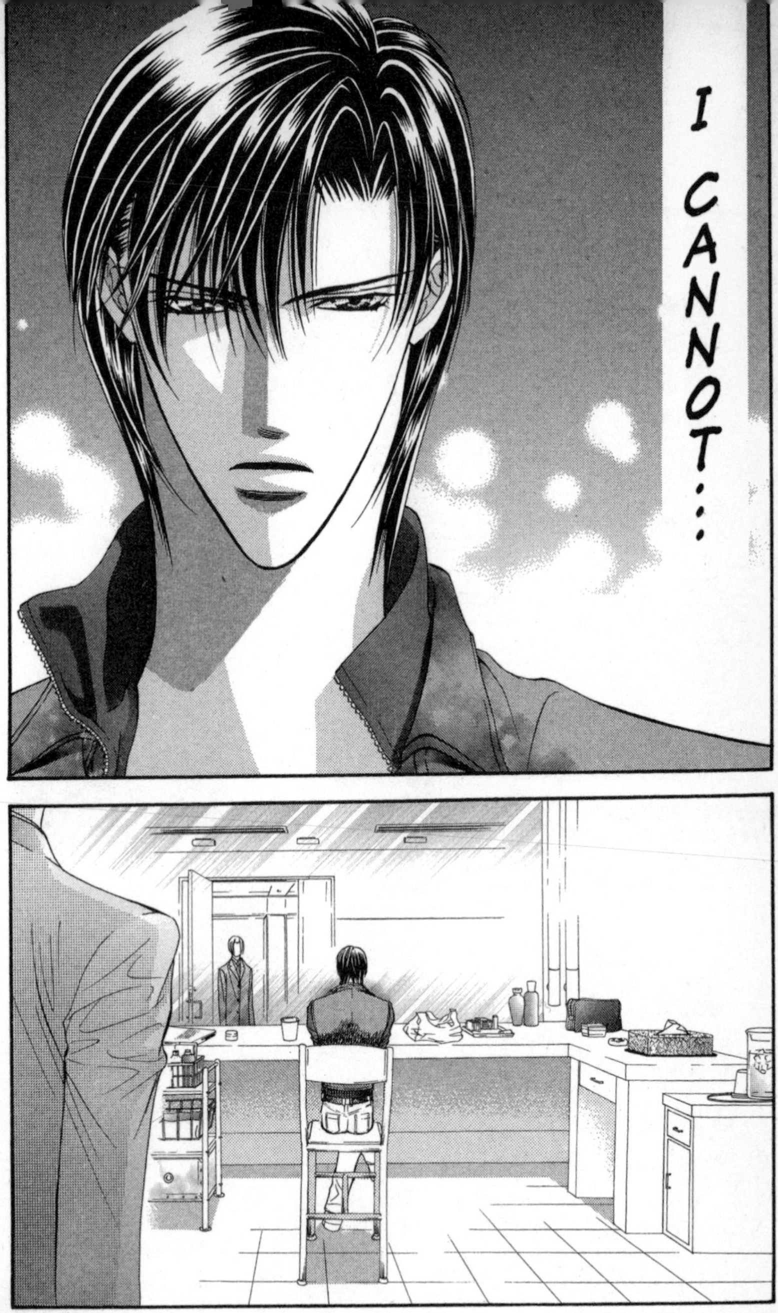
I CANNOT...

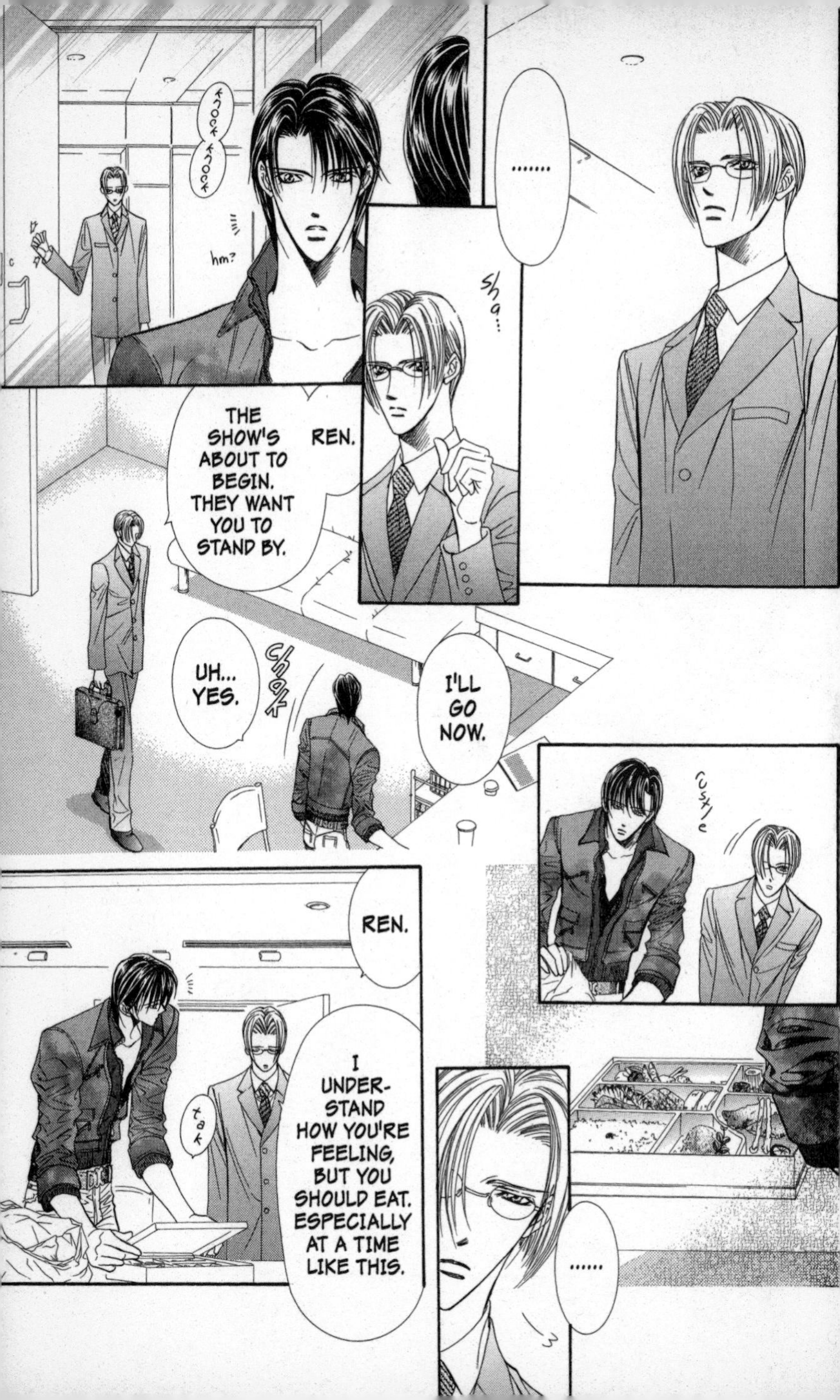

......
knock knock
hm?
Sha...
REN.
THE SHOW'S ABOUT TO BEGIN. THEY WANT YOU TO STAND BY.
UH... YES.
Chak
I'LL GO NOW.
rustle
REN.
tak
I UNDERSTAND HOW YOU'RE FEELING, BUT YOU SHOULD EAT. ESPECIALLY AT A TIME LIKE THIS.
......

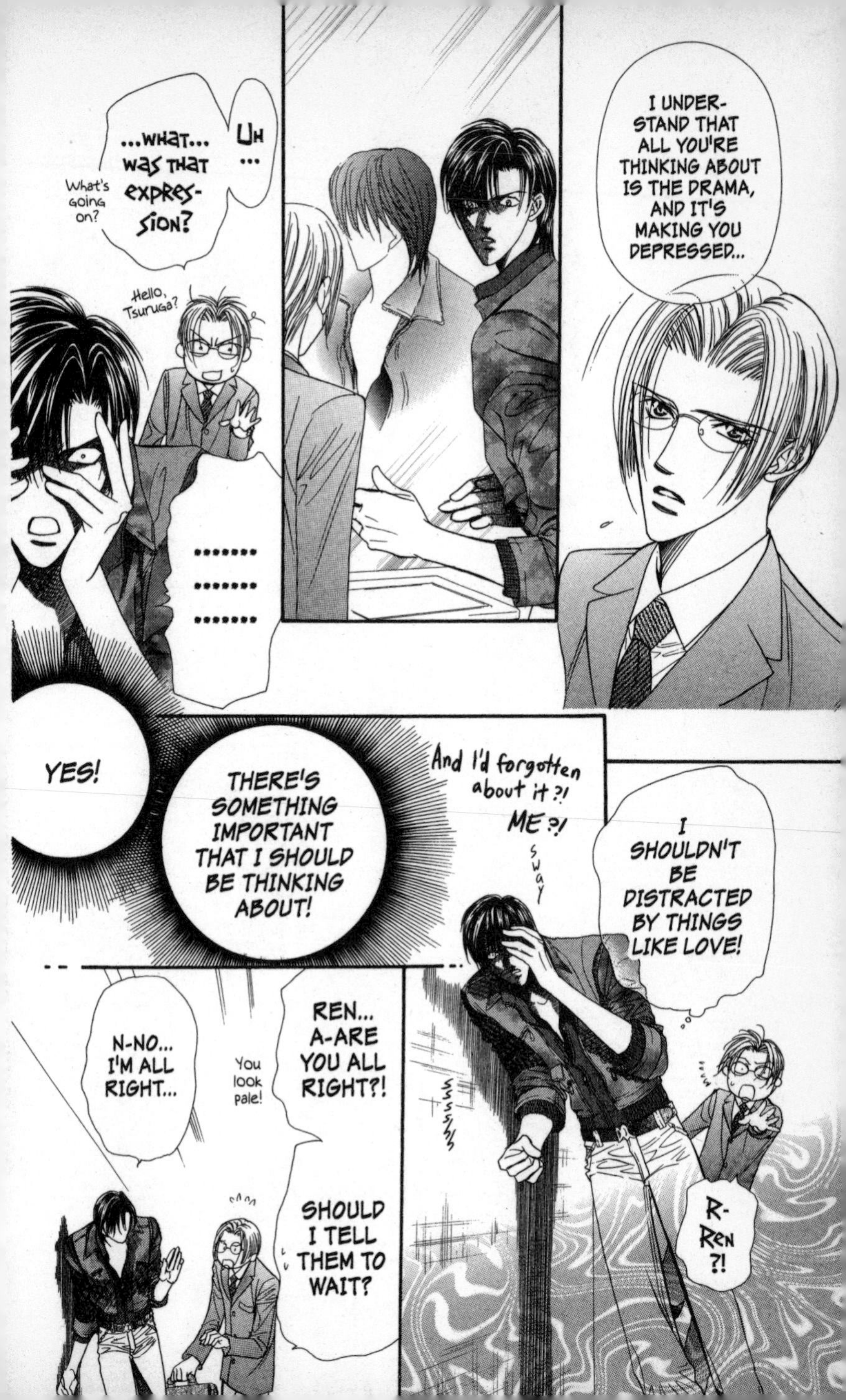
I UNDER-STAND THAT ALL YOU'RE THINKING ABOUT IS THE DRAMA, AND IT'S MAKING YOU DEPRESSED...
UH ...
...WHAT... WAS THAT EXPRES-SION?
What's going on?
Hello, Tsuruga?
....
....
....
And I'd forgotten about it?!
ME?!
THERE'S SOMETHING IMPORTANT THAT I SHOULD BE THINKING ABOUT!
YES!
I SHOULDN'T BE DISTRACTED BY THINGS LIKE LOVE!
SWAY
R-REN?!
REN... A-ARE YOU ALL RIGHT?!
You look pale!
N-NO... I'M ALL RIGHT...
SHOULD I TELL THEM TO WAIT?

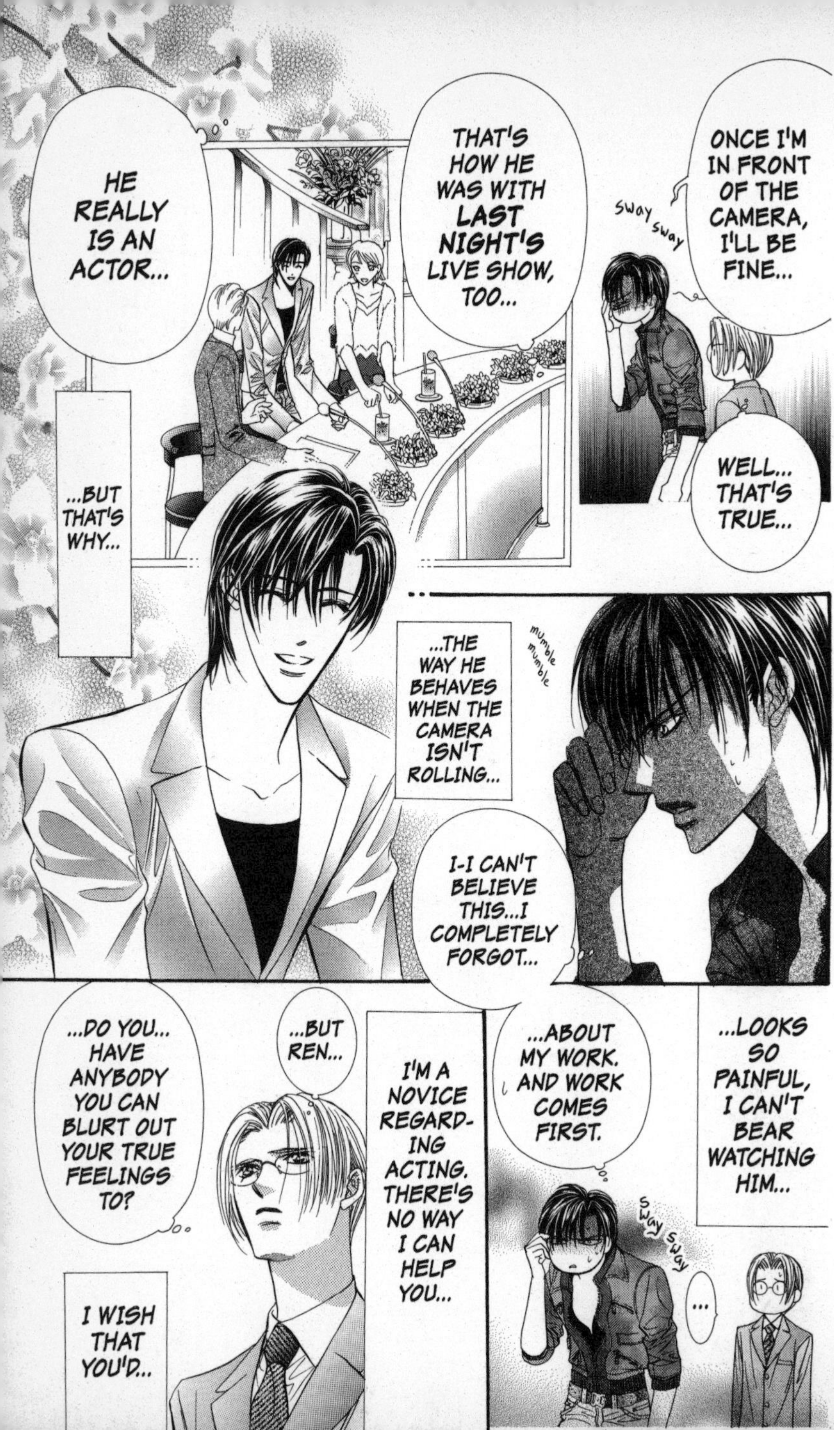
ONCE I'M IN FRONT OF THE CAMERA, I'LL BE FINE...
sway sway
WELL... THAT'S TRUE...
THAT'S HOW HE WAS WITH LAST NIGHT'S LIVE SHOW, TOO...
HE REALLY IS AN ACTOR...
...BUT THAT'S WHY...
mumble mumble
I-I CAN'T BELIEVE THIS...I COMPLETELY FORGOT...
...THE WAY HE BEHAVES WHEN THE CAMERA ISN'T ROLLING...
...LOOKS SO PAINFUL, I CAN'T BEAR WATCHING HIM...
...ABOUT MY WORK. AND WORK COMES FIRST.
sway sway
...
I'M A NOVICE REGARD-ING ACTING. THERE'S NO WAY I CAN HELP YOU...
...BUT REN...
...DO YOU... HAVE ANYBODY YOU CAN BLURT OUT YOUR TRUE FEELINGS TO?
I WISH THAT YOU'D...

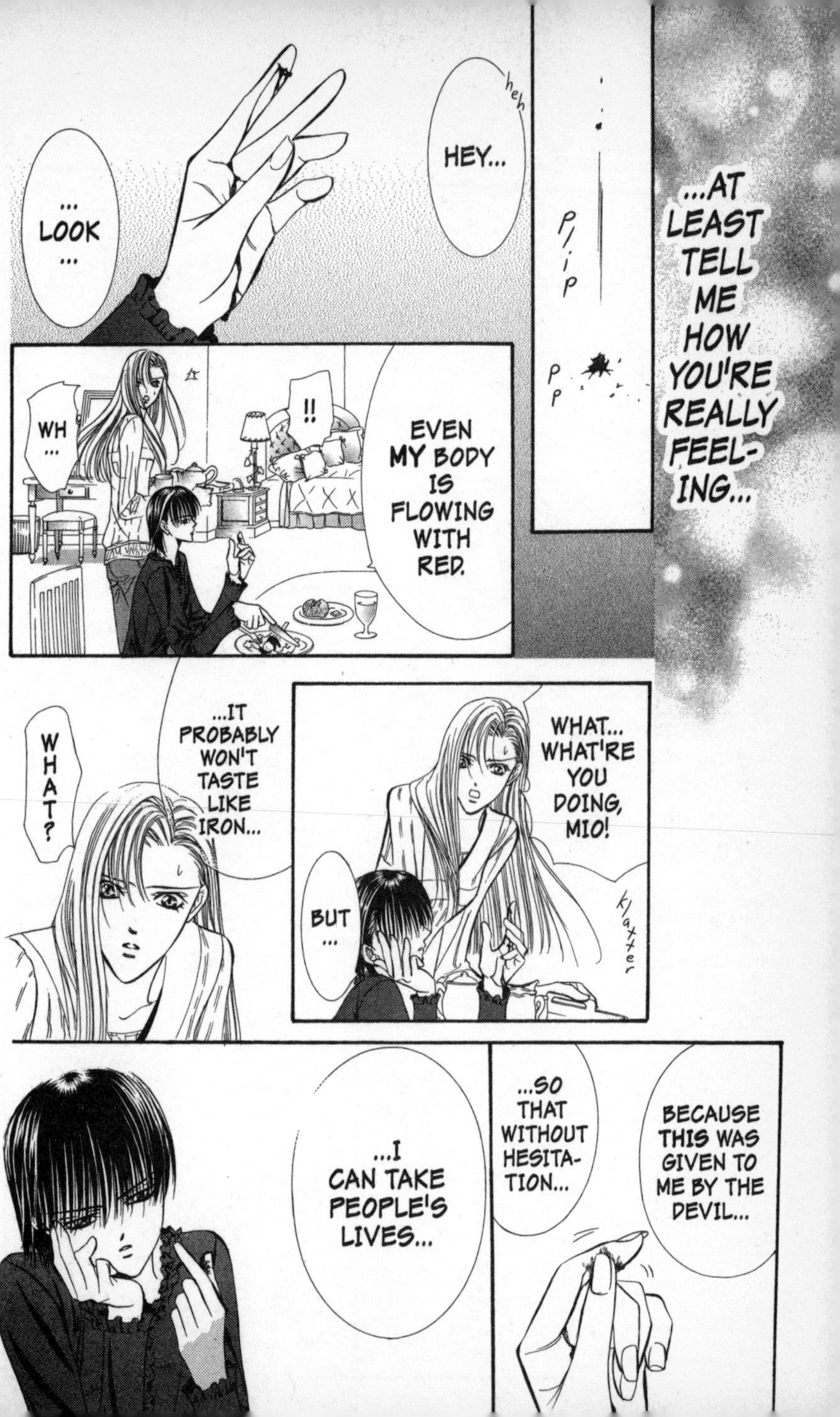
...AT LEAST TELL ME HOW YOU'RE REALLY FEELING...
Plip
pp
heh
HEY...
...LOOK...
EVEN MY BODY IS FLOWING WITH RED.
!!
WH...
WHAT... WHAT'RE YOU DOING, MIO!
klaxter
BUT...
...IT PROBABLY WON'T TASTE LIKE IRON...
WHAT?
BECAUSE THIS WAS GIVEN TO ME BY THE DEVIL...
...SO THAT WITHOUT HESITATION...
...I CAN TAKE PEOPLE'S LIVES...

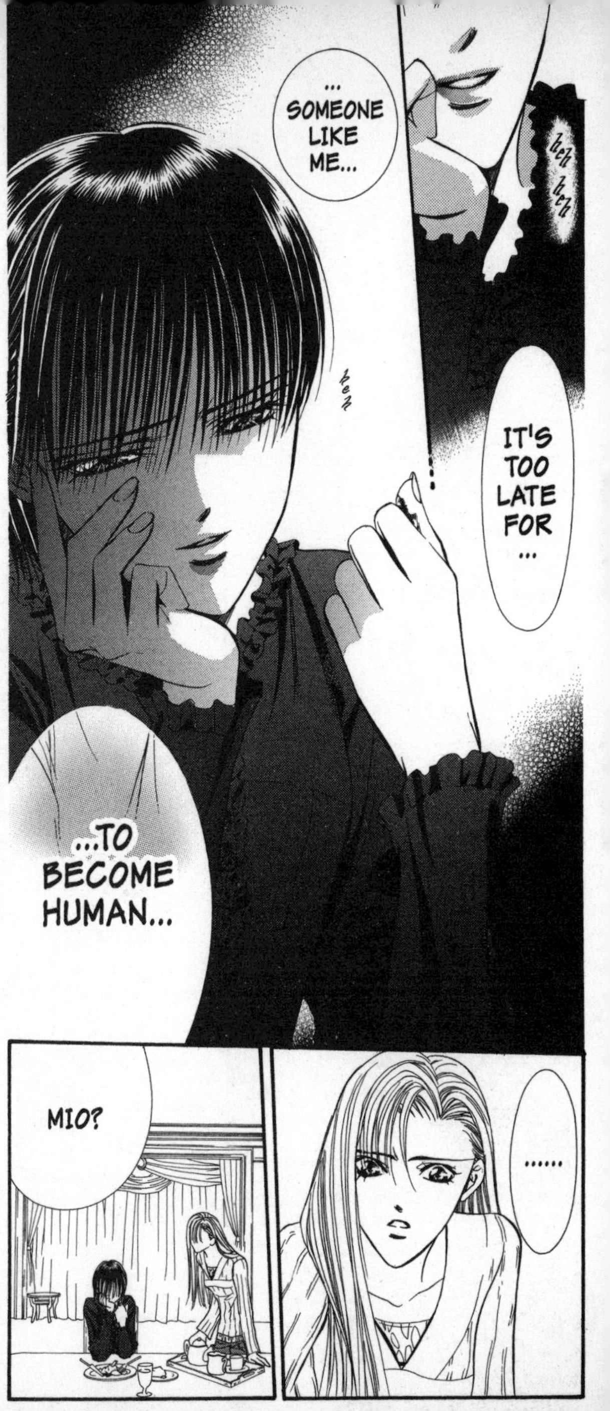
heh heh
...
SOMEONE LIKE ME...
IT'S TOO LATE FOR ...
...TO BECOME HUMAN...
......
MIO?

Itsumi Momose

People think she's a little older than she actually is. This may be because she looks calm before she starts to act. However, she is a young 17-year-old and attends high school.

Until the previous volume, most of her lines were ".....", but this time she finally says something!!

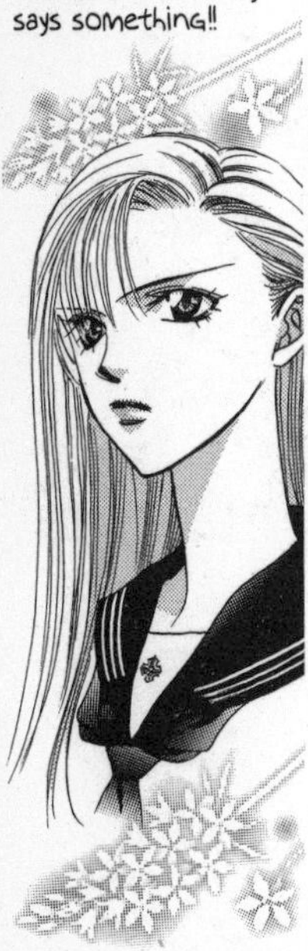

What she says demonstrates her professionalism, and the readers seem to like that. I don't know whether that's still true after she says Kyoko is better than Ren...

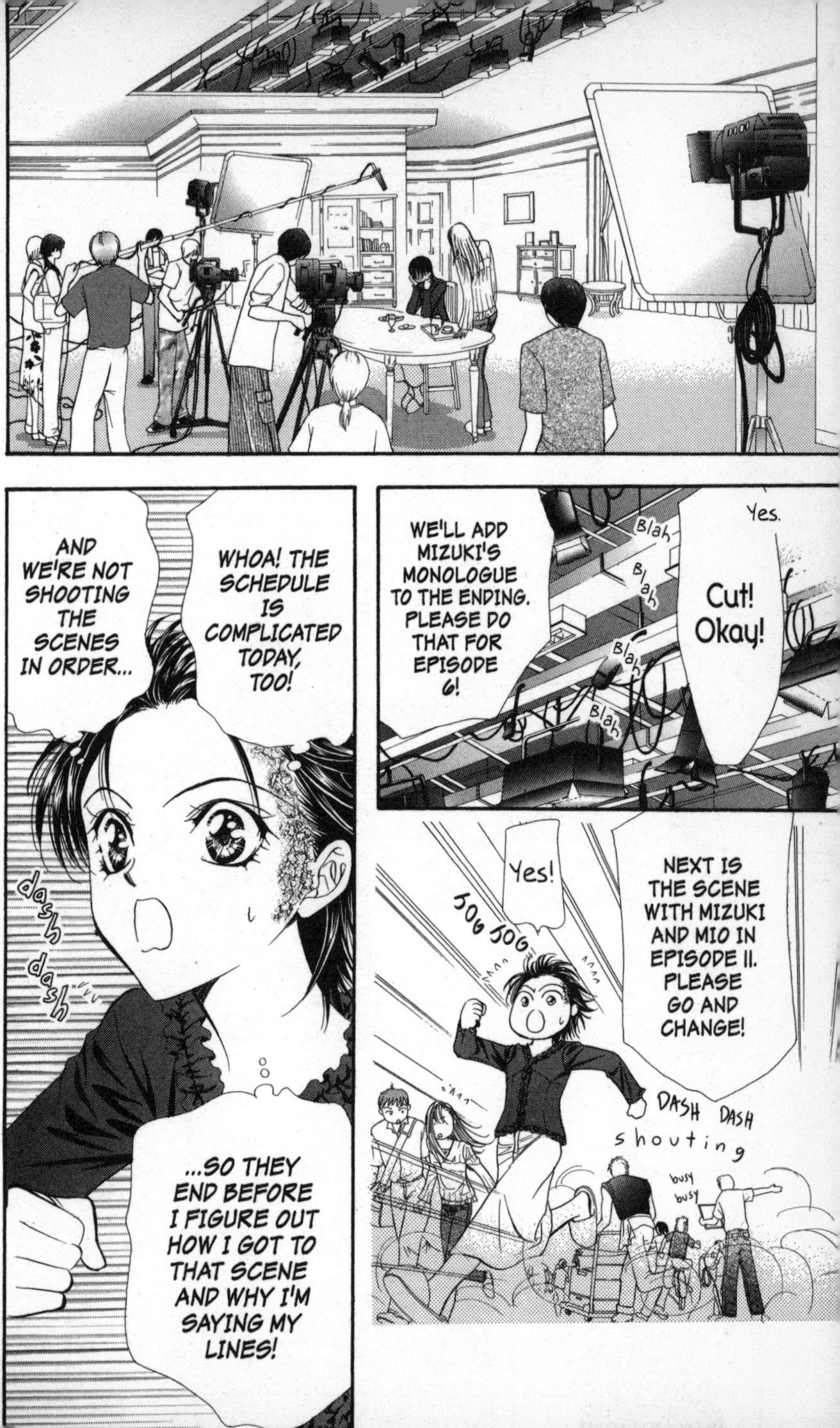
Yes.
Cut! Okay!
WE'LL ADD MIZUKI'S MONOLOGUE TO THE ENDING. PLEASE DO THAT FOR EPISODE 6!
Blah Blah Blah Blah
NEXT IS THE SCENE WITH MIZUKI AND MIO IN EPISODE 11. PLEASE GO AND CHANGE!
Yes!
JOG JOG
DASH DASH
shouting
busy busy
WHOA! THE SCHEDULE IS COMPLICATED TODAY, TOO!
AND WE'RE NOT SHOOTING THE SCENES IN ORDER...
dash dash
...SO THEY END BEFORE I FIGURE OUT HOW I GOT TO THAT SCENE AND WHY I'M SAYING MY LINES!

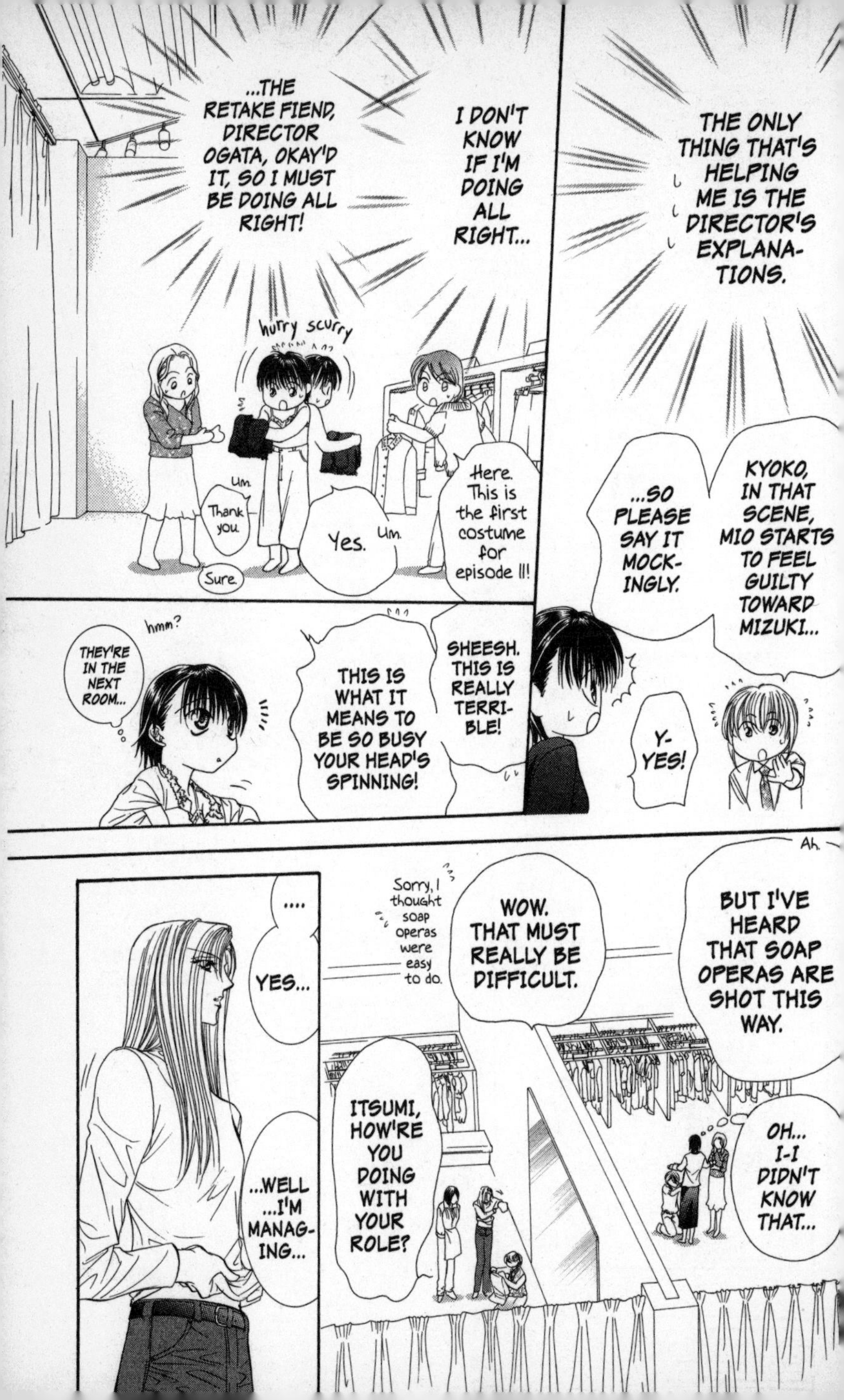
THE ONLY THING THAT'S HELPING ME IS THE DIRECTOR'S EXPLANATIONS.
KYOKO, IN THAT SCENE, MIO STARTS TO FEEL GUILTY TOWARD MIZUKI...
...SO PLEASE SAY IT MOCKINGLY.
Y-YES!
I DON'T KNOW IF I'M DOING ALL RIGHT...
...THE RETAKE FIEND, DIRECTOR OGATA, OKAY'D IT, SO I MUST BE DOING ALL RIGHT!
hurry scurry
Here. This is the first costume for episode 11!
Um.
Yes.
Um.
Thank you.
Sure.
SHEESH. THIS IS REALLY TERRIBLE!
THIS IS WHAT IT MEANS TO BE SO BUSY YOUR HEAD'S SPINNING!
hmm?
THEY'RE IN THE NEXT ROOM...
Ah.
BUT I'VE HEARD THAT SOAP OPERAS ARE SHOT THIS WAY.
WOW. THAT MUST REALLY BE DIFFICULT.
Sorry, I thought soap operas were easy to do.
YES...
....
OH... I-I DIDN'T KNOW THAT...
ITSUMI, HOW'RE YOU DOING WITH YOUR ROLE?
...WELL ...I'M MANAGING...

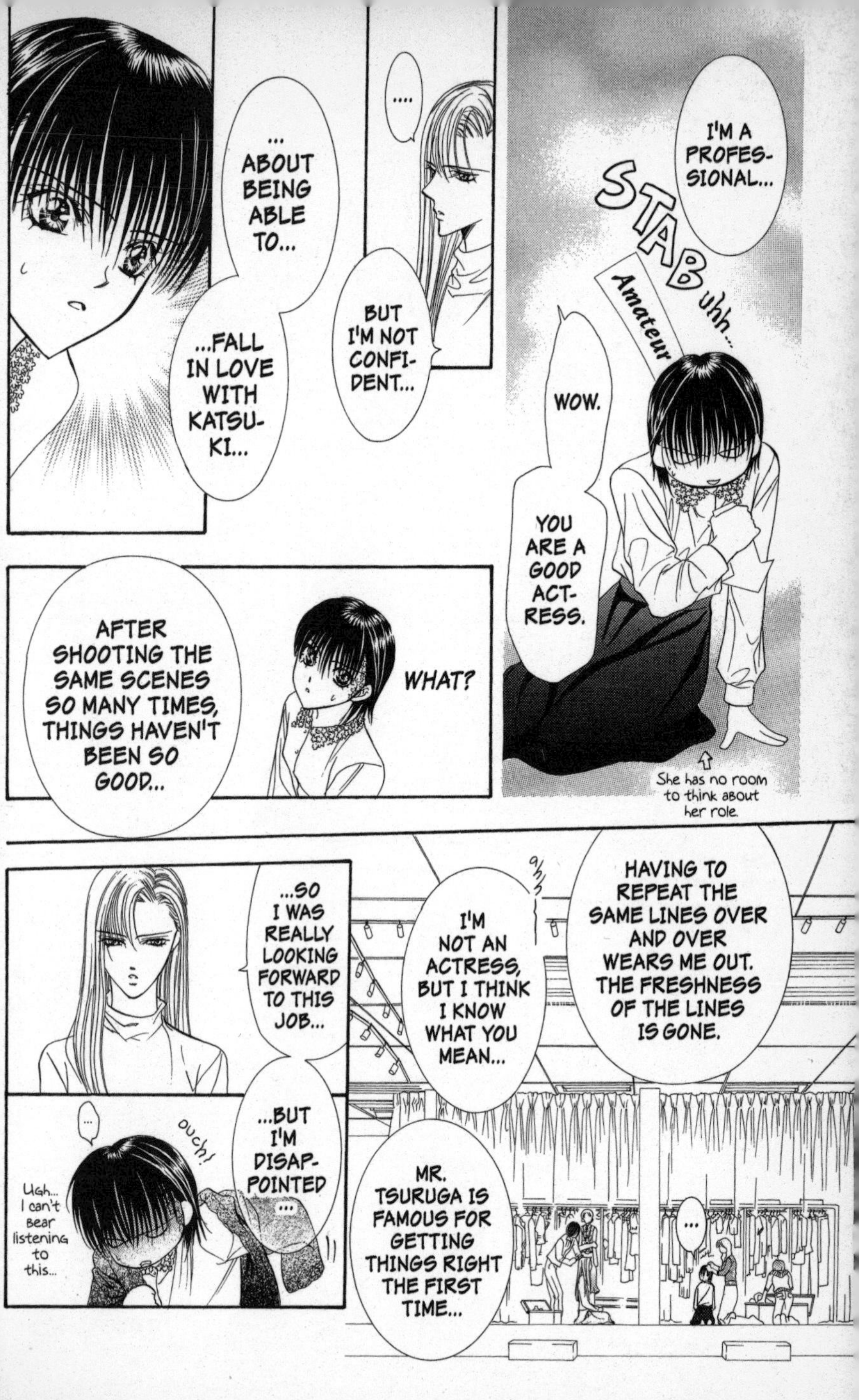
I'M A PROFESSIONAL...
STAB
Amateur
uhh...
WOW.
YOU ARE A GOOD ACTRESS.
She has no room to think about her role.
....
BUT I'M NOT CONFIDENT...
... ABOUT BEING ABLE TO...
...FALL IN LOVE WITH KATSUKI...
WHAT?
AFTER SHOOTING THE SAME SCENES SO MANY TIMES, THINGS HAVEN'T BEEN SO GOOD...
HAVING TO REPEAT THE SAME LINES OVER AND OVER WEARS ME OUT. THE FRESHNESS OF THE LINES IS GONE.
I'M NOT AN ACTRESS, BUT I THINK I KNOW WHAT YOU MEAN...
MR. TSURUGA IS FAMOUS FOR GETTING THINGS RIGHT THE FIRST TIME...
...
...SO I WAS REALLY LOOKING FORWARD TO THIS JOB...
...BUT I'M DISAPPOINTED...
...
ouch!
Ugh... I can't bear listening to this...

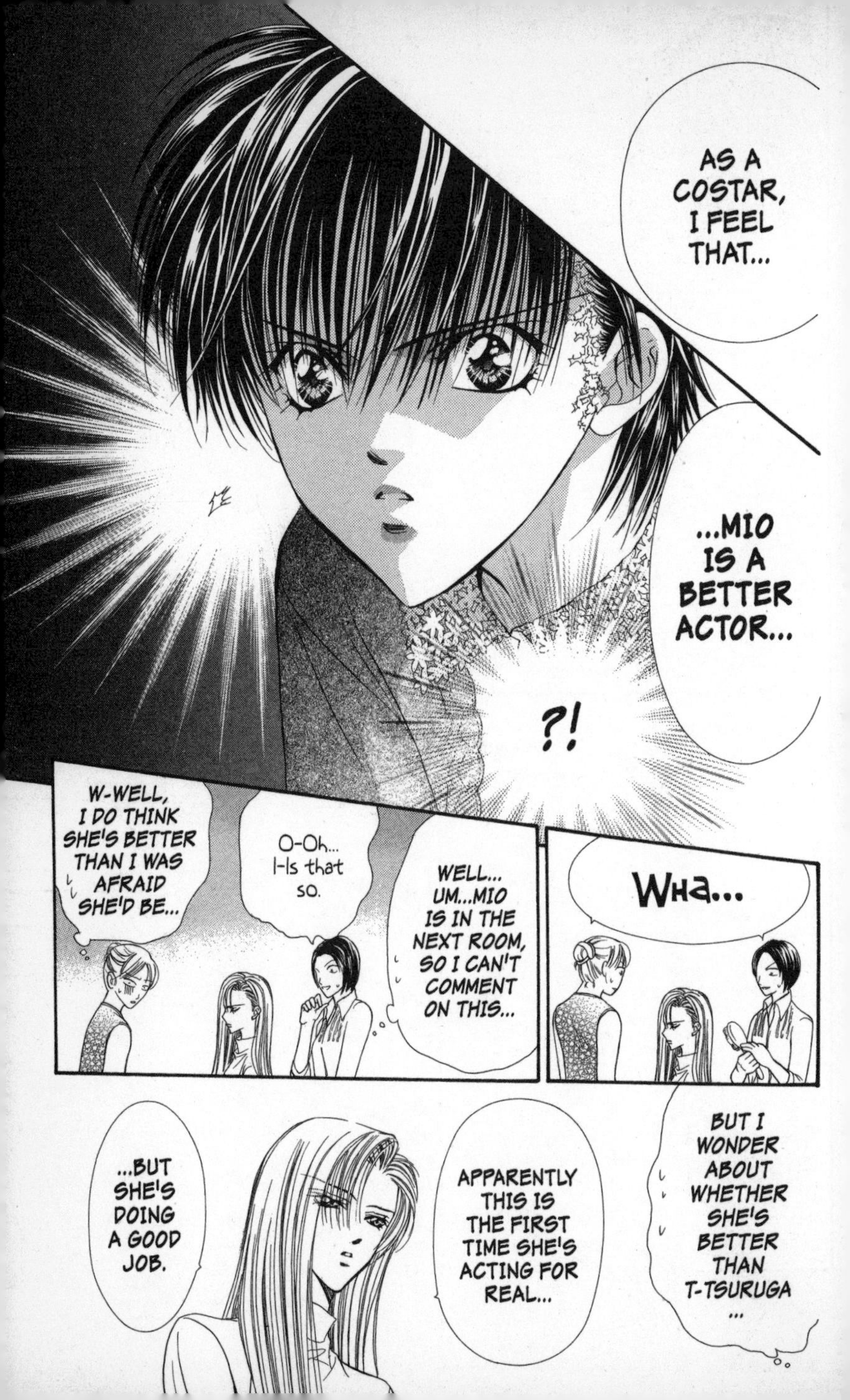

AS A COSTAR, I FEEL THAT...
...MIO IS A BETTER ACTOR...
?!
Wha...
WELL... UM...MIO IS IN THE NEXT ROOM, SO I CAN'T COMMENT ON THIS...
O-Oh... I-Is that so.
W-WELL, I DO THINK SHE'S BETTER THAN I WAS AFRAID SHE'D BE...
BUT I WONDER ABOUT WHETHER SHE'S BETTER THAN T-TSURUGA...
APPARENTLY THIS IS THE FIRST TIME SHE'S ACTING FOR REAL...
...BUT SHE'S DOING A GOOD JOB.

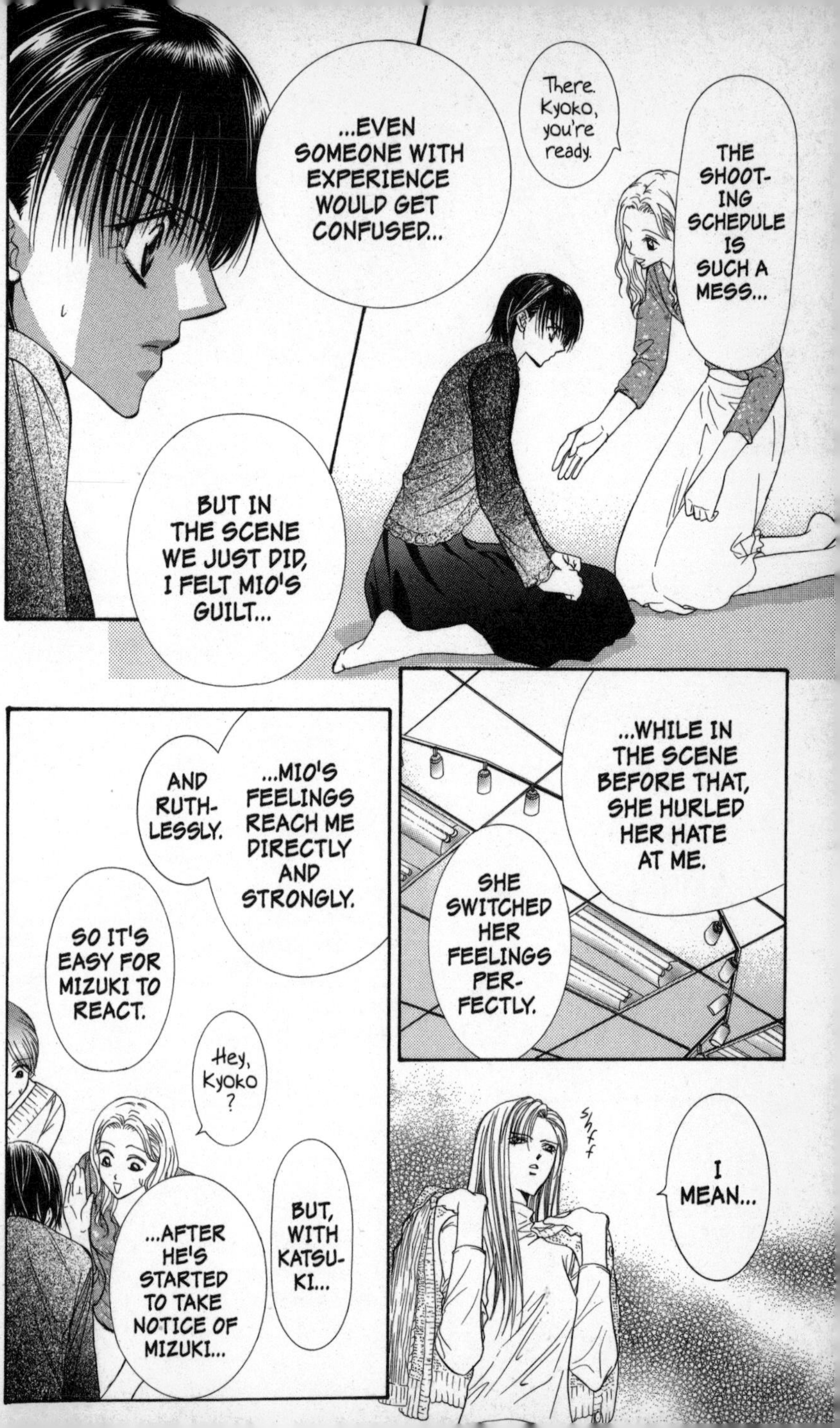
THE SHOOTING SCHEDULE IS SUCH A MESS...
There. Kyoko, you're ready.
...EVEN SOMEONE WITH EXPERIENCE WOULD GET CONFUSED...
BUT IN THE SCENE WE JUST DID, I FELT MIO'S GUILT...
...WHILE IN THE SCENE BEFORE THAT, SHE HURLED HER HATE AT ME.
SHE SWITCHED HER FEELINGS PERFECTLY.
shff
I MEAN...
...MIO'S FEELINGS REACH ME DIRECTLY AND STRONGLY.
AND RUTHLESSLY.
SO IT'S EASY FOR MIZUKI TO REACT.
Hey, Kyoko?
BUT, WITH KATSUKI...
...AFTER HE'S STARTED TO TAKE NOTICE OF MIZUKI...

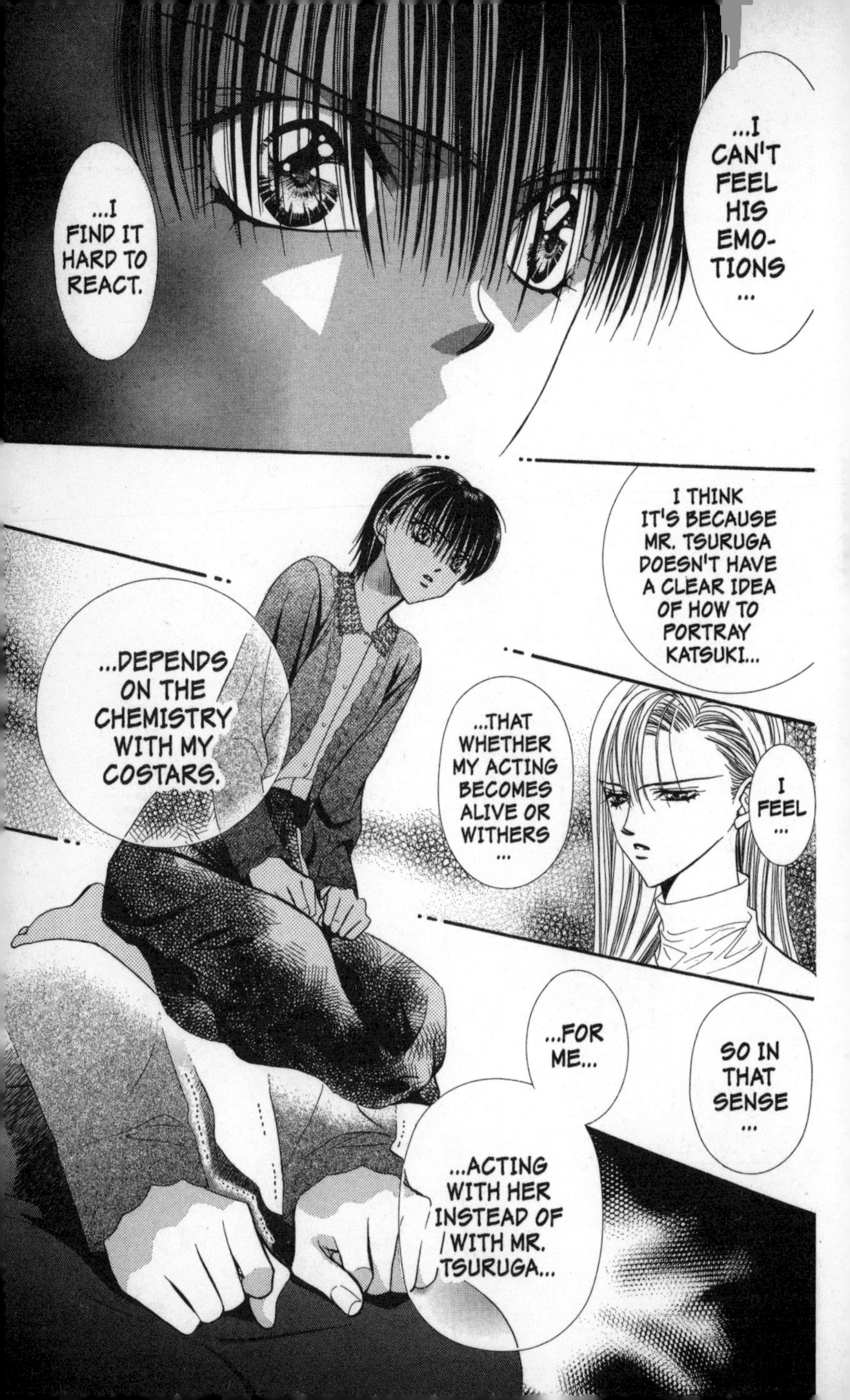
...I CAN'T FEEL HIS EMOTIONS...
...I FIND IT HARD TO REACT.
I THINK IT'S BECAUSE MR. TSURUGA DOESN'T HAVE A CLEAR IDEA OF HOW TO PORTRAY KATSUKI...
I FEEL...
...THAT WHETHER MY ACTING BECOMES ALIVE OR WITHERS...
...DEPENDS ON THE CHEMISTRY WITH MY COSTARS.
SO IN THAT SENSE...
...FOR ME...
...ACTING WITH HER INSTEAD OF WITH MR. TSURUGA...

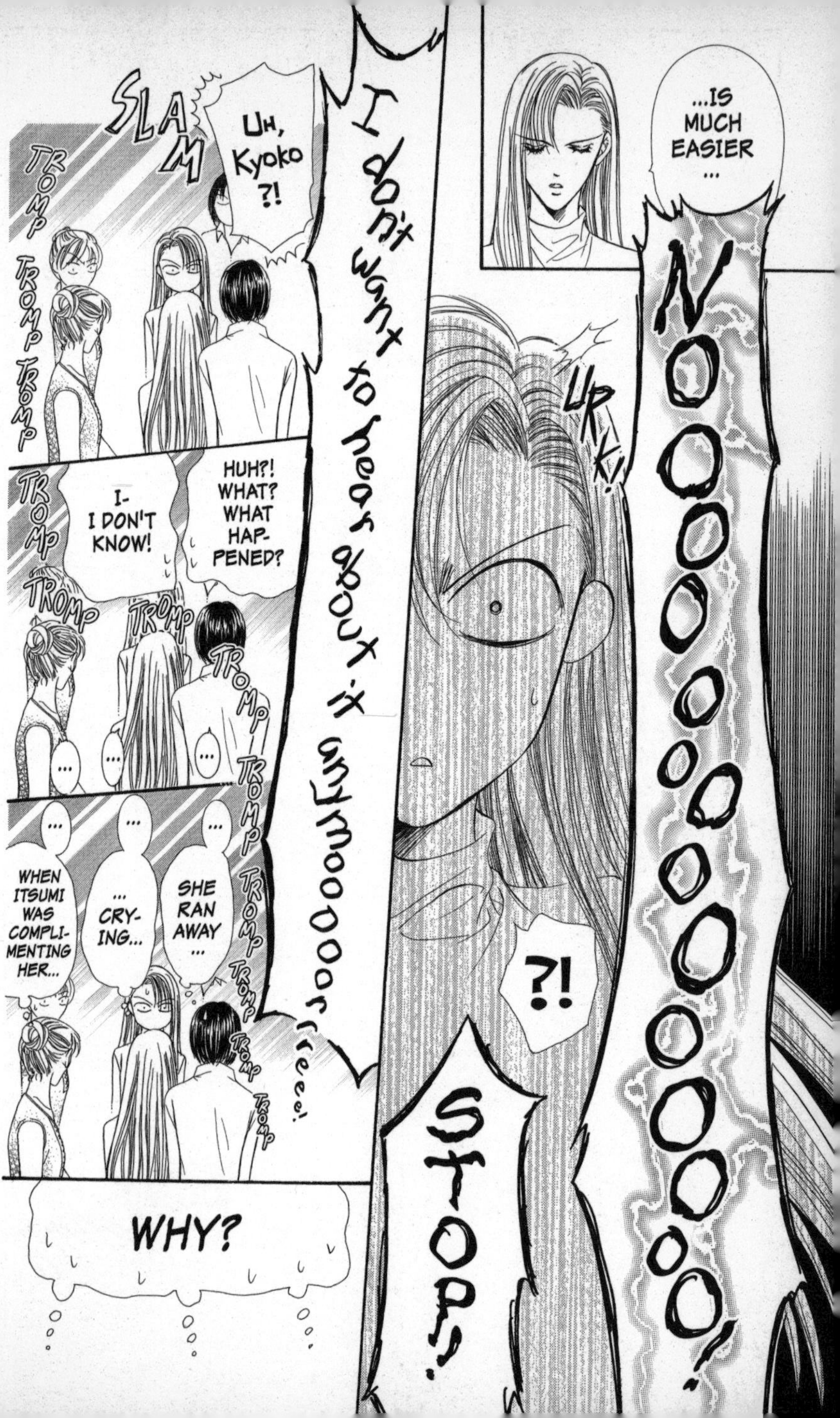
...IS MUCH EASIER ...
NOOOOOOOOOOOOOOO!
URK!
?!
STOP!!
I don't want to hear about it anymooooor reeee!
SLAM
UH, Kyoko?!
TROMP TROMP TROMP TROMP
HUH?! WHAT? WHAT HAP-PENED?
I- I DON'T KNOW!
TROMP TROMP TROMP TROMP TROMP TROMP TROMP TROMP
...
...
...
...
SHE RAN AWAY ...
...
... CRY-ING...
...
WHEN ITSUMI WAS COMPLI-MENTING HER...
WHY?

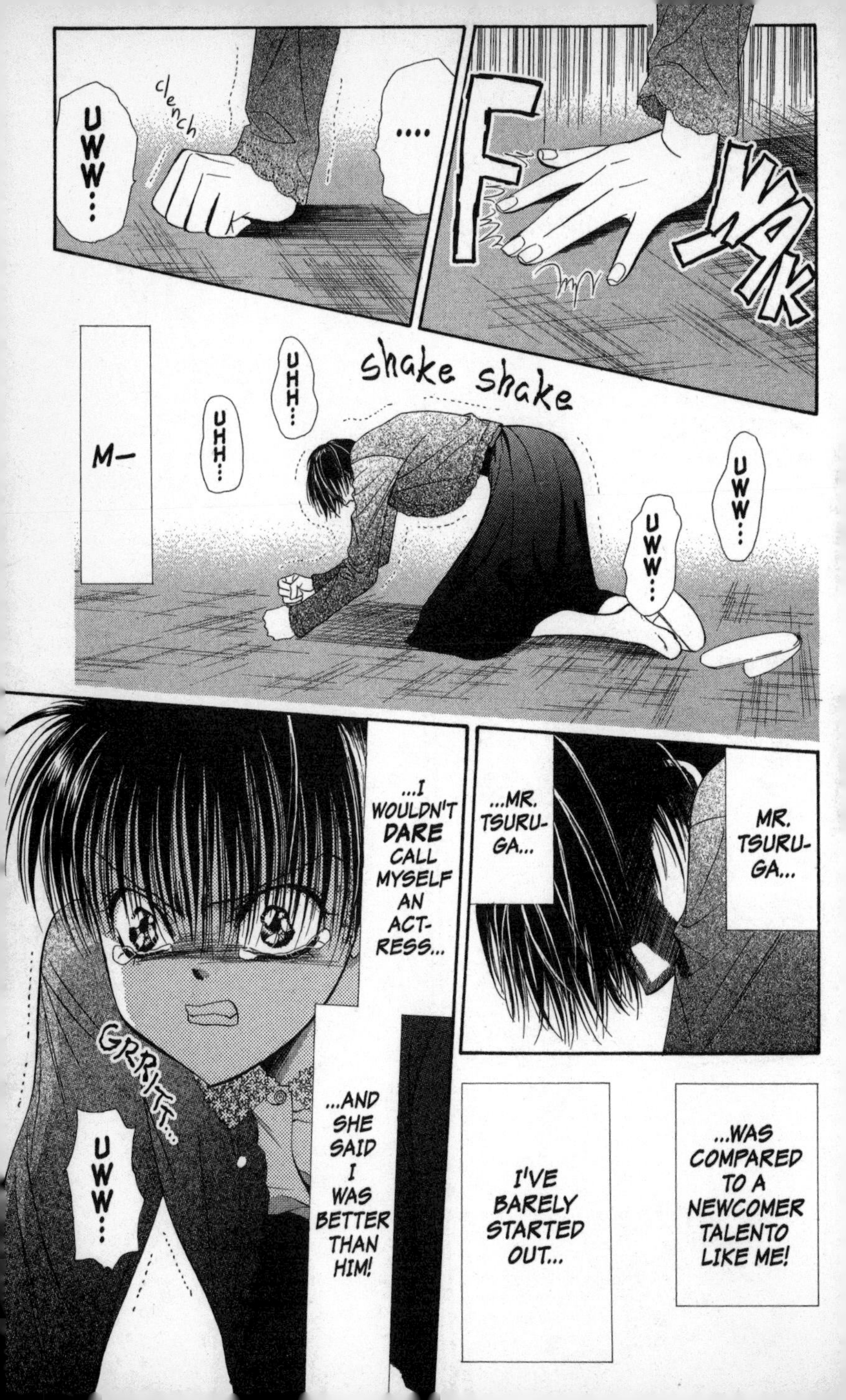
FWAK
....
clench
UWW...
UWW...
UWW...
shake shake
UHH...
UHH...
M—
MR. TSURU-GA...
...MR. TSURU-GA...
...I WOULDN'T DARE CALL MYSELF AN ACT-RESS...
...WAS COMPARED TO A NEWCOMER TALENTO LIKE ME!
I'VE BARELY STARTED OUT...
...AND SHE SAID I WAS BETTER THAN HIM!
GRRITT...
UWW...

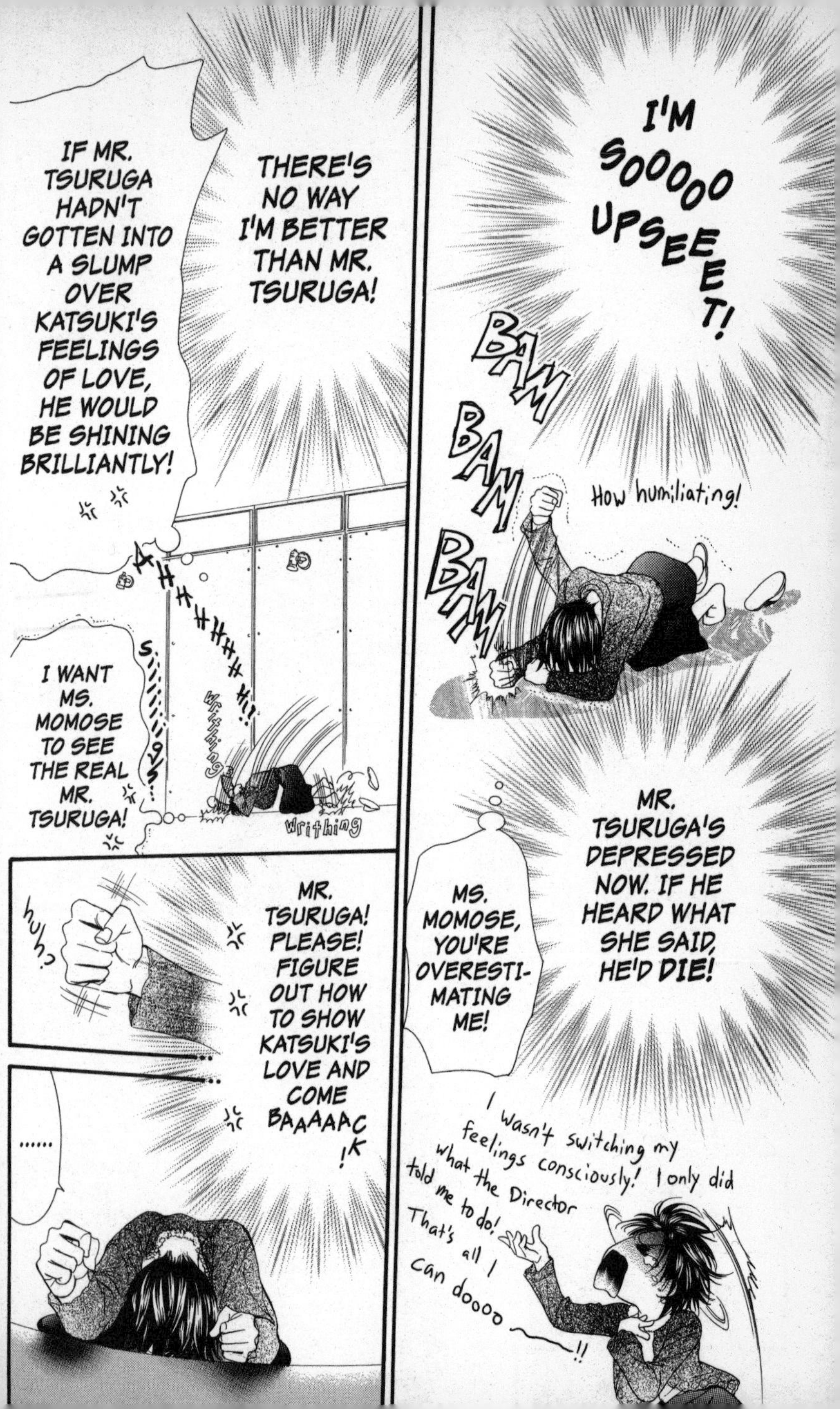

I'M SOOOOOO UPSEEEET!
BAM BAM BAM
How humiliating!
MR. TSURUGA'S DEPRESSED NOW. IF HE HEARD WHAT SHE SAID, HE'D DIE!
MS. MOMOSE, YOU'RE OVERESTI-MATING ME!
I wasn't switching my feelings consciously! I only did what the Director told me to do! That's all I can doooo—!!
THERE'S NO WAY I'M BETTER THAN MR. TSURUGA!
IF MR. TSURUGA HADN'T GOTTEN INTO A SLUMP OVER KATSUKI'S FEELINGS OF LOVE, HE WOULD BE SHINING BRILLIANTLY!
AHHHHHHHH!!
squiggle
writhing
I WANT MS. MOMOSE TO SEE THE REAL MR. TSURUGA!
writhing
huh?
MR. TSURUGA! PLEASE! FIGURE OUT HOW TO SHOW KATSUKI'S LOVE AND COME BAAAAACK!
......

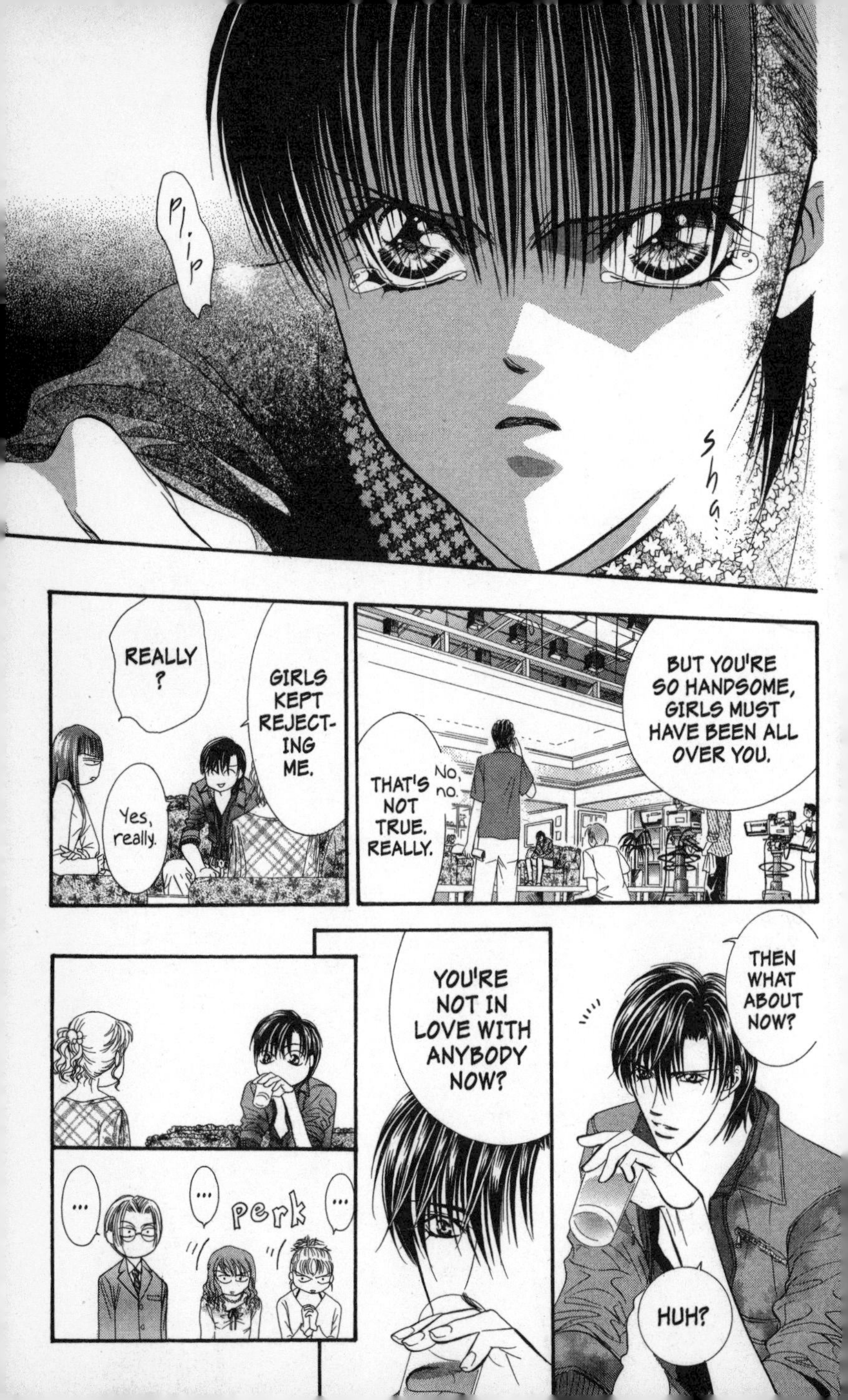

Plip
sha...
BUT YOU'RE SO HANDSOME, GIRLS MUST HAVE BEEN ALL OVER YOU.
No, no.
THAT'S NOT TRUE. REALLY.
GIRLS KEPT REJECT-ING ME.
REALLY?
Yes, really.
THEN WHAT ABOUT NOW?
YOU'RE NOT IN LOVE WITH ANYBODY NOW?
HUH?
...
perk
...
...

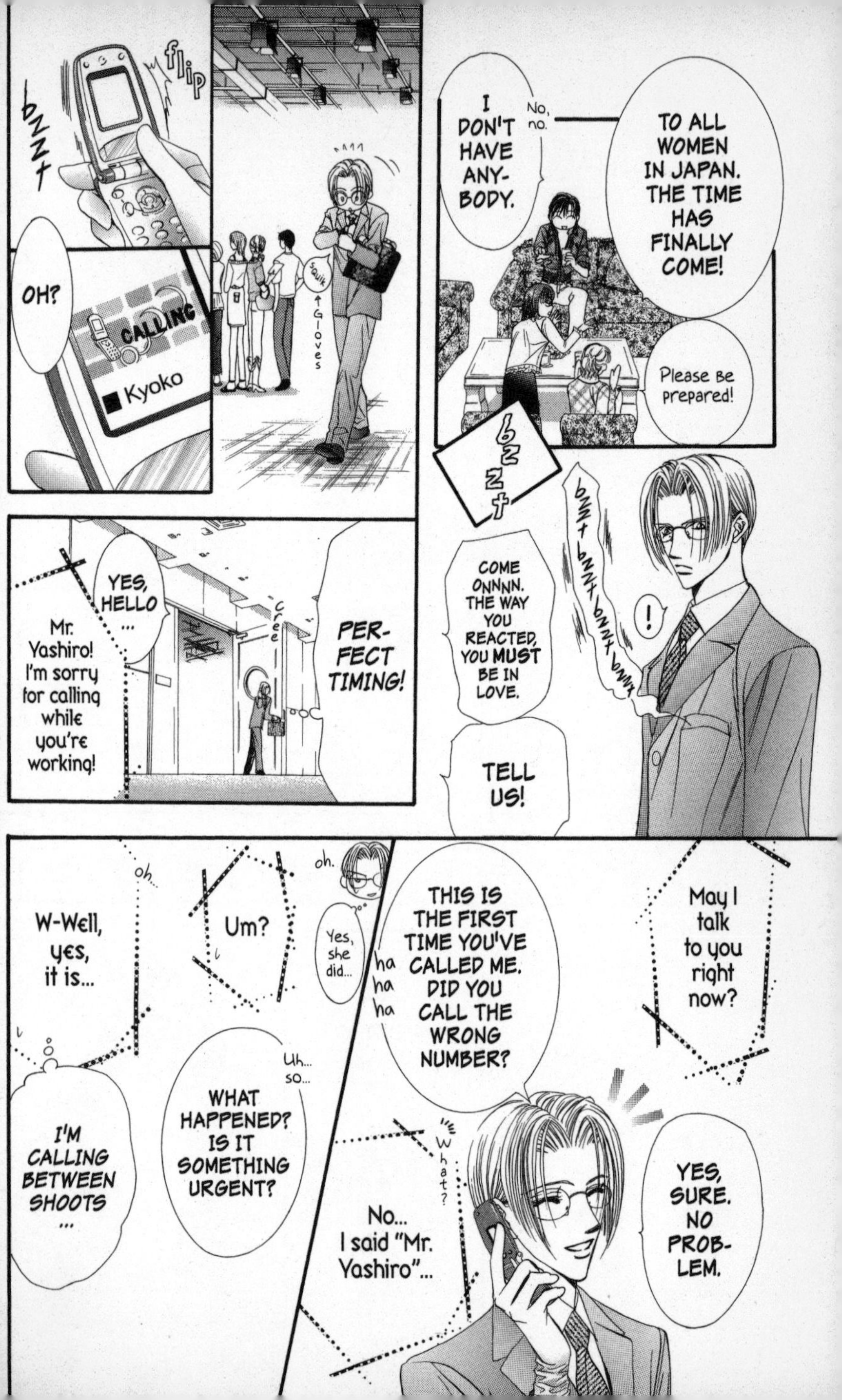
TO ALL WOMEN IN JAPAN. THE TIME HAS FINALLY COME!
Please be prepared!
No, no.
I DON'T HAVE ANYBODY.
bzzt
Squik
↑ Gloves
flip
bzzt
OH?
CALLING
Kyoko
bzzt bzzt bzzt bzzzz
!
COME ONNNN. THE WAY YOU REACTED, YOU MUST BE IN LOVE.
TELL US!
PERFECT TIMING!
Cree
YES, HELLO...
Mr. Yashiro! I'm sorry for calling while you're working!
May I talk to you right now?
YES, SURE. NO PROBLEM.
THIS IS THE FIRST TIME YOU'VE CALLED ME. DID YOU CALL THE WRONG NUMBER?
ha ha ha
oh.
Yes, she did...
What?
No... I said "Mr. Yashiro"...
Um?
oh...
W-Well, yes, it is...
Uh... so...
WHAT HAPPENED? IS IT SOMETHING URGENT?
I'M CALLING BETWEEN SHOOTS...

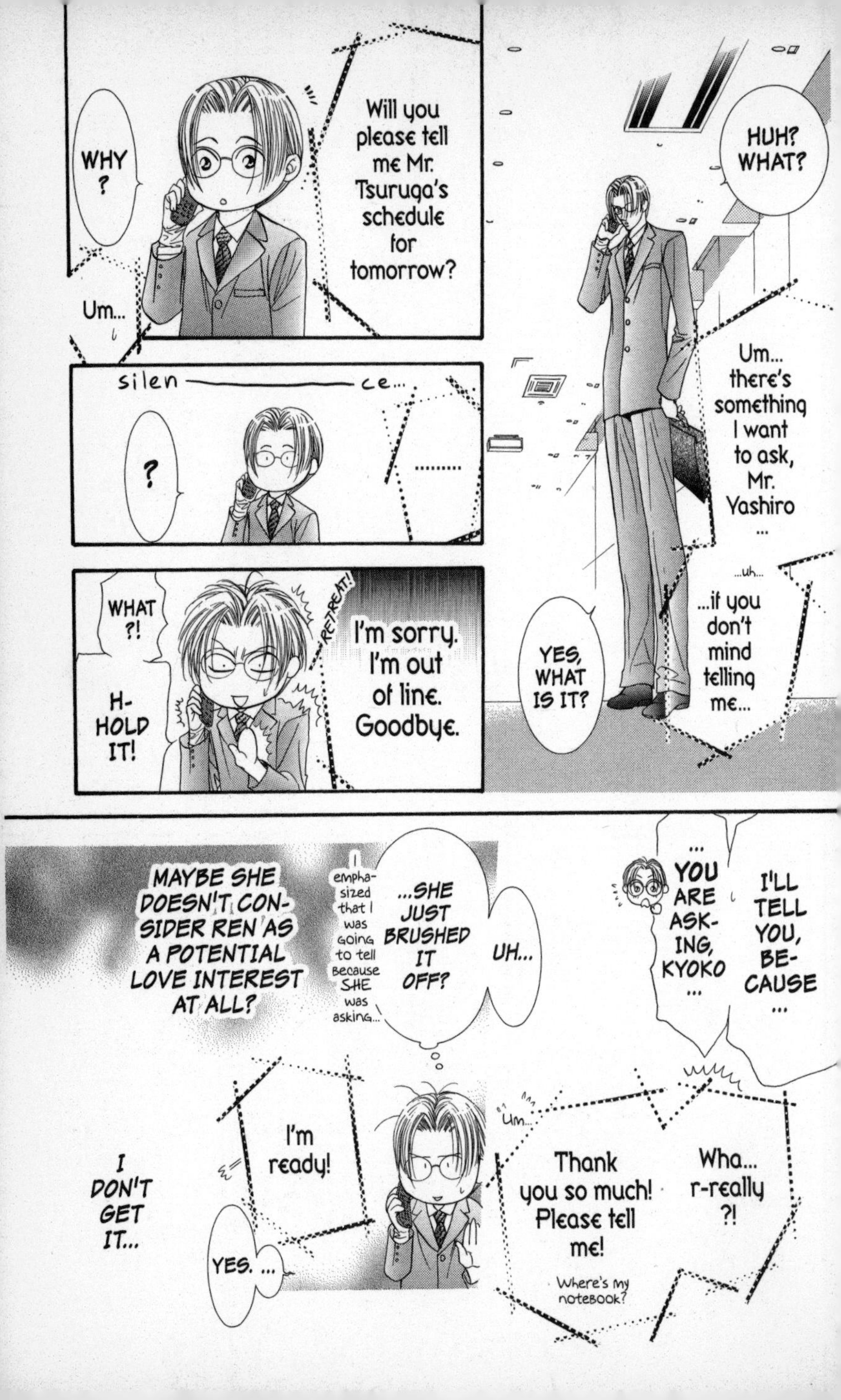
HUH? WHAT?
Um... there's something I want to ask, Mr. Yashiro...
...uh...
...if you don't mind telling me...
YES, WHAT IS IT?
Will you please tell me Mr. Tsuruga's schedule for tomorrow?
WHY?
Um...
silen——ce...
....
?
I'm sorry. I'm out of line. Goodbye.
RETREAT!
WHAT?!
H-HOLD IT!
I'LL TELL YOU, BECAUSE...
...YOU ARE ASKING, KYOKO...
UH...
...SHE JUST BRUSHED IT OFF?
I emphasized that I was going to tell because SHE was asking...
MAYBE SHE DOESN'T CONSIDER REN AS A POTENTIAL LOVE INTEREST AT ALL?
Wha... r-really?!
Thank you so much! Please tell me!
Um...
Where's my notebook?
I'm ready!
YES. ...
I DON'T GET IT...

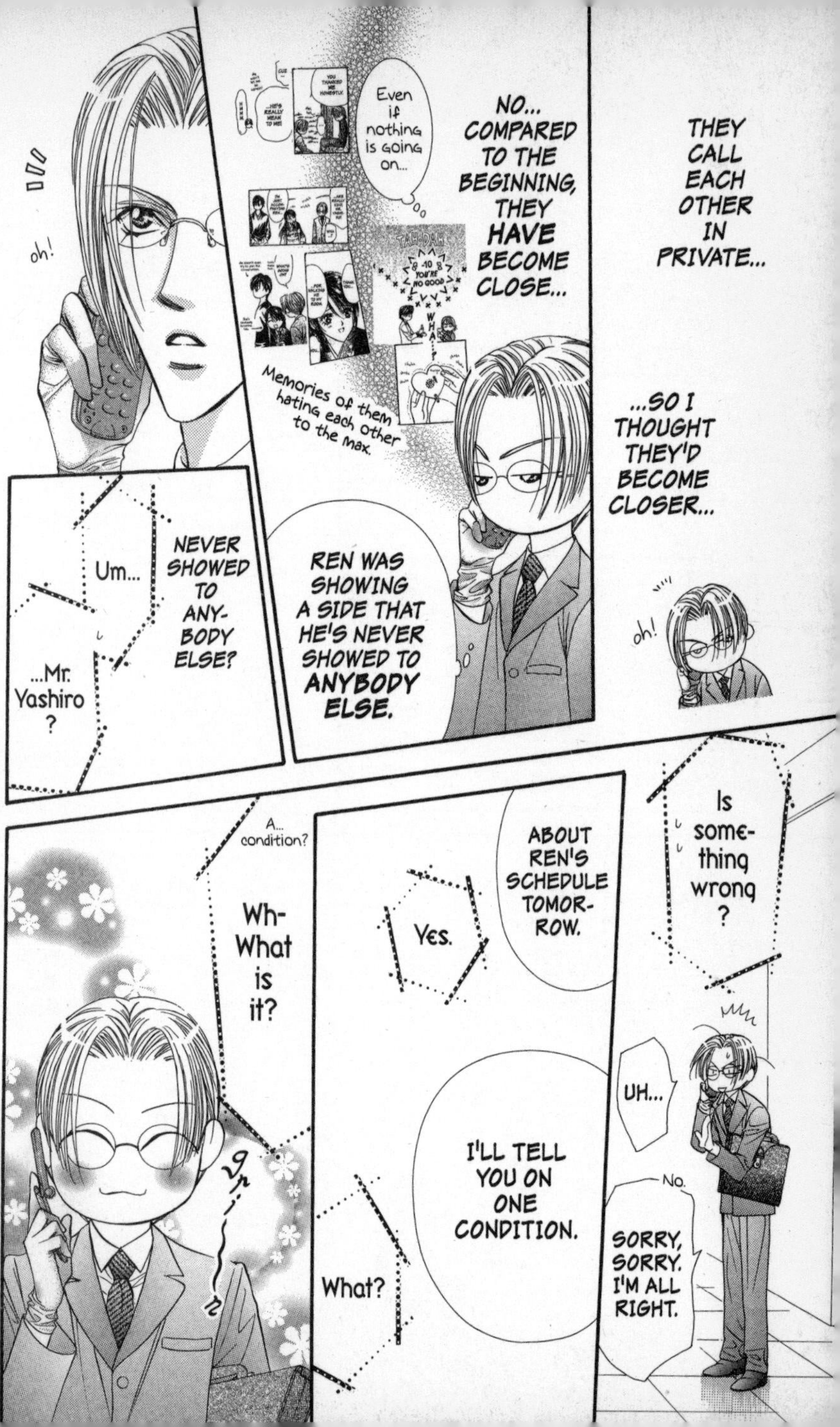
THEY CALL EACH OTHER IN PRIVATE...
...SO I THOUGHT THEY'D BECOME CLOSER...
oh!
NO... COMPARED TO THE BEGINNING, THEY HAVE BECOME CLOSE...
Even if nothing is going on...
TAH-DAH
Memories of them hating each other to the max.
oh!
REN WAS SHOWING A SIDE THAT HE'S NEVER SHOWED TO ANYBODY ELSE.
NEVER SHOWED TO ANYBODY ELSE?
Um...
...Mr. Yashiro ?
Is something wrong ?
UH...
No.
SORRY, SORRY. I'M ALL RIGHT.
ABOUT REN'S SCHEDULE TOMORROW.
Yes.
I'LL TELL YOU ON ONE CONDITION.
What?
A... condition?
Wh-What is it?

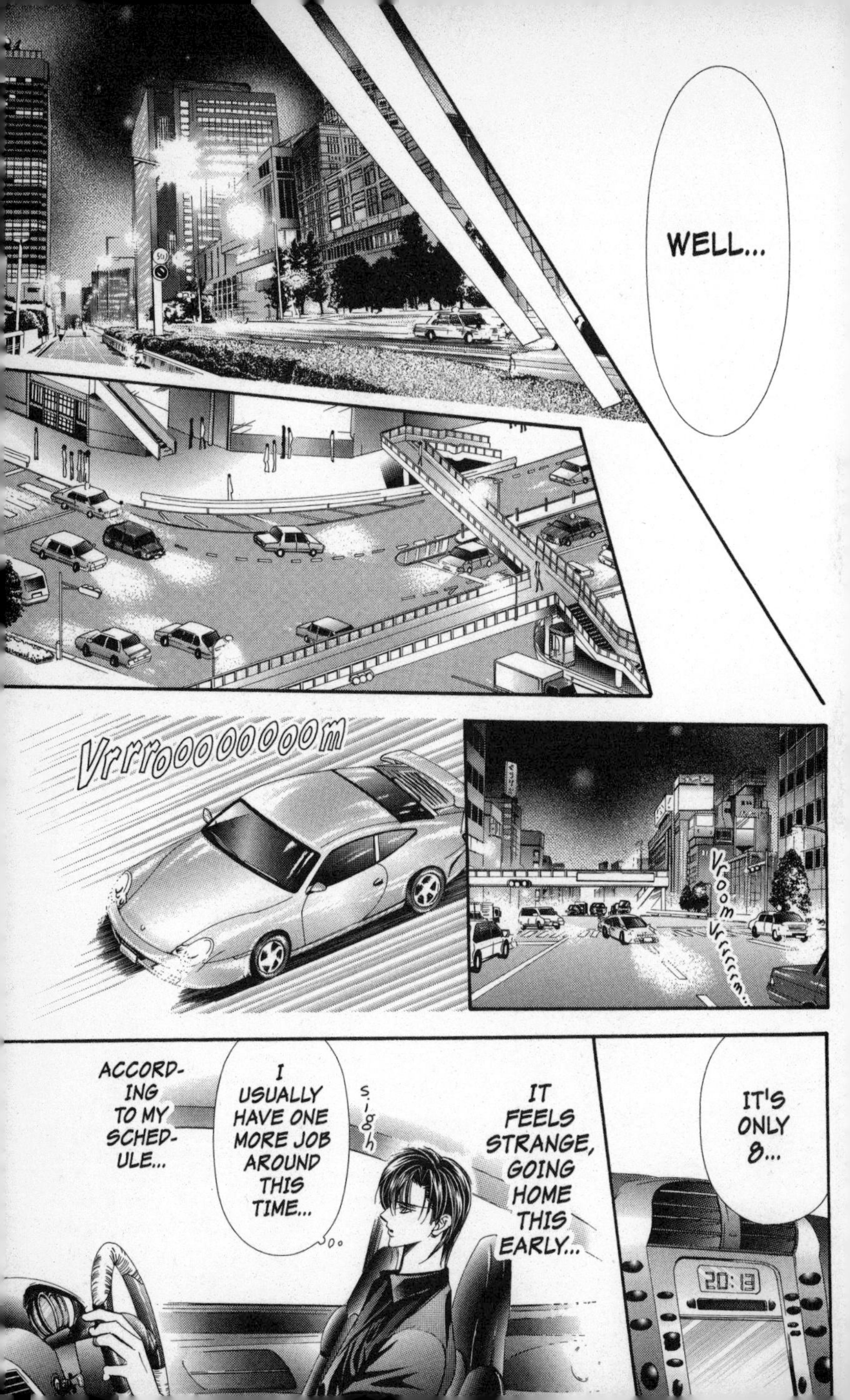
WELL...
Vroom Vrrrrrm...
Vrrroooooooom
IT'S ONLY 8...
20:13
IT FEELS STRANGE, GOING HOME THIS EARLY...
sigh
ACCORD-ING TO MY SCHED-ULE...
I USUALLY HAVE ONE MORE JOB AROUND THIS TIME...

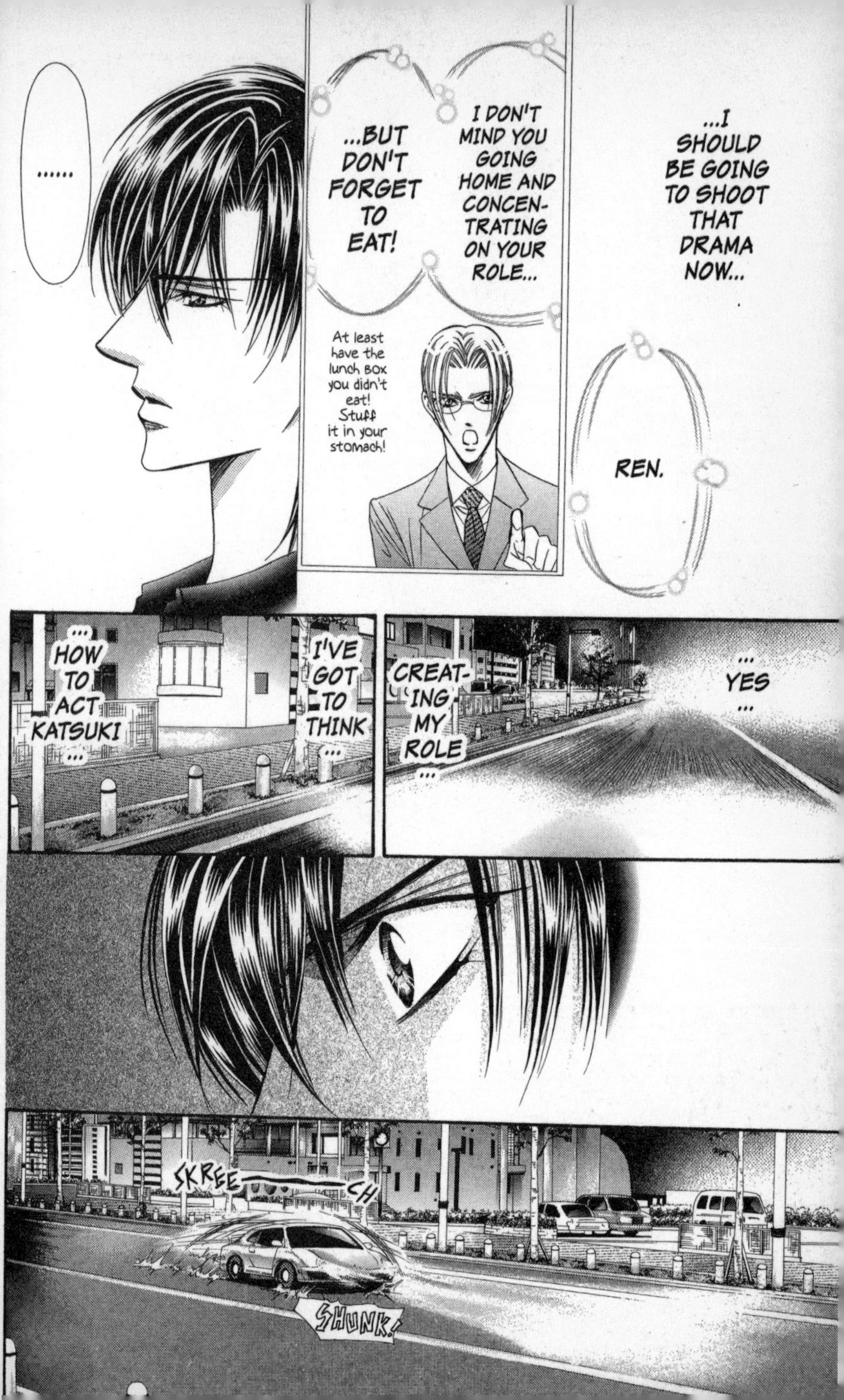

...I SHOULD BE GOING TO SHOOT THAT DRAMA NOW...
REN.
I DON'T MIND YOU GOING HOME AND CONCEN-TRATING ON YOUR ROLE...
...BUT DON'T FORGET TO EAT!
At least have the lunch box you didn't eat! Stuff it in your stomach!
......
...YES...
CREAT-ING MY ROLE...
I'VE GOT TO THINK...
...HOW TO ACT KATSUKI...
SKREE—CH
SHUNK!

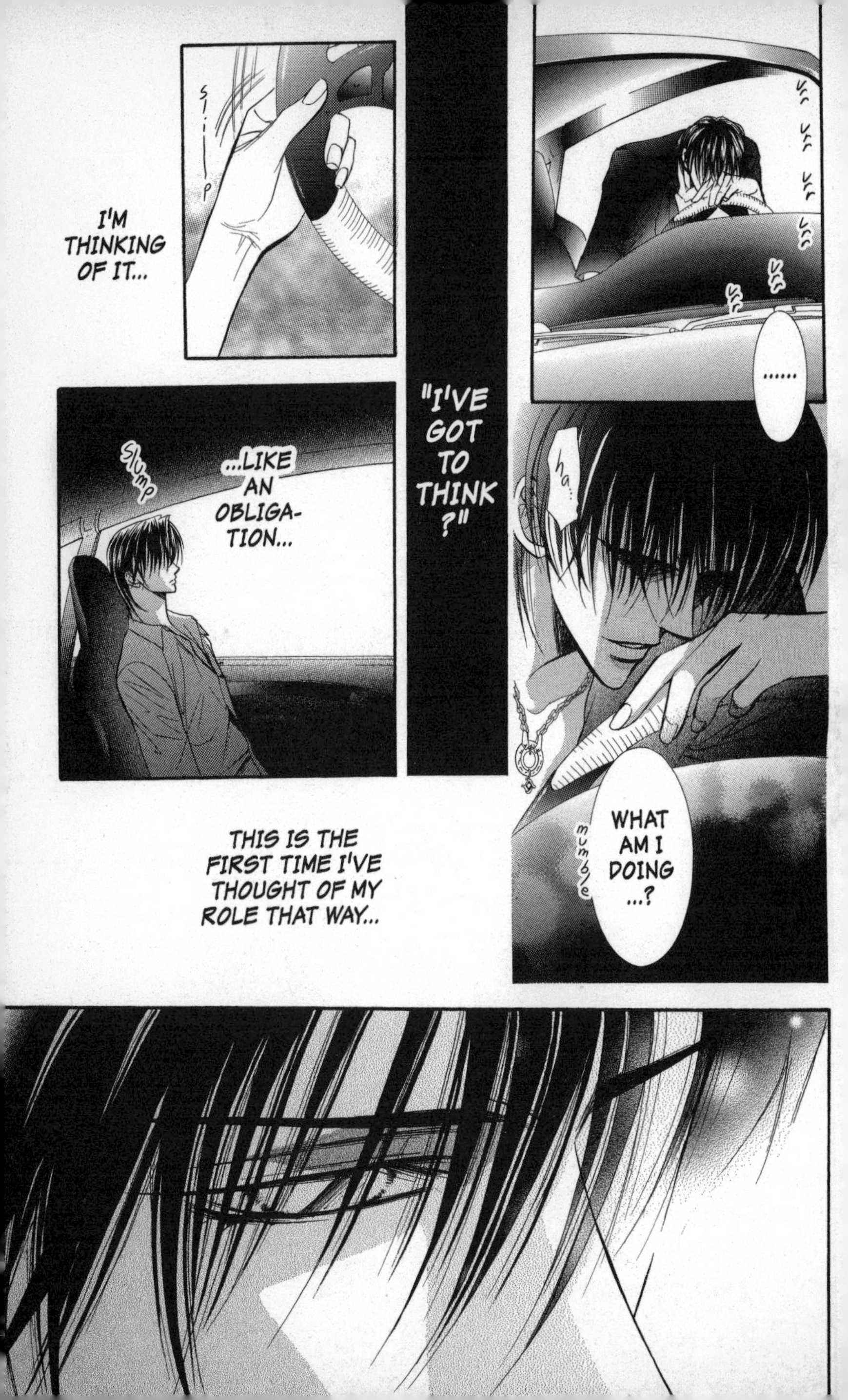
vrr vrr vrr vrr vrr vrr vrr
......
sli-p
I'M THINKING OF IT...
ha...
mumble
WHAT AM I DOING ...?
"I'VE GOT TO THINK?"
slump
...LIKE AN OBLIGATION...
THIS IS THE FIRST TIME I'VE THOUGHT OF MY ROLE THAT WAY...

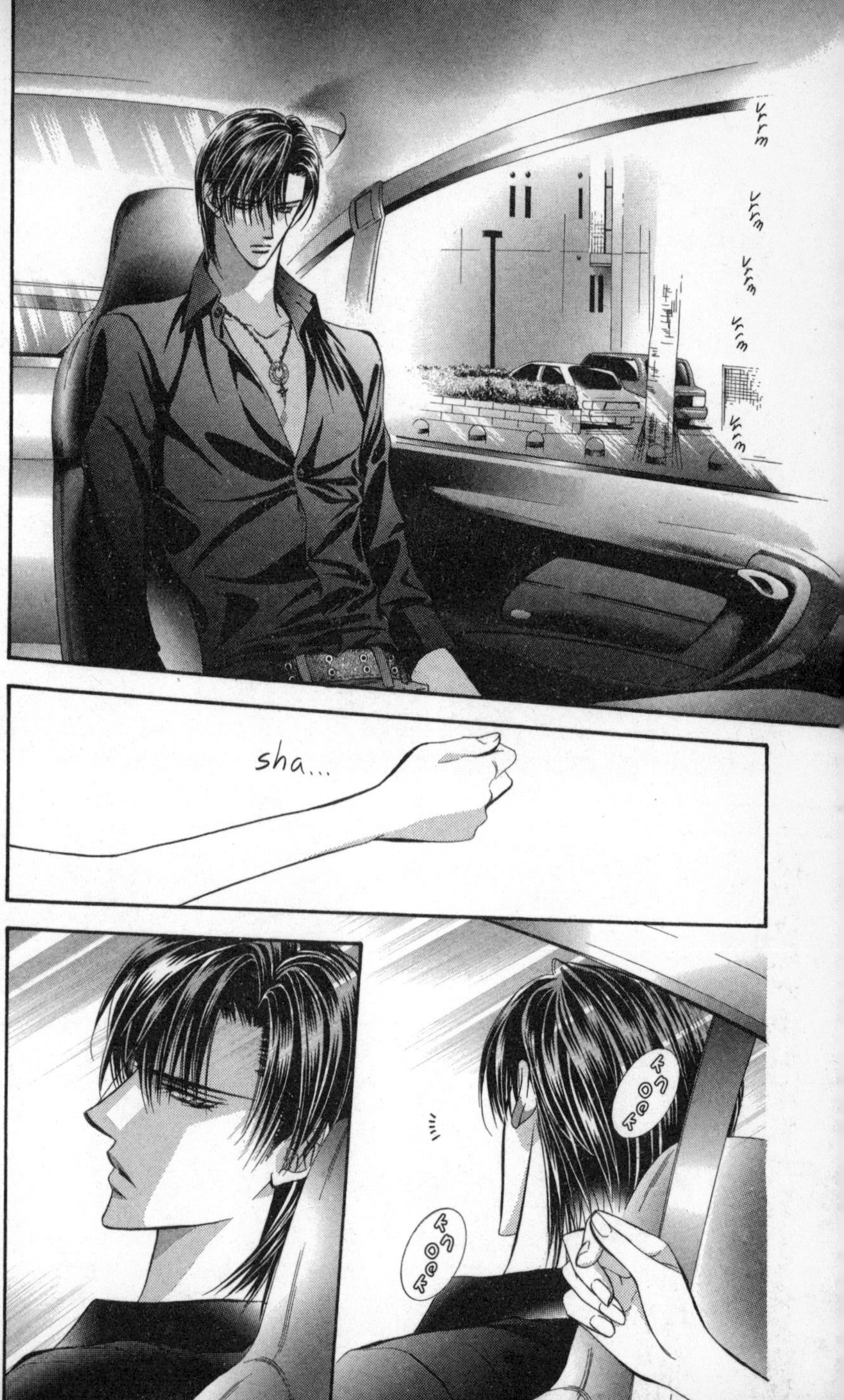
Vrrm
Vrrm
Vrrm
Vrrm
Vrrm
sha...
kroek
kroek

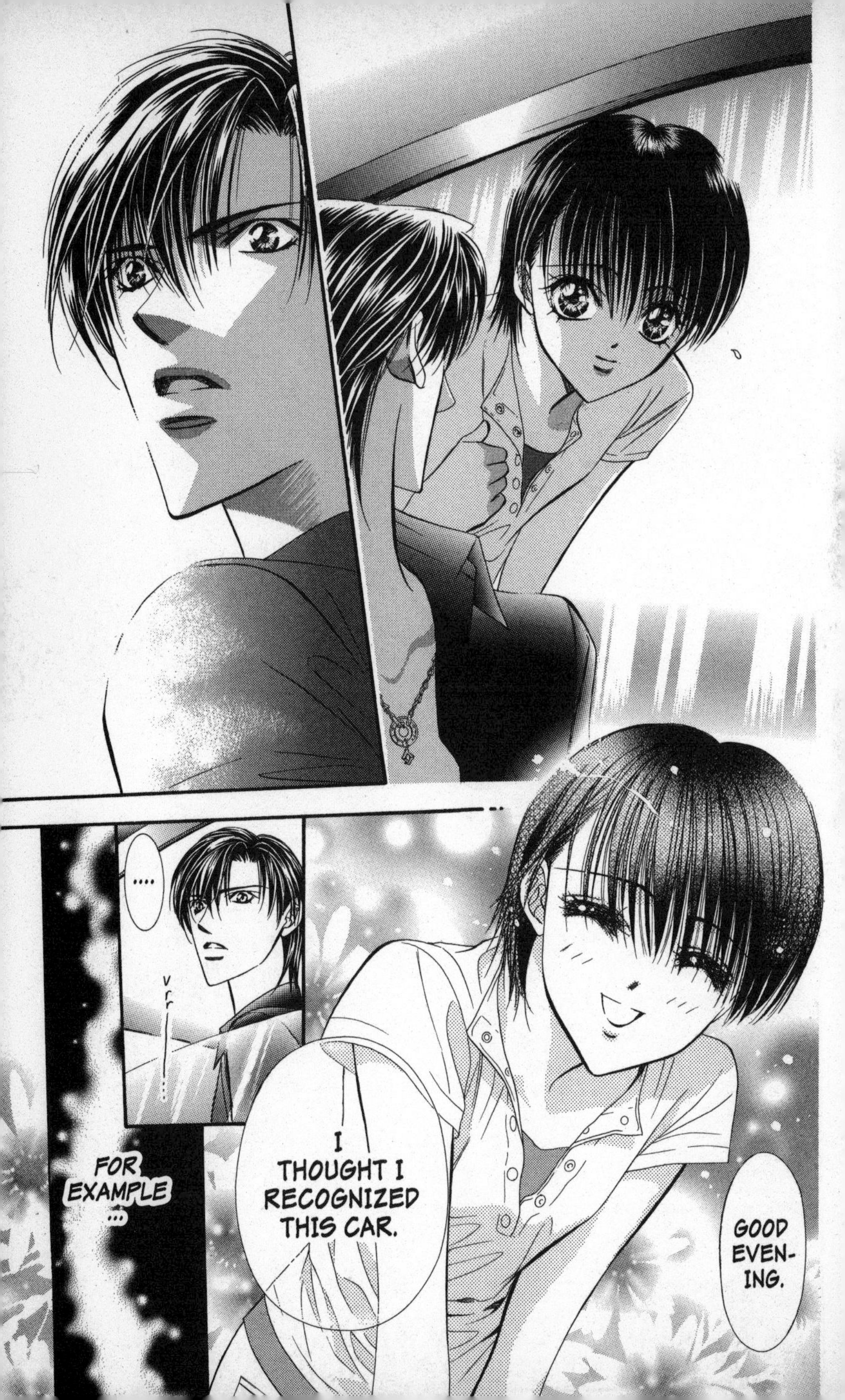
GOOD EVENING.
I THOUGHT I RECOGNIZED THIS CAR.
....
vrr
FOR EXAMPLE...

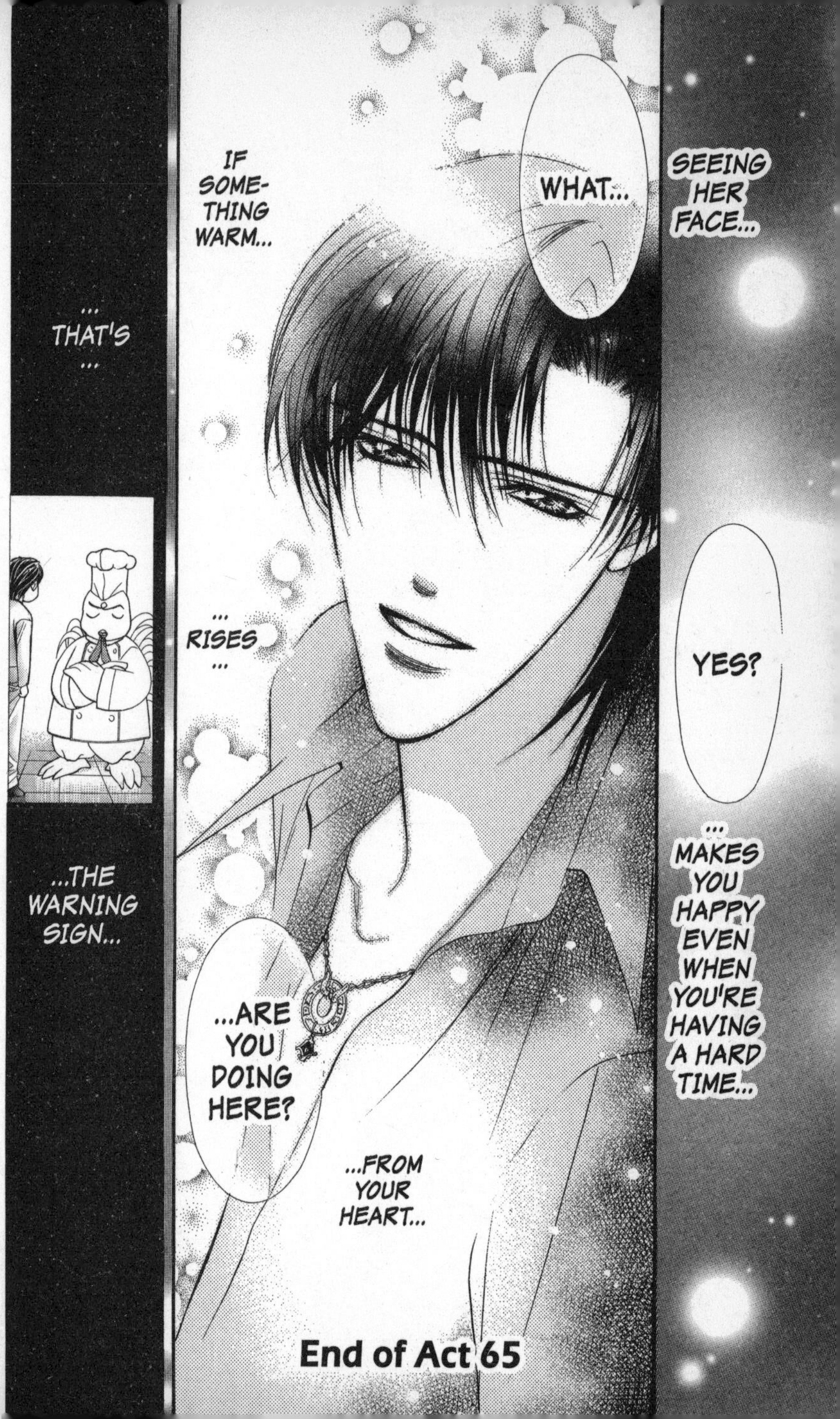
SEEING HER FACE...
YES?
...MAKES YOU HAPPY EVEN WHEN YOU'RE HAVING A HARD TIME...
WHAT...
IF SOMETHING WARM...
...RISES...
...ARE YOU DOING HERE?
...FROM YOUR HEART...
...THAT'S...
...THE WARNING SIGN...

End of Act 65

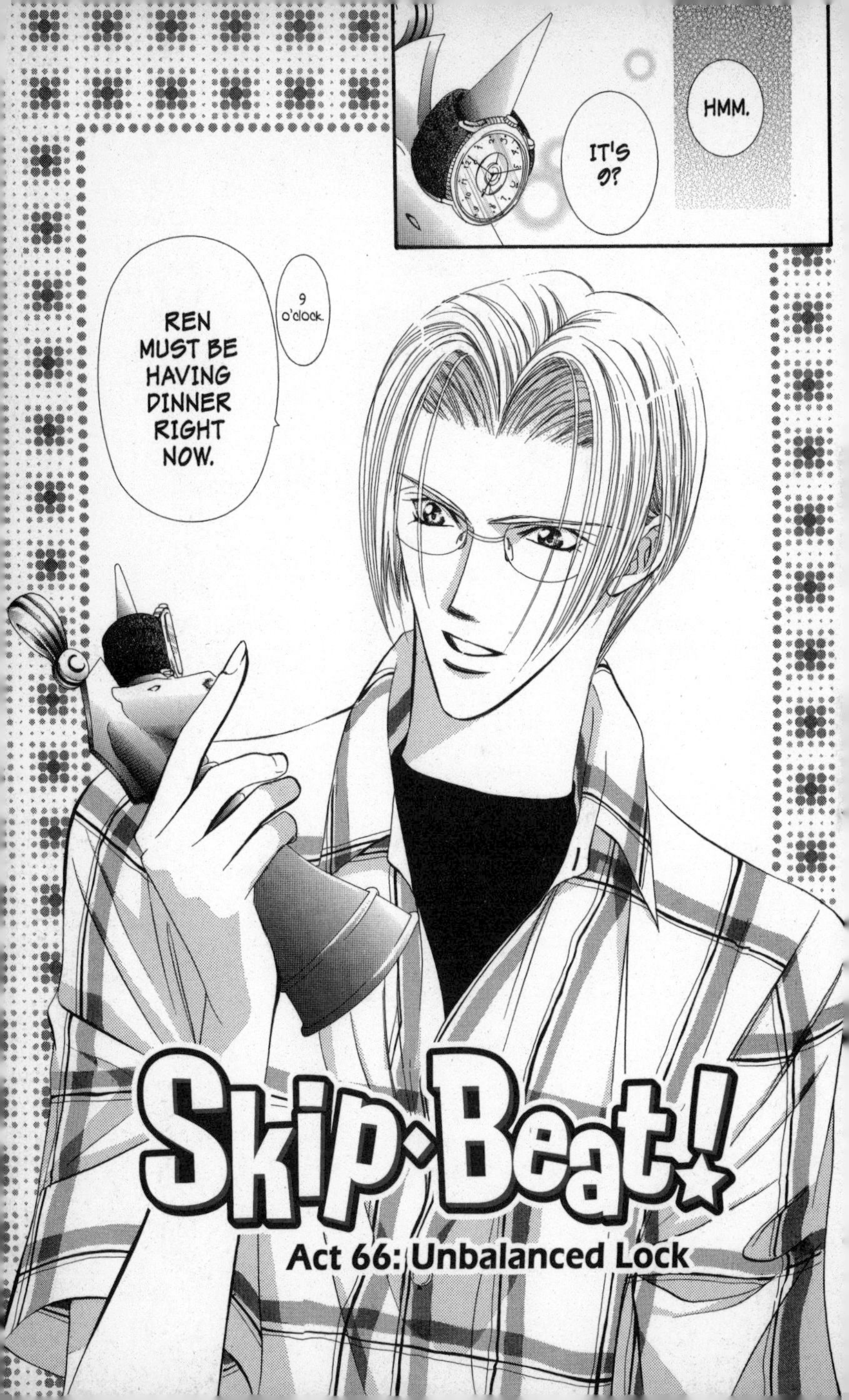
HMM.
IT'S 9?
9 o'clock.
REN MUST BE HAVING DINNER RIGHT NOW.
Skip·Beat!
Act 66: Unbalanced Lock

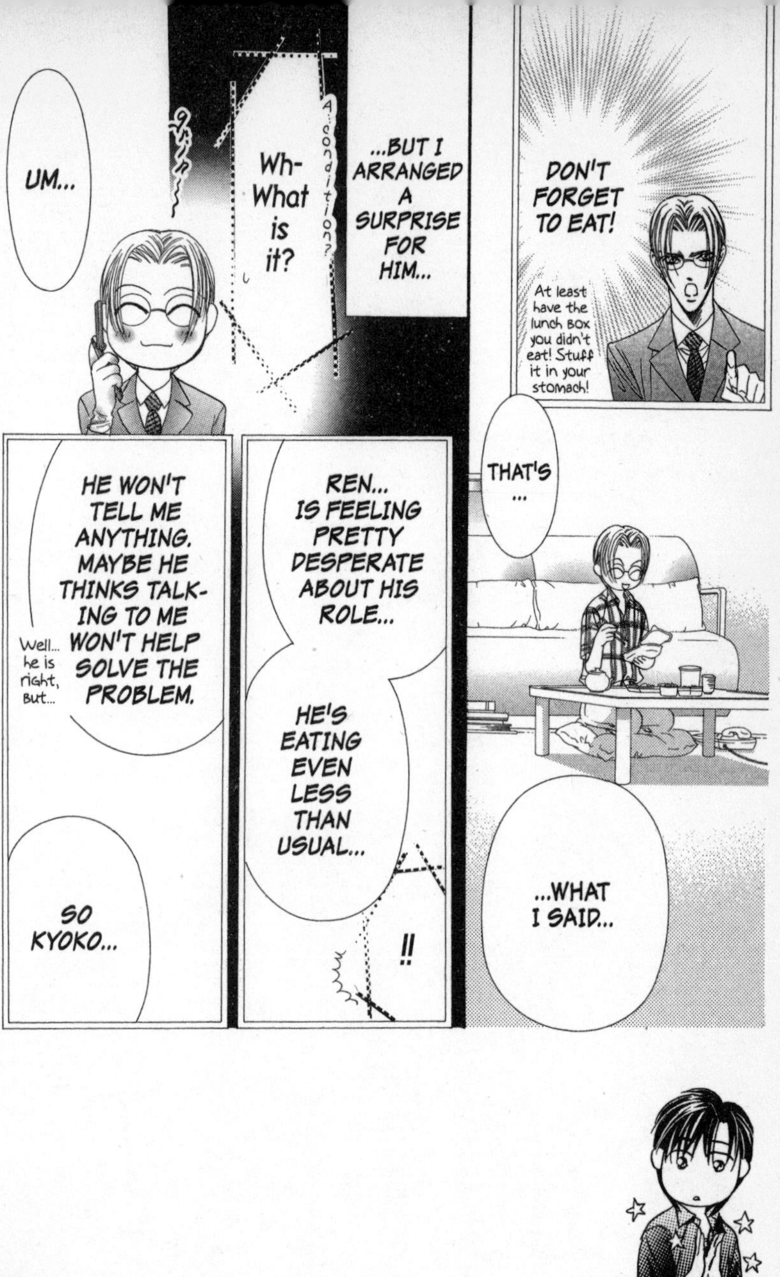
DON'T FORGET TO EAT!
At least have the lunch box you didn't eat! Stuff it in your stomach!
...BUT I ARRANGED A SURPRISE FOR HIM...
A condition?
Wh- What is it?
UM...
THAT'S ...
...WHAT I SAID...
REN... IS FEELING PRETTY DESPERATE ABOUT HIS ROLE...
HE'S EATING EVEN LESS THAN USUAL...
!!
HE WON'T TELL ME ANYTHING. MAYBE HE THINKS TALKING TO ME WON'T HELP SOLVE THE PROBLEM.
Well... he is right, but...
SO KYOKO...

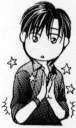

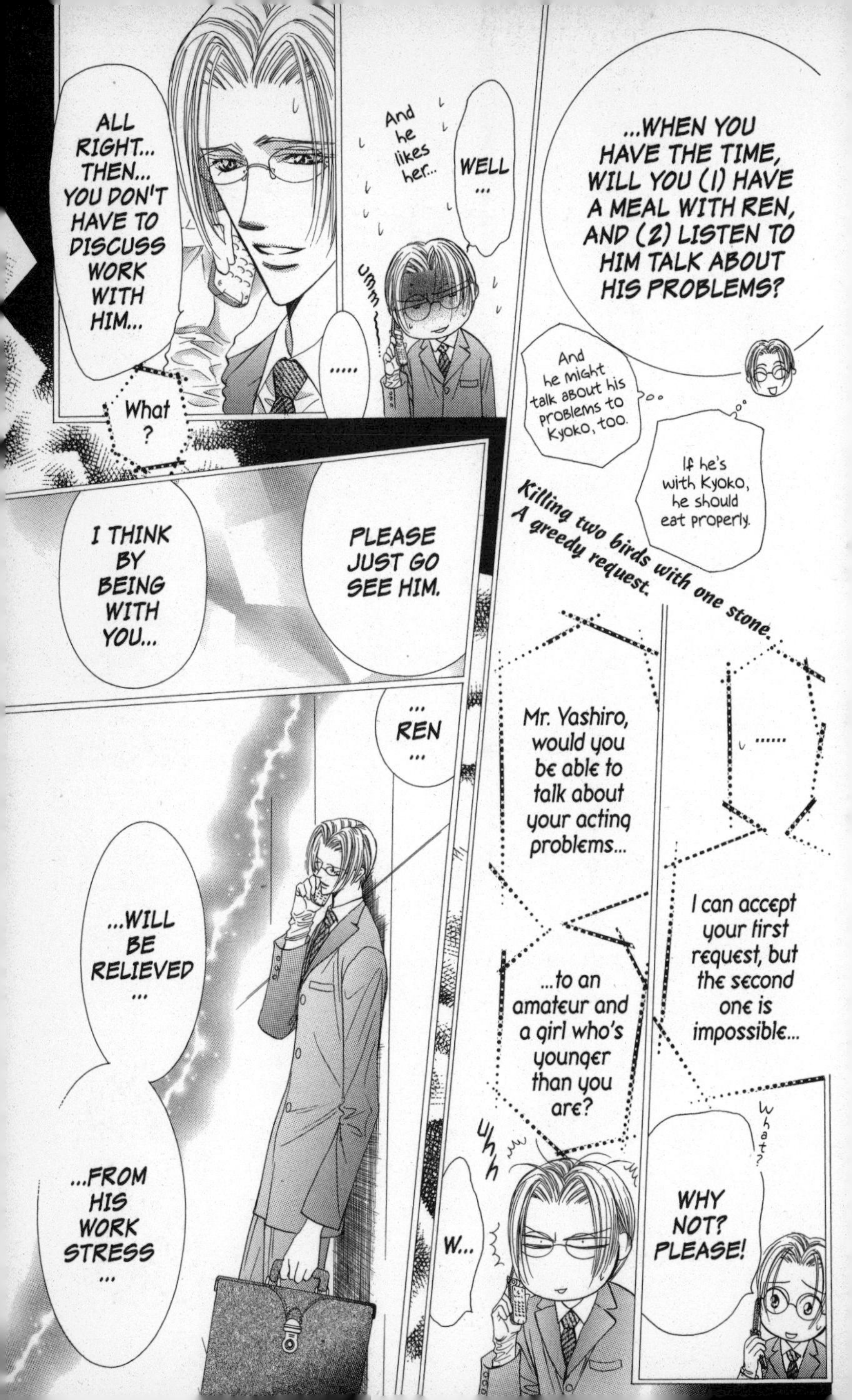

...WHEN YOU HAVE THE TIME, WILL YOU (1) HAVE A MEAL WITH REN, AND (2) LISTEN TO HIM TALK ABOUT HIS PROBLEMS?
And he might talk about his problems to Kyoko, too.
If he's with Kyoko, he should eat properly.
Killing two birds with one stone. A greedy request.
......
Mr. Yashiro, would you be able to talk about your acting problems...
I can accept your first request, but the second one is impossible...
...to an amateur and a girl who's younger than you are?
What?
WHY NOT? PLEASE!
Uhh
W...
And he likes her...
WELL...
Umm~
.....
ALL RIGHT... THEN... YOU DON'T HAVE TO DISCUSS WORK WITH HIM...
What?
PLEASE JUST GO SEE HIM.
I THINK BY BEING WITH YOU...
...REN...
...WILL BE RELIEVED...
...FROM HIS WORK STRESS...

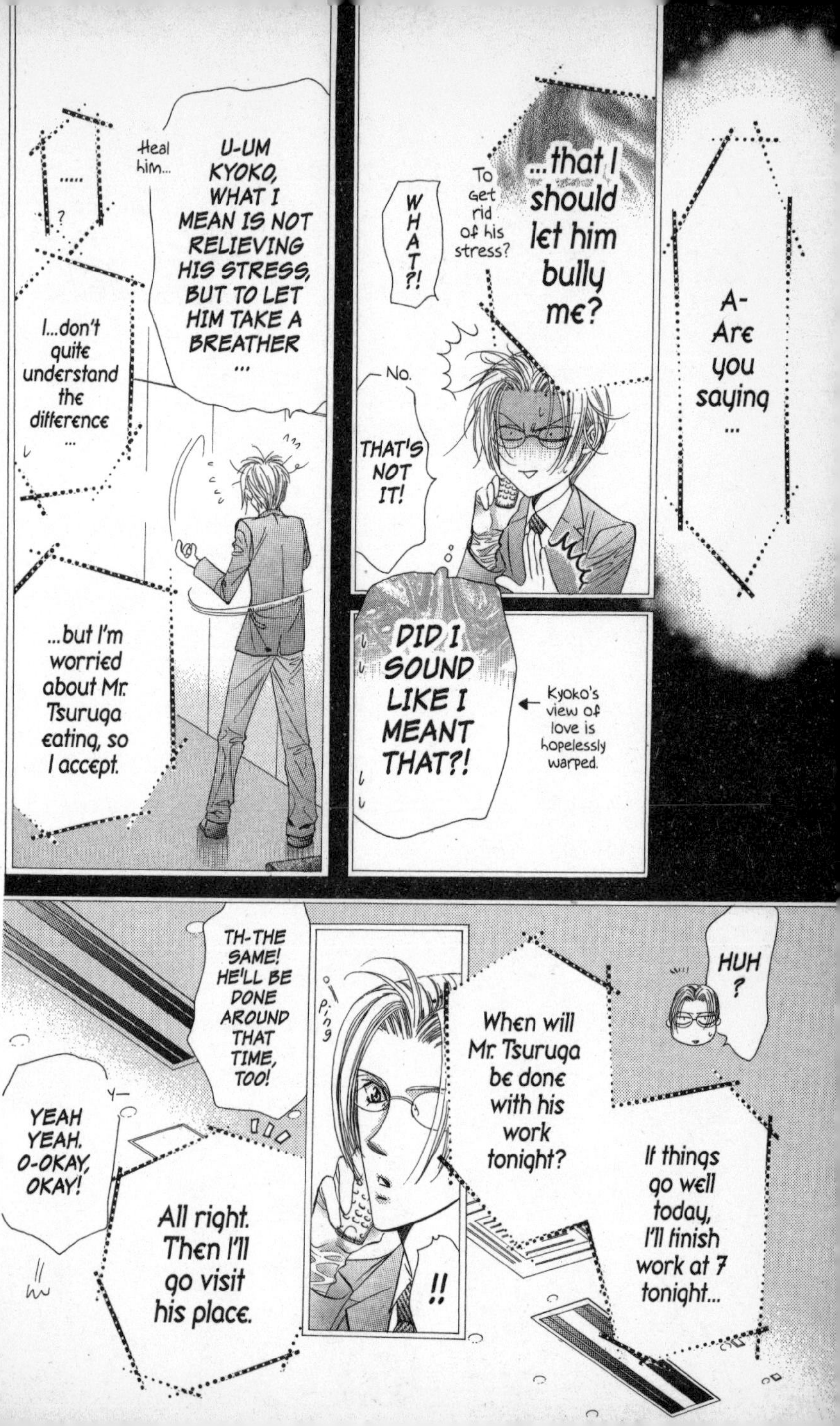
A- Are you saying...
...that I should let him bully me?
To get rid of his stress?
WHAT?!
No.
THAT'S NOT IT!
DID I SOUND LIKE I MEANT THAT?!
Kyoko's view of love is hopelessly warped.
Heal him...
U-UM KYOKO, WHAT I MEAN IS NOT RELIEVING HIS STRESS, BUT TO LET HIM TAKE A BREATHER...
.....?
I...don't quite understand the difference...
...but I'm worried about Mr. Tsuruga eating, so I accept.
HUH?
If things go well today, I'll finish work at 7 tonight...
When will Mr. Tsuruga be done with his work tonight?
Ping
!!
TH-THE SAME! HE'LL BE DONE AROUND THAT TIME, TOO!
All right. Then I'll go visit his place.
Y—
YEAH YEAH. O-OKAY, OKAY!

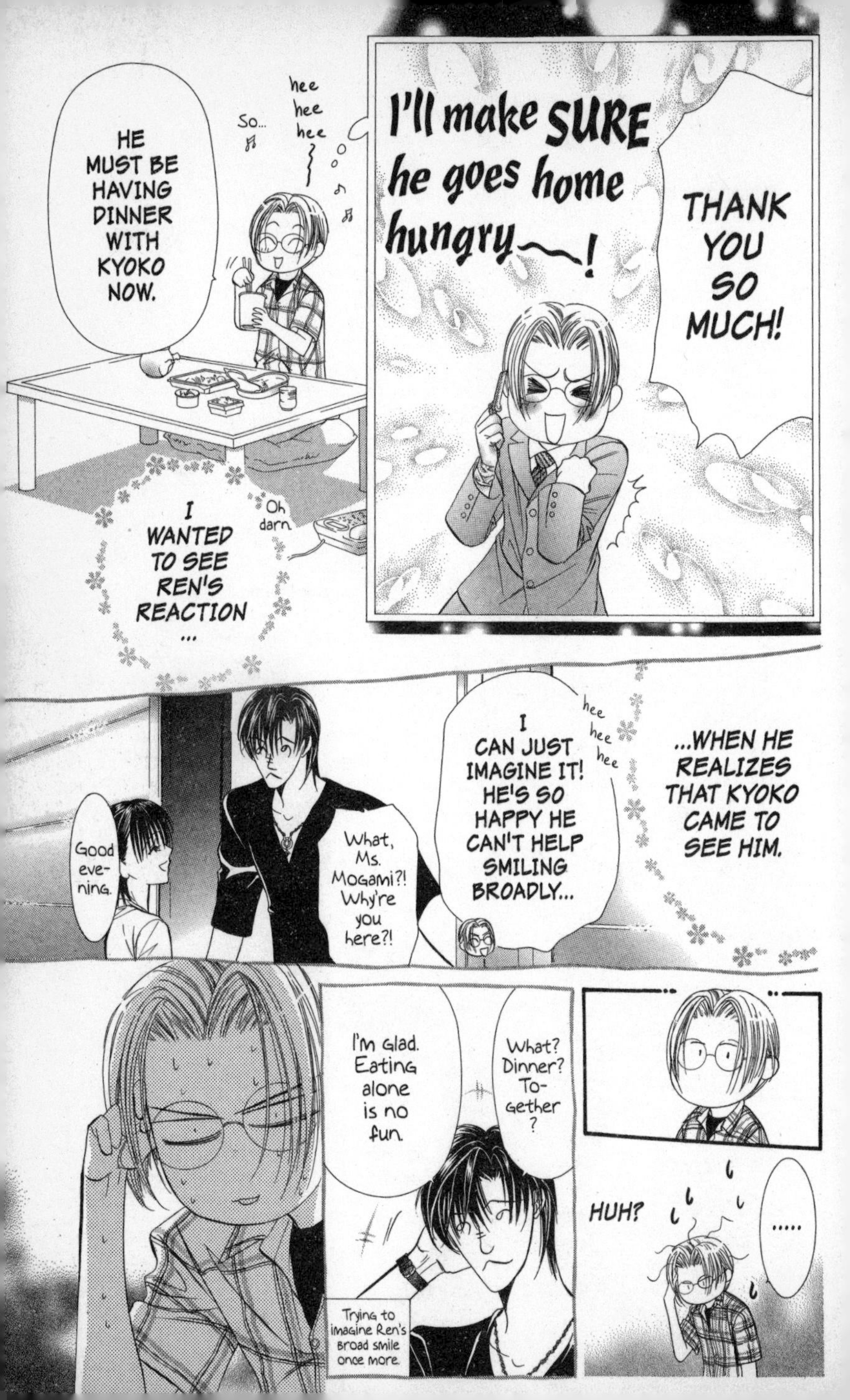
THANK YOU SO MUCH!
I'll make SURE he goes home hungry~~!
So... hee hee hee
HE MUST BE HAVING DINNER WITH KYOKO NOW.
Oh darn.
I WANTED TO SEE REN'S REACTION...
...WHEN HE REALIZES THAT KYOKO CAME TO SEE HIM.
I CAN JUST IMAGINE IT! HE'S SO HAPPY HE CAN'T HELP SMILING BROADLY...
hee hee hee
What, Ms. Mogami?! Why're you here?!
Good evening.
HUH?
.....
What? Dinner? Together?
I'm glad. Eating alone is no fun.
Trying to imagine Ren's broad smile once more.

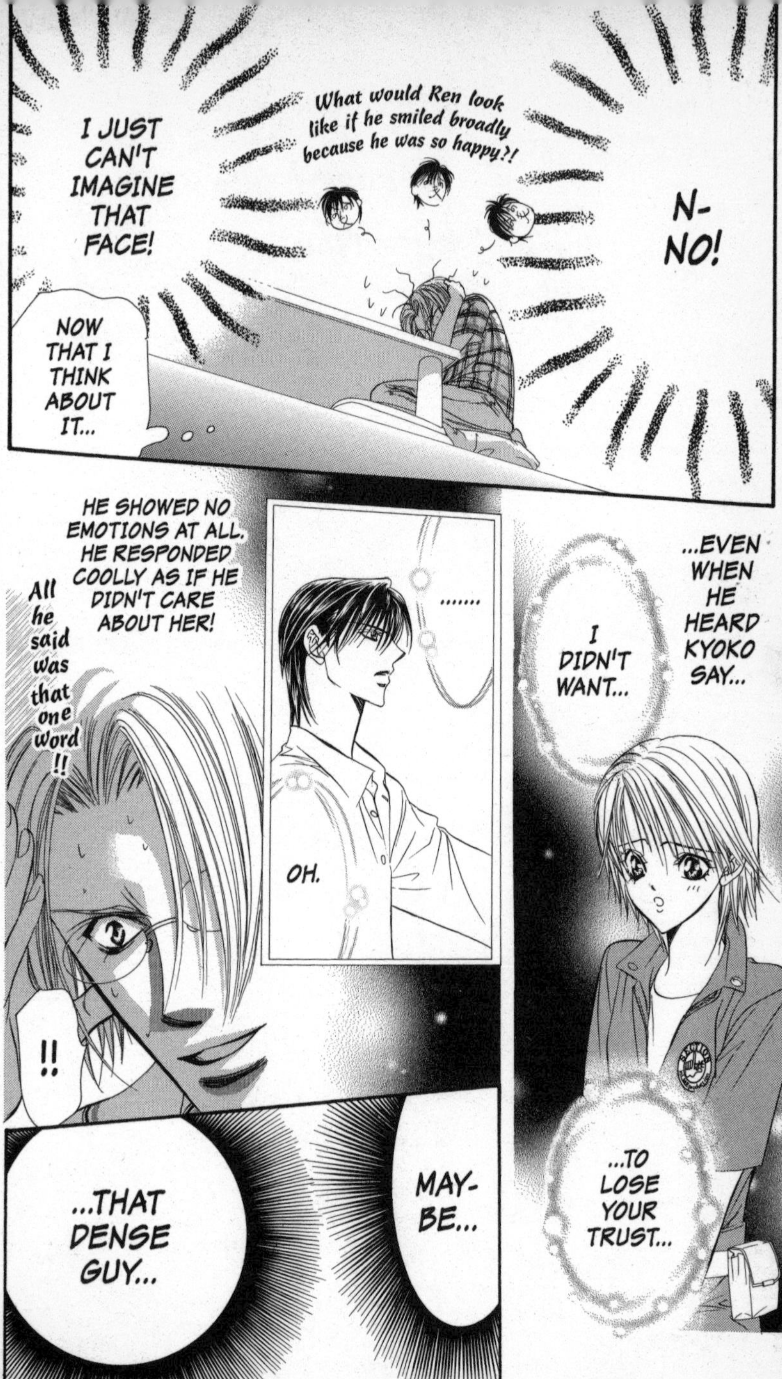
N-NO!
What would Ren look like if he smiled broadly because he was so happy?!
I JUST CAN'T IMAGINE THAT FACE!
NOW THAT I THINK ABOUT IT...
...EVEN WHEN HE HEARD KYOKO SAY...
I DIDN'T WANT...
...TO LOSE YOUR TRUST...
....
OH.
HE SHOWED NO EMOTIONS AT ALL. HE RESPONDED COOLLY AS IF HE DIDN'T CARE ABOUT HER!
All he said was that one word!!
!!
MAY-BE...
...THAT DENSE GUY...

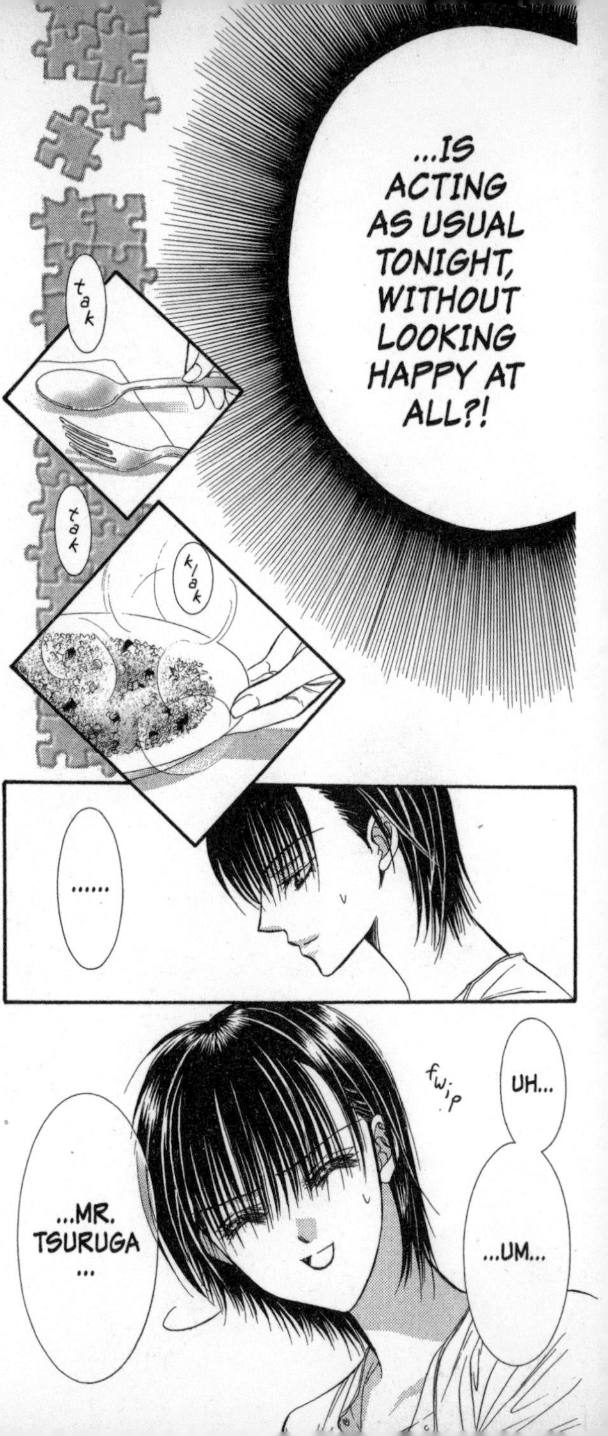
...IS ACTING AS USUAL TONIGHT, WITHOUT LOOKING HAPPY AT ALL?!
tak
tak
klak
......
UH...
...UM...
fwip
...MR. TSURUGA...

You guys are really stupidly in love, with a large age difference.

Please realize your own feelings. Or have someone make him realize it!! The readers were asking for this, almost threateningly. Not Yashiro, not Lory...but these two strangers did it.

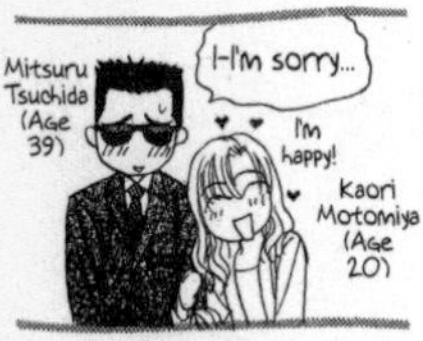
Mitsuru Tsuchida (Age 39)
I-I'm sorry...
I'm happy!
Kaori Motomiya (Age 20)

Mr. Tsuchida's appearance (just the visuals) is based on a teacher at the middle school Nakamura attended. He looked scary, but he was very funny and was popular with the students.

— And...

What that teacher looked like at school.

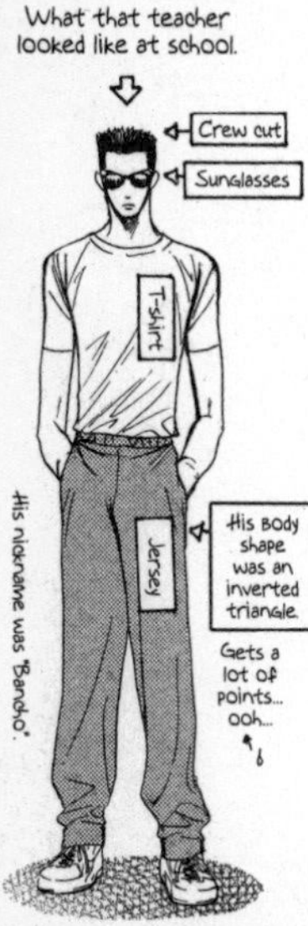
Crew cut
Sunglasses
T-shirt
Jersey
His body shape was an inverted triangle.
Gets a lot of points... ooh...
His nickname was "Bancho".

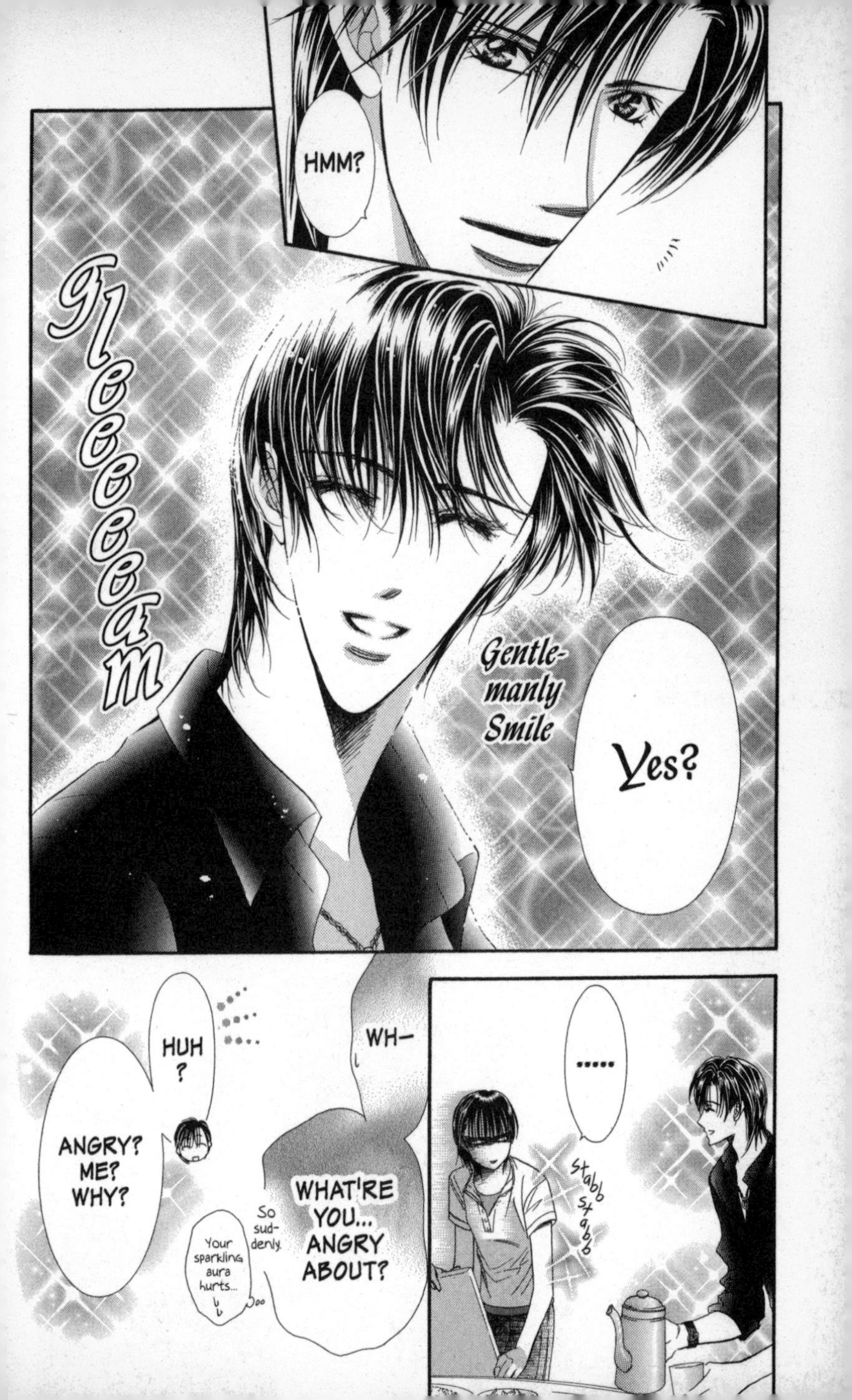
HMM?
Yes?
Gentlemanly Smile
Gleeeeam
......
stabb stabb
WH—
WHAT'RE YOU... ANGRY ABOUT?
So suddenly.
Your sparkling aura hurts...
HUH?
ANGRY? ME? WHY?

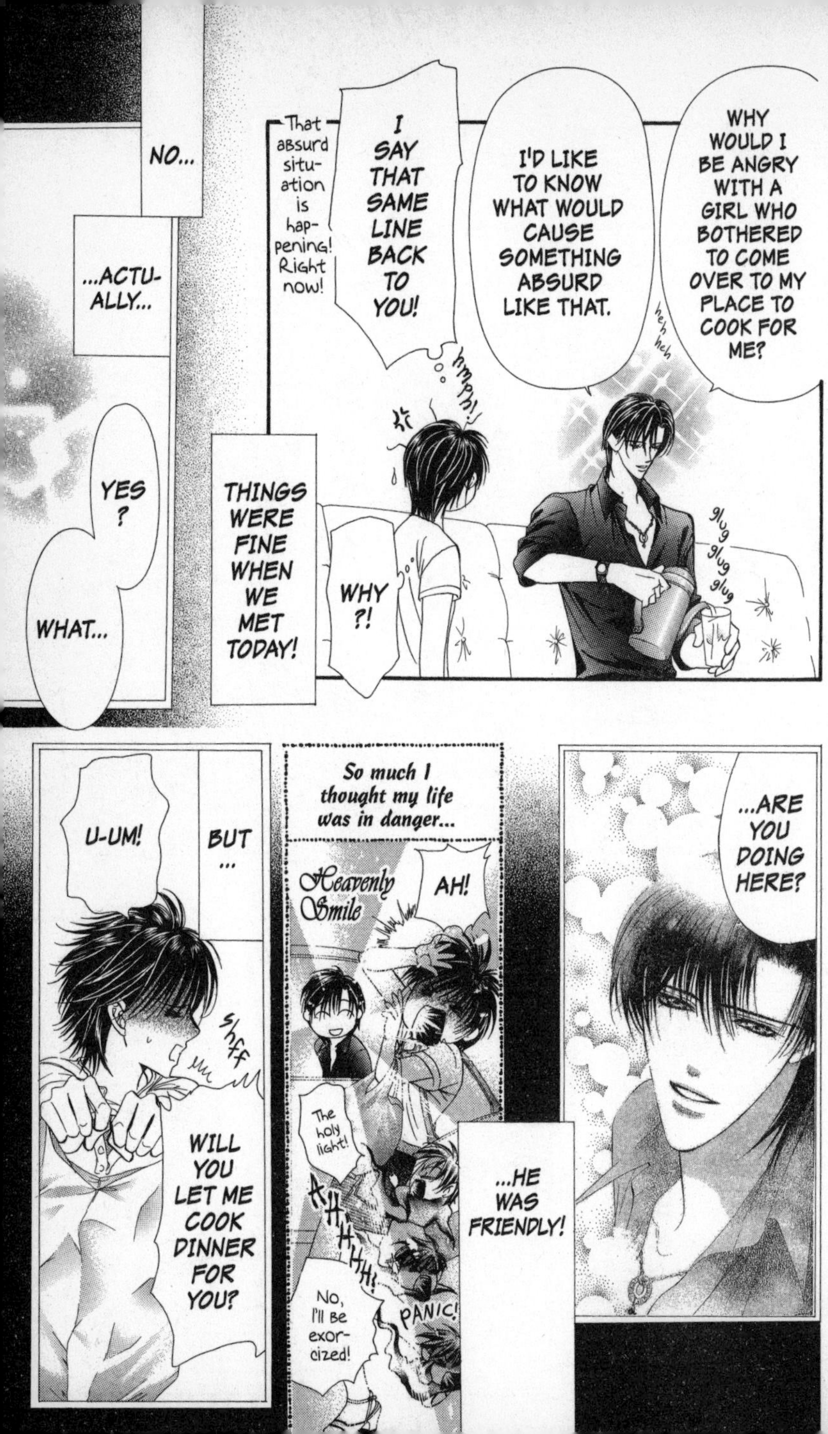
WHY WOULD I BE ANGRY WITH A GIRL WHO BOTHERED TO COME OVER TO MY PLACE TO COOK FOR ME?
heh heh
I'D LIKE TO KNOW WHAT WOULD CAUSE SOMETHING ABSURD LIKE THAT.
I SAY THAT SAME LINE BACK TO YOU!
That absurd situation is happening! Right now!
hmph!
glug glug glug
THINGS WERE FINE WHEN WE MET TODAY!
WHY?!
NO...
...ACTUALLY...
YES?
WHAT...
...ARE YOU DOING HERE?
So much I thought my life was in danger...
Heavenly Smile
AH!
The holy light!
AHHHH!
PANIC!
No, I'll be exorcized!
...HE WAS FRIENDLY!
BUT...
U-UM!
shff
WILL YOU LET ME COOK DINNER FOR YOU?

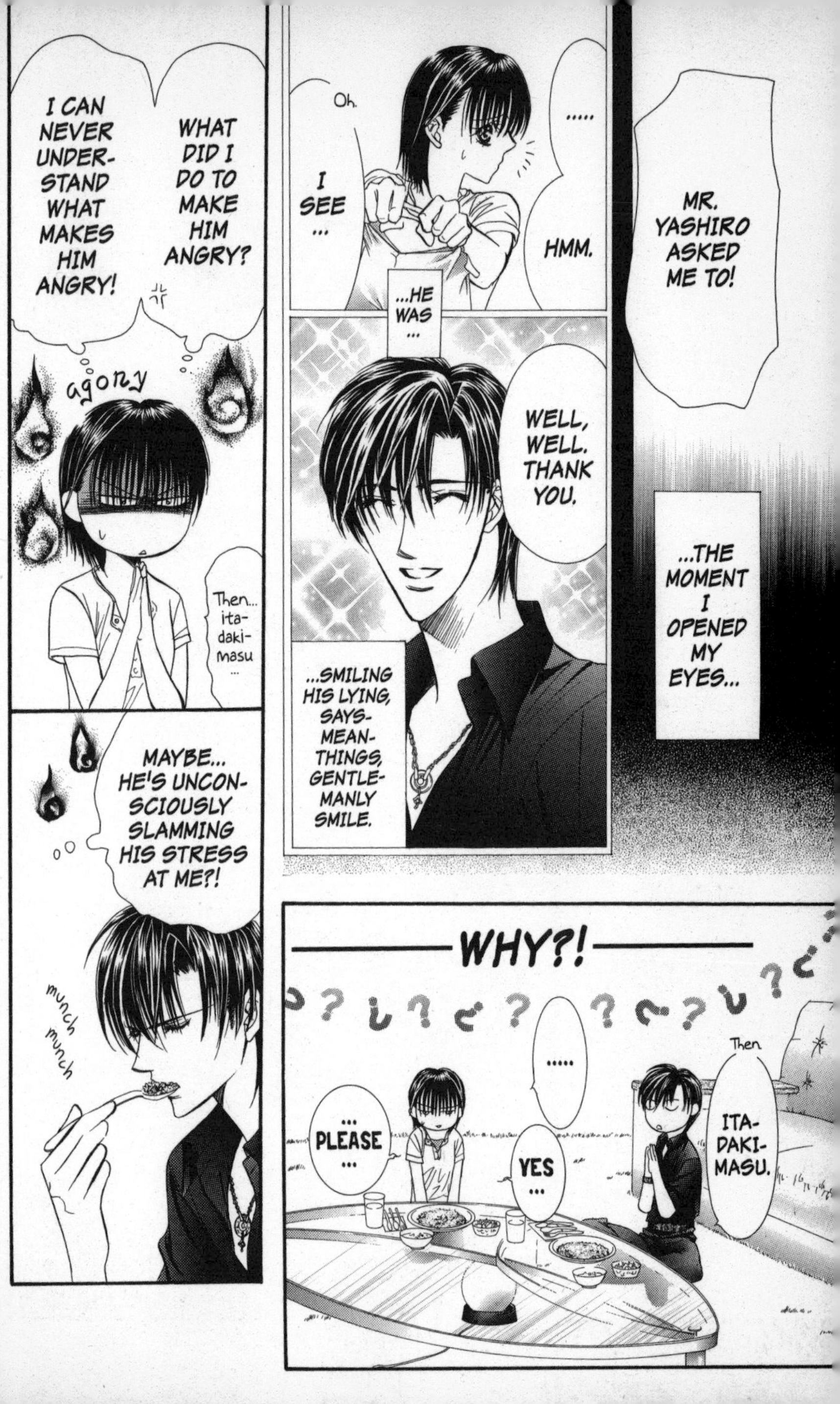
MR. YASHIRO ASKED ME TO!
...THE MOMENT I OPENED MY EYES...
.....
HMM.
Oh.
I SEE ...
...HE WAS ...
WELL, WELL. THANK YOU.
...SMILING HIS LYING, SAYS-MEAN-THINGS, GENTLEMANLY SMILE.
WHAT DID I DO TO MAKE HIM ANGRY?
I CAN NEVER UNDERSTAND WHAT MAKES HIM ANGRY!
agony
Then... itadakimasu ...
MAYBE... HE'S UNCONSCIOUSLY SLAMMING HIS STRESS AT ME?!
munch munch
WHY?!
Then.
ITADAKIMASU.
YES ...
.....
... PLEASE ...

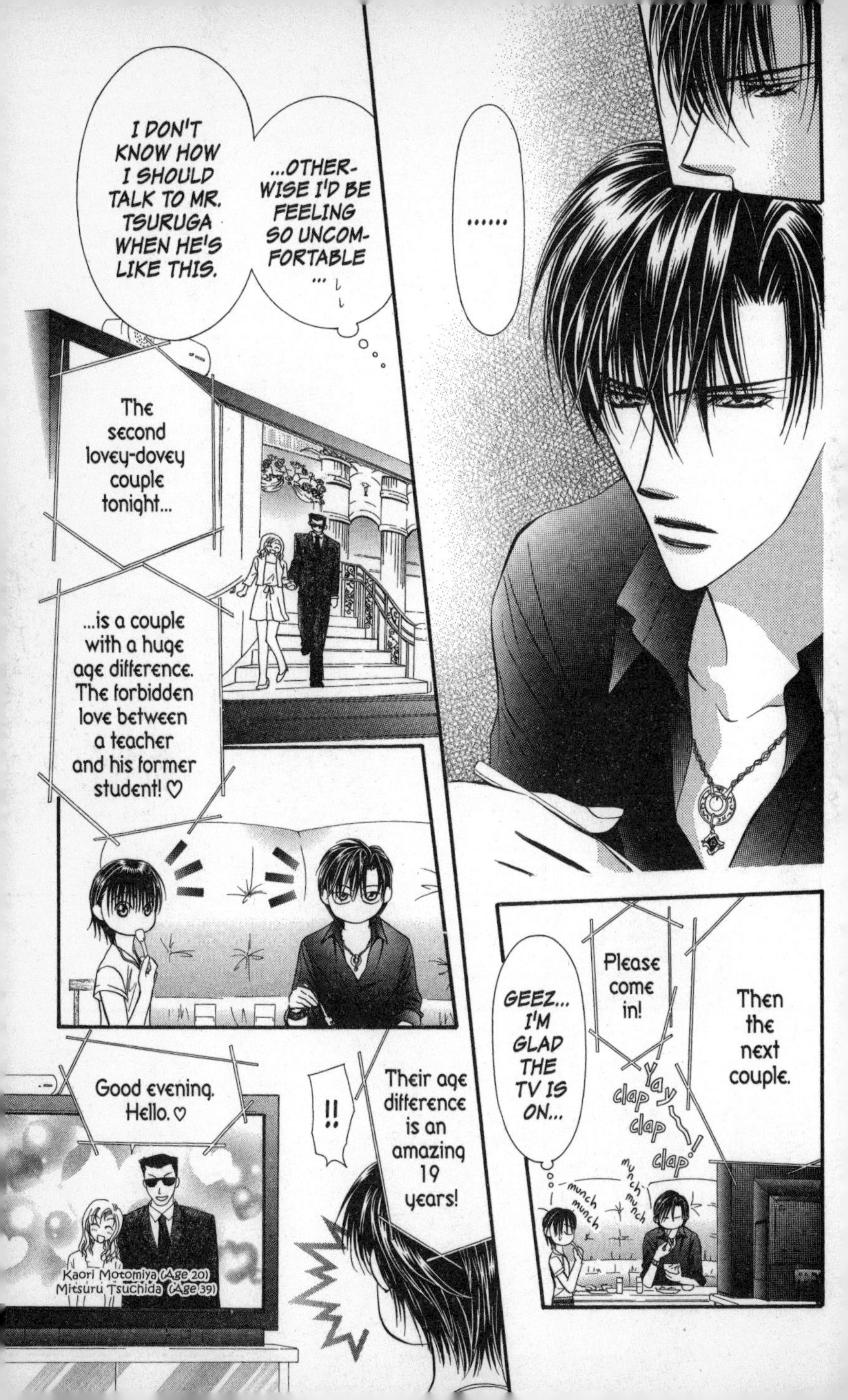
Then the next couple.
Please come in!
Yay
clap clap clap
munch munch
munch munch
GEEZ... I'M GLAD THE TV IS ON...
...OTHER-WISE I'D BE FEELING SO UNCOM-FORTABLE ...
I DON'T KNOW HOW I SHOULD TALK TO MR. TSURUGA WHEN HE'S LIKE THIS.
......
The second lovey-dovey couple tonight...
...is a couple with a huge age difference. The forbidden love between a teacher and his former student! ♡
Good evening. Hello. ♡
Kaori Motomiya (Age 20)
Mitsuru Tsuchida (Age 39)
Their age difference is an amazing 19 years!
!!

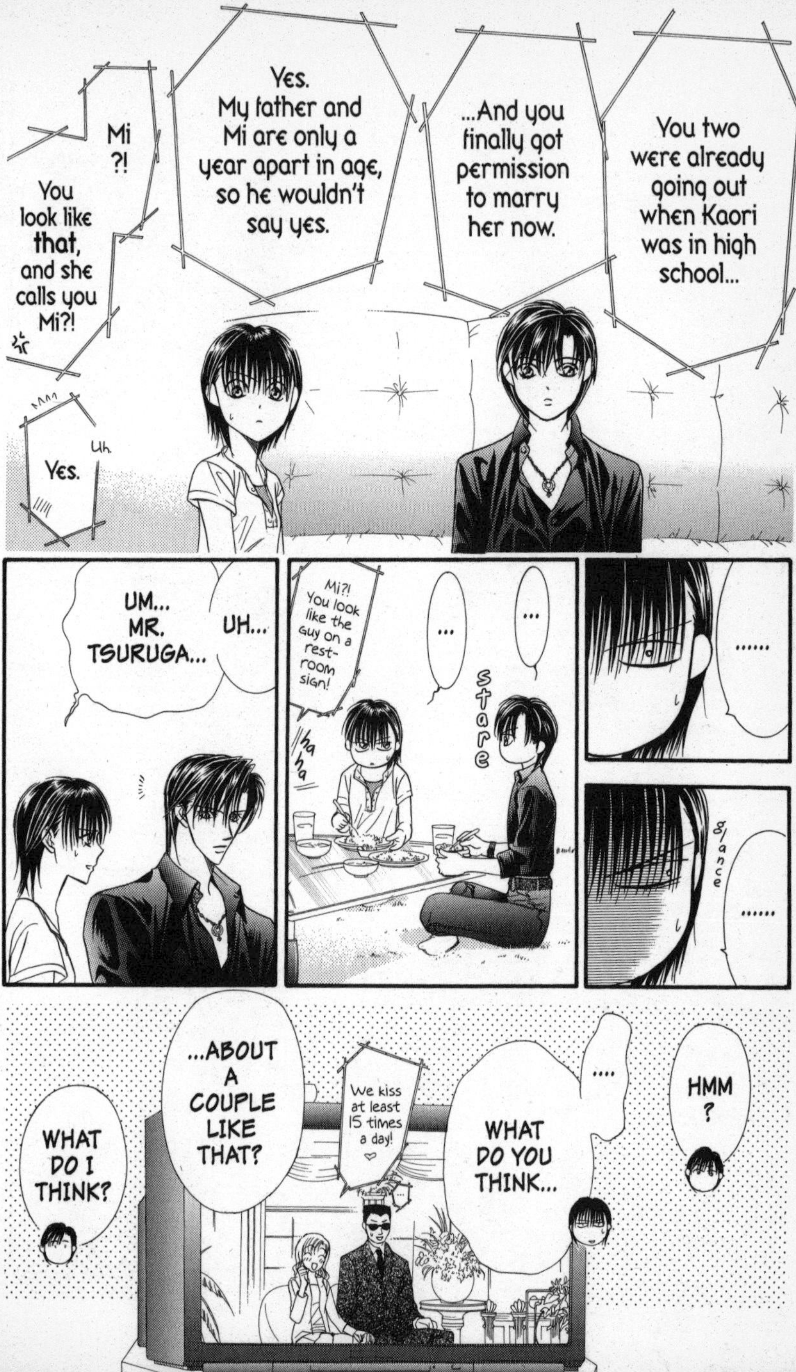
You two were already going out when Kaori was in high school...
...And you finally got permission to marry her now.
Yes. My father and Mi are only a year apart in age, so he wouldn't say yes.
Mi ?!
You look like that, and she calls you Mi?!
Uh.
Yes.
......
glance
......
...
...
stare
Mi?! You look like the guy on a rest-room sign!
ha ha
UH...
UM... MR. TSURUGA...
HMM ?
....
WHAT DO YOU THINK...
We kiss at least 15 times a day!
...ABOUT A COUPLE LIKE THAT?
WHAT DO I THINK?

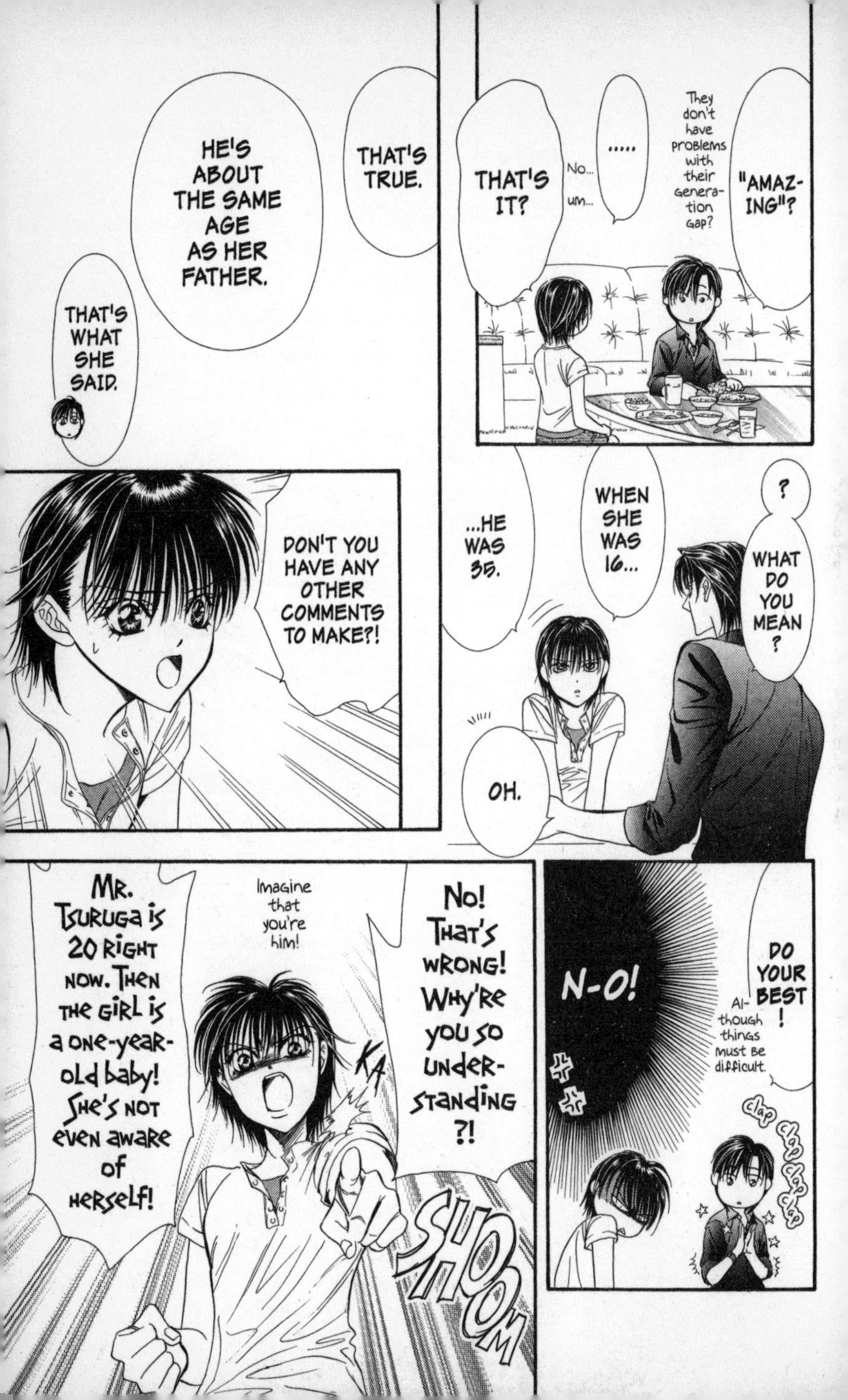
"AMAZ-ING"?
They don't have problems with their generation gap?
.....
No... um...
THAT'S IT?
THAT'S TRUE.
HE'S ABOUT THE SAME AGE AS HER FATHER.
THAT'S WHAT SHE SAID.
? WHAT DO YOU MEAN?
WHEN SHE WAS 16...
...HE WAS 35.
OH.
DON'T YOU HAVE ANY OTHER COMMENTS TO MAKE?!
DO YOUR BEST!
Although things must be difficult.
N-O!
clap clap clap clap
No! That's wrong! Why're you so understanding?!
Imagine that you're him!
Mr. Tsuruga is 20 right now. Then the girl is a one-year-old baby! She's not even aware of herself!
KA
SHOOM

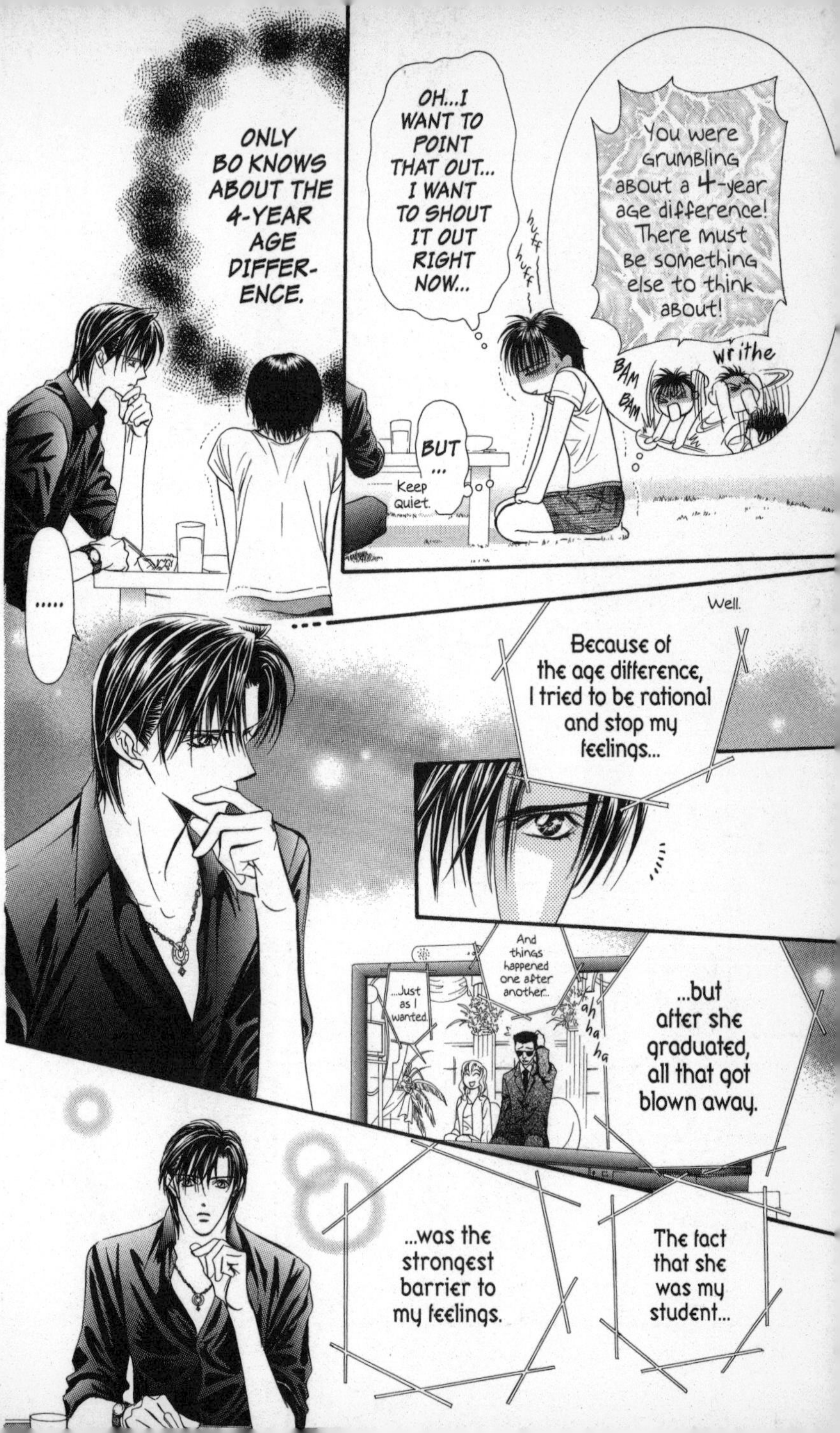

You were grumbling about a 4-year age difference! There must be something else to think about!
writhe
BAM BAM
huff huff
OH...I WANT TO POINT THAT OUT... I WANT TO SHOUT IT OUT RIGHT NOW...
BUT ...
Keep quiet.
ONLY BO KNOWS ABOUT THE 4-YEAR AGE DIFFER-ENCE.
......
Well.
Because of the age difference, I tried to be rational and stop my feelings...
...but after she graduated, all that got blown away.
And things happened one after another...
...Just as I wanted.
ah ha ha ha
The fact that she was my student...
...was the strongest barrier to my feelings.

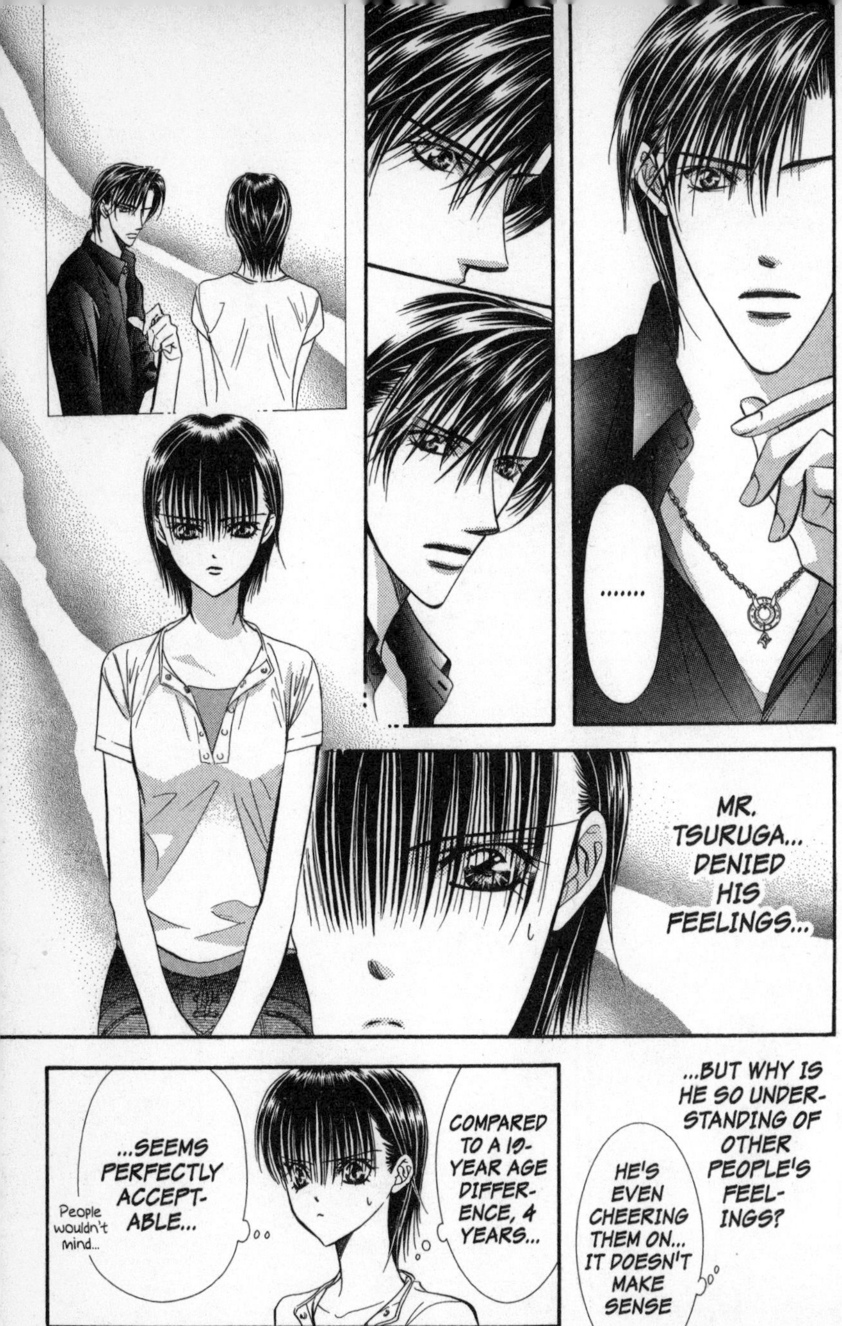
....
MR. TSURUGA... DENIED HIS FEELINGS...
...BUT WHY IS HE SO UNDER-STANDING OF OTHER PEOPLE'S FEEL-INGS?
HE'S EVEN CHEERING THEM ON... IT DOESN'T MAKE SENSE ...
COMPARED TO A 19-YEAR AGE DIFFER-ENCE, 4 YEARS...
...SEEMS PERFECTLY ACCEPT-ABLE...
People wouldn't mind...

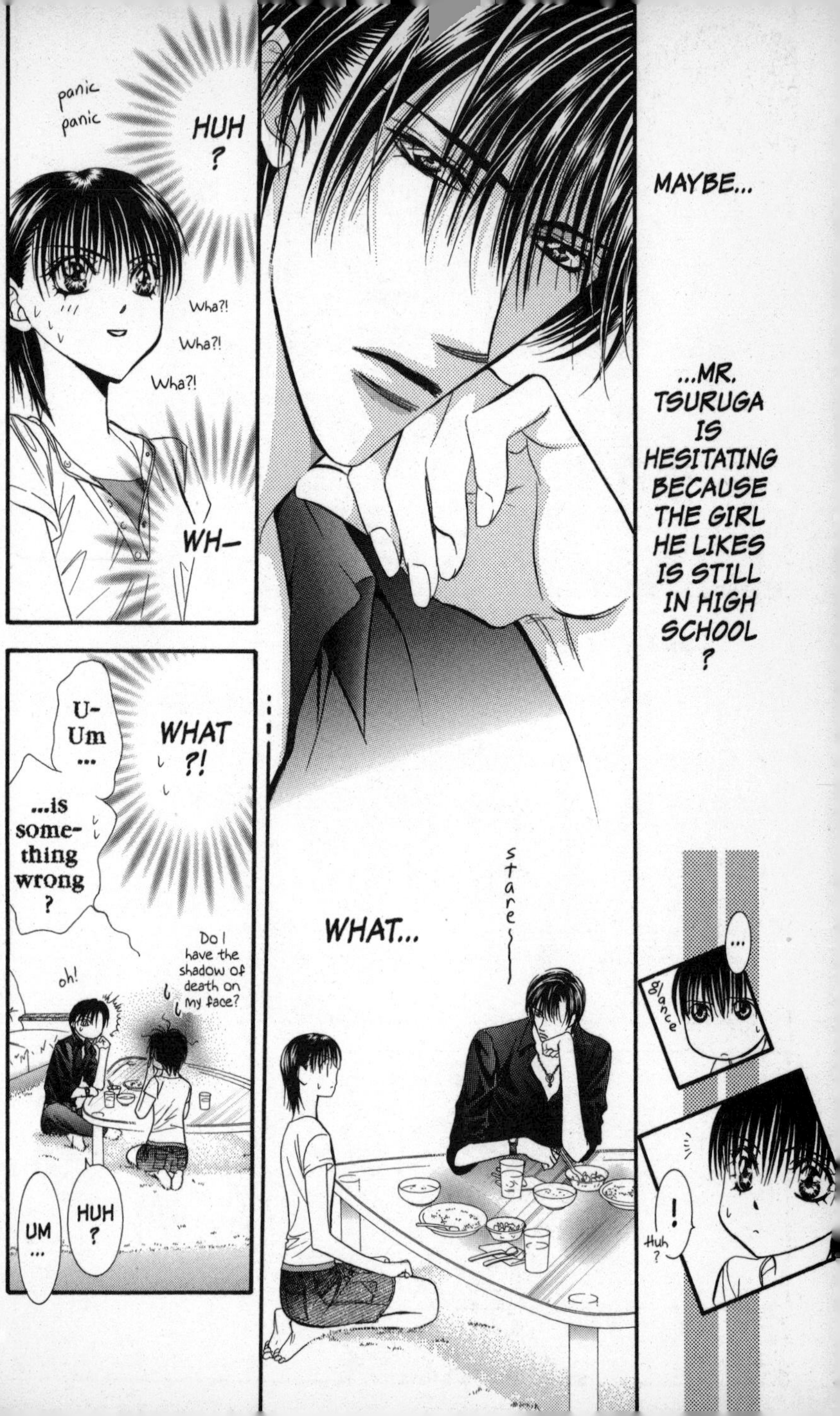

MAYBE...
...MR. TSURUGA IS HESITATING BECAUSE THE GIRL HE LIKES IS STILL IN HIGH SCHOOL?
...
glance
!
Huh?
...
stare~
WHAT...
HUH?
panic panic
Wha?!
Wha?!
Wha?!
WH—
WHAT?!
U-Um...
...is something wrong?
Do I have the shadow of death on my face?
oh!
HUH?
UM...

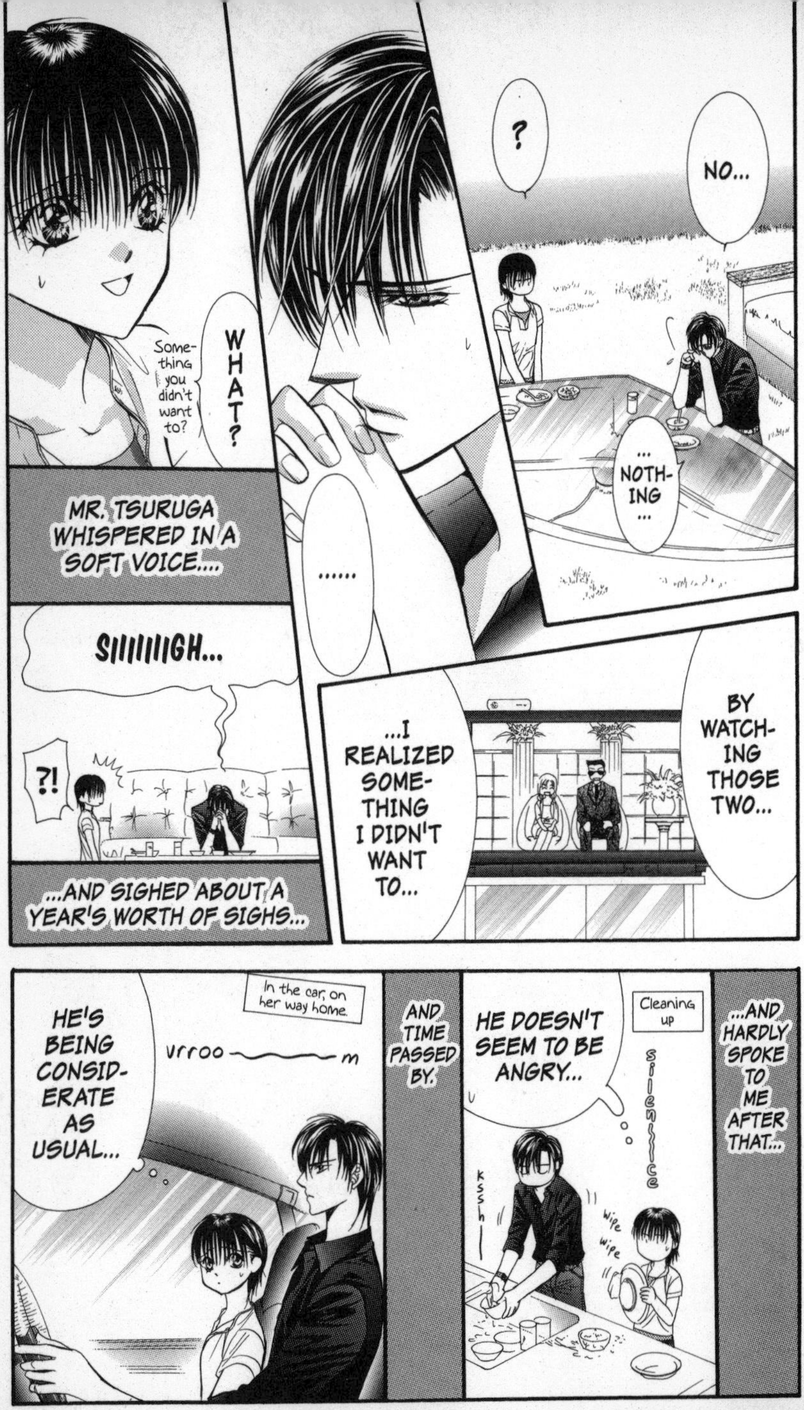
BY WATCHING THOSE TWO...
...I REALIZED SOMETHING I DIDN'T WANT TO...
WHAT?
Something you didn't want to?
......
?
NO...
...NOTHING...
MR. TSURUGA WHISPERED IN A SOFT VOICE....
SIIIIIIGH...
?!
...AND SIGHED ABOUT A YEAR'S WORTH OF SIGHS...
...AND HARDLY SPOKE TO ME AFTER THAT...
Cleaning up
HE DOESN'T SEEM TO BE ANGRY...
silence
kssh
wipe wipe
AND TIME PASSED BY.
In the car, on her way home.
HE'S BEING CONSIDERATE AS USUAL...
vrroo——m

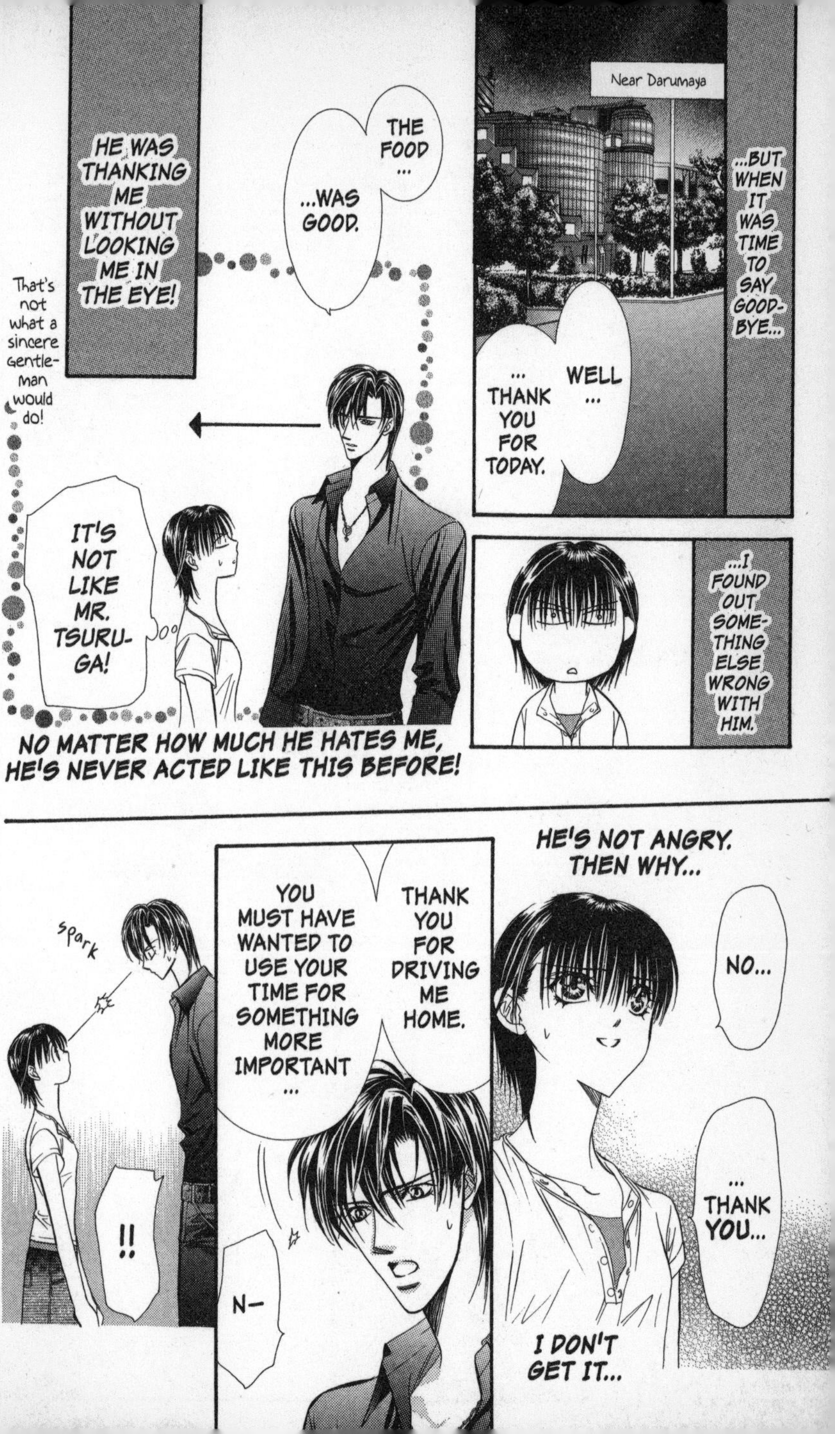
Near Darumaya
...BUT WHEN IT WAS TIME TO SAY GOOD-BYE...
WELL ...
... THANK YOU FOR TODAY.
...I FOUND OUT SOMETHING ELSE WRONG WITH HIM.
THE FOOD ...
...WAS GOOD.
HE WAS THANKING ME WITHOUT LOOKING ME IN THE EYE!
That's not what a sincere gentle-man would do!
IT'S NOT LIKE MR. TSURU-GA!
NO MATTER HOW MUCH HE HATES ME, HE'S NEVER ACTED LIKE THIS BEFORE!
HE'S NOT ANGRY. THEN WHY...
NO...
... THANK YOU...
I DON'T GET IT...
THANK YOU FOR DRIVING ME HOME.
YOU MUST HAVE WANTED TO USE YOUR TIME FOR SOMETHING MORE IMPORTANT ...
N-
spark
!!

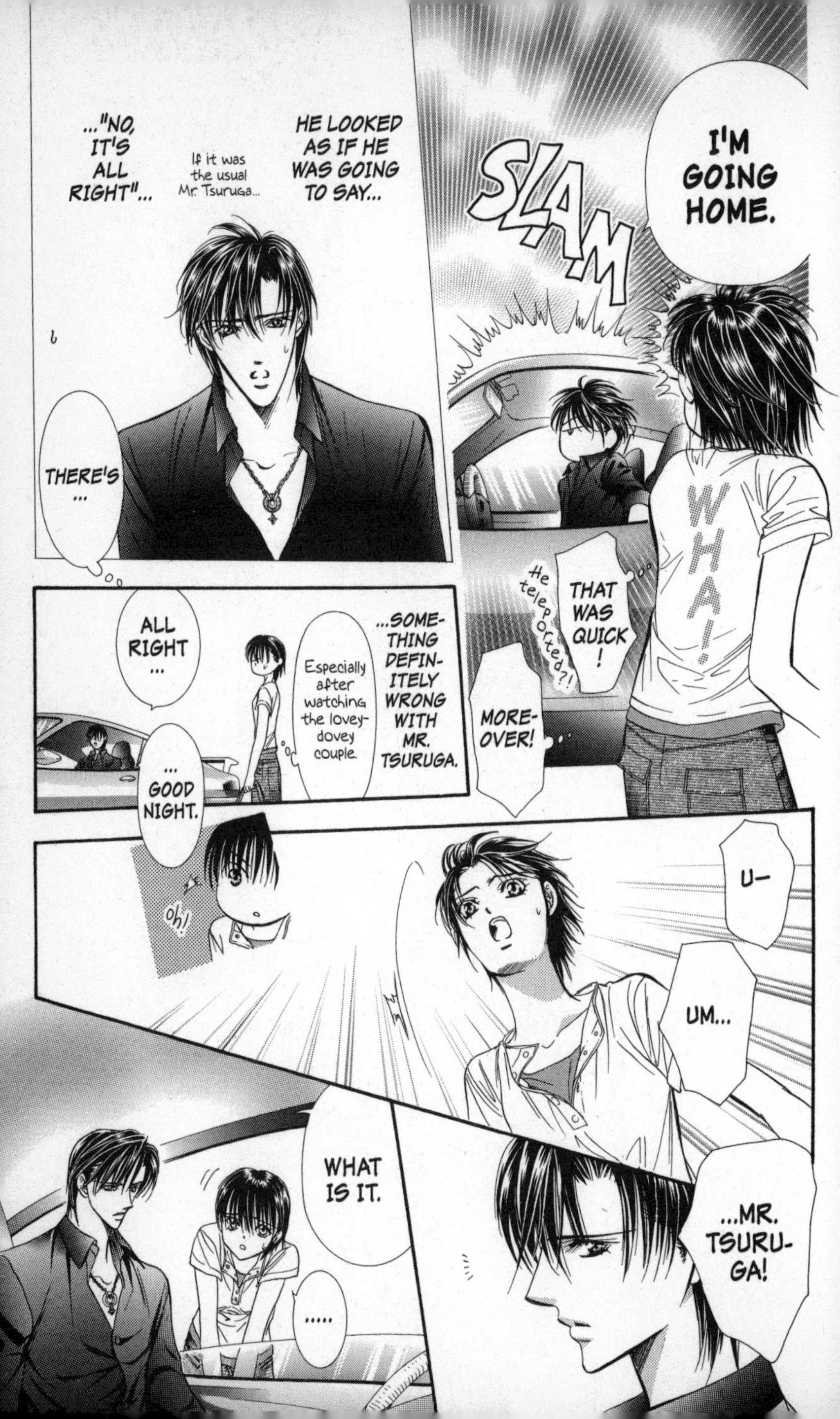
I'M GOING HOME.
SLAM
WHA!
THAT WAS QUICK!
He teleported?!
MORE-OVER!
HE LOOKED AS IF HE WAS GOING TO SAY...
If it was the usual Mr. Tsuruga...
..."NO, IT'S ALL RIGHT"...
THERE'S ...
...SOME-THING DEFIN-ITELY WRONG WITH MR. TSURUGA.
Especially after watching the lovey-dovey couple.
ALL RIGHT ...
... GOOD NIGHT.
U–
UM...
Oh!
...MR. TSURU-GA!
WHAT IS IT.
.....

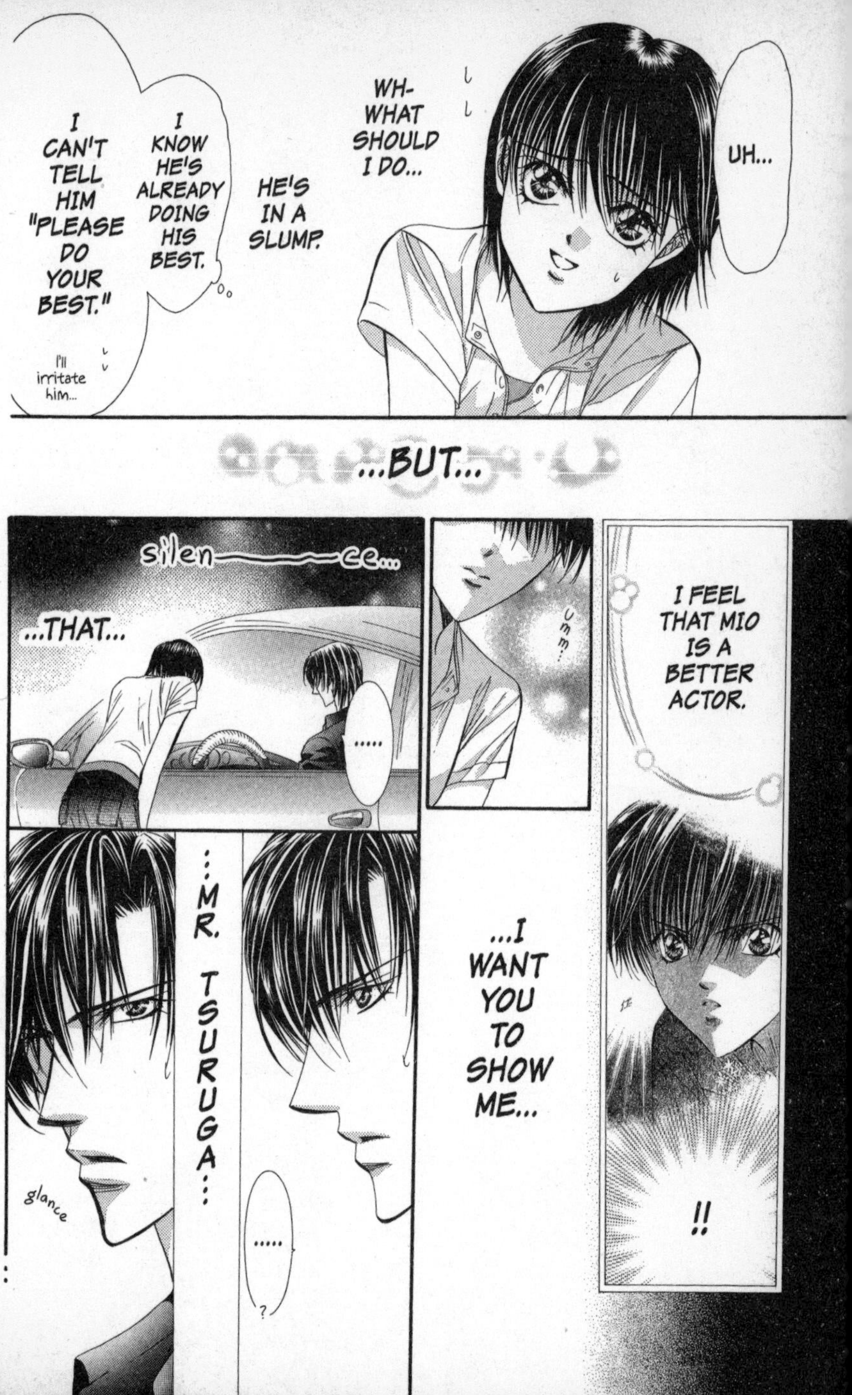
UH...
WH- WHAT SHOULD I DO...
HE'S IN A SLUMP.
I KNOW HE'S ALREADY DOING HIS BEST.
I CAN'T TELL HIM "PLEASE DO YOUR BEST."
I'll irritate him...
...BUT...
I FEEL THAT MIO IS A BETTER ACTOR.
Umm...
silen———ce...
...THAT...
.....
!!
...I WANT YOU TO SHOW ME...
...MR. TSURUGA...
.....
?
glance

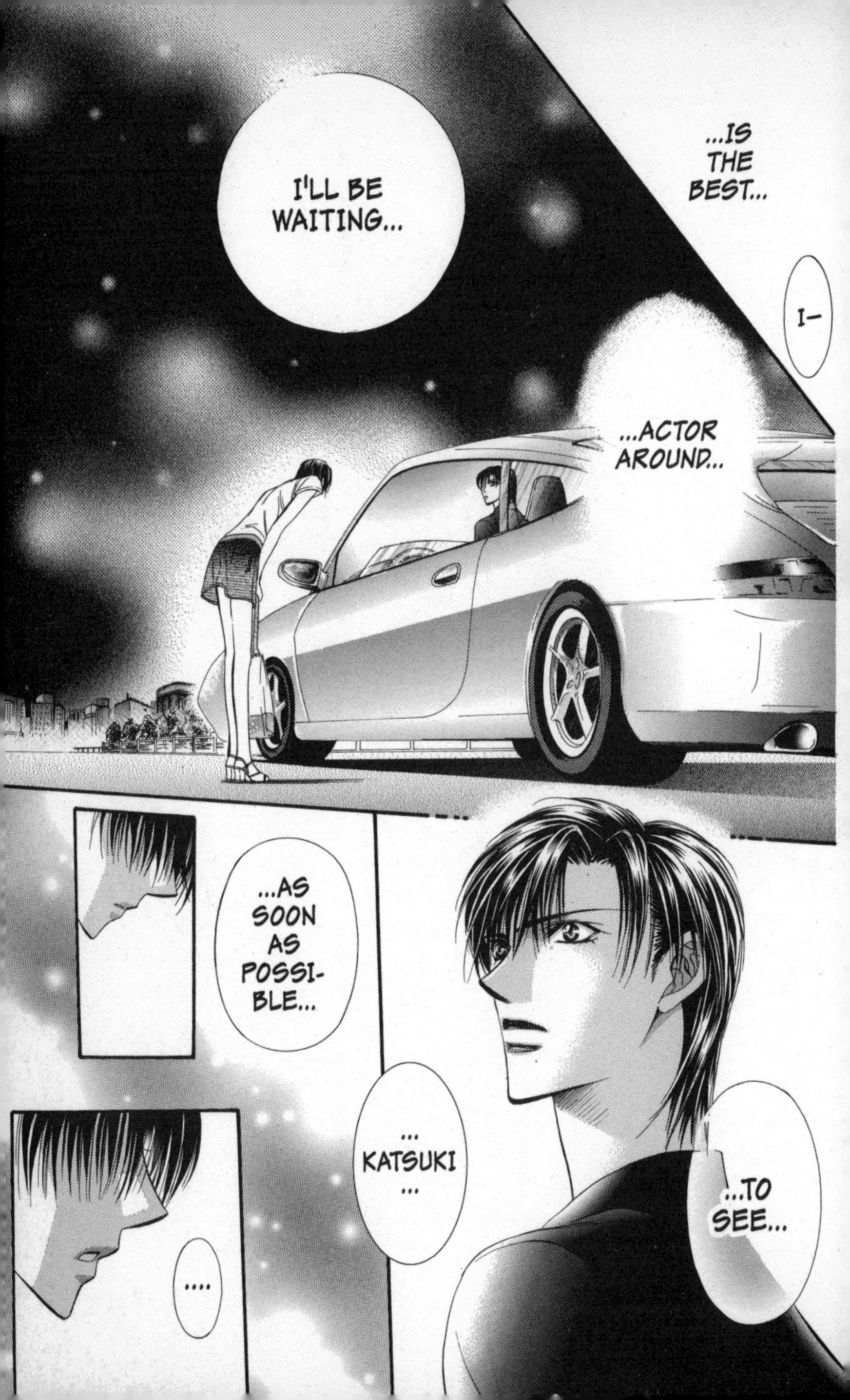
...IS THE BEST...
I—
...ACTOR AROUND...
I'LL BE WAITING...
...TO SEE...
... KATSUKI ...
...AS SOON AS POSSI-BLE...
....

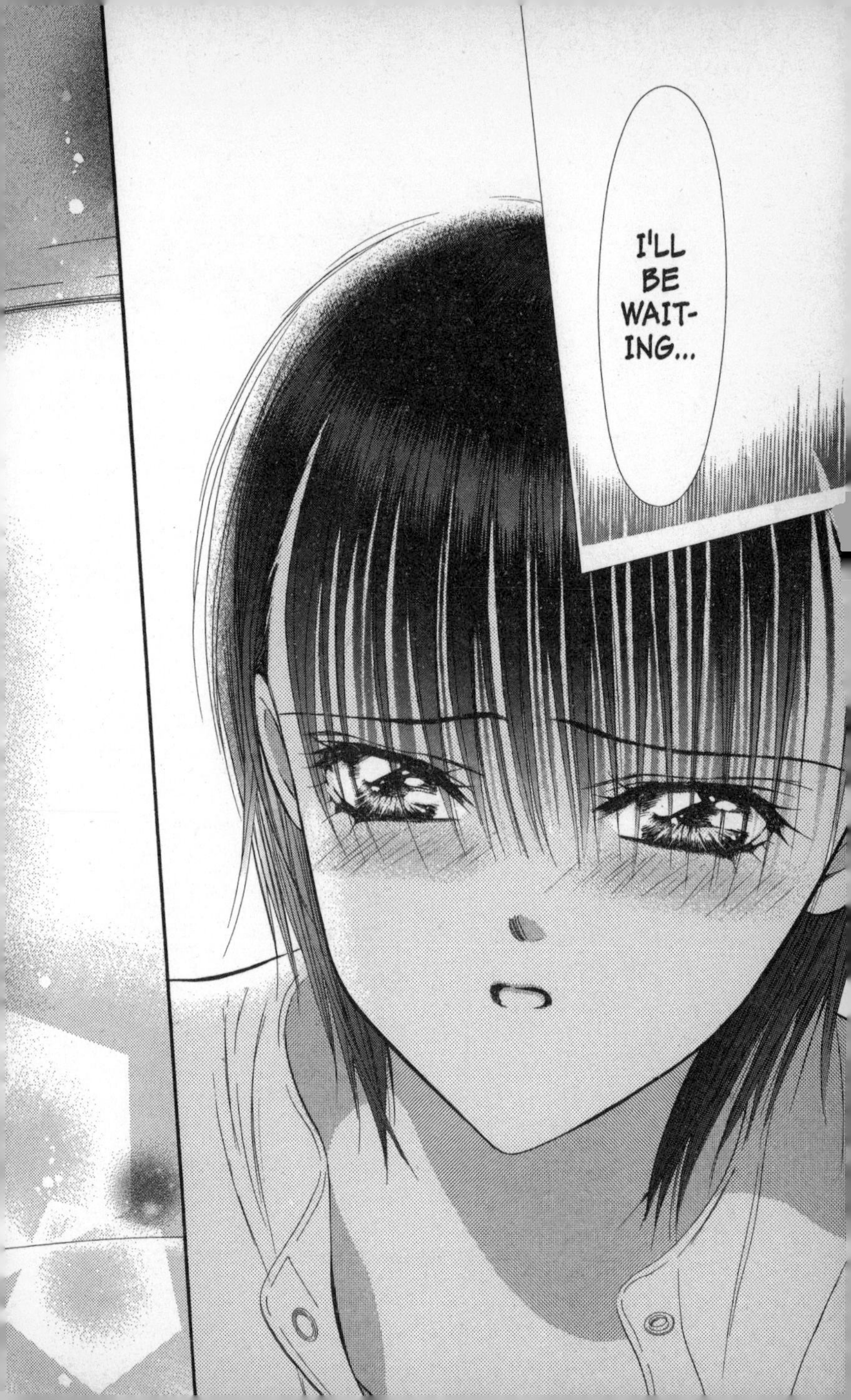
I'LL BE WAIT- ING...

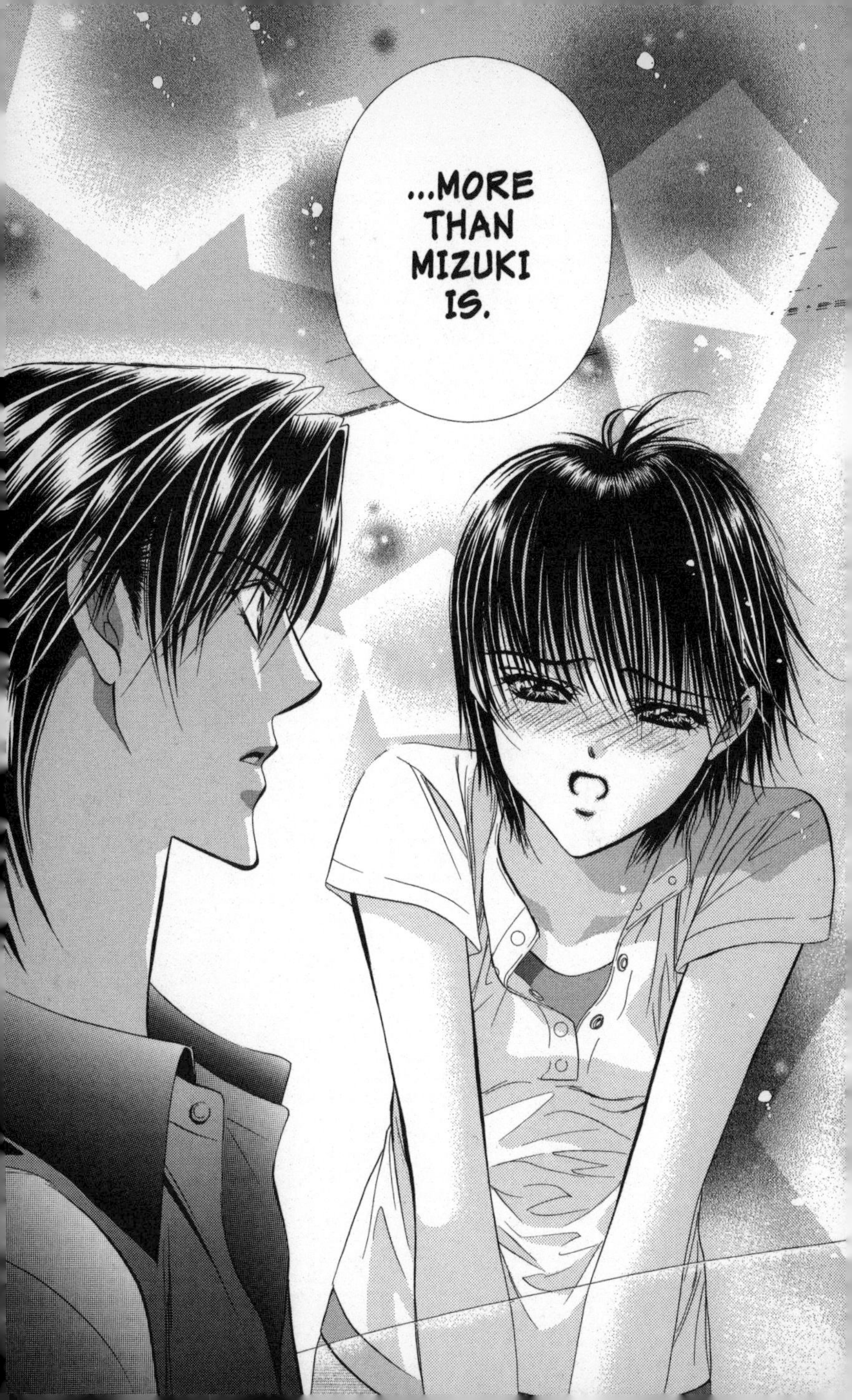
...MORE THAN MIZUKI IS.

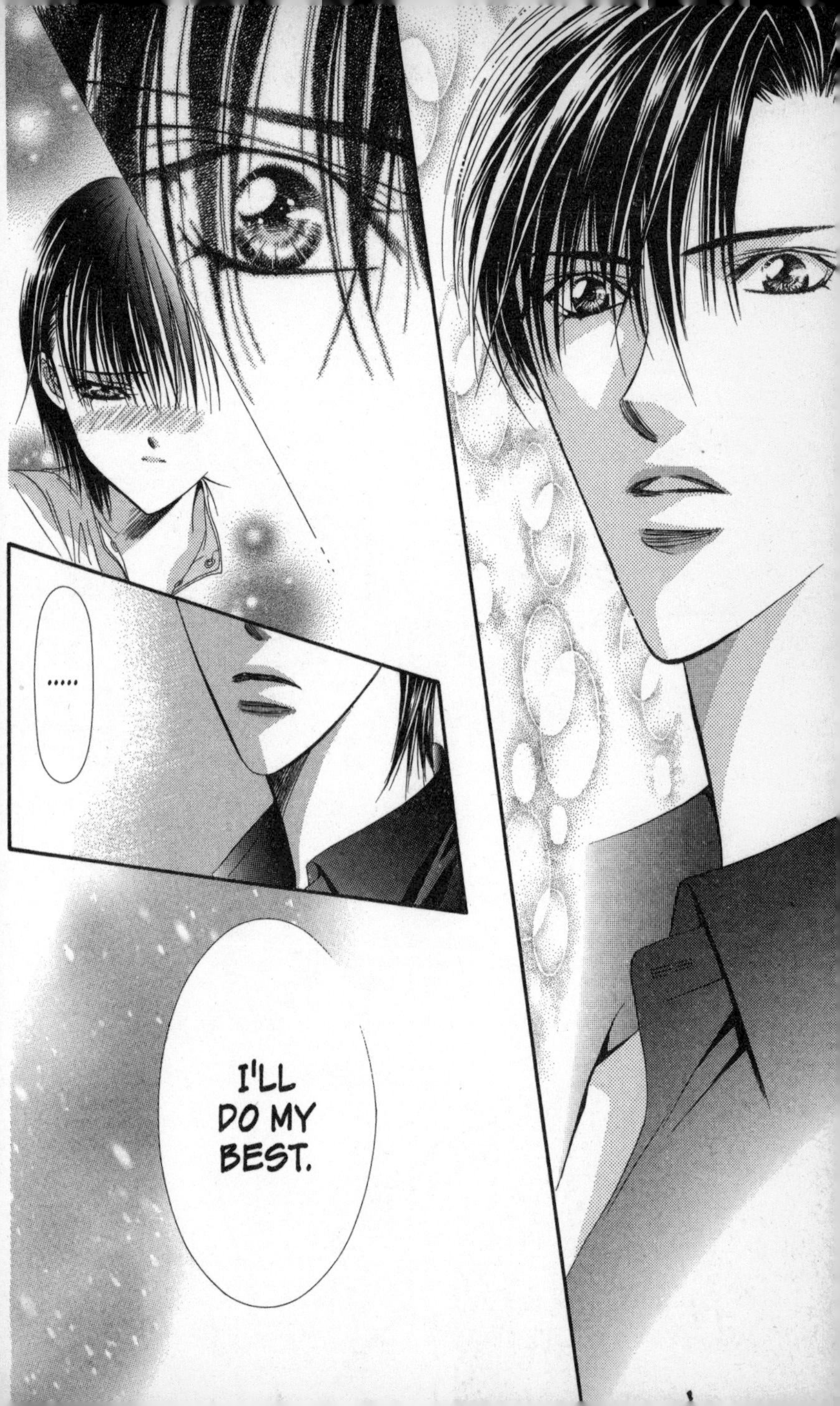
......
I'LL DO MY BEST.

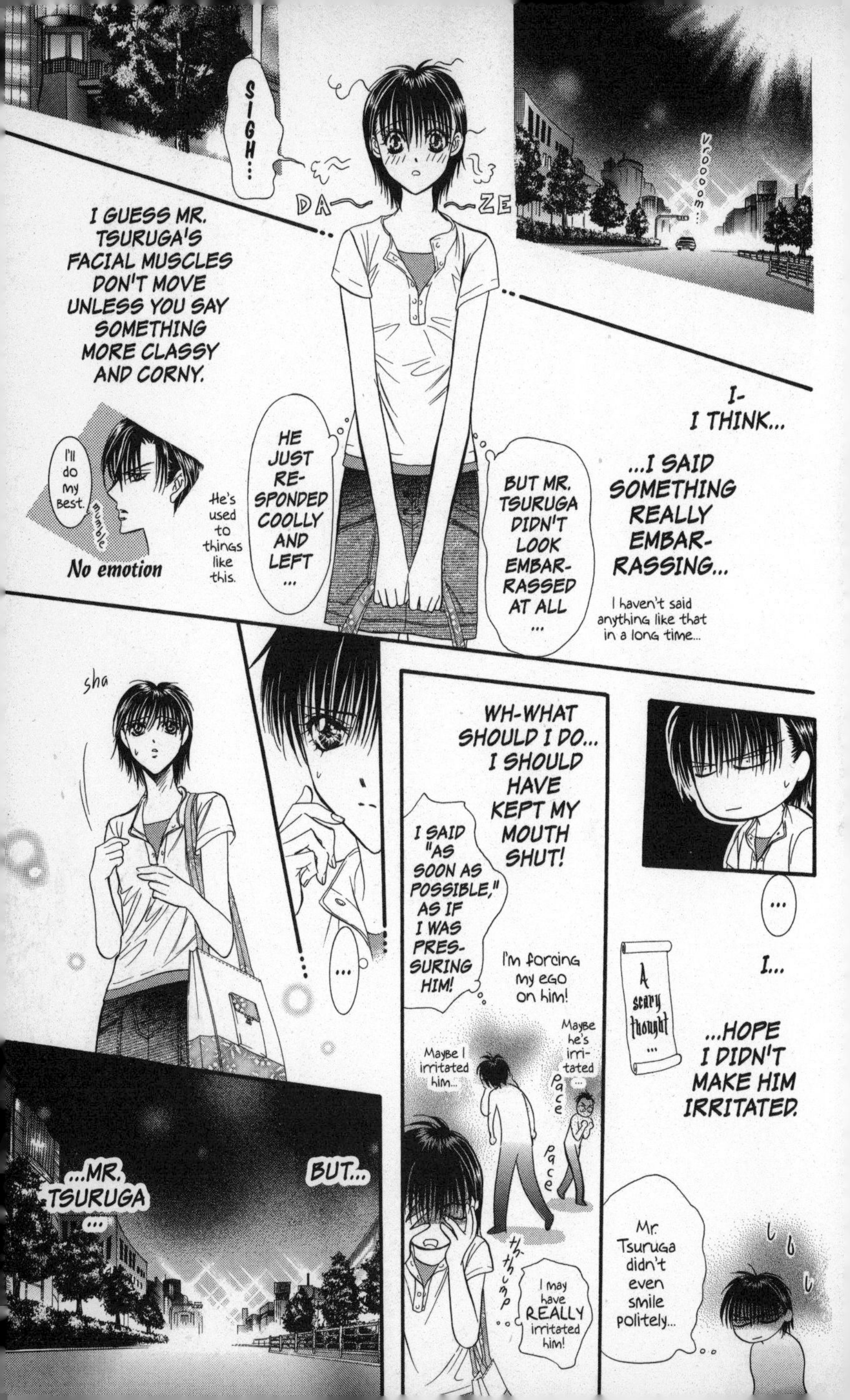
Vroooom...
SIGH...
DA~~ ~~ZE
I GUESS MR. TSURUGA'S FACIAL MUSCLES DON'T MOVE UNLESS YOU SAY SOMETHING MORE CLASSY AND CORNY.
I- I THINK...
...I SAID SOMETHING REALLY EMBARRASSING...
I haven't said anything like that in a long time...
BUT MR. TSURUGA DIDN'T LOOK EMBARRASSED AT ALL...
HE JUST RESPONDED COOLLY AND LEFT...
He's used to things like this.
I'll do my Best.
mumble
No emotion
...
I...
...HOPE I DIDN'T MAKE HIM IRRITATED.
A scary thought...
WH-WHAT SHOULD I DO... I SHOULD HAVE KEPT MY MOUTH SHUT!
I SAID "AS SOON AS POSSIBLE," AS IF I WAS PRESSURING HIM!
I'm forcing my ego on him!
Maybe he's irritated...
Maybe I irritated him...
Pace
Pace
thump
I may have REALLY irritated him!
Mr. Tsuruga didn't even smile politely...
...
sha
BUT...
...MR. TSURUGA...

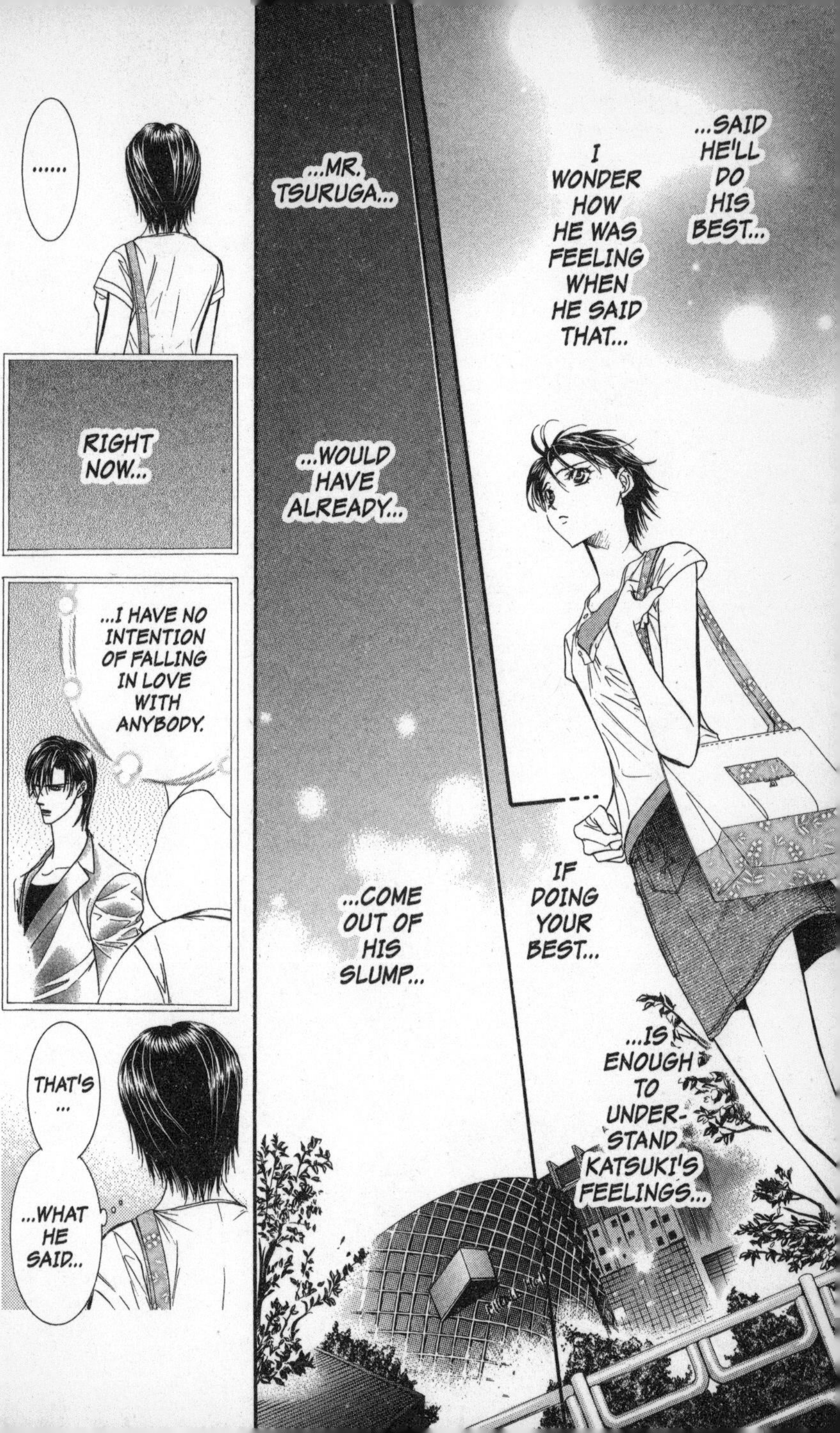
...SAID HE'LL DO HIS BEST...
I WONDER HOW HE WAS FEELING WHEN HE SAID THAT...
IF DOING YOUR BEST...
...IS ENOUGH TO UNDER-STAND KATSUKI'S FEELINGS...
...MR. TSURUGA...
...WOULD HAVE ALREADY...
...COME OUT OF HIS SLUMP...
......
RIGHT NOW...
...I HAVE NO INTENTION OF FALLING IN LOVE WITH ANYBODY.
THAT'S ...
...WHAT HE SAID...

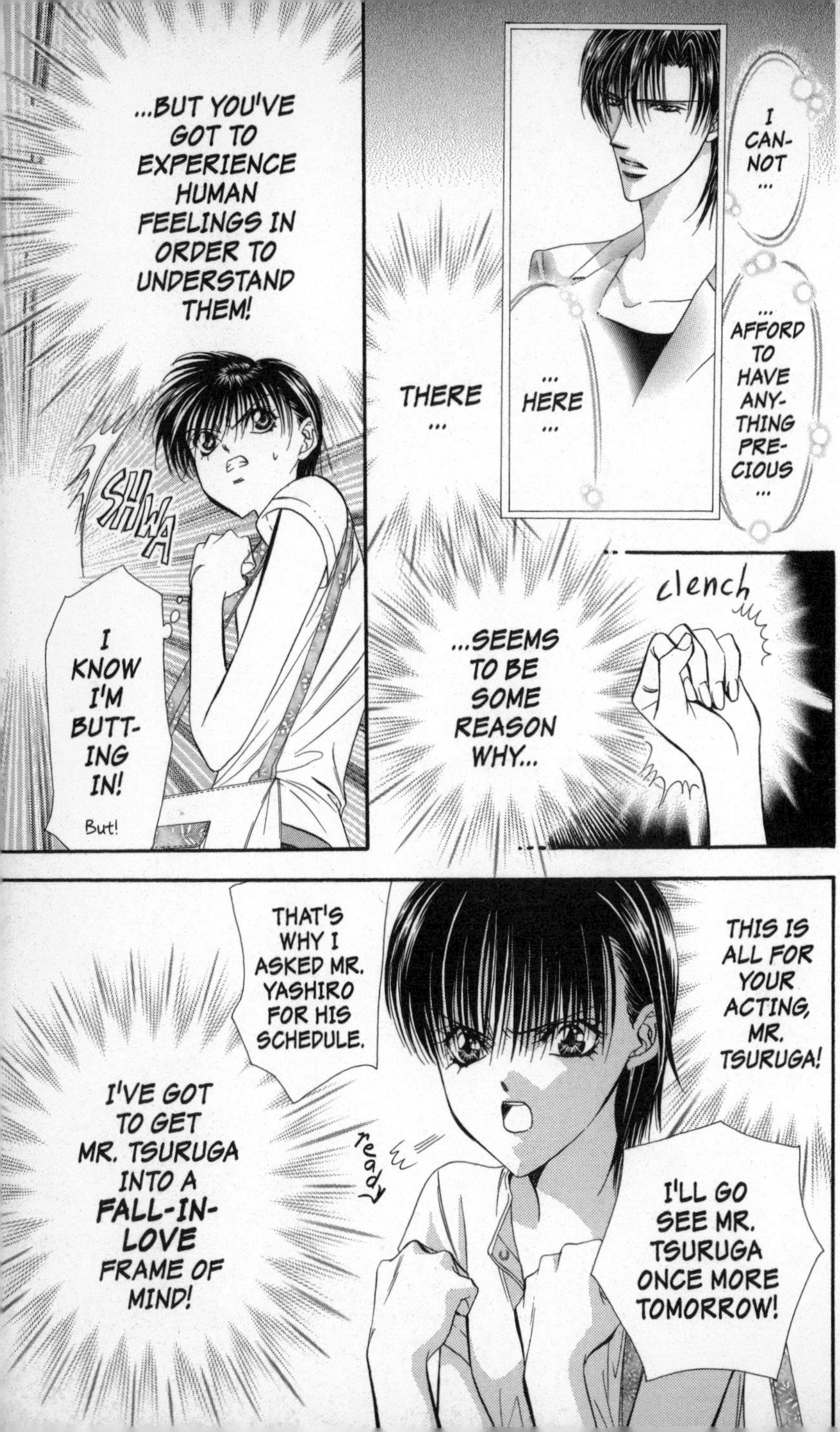
I CANNOT...
...AFFORD TO HAVE ANYTHING PRECIOUS...
...HERE...
THERE...
clench
...SEEMS TO BE SOME REASON WHY...
...BUT YOU'VE GOT TO EXPERIENCE HUMAN FEELINGS IN ORDER TO UNDERSTAND THEM!
SHWA
I KNOW I'M BUTTING IN!
But!
THIS IS ALL FOR YOUR ACTING, MR. TSURUGA!
THAT'S WHY I ASKED MR. YASHIRO FOR HIS SCHEDULE.
I'LL GO SEE MR. TSURUGA ONCE MORE TOMORROW!
ready
I'VE GOT TO GET MR. TSURUGA INTO A FALL-IN-LOVE FRAME OF MIND!

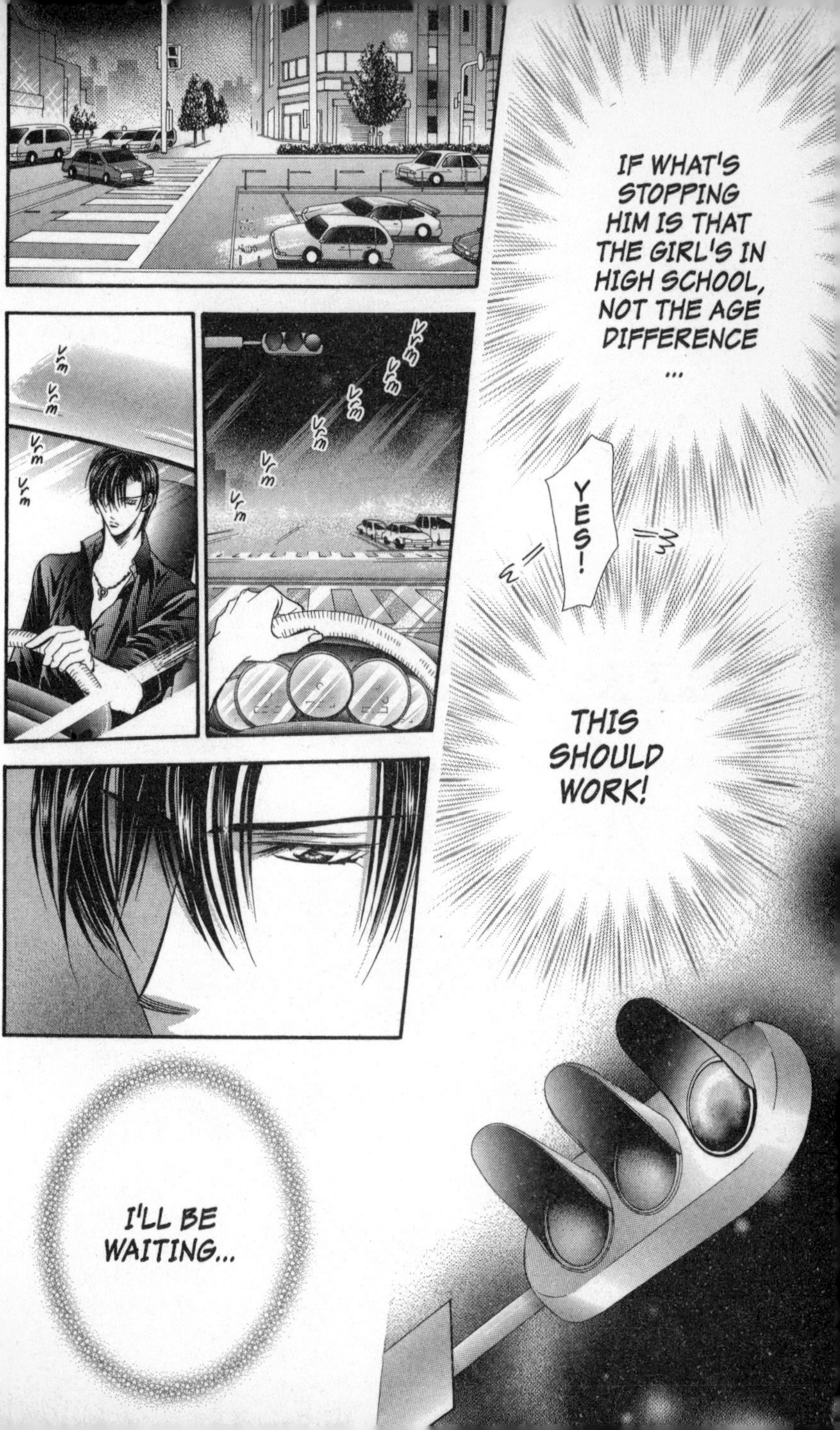
IF WHAT'S STOPPING HIM IS THAT THE GIRL'S IN HIGH SCHOOL, NOT THE AGE DIFFERENCE ...
YES!
THIS SHOULD WORK!
vrm
vrm
vrm
vrm
vrm
vrm
vrm
vrm
vrm
vrm
I'LL BE WAITING...

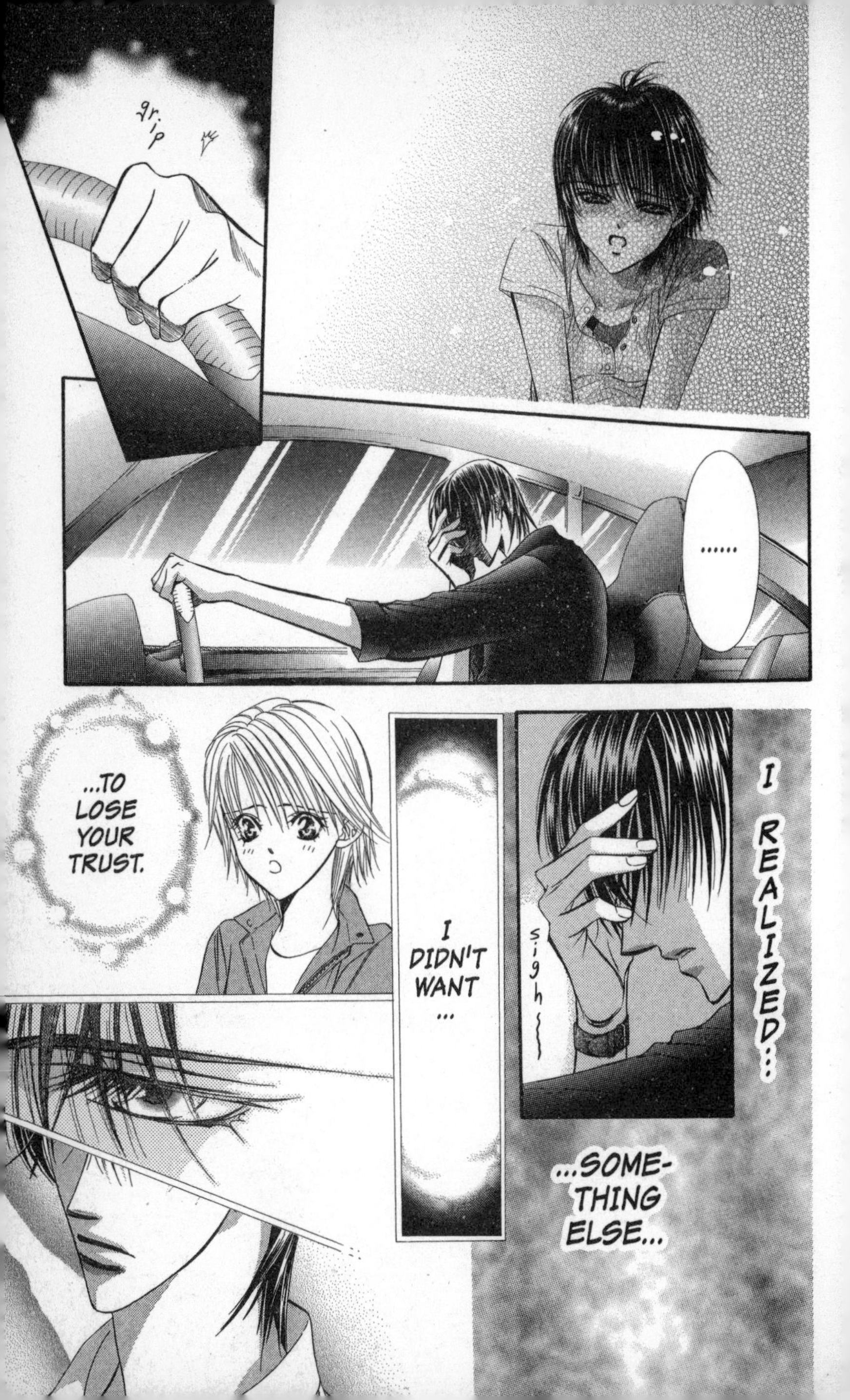
grip
......
I REALIZED...
sigh~~
I DIDN'T WANT...
...TO LOSE YOUR TRUST.
...SOME-THING ELSE...

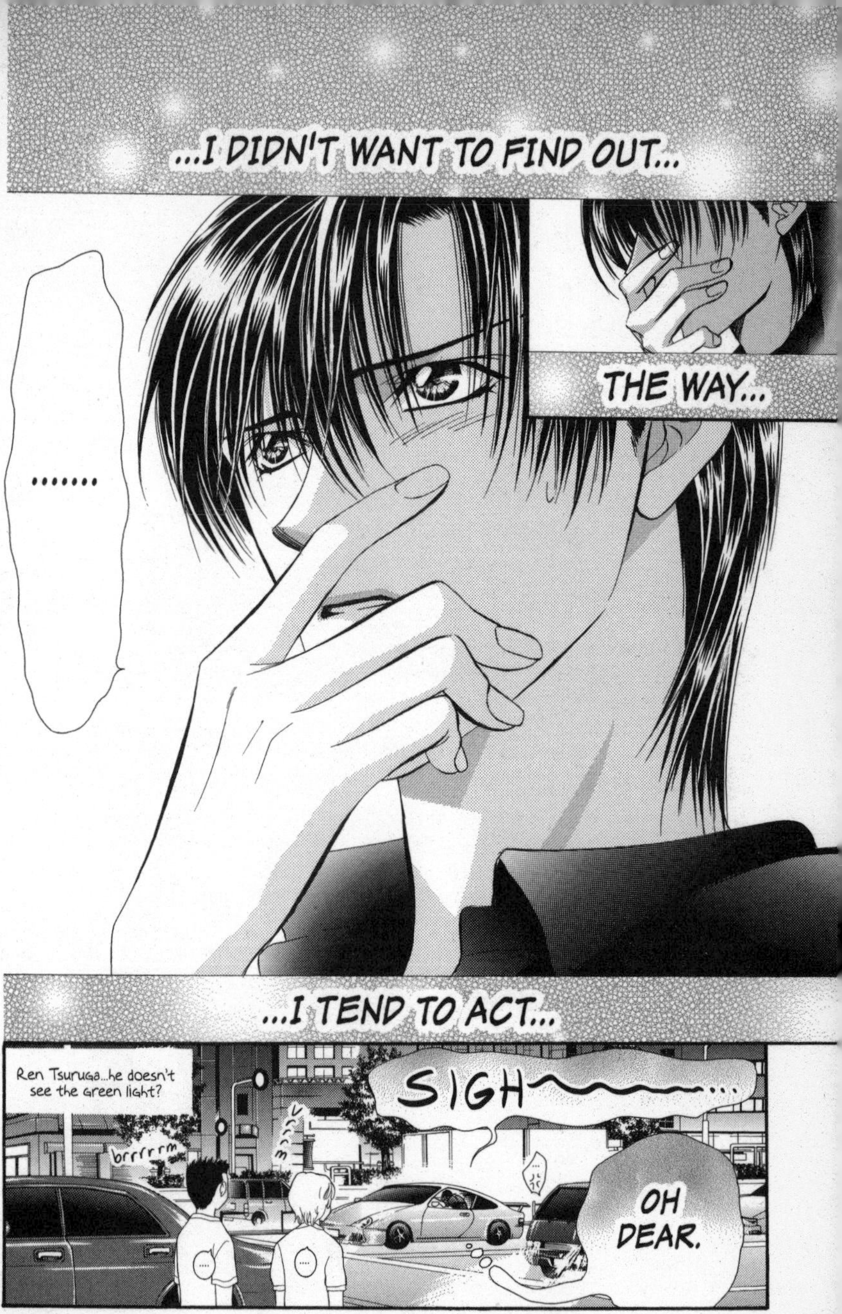
...I DIDN'T WANT TO FIND OUT...
THE WAY...
....
...I TEND TO ACT...
OH DEAR.
SIGH~~~...
brrrrm
....
....
Ren Tsuruga...he doesn't see the green light?

End of Act 66

Skip·Beat! End Notes
Everyone knows how to be a fan, but sometimes cool things from other cultures need a little help crossing the language barrier.

Page 33, panel 3: Rakshasa
Hindu demons known for cannibalism, grave desecration, and human possession. They are also shape shifters and magicians. The females are called *rakshasi*.

Page 59, panel 1: Hoshi Ittetsu
Hoshi Ittetsu is a character from the manga and anime *Kyojin no Hoshi*. When he got angry, he flipped over the dinner table.

Page 75, sidebar: A Stormy Life Always
This is a Japanese TV show where a celebrity is featured each week and the ups and downs of their life are revealed.

Page 103, sidebar: 19-episode series
Modern Japanese dramas only run for about three months or ten episodes. In the past, a six-month run was more common.

Page 134, panel 7: Get married
In Japan, a girl can get married at 16 with her parents' permission.

Page 167, side bar: Bancho
The term for the leader of a juvenile gang.

170, panel 4: Itadakimasu
A word of thanks said before eating.

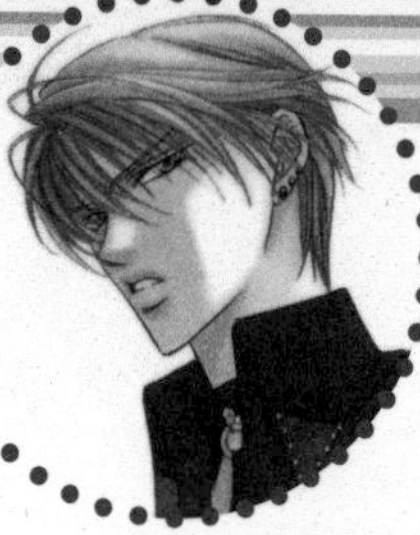

Yoshiki Nakamura is originally from Tokushima prefecture. She started drawing manga in elementary school, which eventually led to her 1993 debut of *Yume de Au yori Suteki* (Better than Seeing in a Dream) in *Hana to Yume* magazine. Her other works include the basketball series *Saint Love*, *MVP wa Yuzurenai* (Can't Give Up MVP), *Blue Wars*, and *Tokyo Crazy Paradise*, a series about a female bodyguard in 2020 Tokyo.

SKIP·BEAT!
Vol. 11
The Shojo Beat Manga Edition

STORY AND ART BY YOSHIKI NAKAMURA

English Translation & Adaptation/Tomo Kimura
Touch-up Art & Lettering/Sabrina Heep
Cover Design/Yukiko Whitley
Interior Design/Izumi Evers
Editor/Pancha Diaz

Editor in Chief, Books/Alvin Lu
Editor in Chief, Magazines/Marc Weidenbaum
VP of Publishing Licensing/Rika Inouye
VP of Sales/Gonzalo Ferreyra
Sr. VP of Marketing/Liza Coppola
Publisher/Hyoe Narita

Published by VIZ Media, LLC
P.O. Box 77010
San Francisco, CA 94107

Shojo Beat Manga Edition
10 9 8 7 6 5 4 3 2 1
First printing, March 2008

store.viz.com

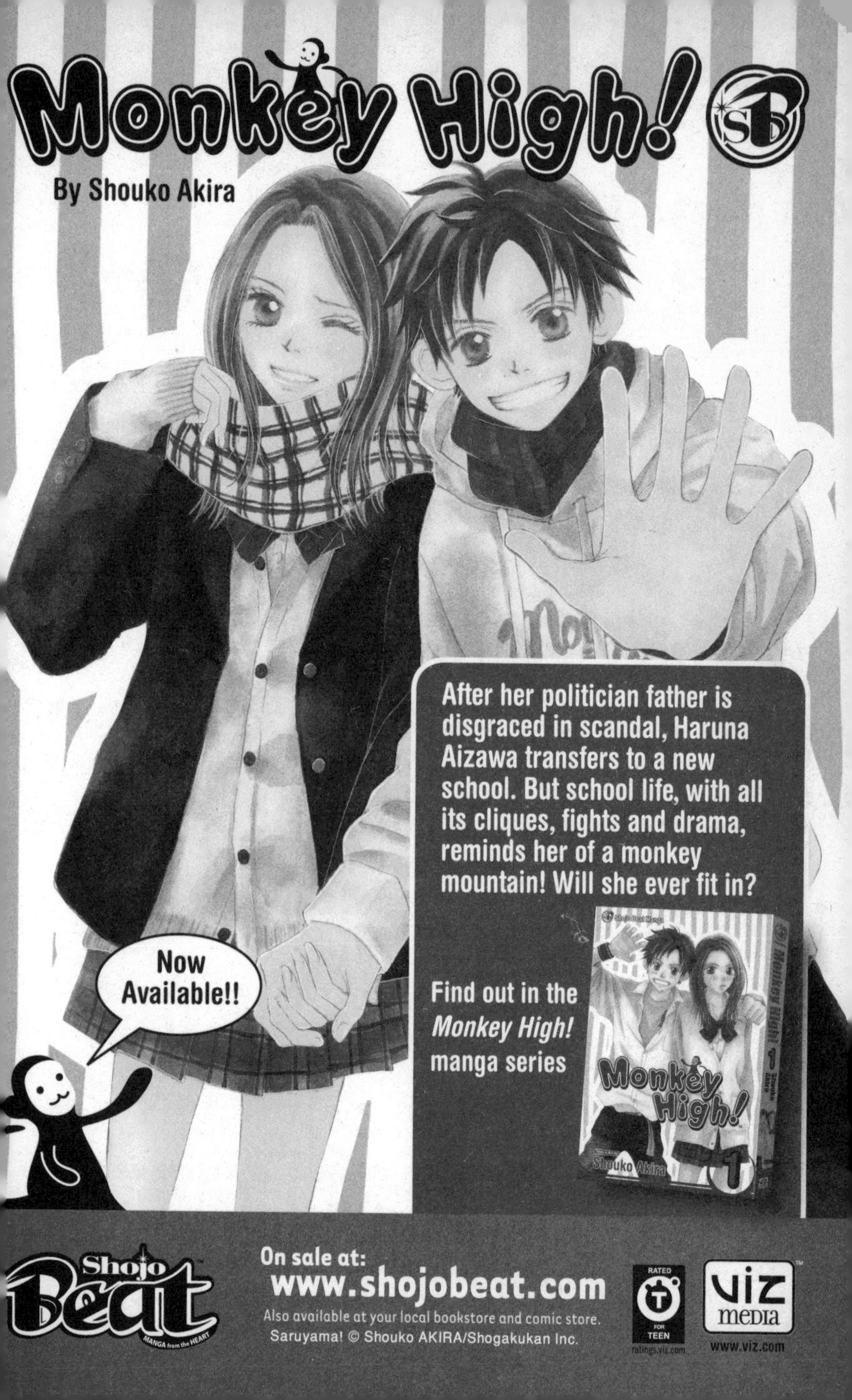
Monkey High!
SB
By Shouko Akira
After her politician father is disgraced in scandal, Haruna Aizawa transfers to a new school. But school life, with all its cliques, fights and drama, reminds her of a monkey mountain! Will she ever fit in?
Find out in the Monkey High! manga series
Now Available!!
Shojo Beat
MANGA from the HEART
On sale at:
www.shojobeat.com
Also available at your local bookstore and comic store.
Saruyama! © Shouko AKIRA/Shogakukan Inc.
RATED T FOR TEEN
ratings.viz.com
VIZ media
www.viz.com

Tell us what you think about Shojo Beat Manga!

Our survey is now
available online. Go to:

shojobeat.com/mangasurvey

Help us make our product offerings better!

Shojo **Beat**
MANGA from the HEART

THE REAL DRAMA BEGINS IN...

Jiu Jiu

Vol. 4

Story & Art by

Touya Tobina

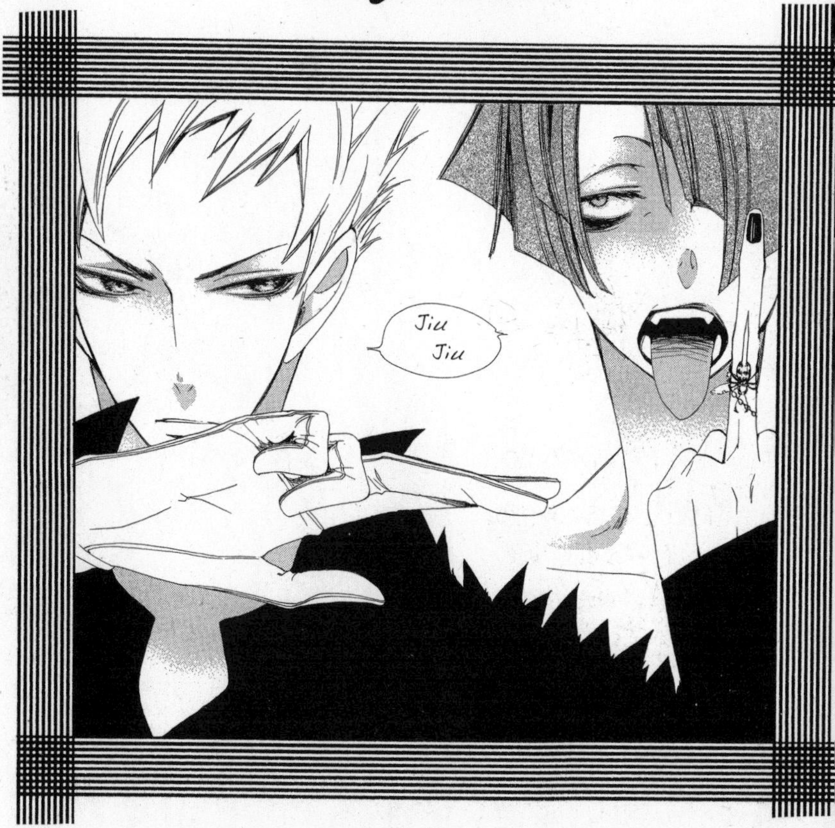
Jiu Jiu

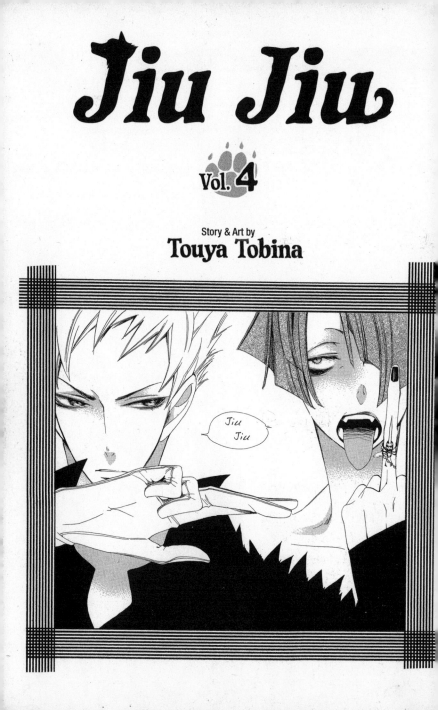

CONTENTS

JIUJIU 4

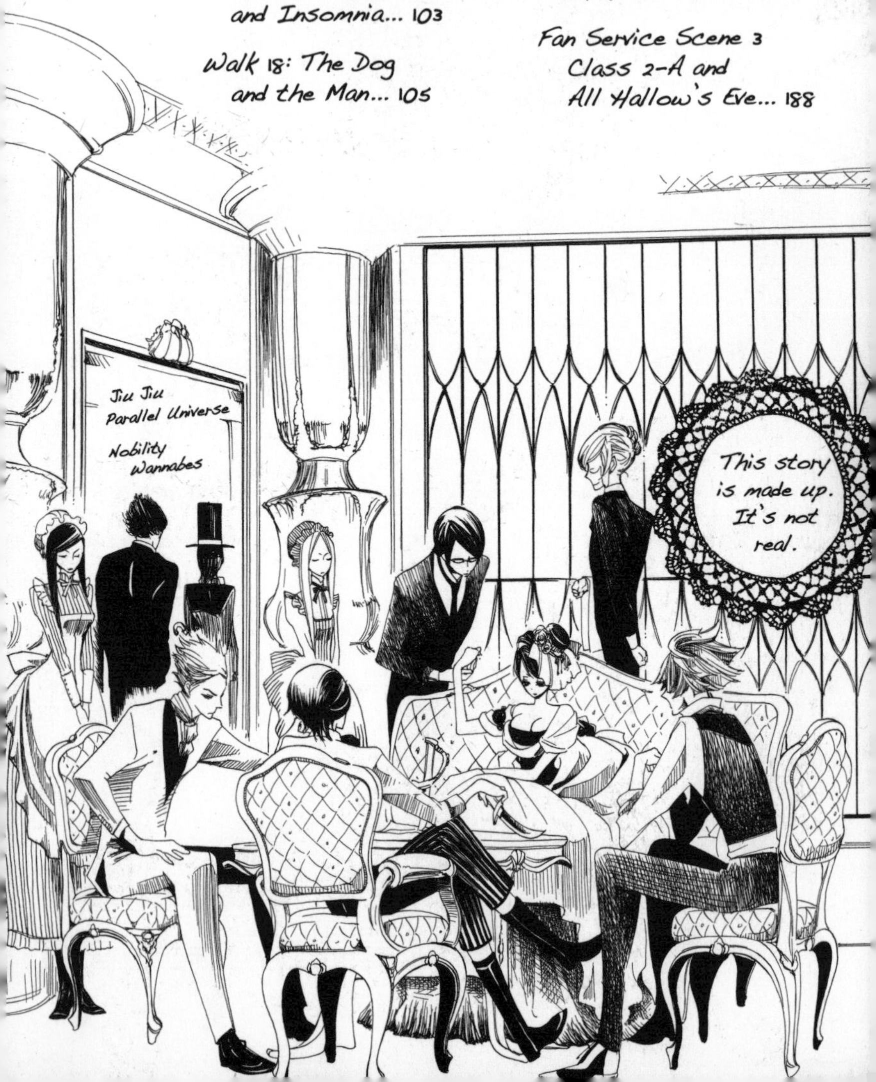

Jiu Jiu Parallel Universe
Nobility Wannabes
This story is made up. It's not real.

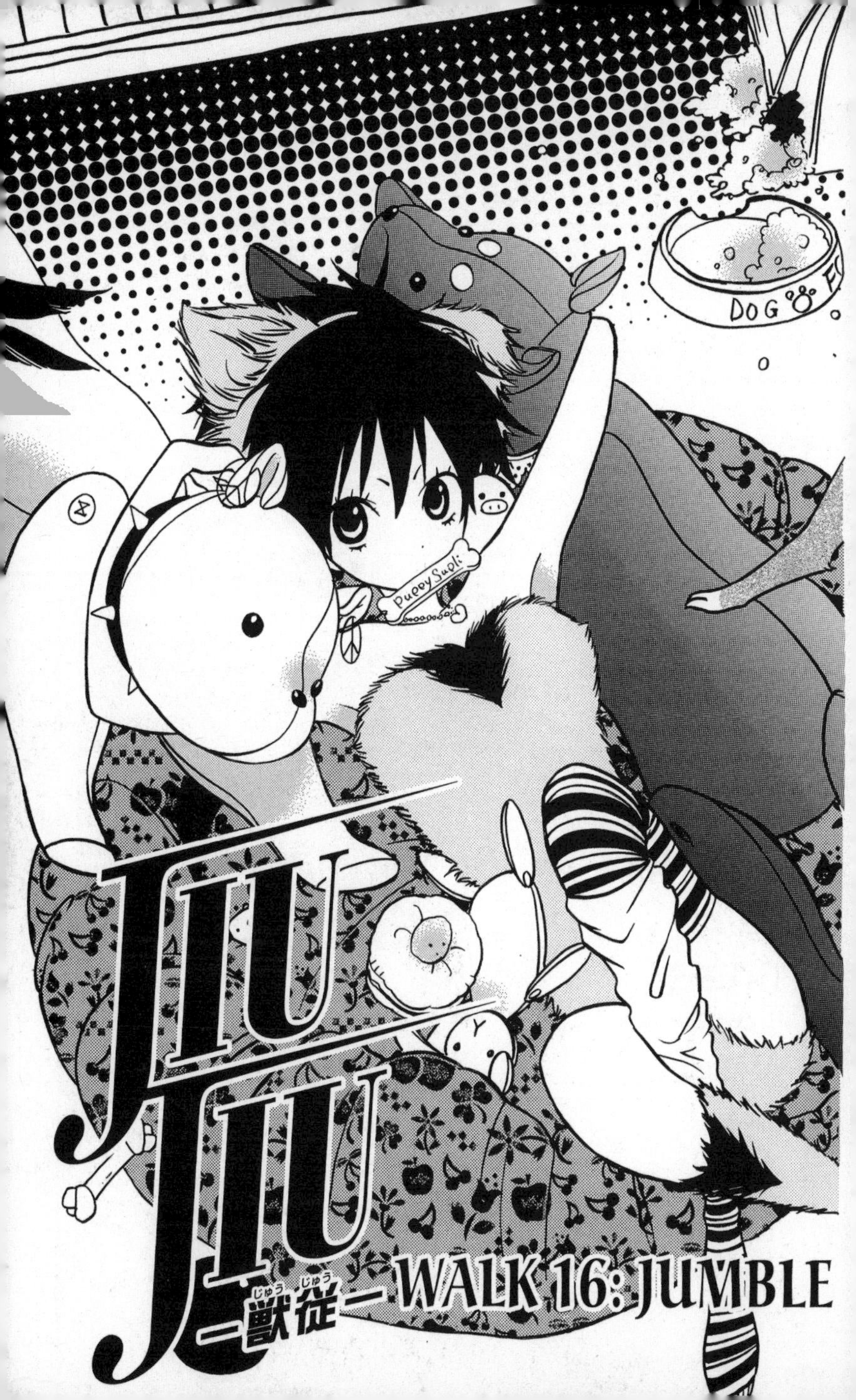
JIU JIU
—獣従—
じゅう じゅう
WALK 16: JUMBLE
DOG
Puppy Supli

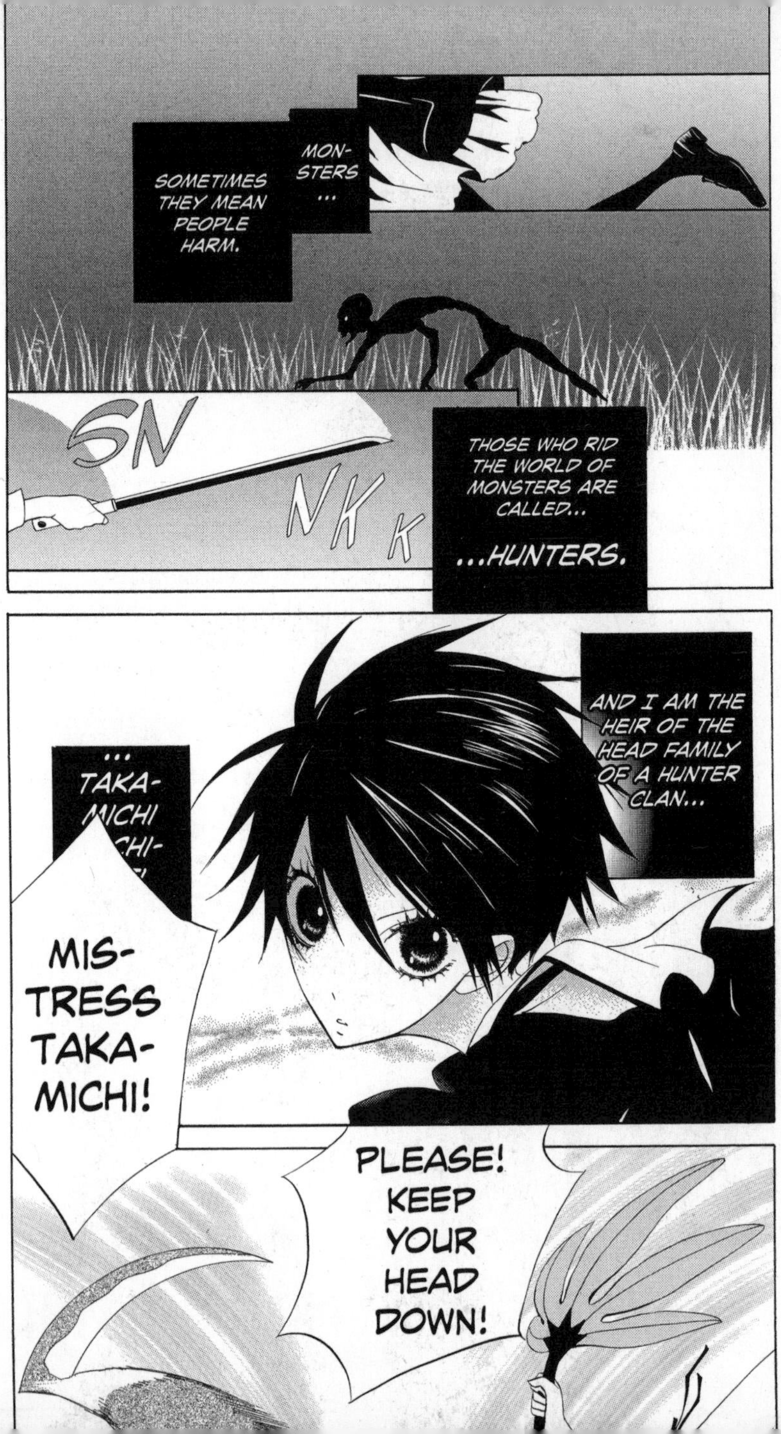
MON-STERS ...
SOMETIMES THEY MEAN PEOPLE HARM.
THOSE WHO RID THE WORLD OF MONSTERS ARE CALLED...
...HUNTERS.
SNNKK
AND I AM THE HEIR OF THE HEAD FAMILY OF A HUNTER CLAN...
... TAKAMICHI
MISTRESS TAKAMICHI!
PLEASE! KEEP YOUR HEAD DOWN!

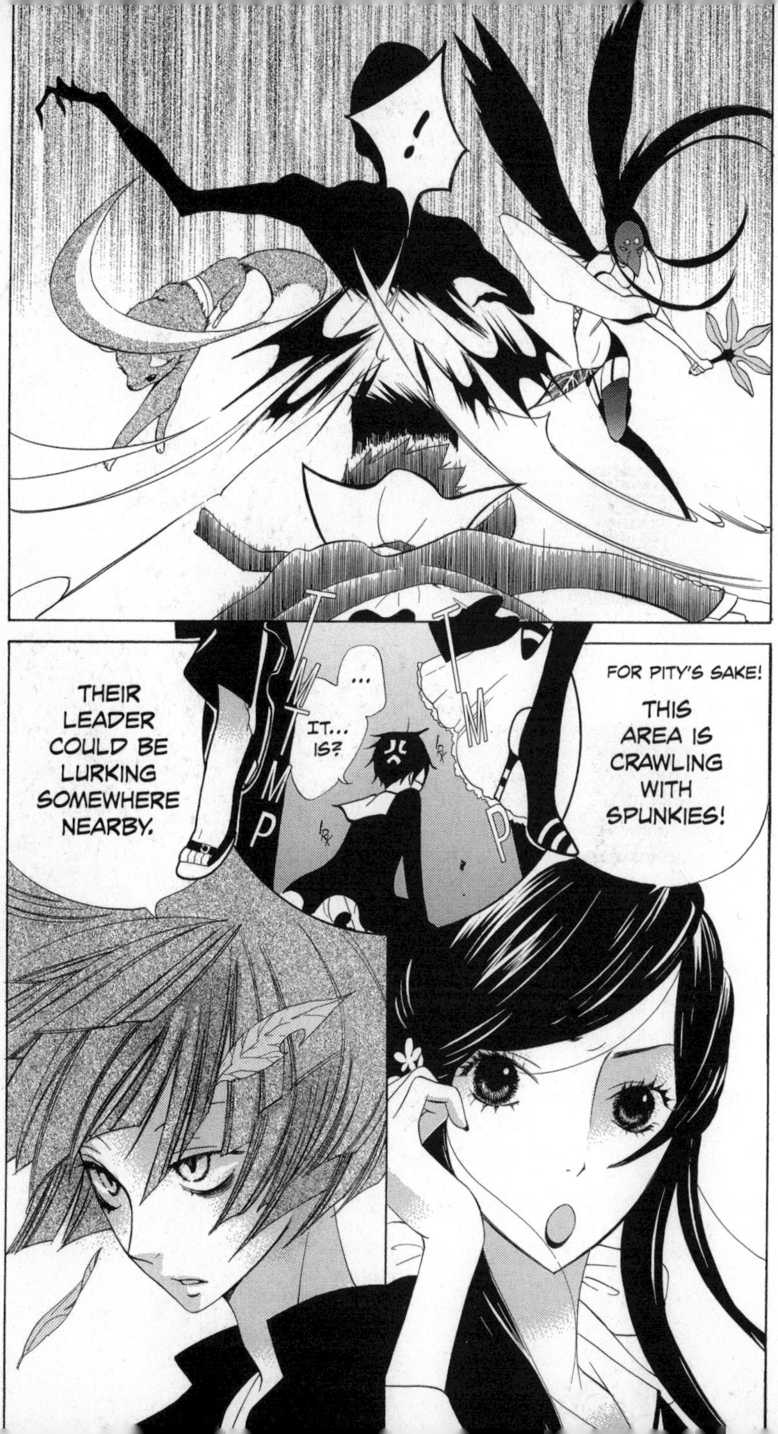
FOR PITY'S SAKE!
THIS AREA IS CRAWLING WITH SPUNKIES!
TMP
TMP
...
IT... IS?
THEIR LEADER COULD BE LURKING SOMEWHERE NEARBY.

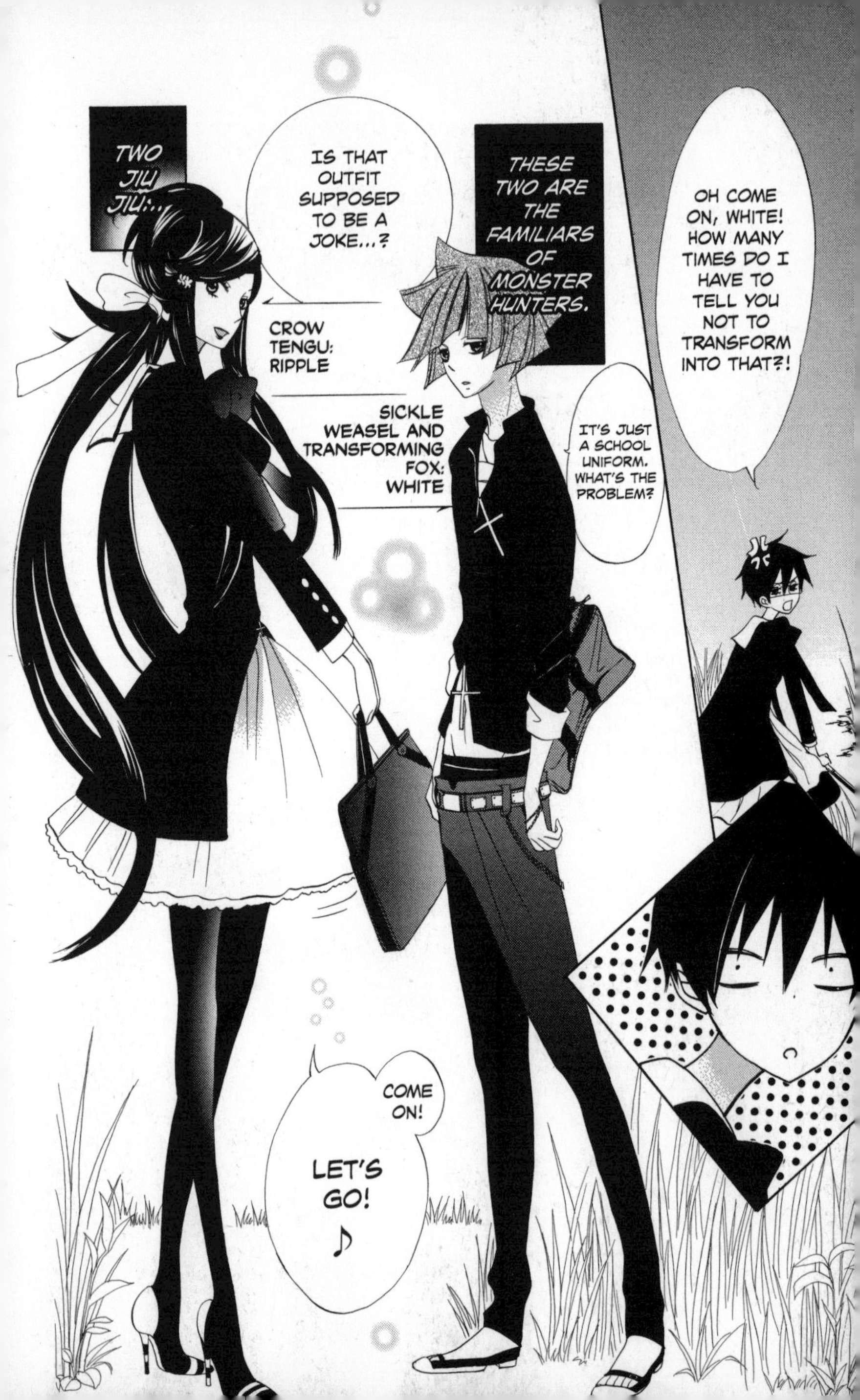

TWO JIU JIU...
THESE TWO ARE THE FAMILIARS OF MONSTER HUNTERS.
IS THAT OUTFIT SUPPOSED TO BE A JOKE...?
CROW TENGU: RIPPLE
SICKLE WEASEL AND TRANSFORMING FOX: WHITE
IT'S JUST A SCHOOL UNIFORM. WHAT'S THE PROBLEM?
OH COME ON, WHITE! HOW MANY TIMES DO I HAVE TO TELL YOU NOT TO TRANSFORM INTO THAT?!
COME ON!
LET'S GO! ♪

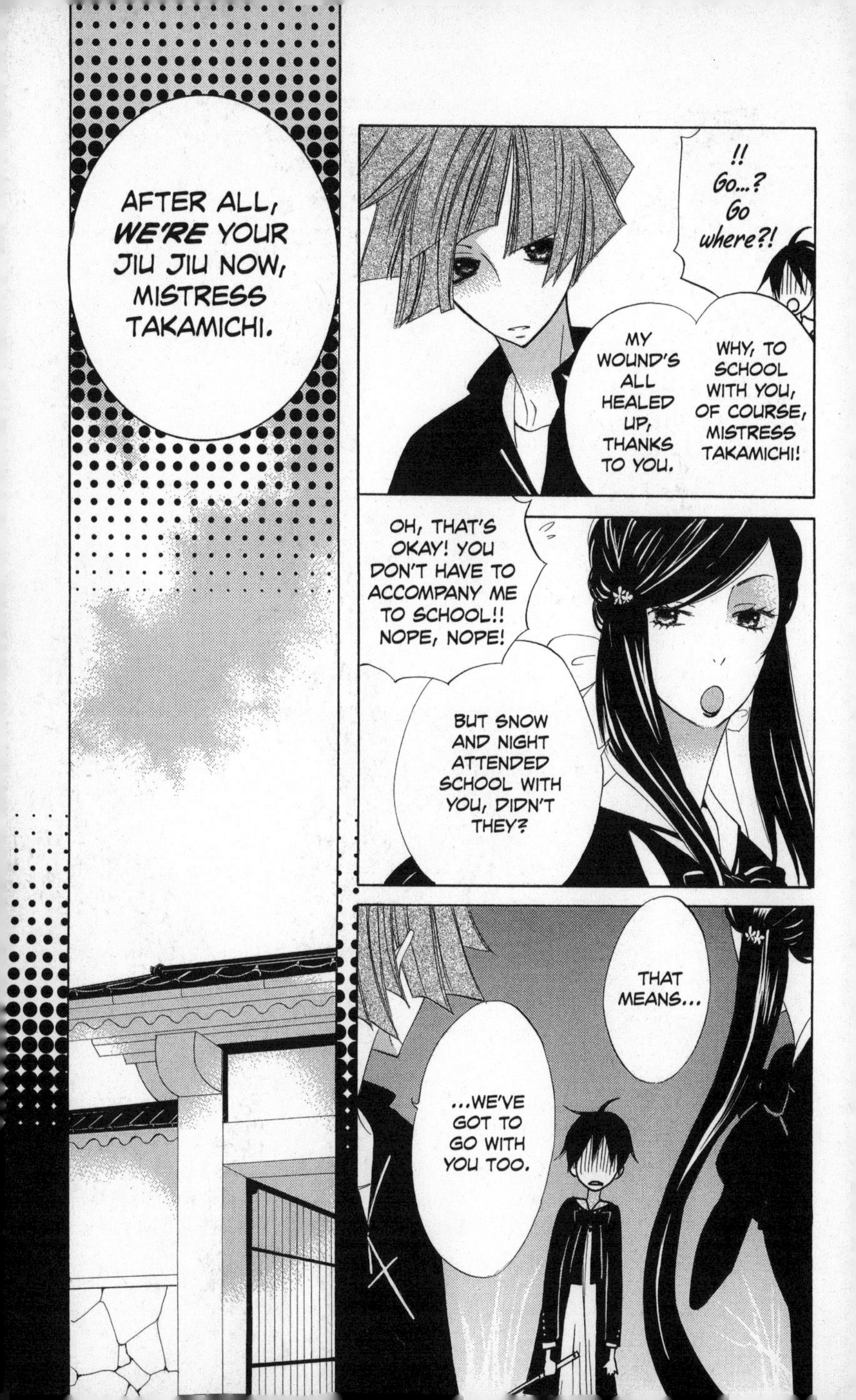
!! Go...? Go where?!
WHY, TO SCHOOL WITH YOU, OF COURSE, MISTRESS TAKAMICHI!
MY WOUND'S ALL HEALED UP, THANKS TO YOU.
OH, THAT'S OKAY! YOU DON'T HAVE TO ACCOMPANY ME TO SCHOOL!! NOPE, NOPE!
BUT SNOW AND NIGHT ATTENDED SCHOOL WITH YOU, DIDN'T THEY?
THAT MEANS...
...WE'VE GOT TO GO WITH YOU TOO.
AFTER ALL, ***WE'RE*** YOUR JIU JIU NOW, MISTRESS TAKAMICHI.

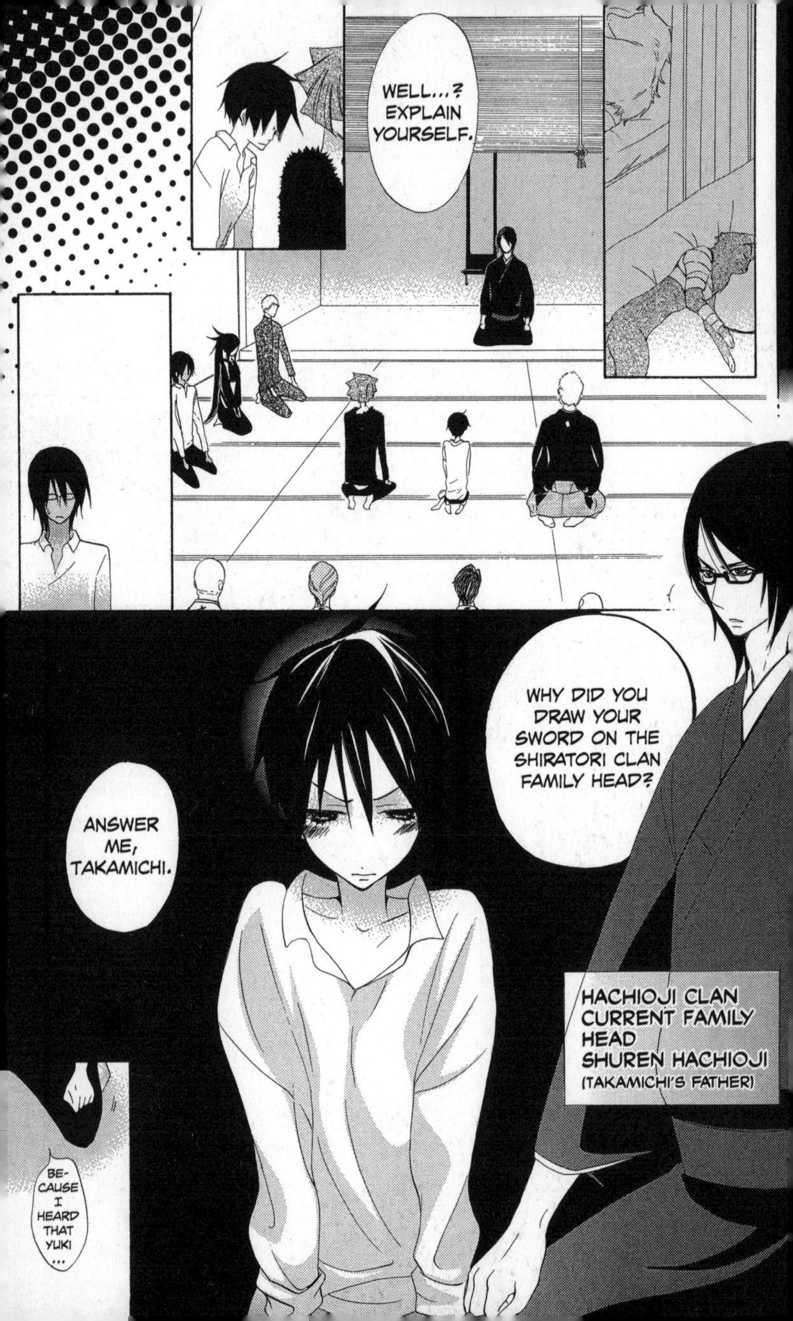
WELL...? EXPLAIN YOURSELF.
WHY DID YOU DRAW YOUR SWORD ON THE SHIRATORI CLAN FAMILY HEAD?
ANSWER ME, TAKAMICHI.
HACHIOJI CLAN CURRENT FAMILY HEAD SHUREN HACHIOJI (TAKAMICHI'S FATHER)
BE-CAUSE I HEARD THAT YUKI...

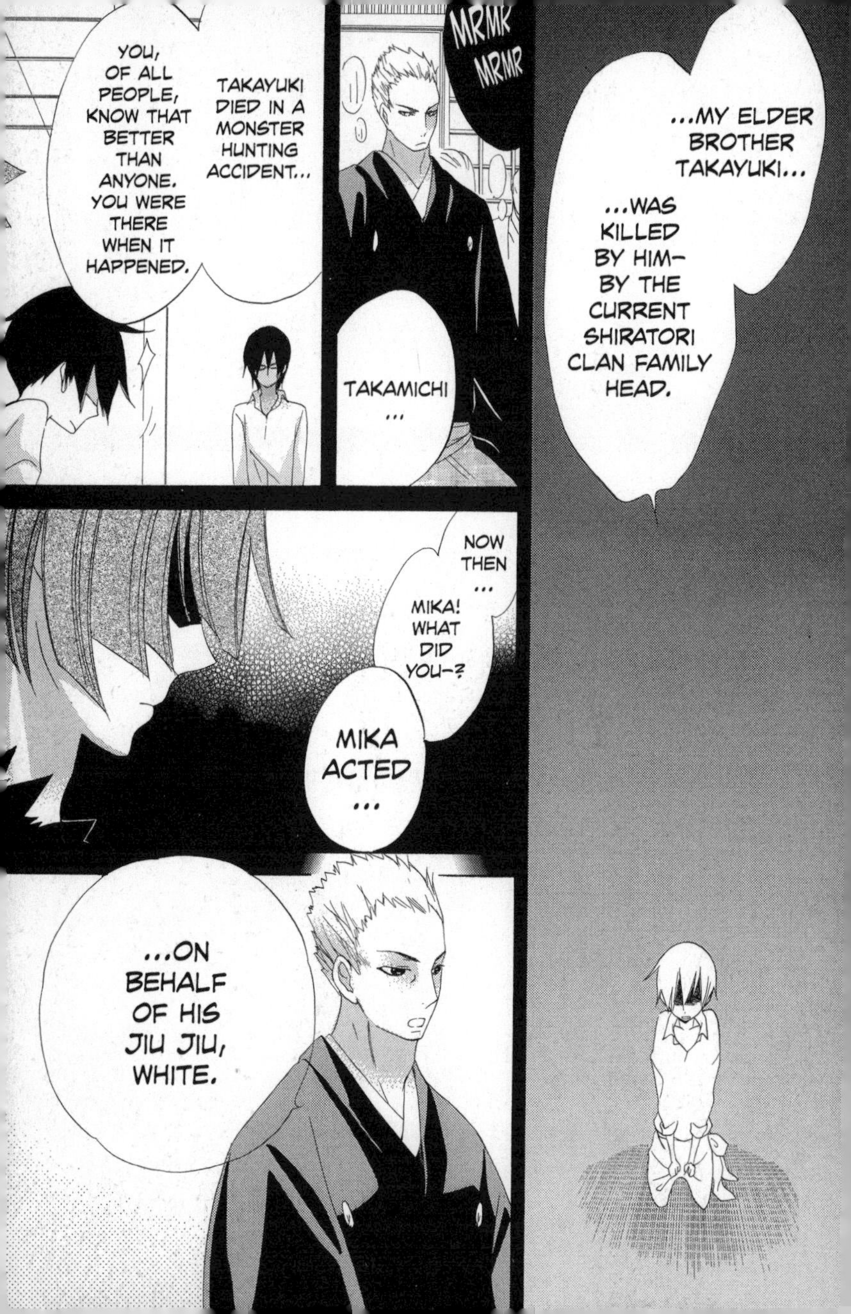
...MY ELDER BROTHER TAKAYUKI...
...WAS KILLED BY HIM-BY THE CURRENT SHIRATORI CLAN FAMILY HEAD.
MRMK MRMR
TAKAMICHI ...
TAKAYUKI DIED IN A MONSTER HUNTING ACCIDENT...
YOU, OF ALL PEOPLE, KNOW THAT BETTER THAN ANYONE. YOU WERE THERE WHEN IT HAPPENED.
NOW THEN ...
MIKA! WHAT DID YOU-?
MIKA ACTED ...
...ON BEHALF OF HIS JIU JIU, WHITE.

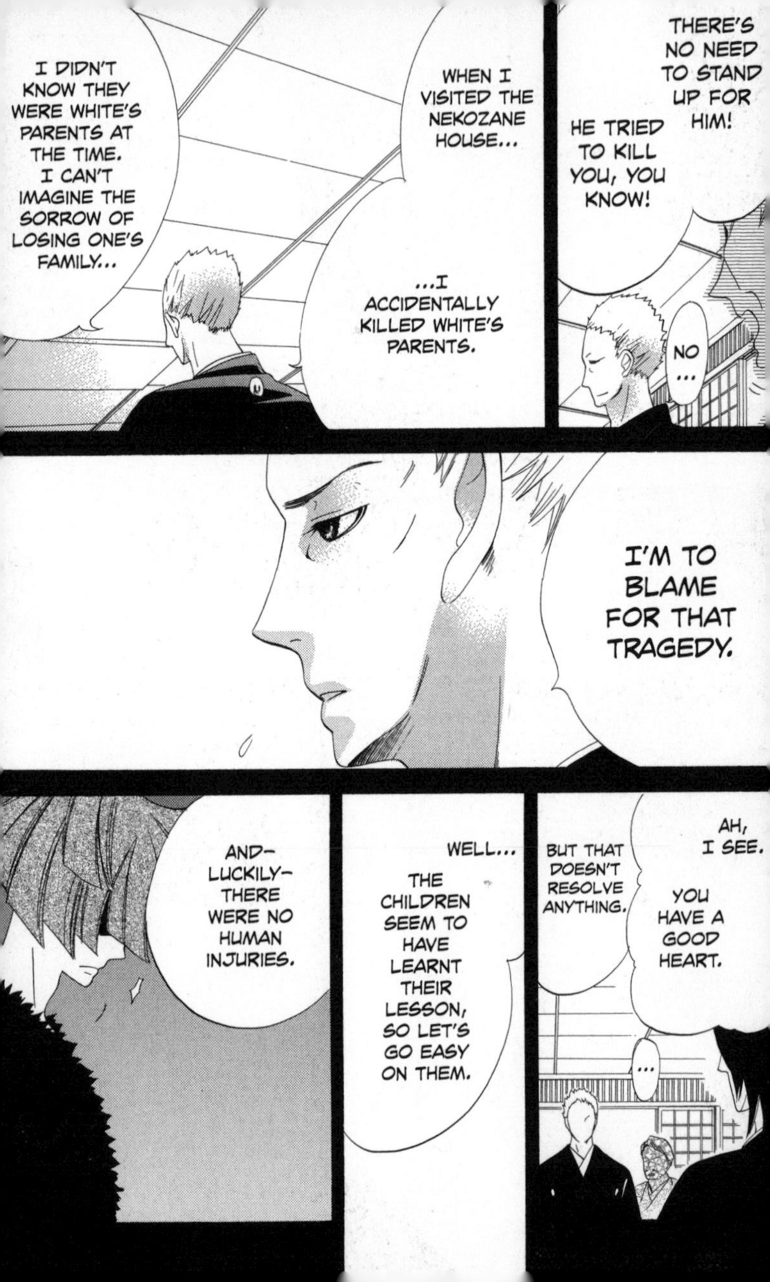
THERE'S NO NEED TO STAND UP FOR HIM!
HE TRIED TO KILL YOU, YOU KNOW!
NO...
WHEN I VISITED THE NEKOZANE HOUSE...
...I ACCIDENTALLY KILLED WHITE'S PARENTS.
I DIDN'T KNOW THEY WERE WHITE'S PARENTS AT THE TIME. I CAN'T IMAGINE THE SORROW OF LOSING ONE'S FAMILY...
I'M TO BLAME FOR THAT TRAGEDY.
AH, I SEE.
YOU HAVE A GOOD HEART.
BUT THAT DOESN'T RESOLVE ANYTHING.
...
WELL...
THE CHILDREN SEEM TO HAVE LEARNT THEIR LESSON, SO LET'S GO EASY ON THEM.
AND—LUCKILY—THERE WERE NO HUMAN INJURIES.

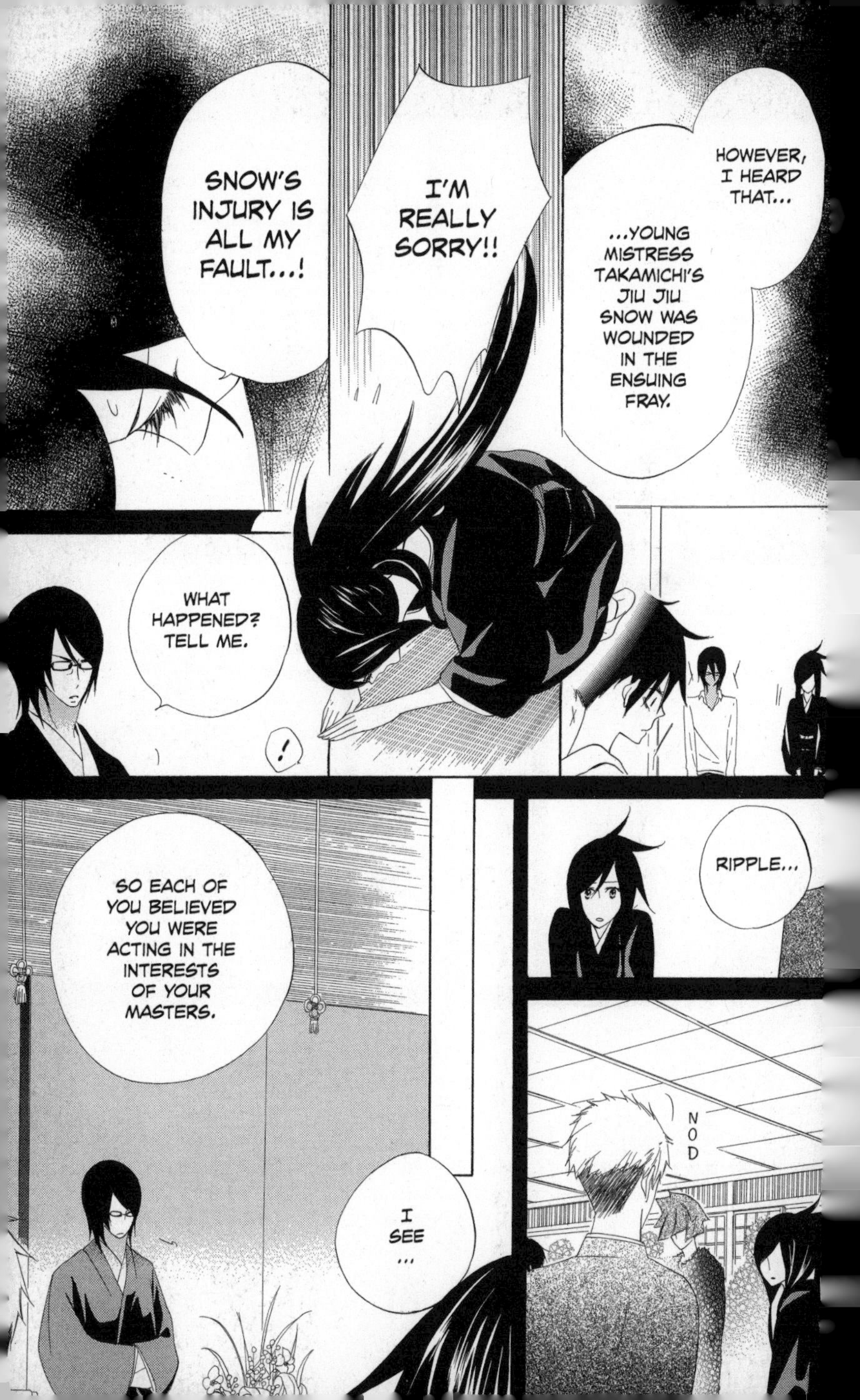
HOWEVER, I HEARD THAT...
...YOUNG MISTRESS TAKAMICHI'S JIU JIU SNOW WAS WOUNDED IN THE ENSUING FRAY.
I'M REALLY SORRY!!
SNOW'S INJURY IS ALL MY FAULT...!
WHAT HAPPENED? TELL ME.
!
RIPPLE...
NOD
SO EACH OF YOU BELIEVED YOU WERE ACTING IN THE INTERESTS OF YOUR MASTERS.
I SEE ...

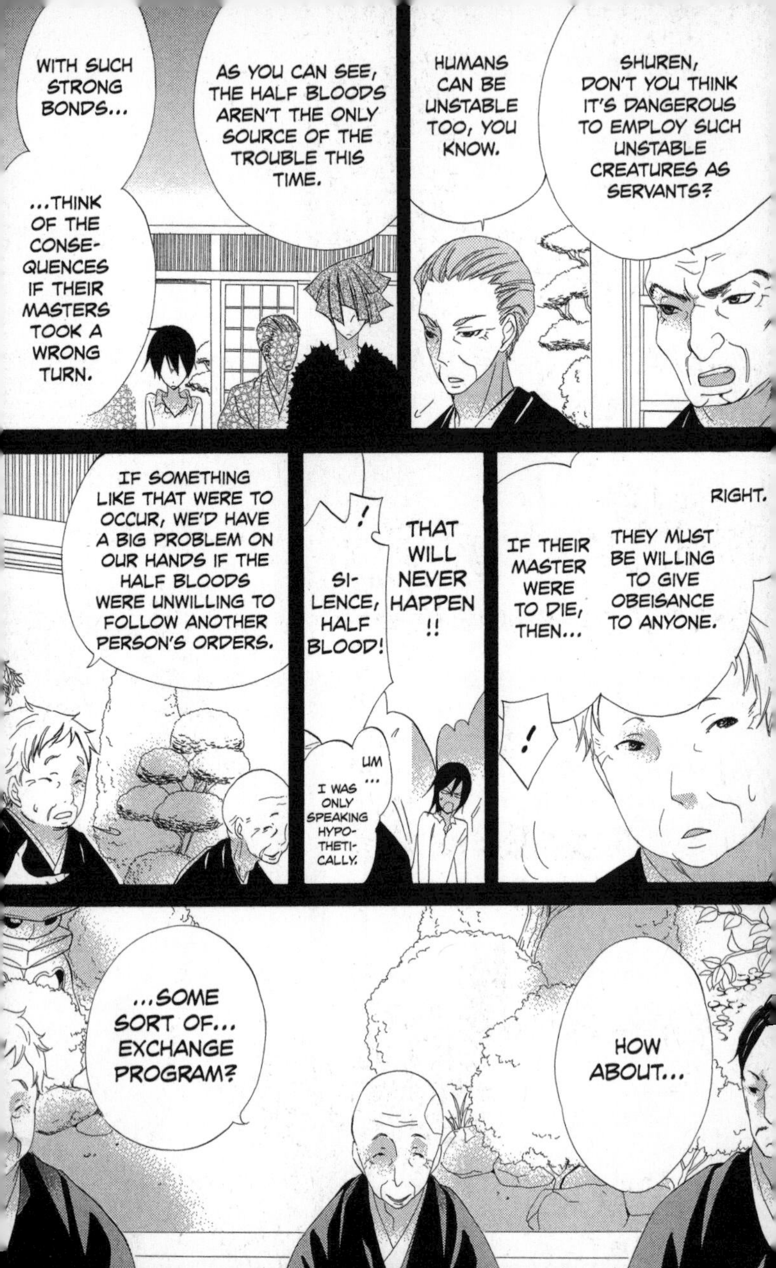
SHUREN, DON'T YOU THINK IT'S DANGEROUS TO EMPLOY SUCH UNSTABLE CREATURES AS SERVANTS?
HUMANS CAN BE UNSTABLE TOO, YOU KNOW.
AS YOU CAN SEE, THE HALF BLOODS AREN'T THE ONLY SOURCE OF THE TROUBLE THIS TIME.
WITH SUCH STRONG BONDS...
...THINK OF THE CONSE-QUENCES IF THEIR MASTERS TOOK A WRONG TURN.
RIGHT.
THEY MUST BE WILLING TO GIVE OBEISANCE TO ANYONE.
IF THEIR MASTER WERE TO DIE, THEN...
!
THAT WILL NEVER HAPPEN!!
!
SI-LENCE, HALF BLOOD!
UM...
I WAS ONLY SPEAKING HYPO-THETI-CALLY.
IF SOMETHING LIKE THAT WERE TO OCCUR, WE'D HAVE A BIG PROBLEM ON OUR HANDS IF THE HALF BLOODS WERE UNWILLING TO FOLLOW ANOTHER PERSON'S ORDERS.
HOW ABOUT...
...SOME SORT OF... EXCHANGE PROGRAM?

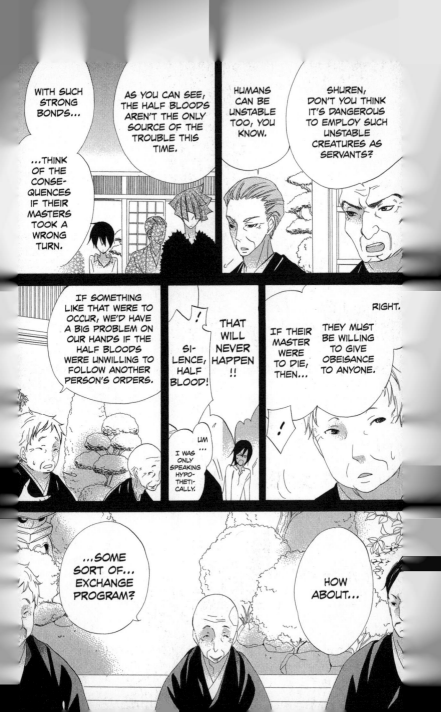

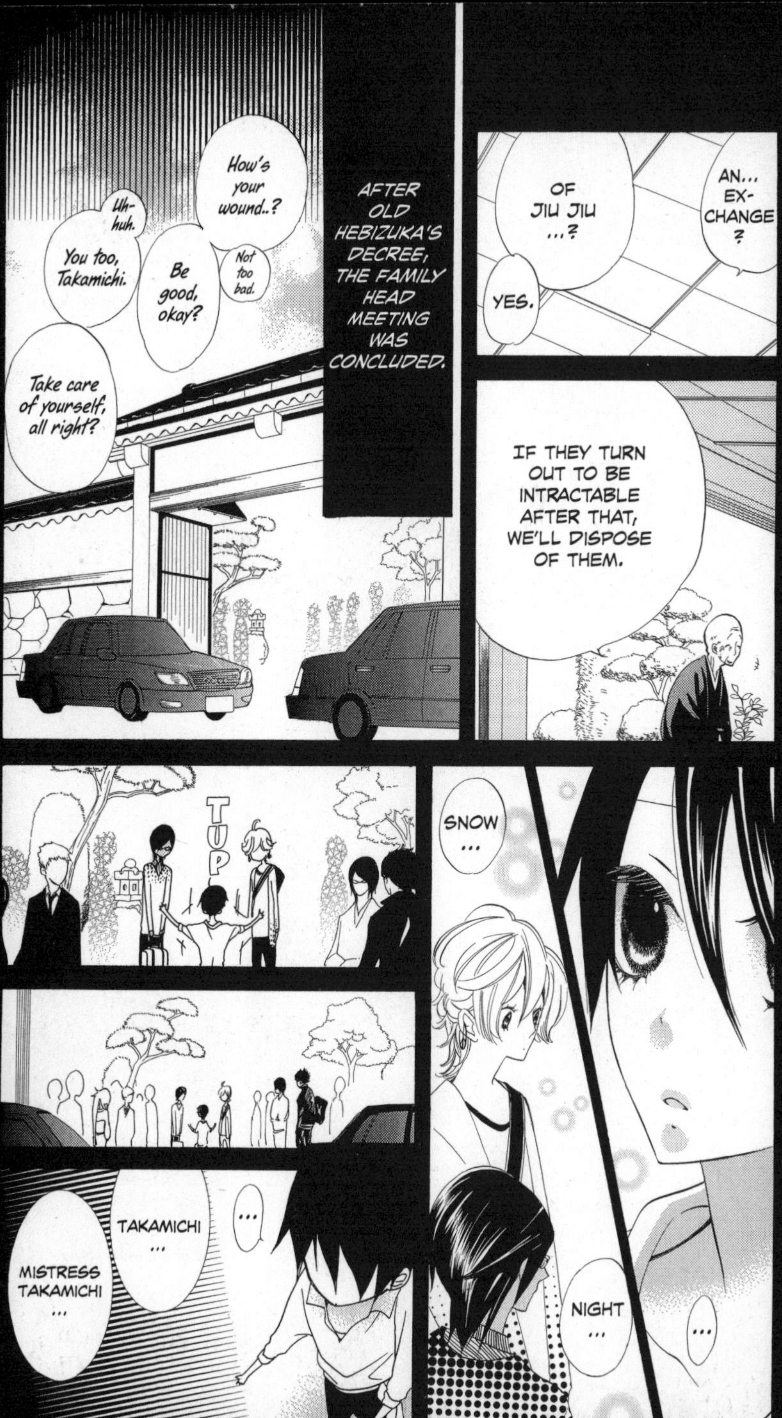
AN... EX-CHANGE?
OF JIU JIU ...?
YES.
IF THEY TURN OUT TO BE INTRACTABLE AFTER THAT, WE'LL DISPOSE OF THEM.
AFTER OLD HEBIZUKA'S DECREE, THE FAMILY HEAD MEETING WAS CONCLUDED.
How's your wound..?
Not too bad.
Uh-huh.
Be good, okay?
You too, Takamichi.
Take care of yourself, all right?
SNOW ...
...
NIGHT ...
TUP
...
TAKAMICHI ...
MISTRESS TAKAMICHI ...

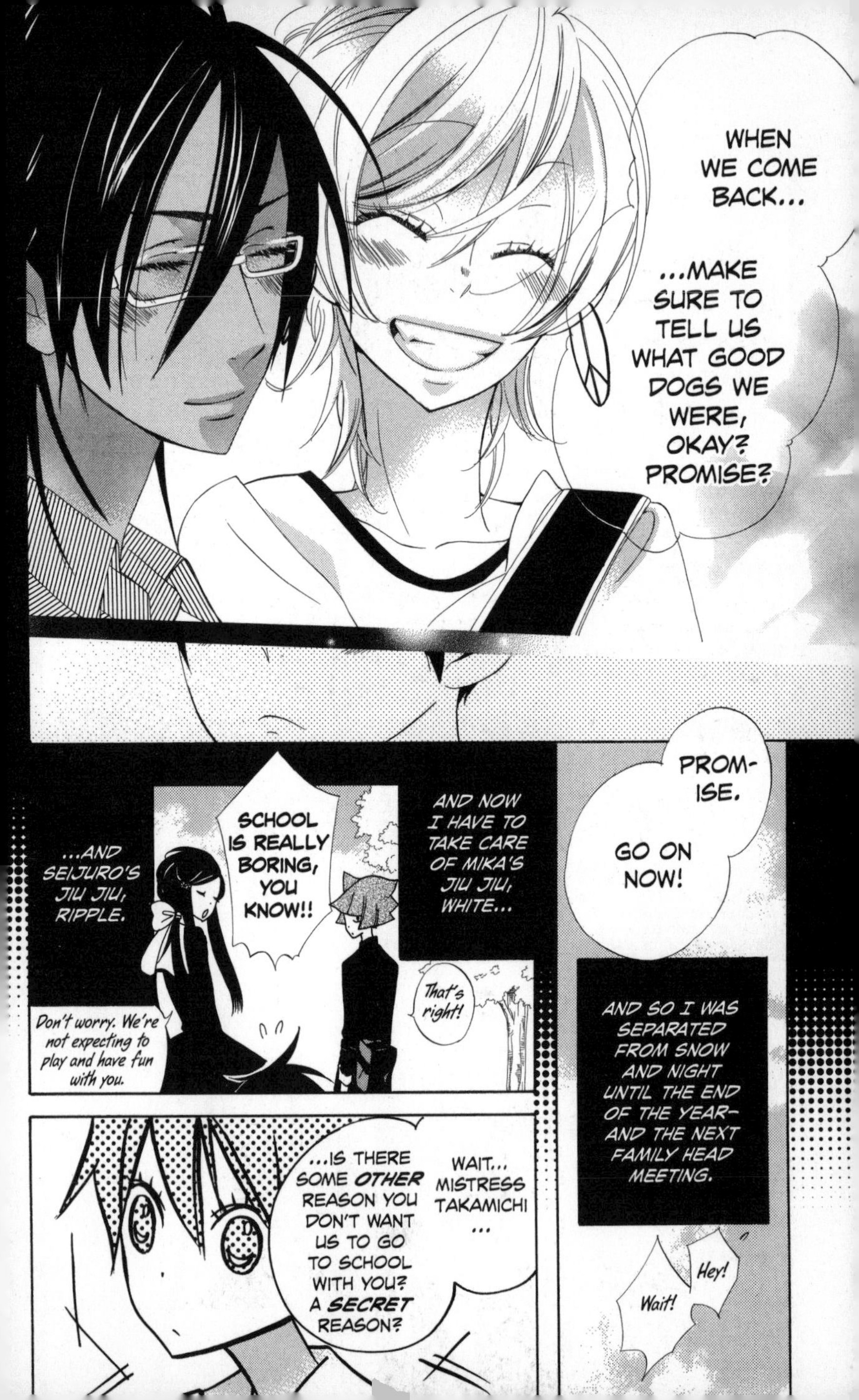
WHEN WE COME BACK...
...MAKE SURE TO TELL US WHAT GOOD DOGS WE WERE, OKAY? PROMISE?
PROMISE.
GO ON NOW!
AND SO I WAS SEPARATED FROM SNOW AND NIGHT UNTIL THE END OF THE YEAR—AND THE NEXT FAMILY HEAD MEETING.
Hey!
Wait!
AND NOW I HAVE TO TAKE CARE OF MIKA'S JIU JIU, WHITE...
SCHOOL IS REALLY BORING, YOU KNOW!!
...AND SEIJURO'S JIU JIU, RIPPLE.
That's right!
Don't worry. We're not expecting to play and have fun with you.
WAIT... MISTRESS TAKAMICHI ...
...IS THERE SOME OTHER REASON YOU DON'T WANT US TO GO TO SCHOOL WITH YOU? A SECRET REASON?

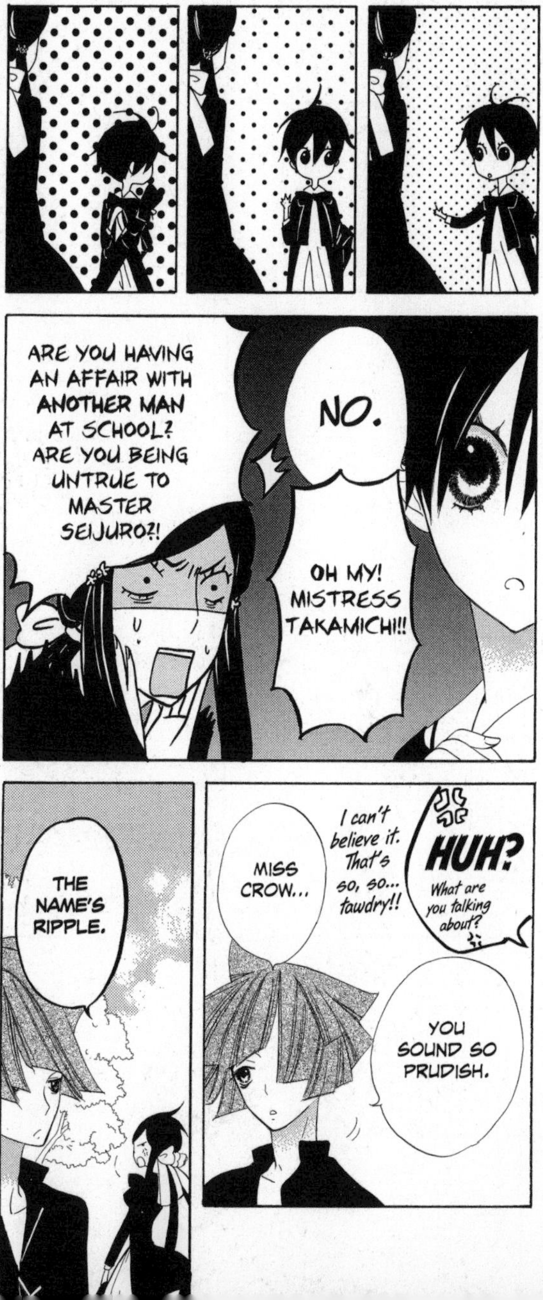
OH MY! MISTRESS TAKAMICHI!!
ARE YOU HAVING AN AFFAIR WITH ANOTHER MAN AT SCHOOL? ARE YOU BEING UNTRUE TO MASTER SEIJURO?!
NO.
I can't believe it. That's so, so... tawdry!!
HUH? What are you talking about?
YOU SOUND SO PRUDISH.
MISS CROW...
THE NAME'S RIPPLE.

One year later, Jiu Jiu volume 4...

Are you guy's comin' after me?!

Uh... Well, to be exact, you ladies!!

?? Well, 80% ladies...!

Snow and Night are almost four years old. That would make them about thirty years old according to the age ratio for large dogs, right? Or would they age differently because they're half human?

Hyogo Prefecture: Chinatty

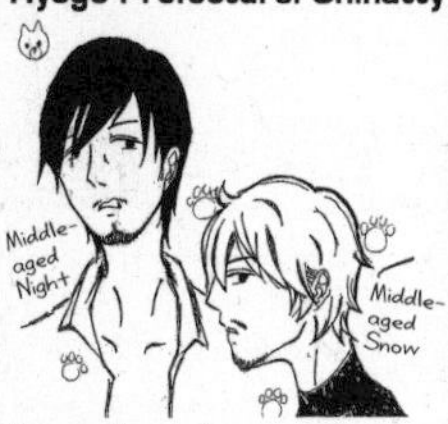
Middle-aged Night
Middle-aged Snow

Um, well, you know, some people do look young for their age. I think that explains it. But then again... I kind of like the idea of middle-aged Night and Snow!

Hello! Tobi-meow here.

What gender are you, Tobina?

Tottori Prefecture: Tobunki and many others

I've received a lot of questions about this. I hope you're not disappointed that I'm female!! Hmph. I have such a strange name!!

From now on, I'll call myself Touya♀Tobina!

But that's kind of awkward. And it looks kind of... you know...

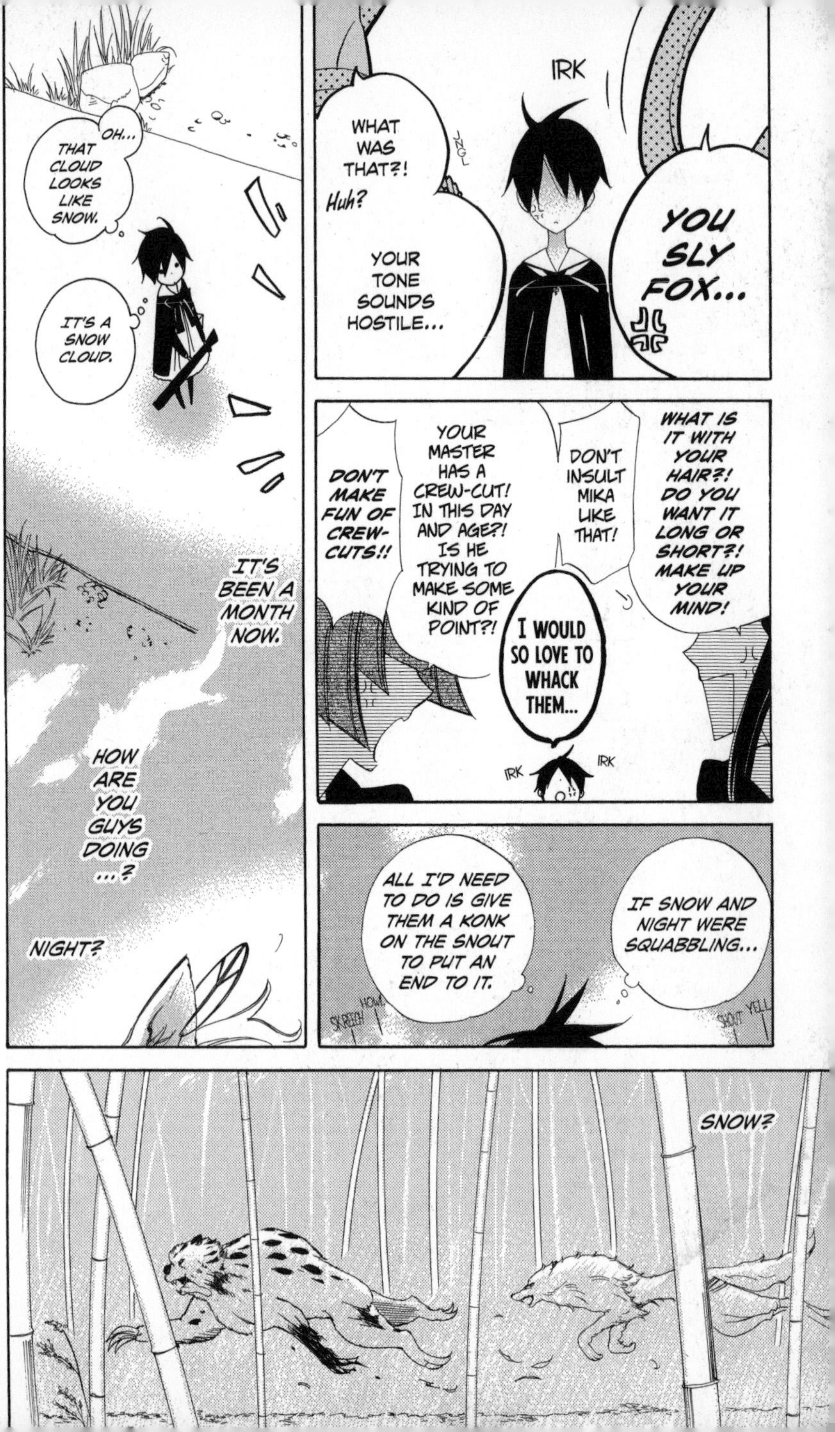
IRK
YOU SLY FOX...
WHAT WAS THAT?!
JNGL
Huh?
YOUR TONE SOUNDS HOSTILE...
WHAT IS IT WITH YOUR HAIR?! DO YOU WANT IT LONG OR SHORT?! MAKE UP YOUR MIND!
DON'T INSULT MIKA LIKE THAT!
YOUR MASTER HAS A CREW-CUT! IN THIS DAY AND AGE?! IS HE TRYING TO MAKE SOME KIND OF POINT?!
DON'T MAKE FUN OF CREW-CUTS!!
I WOULD SO LOVE TO WHACK THEM...
IRK
IRK
IF SNOW AND NIGHT WERE SQUABBLING...
YELL
SHOUT
ALL I'D NEED TO DO IS GIVE THEM A KONK ON THE SNOUT TO PUT AN END TO IT.
HOWL
SKREECH
OH... THAT CLOUD LOOKS LIKE SNOW.
IT'S A SNOW CLOUD.
IT'S BEEN A MONTH NOW.
HOW ARE YOU GUYS DOING ...?
NIGHT?
SNOW?

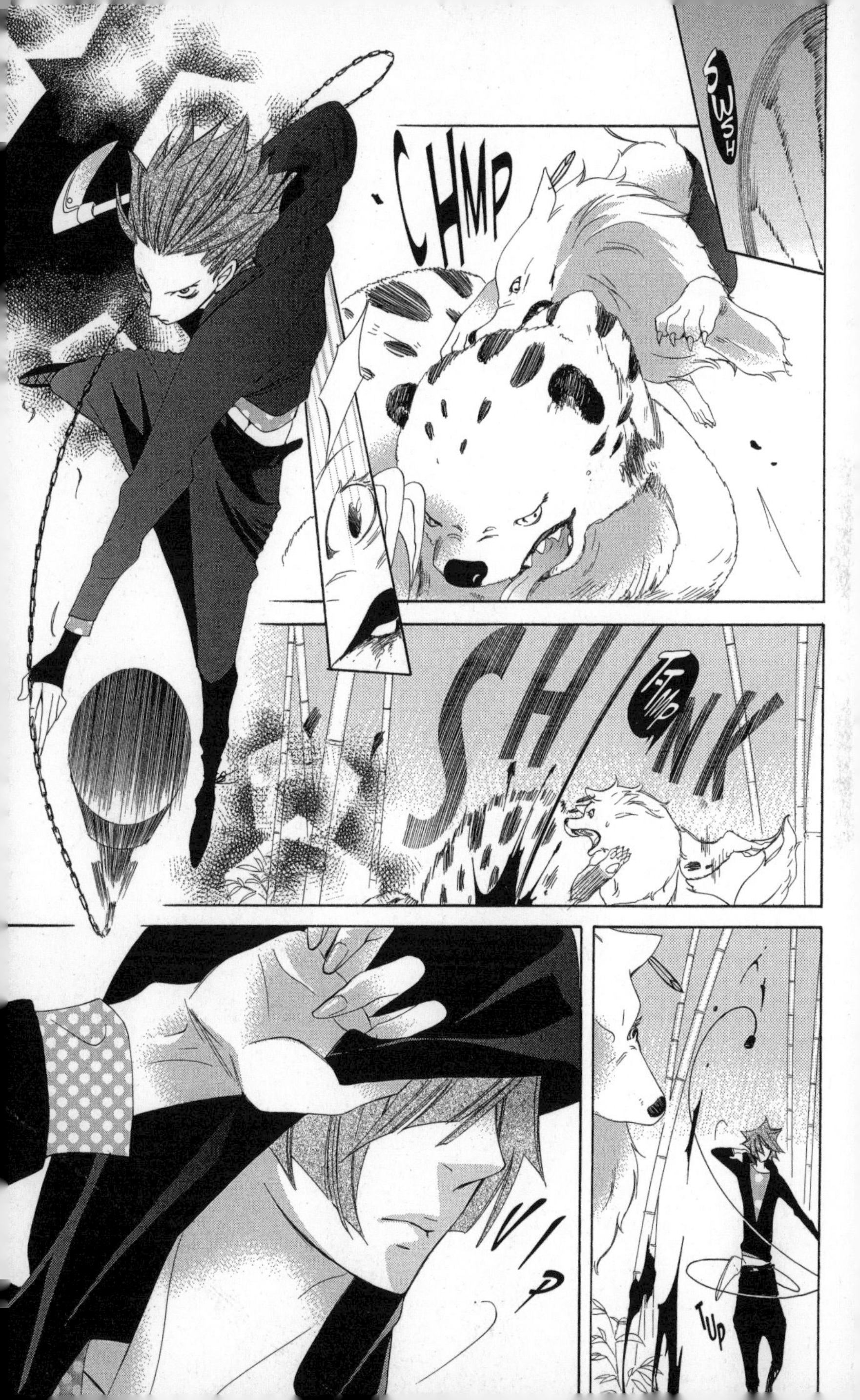
SWSH
CHMP
SCHNK
T-TMP
TUP
!?

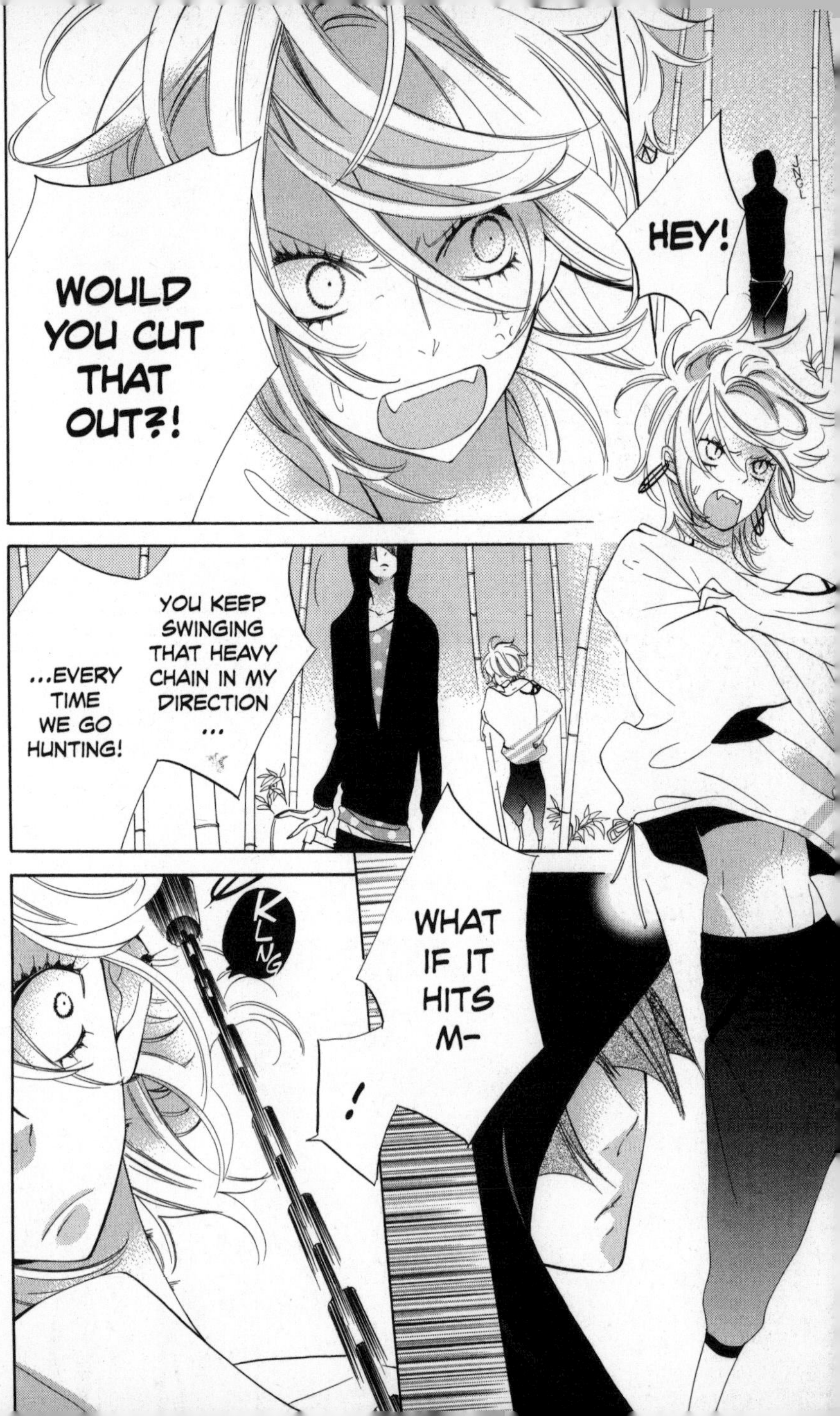
JNGL
HEY!
WOULD YOU CUT THAT OUT?!
YOU KEEP SWINGING THAT HEAVY CHAIN IN MY DIRECTION ...
...EVERY TIME WE GO HUNTING!
WHAT IF IT HITS M-
KLNG
!

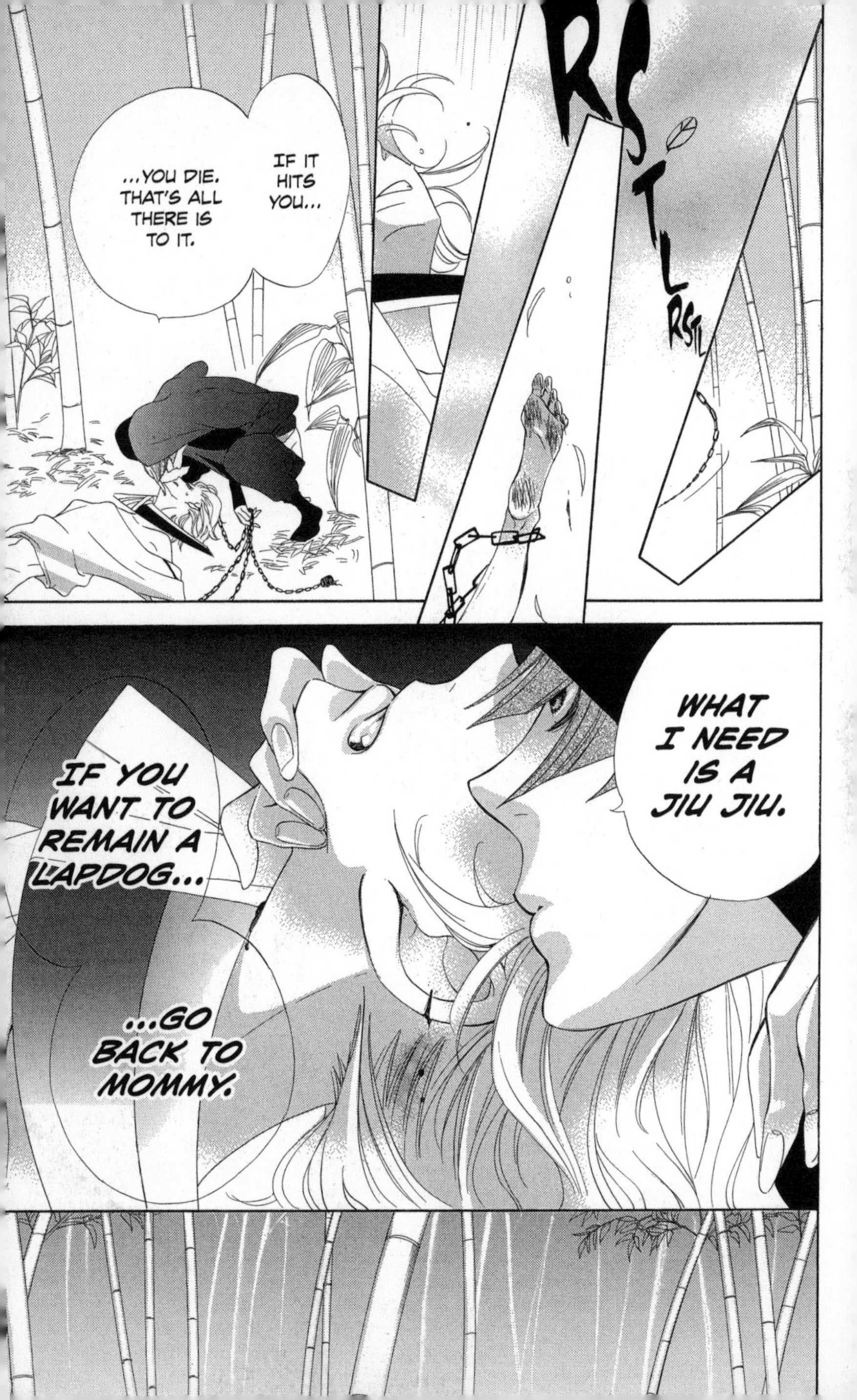
RSTL
RSTL
IF IT HITS YOU...
...YOU DIE. THAT'S ALL THERE IS TO IT.
WHAT I NEED IS A JIU JIU.
IF YOU WANT TO REMAIN A LAPDOG...
...GO BACK TO MOMMY.

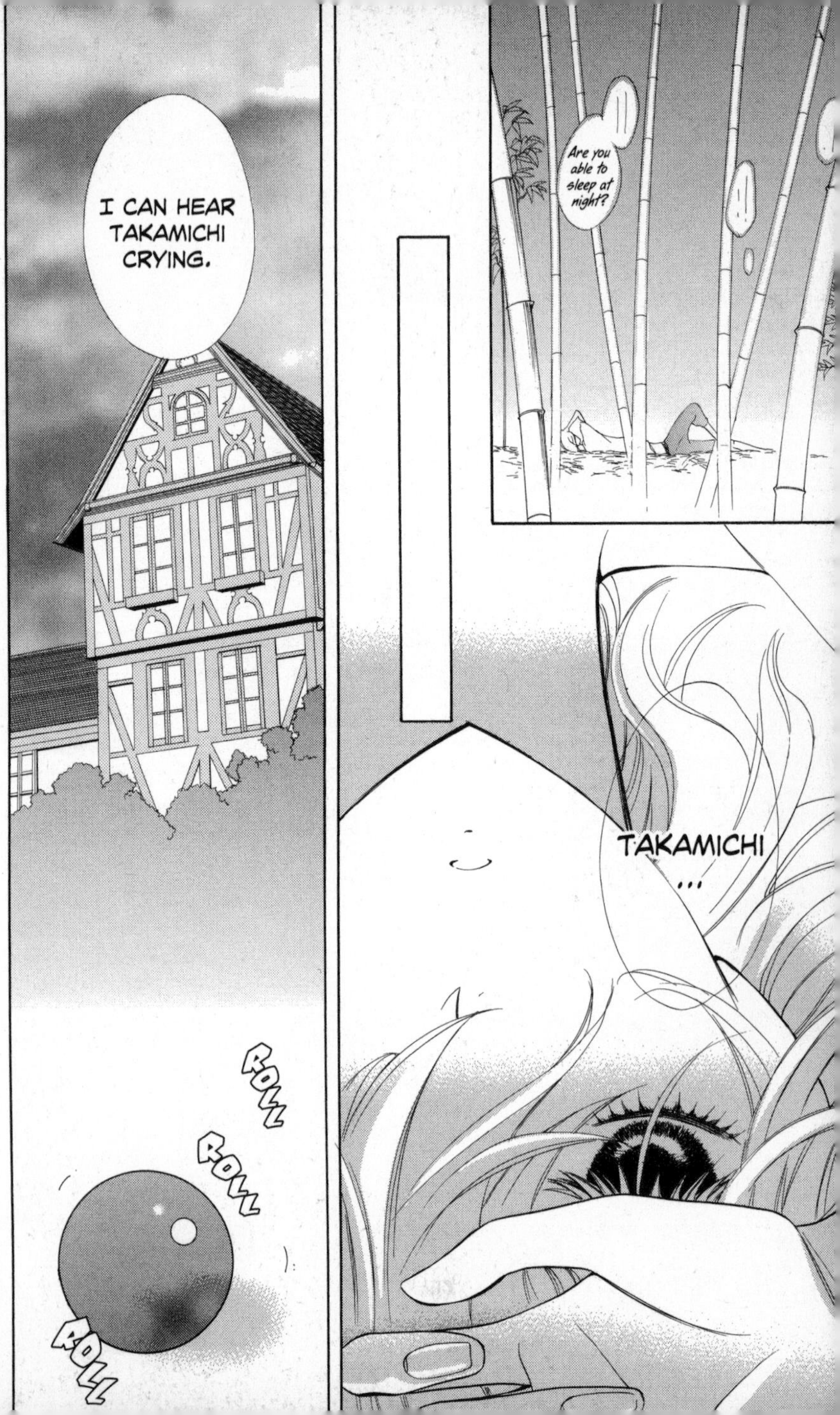
Are you able to sleep at night?
TAKAMICHI ...
I CAN HEAR TAKAMICHI CRYING.
ROLL
ROLL
ROLL

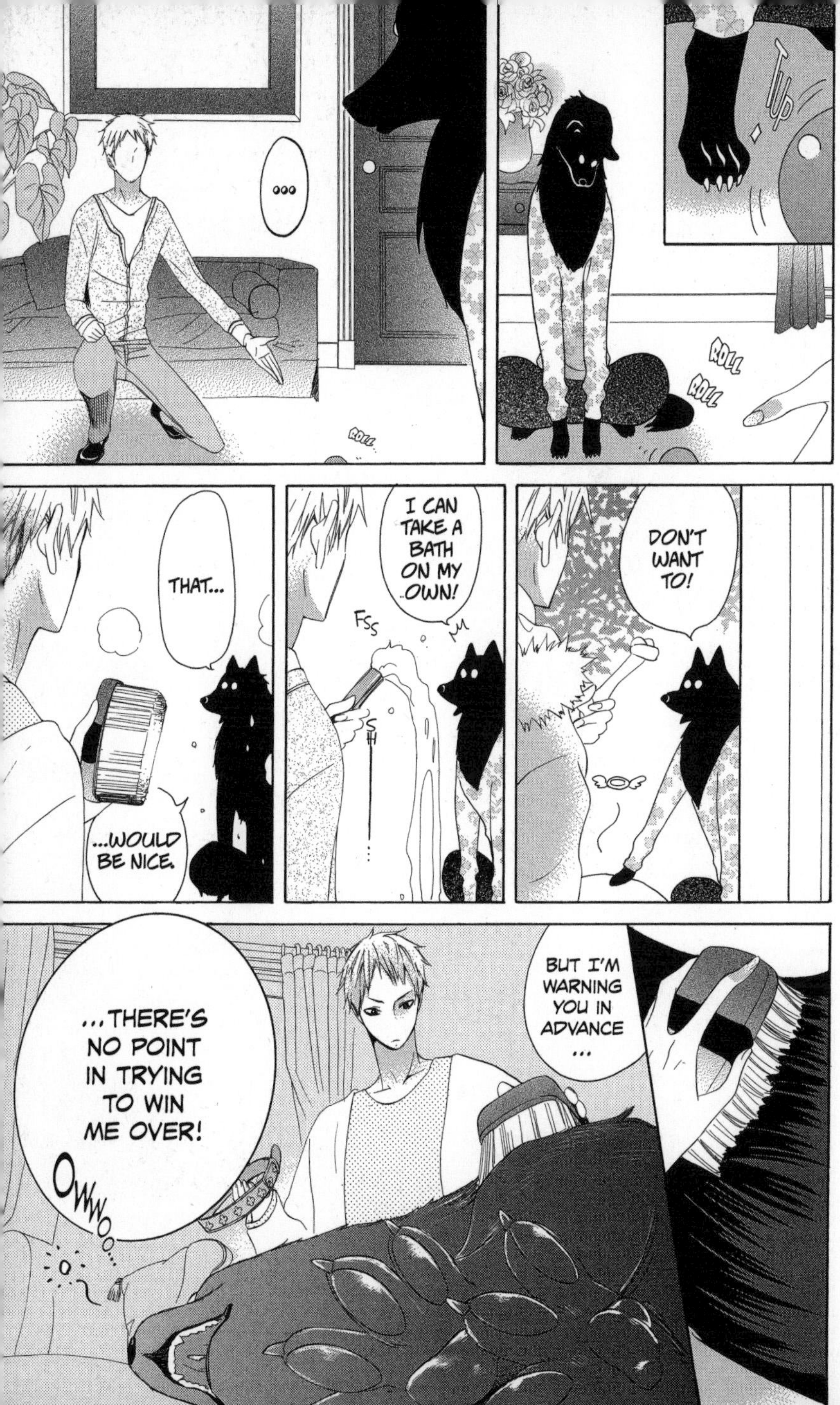
TUP
ROLL
ROLL
...
ROLL
DON'T WANT TO!
I CAN TAKE A BATH ON MY OWN!
FSS
SH
THAT...
...WOULD BE NICE.
BUT I'M WARNING YOU IN ADVANCE...
...THERE'S NO POINT IN TRYING TO WIN ME OVER!
OWWOO...

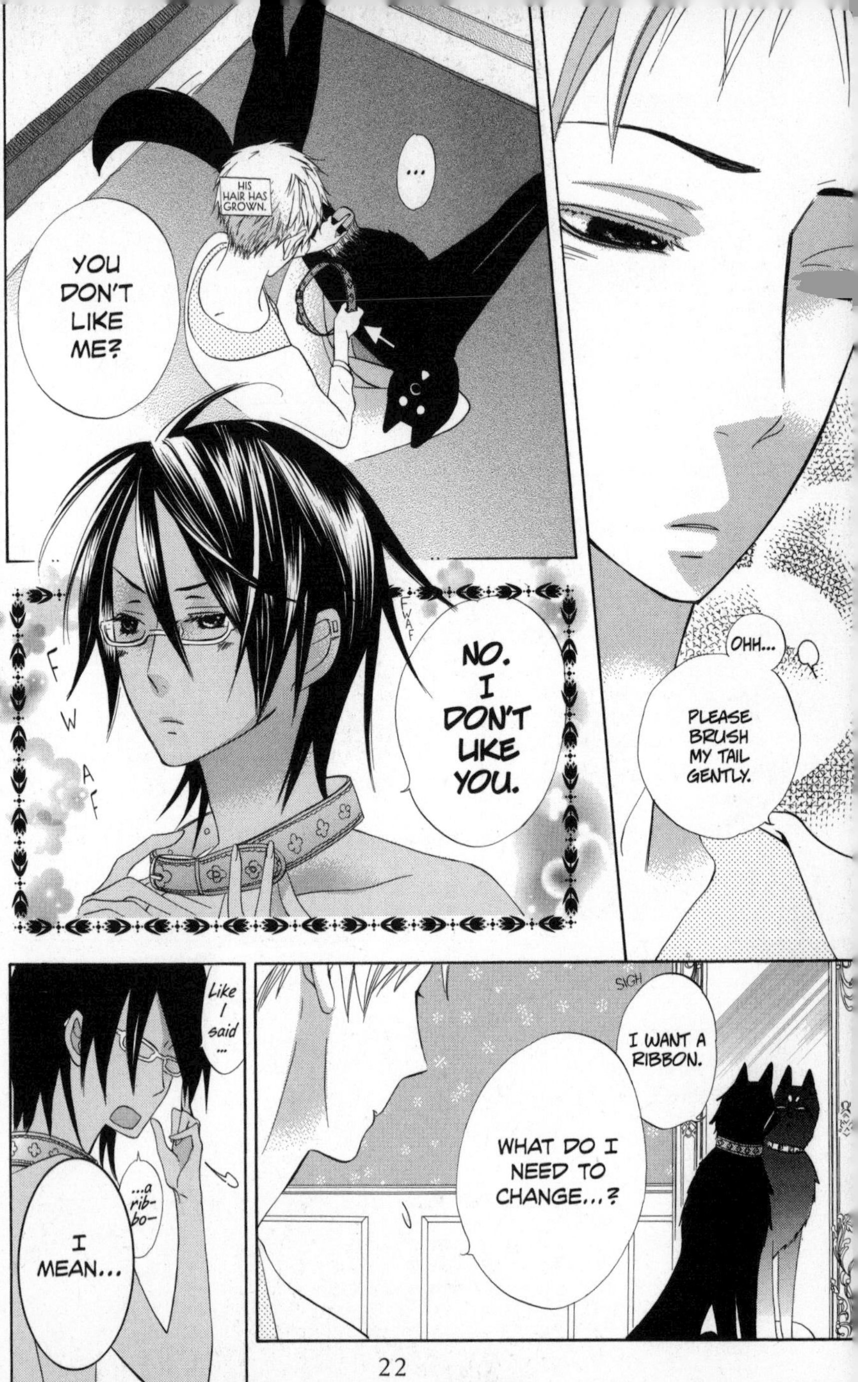
OHH...
PLEASE BRUSH MY TAIL GENTLY.
...
HIS HAIR HAS GROWN.
YOU DON'T LIKE ME?
FWAF
FWAF
NO. I DON'T LIKE YOU.
SIGH
I WANT A RIBBON.
WHAT DO I NEED TO CHANGE...?
Like I said...
...a rib-bo—
I MEAN...

What's wrong with a crew-cut?

Seijuro naturally ended up with bi-colored hair after I initially established his character as a partially fledged swan.

But when I was drawing him, I noticed... Hey, this isn't a crew-cut after all!! He ended up looking like Takamichi's doctor, Gen. (Although Gen actually has white hair.)

The reason his hair is growing out now isn't because he changed his mind about liking crew-cuts! It's just because he's so busy with Night that he doesn't have time to get a haircut!

After all, **personally**, I love crew-cuts.♡

Why does Ripple like the color white so much?

Gunma Prefecture: Myoya

Okay, I'm going to keep answering your questions (from time to time).

As a member of the Shiratori* clan, Ripple has always wanted to be white. But since that will never happen...she at least wants her progeny to be white. I haven't written anything about it yet, but Seijuro's elder brother Kankuro, the family head of the Shiratori clan, has an albino Jiu Jiu named Tsunami. And that's why she's so hung up on the color white.

Oh, wow. I've written such a proper answer.

*WHITE BIRD

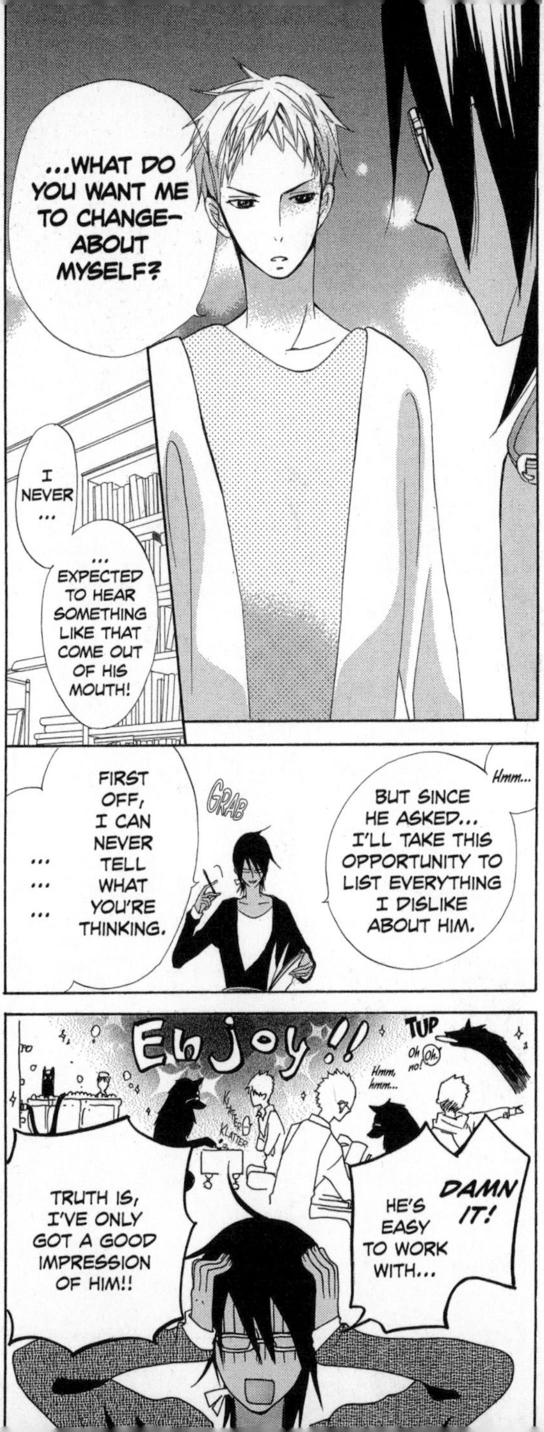
...WHAT DO YOU WANT ME TO CHANGE—ABOUT MYSELF?
I NEVER ...
... EXPECTED TO HEAR SOMETHING LIKE THAT COME OUT OF HIS MOUTH!
Hmm...
BUT SINCE HE ASKED... I'LL TAKE THIS OPPORTUNITY TO LIST EVERYTHING I DISLIKE ABOUT HIM.
GRAB
FIRST OFF, I CAN NEVER TELL WHAT YOU'RE THINKING.
... ...
TUP
Oh no!
Oh
Hmm, hmm...
Enjoy!!
KLATTER
KLATTER
DAMN IT!
HE'S EASY TO WORK WITH...
TRUTH IS, I'VE ONLY GOT A GOOD IMPRESSION OF HIM!!

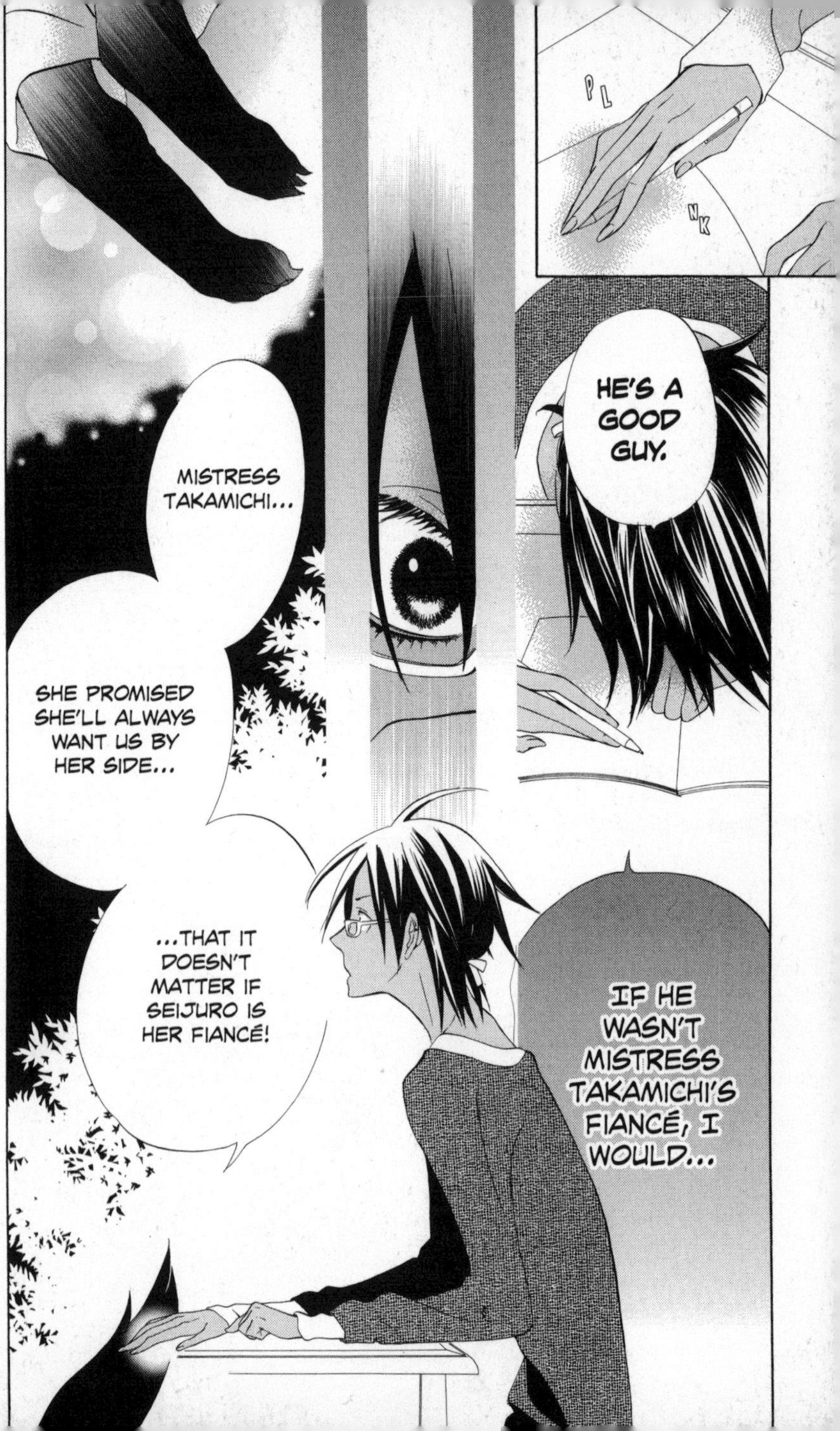
PL
NK
HE'S A GOOD GUY.
IF HE WASN'T MISTRESS TAKAMICHI'S FIANCÉ, I WOULD...
MISTRESS TAKAMICHI...
SHE PROMISED SHE'LL ALWAYS WANT US BY HER SIDE...
...THAT IT DOESN'T MATTER IF SEIJURO IS HER FIANCÉ!

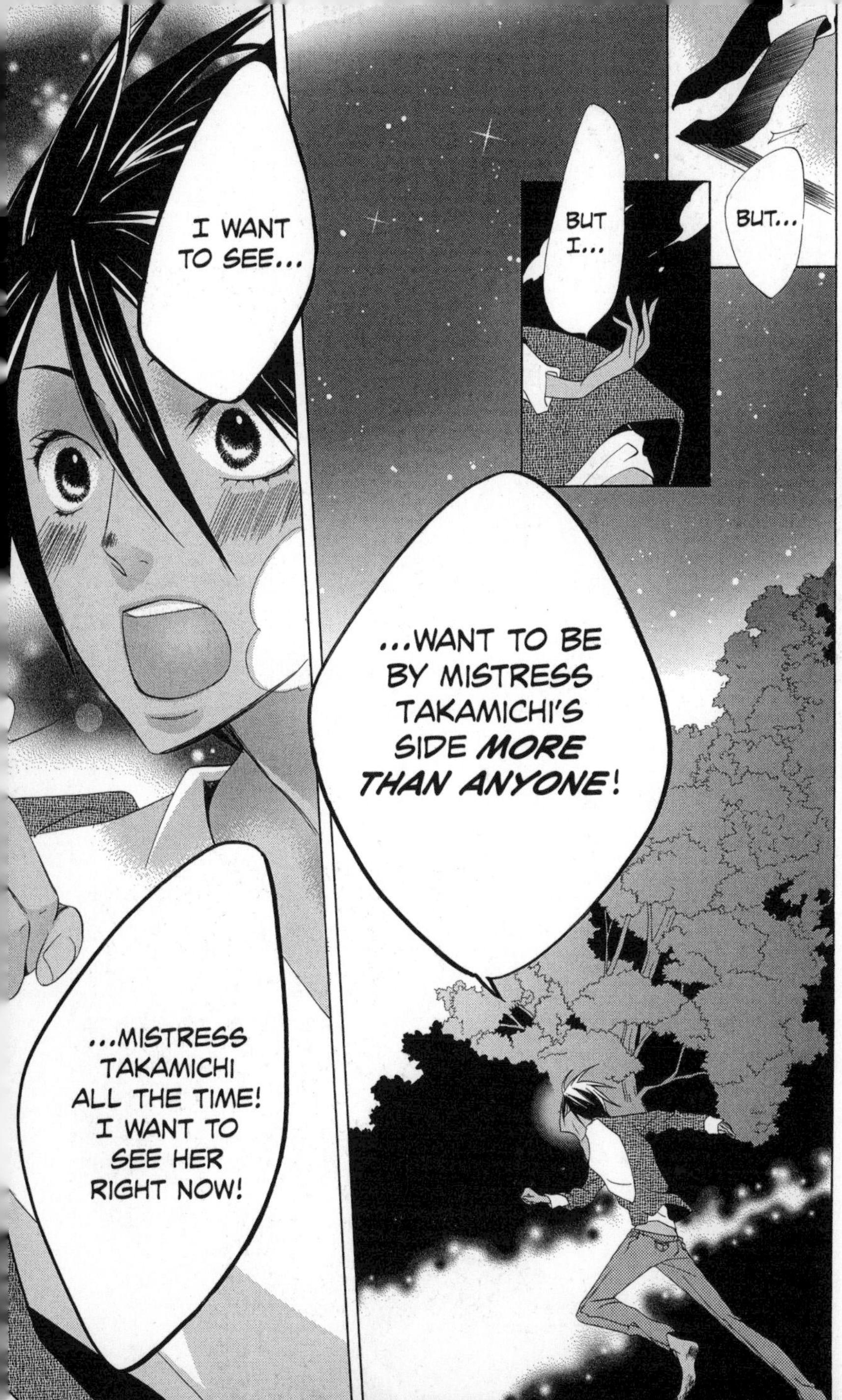
BUT...
BUT I...
...WANT TO BE BY MISTRESS TAKAMICHI'S SIDE *MORE THAN ANYONE*!
I WANT TO SEE...
...MISTRESS TAKAMICHI ALL THE TIME! I WANT TO SEE HER RIGHT NOW!

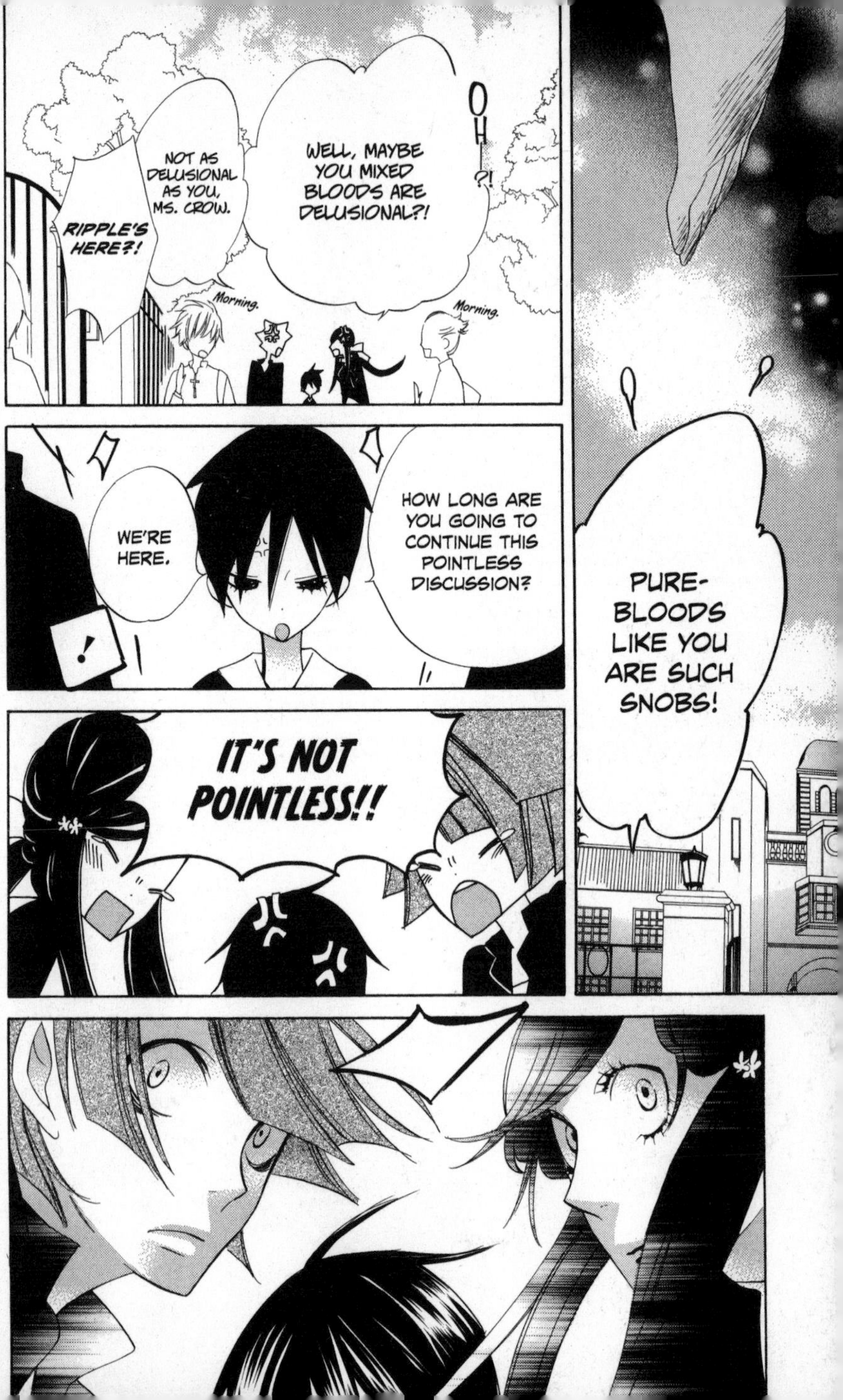
PURE-BLOODS LIKE YOU ARE SUCH SNOBS!
OH!?!
WELL, MAYBE YOU MIXED BLOODS ARE DELUSIONAL?!
NOT AS DELUSIONAL AS YOU, MS. CROW.
Morning.
RIPPLE'S HERE?!
Morning.
HOW LONG ARE YOU GOING TO CONTINUE THIS POINTLESS DISCUSSION?
WE'RE HERE.
!
IT'S NOT POINTLESS!!

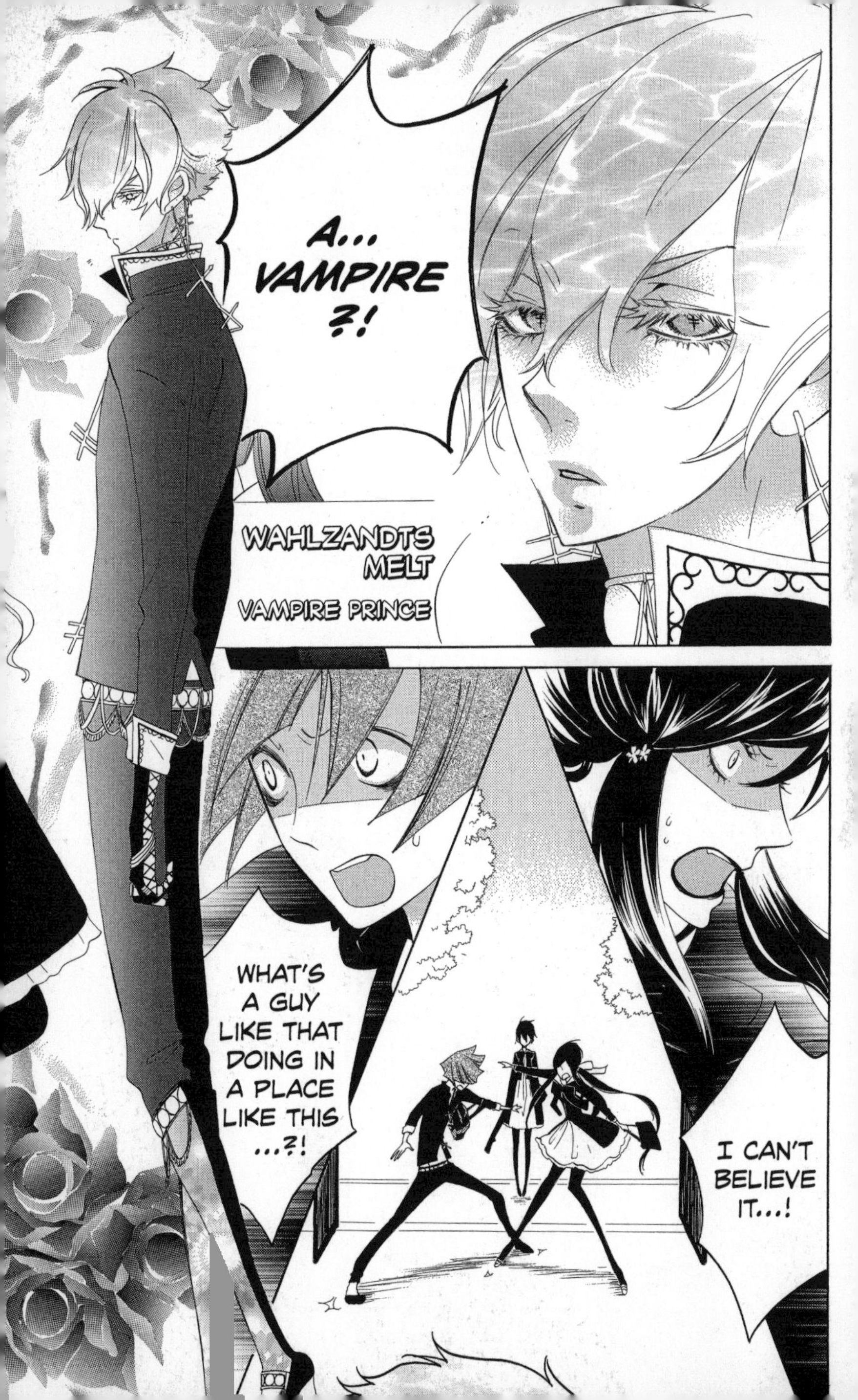
A... VAMPIRE ?!
WAHLZANDTS MELT
VAMPIRE PRINCE
I CAN'T BELIEVE IT...!
WHAT'S A GUY LIKE THAT DOING IN A PLACE LIKE THIS ...?!

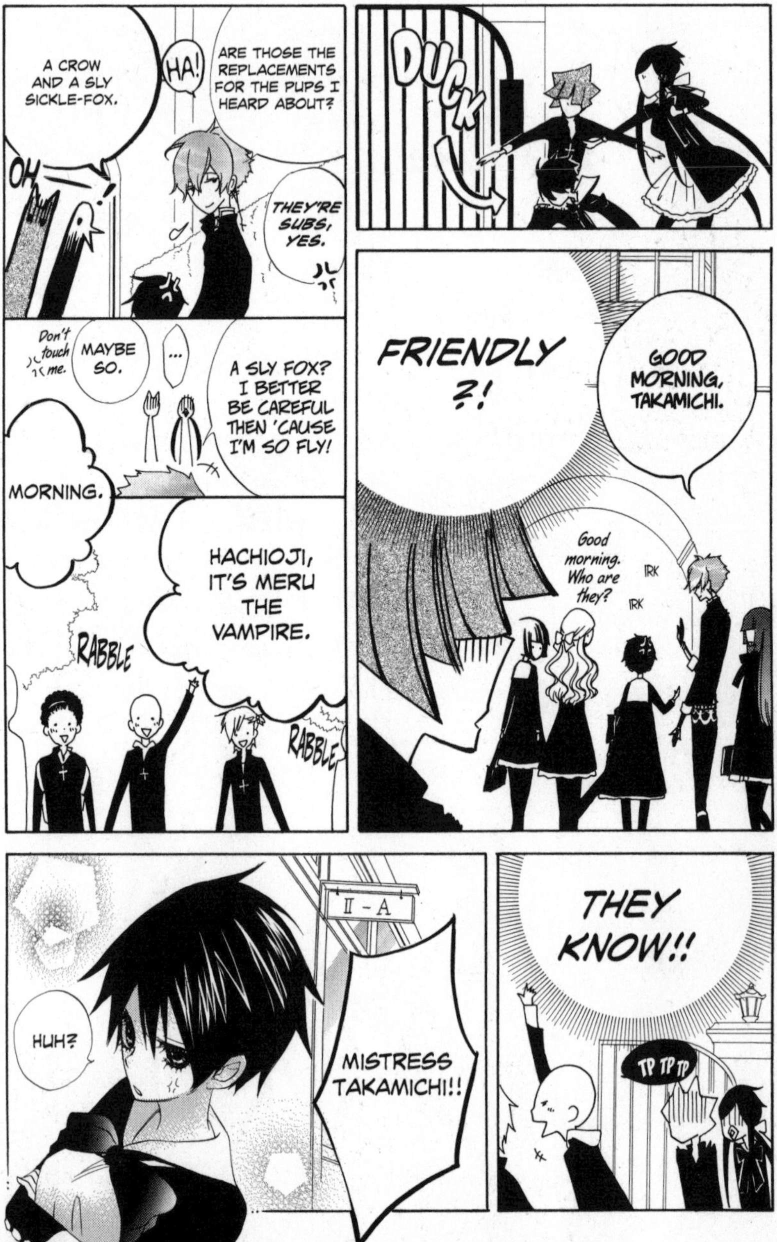
DUCK
ARE THOSE THE REPLACEMENTS FOR THE PUPS I HEARD ABOUT?
HA!
A CROW AND A SLY SICKLE-FOX.
OH—
THEY'RE SUBS, YES.
GOOD MORNING, TAKAMICHI.
FRIENDLY ?!
Good morning. Who are they?
IRK
IRK
A SLY FOX? I BETTER BE CAREFUL THEN 'CAUSE I'M SO FLY!
...
MAYBE SO.
Don't touch me.
MORNING.
HACHIOJI, IT'S MERU THE VAMPIRE.
RABBLE
RABBLE
THEY KNOW!!
TP TP TP
II - A
MISTRESS TAKAMICHI!!
HUH?

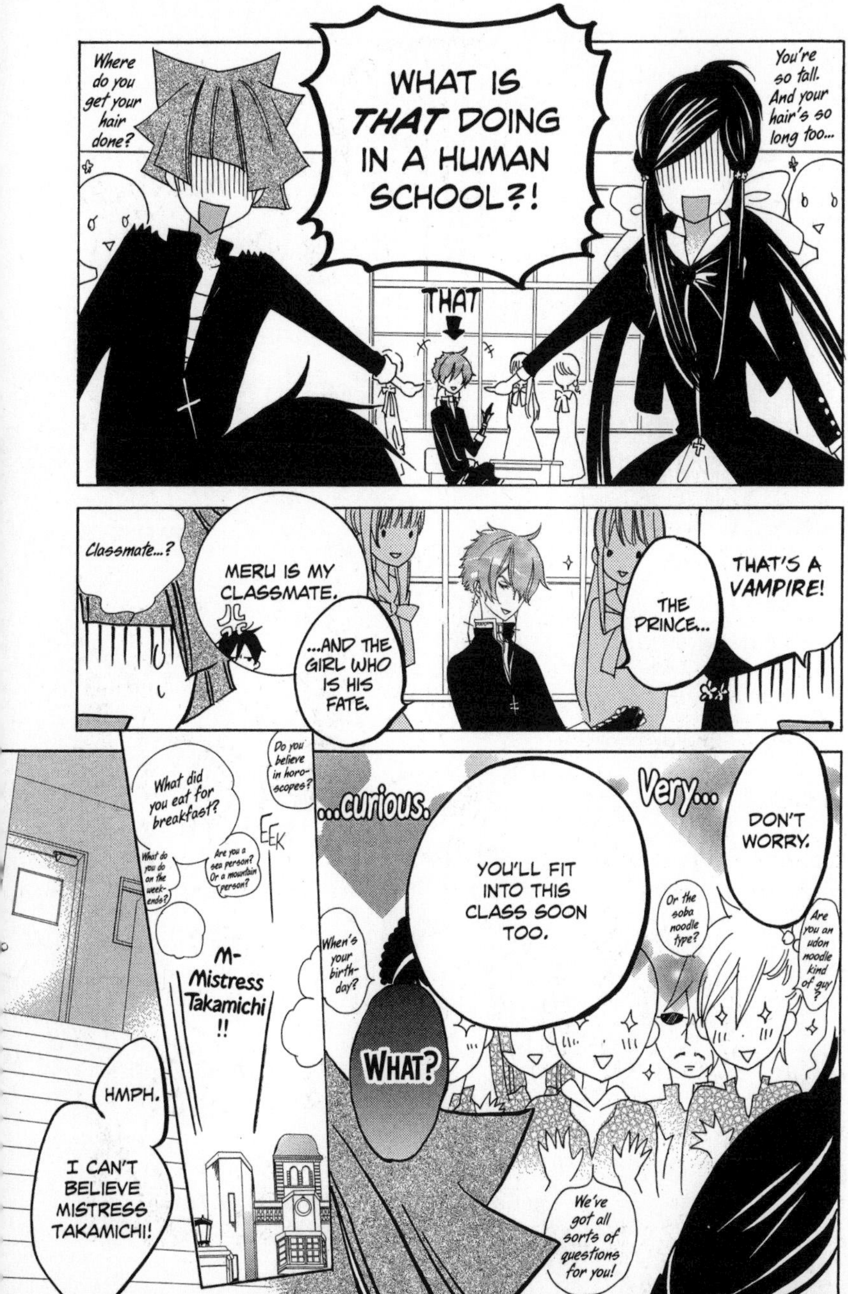
You're so tall. And your hair's so long too...
WHAT IS *THAT* DOING IN A HUMAN SCHOOL?!
THAT
Where do you get your hair done?
THAT'S A VAMPIRE!
THE PRINCE...
...AND THE GIRL WHO IS HIS FATE.
MERU IS MY CLASSMATE.
Classmate...?
DON'T WORRY.
Very...
...curious.
YOU'LL FIT INTO THIS CLASS SOON TOO.
Are you an udon noodle kind of guy?
Or the soba noodle type?
When's your birthday?
WHAT?
We've got all sorts of questions for you!
Do you believe in horoscopes?
What did you eat for breakfast?
Are you a sea person? Or a mountain person?
What do you do on the weekends?
EEK
M-Mistress Takamichi!!
HMPH.
I CAN'T BELIEVE MISTRESS TAKAMICHI!

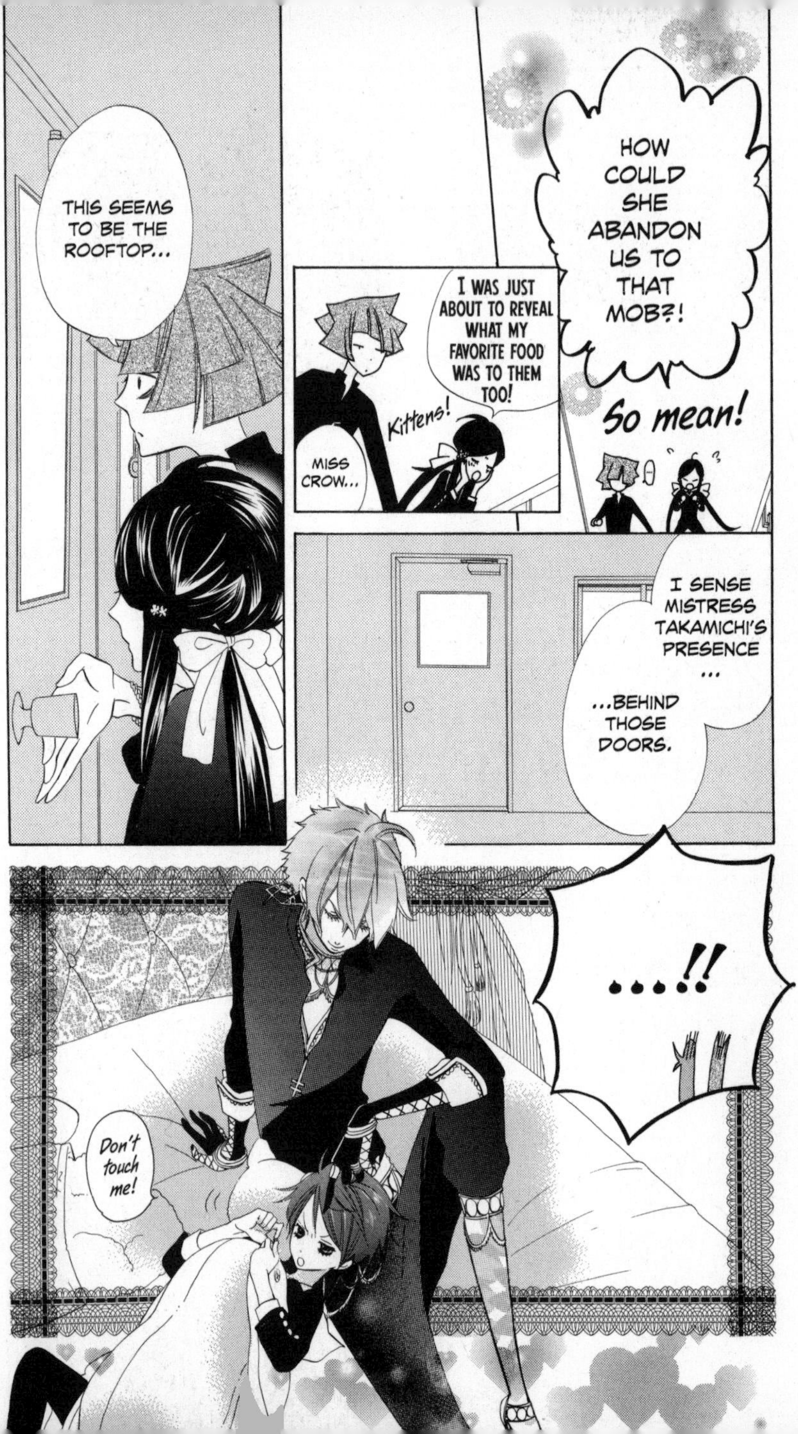

HOW COULD SHE ABANDON US TO THAT MOB?!
So mean!
I WAS JUST ABOUT TO REVEAL WHAT MY FAVORITE FOOD WAS TO THEM TOO!
Kittens!
MISS CROW...
I SENSE MISTRESS TAKAMICHI'S PRESENCE...
...BEHIND THOSE DOORS.
THIS SEEMS TO BE THE ROOFTOP...
...!!
Don't touch me!

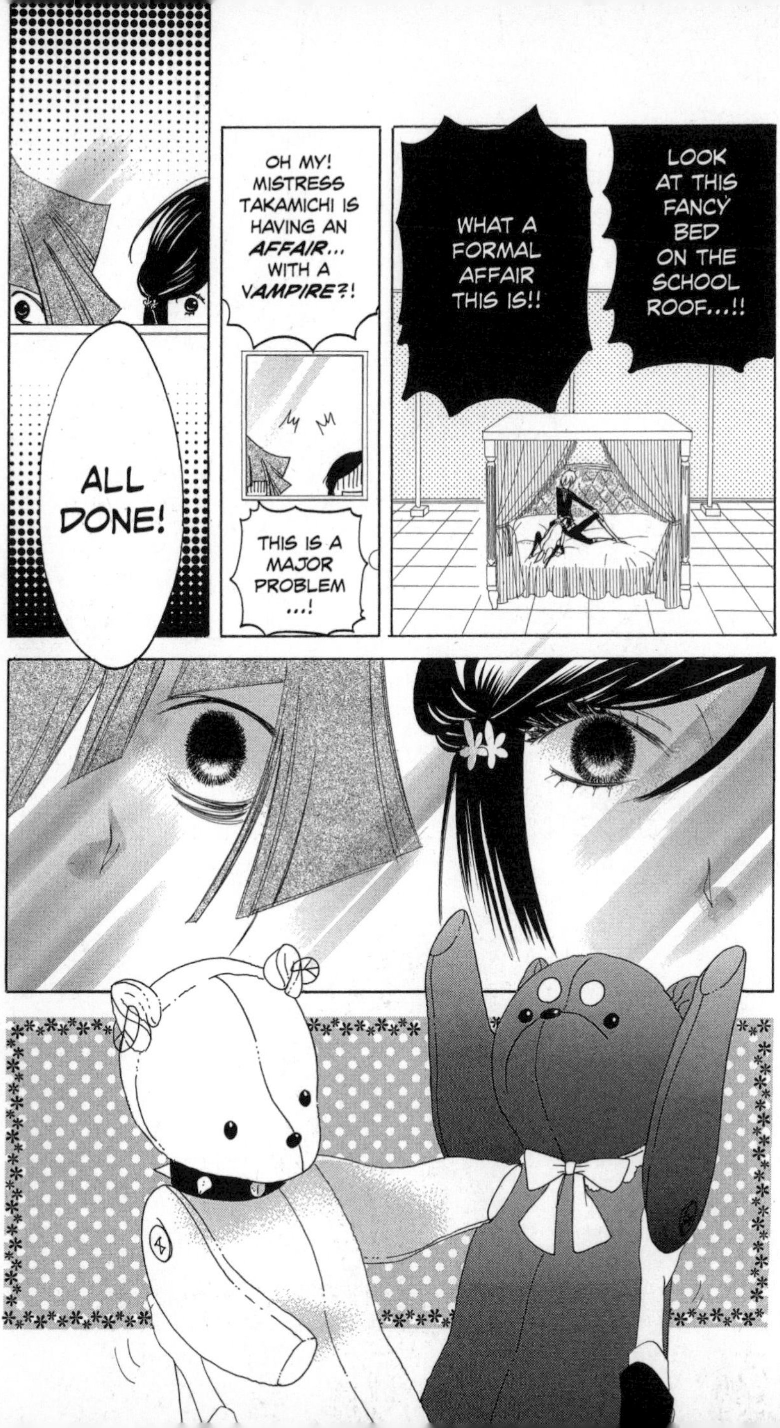
LOOK AT THIS FANCY BED ON THE SCHOOL ROOF...!!
WHAT A FORMAL AFFAIR THIS IS!!
OH MY! MISTRESS TAKAMICHI IS HAVING AN AFFAIR... WITH A VAMPIRE?!
THIS IS A MAJOR PROBLEM ...!
ALL DONE!

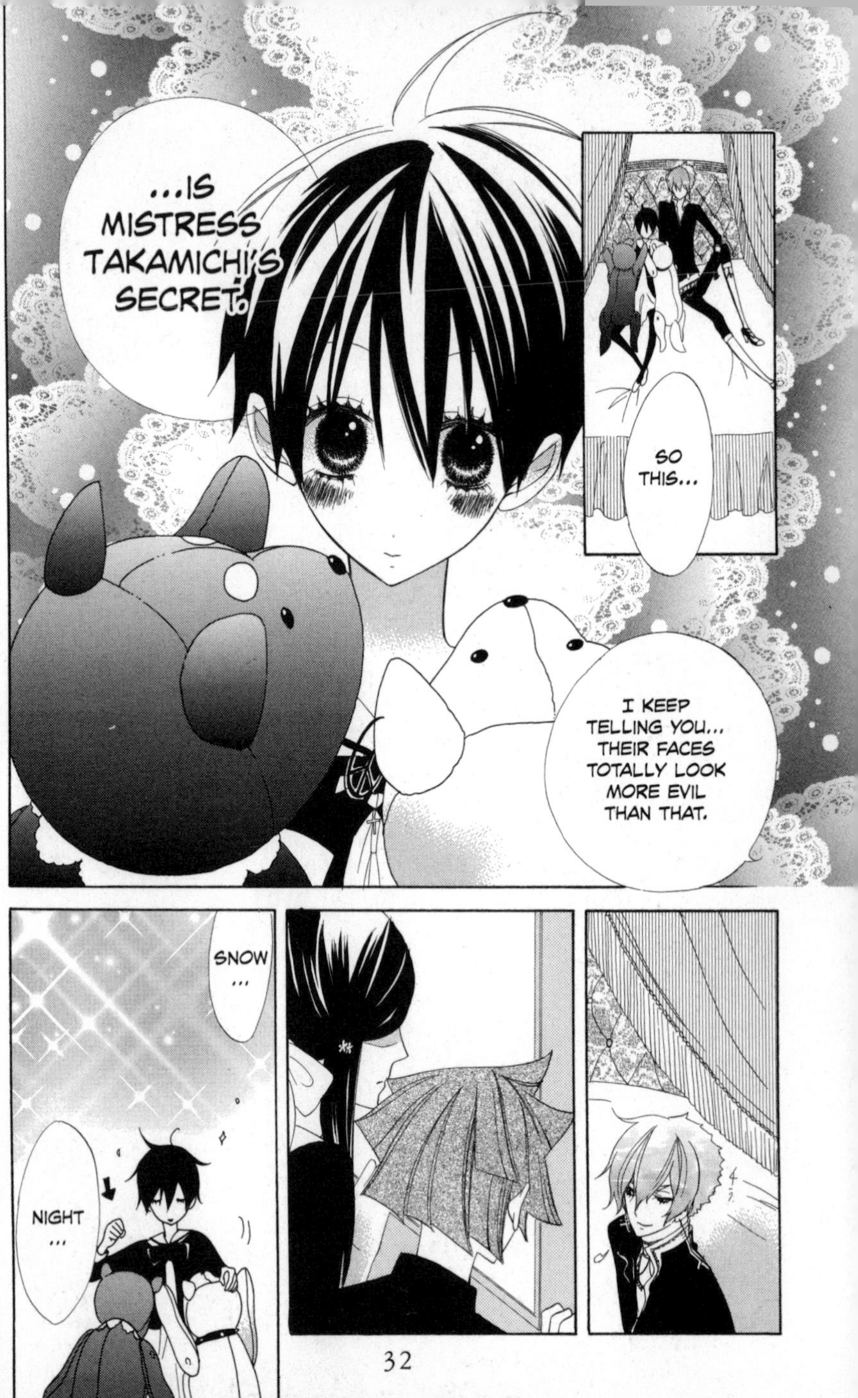
SO THIS...
...IS MISTRESS TAKAMICHI'S SECRET.
I KEEP TELLING YOU... THEIR FACES TOTALLY LOOK MORE EVIL THAN THAT.
SNOW ...
NIGHT ...

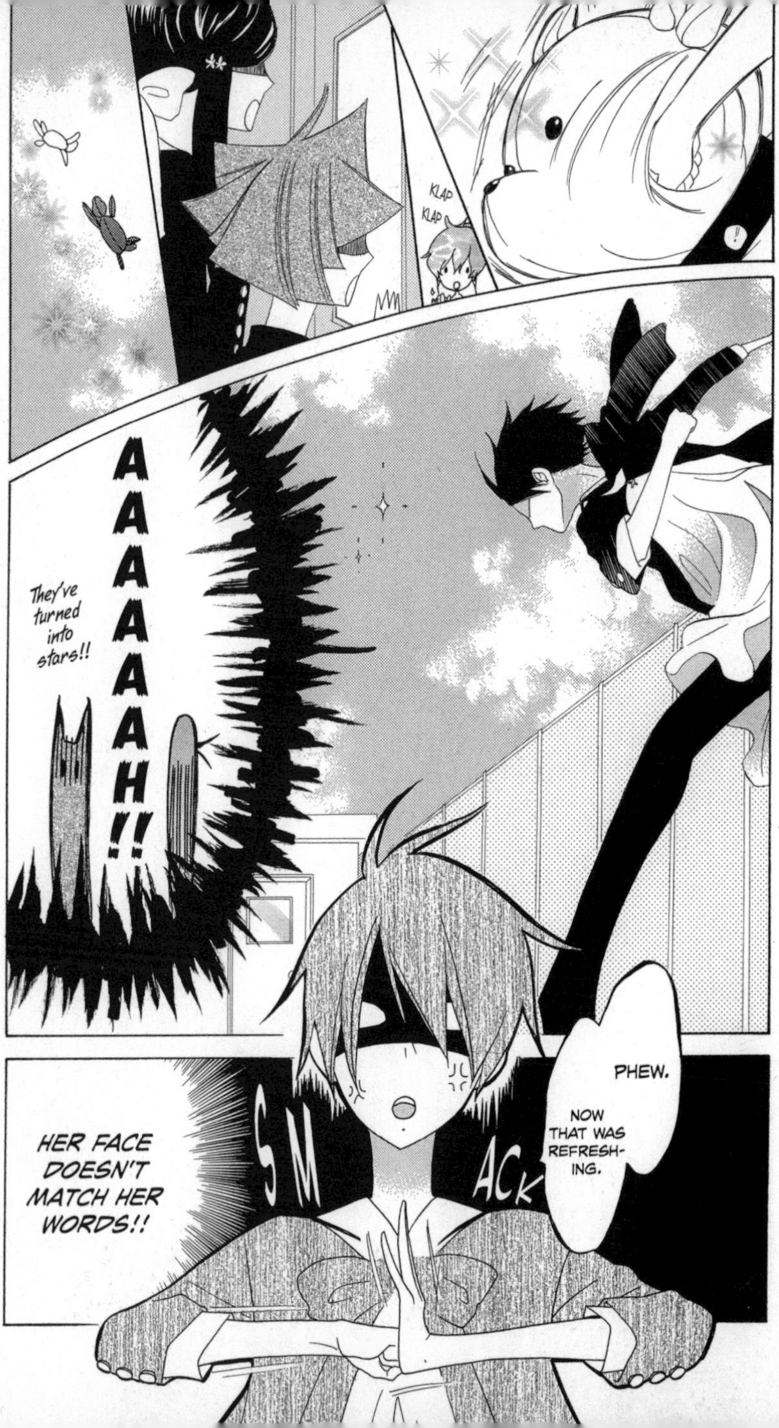

KLAP
KLAP
AAAAAAAH!!
They've turned into stars!!
PHEW.
NOW THAT WAS REFRESHING.
SMACK
HER FACE DOESN'T MATCH HER WORDS!!

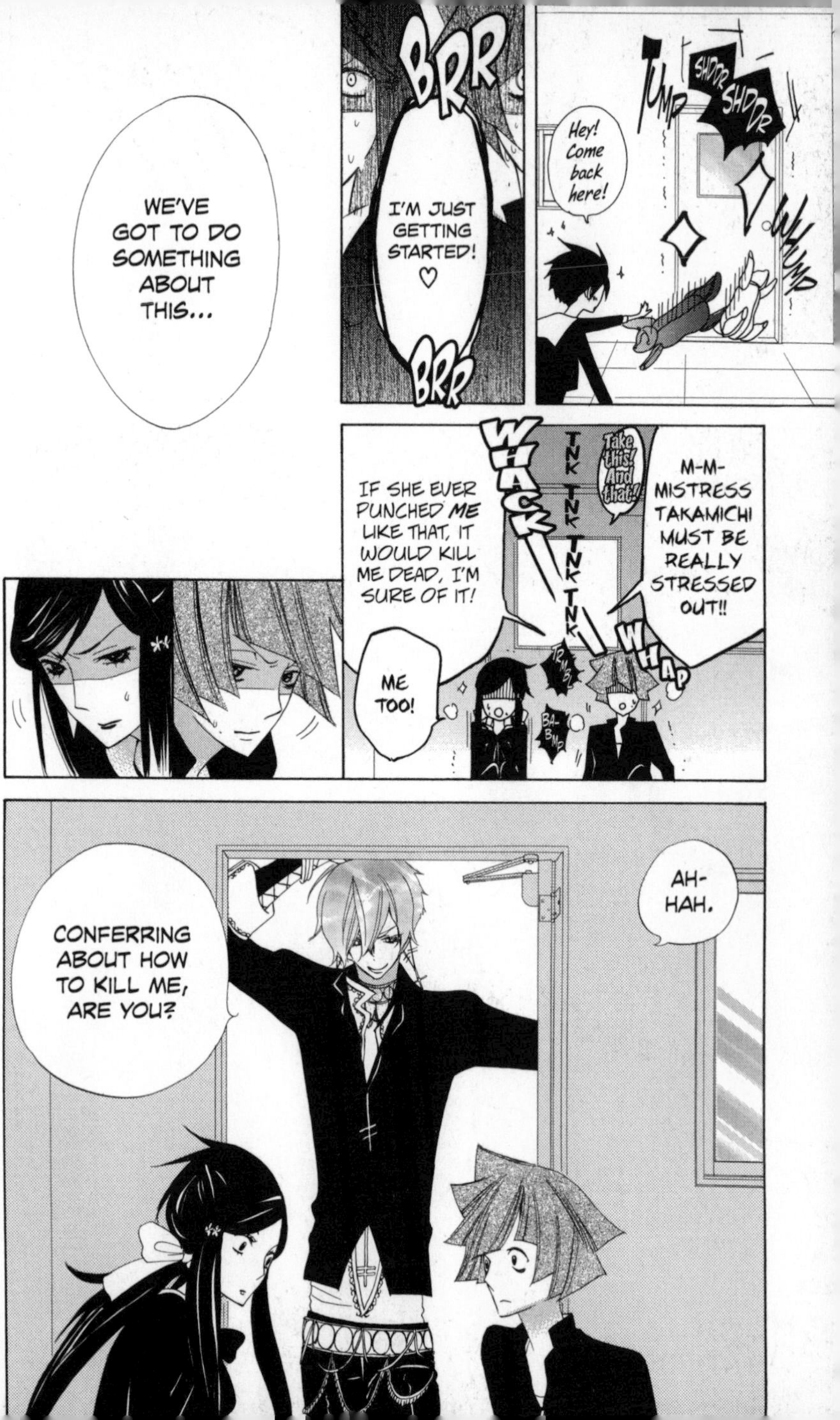
TUMP
SHDDR SHDDR
Hey! Come back here!
WHUMP
BRR
I'M JUST GETTING STARTED! ♡
BRR
Take this! And that!!
M-M-MISTRESS TAKAMICHI MUST BE REALLY STRESSED OUT!!
WHACK
TNK TNK TNK TNK TNK
IF SHE EVER PUNCHED *ME* LIKE THAT, IT WOULD KILL ME DEAD, I'M SURE OF IT!
ME TOO!
TRMBL
BA-BMP
WHAP
WE'VE GOT TO DO SOMETHING ABOUT THIS...
AH-HAH.
CONFERRING ABOUT HOW TO KILL ME, ARE YOU?

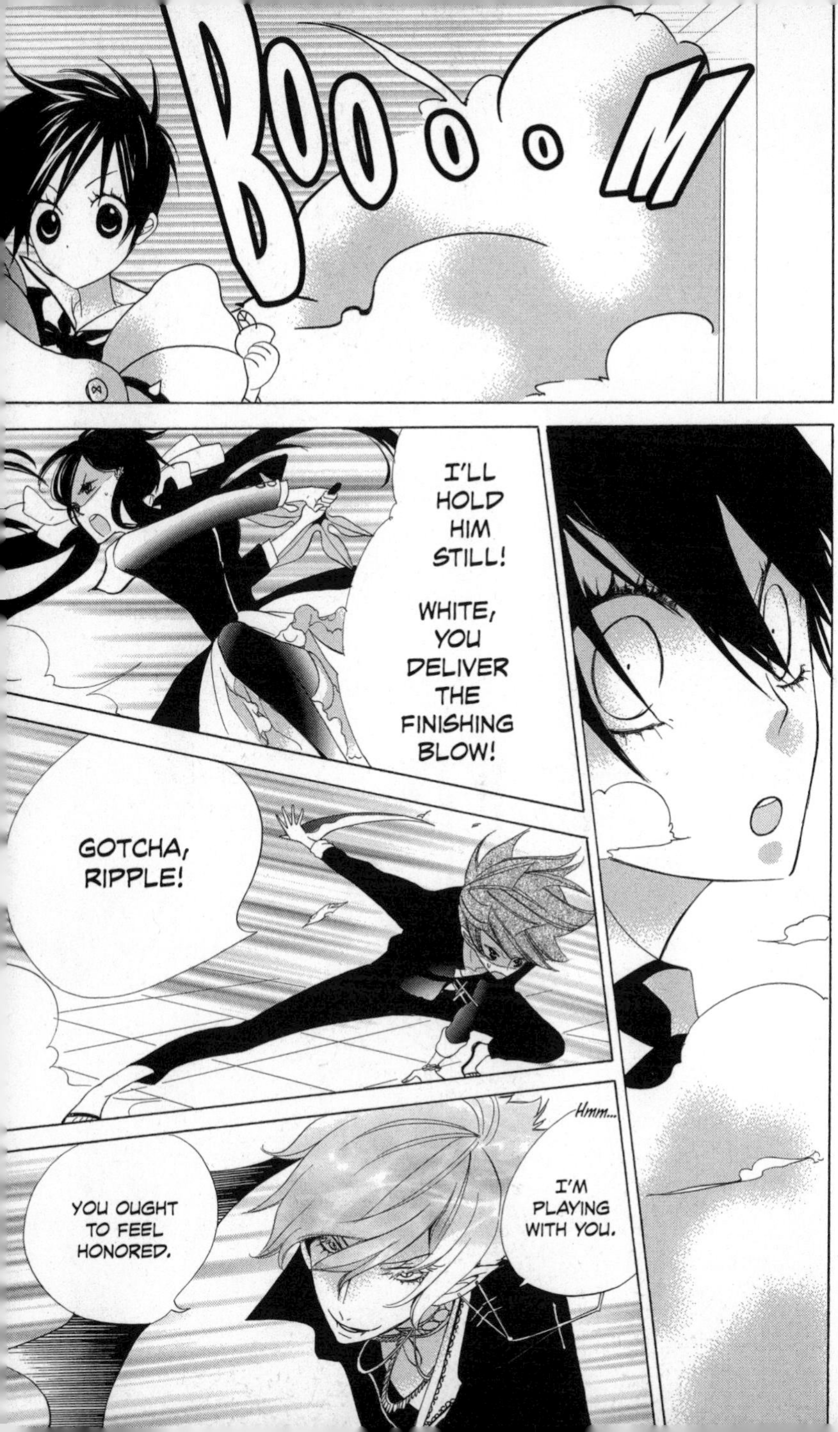
BOOOOOM
I'LL HOLD HIM STILL!
WHITE, YOU DELIVER THE FINISHING BLOW!
GOTCHA, RIPPLE!
Hmm...
I'M PLAYING WITH YOU.
YOU OUGHT TO FEEL HONORED.

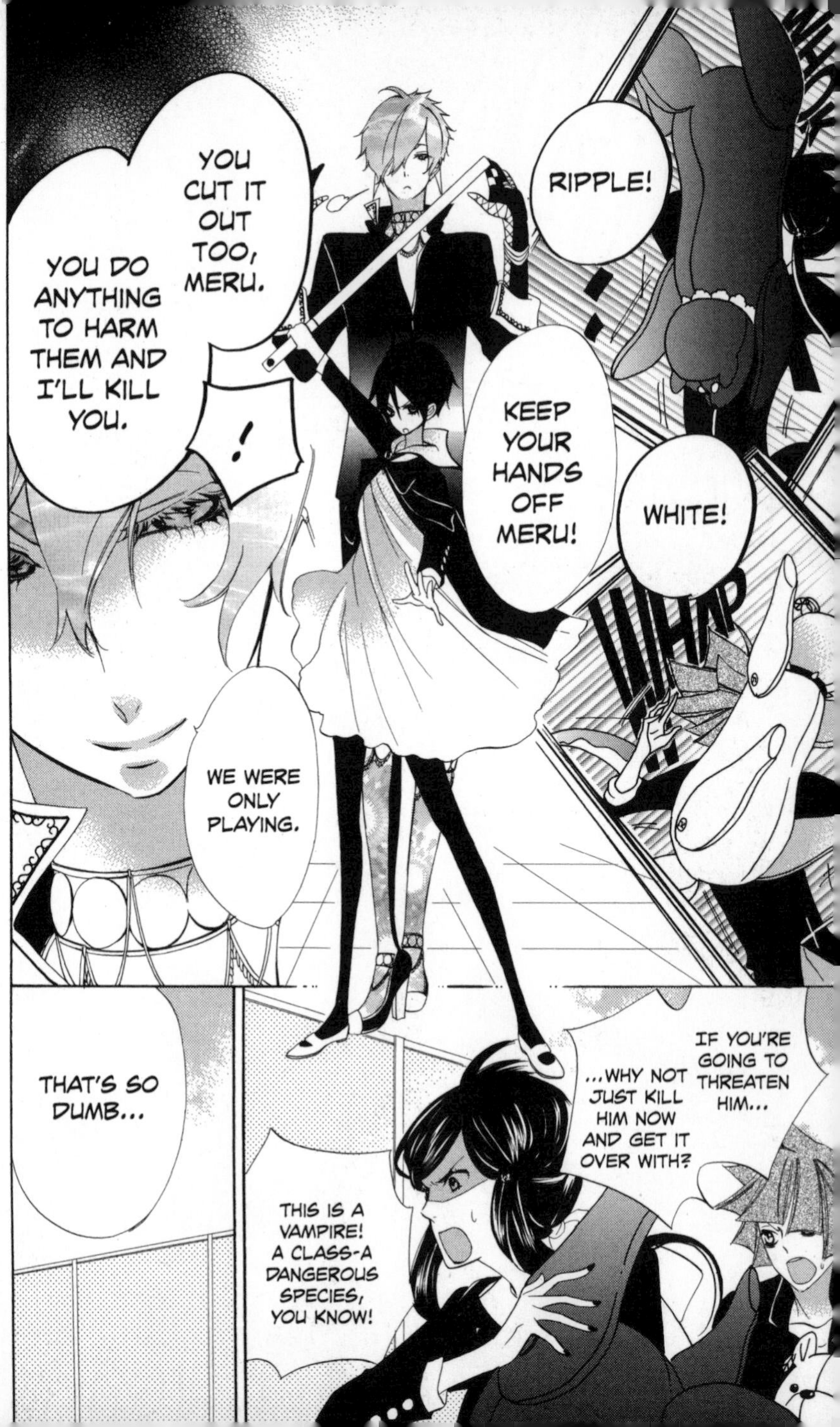
WHACK
RIPPLE!
!
WHITE!
WHAP
KEEP YOUR HANDS OFF MERU!
YOU CUT IT OUT TOO, MERU.
YOU DO ANYTHING TO HARM THEM AND I'LL KILL YOU.
!
WE WERE ONLY PLAYING.
IF YOU'RE GOING TO THREATEN HIM...
...WHY NOT JUST KILL HIM NOW AND GET IT OVER WITH?
THIS IS A VAMPIRE! A CLASS-A DANGEROUS SPECIES, YOU KNOW!
THAT'S SO DUMB...

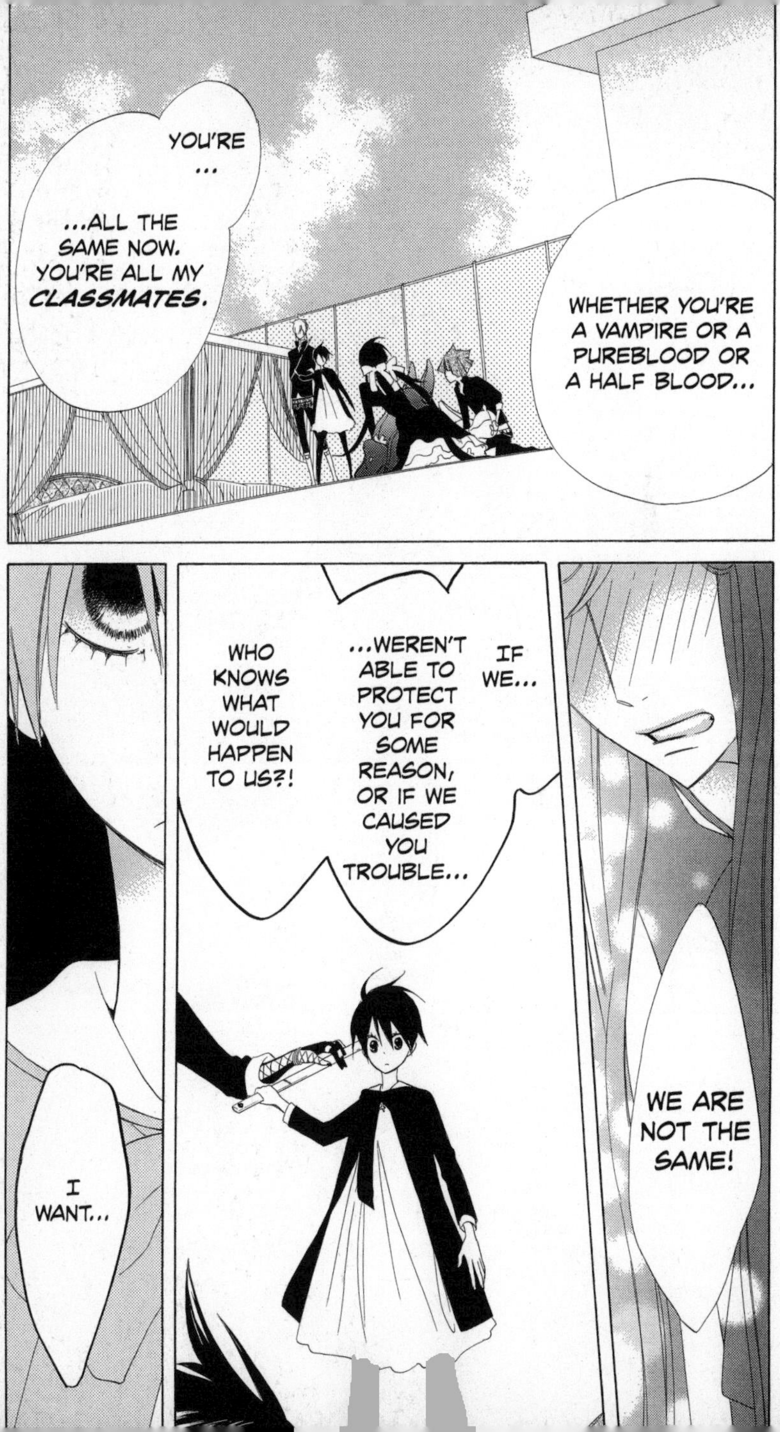
WHETHER YOU'RE A VAMPIRE OR A PUREBLOOD OR A HALF BLOOD...
YOU'RE ...
...ALL THE SAME NOW. YOU'RE ALL MY *CLASSMATES*.
WE ARE NOT THE SAME!
IF WE...
...WEREN'T ABLE TO PROTECT YOU FOR SOME REASON, OR IF WE CAUSED YOU TROUBLE...
WHO KNOWS WHAT WOULD HAPPEN TO US?!
I WANT...

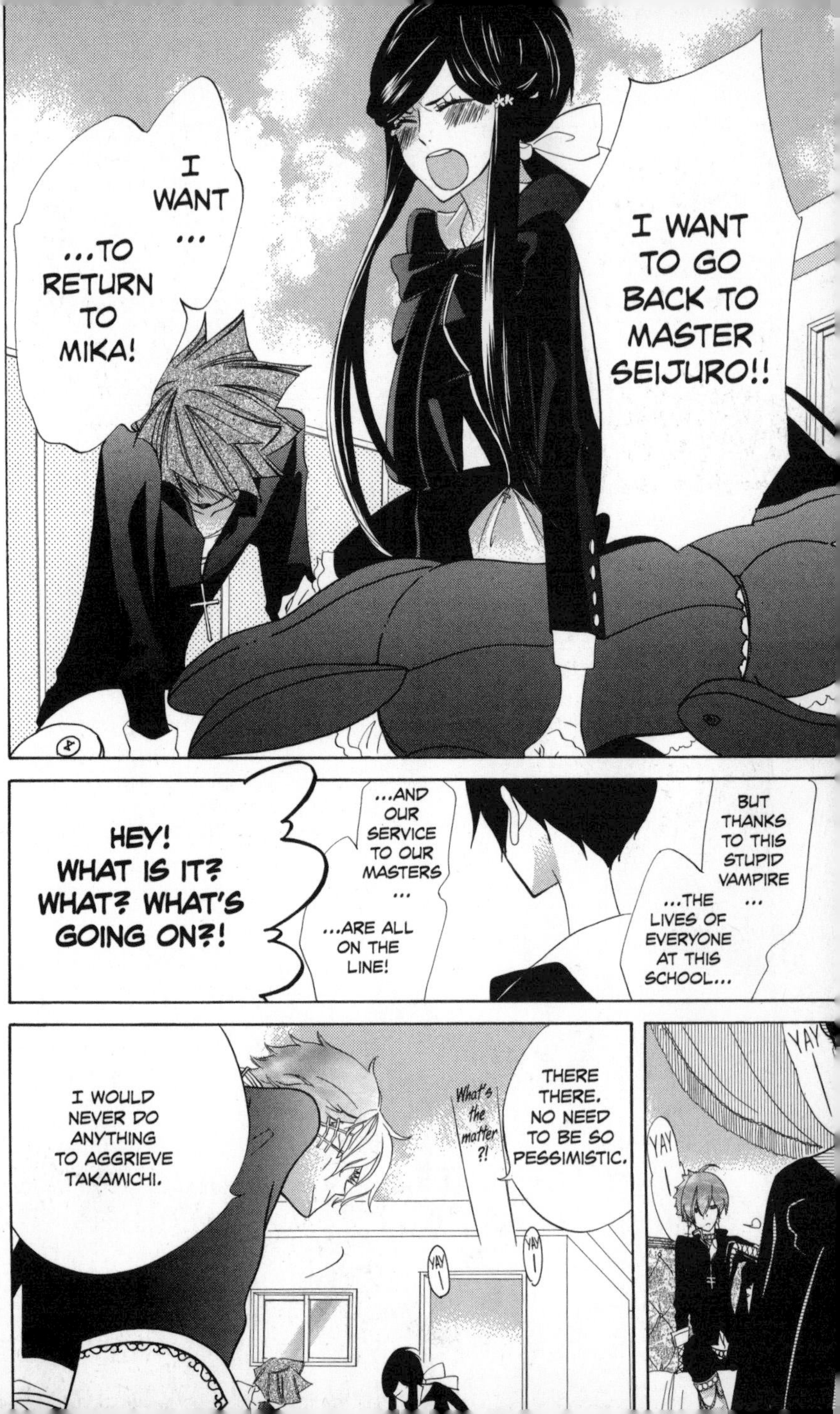
I WANT TO GO BACK TO MASTER SEIJURO!!
I WANT ...
...TO RETURN TO MIKA!
BUT THANKS TO THIS STUPID VAMPIRE ...
...THE LIVES OF EVERYONE AT THIS SCHOOL...
...AND OUR SERVICE TO OUR MASTERS ...
...ARE ALL ON THE LINE!
HEY! WHAT IS IT? WHAT? WHAT'S GOING ON?!
YAY
YAY
THERE THERE. NO NEED TO BE SO PESSIMISTIC.
What's the matter?!
I WOULD NEVER DO ANYTHING TO AGGRIEVE TAKAMICHI.
YAY
YAY

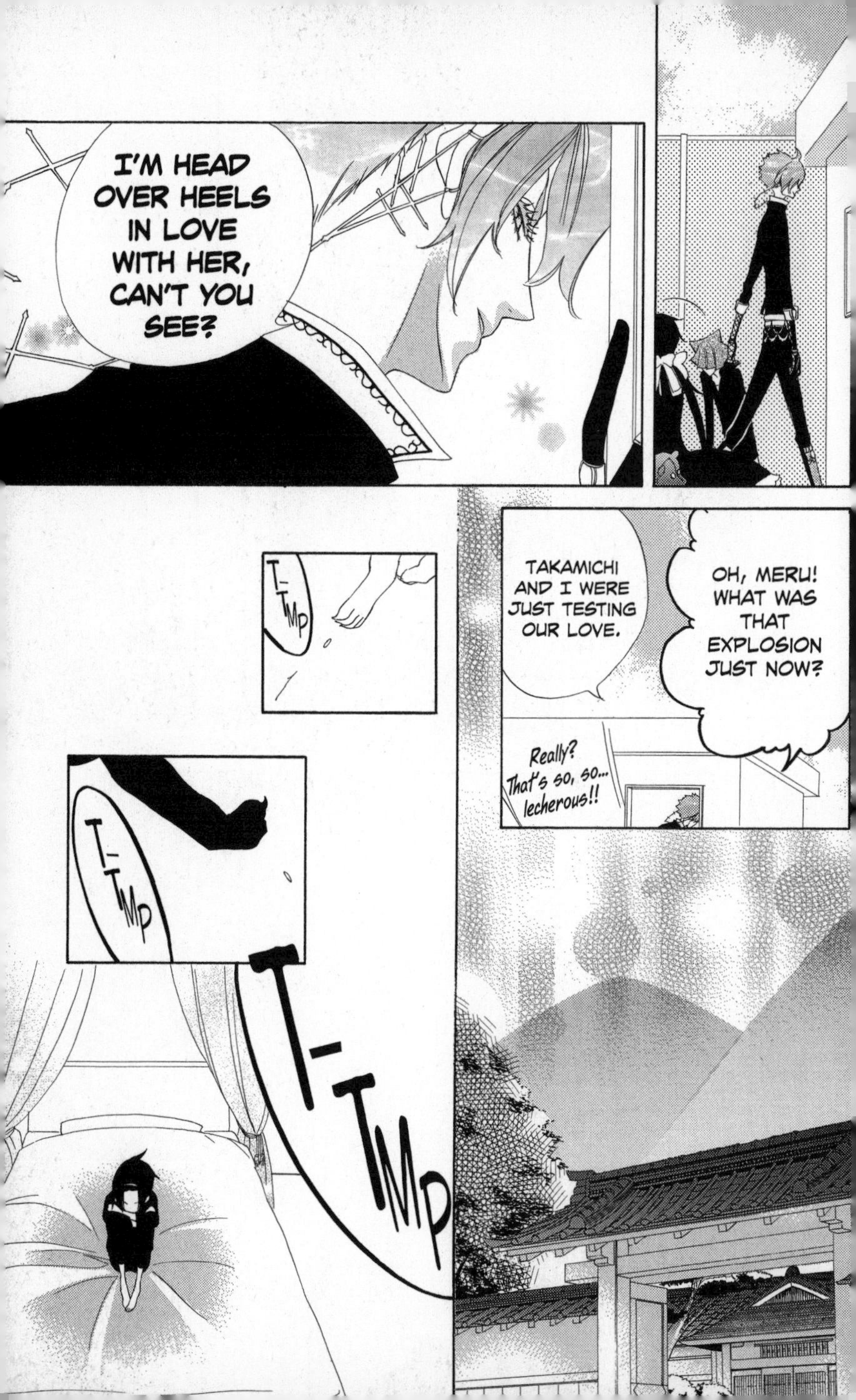
I'M HEAD OVER HEELS IN LOVE WITH HER, CAN'T YOU SEE?
OH, MERU! WHAT WAS THAT EXPLOSION JUST NOW?
TAKAMICHI AND I WERE JUST TESTING OUR LOVE.
Really? That's so, so... lecherous!!
T-TMP
T-TMP
T-TMP

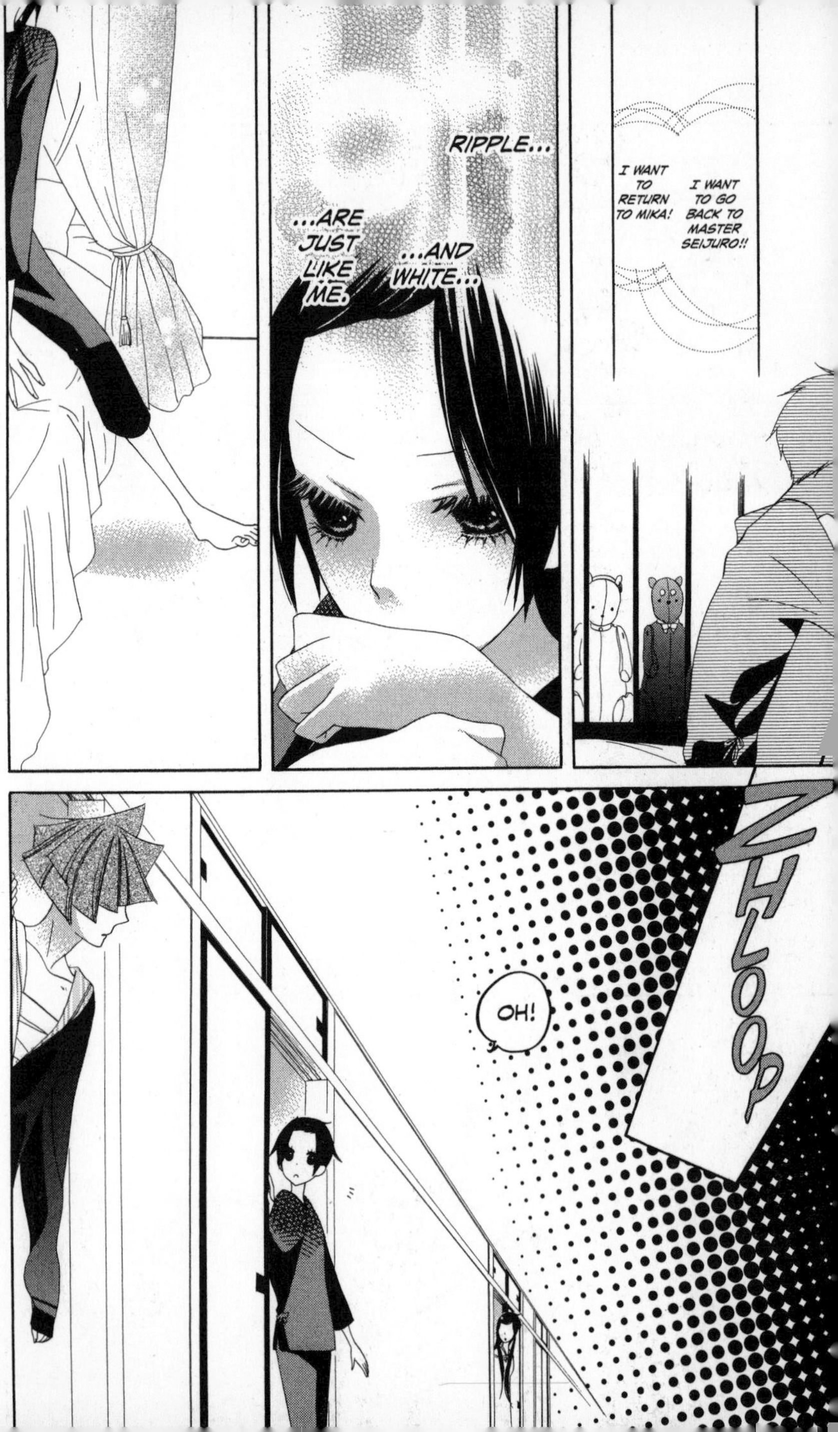

I WANT TO GO BACK TO MASTER SEIJURO!!
I WANT TO RETURN TO MIKA!
RIPPLE...
...AND WHITE...
...ARE JUST LIKE ME.
WHLOOP
OH!

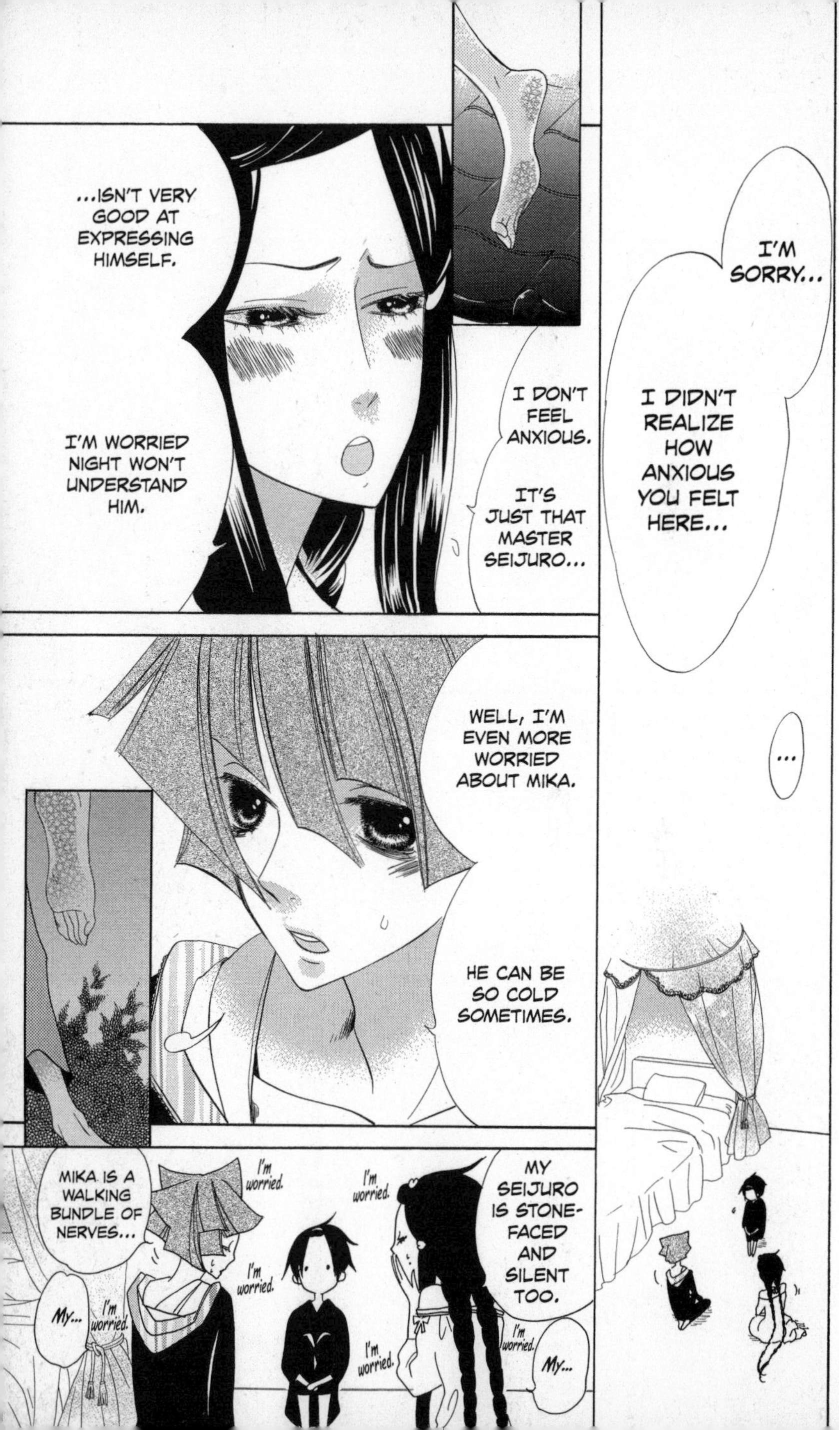
I'M SORRY...
I DIDN'T REALIZE HOW ANXIOUS YOU FELT HERE...
...
I DON'T FEEL ANXIOUS.
IT'S JUST THAT MASTER SEIJURO...
...ISN'T VERY GOOD AT EXPRESSING HIMSELF.
I'M WORRIED NIGHT WON'T UNDERSTAND HIM.
WELL, I'M EVEN MORE WORRIED ABOUT MIKA.
HE CAN BE SO COLD SOMETIMES.
MY SEIJURO IS STONE-FACED AND SILENT TOO.
I'm worried.
My...
I'm worried.
I'm worried.
I'm worried.
I'm worried.
MIKA IS A WALKING BUNDLE OF NERVES...
I'm worried.
My...

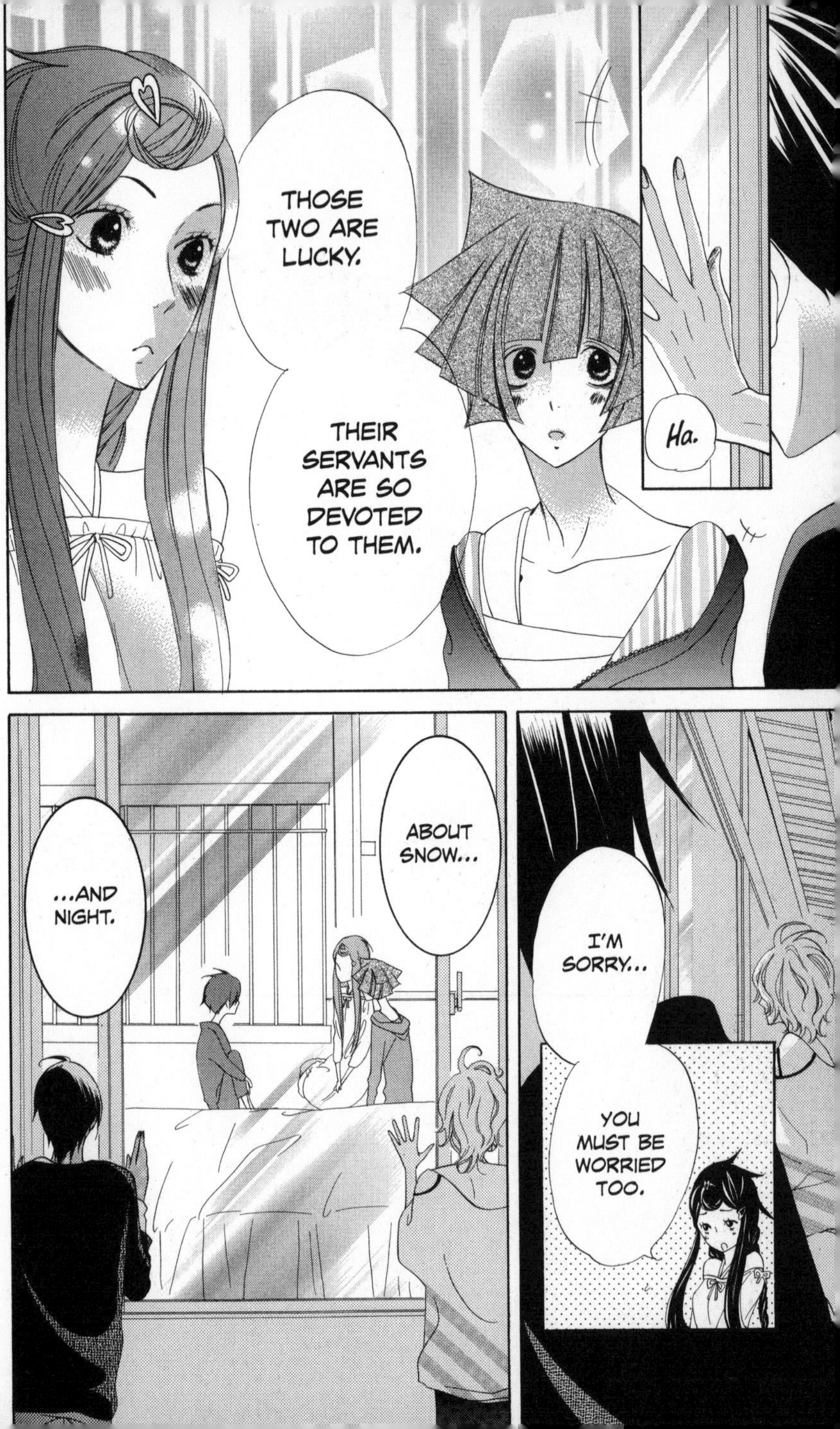
Ha.
THOSE TWO ARE LUCKY.
THEIR SERVANTS ARE SO DEVOTED TO THEM.
I'M SORRY...
YOU MUST BE WORRIED TOO.
ABOUT SNOW...
...AND NIGHT.

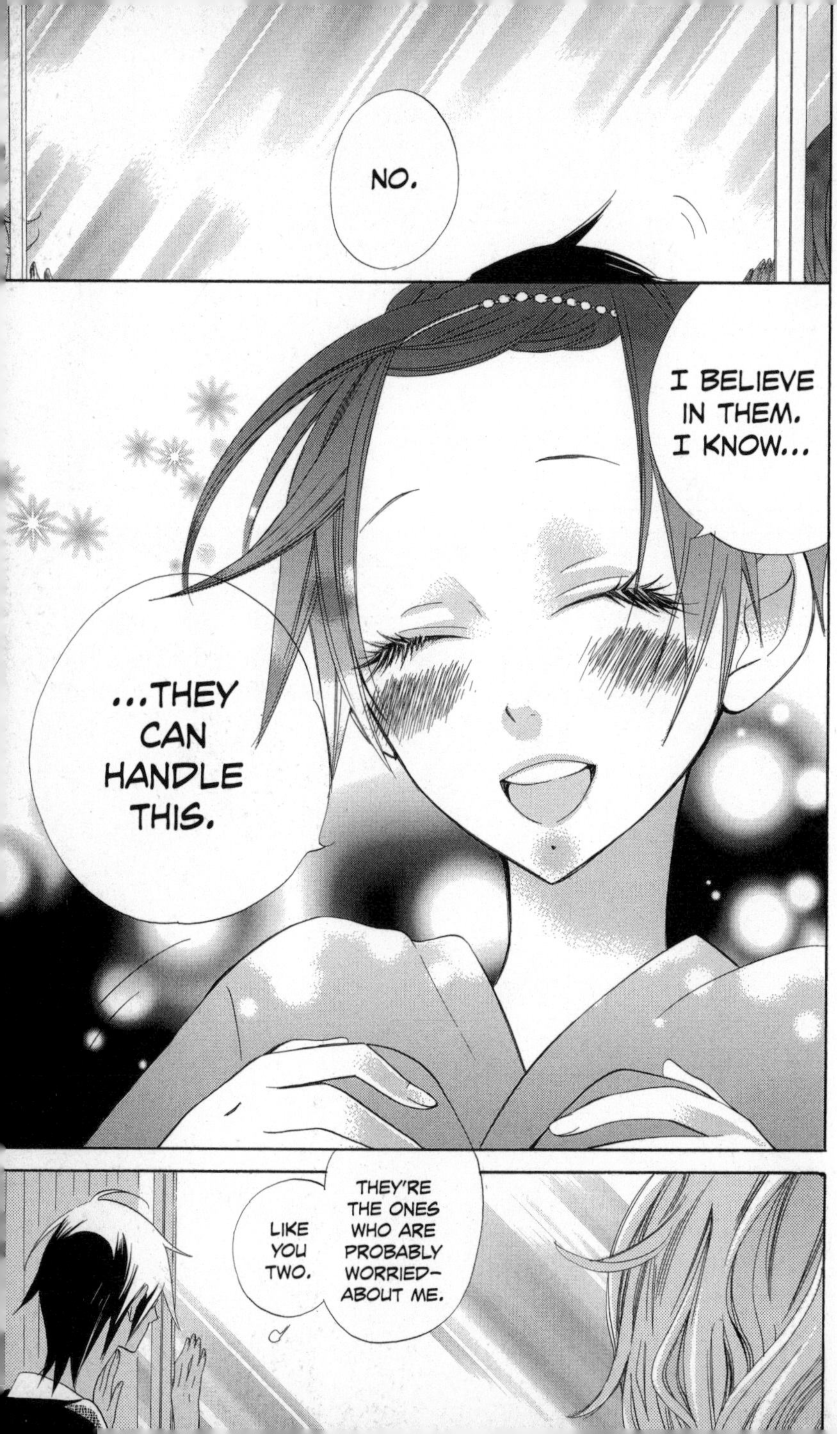
NO.
I BELIEVE IN THEM. I KNOW...
...THEY CAN HANDLE THIS.
THEY'RE THE ONES WHO ARE PROBABLY WORRIED-ABOUT ME.
LIKE YOU TWO.

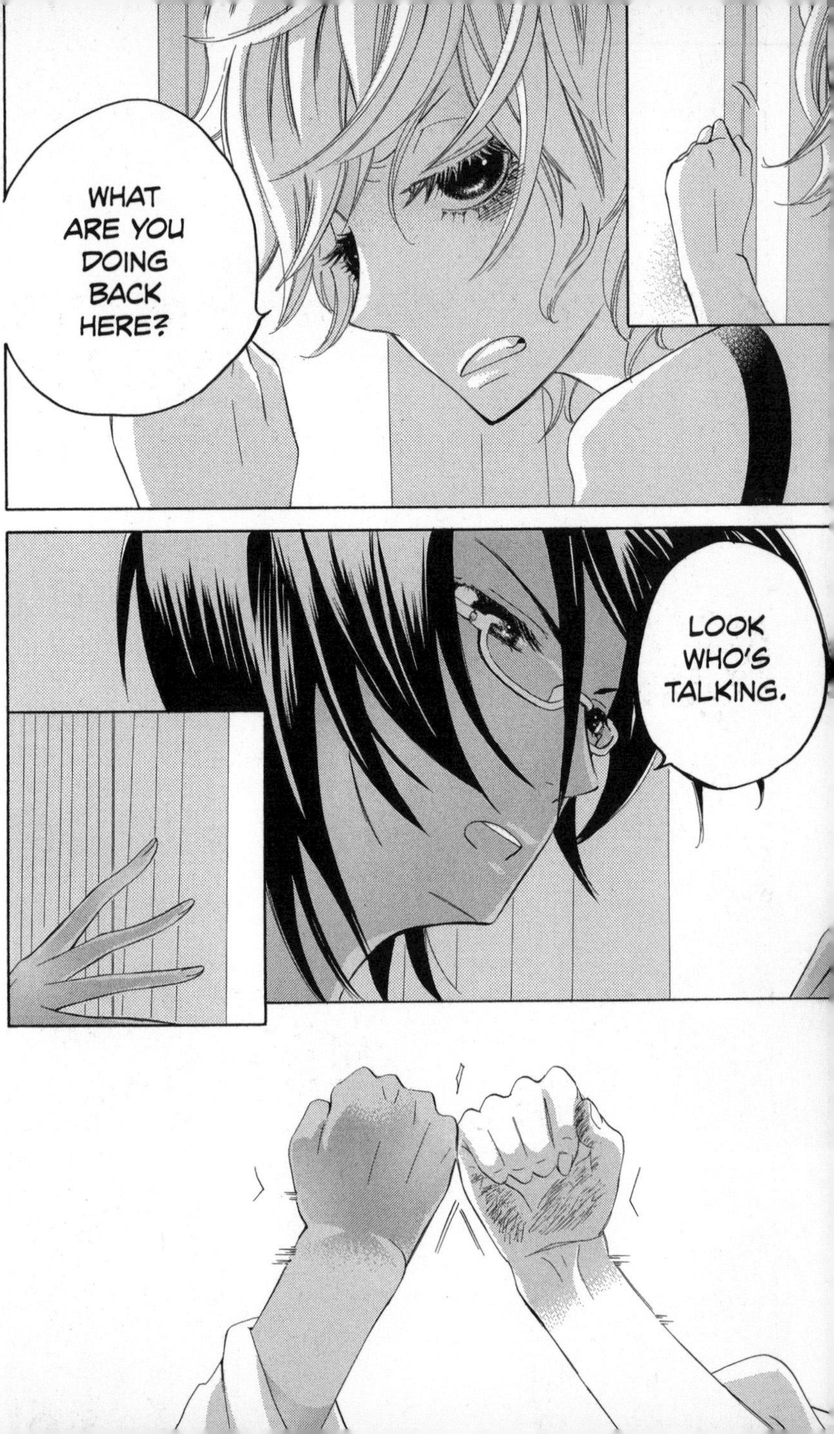
WHAT ARE YOU DOING BACK HERE?
LOOK WHO'S TALKING.

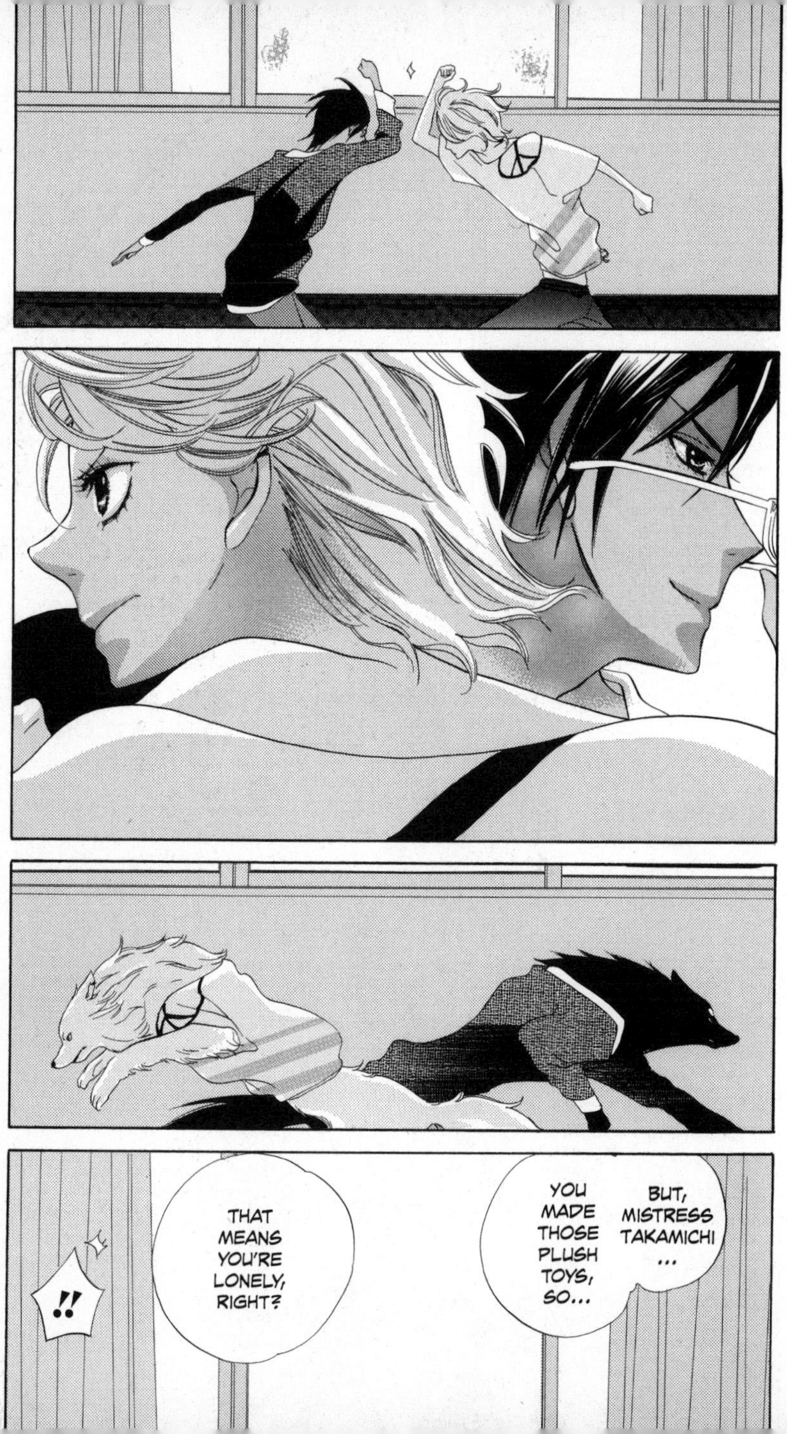
BUT, MISTRESS TAKAMICHI...
YOU MADE THOSE PLUSH TOYS, SO...
THAT MEANS YOU'RE LONELY, RIGHT?
!!

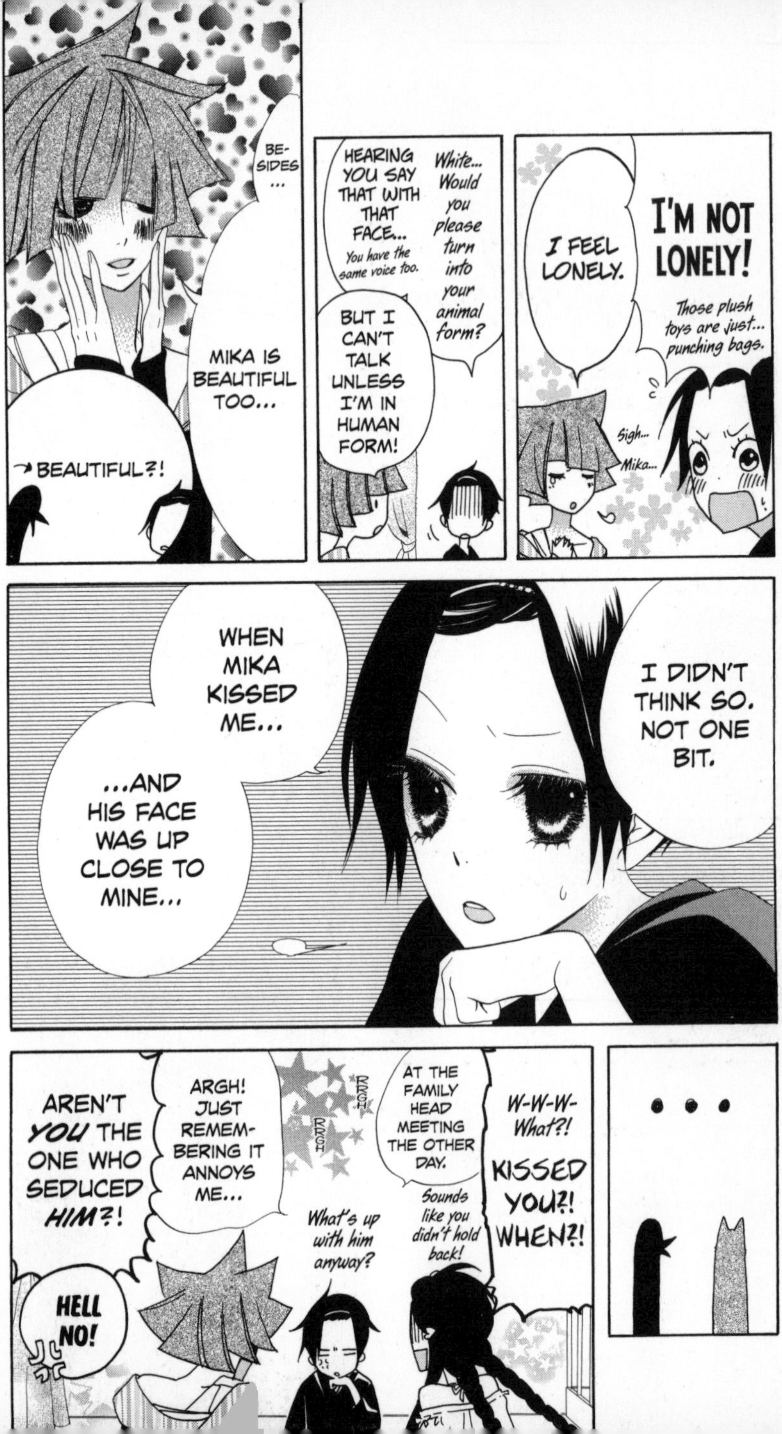
I'M NOT LONELY!
I FEEL LONELY.
Those plush toys are just... punching bags.
Sigh... Mika...
White... Would you please turn into your animal form?
HEARING YOU SAY THAT WITH THAT FACE...
You have the same voice too.
BUT I CAN'T TALK UNLESS I'M IN HUMAN FORM!
BE-SIDES...
MIKA IS BEAUTIFUL TOO...
BEAUTIFUL?!
I DIDN'T THINK SO. NOT ONE BIT.
WHEN MIKA KISSED ME...
...AND HIS FACE WAS UP CLOSE TO MINE...
• • •
W-W-W-What?!
KISSED YOU?! WHEN?!
AT THE FAMILY HEAD MEETING THE OTHER DAY.
RRGH RRGH
Sounds like you didn't hold back!
ARGH! JUST REMEMBERING IT ANNOYS ME...
What's up with him anyway?
AREN'T YOU THE ONE WHO SEDUCED HIM?!
HELL NO!

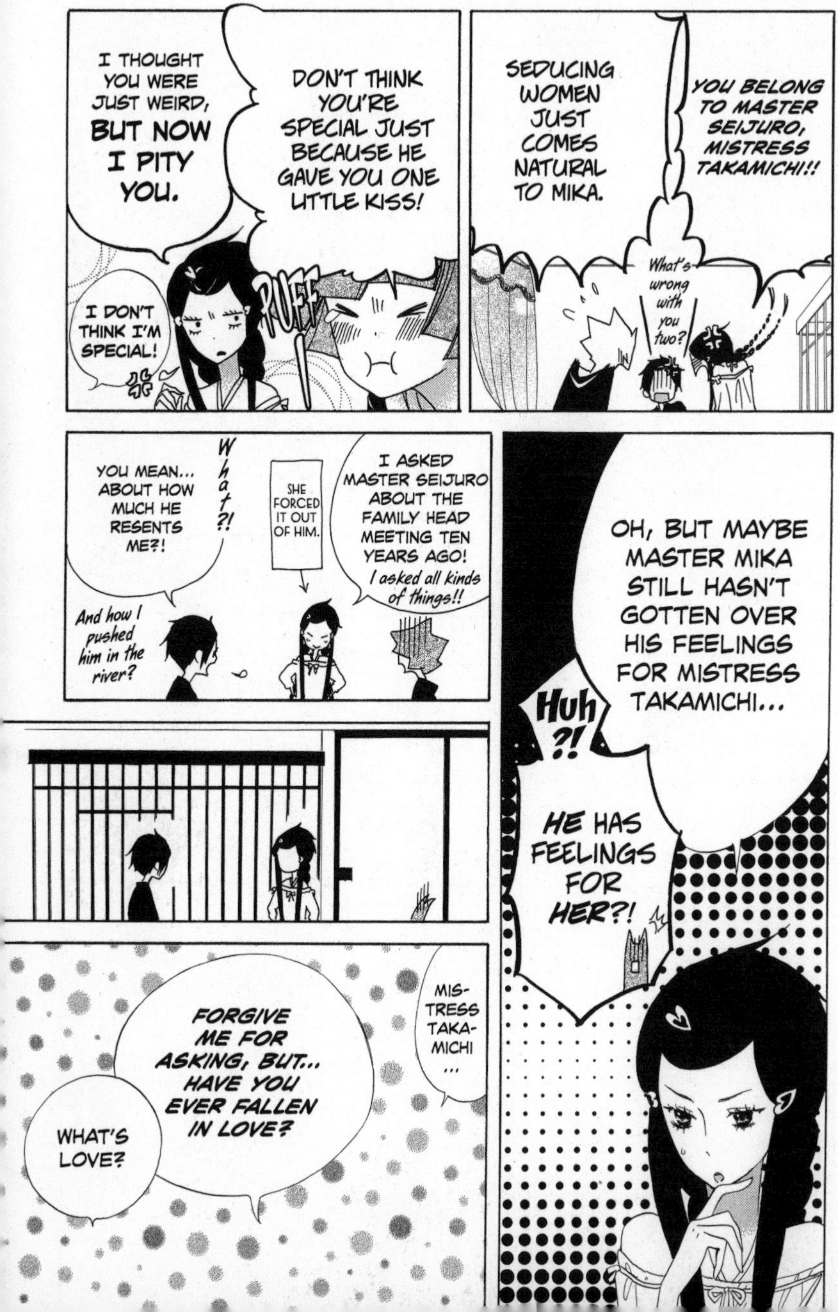
YOU BELONG TO MASTER SEIJURO, MISTRESS TAKAMICHI!!
SEDUCING WOMEN JUST COMES NATURAL TO MIKA.
What's wrong with you two?
DON'T THINK YOU'RE SPECIAL JUST BECAUSE HE GAVE YOU ONE LITTLE KISS!
I THOUGHT YOU WERE JUST WEIRD, BUT NOW I PITY YOU.
RUFF
I DON'T THINK I'M SPECIAL!
OH, BUT MAYBE MASTER MIKA STILL HASN'T GOTTEN OVER HIS FEELINGS FOR MISTRESS TAKAMICHI...
Huh?!
HE HAS FEELINGS FOR HER?!
I ASKED MASTER SEIJURO ABOUT THE FAMILY HEAD MEETING TEN YEARS AGO!
I asked all kinds of things!!
SHE FORCED IT OUT OF HIM.
What?!
YOU MEAN... ABOUT HOW MUCH HE RESENTS ME?!
And how I pushed him in the river?
MISTRESS TAKAMICHI...
FORGIVE ME FOR ASKING, BUT... HAVE YOU EVER FALLEN IN LOVE?
WHAT'S LOVE?

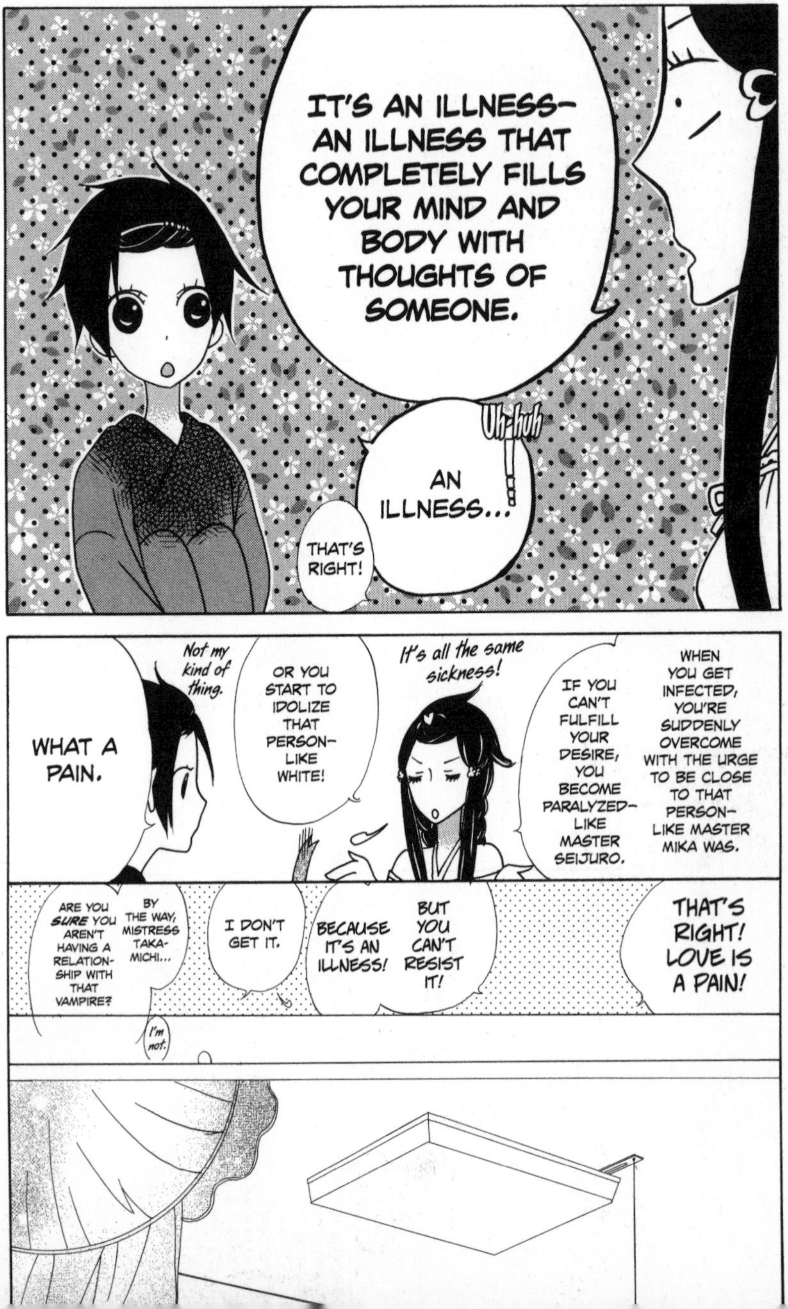
IT'S AN ILLNESS— AN ILLNESS THAT COMPLETELY FILLS YOUR MIND AND BODY WITH THOUGHTS OF SOMEONE.
Uh-huh
AN ILLNESS...
THAT'S RIGHT!
WHEN YOU GET INFECTED, YOU'RE SUDDENLY OVERCOME WITH THE URGE TO BE CLOSE TO THAT PERSON— LIKE MASTER MIKA WAS.
IF YOU CAN'T FULFILL YOUR DESIRE, YOU BECOME PARALYZED— LIKE MASTER SEIJURO.
It's all the same sickness!
OR YOU START TO IDOLIZE THAT PERSON— LIKE WHITE!
Not my kind of thing.
WHAT A PAIN.
THAT'S RIGHT! LOVE IS A PAIN!
BUT YOU CAN'T RESIST IT!
BECAUSE IT'S AN ILLNESS!
I DON'T GET IT.
BY THE WAY, MISTRESS TAKAMICHI...
ARE YOU *SURE* YOU AREN'T HAVING A RELATIONSHIP WITH THAT VAMPIRE?
I'm not.

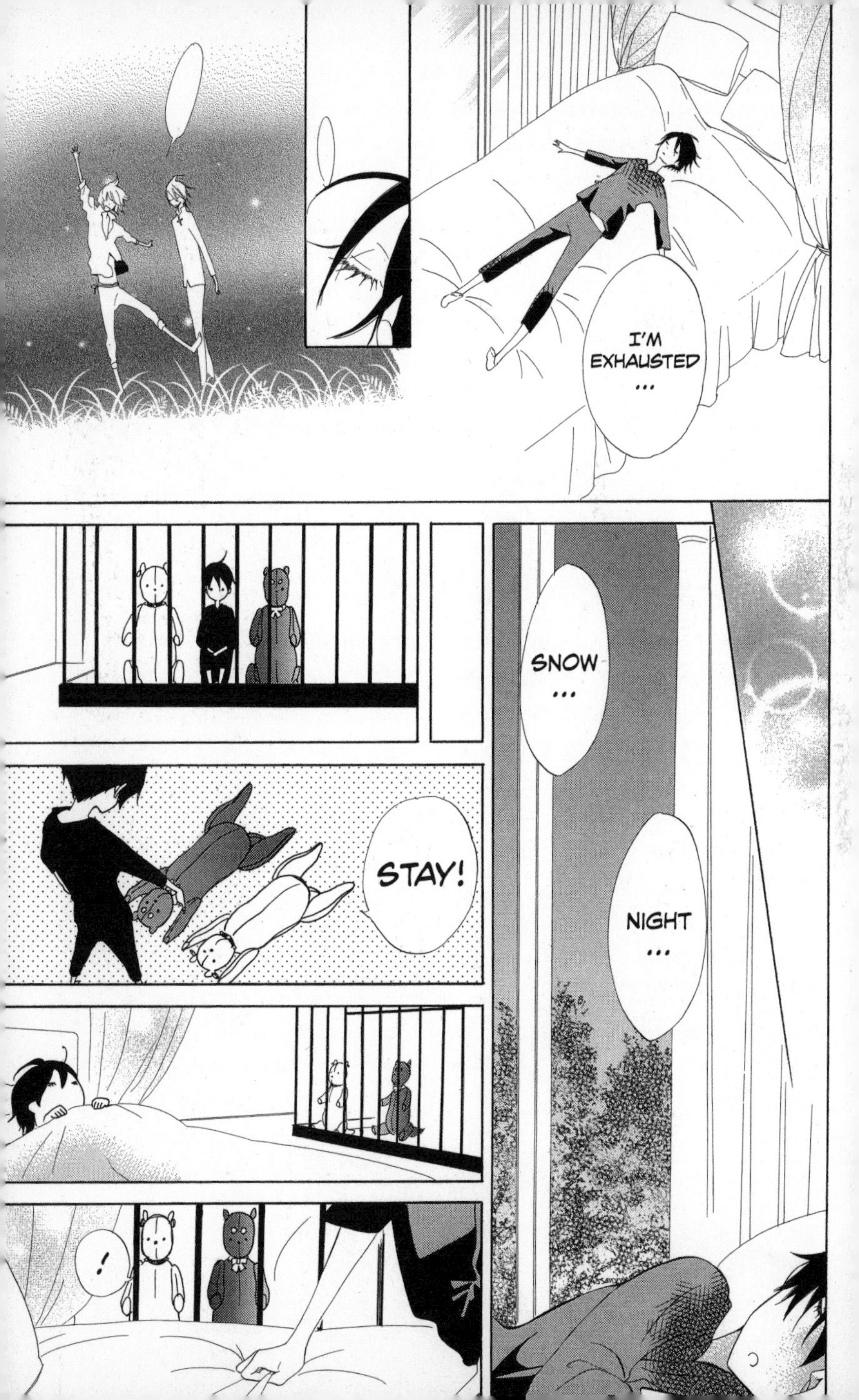
I'M EXHAUSTED...
SNOW...
NIGHT...
STAY!
!

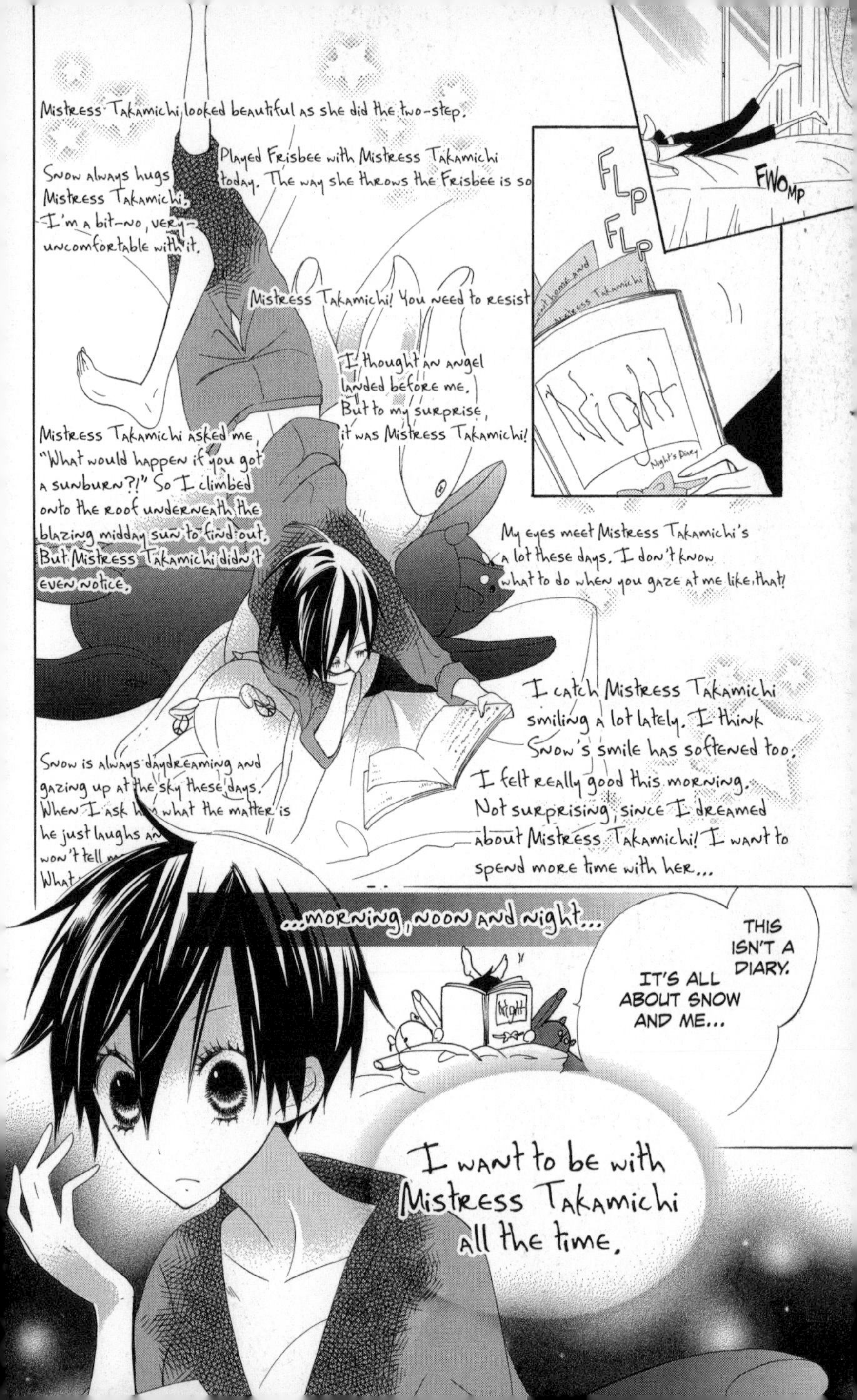
FWOMP
FLP
FLP
Night
Night's Diary
Mistress Takamichi looked beautiful as she did the two-step.
Played Frisbee with Mistress Takamichi today. The way she throws the Frisbee is so
Snow always hugs Mistress Takamichi. I'm a bit—no, very—uncomfortable with it.
Mistress Takamichi! You need to resist
I thought an angel landed before me. But to my surprise, it was Mistress Takamichi!
Mistress Takamichi asked me, "What would happen if you got a sunburn?!" So I climbed onto the roof underneath the blazing midday sun to find out. But Mistress Takamichi didn't even notice.
My eyes meet Mistress Takamichi's a lot these days. I don't know what to do when you gaze at me like that!
I catch Mistress Takamichi smiling a lot lately. I think Snow's smile has softened too.
Snow is always daydreaming and gazing up at the sky these days. When I ask h m what the matter is he just laughs an won't tell m What
I felt really good this morning. Not surprising, since I dreamed about Mistress Takamichi! I want to spend more time with her...
...morning, noon and night...
THIS ISN'T A DIARY.
IT'S ALL ABOUT SNOW AND ME...
I want to be with Mistress Takamichi all the time.

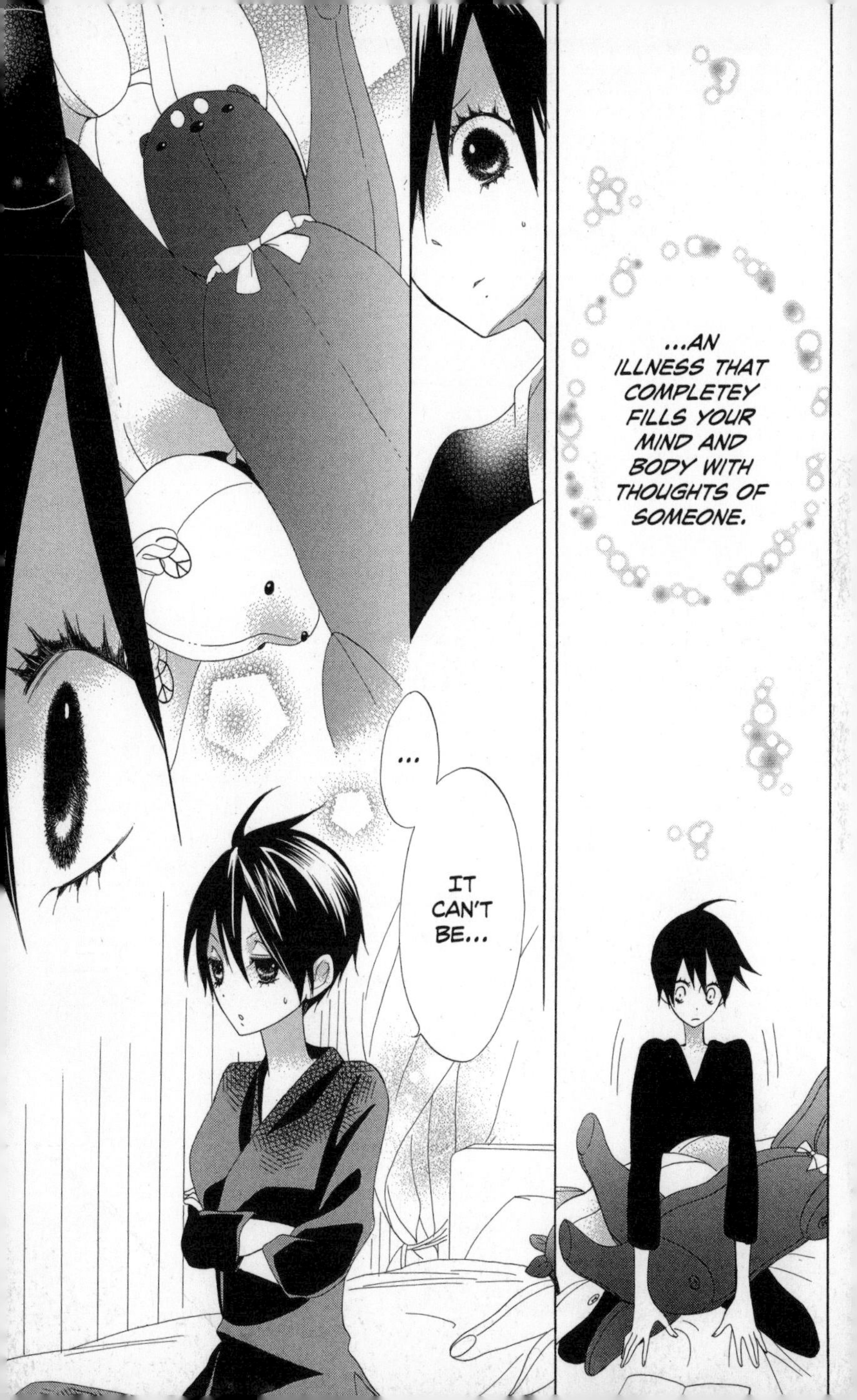
...AN ILLNESS THAT COMPLETEY FILLS YOUR MIND AND BODY WITH THOUGHTS OF SOMEONE.
...
IT CAN'T BE...

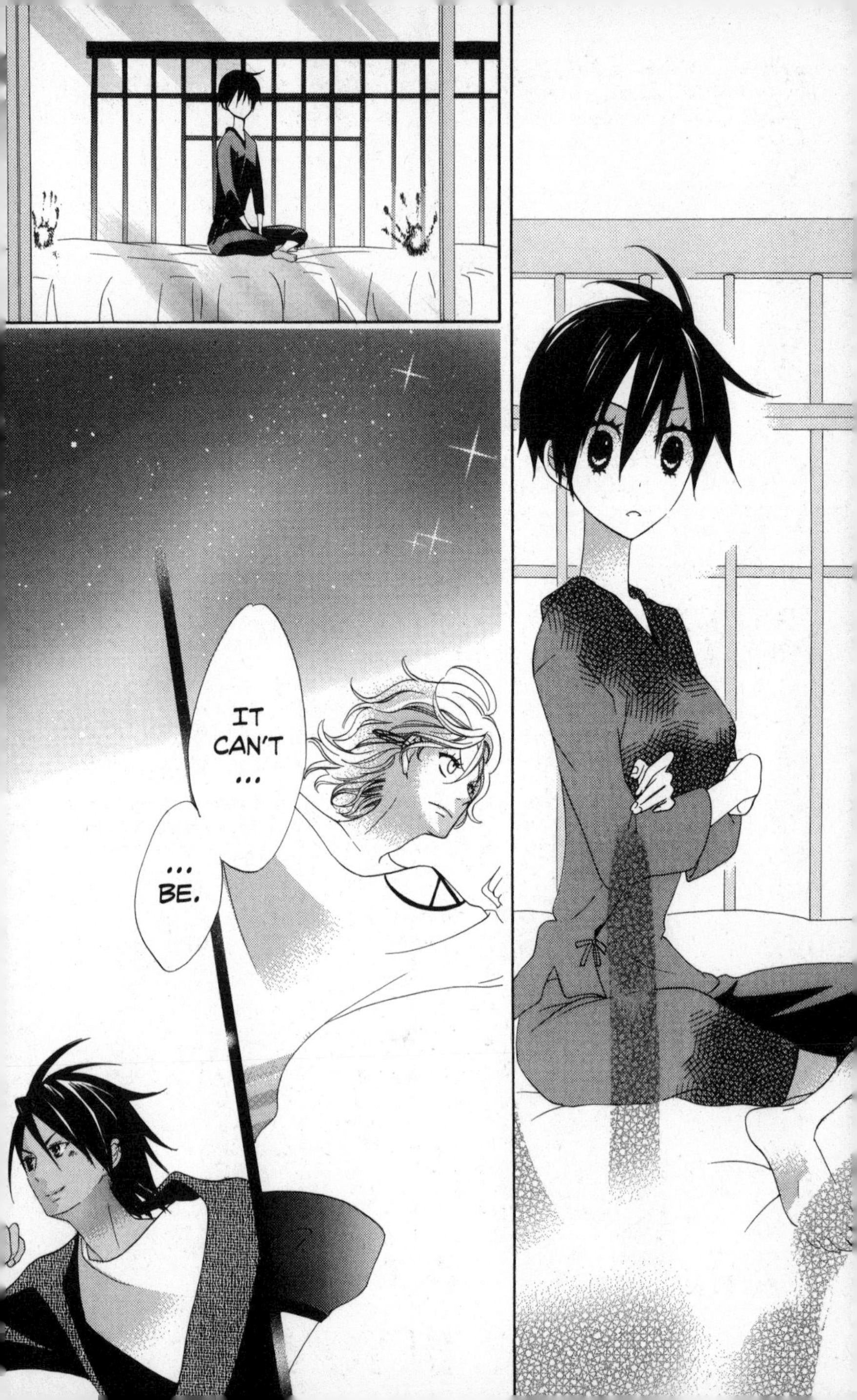
IT CAN'T ...
... BE.

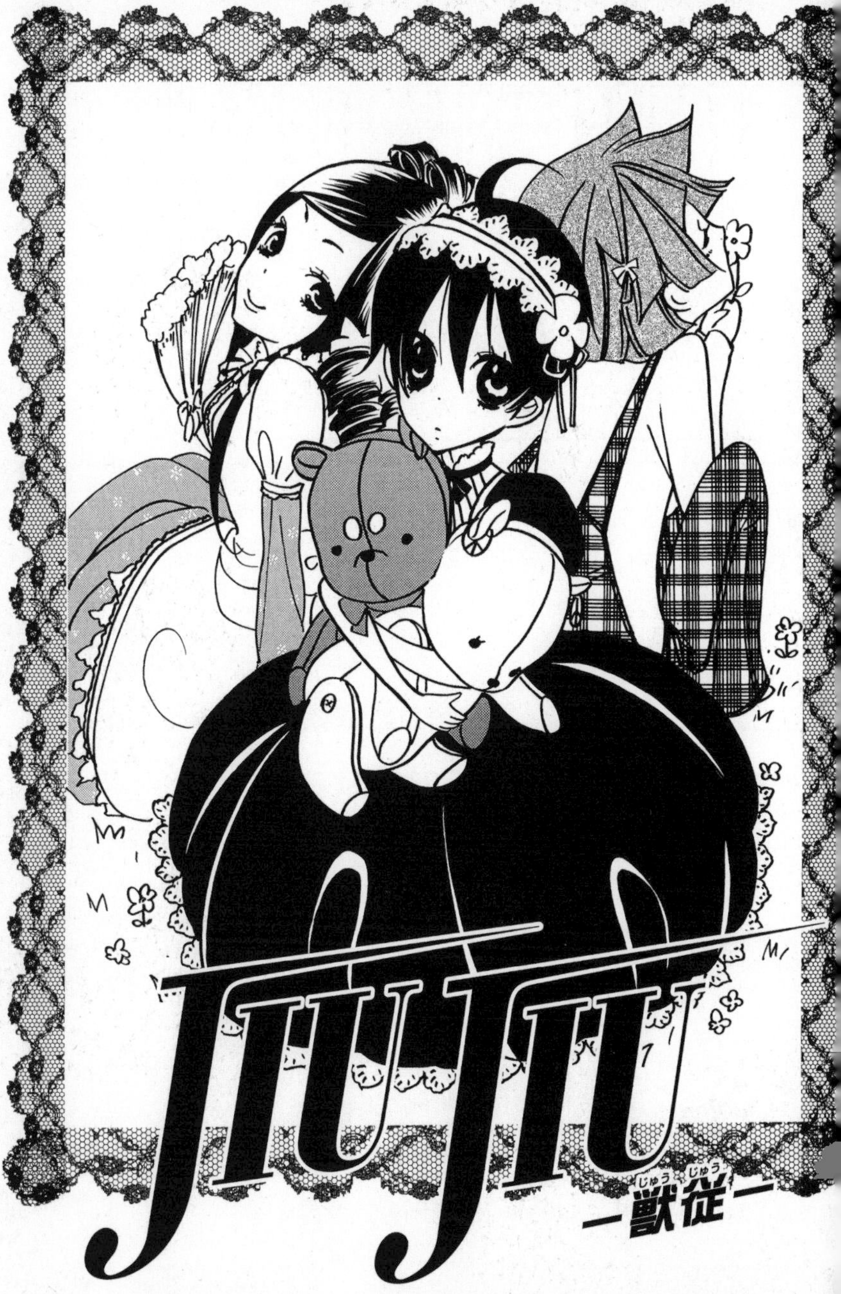
JIUJIU
獣従

WALK 17: BEYOND LOVE?

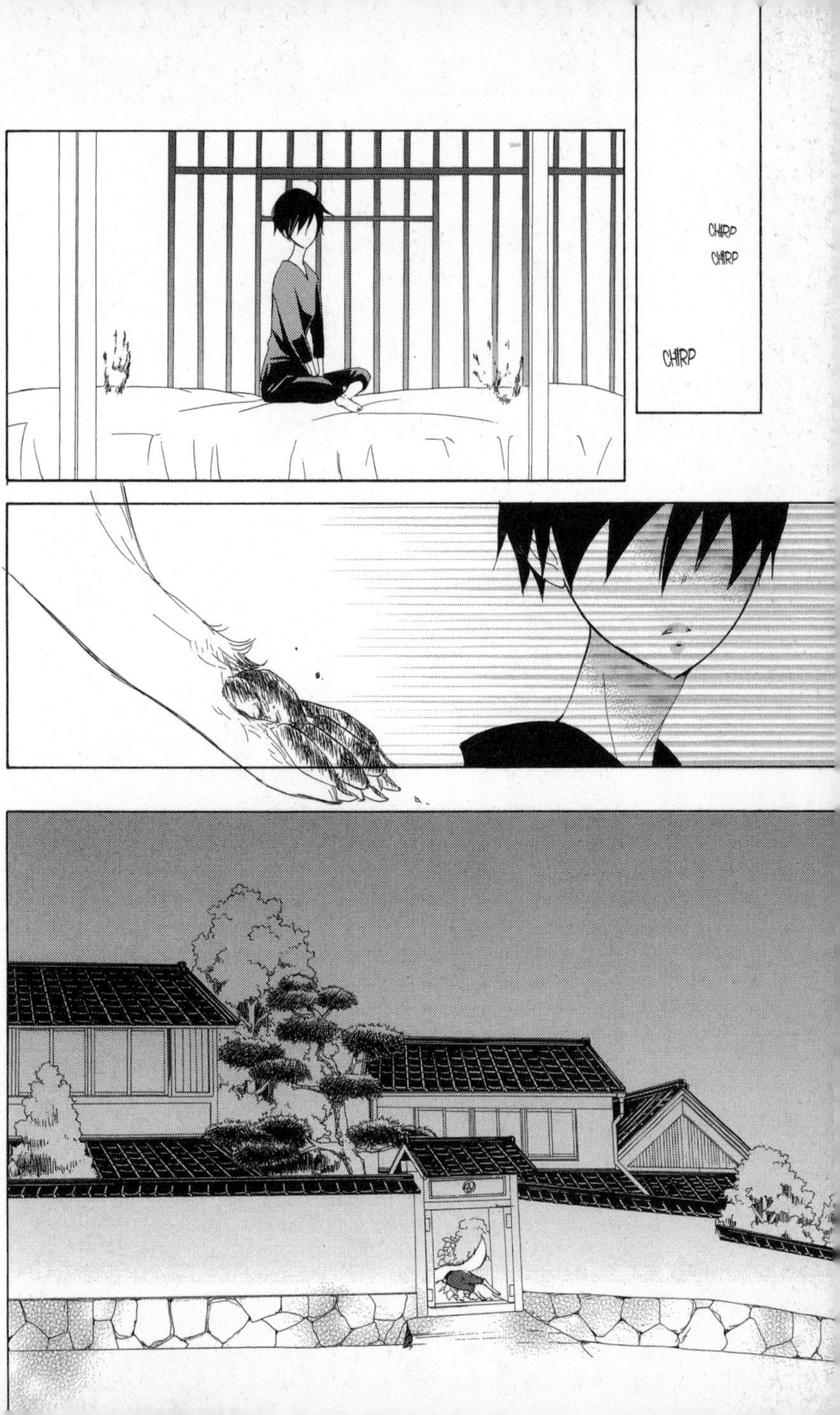
CHIRP
CHIRP
CHIRP

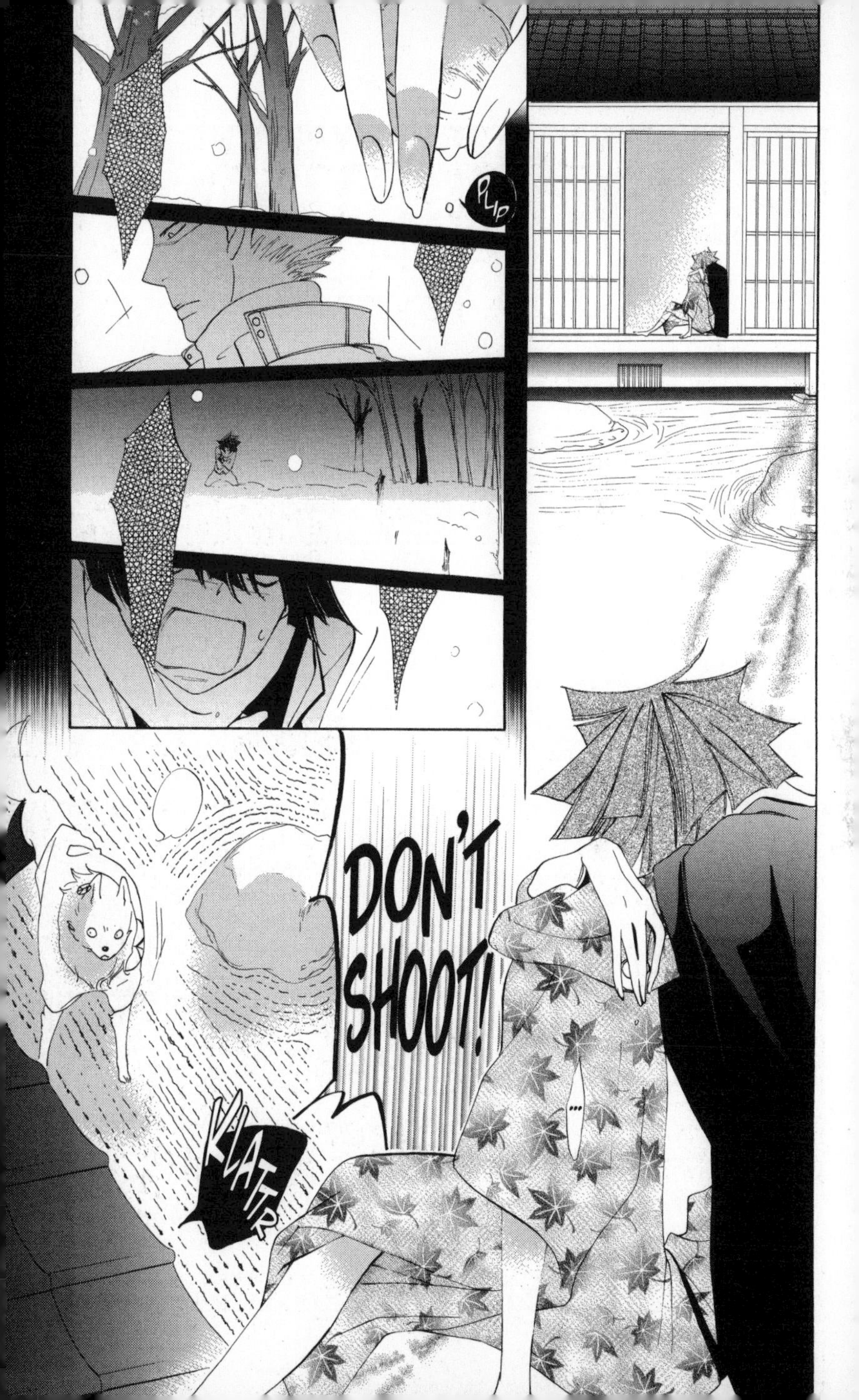
PLIP
DON'T SHOOT!
...
KLATTR

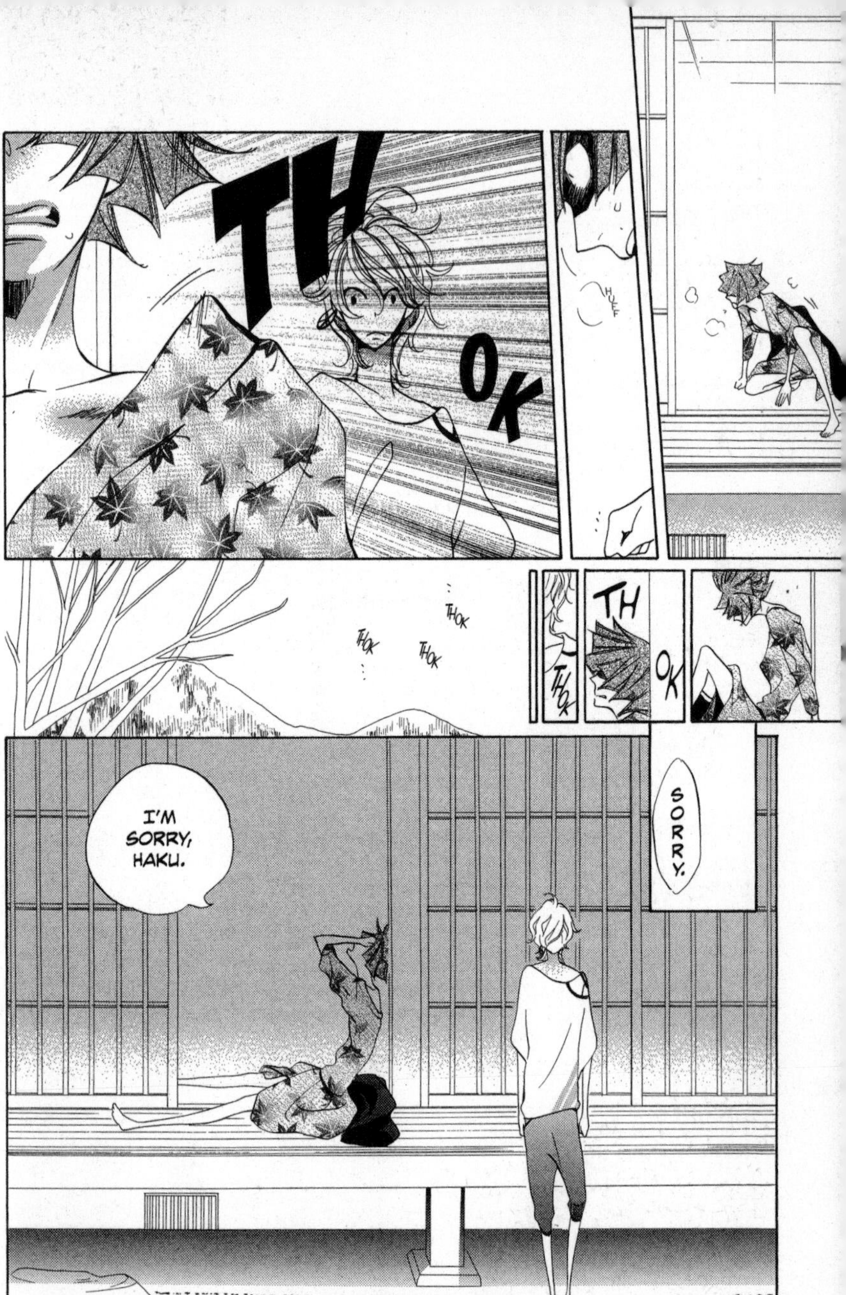
HUFF
THOK
THOK
THOK
THOK
THOK
THOK
SORRY.
I'M SORRY, HAKU.

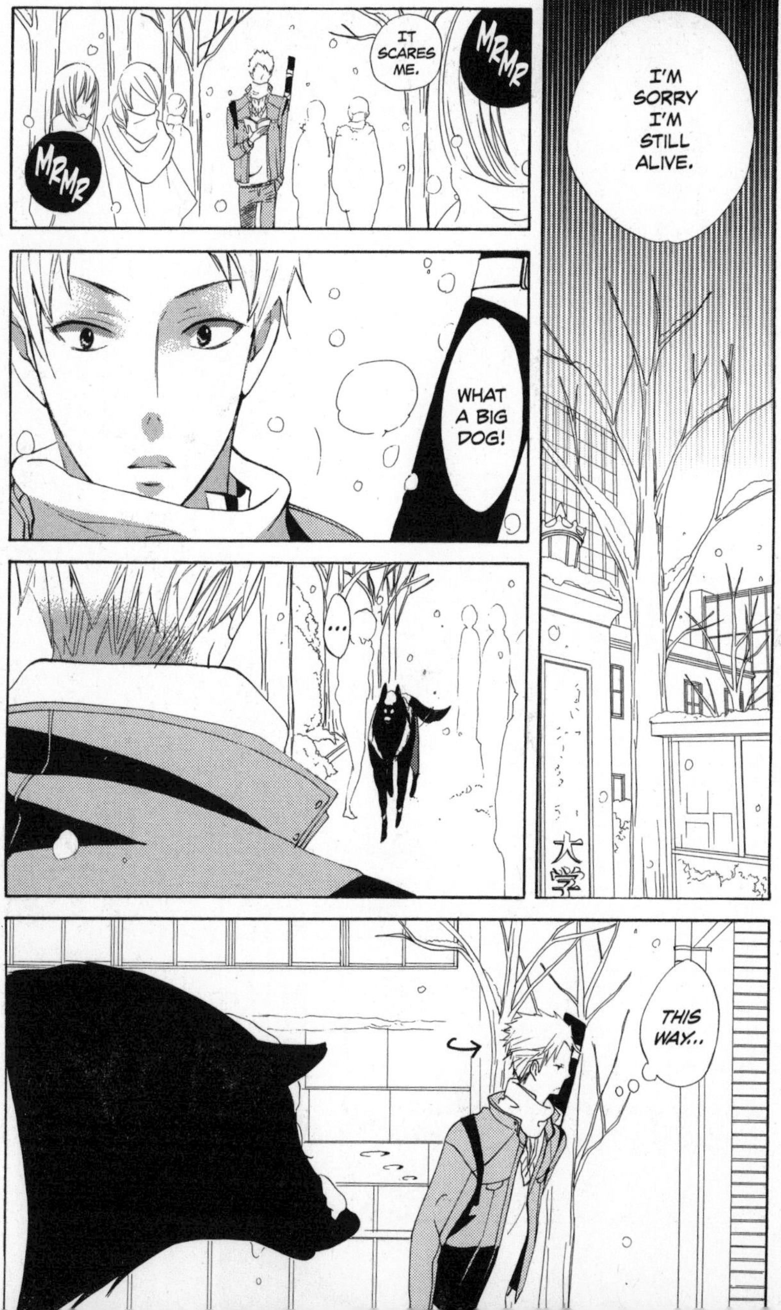
I'M SORRY I'M STILL ALIVE.
大学
MRMR
IT SCARES ME.
MRMR
WHAT A BIG DOG!
...
THIS WAY...

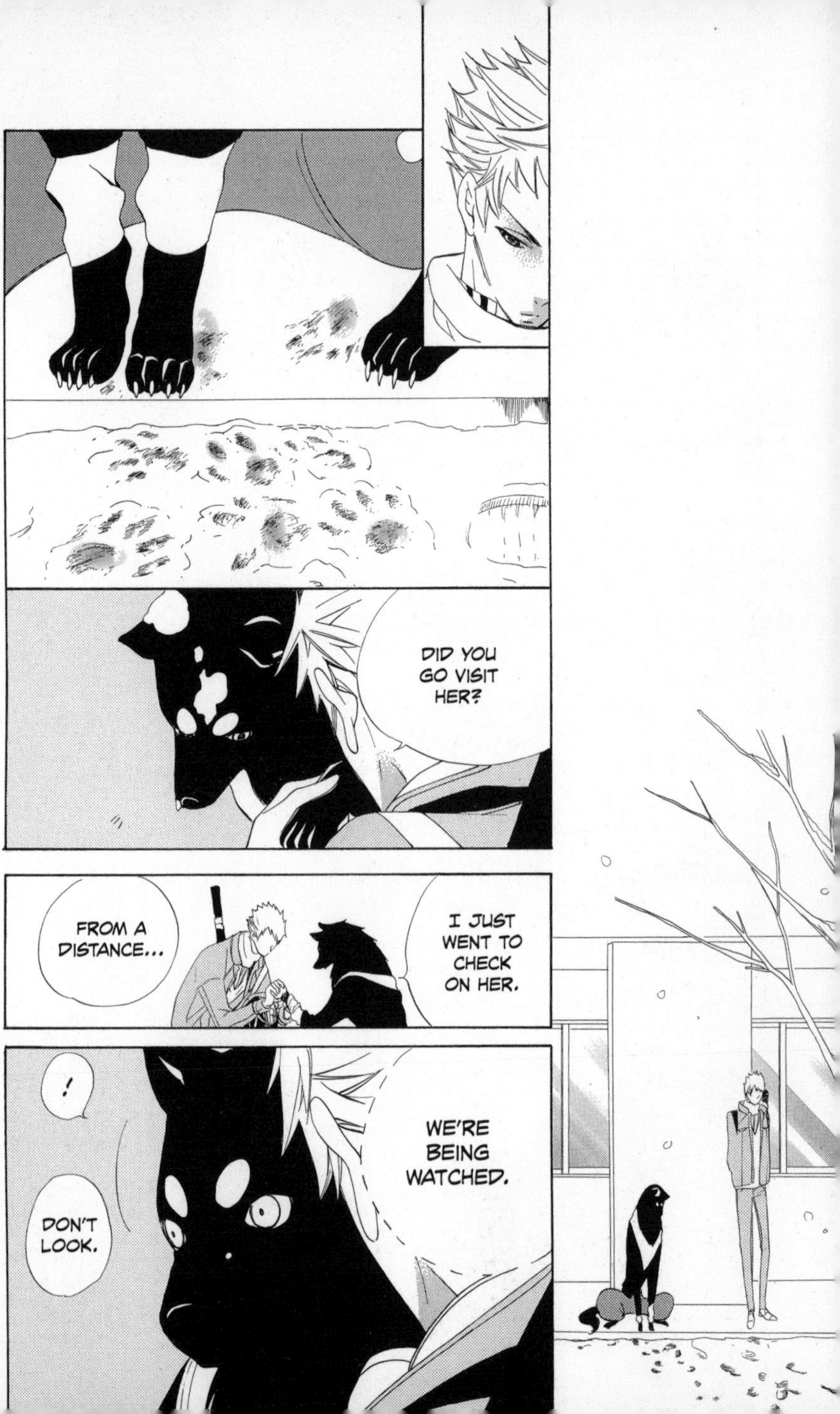

DID YOU GO VISIT HER?
I JUST WENT TO CHECK ON HER.
FROM A DISTANCE...
WE'RE BEING WATCHED.
!
DON'T LOOK.

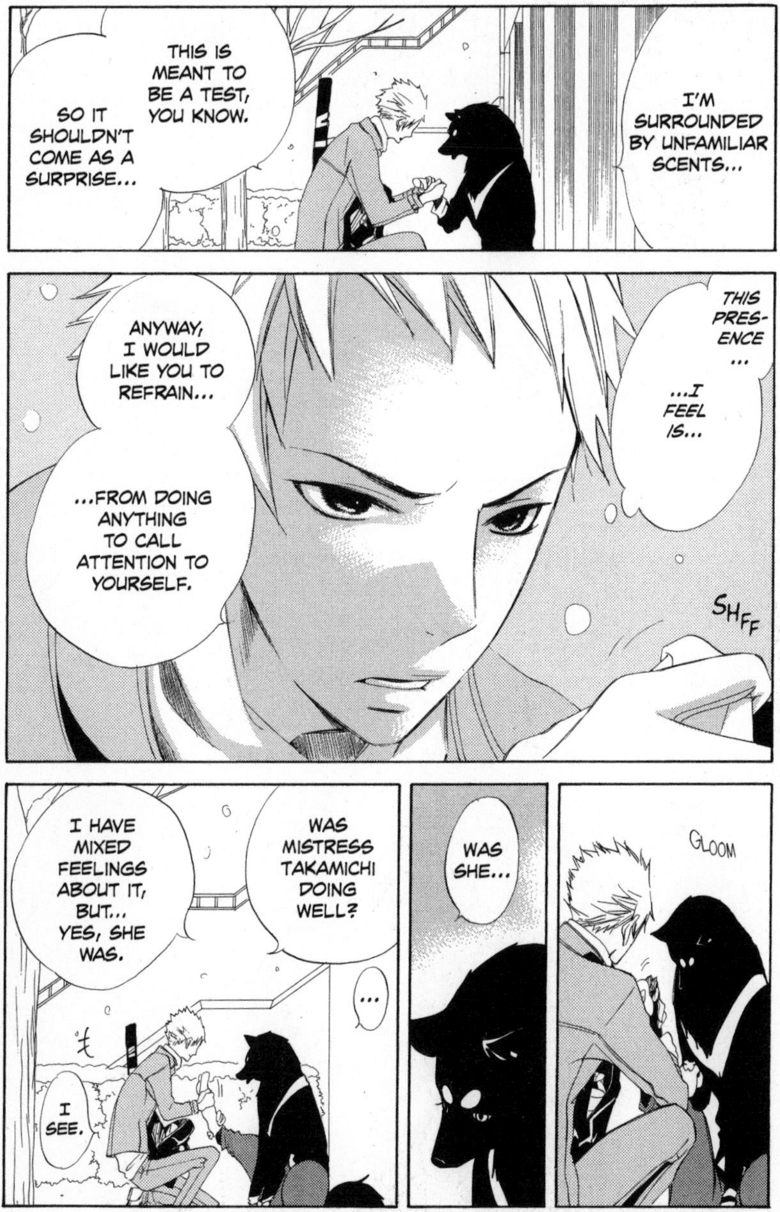
I'M SURROUNDED BY UNFAMILIAR SCENTS...
THIS IS MEANT TO BE A TEST, YOU KNOW.
SO IT SHOULDN'T COME AS A SURPRISE...
THIS PRESENCE...
...I FEEL IS...
ANYWAY, I WOULD LIKE YOU TO REFRAIN...
...FROM DOING ANYTHING TO CALL ATTENTION TO YOURSELF.
SHFF
GLOOM
WAS SHE...
WAS MISTRESS TAKAMICHI DOING WELL?
I HAVE MIXED FEELINGS ABOUT IT, BUT... YES, SHE WAS.
...
I SEE.

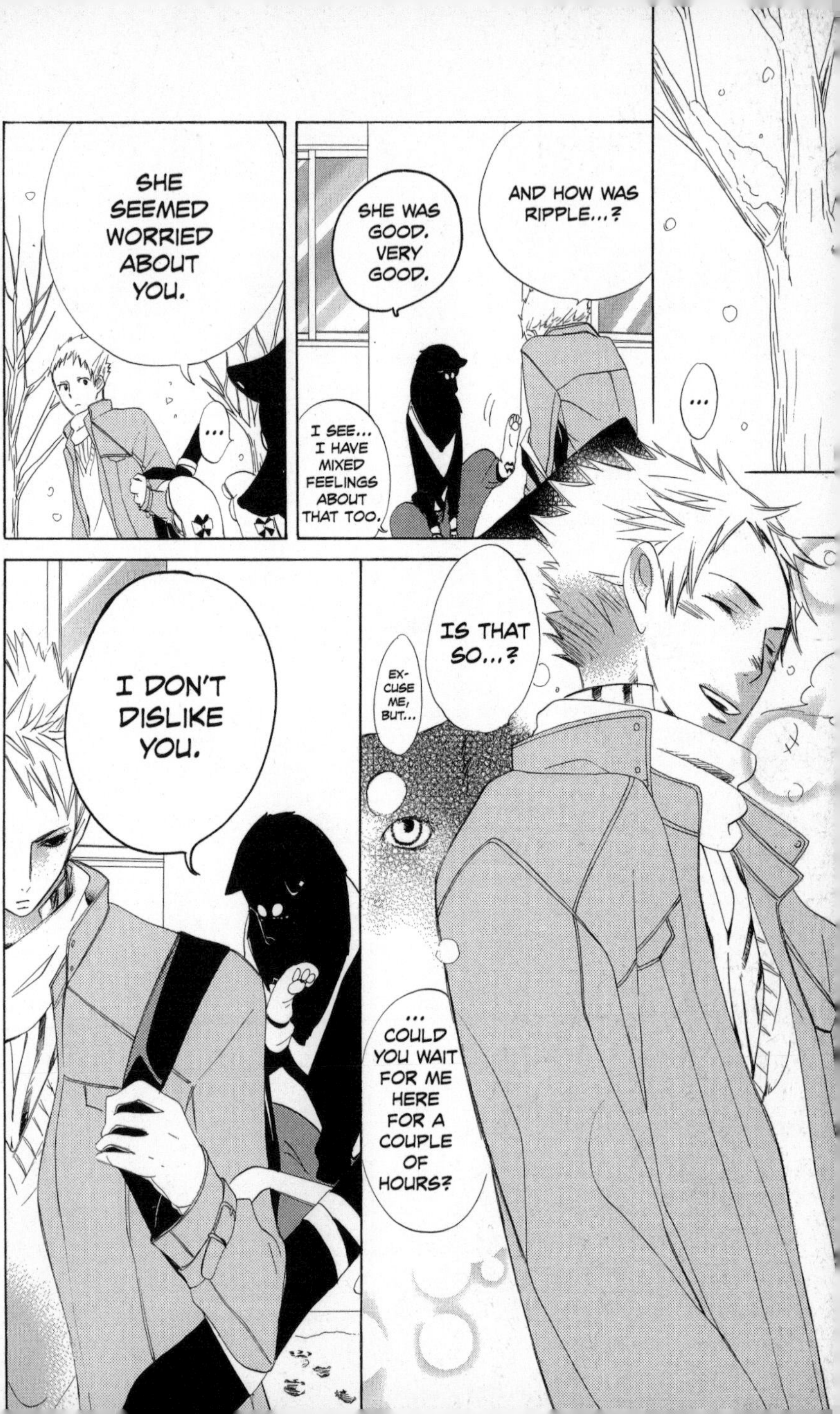
...
AND HOW WAS RIPPLE...?
SHE WAS GOOD. VERY GOOD.
I SEE... I HAVE MIXED FEELINGS ABOUT THAT TOO.
SHE SEEMED WORRIED ABOUT YOU.
...
IS THAT SO...?
EX-CUSE ME, BUT...
...COULD YOU WAIT FOR ME HERE FOR A COUPLE OF HOURS?
I DON'T DISLIKE YOU.

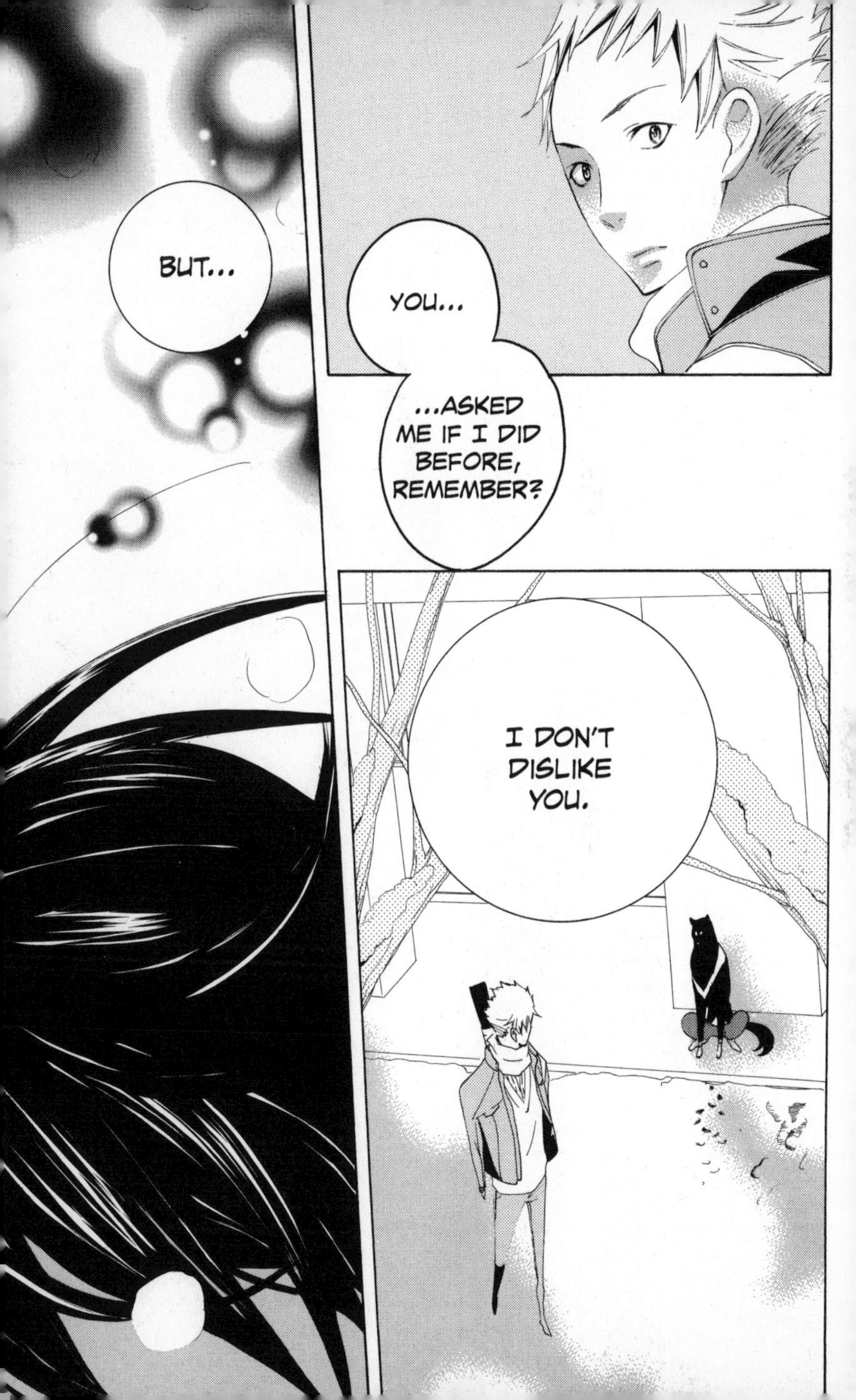
YOU...
...ASKED ME IF I DID BEFORE, REMEMBER?
I DON'T DISLIKE YOU.
BUT...

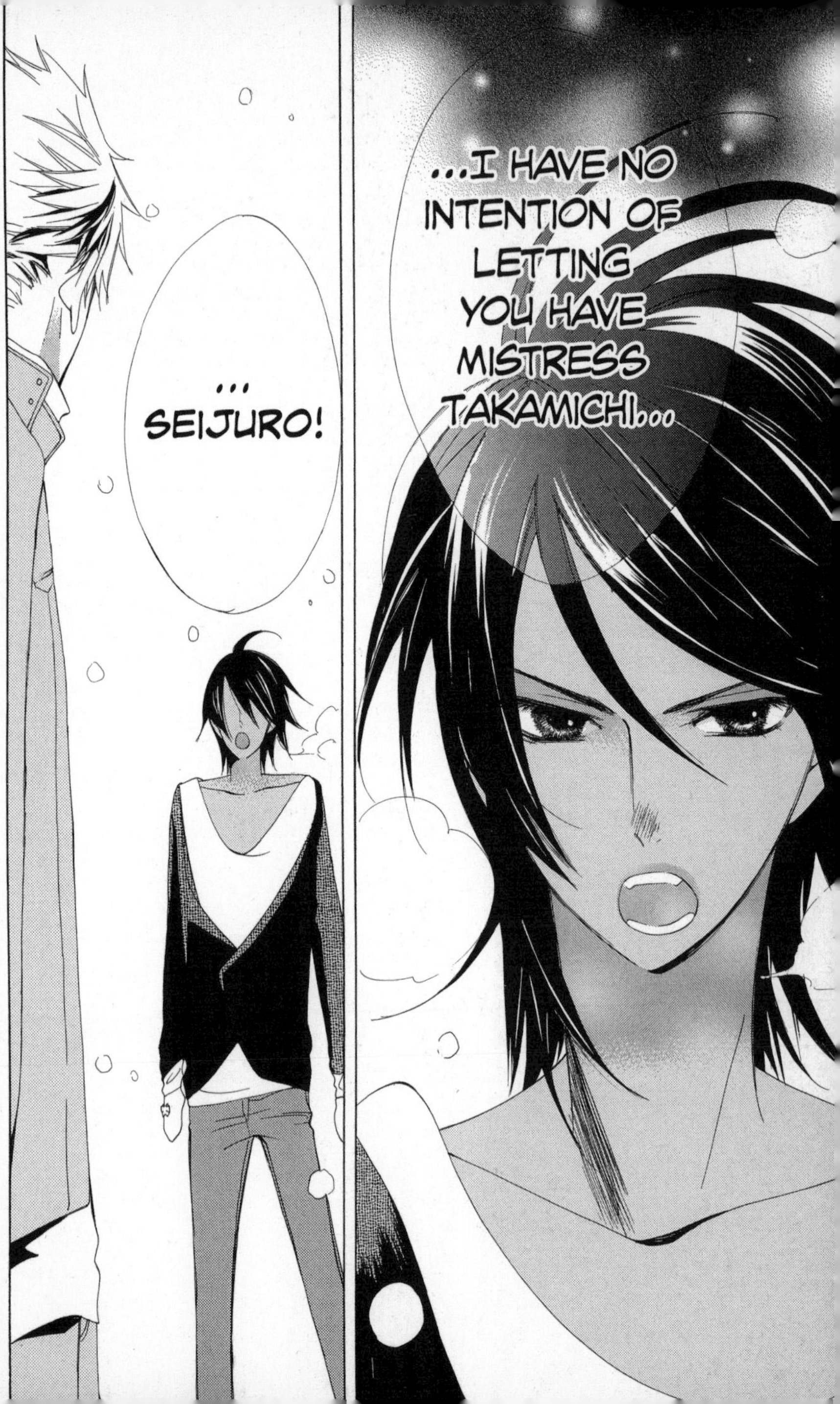
...I HAVE NO INTENTION OF LETTING YOU HAVE MISTRESS TAKAMICHI...
... SEIJURO!

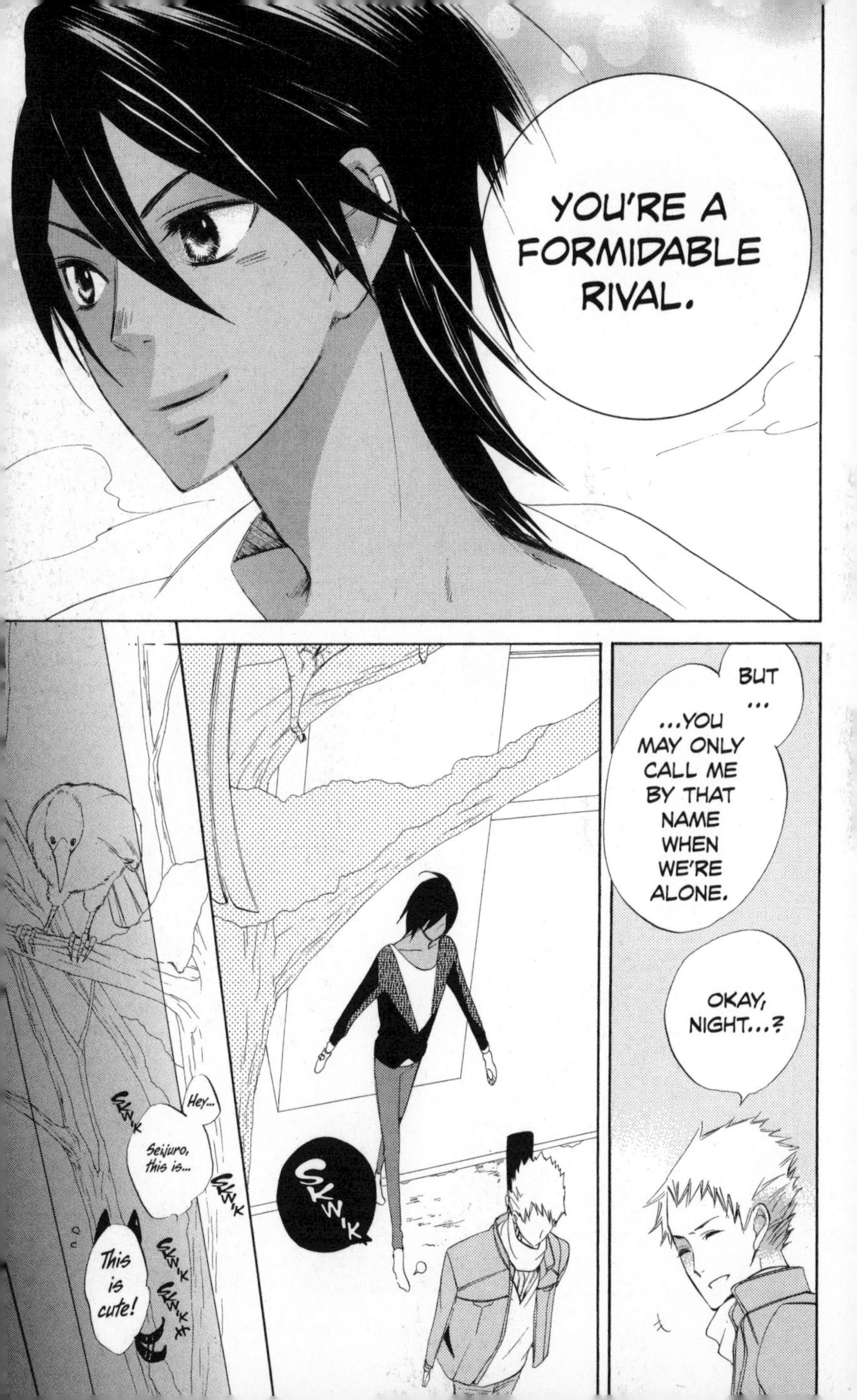
YOU'RE A FORMIDABLE RIVAL.
BUT ...
...YOU MAY ONLY CALL ME BY THAT NAME WHEN WE'RE ALONE.
OKAY, NIGHT...?
Hey...
Seijuro, this is...
SKWIK
SKWIK
SKWIK
This is cute!
SKWIK
SKWIK
SKWIK

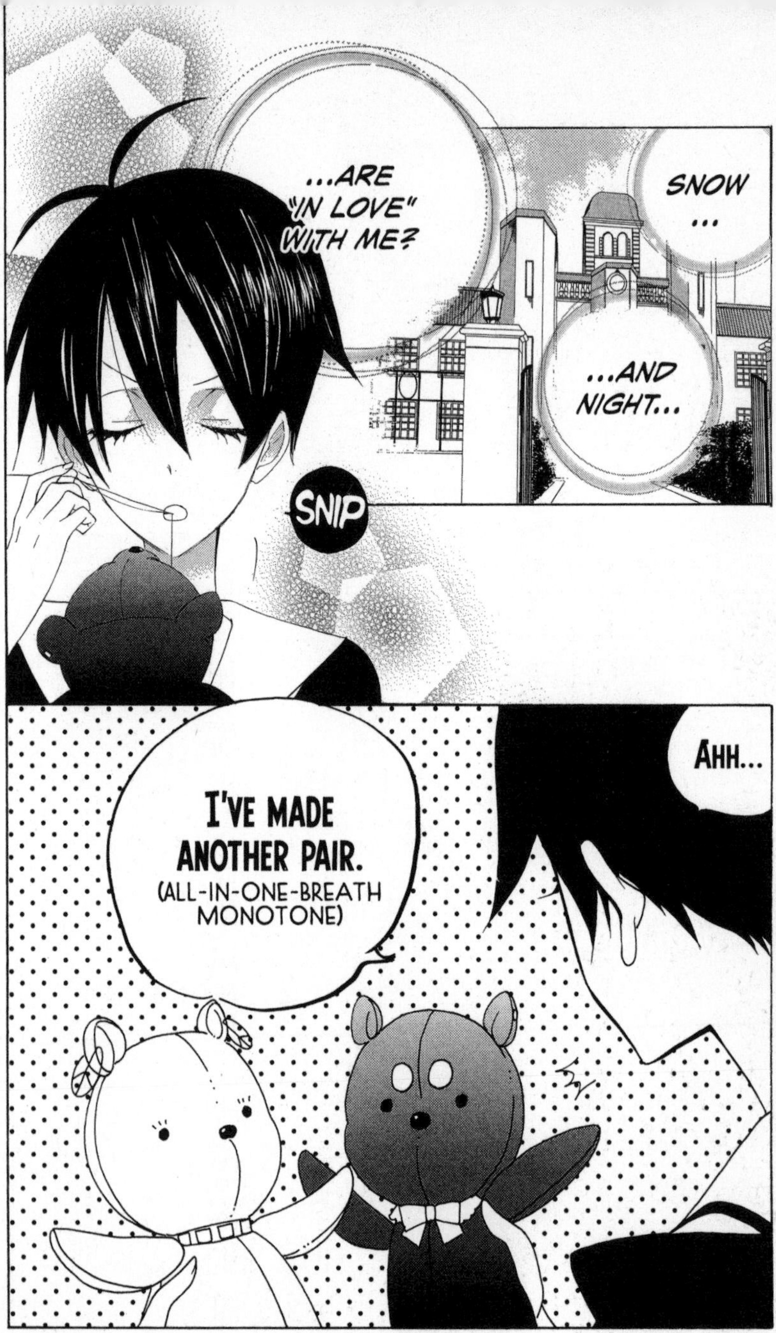
SNOW ...
...AND NIGHT...
...ARE "IN LOVE" WITH ME?
SNIP
AHH...
I'VE MADE ANOTHER PAIR.
(ALL-IN-ONE-BREATH MONOTONE)

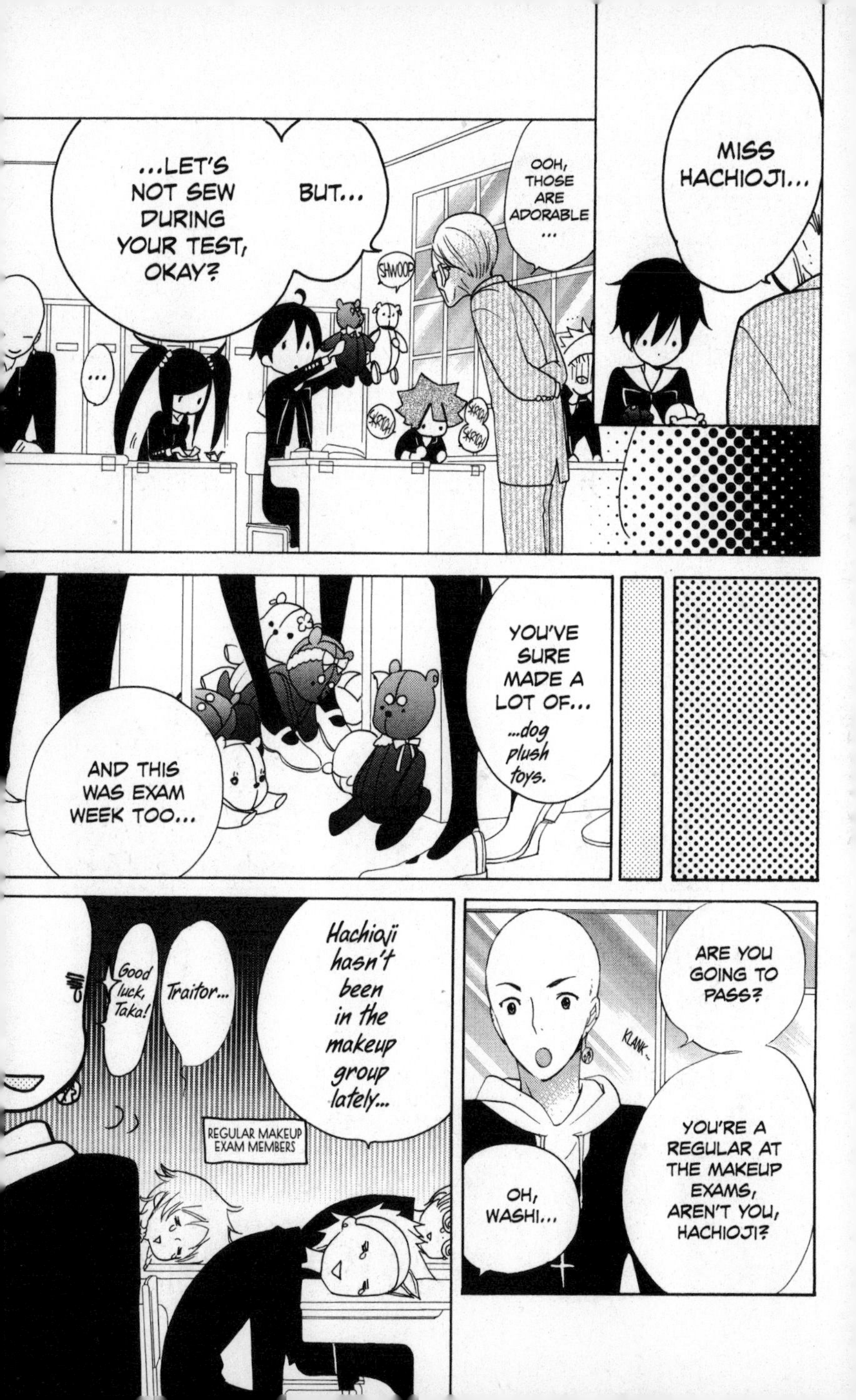
MISS HACHIOJI...
OOH, THOSE ARE ADORABLE...
BUT...
...LET'S NOT SEW DURING YOUR TEST, OKAY?
SHWOOP
...
SKRTCH
SKRTCH SKRTCH
YOU'VE SURE MADE A LOT OF... ...dog plush toys.
AND THIS WAS EXAM WEEK TOO...
ARE YOU GOING TO PASS?
KLANK
YOU'RE A REGULAR AT THE MAKEUP EXAMS, AREN'T YOU, HACHIOJI?
OH, WASHI...
Hachioji hasn't been in the makeup group lately...
Traitor...
Good luck, Taka!
REGULAR MAKEUP EXAM MEMBERS

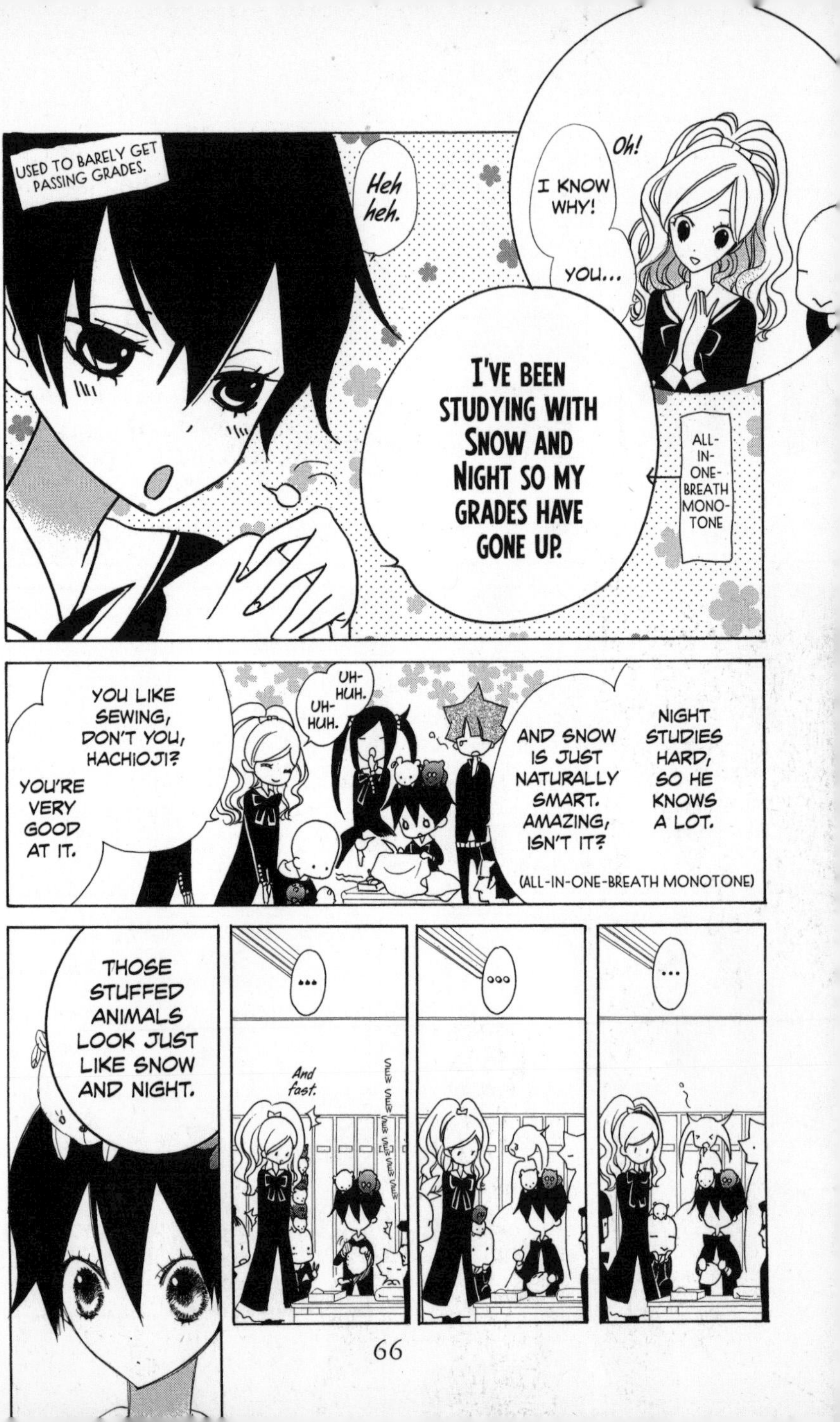
Oh!
I KNOW WHY!
YOU...
I'VE BEEN STUDYING WITH SNOW AND NIGHT SO MY GRADES HAVE GONE UP.
ALL-IN-ONE-BREATH MONOTONE
Heh heh.
USED TO BARELY GET PASSING GRADES.
NIGHT STUDIES HARD, SO HE KNOWS A LOT.
AND SNOW IS JUST NATURALLY SMART. AMAZING, ISN'T IT?
(ALL-IN-ONE-BREATH MONOTONE)
UH-HUH.
UH-HUH.
YOU LIKE SEWING, DON'T YOU, HACHIOJI?
YOU'RE VERY GOOD AT IT.
...
ooo
...
And fast.
SEW SEW SEW SEW SEW SEW
THOSE STUFFED ANIMALS LOOK JUST LIKE SNOW AND NIGHT.

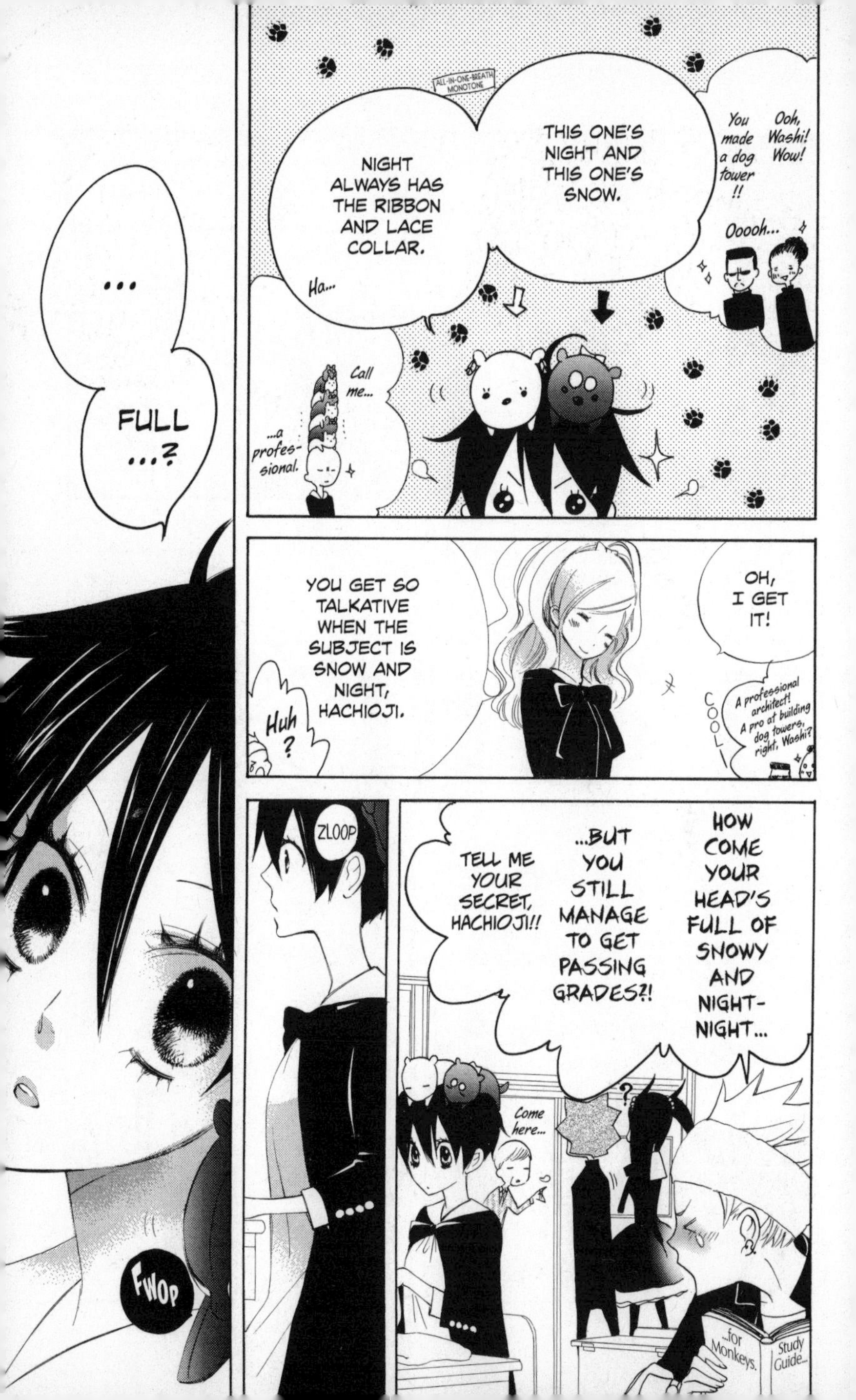
Ooh, Washi! Wow!
You made a dog tower!!
Ooooh...
ALL-IN-ONE-BREATH MONOTONE
THIS ONE'S NIGHT AND THIS ONE'S SNOW.
NIGHT ALWAYS HAS THE RIBBON AND LACE COLLAR.
Ha...
Call me...
...a profes-sional.
OH, I GET IT!
A professional architect! A pro at building dog towers, right, Washi?
COOL
YOU GET SO TALKATIVE WHEN THE SUBJECT IS SNOW AND NIGHT, HACHIOJI.
Huh?
HOW COME YOUR HEAD'S FULL OF SNOWY AND NIGHT-NIGHT...
...BUT YOU STILL MANAGE TO GET PASSING GRADES?!
TELL ME YOUR SECRET, HACHIOJI!!
Come here...
Study Guide...
...for Monkeys.
ZLOOP
...
FULL ...?
FWOP

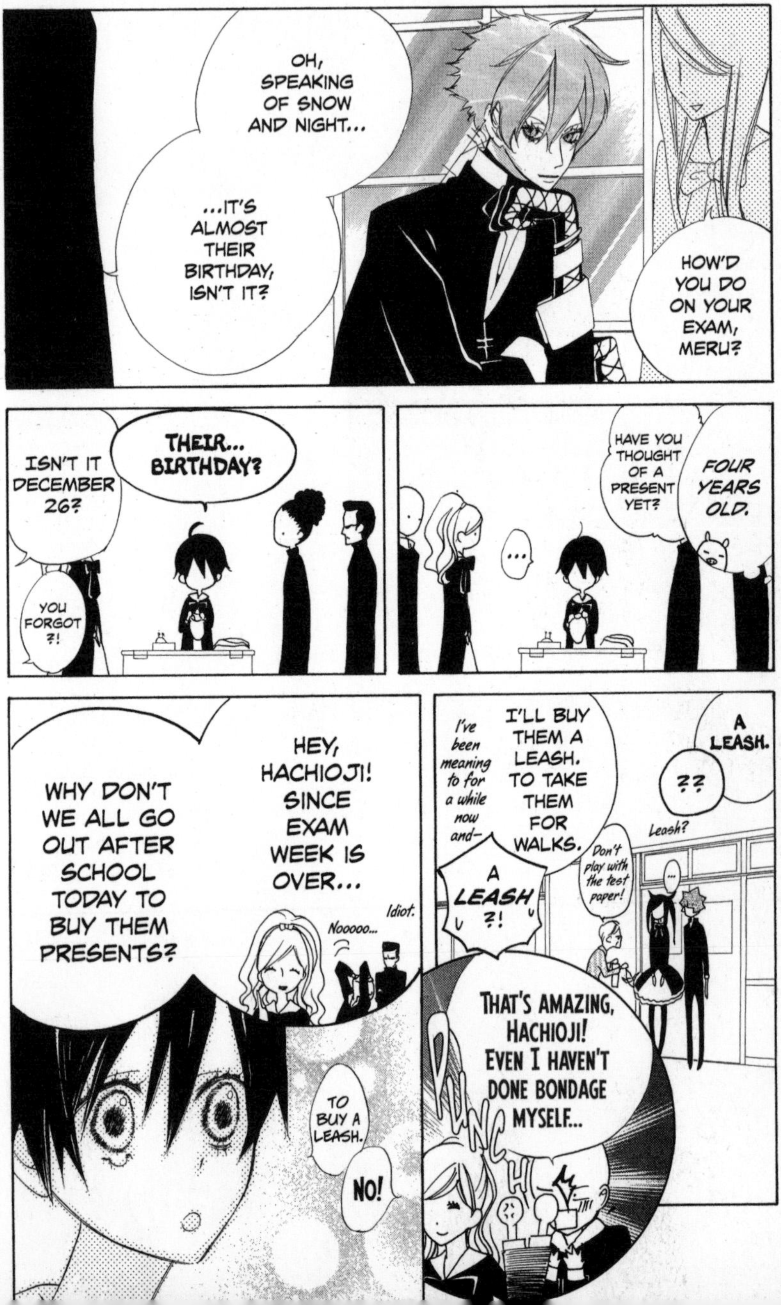
HOW'D YOU DO ON YOUR EXAM, MERU?
OH, SPEAKING OF SNOW AND NIGHT...
...IT'S ALMOST THEIR BIRTHDAY, ISN'T IT?
FOUR YEARS OLD.
HAVE YOU THOUGHT OF A PRESENT YET?
...
THEIR... BIRTHDAY?
ISN'T IT DECEMBER 26?
YOU FORGOT?!
A LEASH.
??
I'LL BUY THEM A LEASH. TO TAKE THEM FOR WALKS.
I've been meaning to for a while now and—
Leash?
Don't play with the test paper!
...
A LEASH?!
THAT'S AMAZING, HACHIOJI! EVEN I HAVEN'T DONE BONDAGE MYSELF...
PUNCH
HEY, HACHIOJI! SINCE EXAM WEEK IS OVER...
WHY DON'T WE ALL GO OUT AFTER SCHOOL TODAY TO BUY THEM PRESENTS?
Idiot.
Nooooo...
TO BUY A LEASH.
NO!

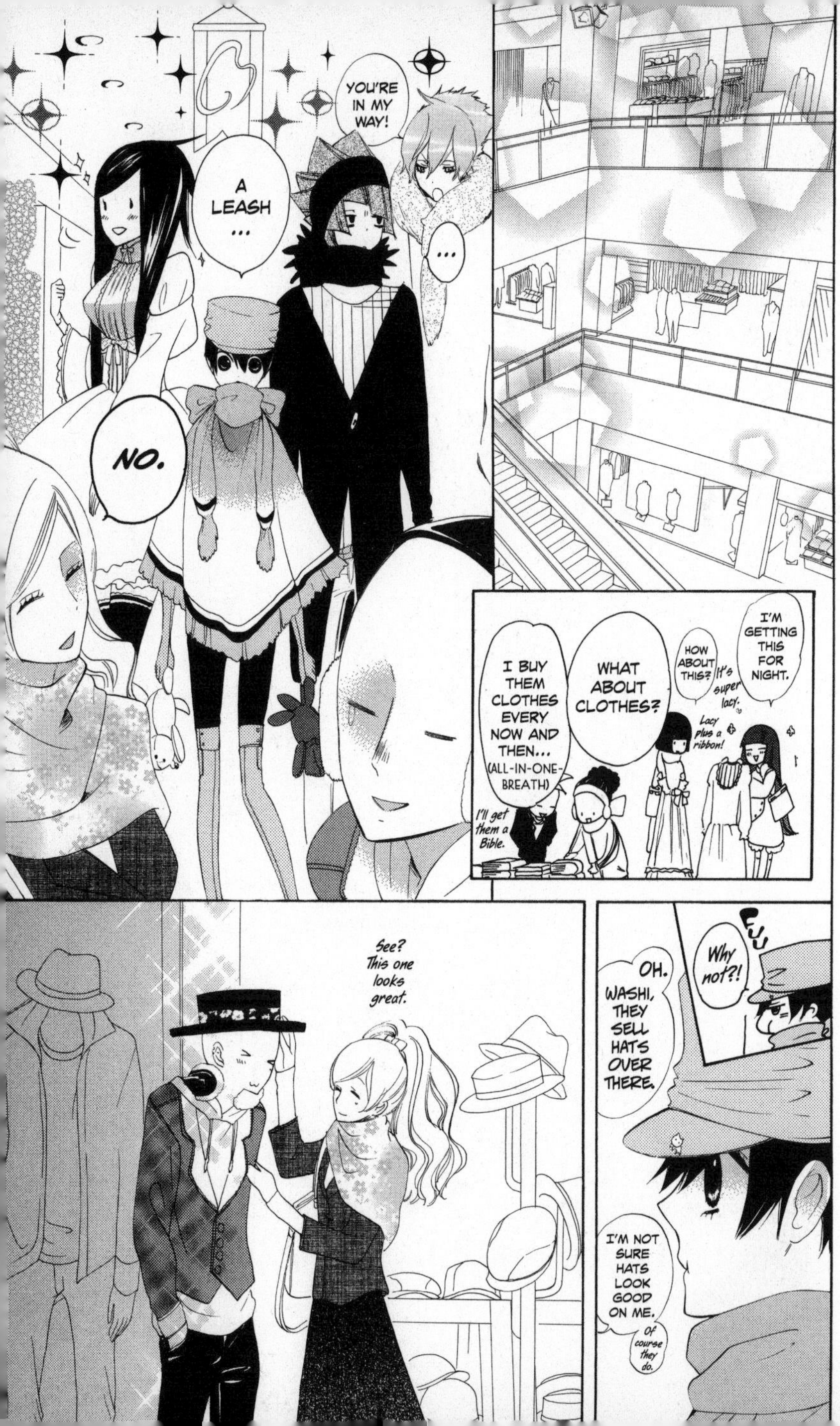
I'M GETTING THIS FOR NIGHT.
HOW ABOUT THIS?
It's super lacy.
Lacy plus a ribbon!
WHAT ABOUT CLOTHES?
I BUY THEM CLOTHES EVERY NOW AND THEN... (ALL-IN-ONE-BREATH)
I'll get them a Bible.
YOU'RE IN MY WAY!
...
A LEASH ...
NO.
Why not?!
OH. WASHI, THEY SELL HATS OVER THERE.
I'M NOT SURE HATS LOOK GOOD ON ME.
Of course they do.
See? This one looks great.

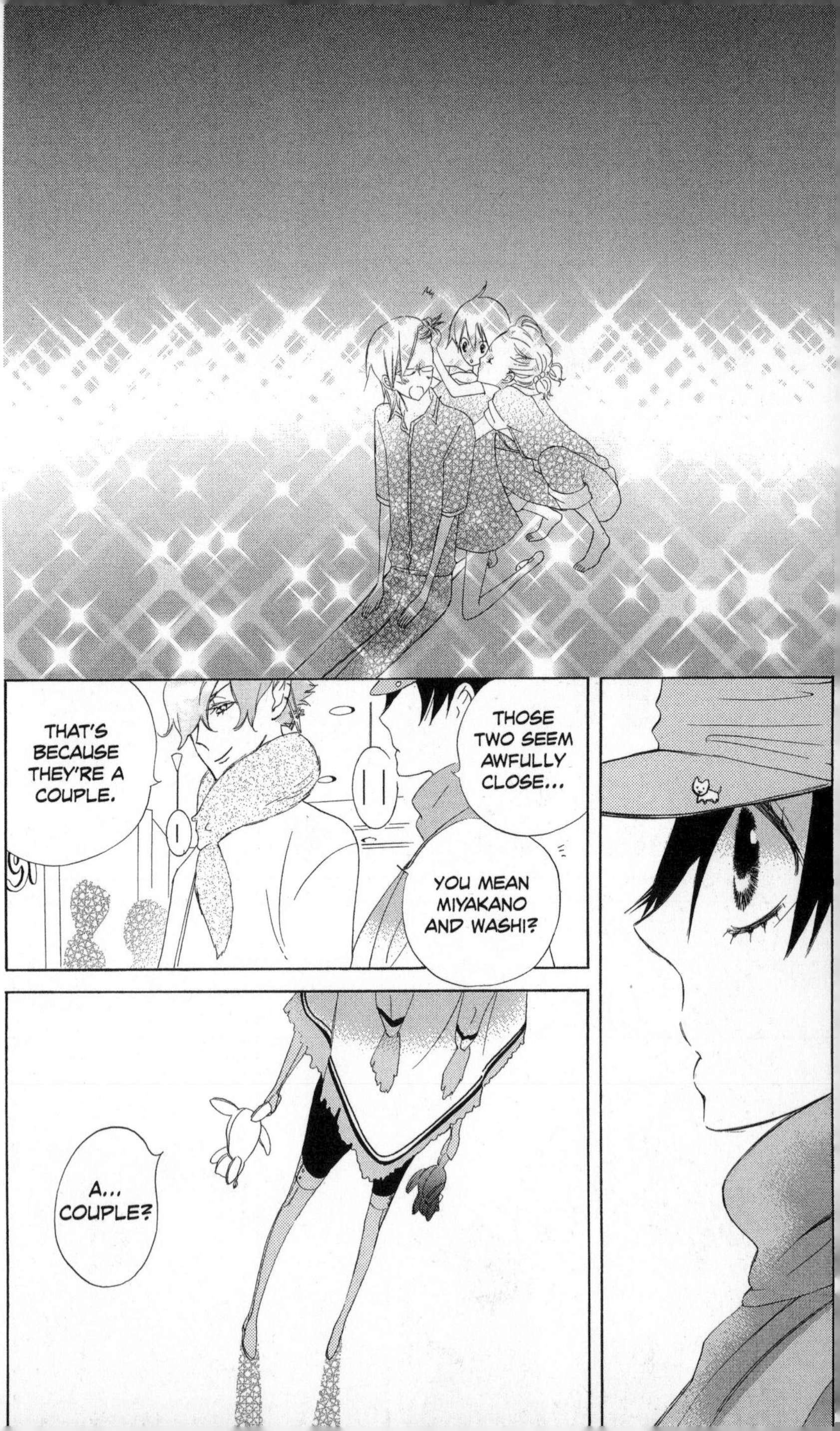
THOSE TWO SEEM AWFULLY CLOSE...
THAT'S BECAUSE THEY'RE A COUPLE.
YOU MEAN MIYAKANO AND WASHI?
A... COUPLE?

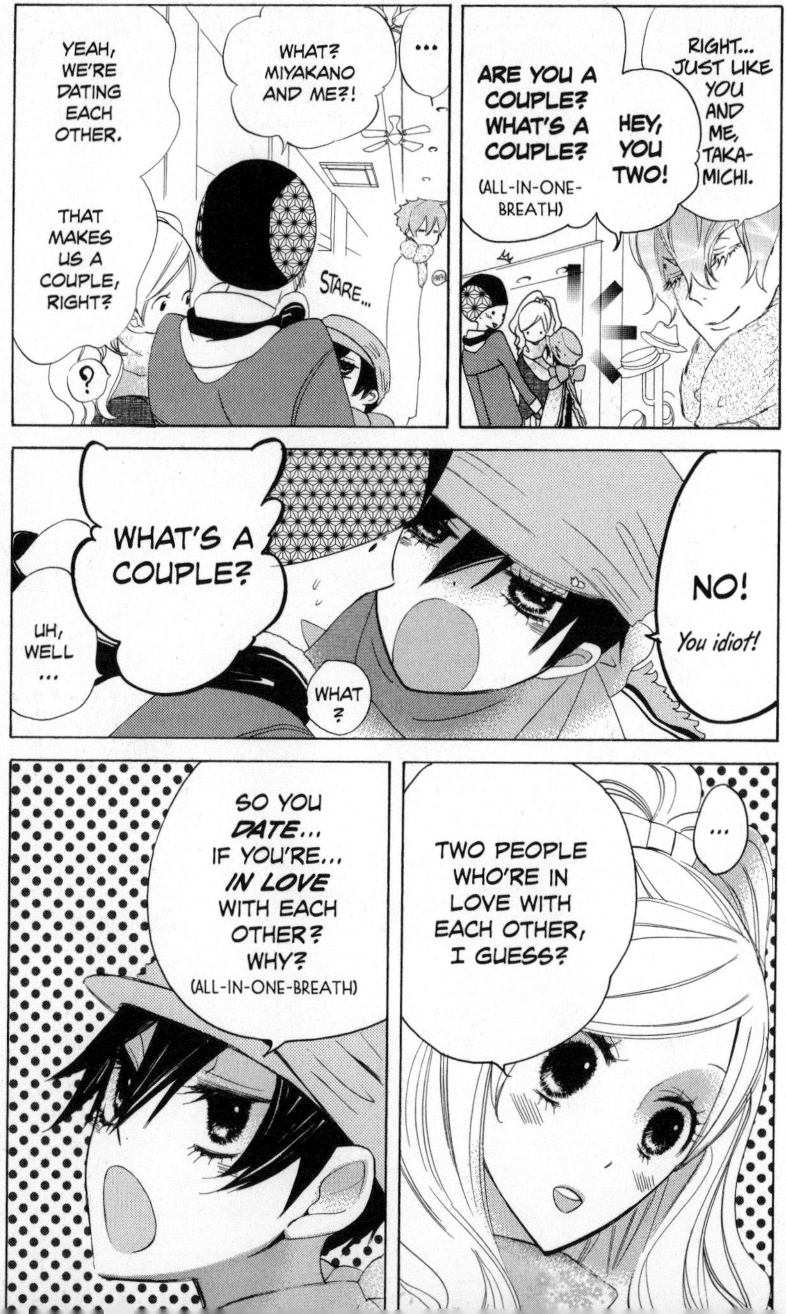
RIGHT... JUST LIKE YOU AND ME, TAKAMICHI.
HEY, YOU TWO!
ARE YOU A COUPLE? WHAT'S A COUPLE?
(ALL-IN-ONE-BREATH)
...
WHAT? MIYAKANO AND ME?!
STARE...
YEAH, WE'RE DATING EACH OTHER.
THAT MAKES US A COUPLE, RIGHT?
?
NO! You idiot!
WHAT?
WHAT'S A COUPLE?
UH, WELL...
...
TWO PEOPLE WHO'RE IN LOVE WITH EACH OTHER, I GUESS?
SO YOU DATE... IF YOU'RE... IN LOVE WITH EACH OTHER? WHY?
(ALL-IN-ONE-BREATH)

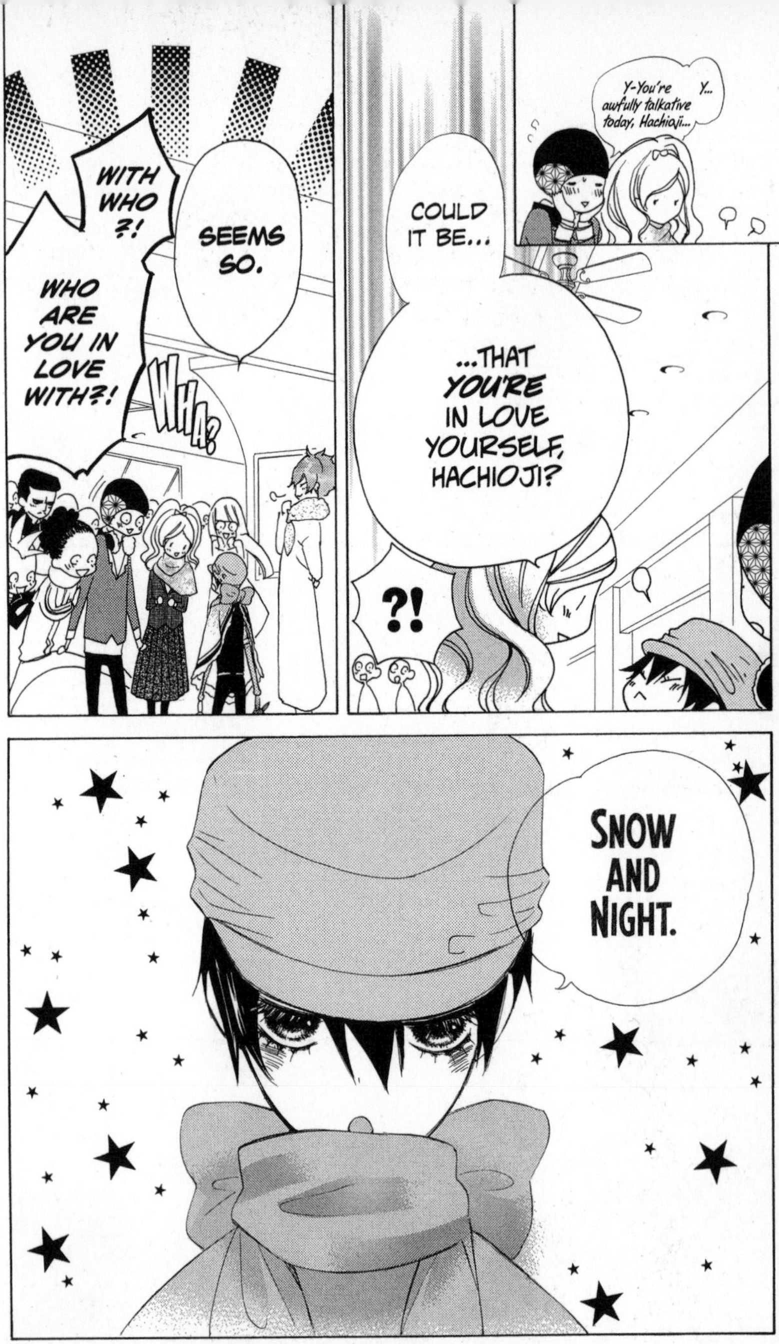
Y-You're awfully talkative today, Hachioji...
Y...
COULD IT BE...
...THAT YOU'RE IN LOVE YOURSELF, HACHIOJI?
?!
SEEMS SO.
WITH WHO?!
WHO ARE YOU IN LOVE WITH?!
WHA?!
SNOW AND NIGHT.

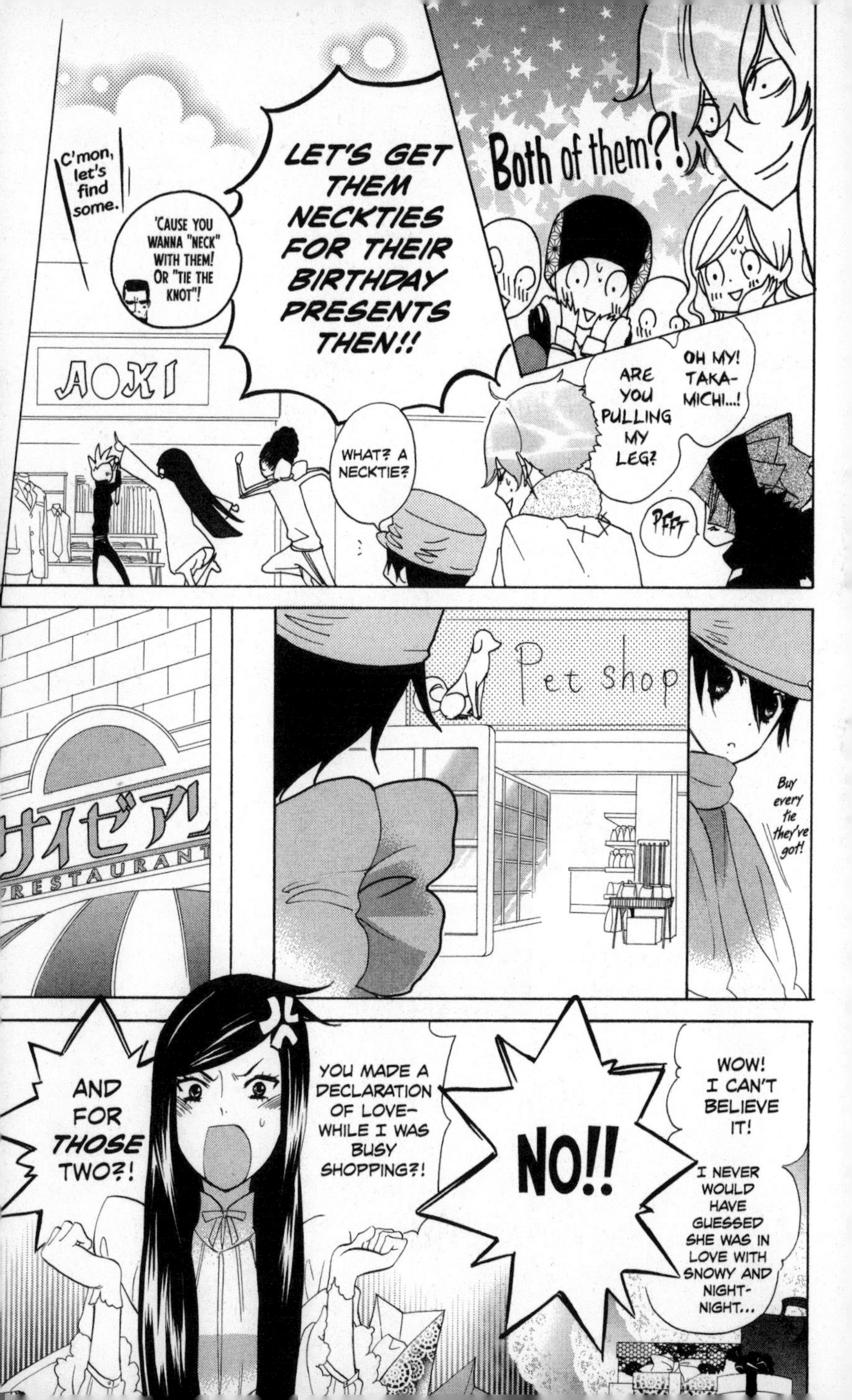

Both of them?!
OH MY! TAKAMICHI...!
ARE YOU PULLING MY LEG?
PFFT
WHAT? A NECKTIE?
LET'S GET THEM NECKTIES FOR THEIR BIRTHDAY PRESENTS THEN!!
'CAUSE YOU WANNA "NECK" WITH THEM! OR "TIE THE KNOT"!
C'mon, let's find some.
AOKI
Buy every tie they've got!
Pet shop
サイゼアリ
RESTAURANT
WOW! I CAN'T BELIEVE IT!
I NEVER WOULD HAVE GUESSED SHE WAS IN LOVE WITH SNOWY AND NIGHT-NIGHT...
NO!!
YOU MADE A DECLARATION OF LOVE—WHILE I WAS BUSY SHOPPING?!
AND FOR *THOSE* TWO?!

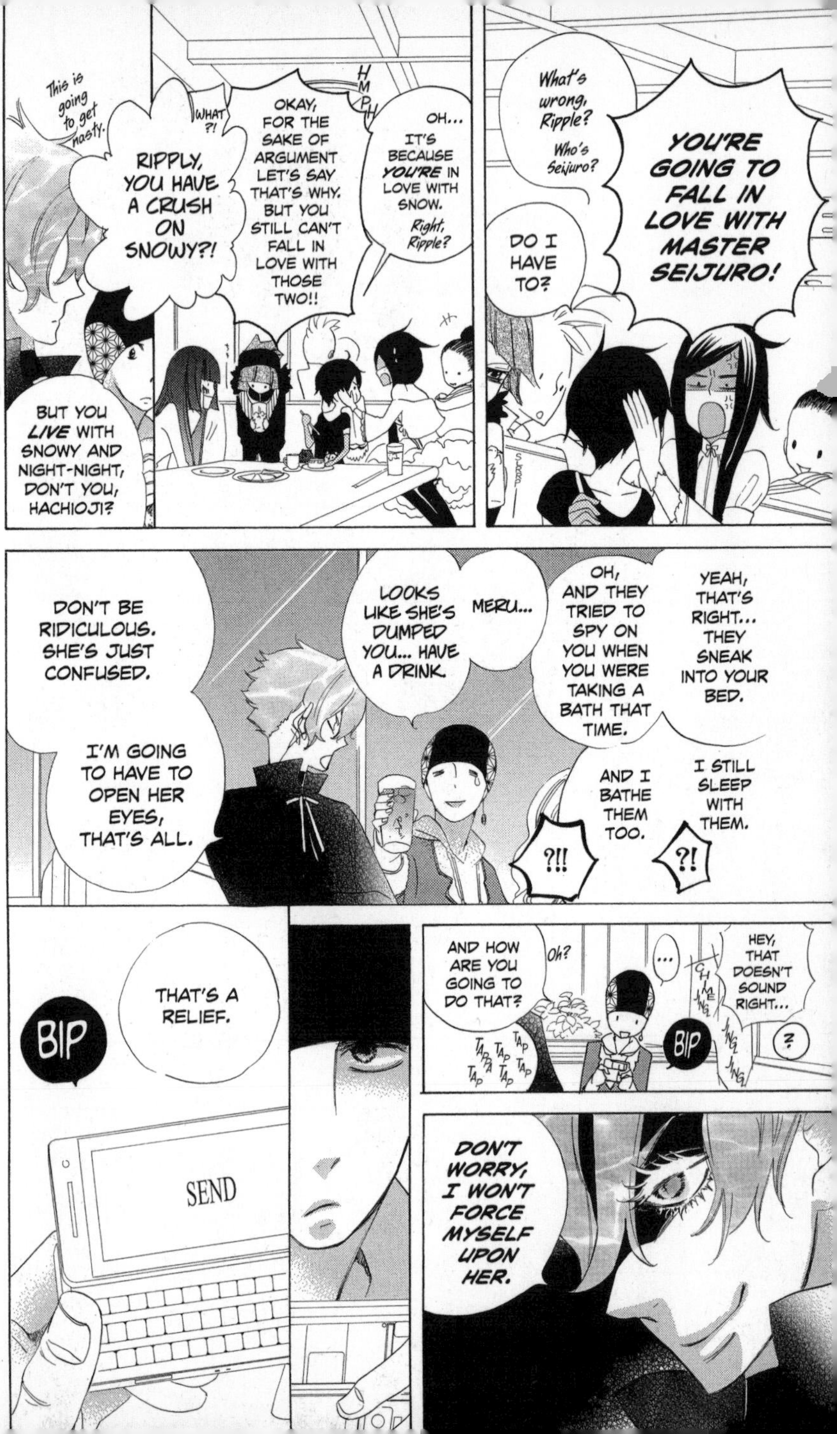
YOU'RE GOING TO FALL IN LOVE WITH MASTER SEIJURO!
What's wrong, Ripple?
Who's Seijuro?
DO I HAVE TO?
OH... IT'S BECAUSE YOU'RE IN LOVE WITH SNOW.
Right, Ripple?
HMPH
OKAY, FOR THE SAKE OF ARGUMENT LET'S SAY THAT'S WHY. BUT YOU STILL CAN'T FALL IN LOVE WITH THOSE TWO!!
WHAT?!
RIPPLY, YOU HAVE A CRUSH ON SNOWY?!
This is going to get nasty.
BUT YOU LIVE WITH SNOWY AND NIGHT-NIGHT, DON'T YOU, HACHIOJI?
YEAH, THAT'S RIGHT... THEY SNEAK INTO YOUR BED.
OH, AND THEY TRIED TO SPY ON YOU WHEN YOU WERE TAKING A BATH THAT TIME.
MERU...
LOOKS LIKE SHE'S DUMPED YOU... HAVE A DRINK.
DON'T BE RIDICULOUS. SHE'S JUST CONFUSED.
I STILL SLEEP WITH THEM.
?!
AND I BATHE THEM TOO.
?!!
I'M GOING TO HAVE TO OPEN HER EYES, THAT'S ALL.
HEY, THAT DOESN'T SOUND RIGHT...
?
JINGLE JINGLE
CHIME
...
BIP
Oh?
AND HOW ARE YOU GOING TO DO THAT?
TAP TAP TAPPA TAP TAP TAP TAP
DON'T WORRY, I WON'T FORCE MYSELF UPON HER.
THAT'S A RELIEF.
BIP
SEND

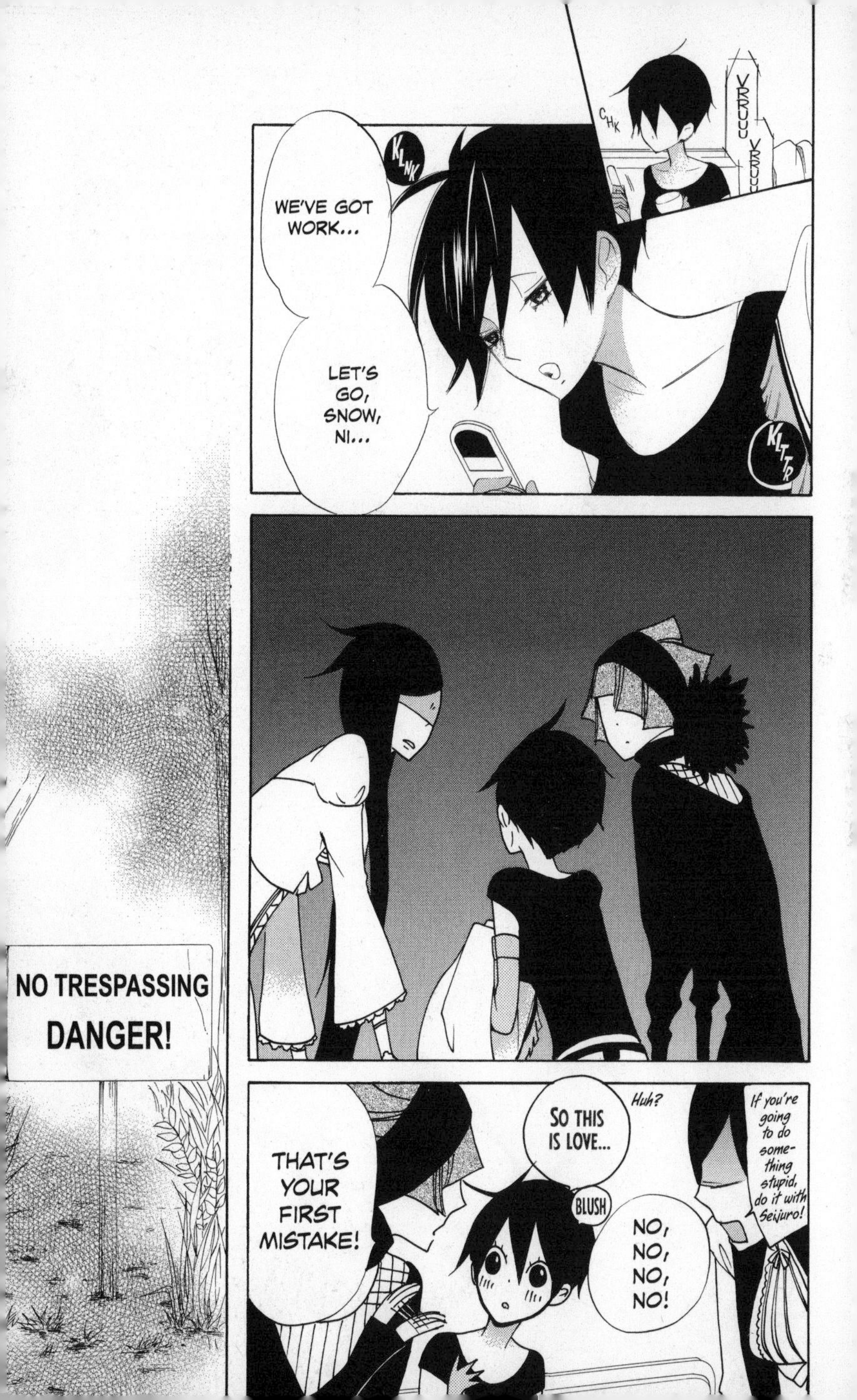
VRUUU
VRUUU
CHK
KLNK
WE'VE GOT WORK...
KLTTR
LET'S GO, SNOW, NI...
If you're going to do something stupid, do it with Seijuro!
Huh?
SO THIS IS LOVE...
BLUSH
NO, NO, NO, NO!
THAT'S YOUR FIRST MISTAKE!
NO TRESPASSING
DANGER!

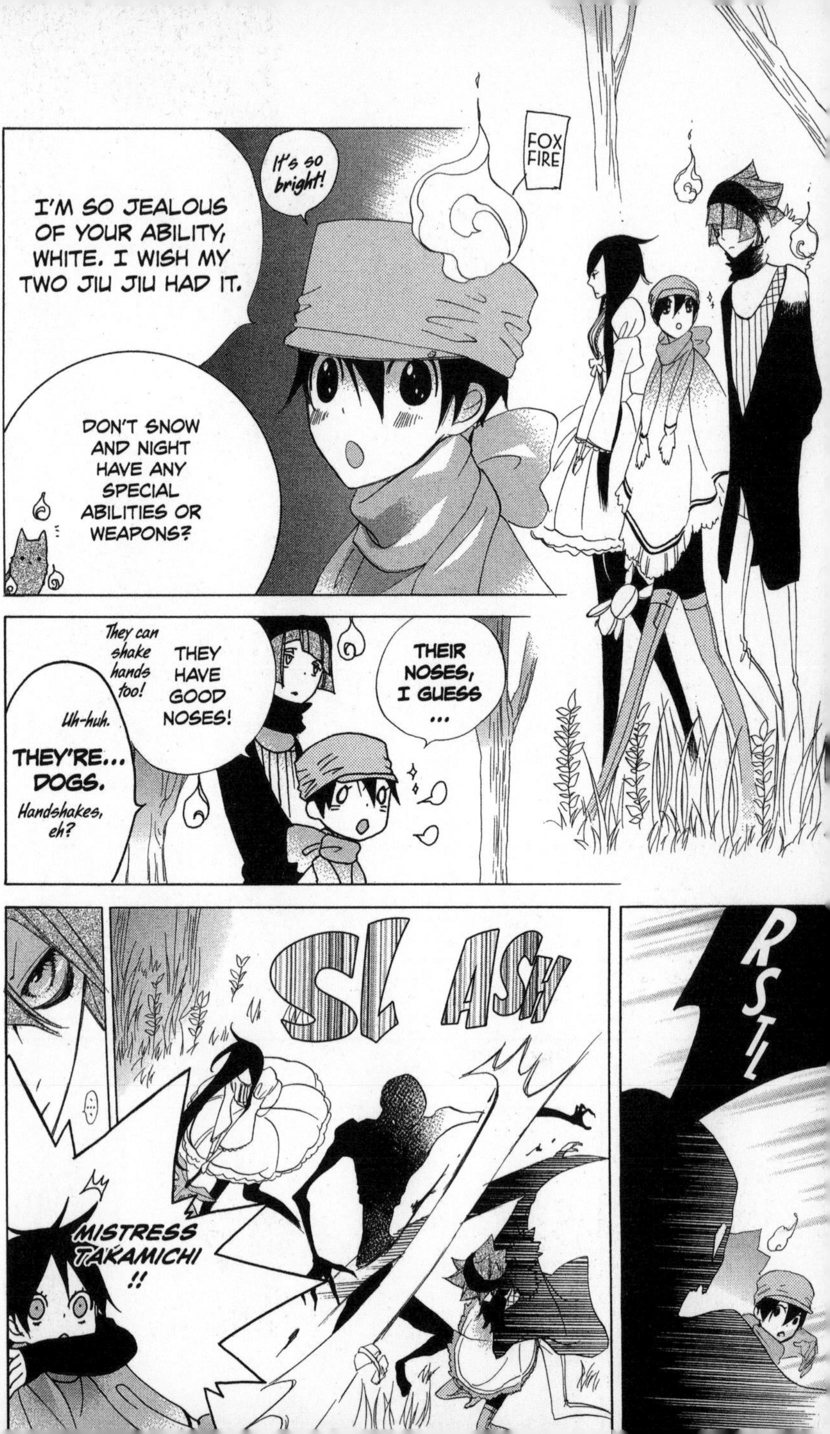
FOX FIRE
It's so bright!
I'M SO JEALOUS OF YOUR ABILITY, WHITE. I WISH MY TWO JIU JIU HAD IT.
DON'T SNOW AND NIGHT HAVE ANY SPECIAL ABILITIES OR WEAPONS?
THEIR NOSES, I GUESS ...
THEY HAVE GOOD NOSES!
They can shake hands too!
Uh-huh.
THEY'RE... DOGS.
Handshakes, eh?
RSTL
SLASH
...
MISTRESS TAKAMICHI !!

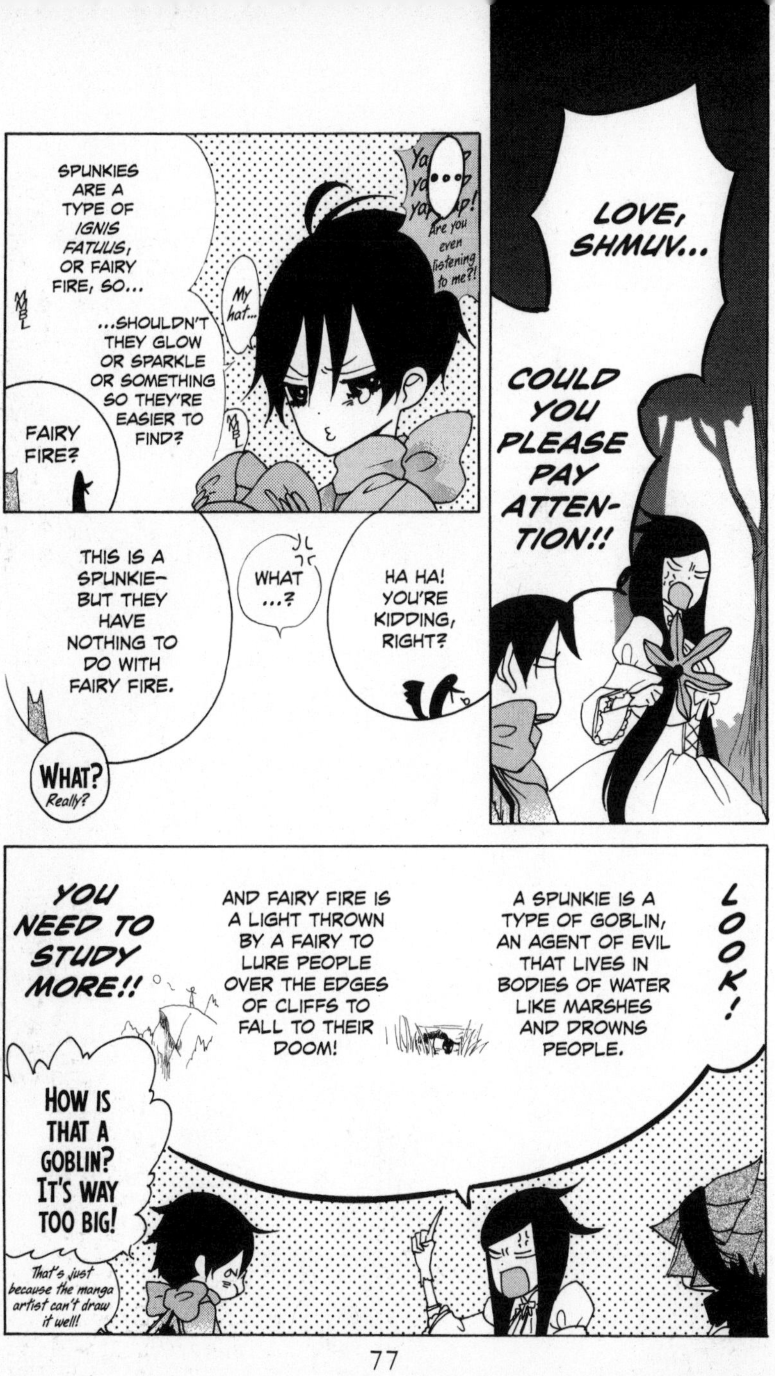
LOVE, SHMUV...
COULD YOU PLEASE PAY ATTEN-TION!!
...
Are you even listening to me?!
My hat...
SPUNKIES ARE A TYPE OF *IGNIS FATUUS*, OR FAIRY FIRE, SO...
MMBL
...SHOULDN'T THEY GLOW OR SPARKLE OR SOMETHING SO THEY'RE EASIER TO FIND?
MMBL
FAIRY FIRE?
HA HA! YOU'RE KIDDING, RIGHT?
WHAT ...?
THIS IS A SPUNKIE— BUT THEY HAVE NOTHING TO DO WITH FAIRY FIRE.
WHAT? Really?
LOOK!
A SPUNKIE IS A TYPE OF GOBLIN, AN AGENT OF EVIL THAT LIVES IN BODIES OF WATER LIKE MARSHES AND DROWNS PEOPLE.
AND FAIRY FIRE IS A LIGHT THROWN BY A FAIRY TO LURE PEOPLE OVER THE EDGES OF CLIFFS TO FALL TO THEIR DOOM!
YOU NEED TO STUDY MORE!!
HOW IS THAT A GOBLIN? IT'S WAY TOO BIG!
That's just because the manga artist can't draw it well!

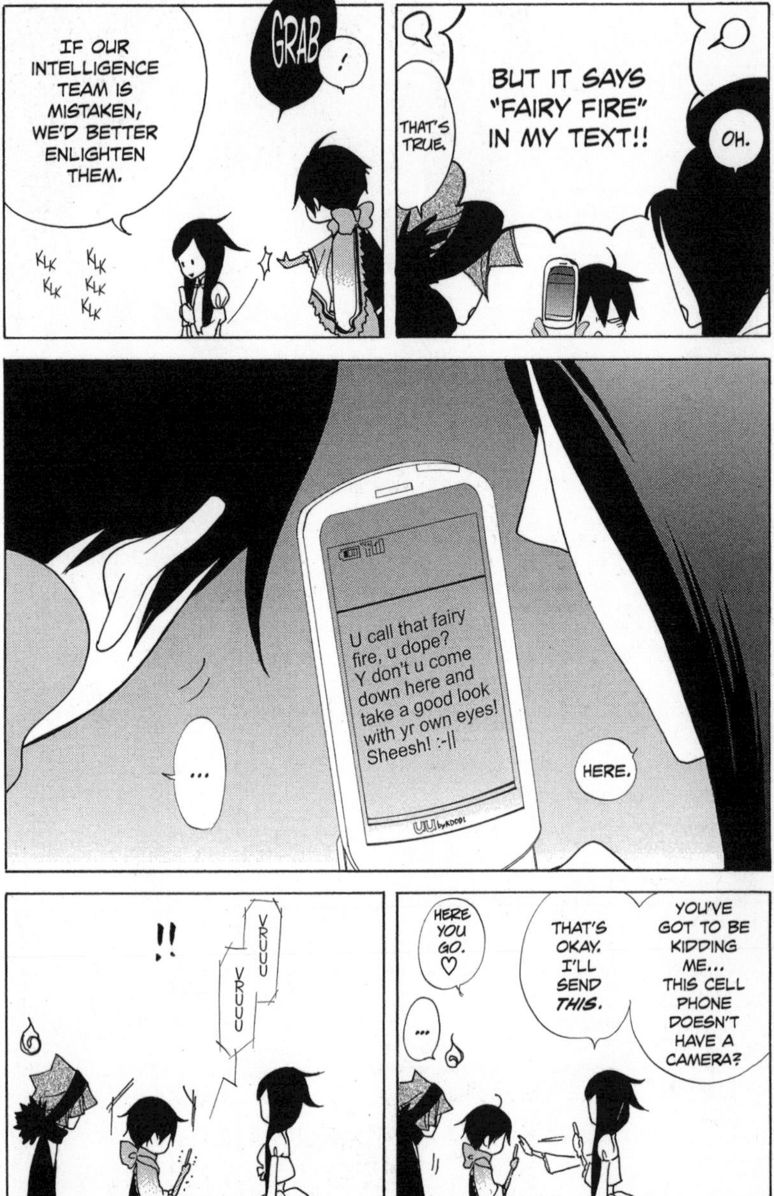
OH.
BUT IT SAYS "FAIRY FIRE" IN MY TEXT!!
THAT'S TRUE.
GRAB
!
IF OUR INTELLIGENCE TEAM IS MISTAKEN, WE'D BETTER ENLIGHTEN THEM.
KLK KLK KLK KLK KLK
HERE.
U call that fairy fire, u dope? Y don't u come down here and take a good look with yr own eyes! Sheesh! :-||
...
YOU'VE GOT TO BE KIDDING ME... THIS CELL PHONE DOESN'T HAVE A CAMERA?
THAT'S OKAY. I'LL SEND *THIS*.
HERE YOU GO. ♡
...
VRUUU
VRUUU
!!

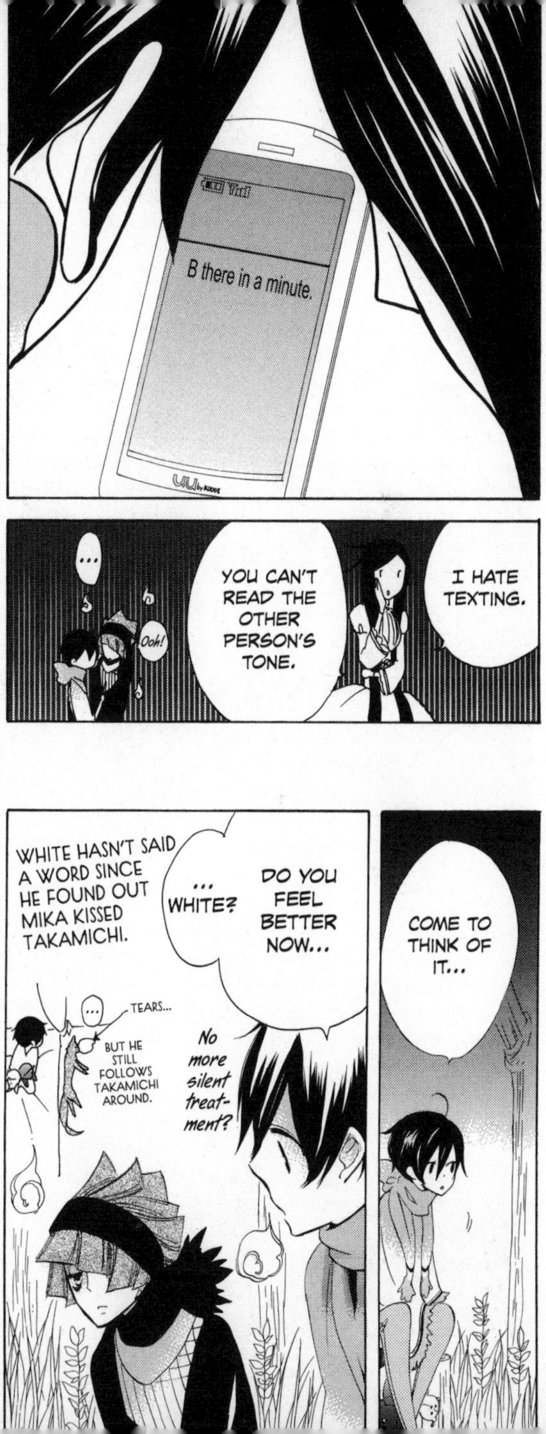
B there in a minute.
I HATE TEXTING.
YOU CAN'T READ THE OTHER PERSON'S TONE.
...
Ooh!
COME TO THINK OF IT...
DO YOU FEEL BETTER NOW...
...WHITE?
WHITE HASN'T SAID A WORD SINCE HE FOUND OUT MIKA KISSED TAKAMICHI.
No more silent treat-ment?
TEARS...
...
BUT HE STILL FOLLOWS TAKAMICHI AROUND.

Exam results.

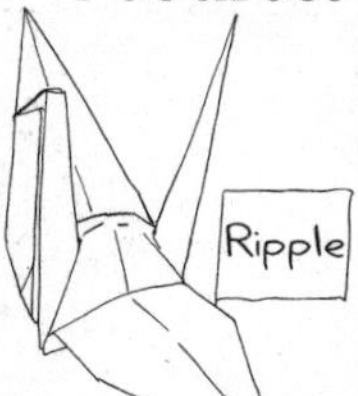
Ripple

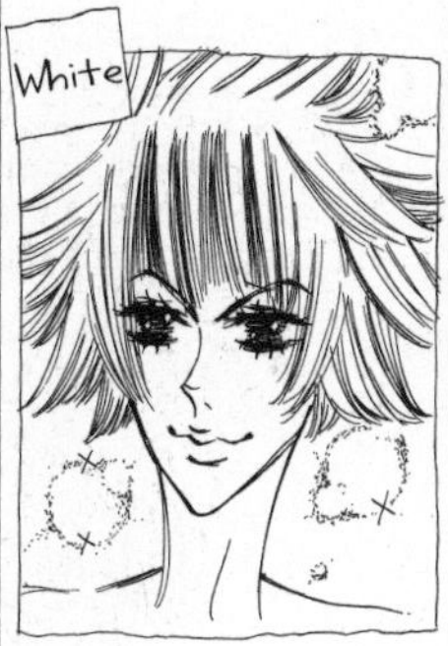
White

Is White a guy?
With the heart of a girl??
Is White a ♀ when in animal form?

Gifu Prefecture: Satomo

Yes, White is a boy. I referred to the trio of Mistress Takamichi, Ripple, and White as the "Girl Team" because White's behavior with Master Mika is so girlish.

There's nothing wrong with falling in love.

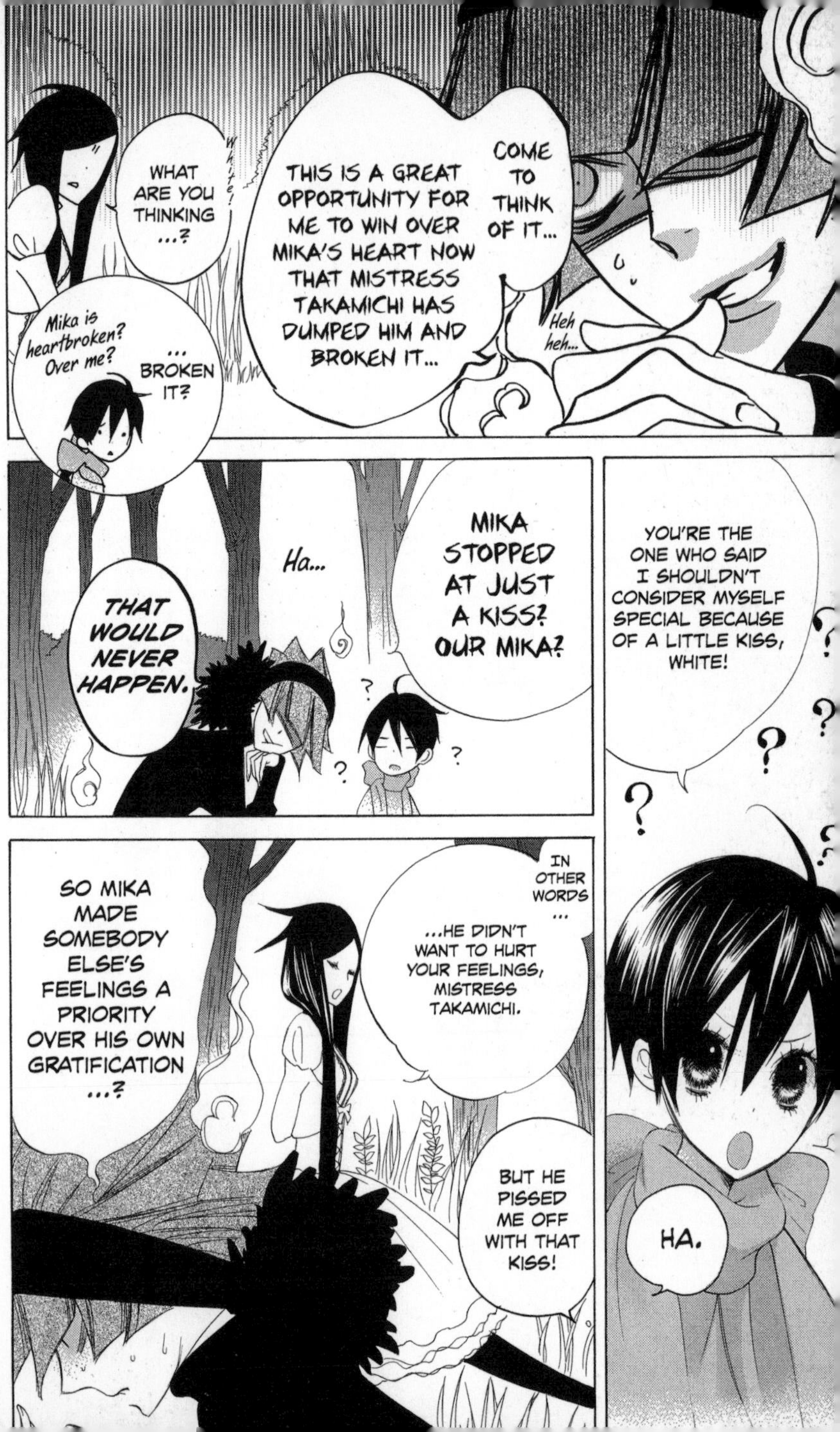
COME TO THINK OF IT...
THIS IS A GREAT OPPORTUNITY FOR ME TO WIN OVER MIKA'S HEART NOW THAT MISTRESS TAKAMICHI HAS DUMPED HIM AND BROKEN IT...
Heh heh...
White!
WHAT ARE YOU THINKING ...?
... BROKEN IT?
Mika is heartbroken? Over me?
YOU'RE THE ONE WHO SAID I SHOULDN'T CONSIDER MYSELF SPECIAL BECAUSE OF A LITTLE KISS, WHITE!
MIKA STOPPED AT JUST A KISS? OUR MIKA?
Ha...
THAT WOULD NEVER HAPPEN.
HA.
IN OTHER WORDS ...
...HE DIDN'T WANT TO HURT YOUR FEELINGS, MISTRESS TAKAMICHI.
SO MIKA MADE SOMEBODY ELSE'S FEELINGS A PRIORITY OVER HIS OWN GRATIFICATION ...?
BUT HE PISSED ME OFF WITH THAT KISS!

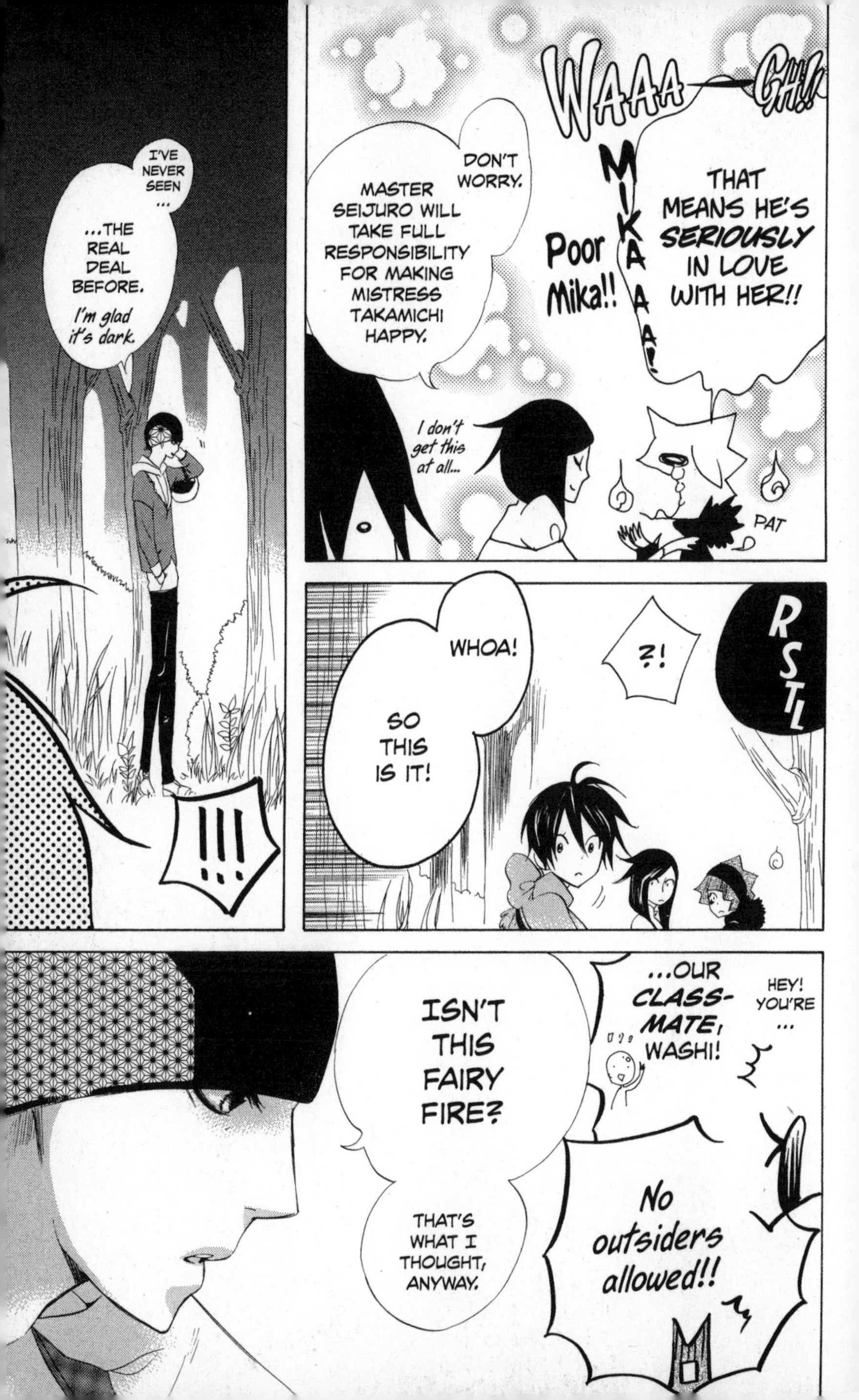

WAAAA-GH!!
THAT MEANS HE'S SERIOUSLY IN LOVE WITH HER!!
MIKAAAA!
Poor Mika!!
DON'T WORRY.
MASTER SEIJURO WILL TAKE FULL RESPONSIBILITY FOR MAKING MISTRESS TAKAMICHI HAPPY.
I don't get this at all...
PAT
RSTL
?!
WHOA!
SO THIS IS IT!
I'VE NEVER SEEN ...
...THE REAL DEAL BEFORE.
I'm glad it's dark.
!!!
HEY! YOU'RE ...
...OUR CLASSMATE, WASHI!
No outsiders allowed!!
ISN'T THIS FAIRY FIRE?
THAT'S WHAT I THOUGHT, ANYWAY.

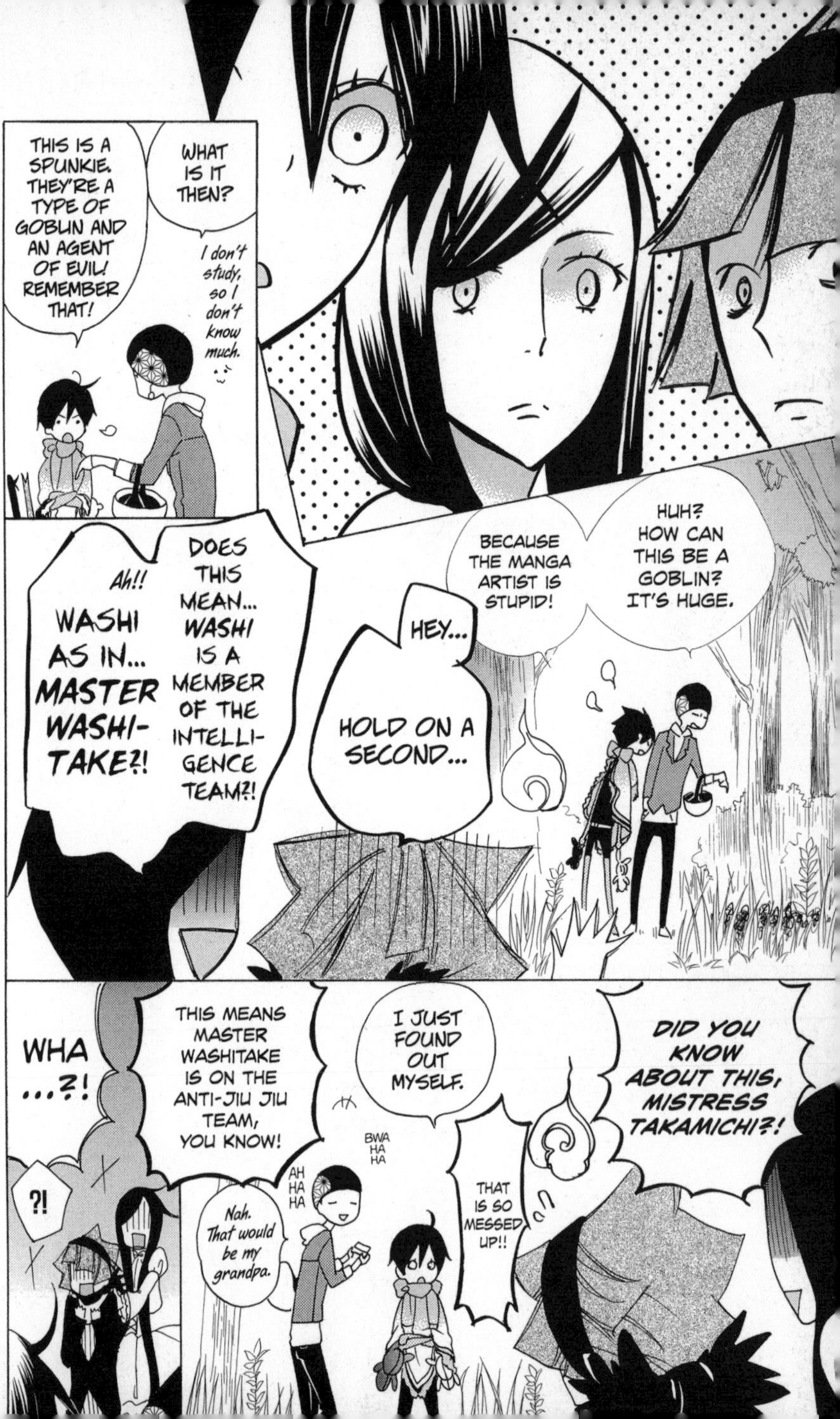
WHAT IS IT THEN?
THIS IS A SPUNKIE. THEY'RE A TYPE OF GOBLIN AND AN AGENT OF EVIL! REMEMBER THAT!
I don't study, so I don't know much.
HUH? HOW CAN THIS BE A GOBLIN? IT'S HUGE.
BECAUSE THE MANGA ARTIST IS STUPID!
HEY...
HOLD ON A SECOND...
DOES THIS MEAN... WASHI IS A MEMBER OF THE INTELLIGENCE TEAM?!
Ah!! WASHI AS IN... MASTER WASHITAKE?!
DID YOU KNOW ABOUT THIS, MISTRESS TAKAMICHI?!
I JUST FOUND OUT MYSELF.
THAT IS SO MESSED UP!!
BWA HA HA
AH HA HA
Nah. That would be my grandpa.
THIS MEANS MASTER WASHITAKE IS ON THE ANTI-JIU JIU TEAM, YOU KNOW!
WHA ...?!
?!

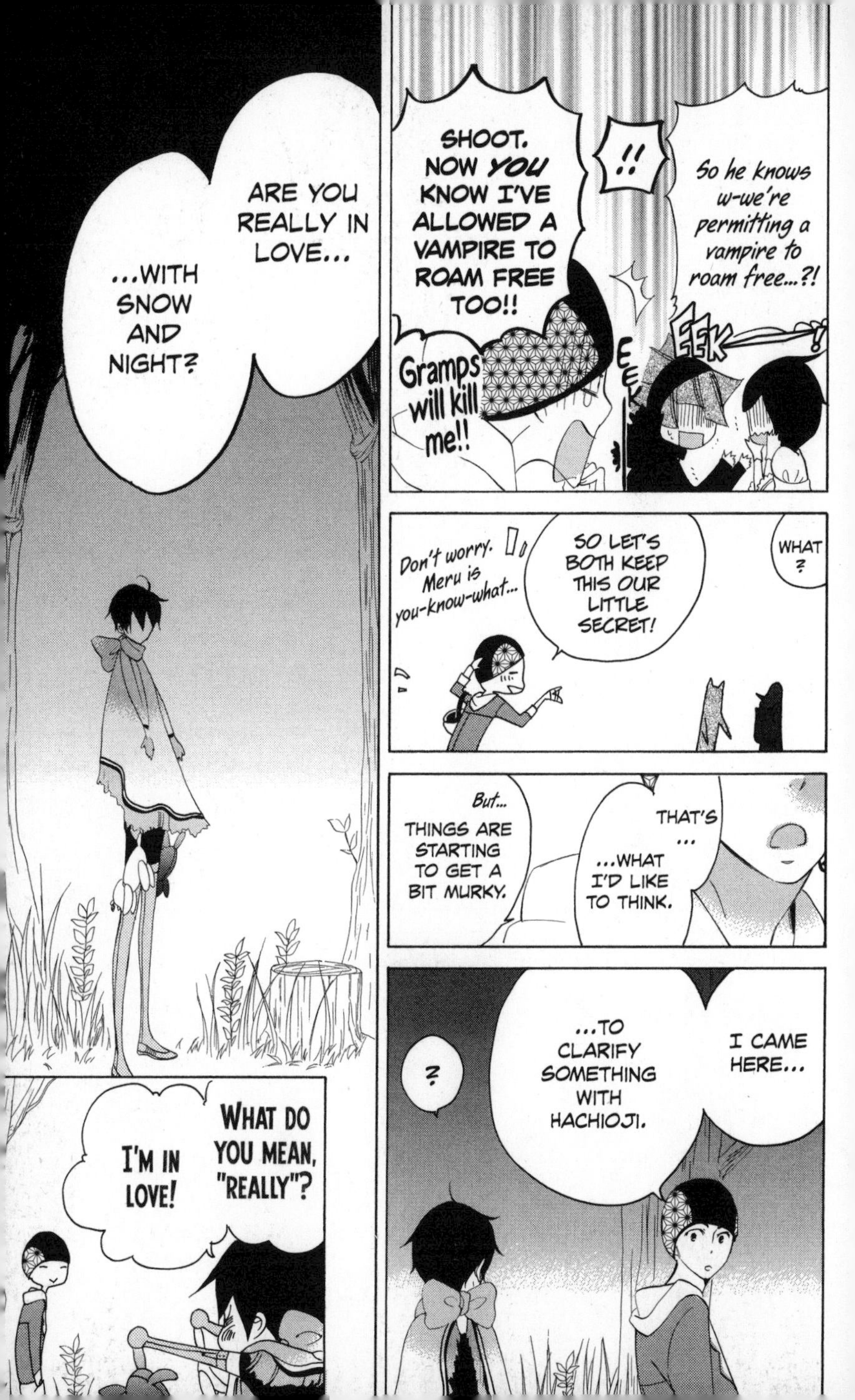

So he knows w-we're permitting a vampire to roam free...?!
!!
SHOOT. NOW YOU KNOW I'VE ALLOWED A VAMPIRE TO ROAM FREE TOO!!
EEK
EEK
Gramps will kill me!!
WHAT?
SO LET'S BOTH KEEP THIS OUR LITTLE SECRET!
Don't worry. Meru is you-know-what...
THAT'S...
...WHAT I'D LIKE TO THINK.
But... THINGS ARE STARTING TO GET A BIT MURKY.
I CAME HERE...
...TO CLARIFY SOMETHING WITH HACHIOJI.
?
ARE YOU REALLY IN LOVE...
...WITH SNOW AND NIGHT?
WHAT DO YOU MEAN, "REALLY"?
I'M IN LOVE!

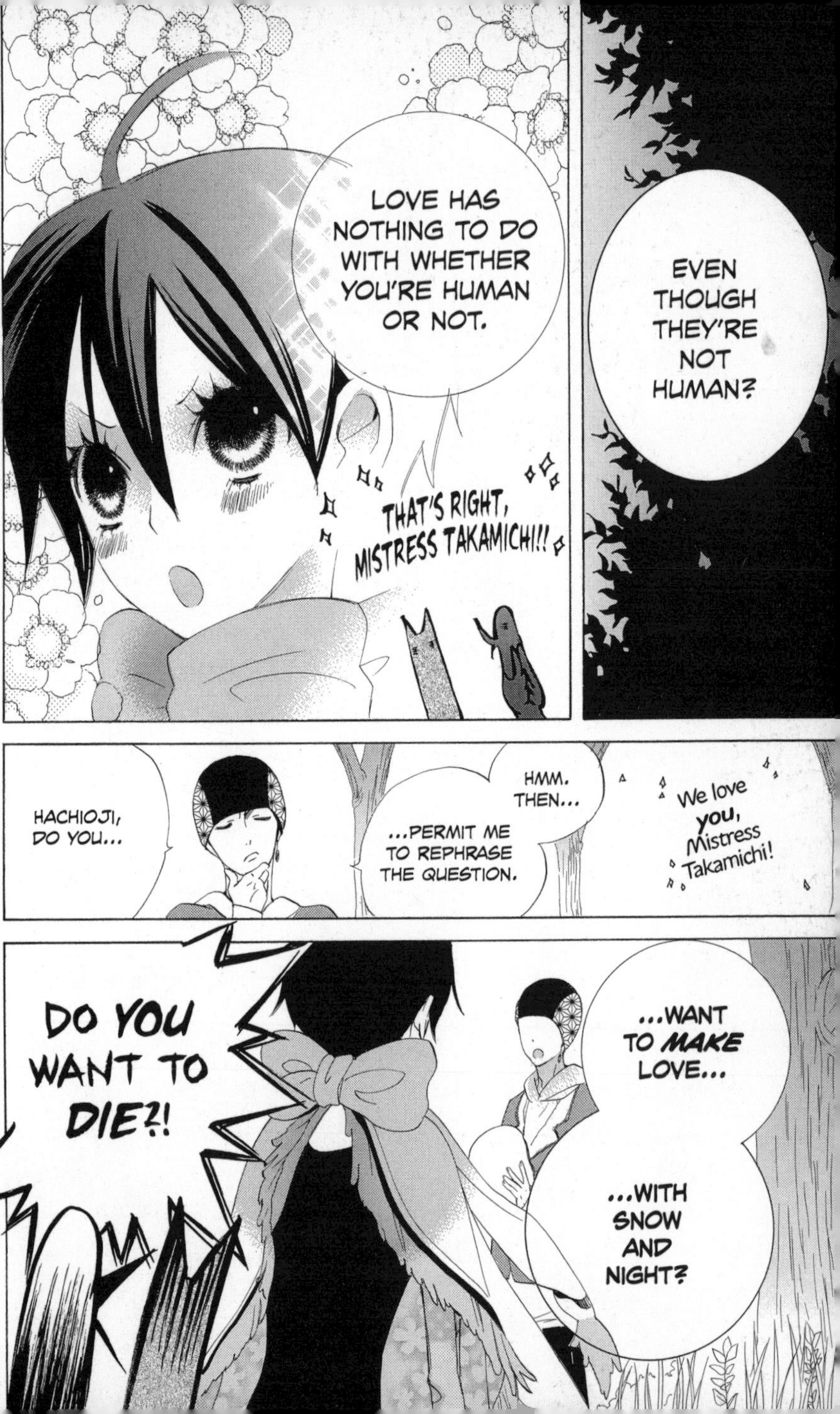
EVEN THOUGH THEY'RE NOT HUMAN?
LOVE HAS NOTHING TO DO WITH WHETHER YOU'RE HUMAN OR NOT.
THAT'S RIGHT, MISTRESS TAKAMICHI!!
We love you, Mistress Takamichi!
HMM. THEN...
...PERMIT ME TO REPHRASE THE QUESTION.
HACHIOJI, DO YOU...
...WANT TO MAKE LOVE...
...WITH SNOW AND NIGHT?
DO YOU WANT TO DIE?!

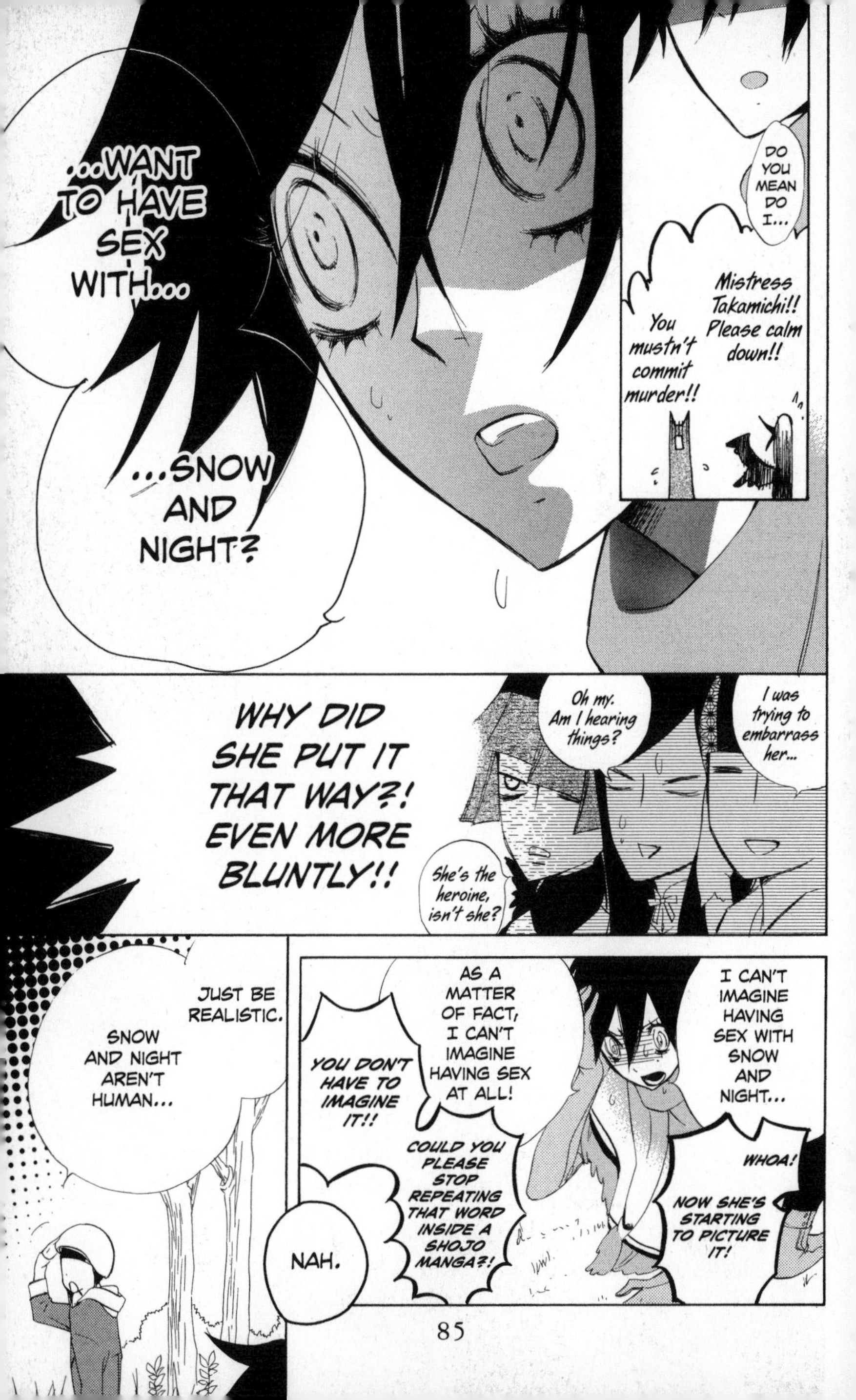
DO YOU MEAN DO I...
...WANT TO HAVE SEX WITH...
...SNOW AND NIGHT?
Mistress Takamichi!! Please calm down!!
You mustn't commit murder!!
I was trying to embarrass her...
Oh my. Am I hearing things?
She's the heroine, isn't she?
WHY DID SHE PUT IT THAT WAY?! EVEN MORE BLUNTLY!!
I CAN'T IMAGINE HAVING SEX WITH SNOW AND NIGHT...
AS A MATTER OF FACT, I CAN'T IMAGINE HAVING SEX AT ALL!
WHOA!
NOW SHE'S STARTING TO PICTURE IT!
YOU DON'T HAVE TO IMAGINE IT!!
COULD YOU PLEASE STOP REPEATING THAT WORD INSIDE A SHOJO MANGA?!
NAH.
JUST BE REALISTIC.
SNOW AND NIGHT AREN'T HUMAN...

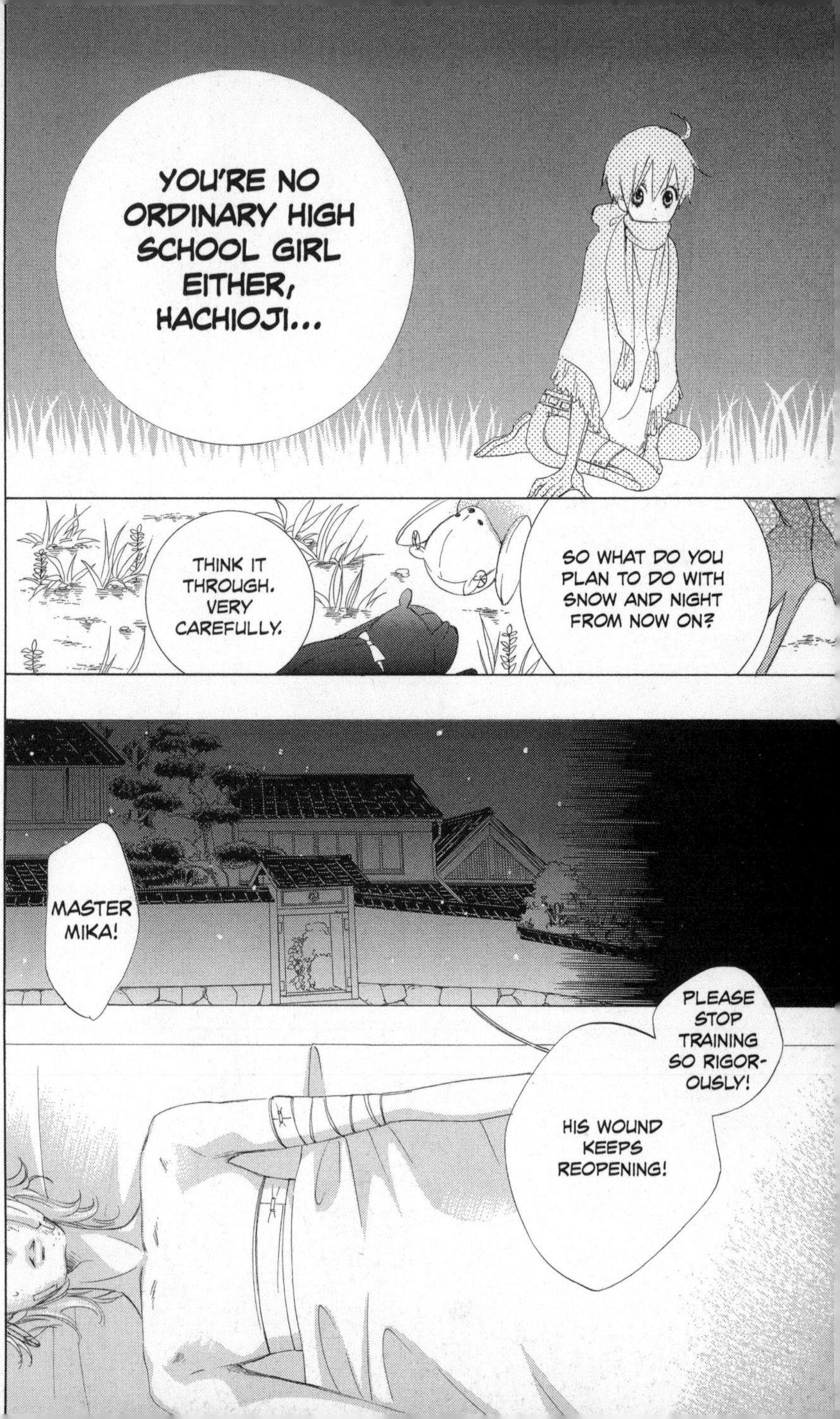
YOU'RE NO ORDINARY HIGH SCHOOL GIRL EITHER, HACHIOJI...
SO WHAT DO YOU PLAN TO DO WITH SNOW AND NIGHT FROM NOW ON?
THINK IT THROUGH. VERY CAREFULLY.
MASTER MIKA!
PLEASE STOP TRAINING SO RIGOR-OUSLY!
HIS WOUND KEEPS REOPENING!

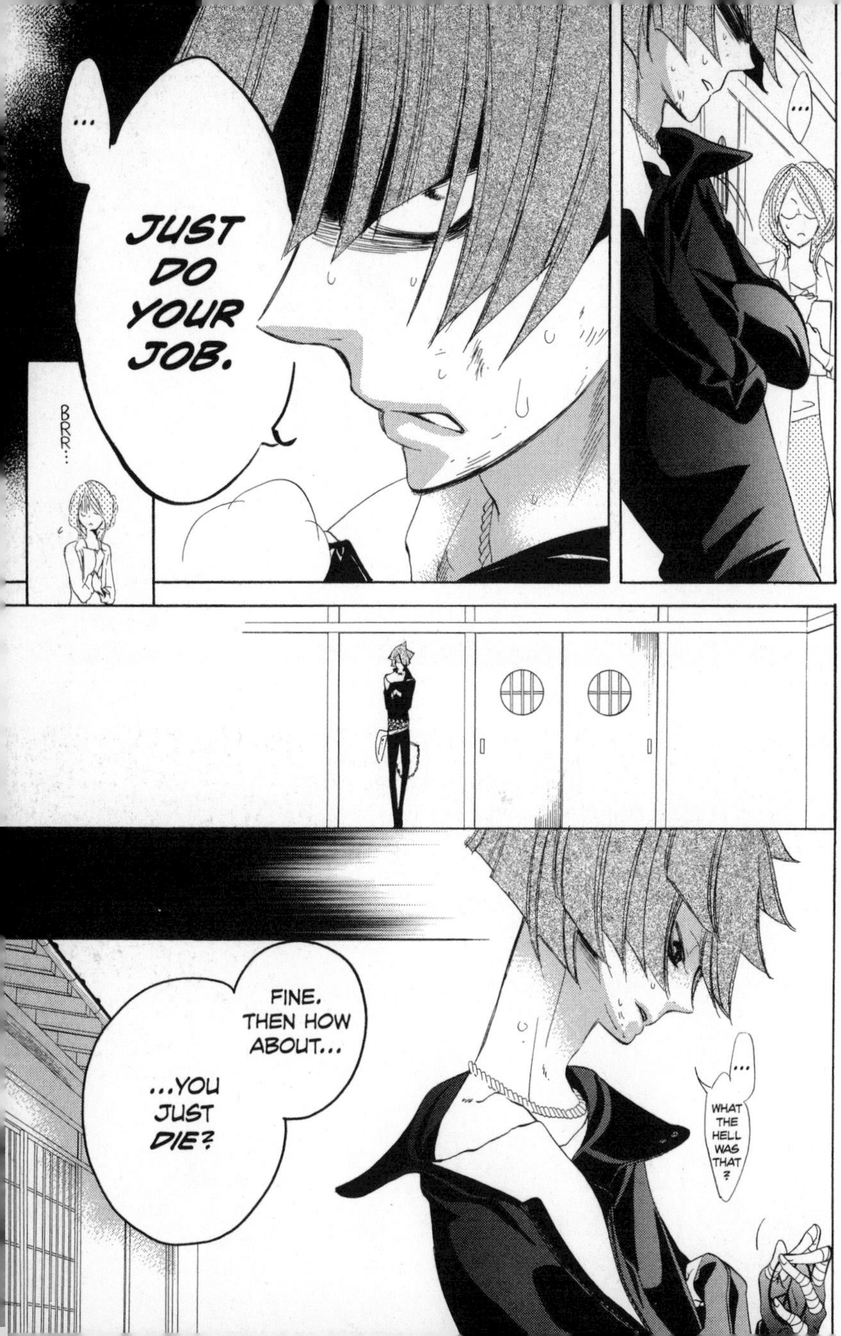
...
...
JUST DO YOUR JOB.
BRR...
FINE. THEN HOW ABOUT...
...YOU JUST DIE?
...
WHAT THE HELL WAS THAT?

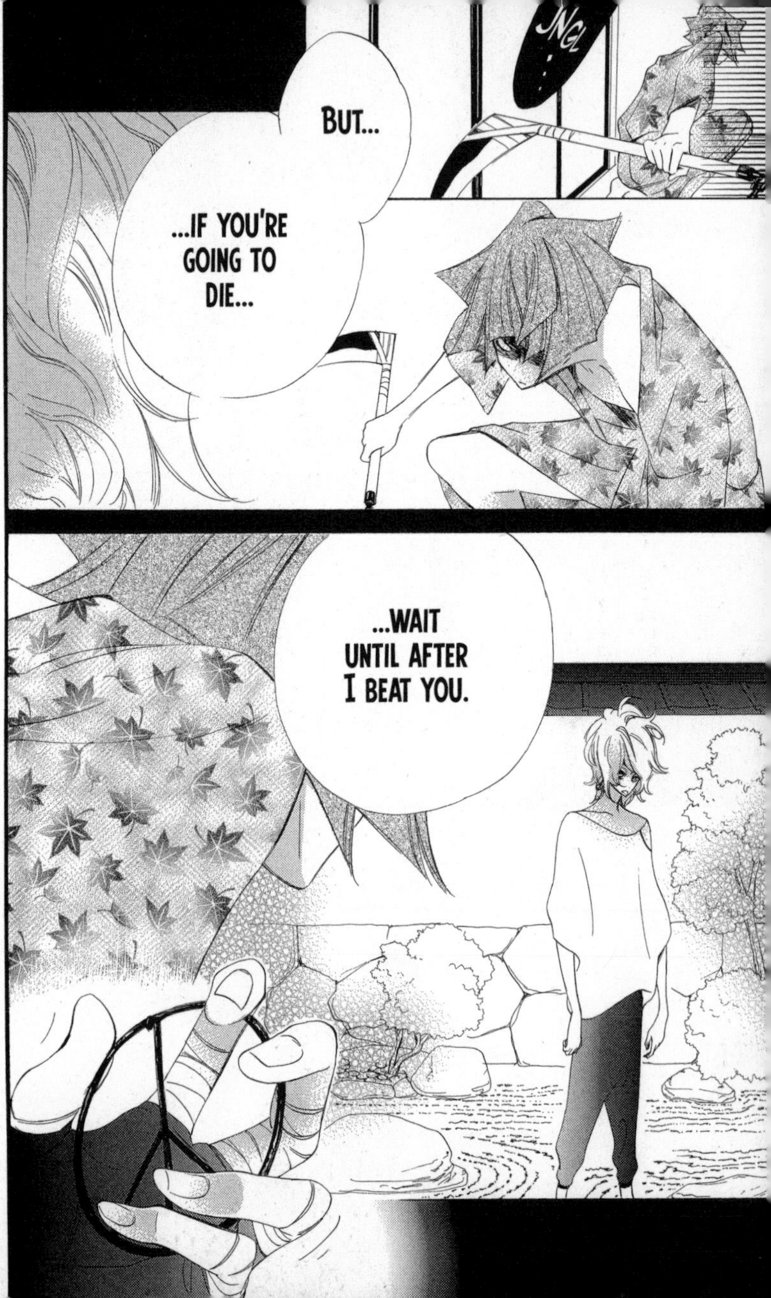
JNGL
BUT...
...IF YOU'RE GOING TO DIE...
...WAIT UNTIL AFTER I BEAT YOU.

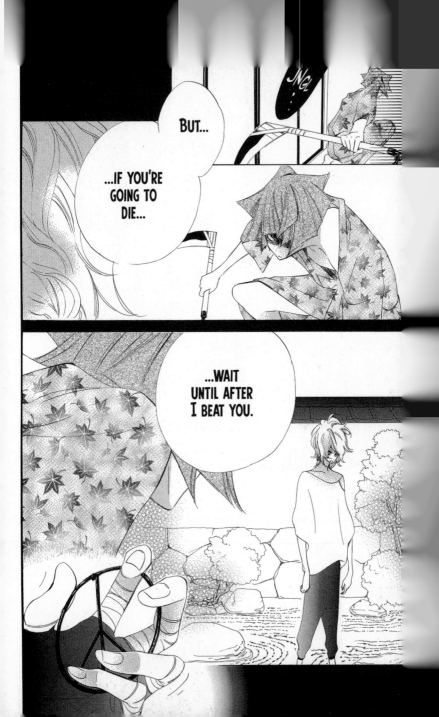

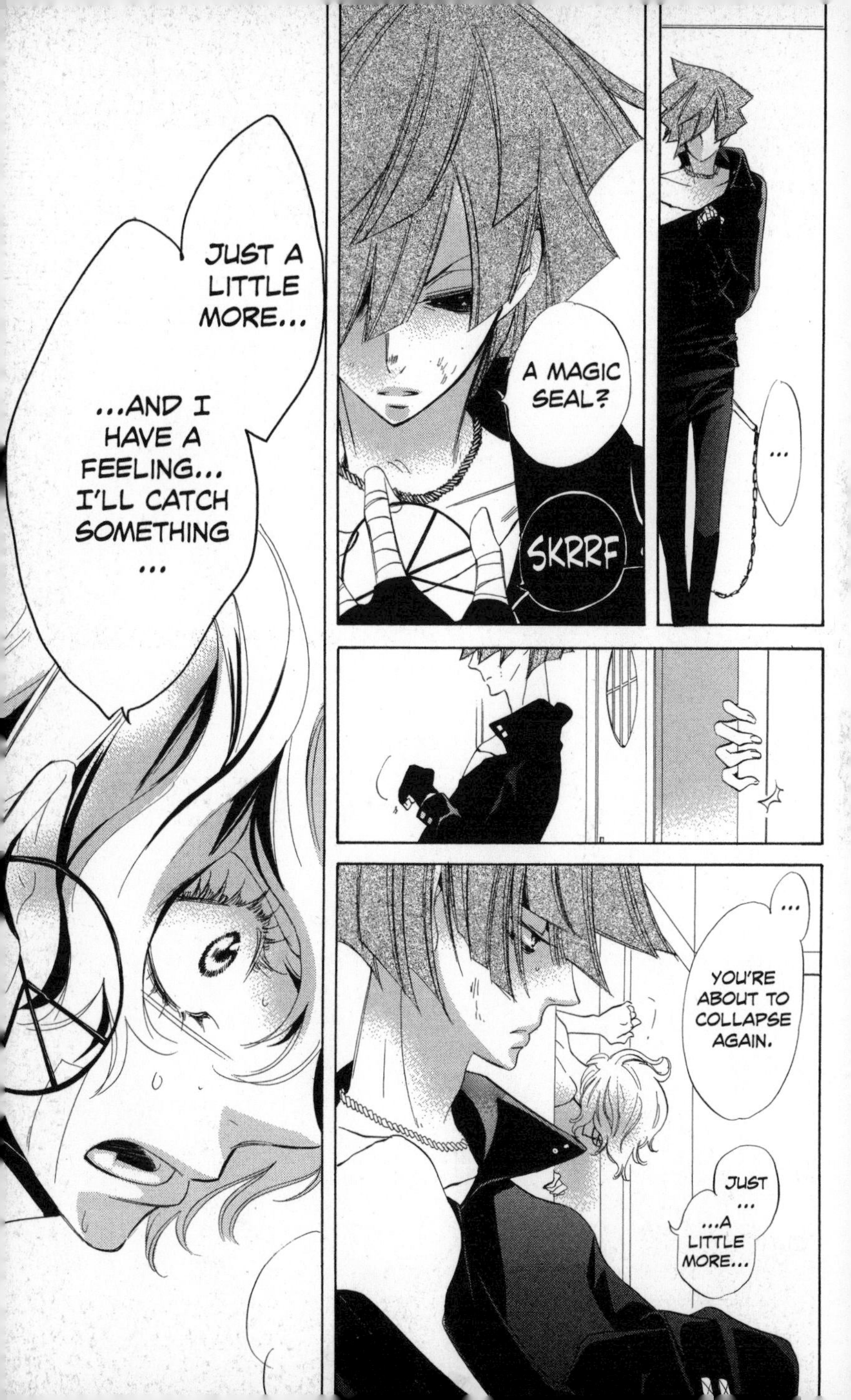
...
A MAGIC SEAL?
SKRRF
...
YOU'RE ABOUT TO COLLAPSE AGAIN.
JUST ... ...A LITTLE MORE...
JUST A LITTLE MORE...
...AND I HAVE A FEELING... I'LL CATCH SOMETHING ...

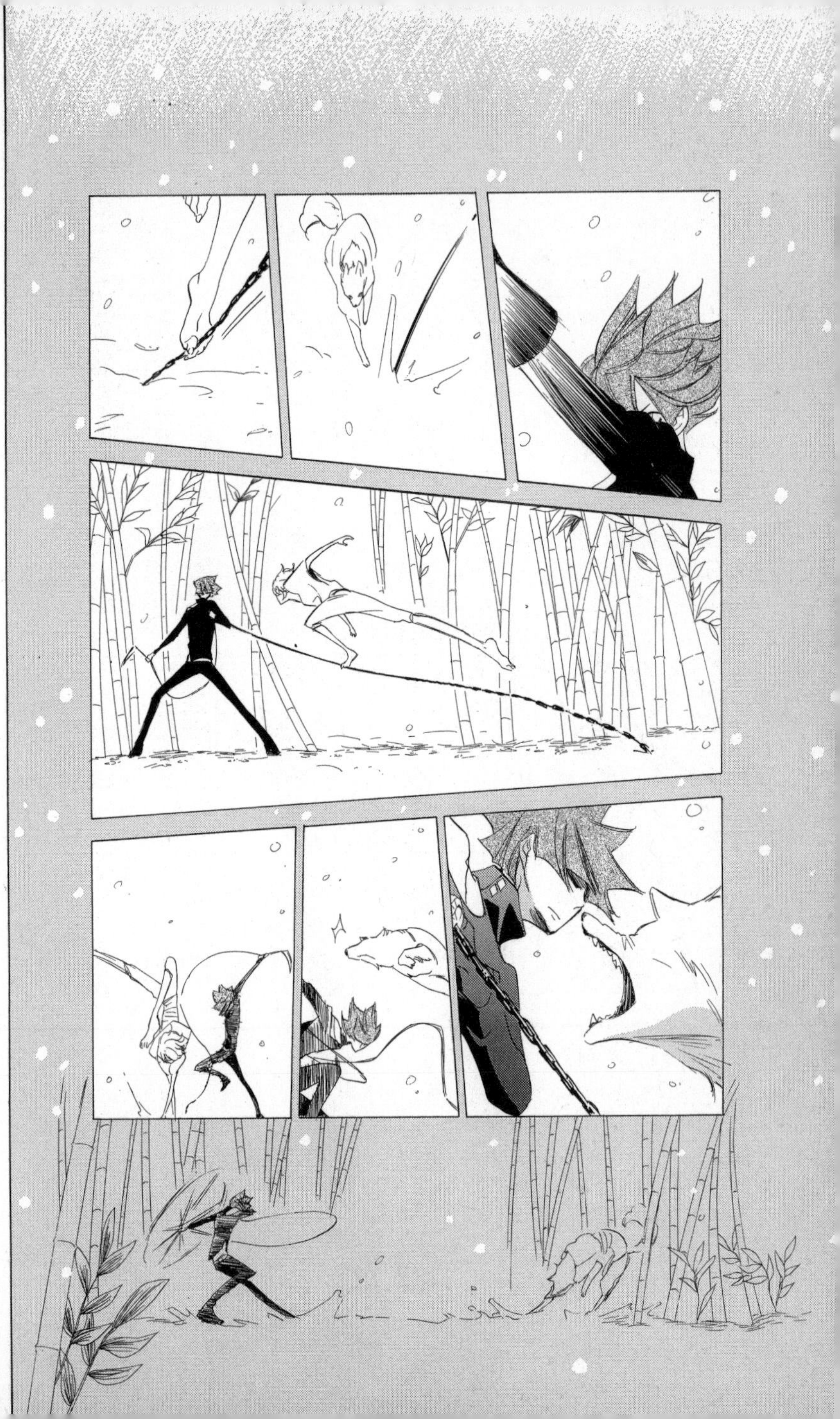

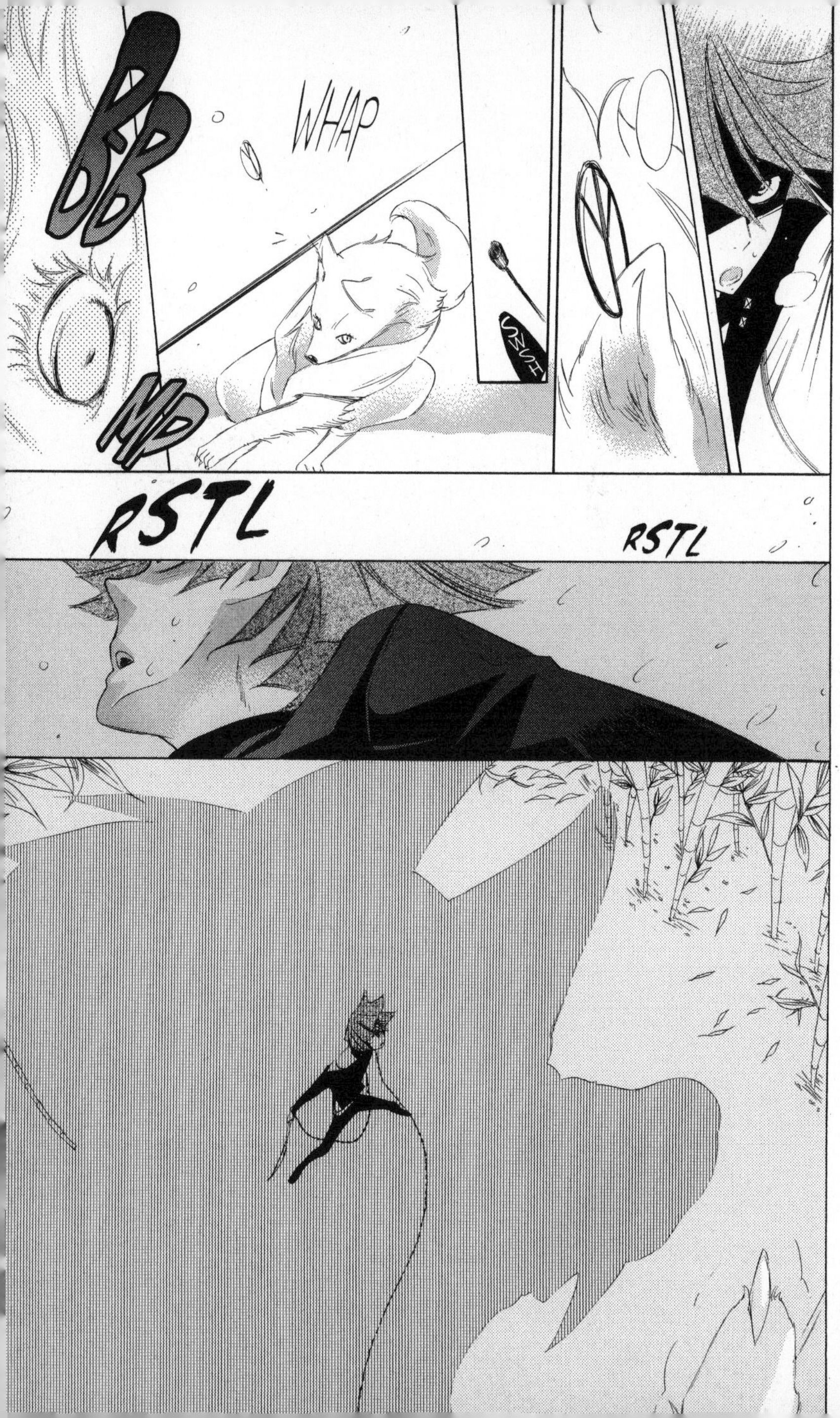
SWSH
WHAP
B-D BD MP
RSTL
RSTL

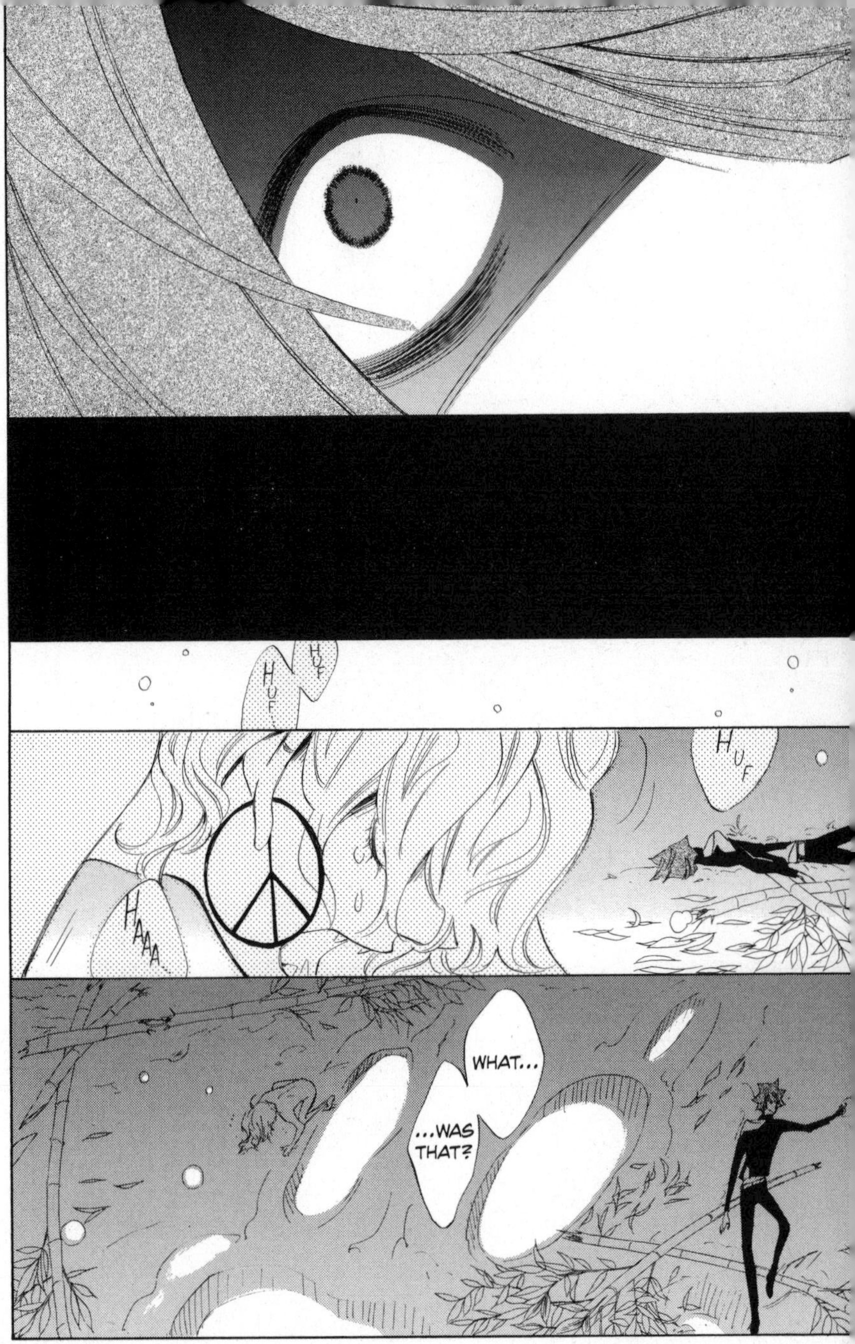
HUF
HUF
HUF
HAAA
WHAT...
...WAS THAT?

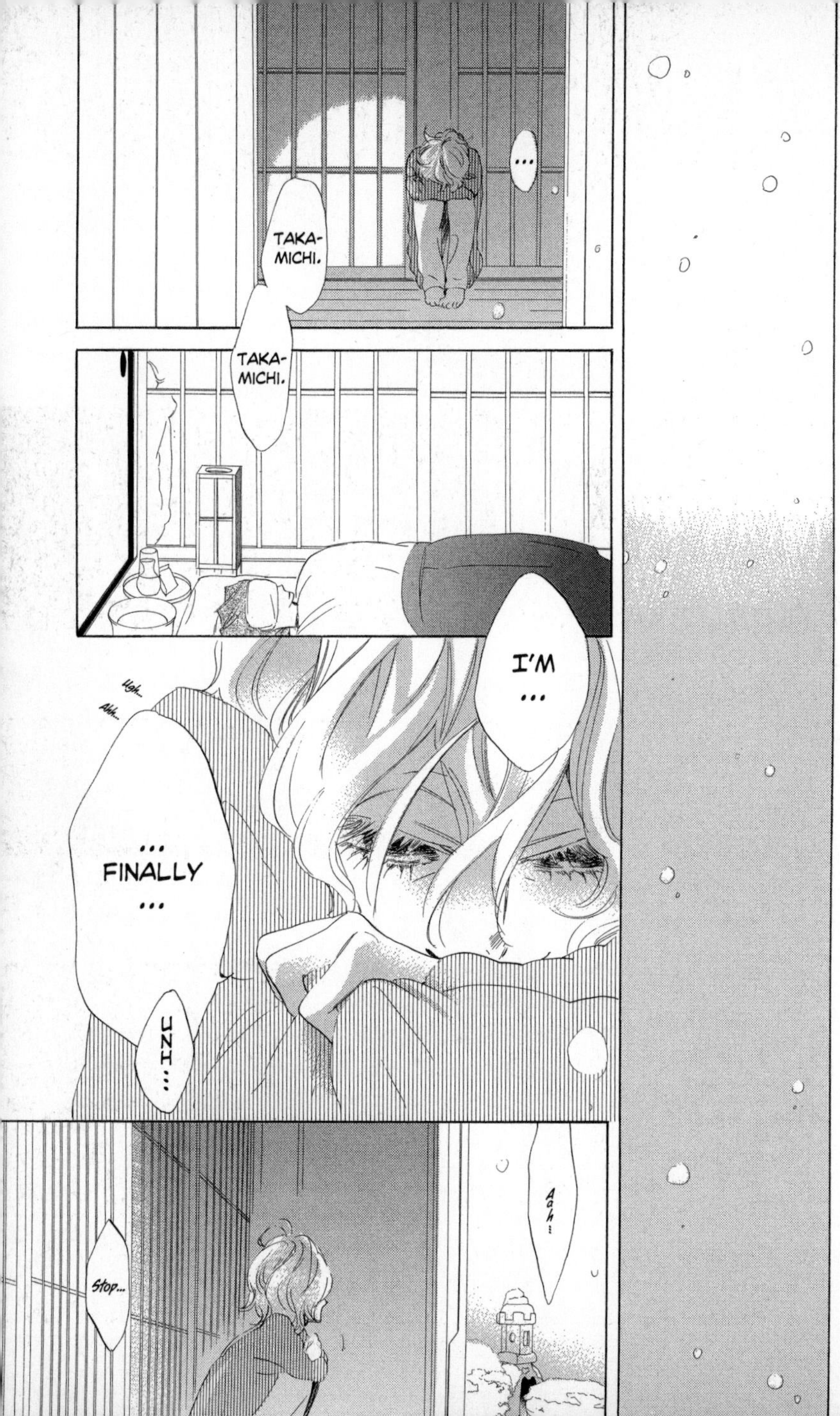
...
TAKA-MICHI.
TAKA-MICHI.
I'M ...
Ugh...
Ahh...
... FINALLY ...
UNH...
Aah...
Stop...

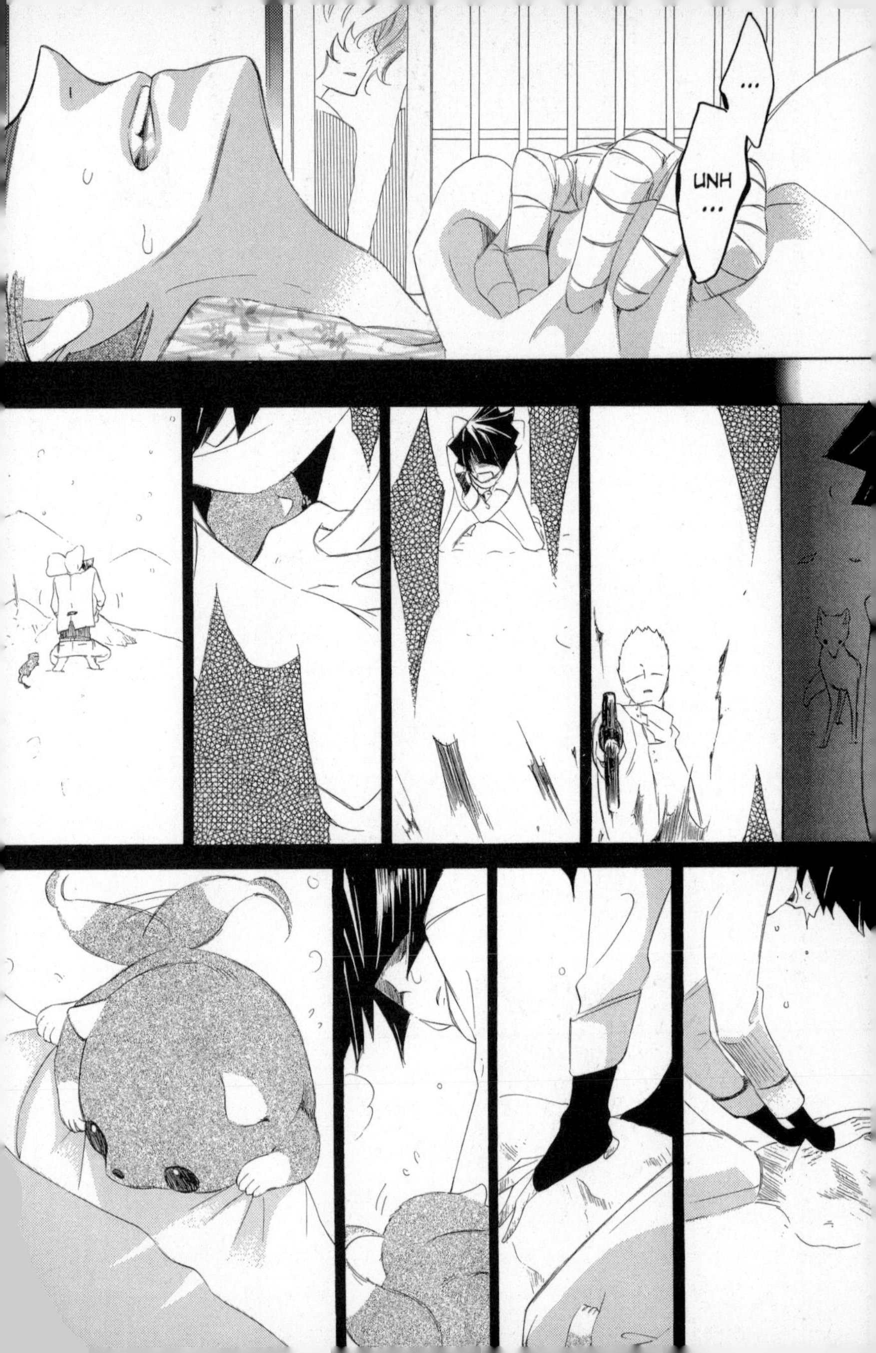
... UNH ...

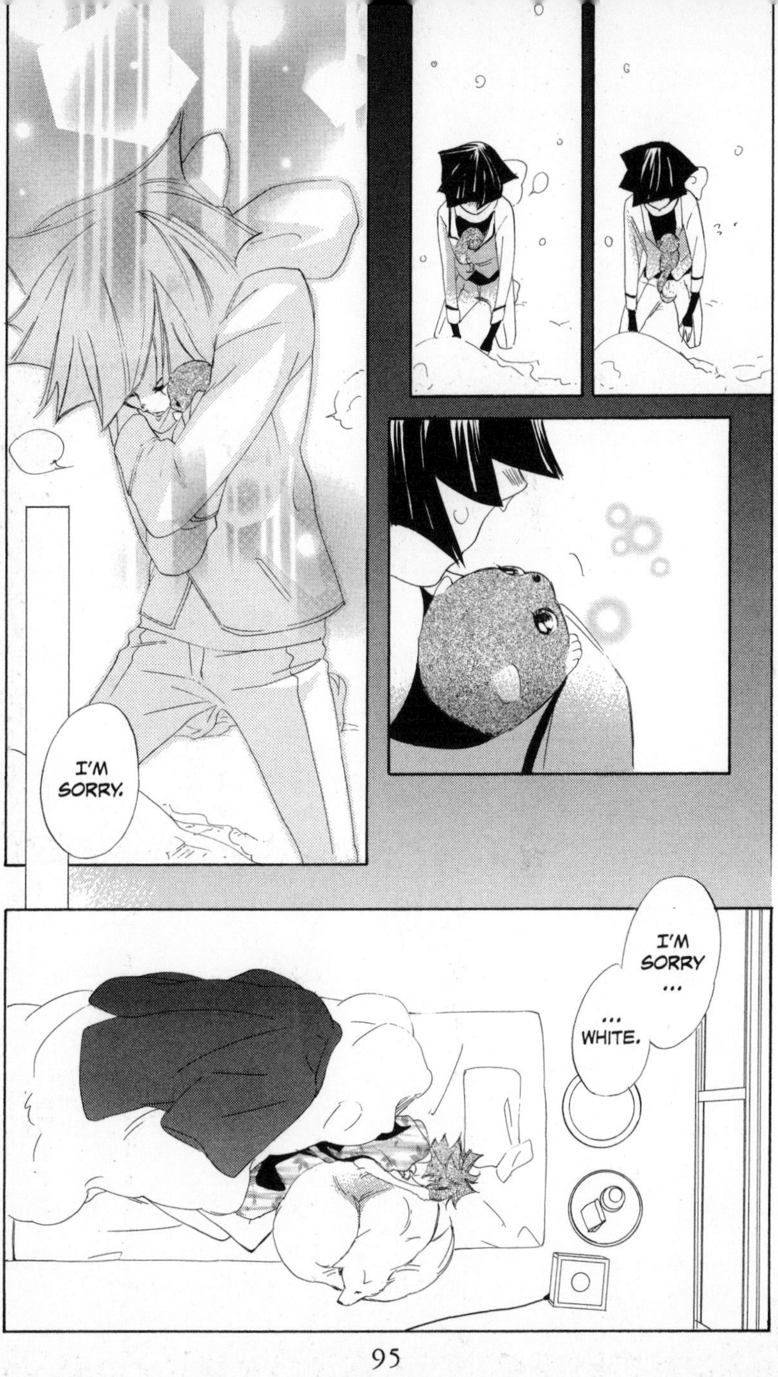
I'M SORRY.
I'M SORRY ...
... WHITE.

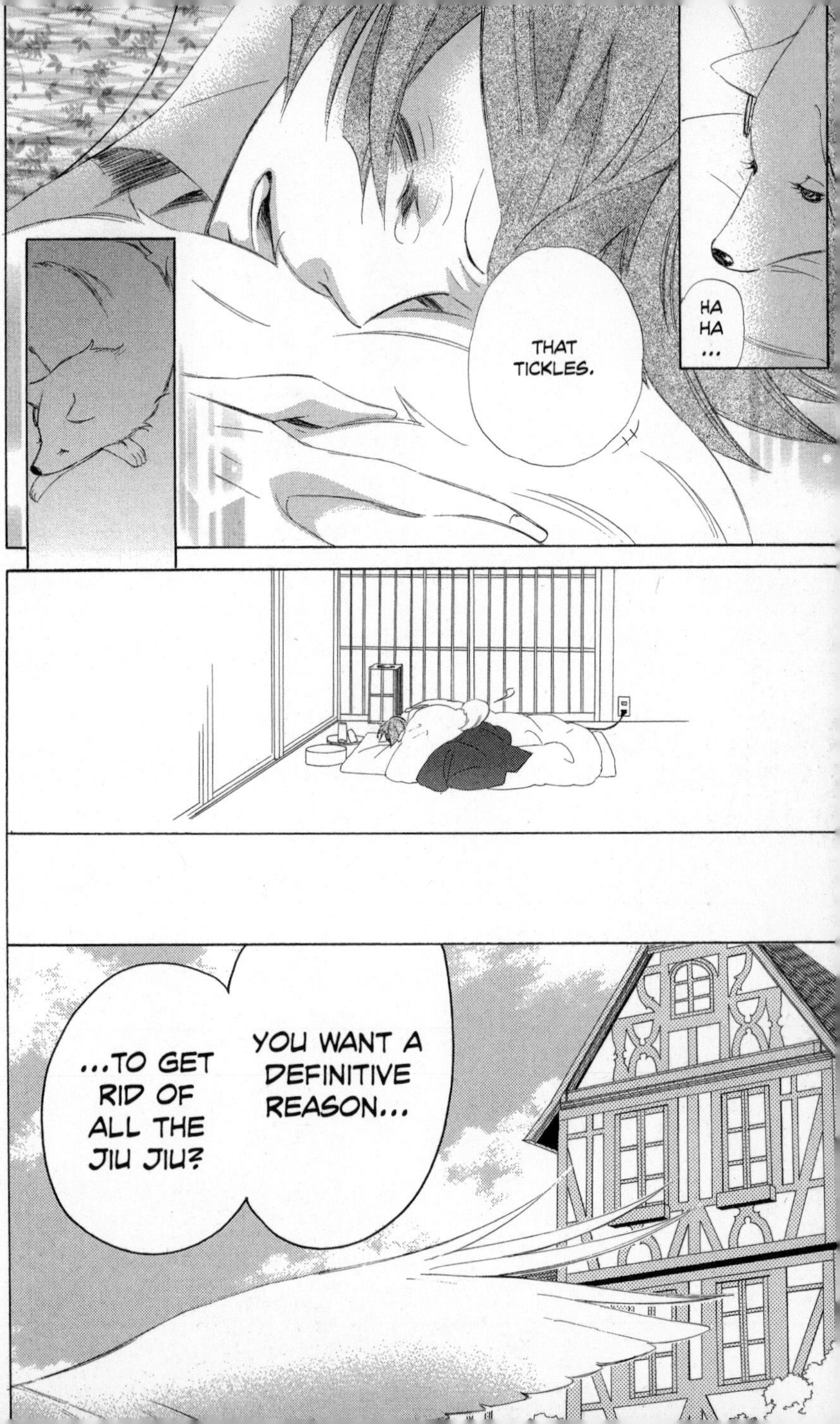
HA HA ...
THAT TICKLES.
YOU WANT A DEFINITIVE REASON...
...TO GET RID OF ALL THE JIU JIU?

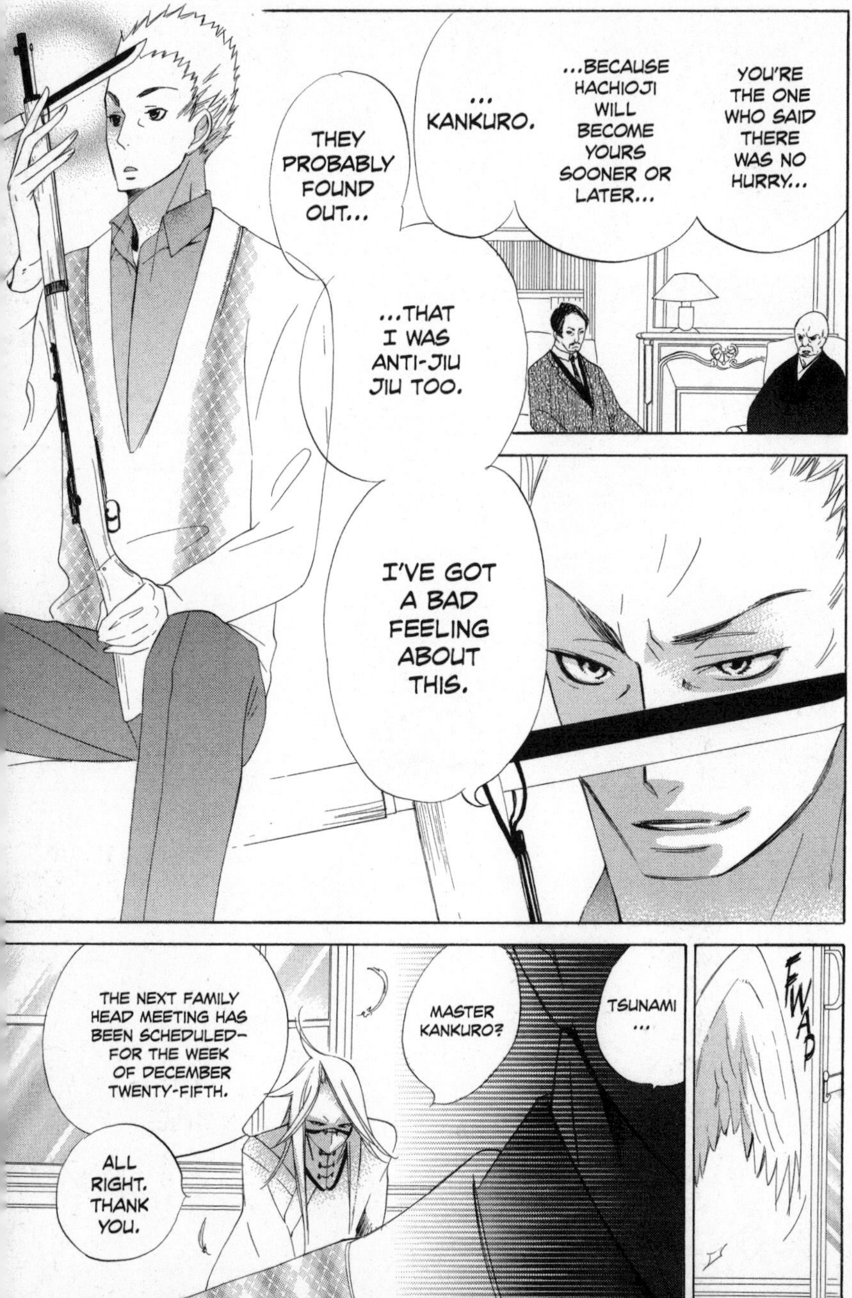
YOU'RE THE ONE WHO SAID THERE WAS NO HURRY...
...BECAUSE HACHIOJI WILL BECOME YOURS SOONER OR LATER...
... KANKURO.
THEY PROBABLY FOUND OUT...
...THAT I WAS ANTI-JIU JIU TOO.
I'VE GOT A BAD FEELING ABOUT THIS.
FWAP
TSUNAMI ...
MASTER KANKURO?
THE NEXT FAMILY HEAD MEETING HAS BEEN SCHEDULED— FOR THE WEEK OF DECEMBER TWENTY-FIFTH.
ALL RIGHT. THANK YOU.

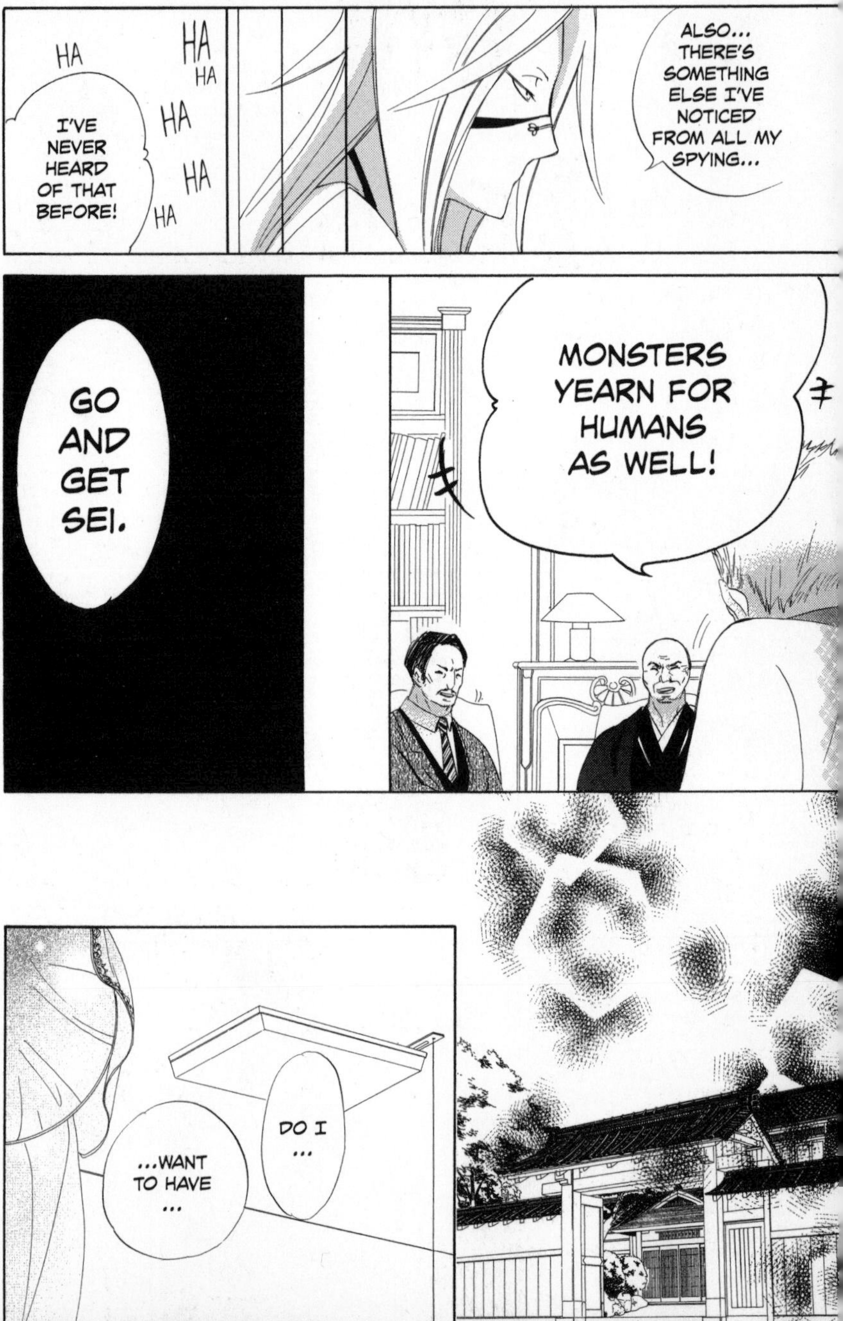
ALSO... THERE'S SOMETHING ELSE I'VE NOTICED FROM ALL MY SPYING...
HA HA HA HA HA HA
I'VE NEVER HEARD OF THAT BEFORE!
MONSTERS YEARN FOR HUMANS AS WELL!
GO AND GET SEI.
DO I ...
...WANT TO HAVE ...

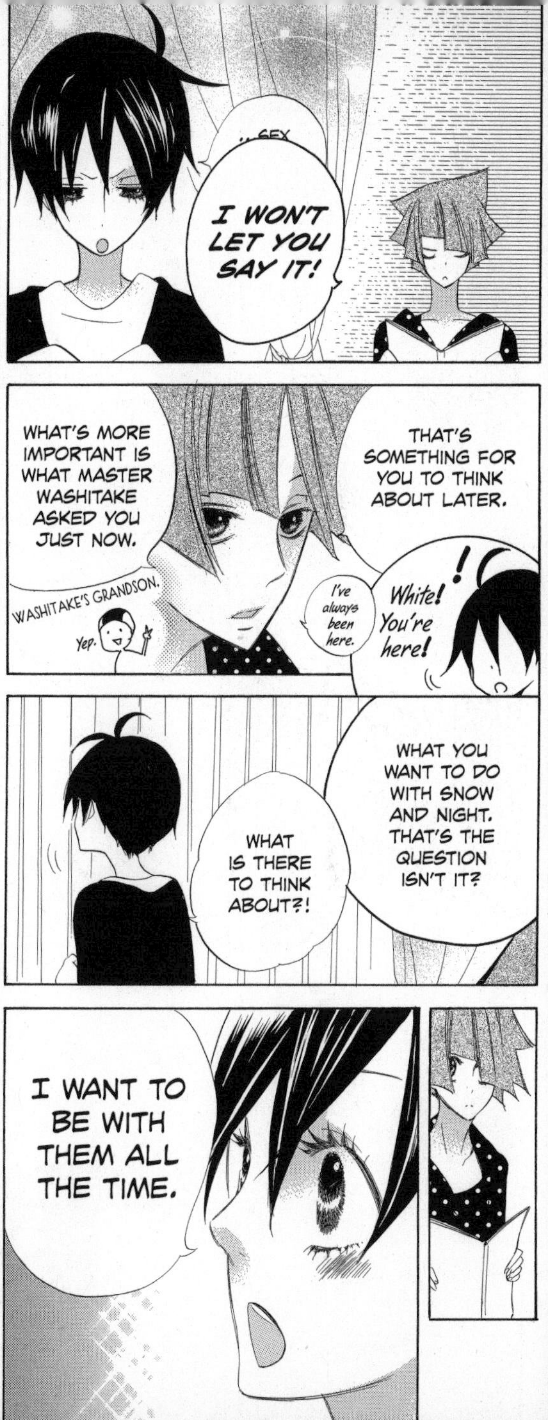
...SEX
I WON'T LET YOU SAY IT!
THAT'S SOMETHING FOR YOU TO THINK ABOUT LATER.
White! You're here!
I've always been here.
WHAT'S MORE IMPORTANT IS WHAT MASTER WASHITAKE ASKED YOU JUST NOW.
WASHITAKE'S GRANDSON.
Yep.
WHAT YOU WANT TO DO WITH SNOW AND NIGHT. THAT'S THE QUESTION ISN'T IT?
WHAT IS THERE TO THINK ABOUT?!
I WANT TO BE WITH THEM ALL THE TIME.

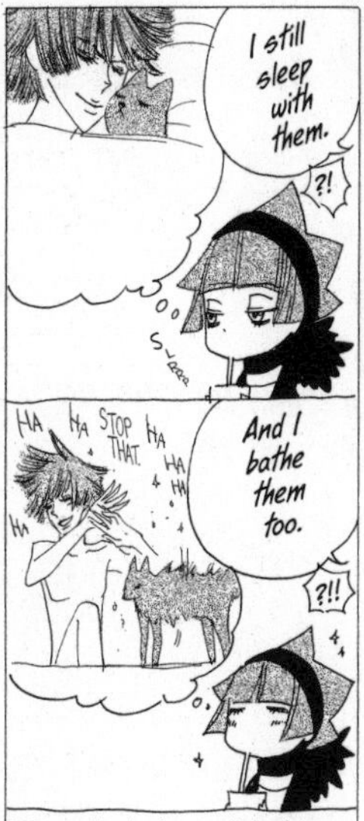
I still sleep with them.
?!
HA HA STOP THAT. HA HA HA HA
And I bathe them too.
?!!

This is kind of out of the blue, but...I wish they had more TV shows about ghosts.
I love ghost stories!
I haven't had much experience with the supernatural myself, and I'm a scaredy-cat, but...
I still love a good ghost story!

One of my assistants, Kikitsu, has suddenly developed the ability to sense ghostly presences.

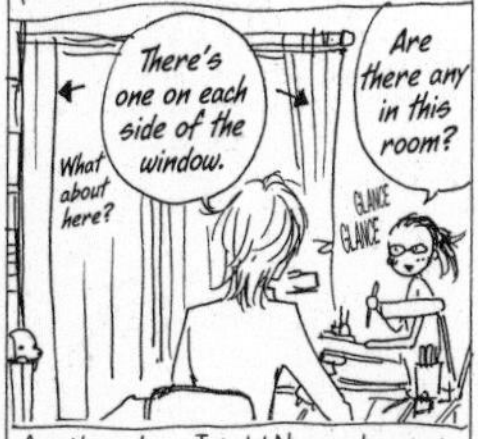
Are there any in this room?
There's one on each side of the window.
What about here?
GLANCE GLANCE

Another day, I told Nana about it.

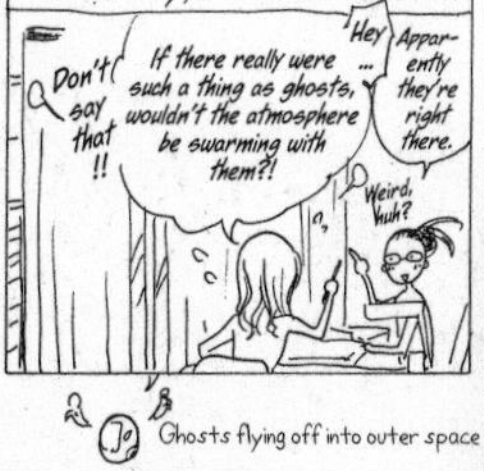
Apparently they're right there.
Hey...
If there really were such a thing as ghosts, wouldn't the atmosphere be swarming with them?!
Don't say that!!
Weird, huh?

Ghosts flying off into outer space

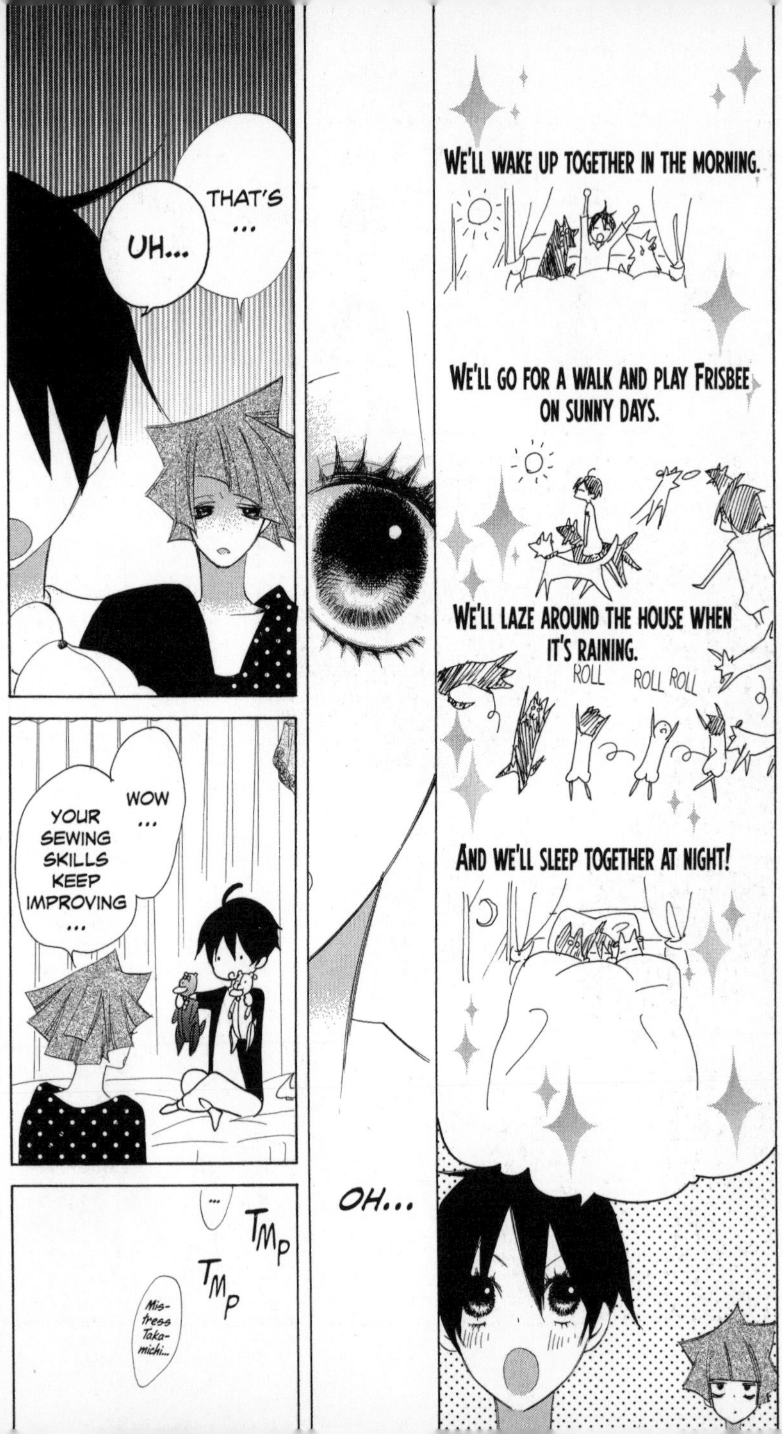

WE'LL WAKE UP TOGETHER IN THE MORNING.
WE'LL GO FOR A WALK AND PLAY FRISBEE ON SUNNY DAYS.
WE'LL LAZE AROUND THE HOUSE WHEN IT'S RAINING.
ROLL ROLL ROLL
AND WE'LL SLEEP TOGETHER AT NIGHT!
OH...
THAT'S ...
UH...
WOW ...
YOUR SEWING SKILLS KEEP IMPROVING ...
...
TMP
TMP
Mis-tress Taka-michi...

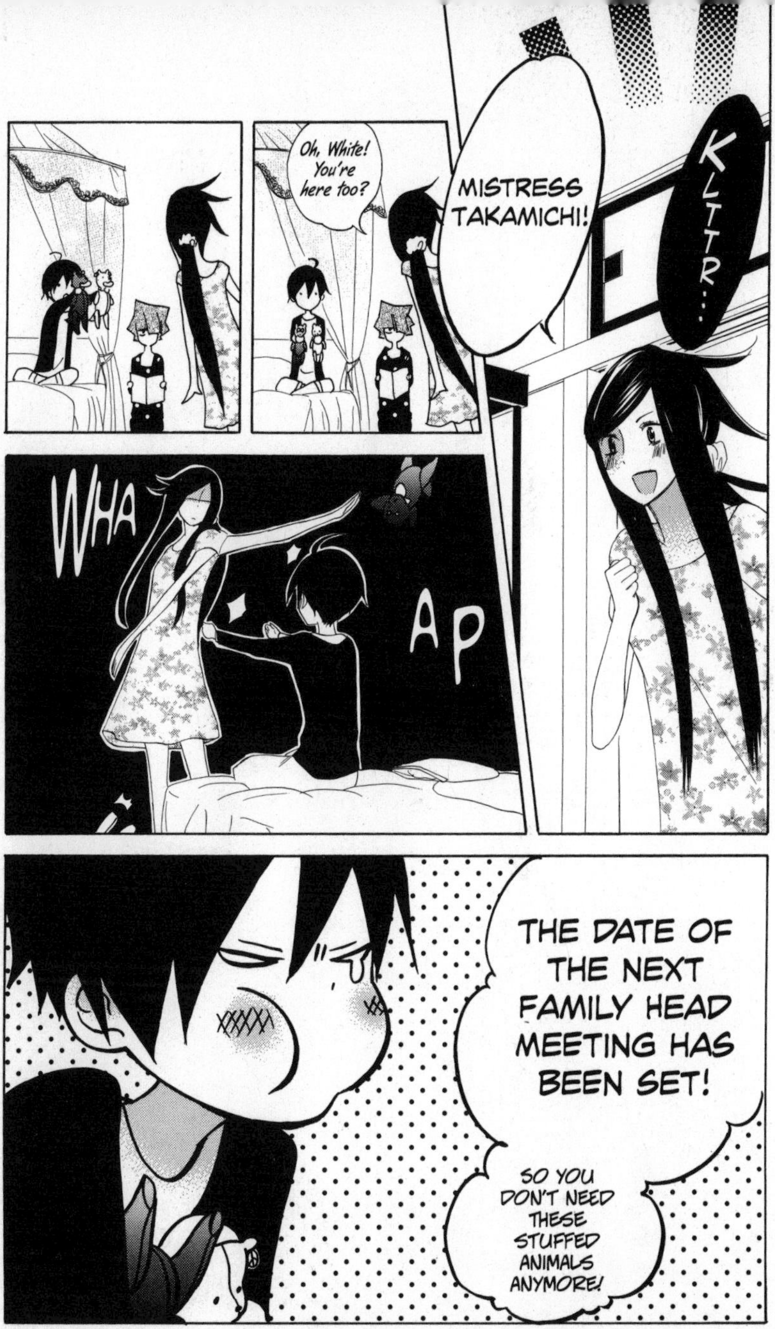
KLTTR...
MISTRESS TAKAMICHI!
Oh, White! You're here too?
WHA AP
THE DATE OF THE NEXT FAMILY HEAD MEETING HAS BEEN SET!
SO YOU DON'T NEED THESE STUFFED ANIMALS ANYMORE!

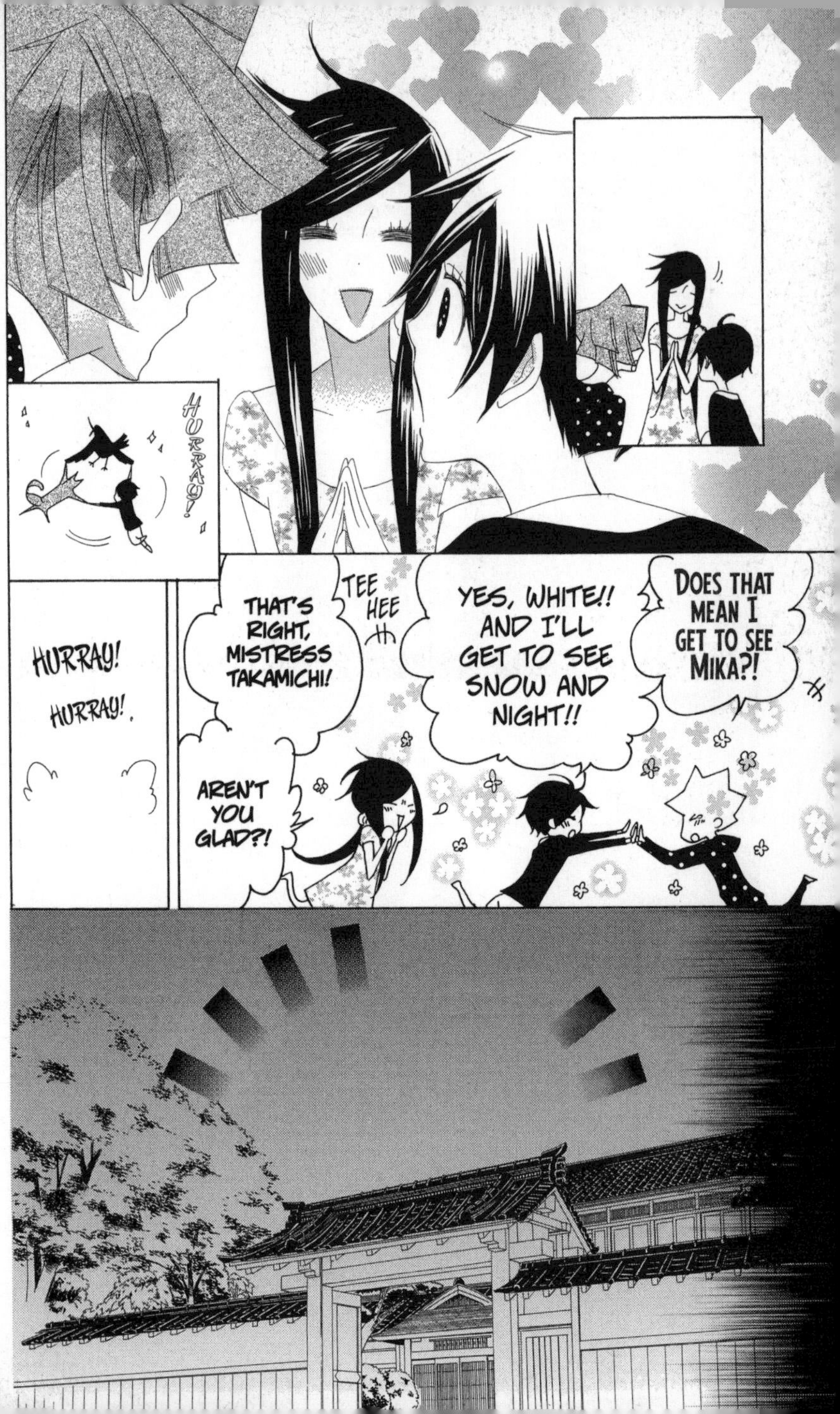
HURRAY!
DOES THAT MEAN I GET TO SEE MIKA?!
YES, WHITE!! AND I'LL GET TO SEE SNOW AND NIGHT!!
TEE HEE
THAT'S RIGHT, MISTRESS TAKAMICHI!
AREN'T YOU GLAD?!
HURRAY!
HURRAY!

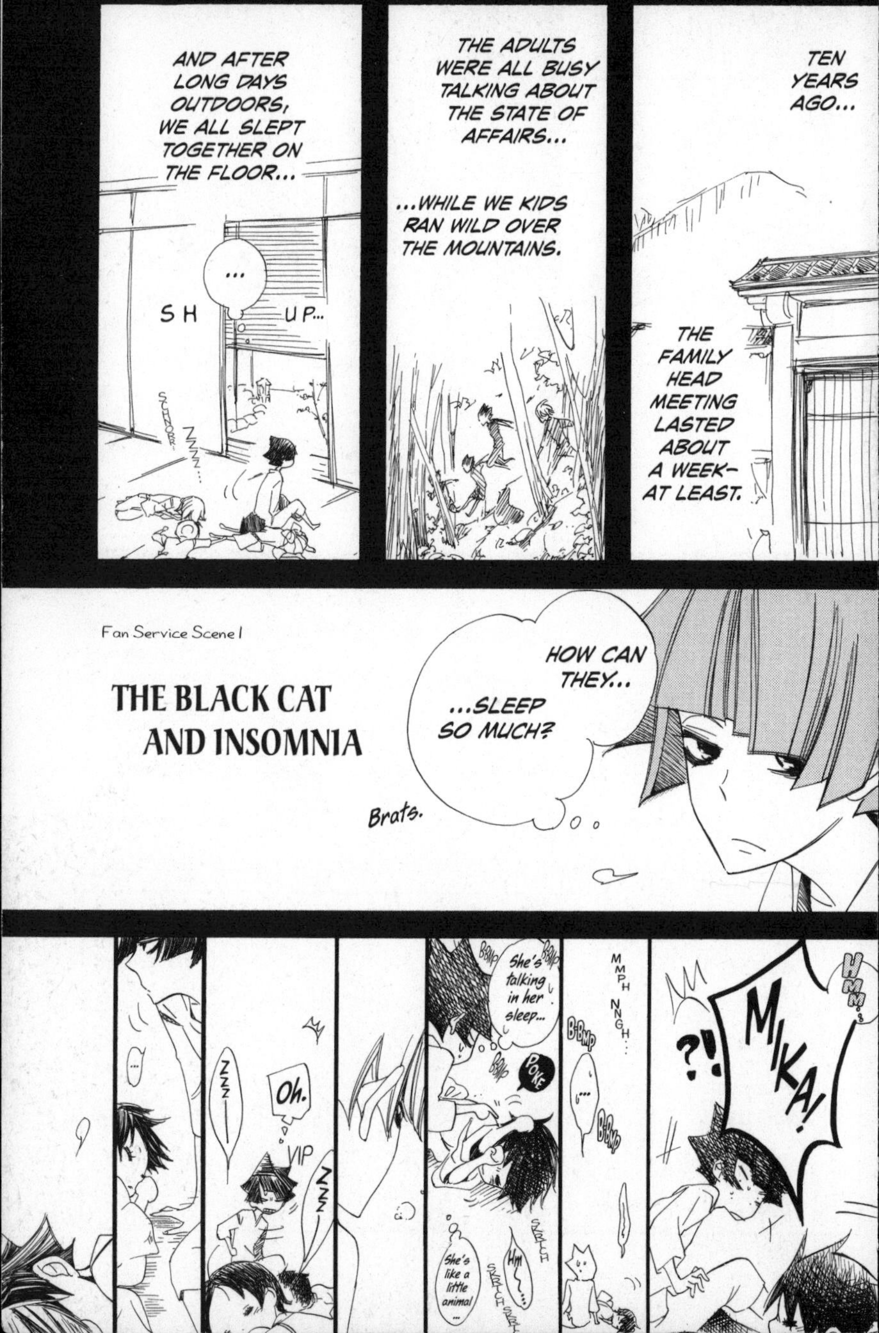
TEN YEARS AGO...
THE FAMILY HEAD MEETING LASTED ABOUT A WEEK-AT LEAST.
THE ADULTS WERE ALL BUSY TALKING ABOUT THE STATE OF AFFAIRS...
...WHILE WE KIDS RAN WILD OVER THE MOUNTAINS.
AND AFTER LONG DAYS OUTDOORS, WE ALL SLEPT TOGETHER ON THE FLOOR...
...
SH UP...
SCHNORR
ZZZZ...
HOW CAN THEY...
...SLEEP SO MUCH?
Brats.
Fan Service Scene 1
THE BLACK CAT AND INSOMNIA
HMM
MIKA!
?!
MMPH NNGH...
B-BMP
...
B-BMP
BBMP
She's talking in her sleep...
BBMP
POKE
HM...
SKRITCH
She's like a little animal...
SKRITCH SKRITCH
Oh.
VIP
ZZZ
ZZZ
...

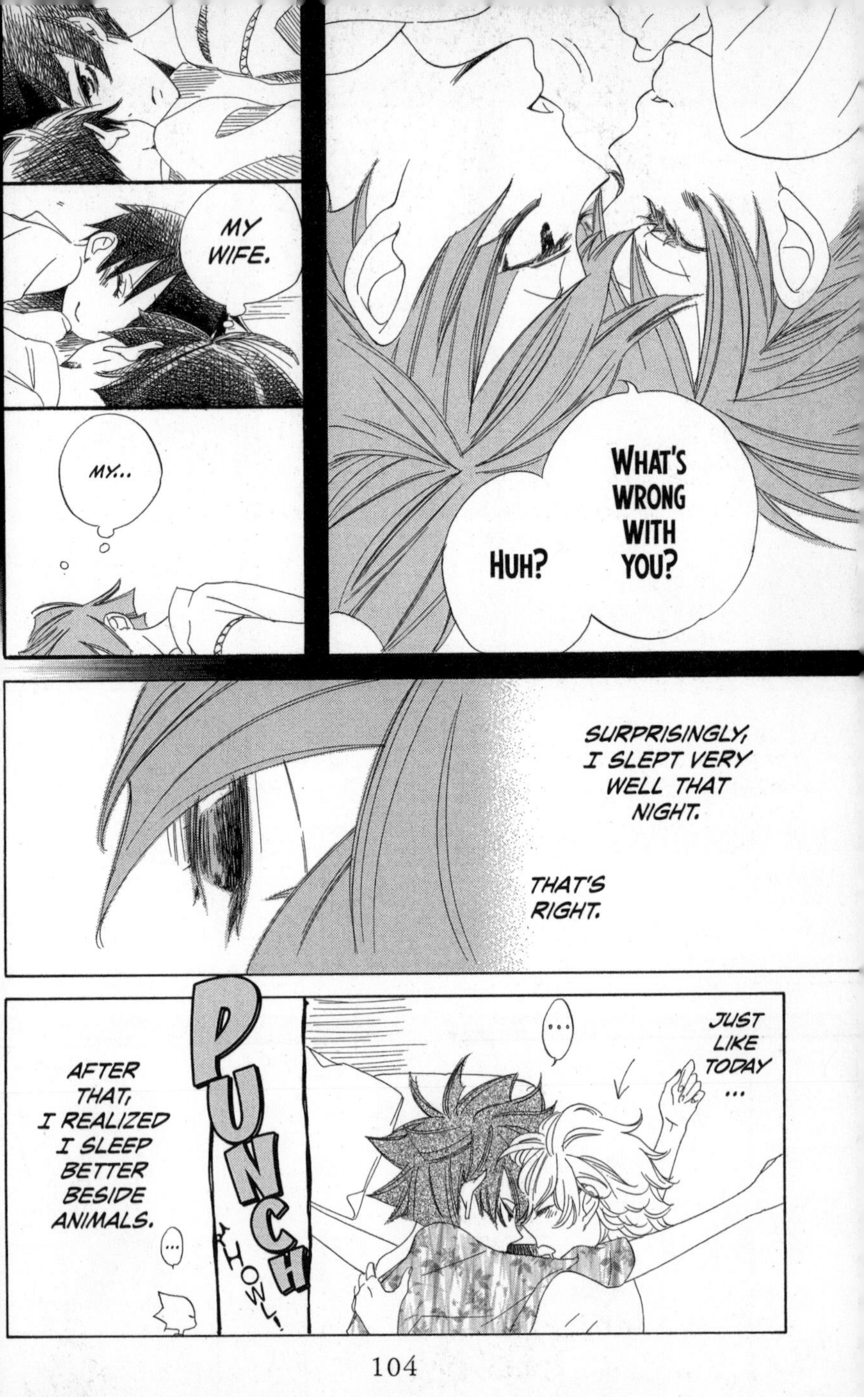
WHAT'S WRONG WITH YOU?
HUH?
MY WIFE.
MY...
SURPRISINGLY, I SLEPT VERY WELL THAT NIGHT.
THAT'S RIGHT.
JUST LIKE TODAY ...
...
PUNCH
HOWL!
AFTER THAT, I REALIZED I SLEEP BETTER BESIDE ANIMALS.
...

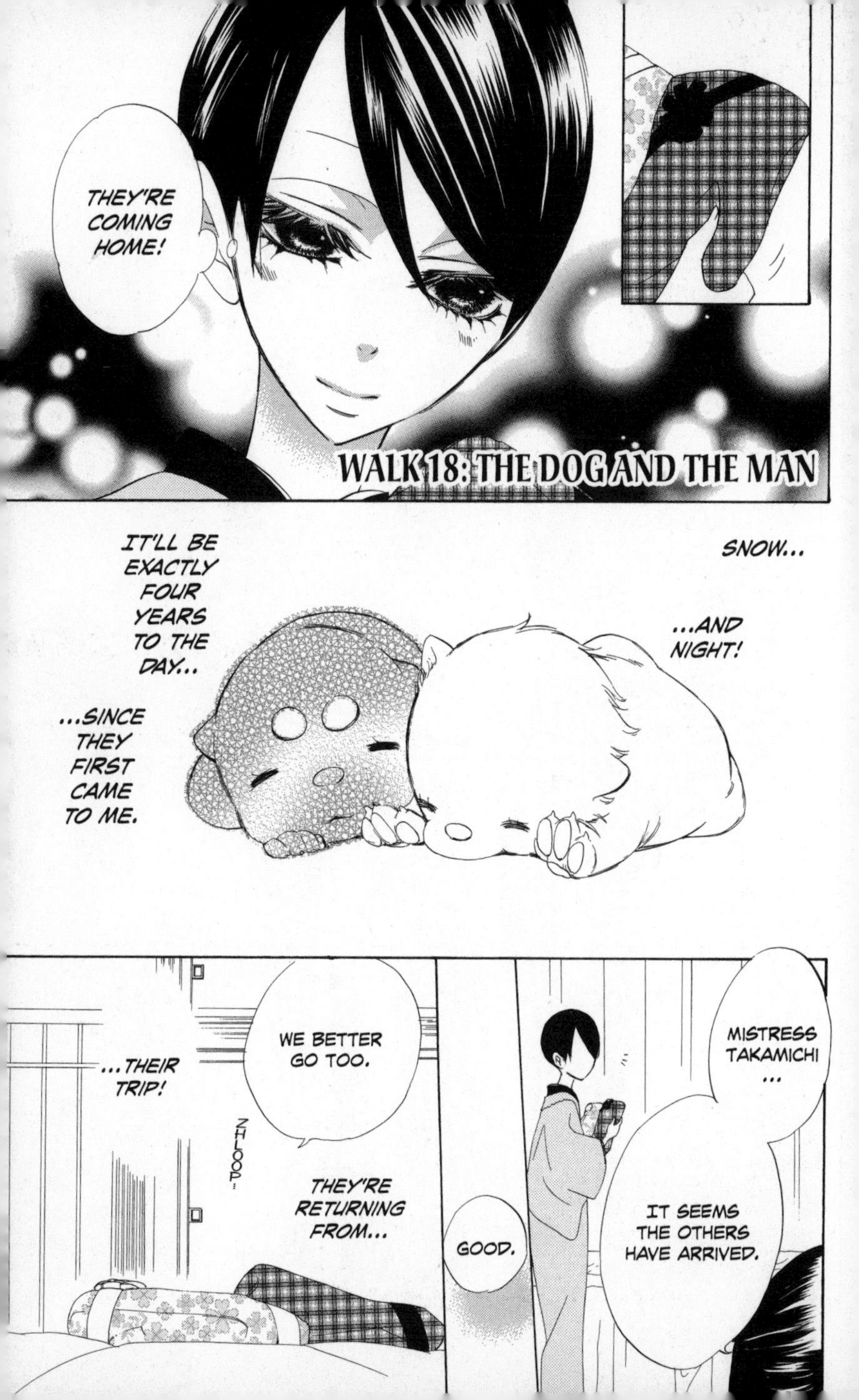
THEY'RE COMING HOME!
WALK 18: THE DOG AND THE MAN
SNOW...
...AND NIGHT!
IT'LL BE EXACTLY FOUR YEARS TO THE DAY...
...SINCE THEY FIRST CAME TO ME.
MISTRESS TAKAMICHI...
IT SEEMS THE OTHERS HAVE ARRIVED.
GOOD.
WE BETTER GO TOO.
ZHLOOP...
THEY'RE RETURNING FROM...
...THEIR TRIP!

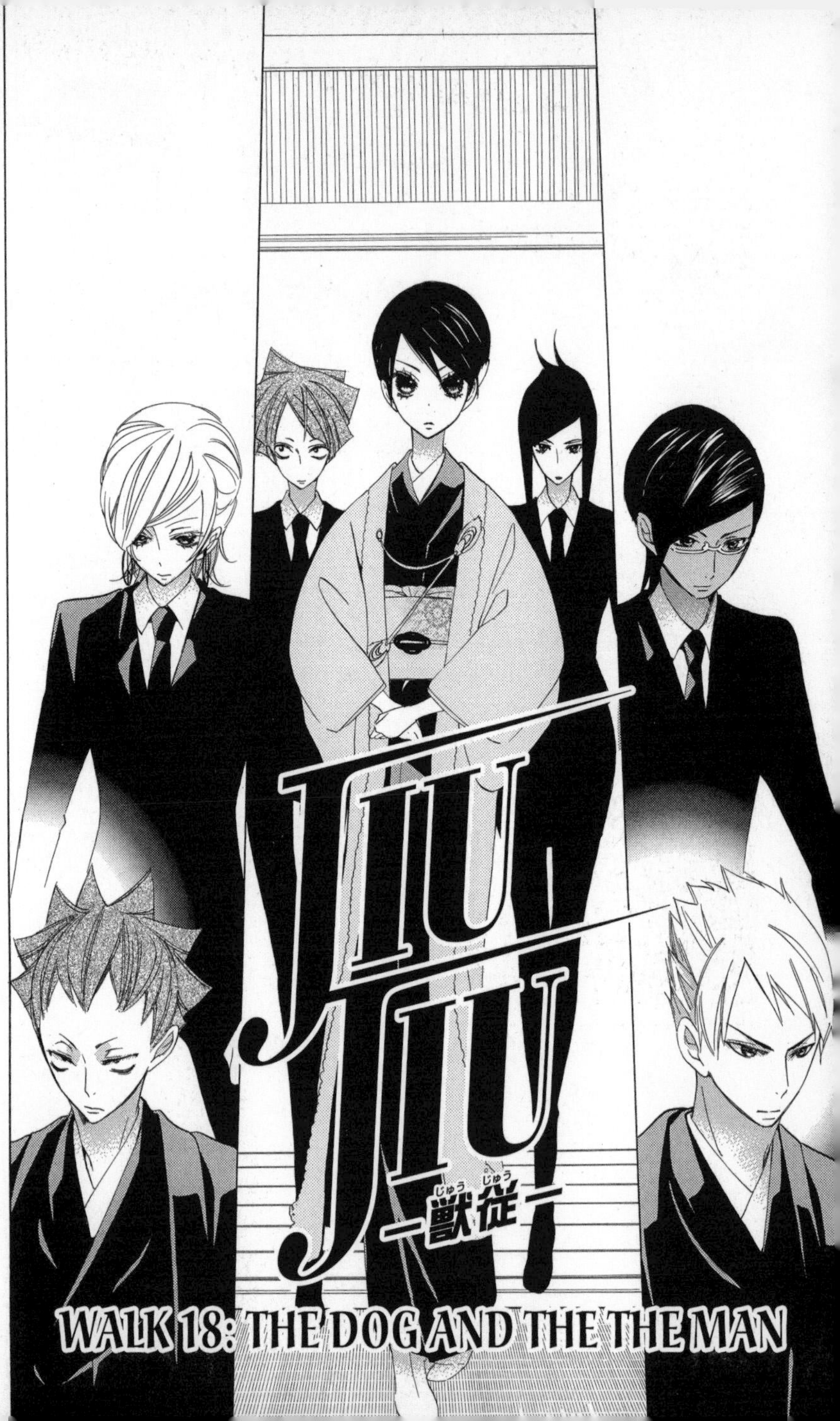
JIU JIU
獣従
WALK 18: THE DOG AND THE THE MAN

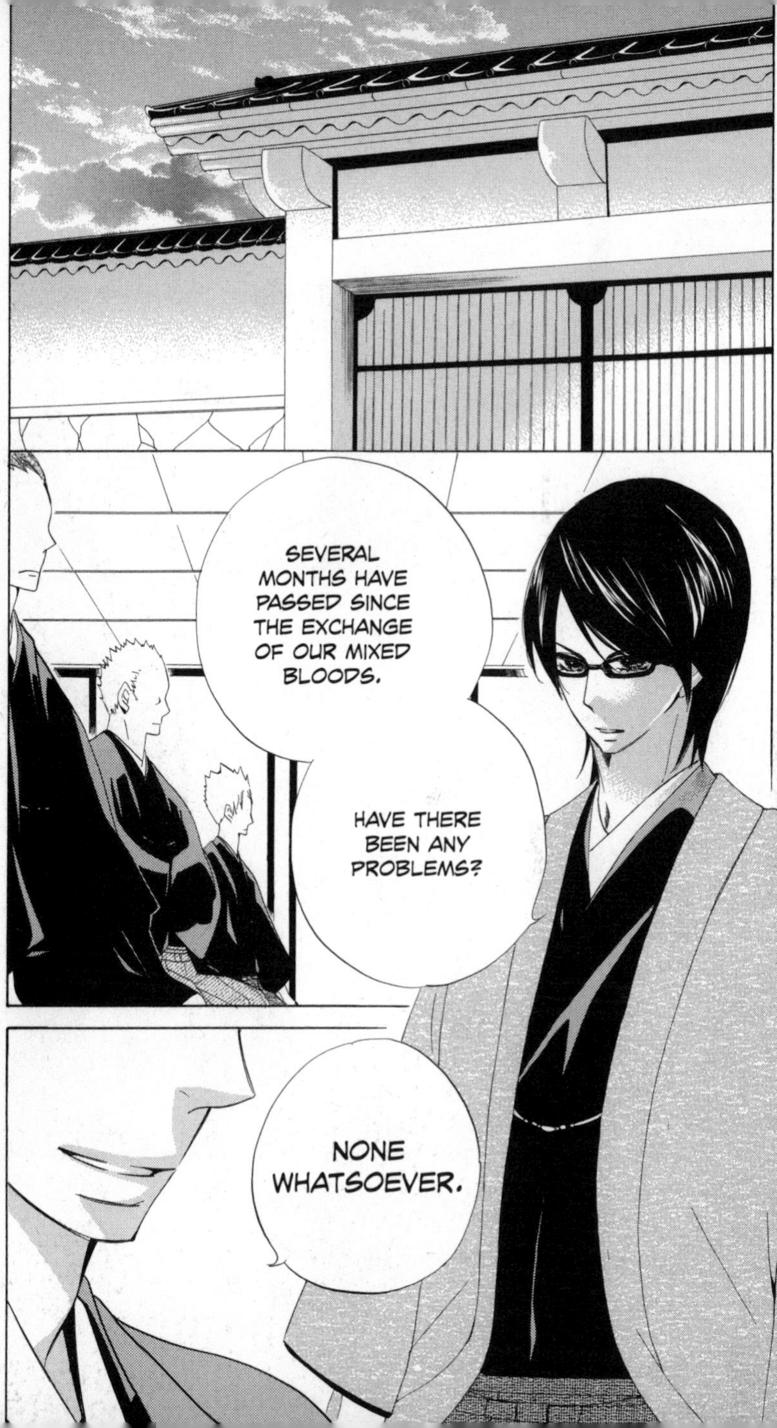
SEVERAL MONTHS HAVE PASSED SINCE THE EXCHANGE OF OUR MIXED BLOODS.
HAVE THERE BEEN ANY PROBLEMS?
NONE WHATSOEVER.

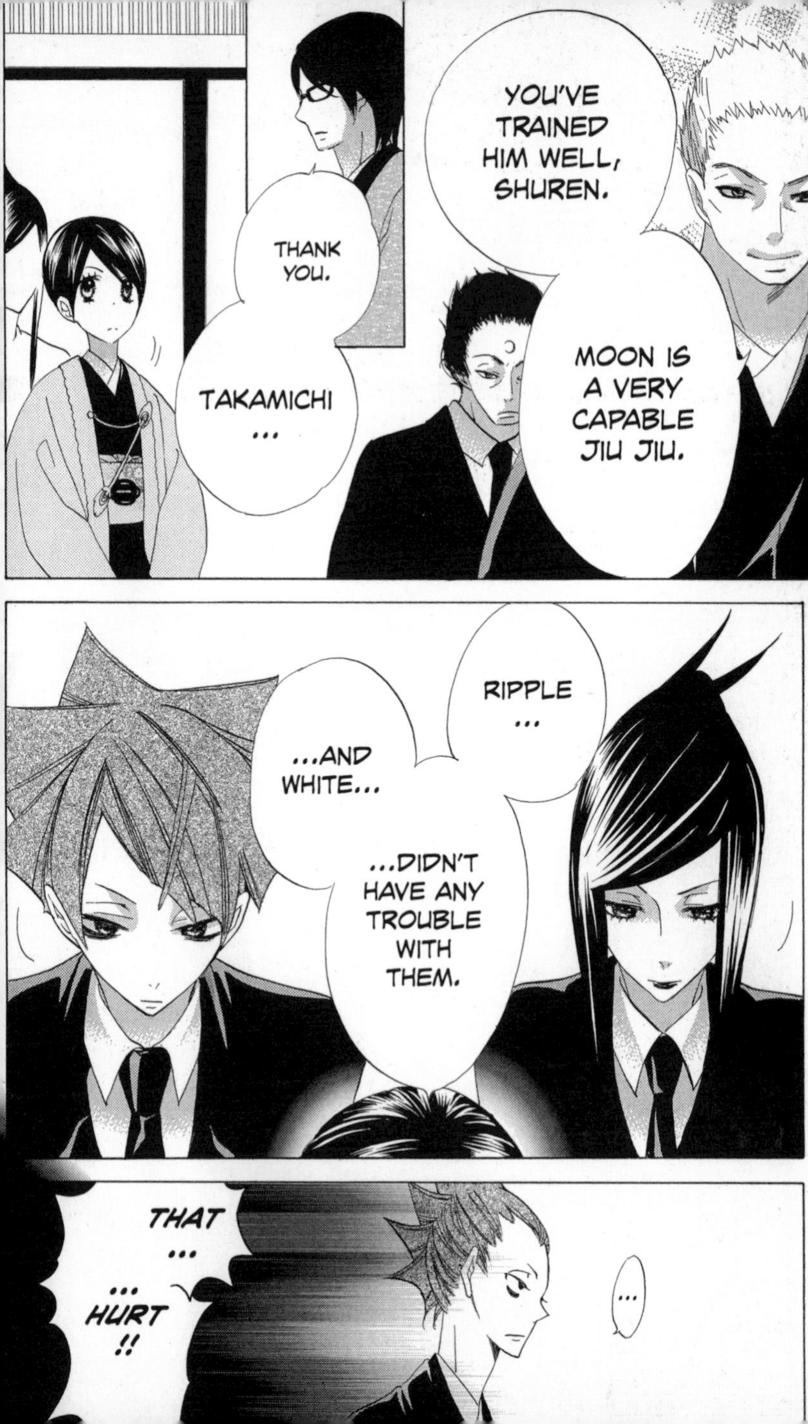
YOU'VE TRAINED HIM WELL, SHUREN.
MOON IS A VERY CAPABLE JIU JIU.
THANK YOU.
TAKAMICHI ...
RIPPLE ...
...AND WHITE...
...DIDN'T HAVE ANY TROUBLE WITH THEM.
...
THAT ...
... HURT !!

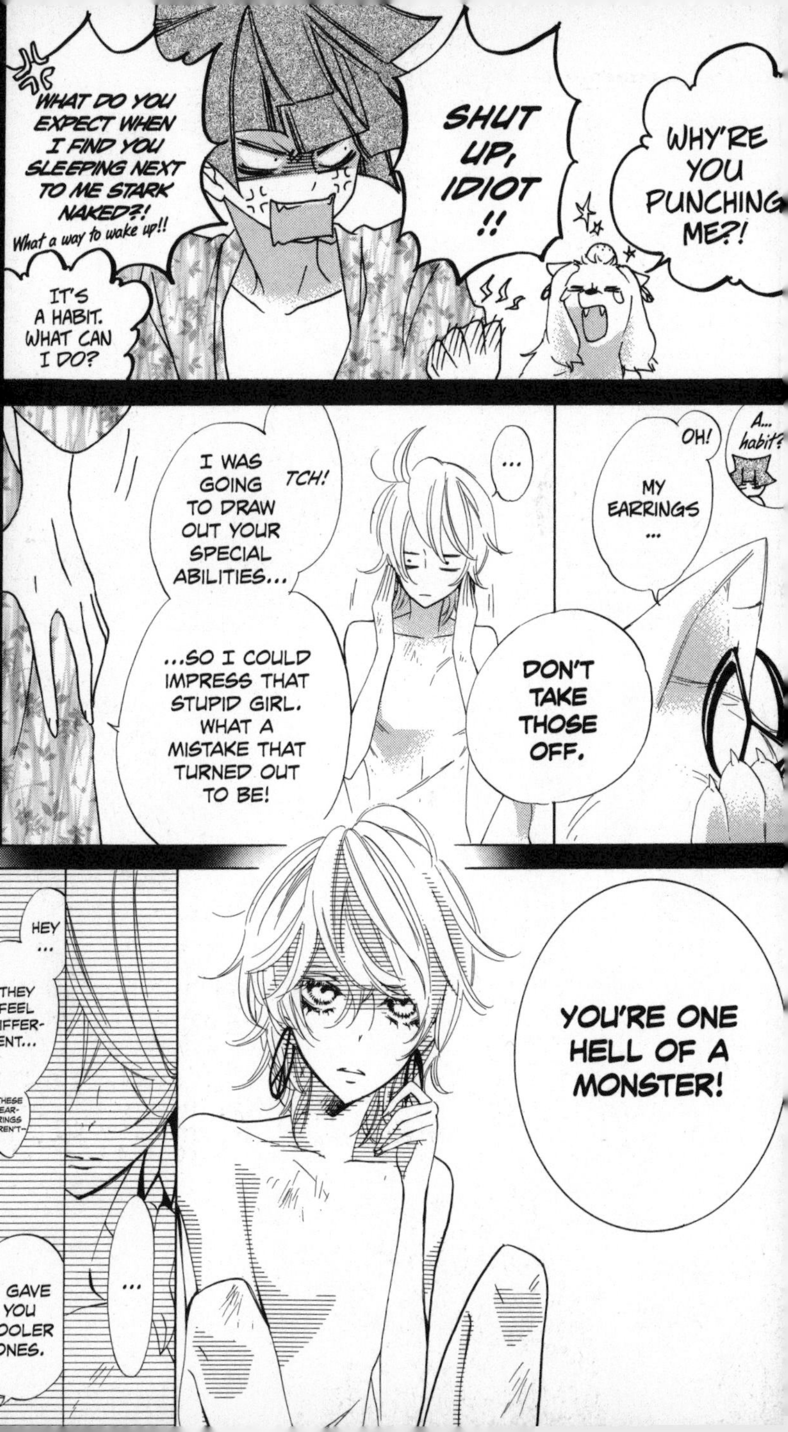
WHY'RE YOU PUNCHING ME?!
SHUT UP, IDIOT!!
WHAT DO YOU EXPECT WHEN I FIND YOU SLEEPING NEXT TO ME STARK NAKED?!
What a way to wake up!!
IT'S A HABIT. WHAT CAN I DO?
A... habit?
OH!
MY EARRINGS...
DON'T TAKE THOSE OFF.
...
TCH!
I WAS GOING TO DRAW OUT YOUR SPECIAL ABILITIES...
...SO I COULD IMPRESS THAT STUPID GIRL. WHAT A MISTAKE THAT TURNED OUT TO BE!
YOU'RE ONE HELL OF A MONSTER!
HEY...
THEY FEEL DIFFER-ENT...
THESE EAR-RINGS AREN'T—
...
I GAVE YOU COOLER ONES.

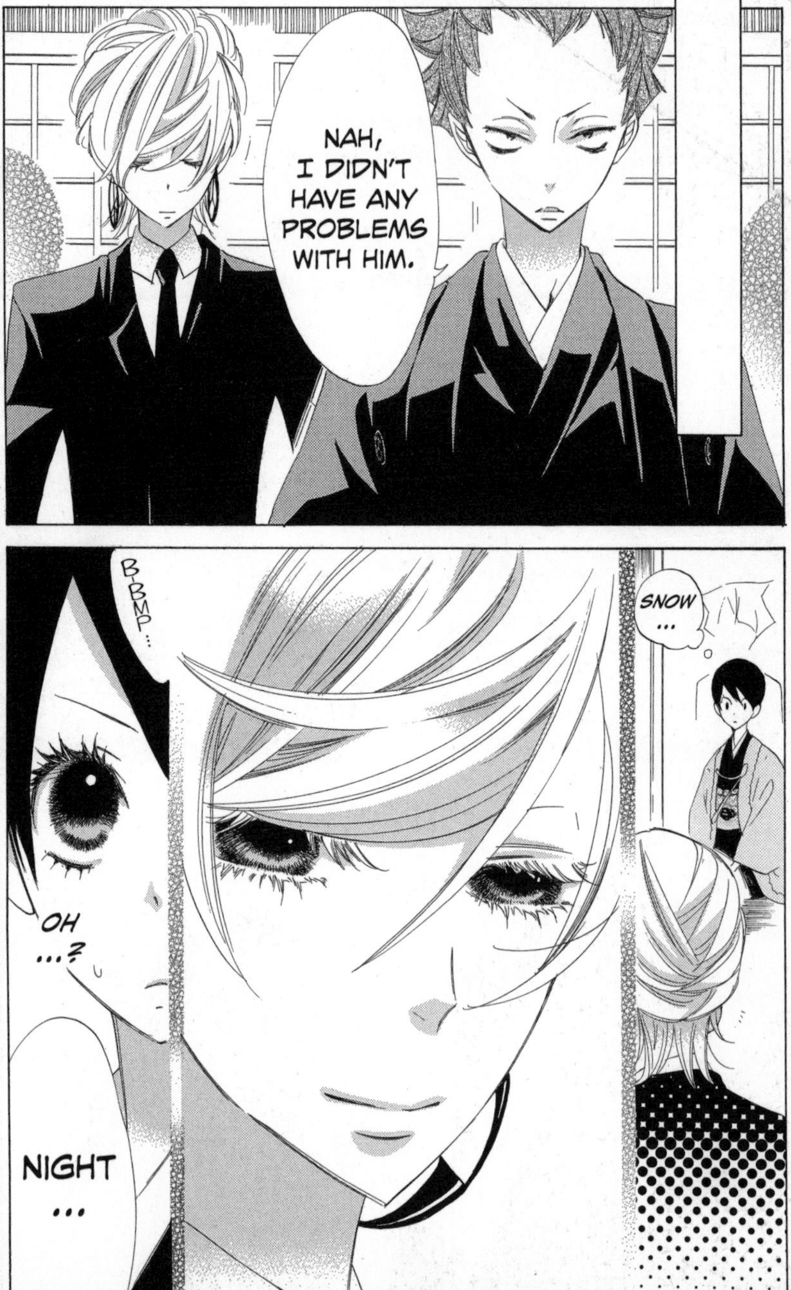
NAH, I DIDN'T HAVE ANY PROBLEMS WITH HIM.
SNOW ...
B-BMP...
OH ...?
NIGHT ...

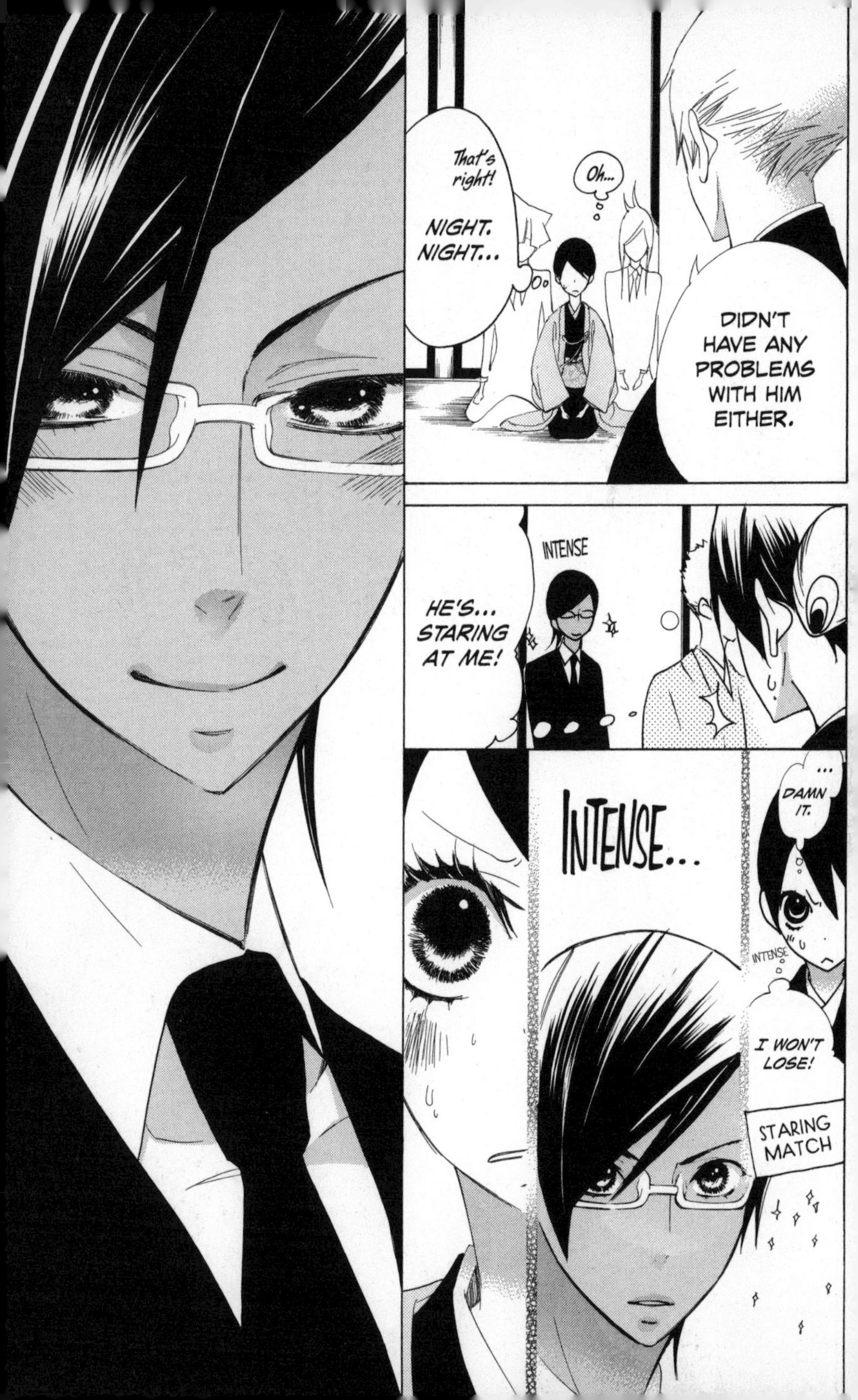
DIDN'T HAVE ANY PROBLEMS WITH HIM EITHER.
Oh...
That's right!
NIGHT. NIGHT...
INTENSE
HE'S... STARING AT ME!
... DAMN IT.
INTENSE
I WON'T LOSE!
STARING MATCH
INTENSE...

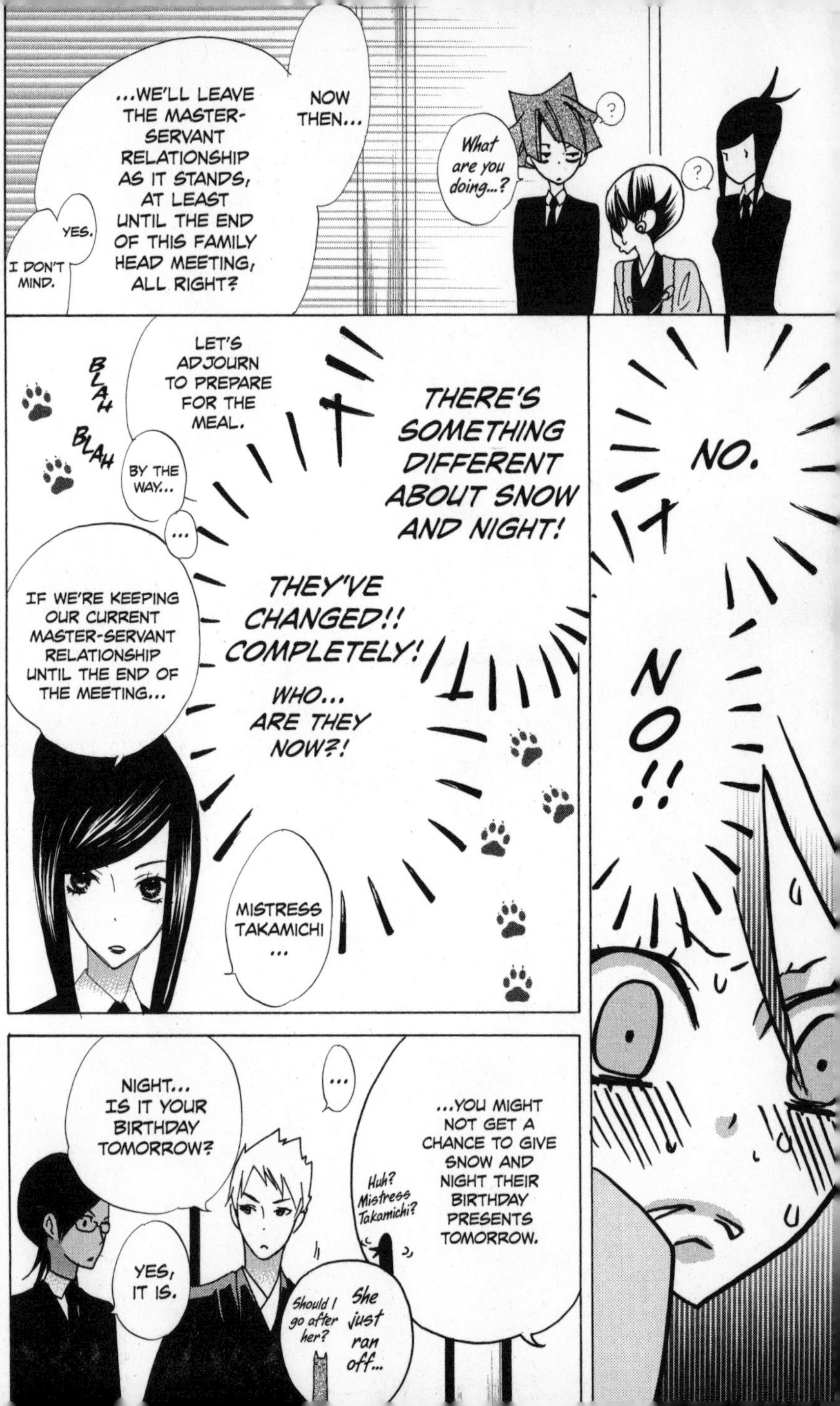
?
?
What are you doing...?
NOW THEN...
...WE'LL LEAVE THE MASTER-SERVANT RELATIONSHIP AS IT STANDS, AT LEAST UNTIL THE END OF THIS FAMILY HEAD MEETING, ALL RIGHT?
YES.
I DON'T MIND.
NO.
NO NO!!
THERE'S SOMETHING DIFFERENT ABOUT SNOW AND NIGHT!
LET'S ADJOURN TO PREPARE FOR THE MEAL.
BLAH BLAH
BY THE WAY...
...
THEY'VE CHANGED!! COMPLETELY!
WHO... ARE THEY NOW?!
IF WE'RE KEEPING OUR CURRENT MASTER-SERVANT RELATIONSHIP UNTIL THE END OF THE MEETING...
MISTRESS TAKAMICHI...
...YOU MIGHT NOT GET A CHANCE TO GIVE SNOW AND NIGHT THEIR BIRTHDAY PRESENTS TOMORROW.
...
Huh? Mistress Takamichi?
NIGHT... IS IT YOUR BIRTHDAY TOMORROW?
She just ran off...
Should I go after her?
YES, IT IS.

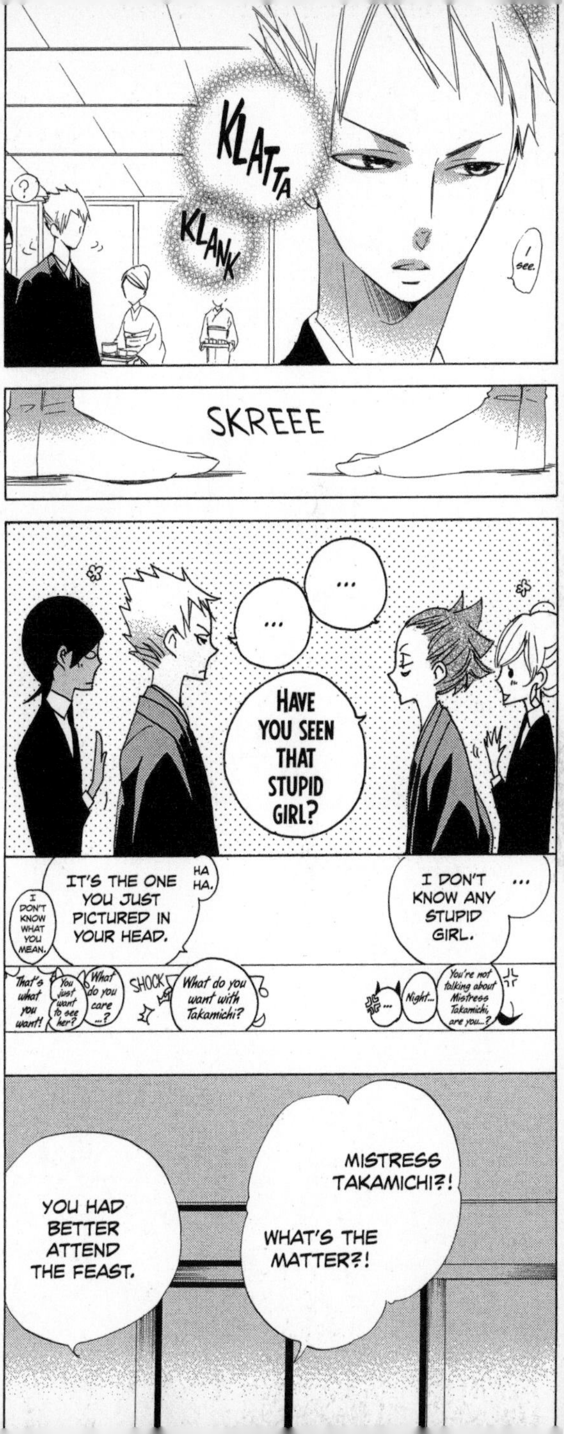
KLATTA
KLANK
?
I see.
SKREEE
...
...
HAVE YOU SEEN THAT STUPID GIRL?
I DON'T KNOW ANY STUPID GIRL.
...
HA HA.
IT'S THE ONE YOU JUST PICTURED IN YOUR HEAD.
I DON'T KNOW WHAT YOU MEAN.
You're not talking about Mistress Takamichi, are you...?
Night...
...
What do you want with Takamichi?
SHOCK
What do you care...?
You just want to see her?
That's what you want!
MISTRESS TAKAMICHI?!
WHAT'S THE MATTER?!
YOU HAD BETTER ATTEND THE FEAST.

March 11, 2011.

The Great East Japan Earthquake occurred as I was working on Chapter 18.

The house and my hand kept shaking. I forced myself to complete the chapter, despite the circumstances. But for a while I couldn't even draw scribbles.

Because it was dark!
↑
We weren't in a scheduled blackout area, but I felt bad about turning the lights on.

Actually, I really couldn't draw anything for about two months after that. The only thing I managed was a message of support and rough sketches of the characters for a joint piece I was working on.
↑
I'd calmed down a lot by the time I worked on this.

I just hope someday people will be able to talk about it calmly... someday...

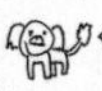
← My dog. Summer version.

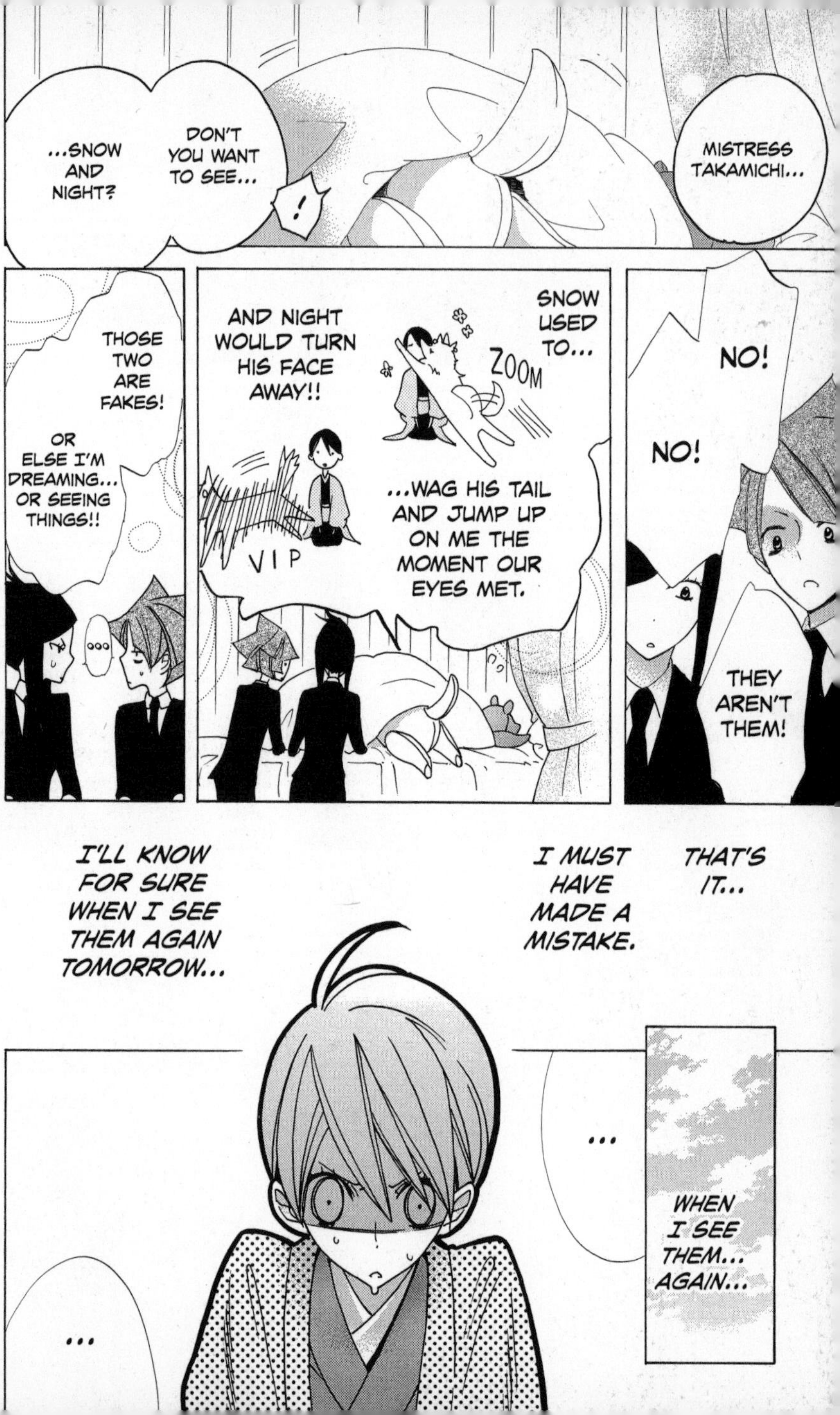
MISTRESS TAKAMICHI...
!
DON'T YOU WANT TO SEE...
...SNOW AND NIGHT?
NO!
NO!
THEY AREN'T THEM!
SNOW USED TO...
ZOOM
...WAG HIS TAIL AND JUMP UP ON ME THE MOMENT OUR EYES MET.
AND NIGHT WOULD TURN HIS FACE AWAY!!
VIP
THOSE TWO ARE FAKES!
OR ELSE I'M DREAMING... OR SEEING THINGS!!
THAT'S IT...
I MUST HAVE MADE A MISTAKE.
I'LL KNOW FOR SURE WHEN I SEE THEM AGAIN TOMORROW...
WHEN I SEE THEM... AGAIN...
...
...

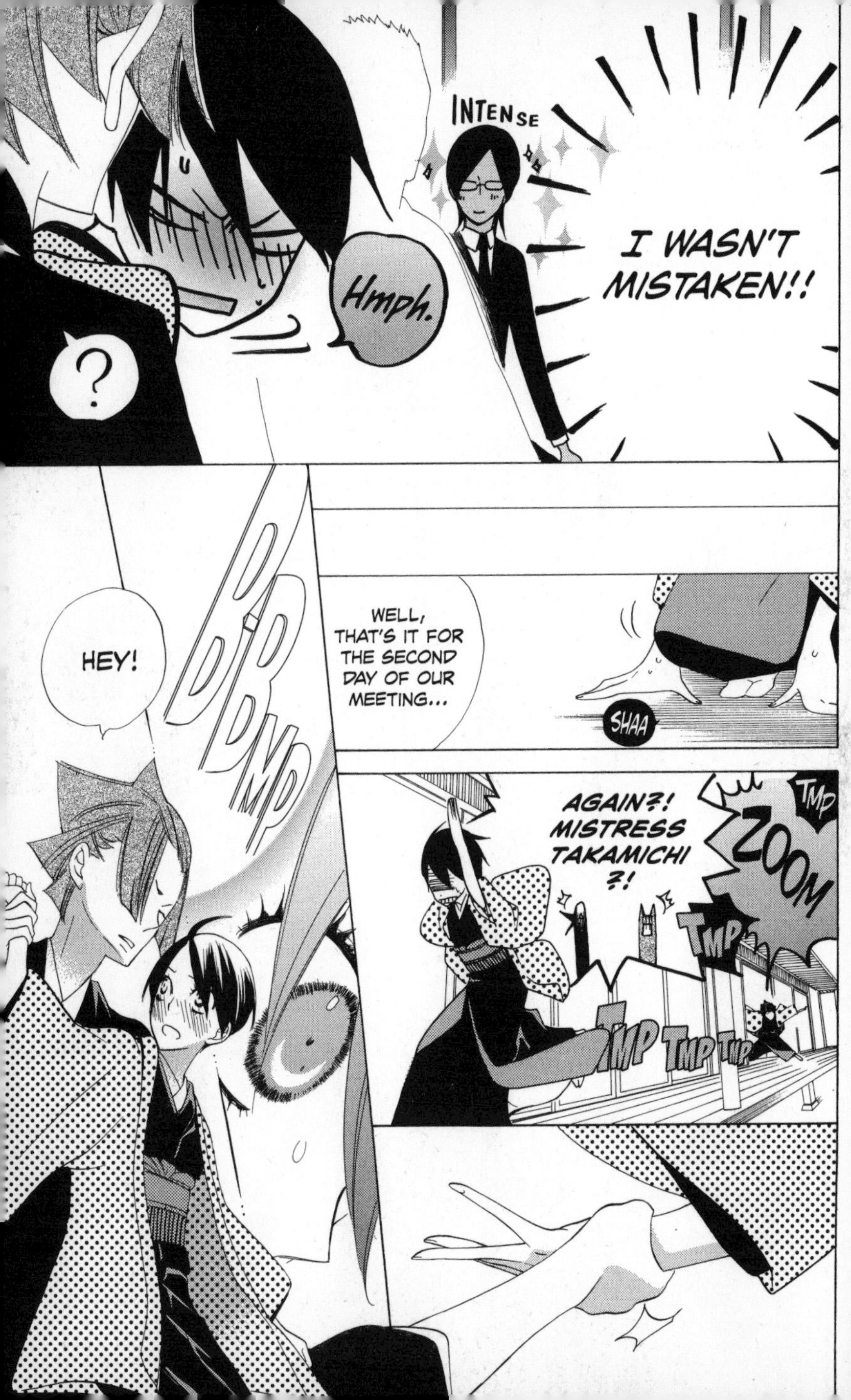
INTENSE
I WASN'T MISTAKEN!!
Hmph.
?
SHAA
WELL, THAT'S IT FOR THE SECOND DAY OF OUR MEETING...
TMP
ZOOM
AGAIN?! MISTRESS TAKAMICHI?!
TMP
TMP TMP TMP
HEY!

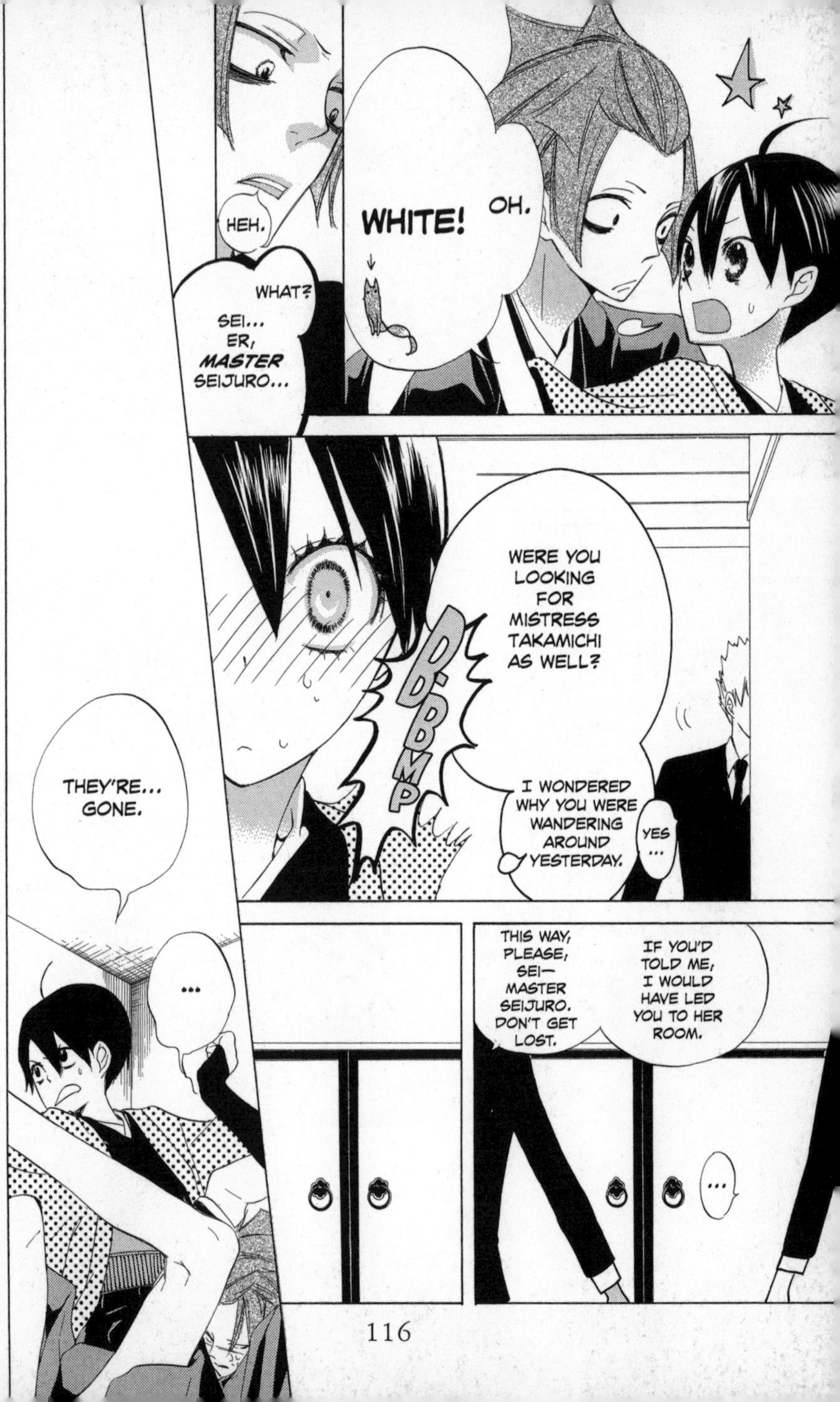
OH.
WHITE!
HEH.
WHAT?
SEI... ER, MASTER SEIJURO...
WERE YOU LOOKING FOR MISTRESS TAKAMICHI AS WELL?
B-BDMP
I WONDERED WHY YOU WERE WANDERING AROUND YESTERDAY.
YES ...
IF YOU'D TOLD ME, I WOULD HAVE LED YOU TO HER ROOM.
THIS WAY, PLEASE, SEI— MASTER SEIJURO. DON'T GET LOST.
...
THEY'RE... GONE.
...

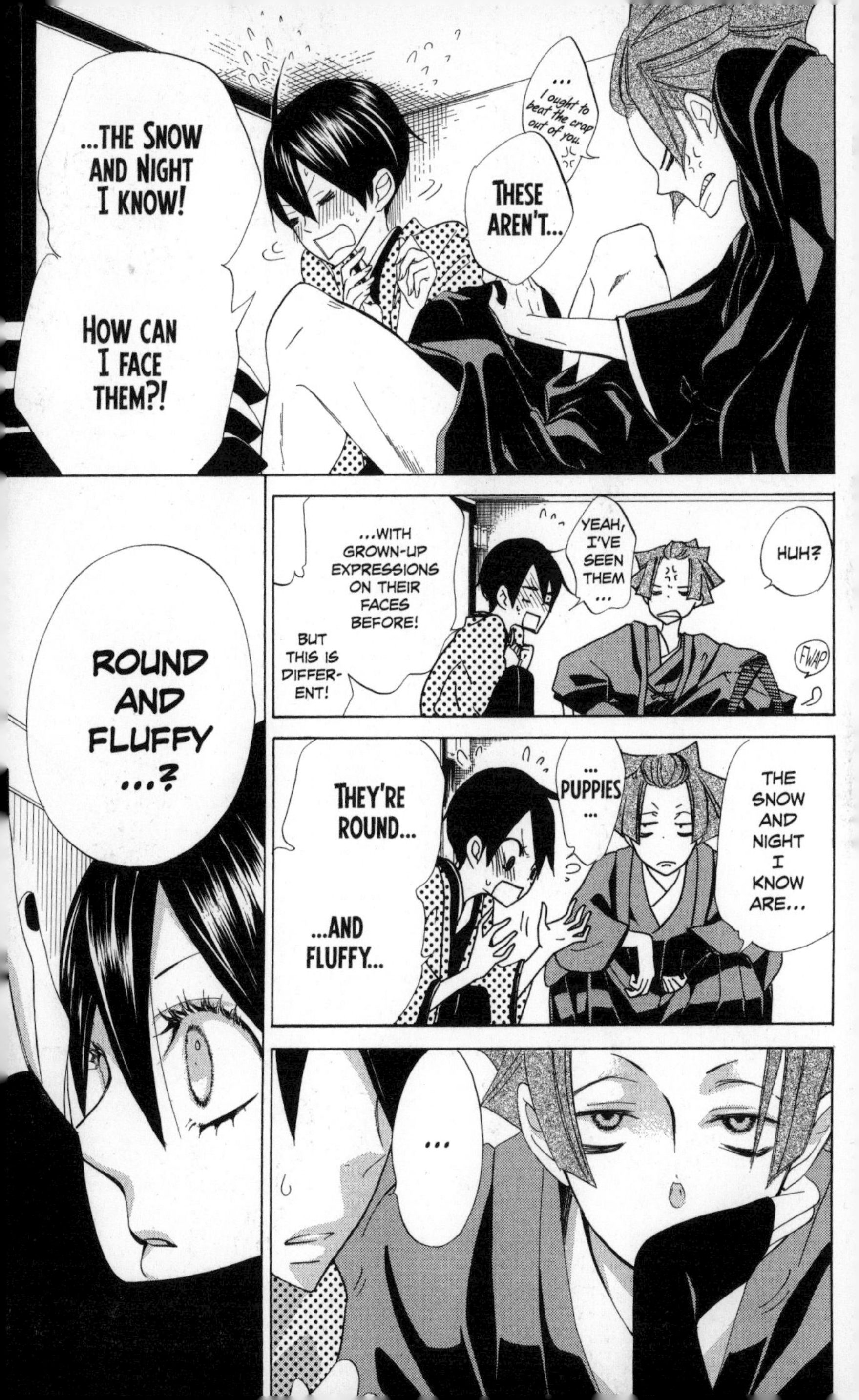
... I ought to beat the crap out of you.
THESE AREN'T...
...THE SNOW AND NIGHT I KNOW!
HOW CAN I FACE THEM?!
HUH?
FWAP
YEAH, I'VE SEEN THEM ...
...WITH GROWN-UP EXPRESSIONS ON THEIR FACES BEFORE!
BUT THIS IS DIFFER-ENT!
THE SNOW AND NIGHT I KNOW ARE...
... PUPPIES ...
THEY'RE ROUND...
...AND FLUFFY...
...
ROUND AND FLUFFY ...?

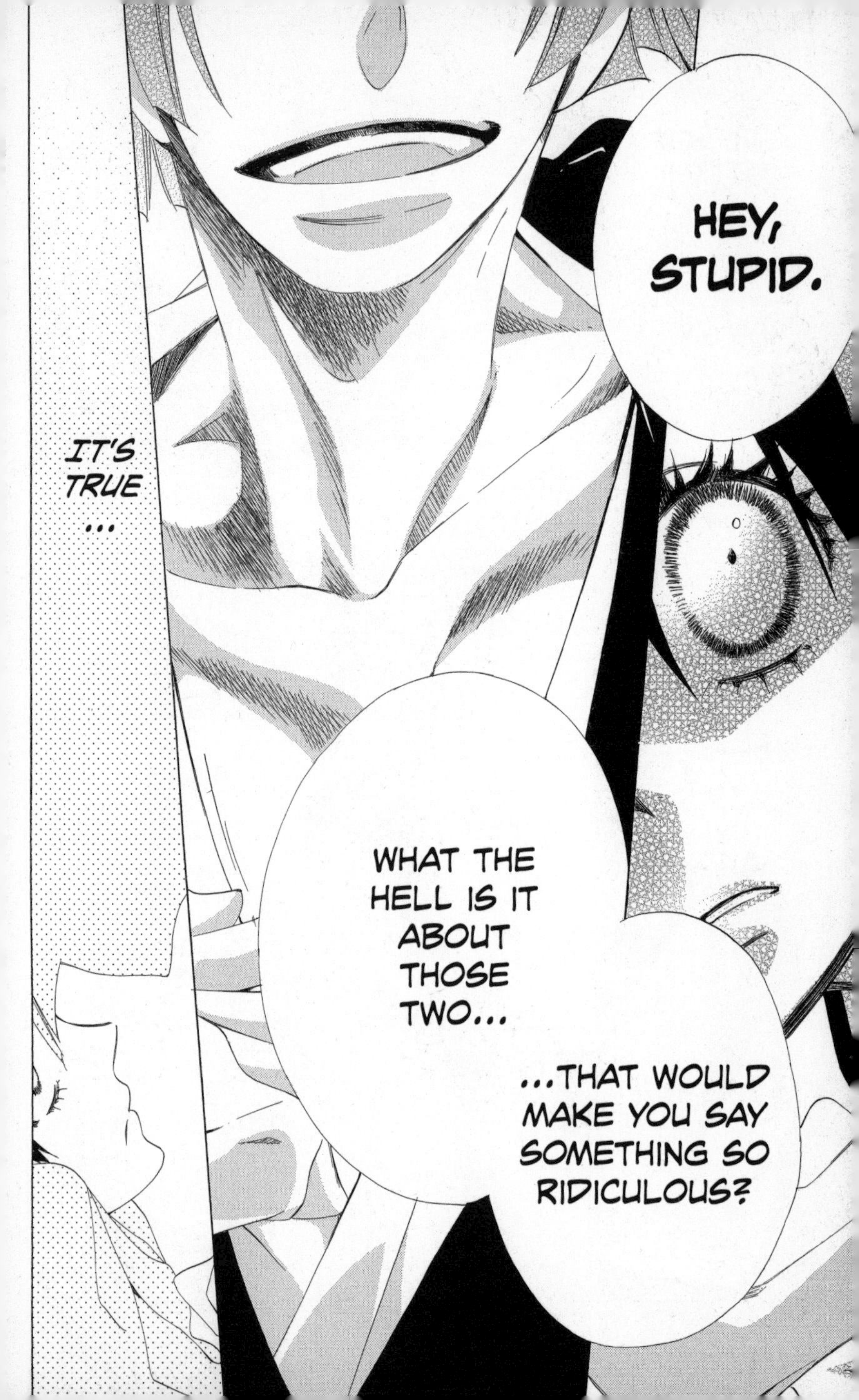
HEY, STUPID.
WHAT THE HELL IS IT ABOUT THOSE TWO...
...THAT WOULD MAKE YOU SAY SOMETHING SO RIDICULOUS?
IT'S TRUE...

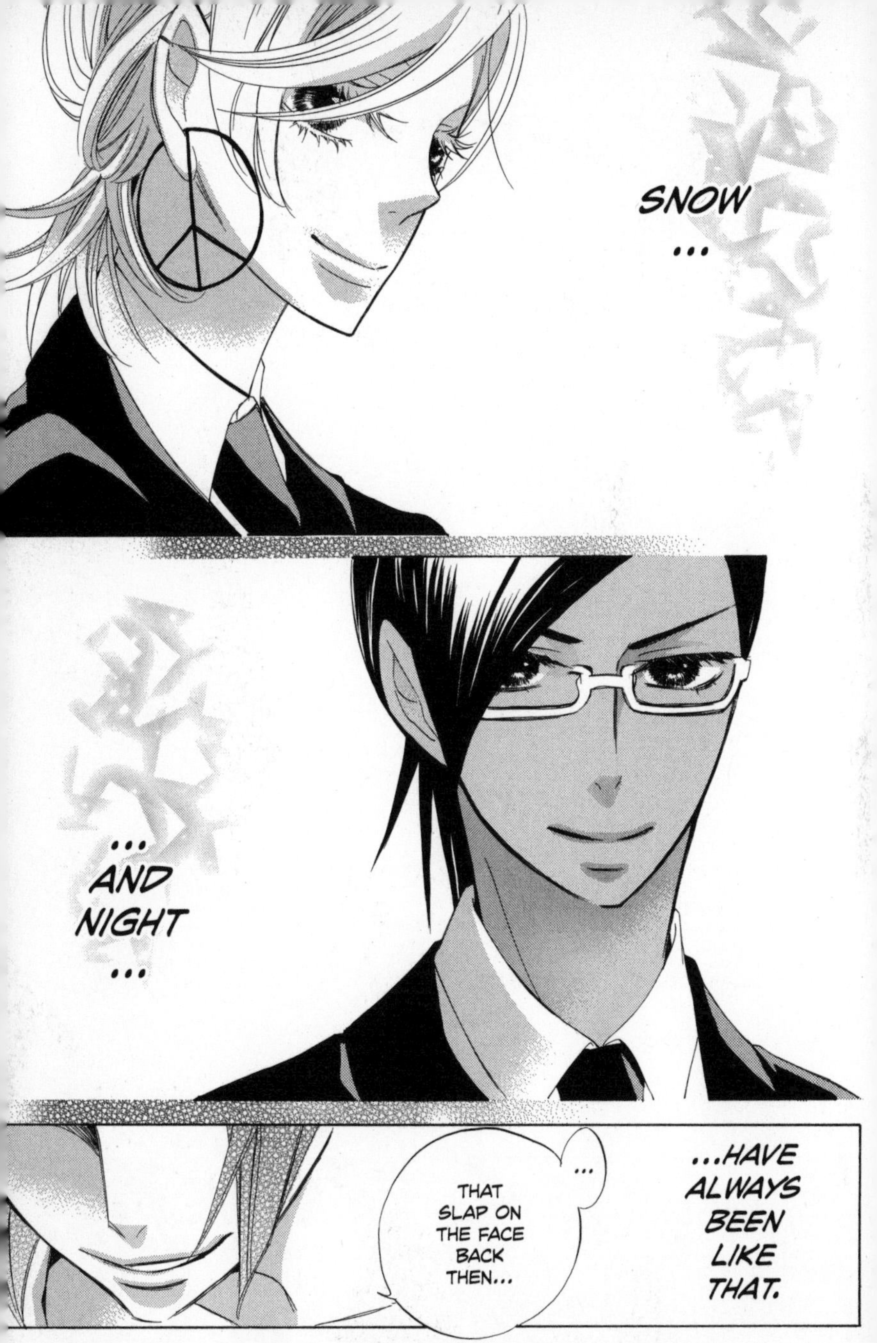
SNOW ...
... AND NIGHT ...
...HAVE ALWAYS BEEN LIKE THAT.
...
THAT SLAP ON THE FACE BACK THEN...

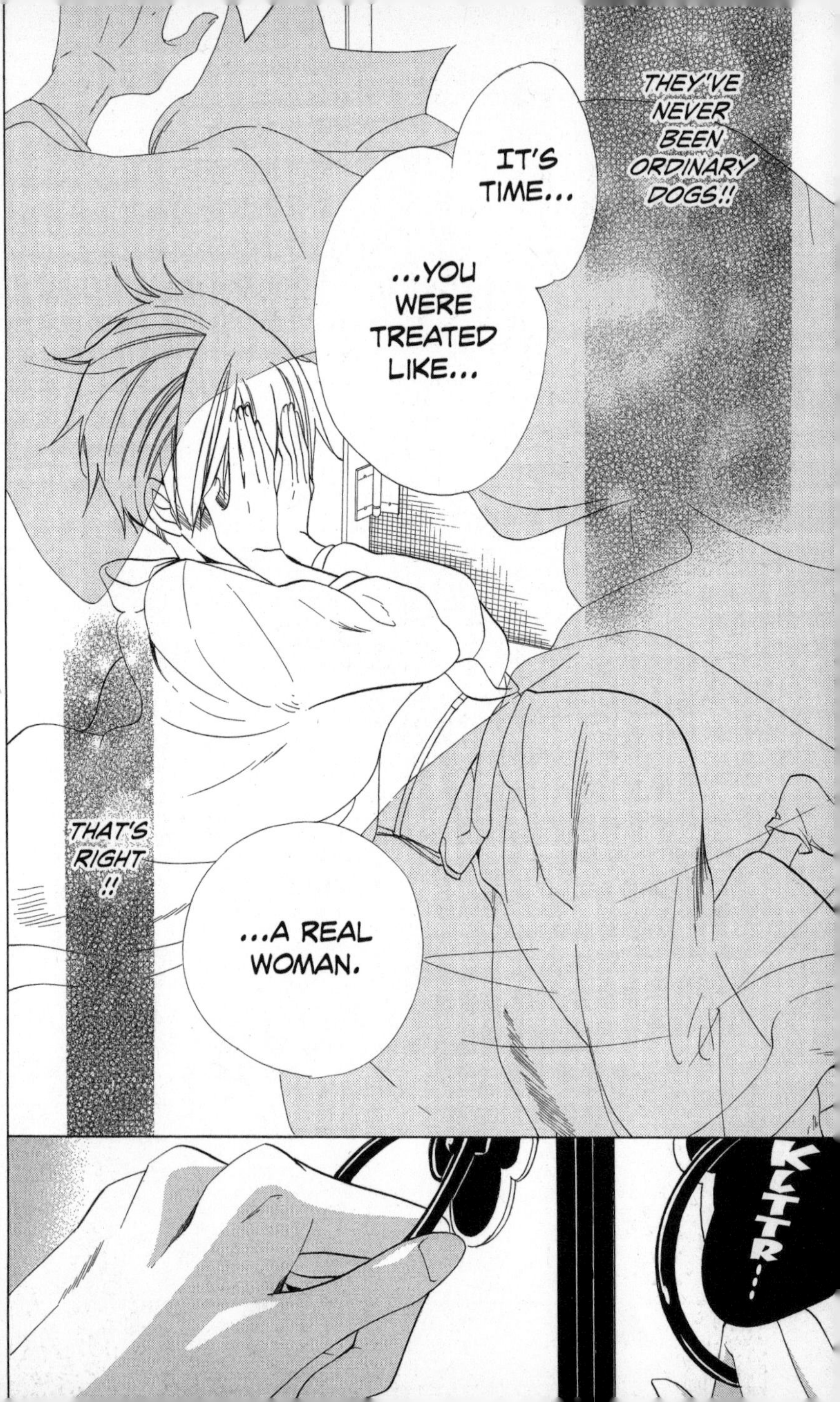
THEY'VE NEVER BEEN ORDINARY DOGS!!
IT'S TIME...
...YOU WERE TREATED LIKE...
THAT'S RIGHT!!
...A REAL WOMAN.
KLTTR...

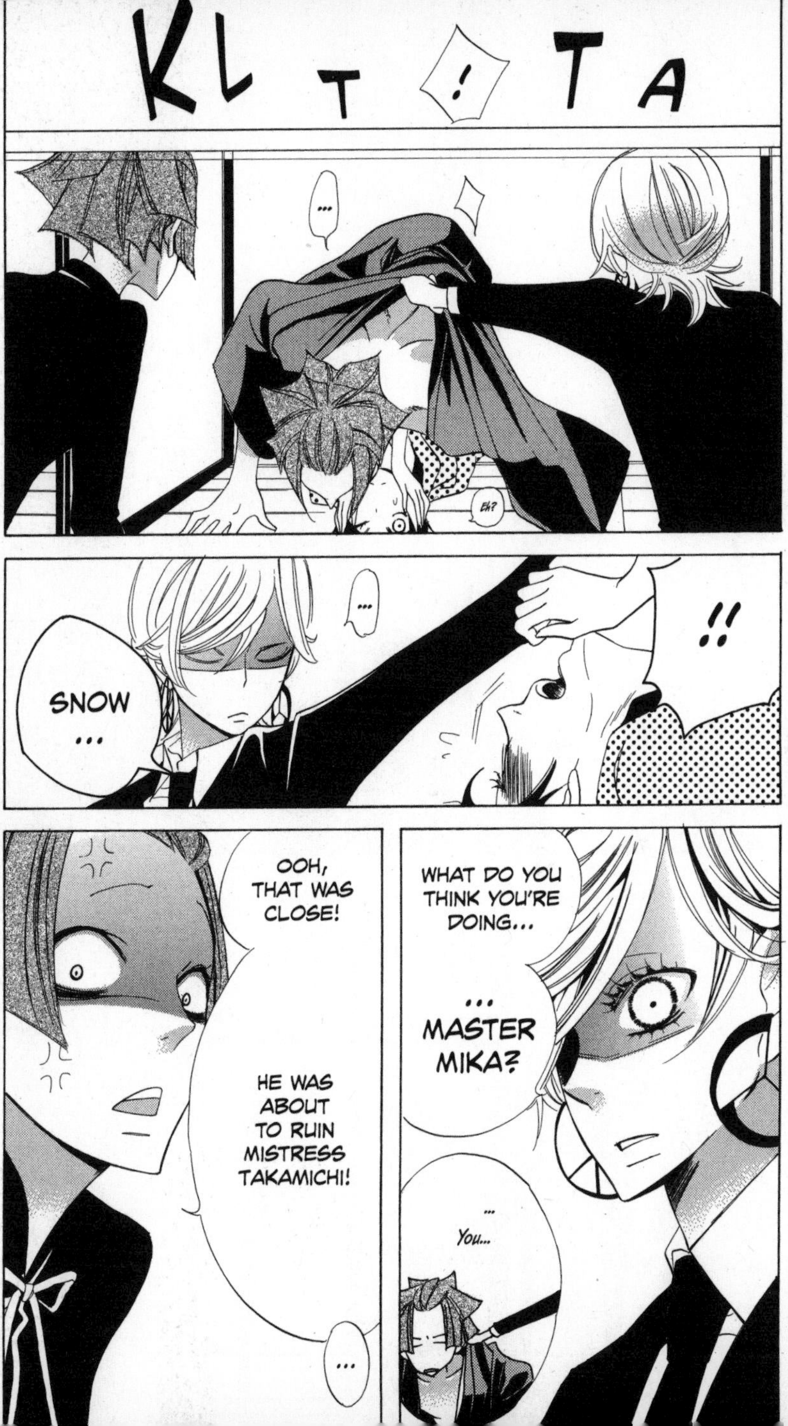
KLTTA
!
...
Eh?
!!
...
SNOW ...
WHAT DO YOU THINK YOU'RE DOING...
... MASTER MIKA?
... You...
OOH, THAT WAS CLOSE!
HE WAS ABOUT TO RUIN MISTRESS TAKAMICHI!
...

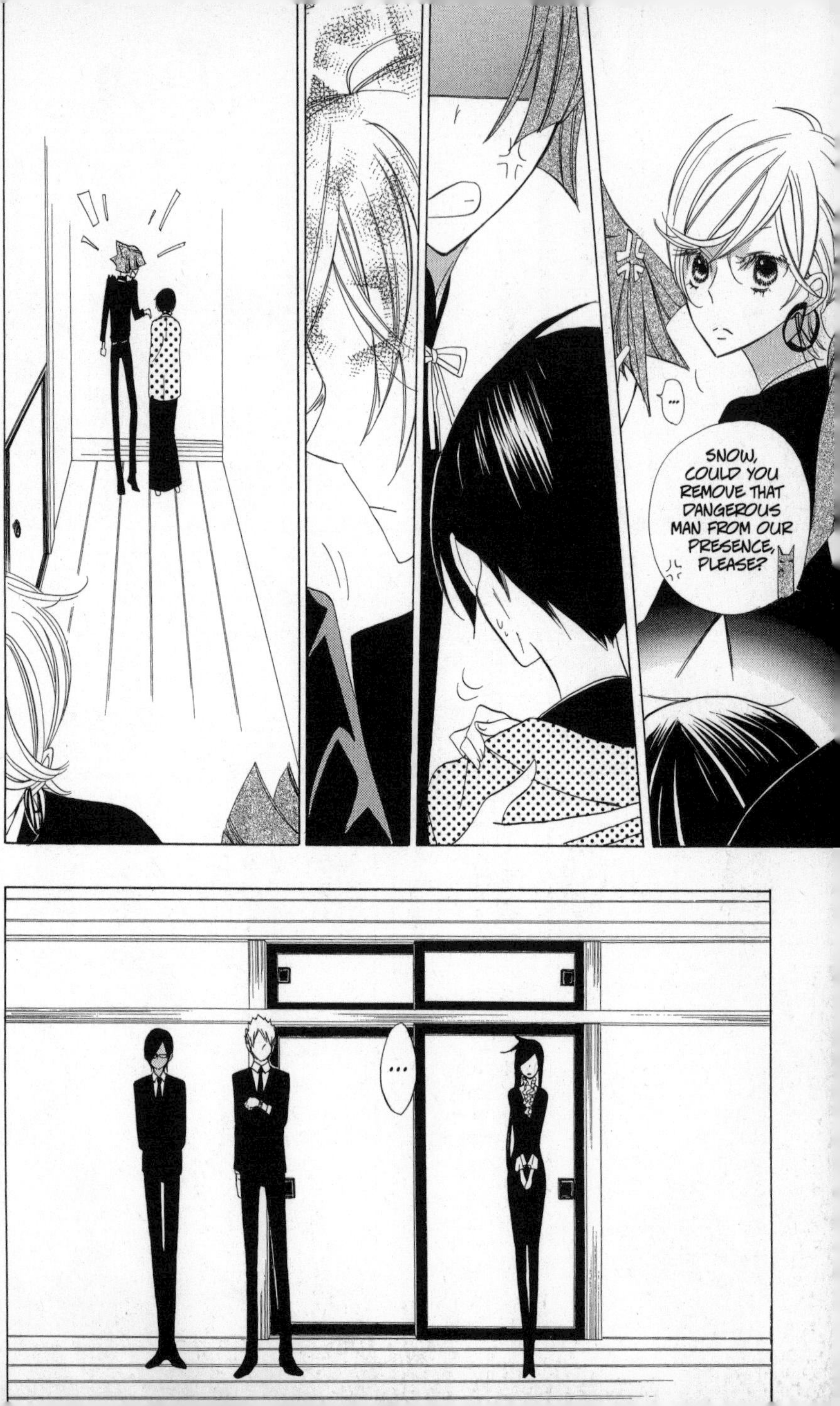
...
SNOW, COULD YOU REMOVE THAT DANGEROUS MAN FROM OUR PRESENCE, PLEASE?
...

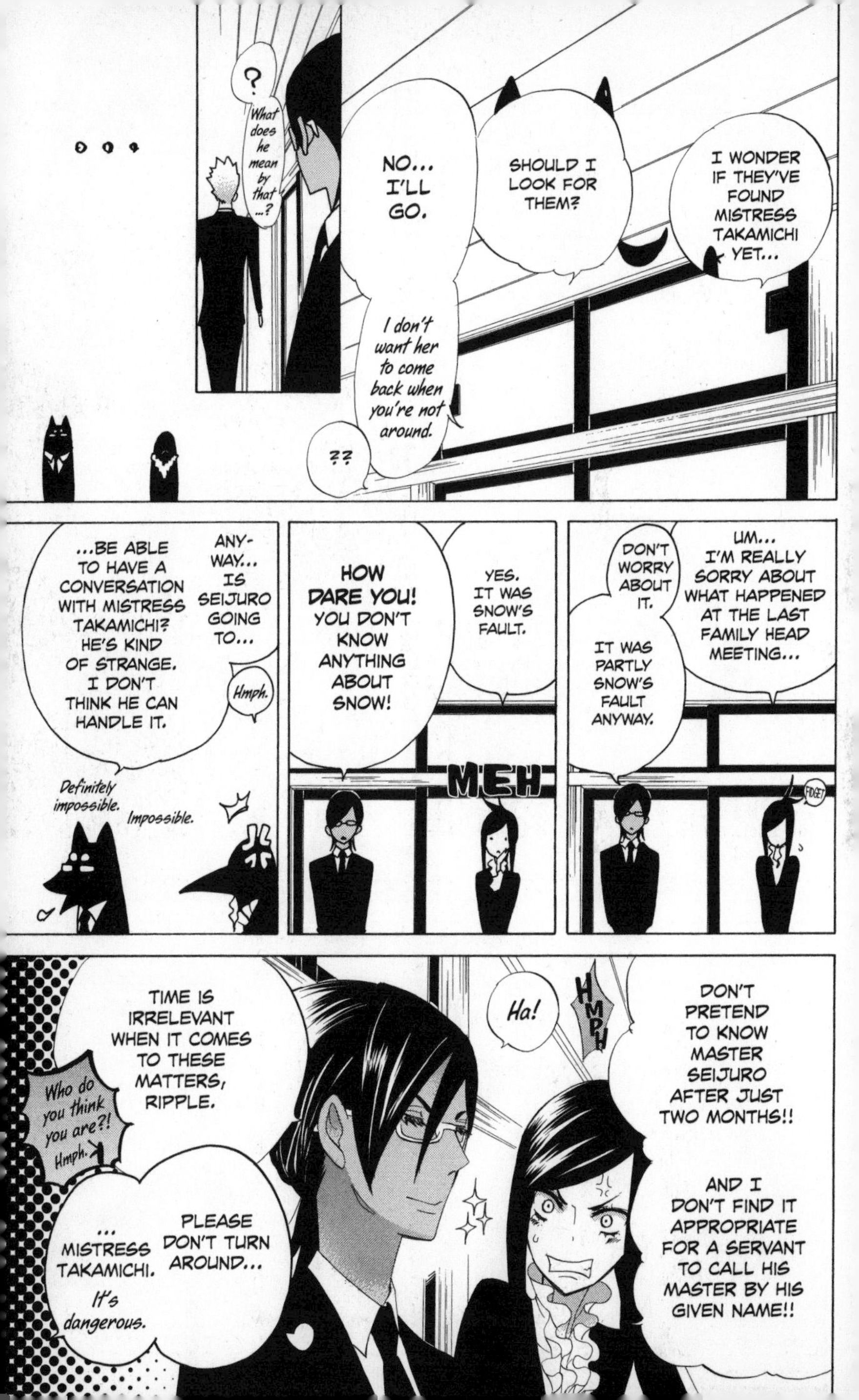
I WONDER IF THEY'VE FOUND MISTRESS TAKAMICHI YET...
SHOULD I LOOK FOR THEM?
NO... I'LL GO.
I don't want her to come back when you're not around.
??
?
What does he mean by that...?
...
UM... I'M REALLY SORRY ABOUT WHAT HAPPENED AT THE LAST FAMILY HEAD MEETING...
DON'T WORRY ABOUT IT.
IT WAS PARTLY SNOW'S FAULT ANYWAY.
FIDGET
YES. IT WAS SNOW'S FAULT.
HOW DARE YOU! YOU DON'T KNOW ANYTHING ABOUT SNOW!
MEH
ANYWAY... IS SEIJURO GOING TO...
...BE ABLE TO HAVE A CONVERSATION WITH MISTRESS TAKAMICHI? HE'S KIND OF STRANGE. I DON'T THINK HE CAN HANDLE IT.
Hmph.
Impossible.
Definitely impossible.
DON'T PRETEND TO KNOW MASTER SEIJURO AFTER JUST TWO MONTHS!!
AND I DON'T FIND IT APPROPRIATE FOR A SERVANT TO CALL HIS MASTER BY HIS GIVEN NAME!!
HMPH
Ha!
TIME IS IRRELEVANT WHEN IT COMES TO THESE MATTERS, RIPPLE.
Who do you think you are?! Hmph.
PLEASE DON'T TURN AROUND...
...MISTRESS TAKAMICHI.
It's dangerous.

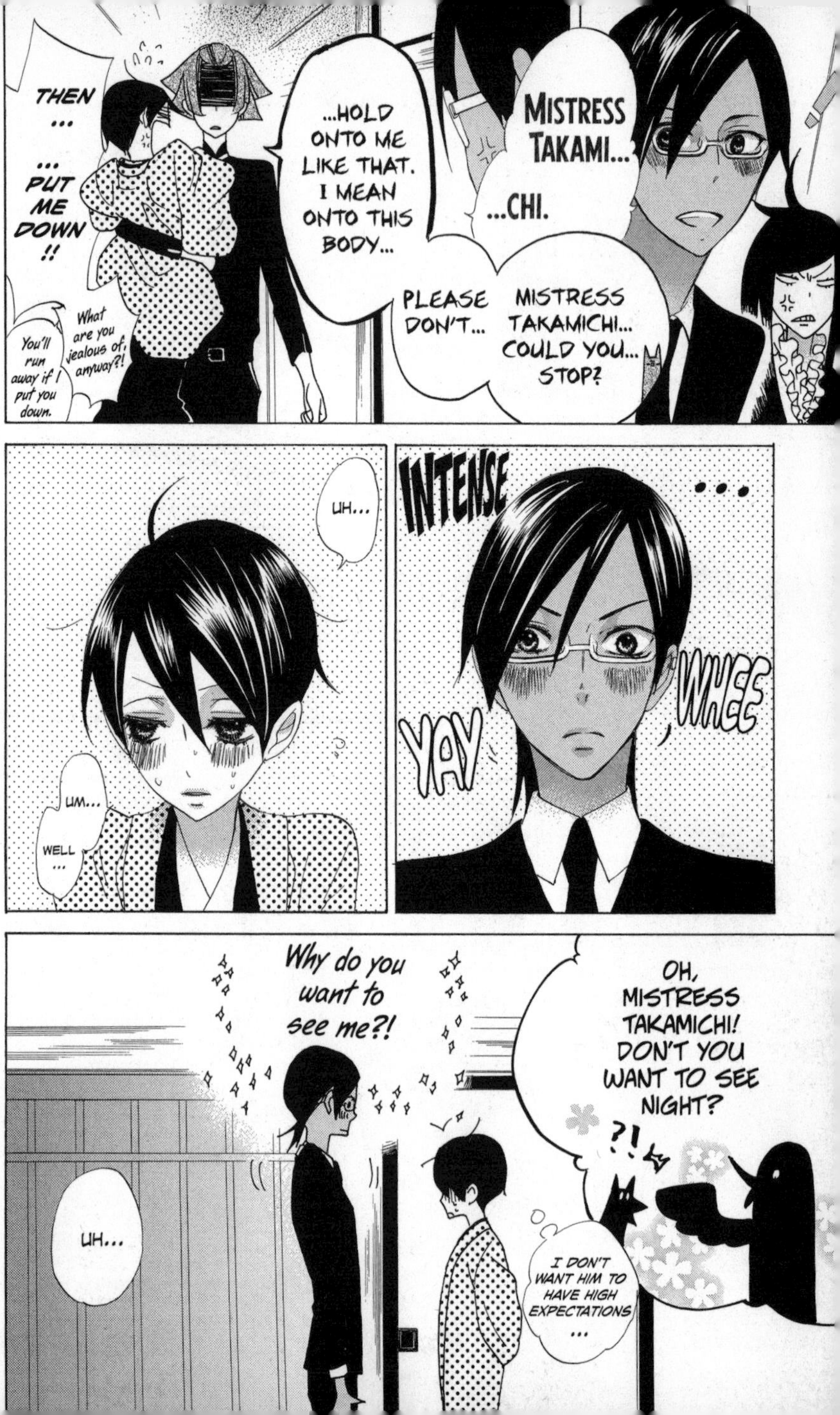
MISTRESS TAKAMI...
...CHI.
MISTRESS TAKAMICHI... COULD YOU... STOP?
PLEASE DON'T...
...HOLD ONTO ME LIKE THAT. I MEAN ONTO THIS BODY...
THEN... ...PUT ME DOWN!!
What are you jealous of, anyway?!
You'll run away if I put you down.
INTENSE
...
WHEE
YAY
UH...
UM...
WELL...
OH, MISTRESS TAKAMICHI! DON'T YOU WANT TO SEE NIGHT?
?!
Why do you want to see me?!
I DON'T WANT HIM TO HAVE HIGH EXPECTATIONS...
UH...

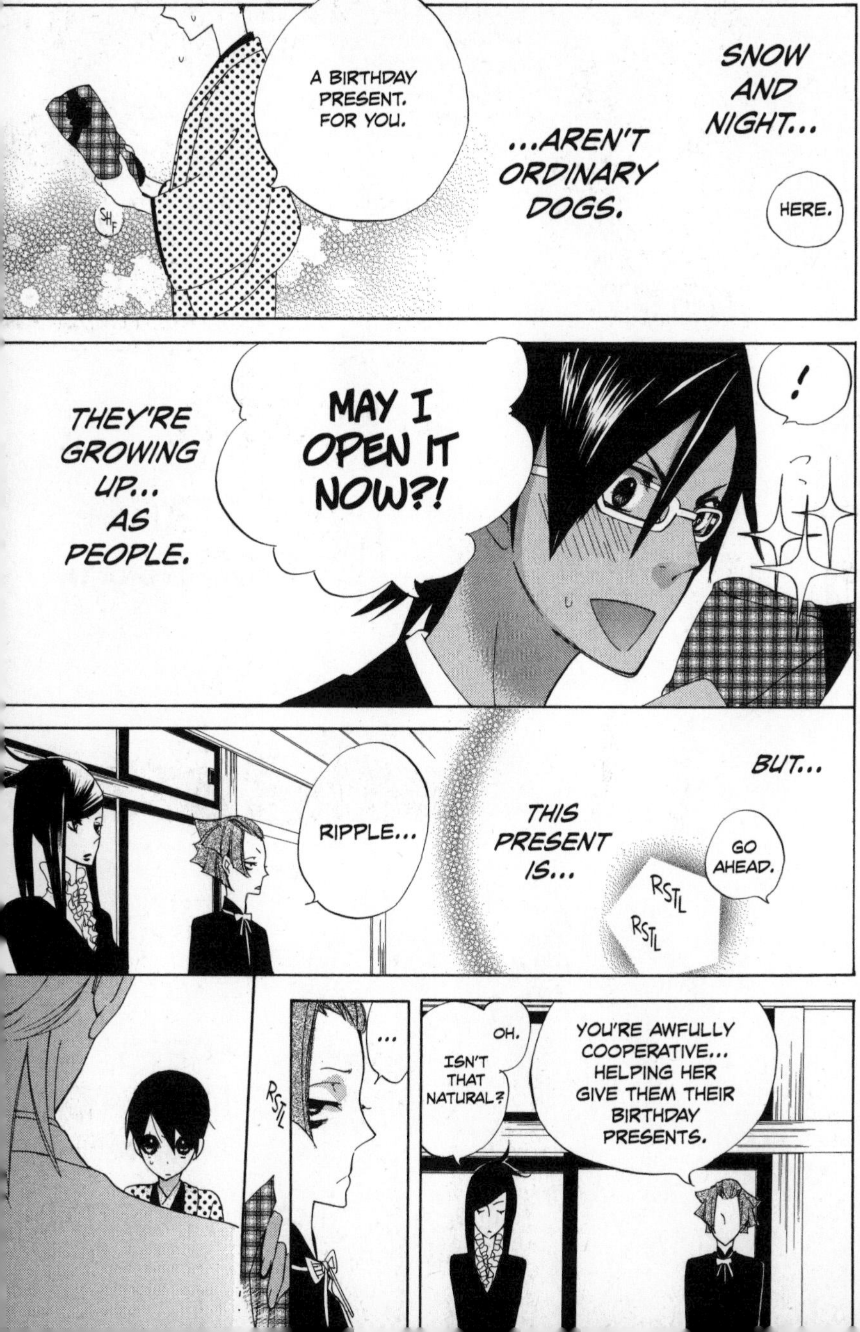
SNOW AND NIGHT...
HERE.
...AREN'T ORDINARY DOGS.
A BIRTHDAY PRESENT. FOR YOU.
SHF
!
MAY I OPEN IT NOW?!
THEY'RE GROWING UP... AS PEOPLE.
BUT...
GO AHEAD.
RSTL
RSTL
THIS PRESENT IS...
RIPPLE...
YOU'RE AWFULLY COOPERATIVE... HELPING HER GIVE THEM THEIR BIRTHDAY PRESENTS.
OH.
ISN'T THAT NATURAL?
...
RSTL

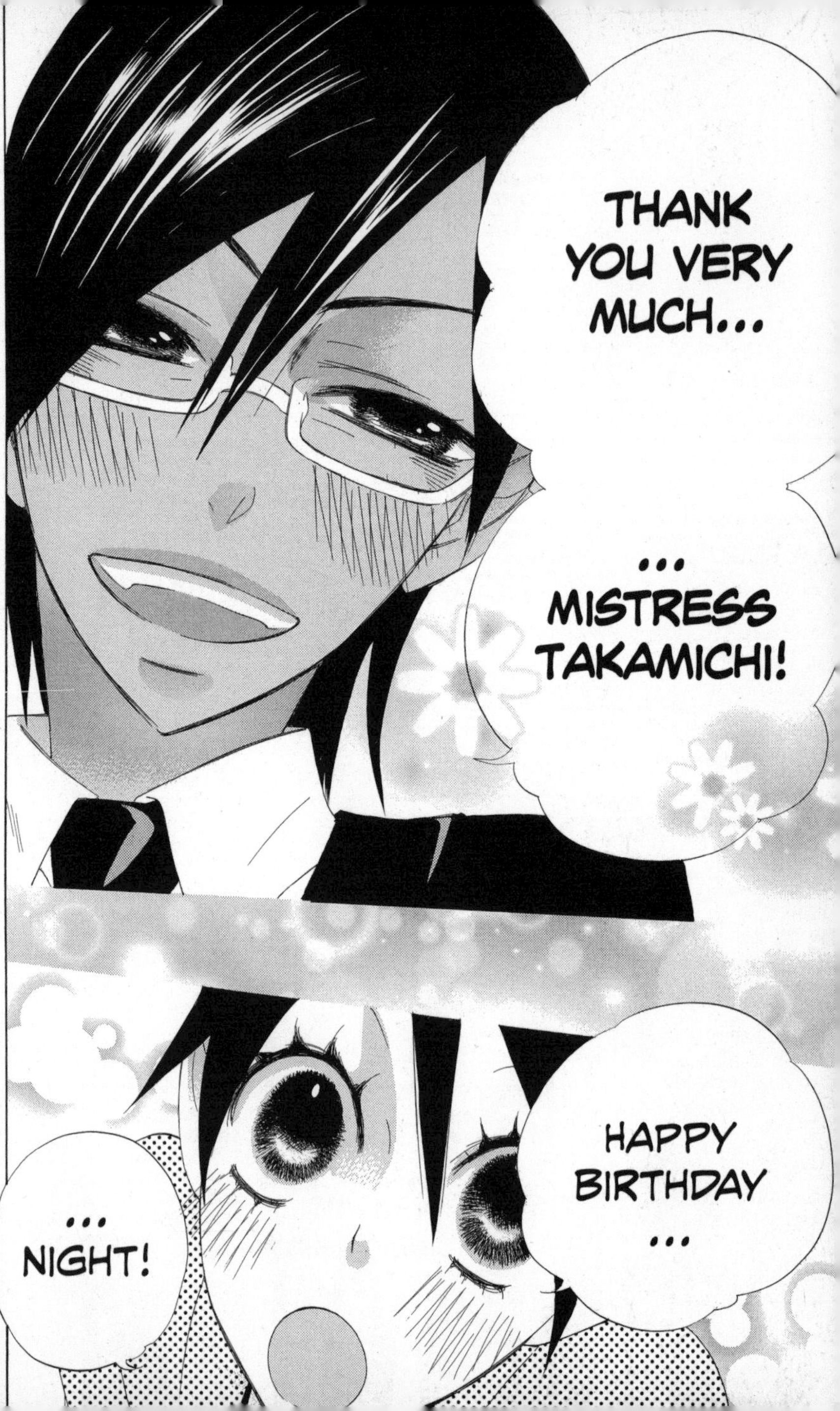
THANK YOU VERY MUCH...
...MISTRESS TAKAMICHI!
HAPPY BIRTHDAY...
...NIGHT!

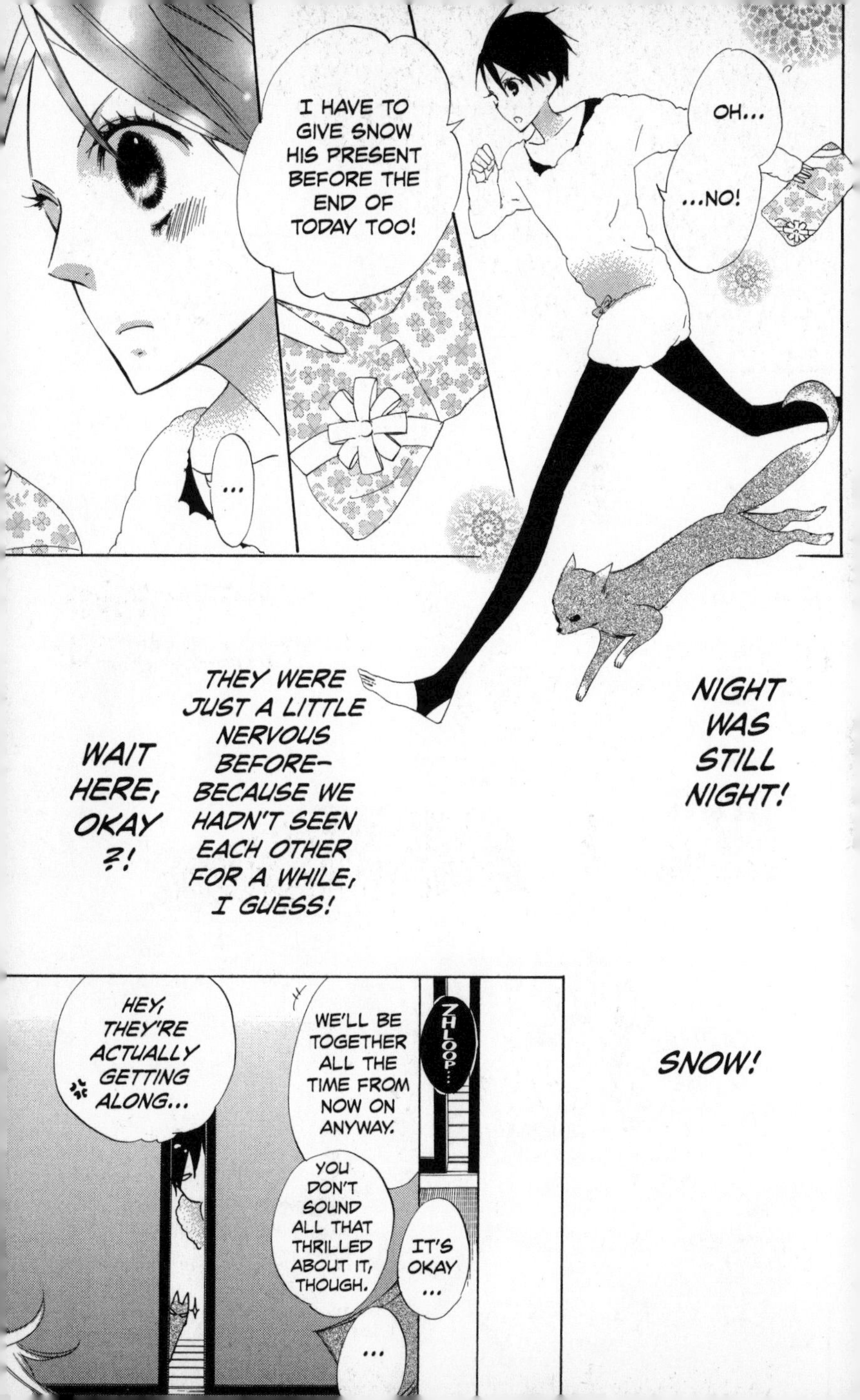
OH...
...NO!
I HAVE TO GIVE SNOW HIS PRESENT BEFORE THE END OF TODAY TOO!
...
NIGHT WAS STILL NIGHT!
THEY WERE JUST A LITTLE NERVOUS BEFORE— BECAUSE WE HADN'T SEEN EACH OTHER FOR A WHILE, I GUESS!
WAIT HERE, OKAY ?!
SNOW!
ZHLOOP...
WE'LL BE TOGETHER ALL THE TIME FROM NOW ON ANYWAY.
YOU DON'T SOUND ALL THAT THRILLED ABOUT IT, THOUGH.
IT'S OKAY ...
...
HEY, THEY'RE ACTUALLY GETTING ALONG...

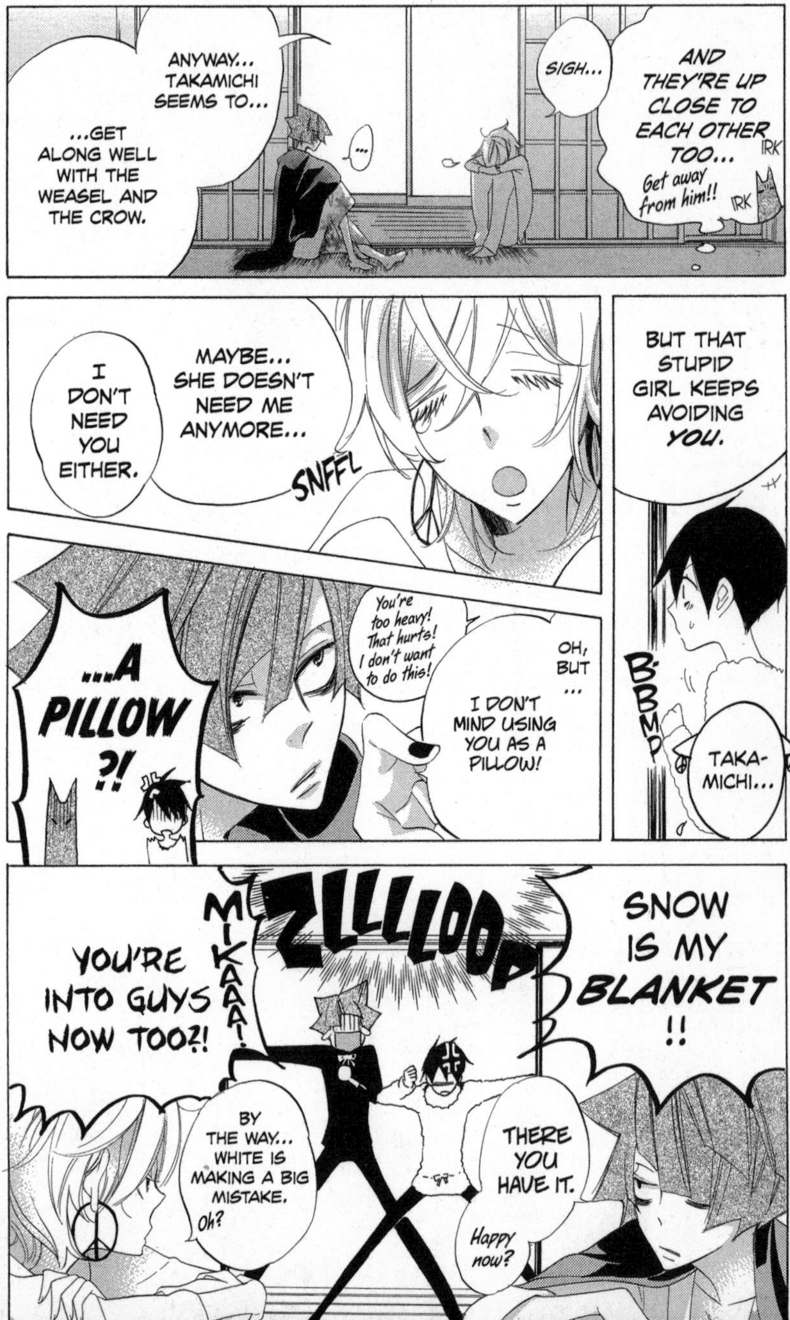
AND THEY'RE UP CLOSE TO EACH OTHER TOO...
IRK
Get away from him!!
IRK
SIGH...
...
ANYWAY... TAKAMICHI SEEMS TO...
...GET ALONG WELL WITH THE WEASEL AND THE CROW.
BUT THAT STUPID GIRL KEEPS AVOIDING YOU.
BBMP
TAKA-MICHI...
MAYBE... SHE DOESN'T NEED ME ANYMORE...
SNFFL
I DON'T NEED YOU EITHER.
OH, BUT ...
I DON'T MIND USING YOU AS A PILLOW!
You're too heavy! That hurts! I don't want to do this!
...A PILLOW ?!
SNOW IS MY BLANKET !!
ZLLLLOOP
MIKAAAA!
YOU'RE INTO GUYS NOW TOO?!
THERE YOU HAVE IT.
Happy now?
BY THE WAY... WHITE IS MAKING A BIG MISTAKE.
Oh?

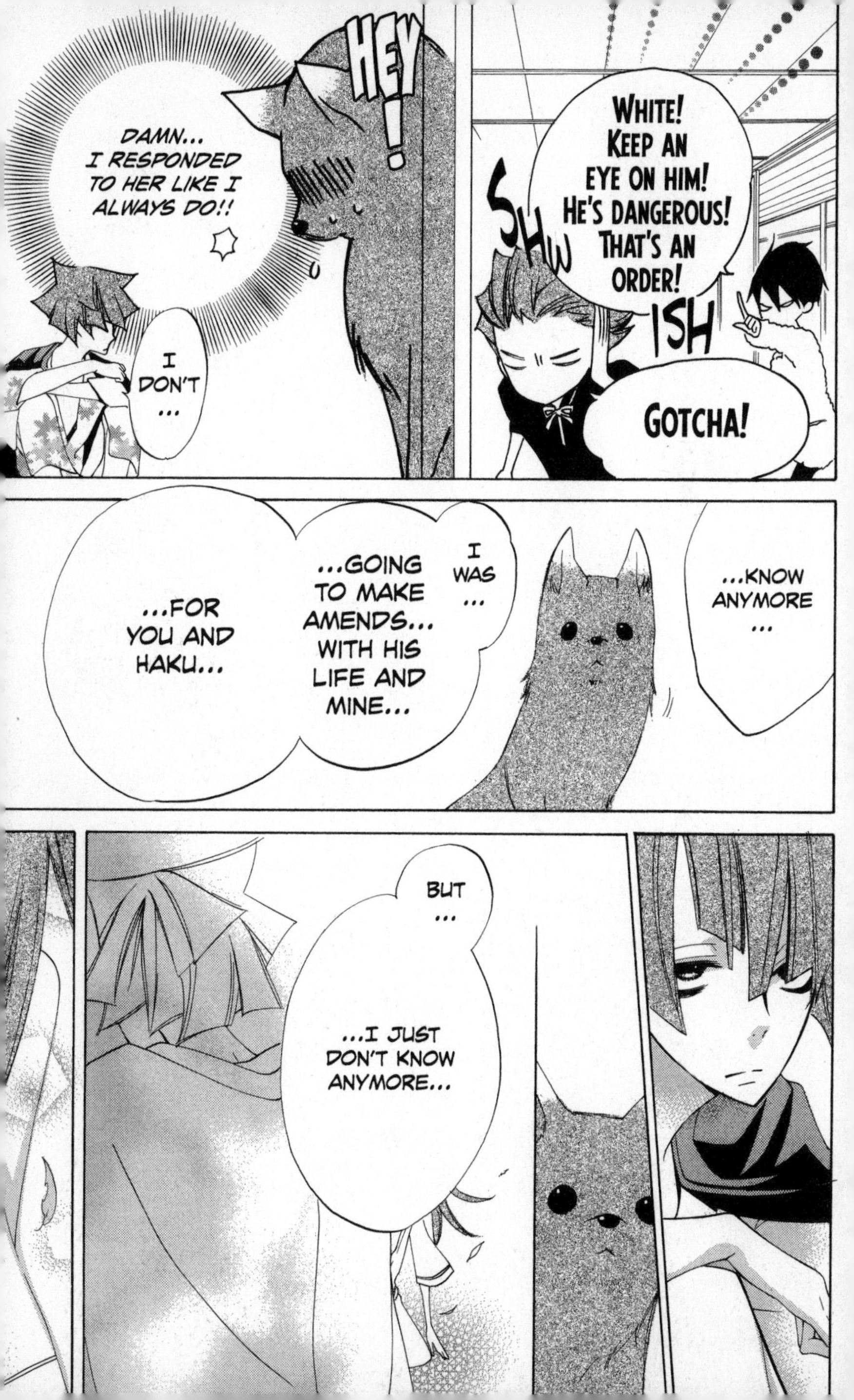
WHITE! KEEP AN EYE ON HIM! HE'S DANGEROUS! THAT'S AN ORDER!
SHWISH
GOTCHA!
HEY!
DAMN... I RESPONDED TO HER LIKE I ALWAYS DO!!
I DON'T ...
...KNOW ANYMORE ...
I WAS ...
...GOING TO MAKE AMENDS... WITH HIS LIFE AND MINE...
...FOR YOU AND HAKU...
BUT ...
...I JUST DON'T KNOW ANYMORE...

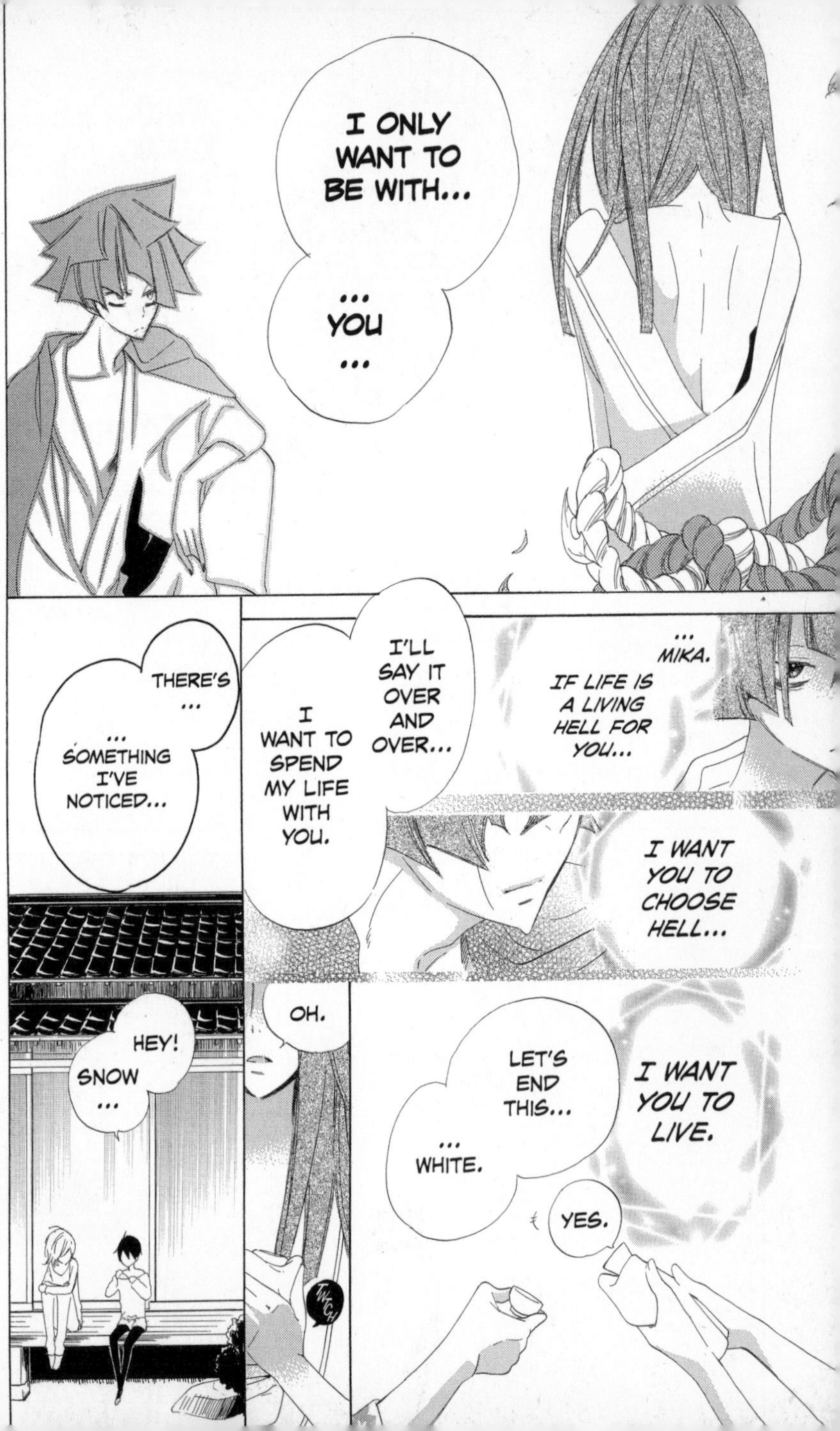
I ONLY WANT TO BE WITH...
... YOU ...
... MIKA.
IF LIFE IS A LIVING HELL FOR YOU...
I'LL SAY IT OVER AND OVER...
I WANT TO SPEND MY LIFE WITH YOU.
I WANT YOU TO CHOOSE HELL...
THERE'S ...
... SOMETHING I'VE NOTICED...
I WANT YOU TO LIVE.
LET'S END THIS...
... WHITE.
YES.
OH.
TWITCH
HEY!
SNOW ...

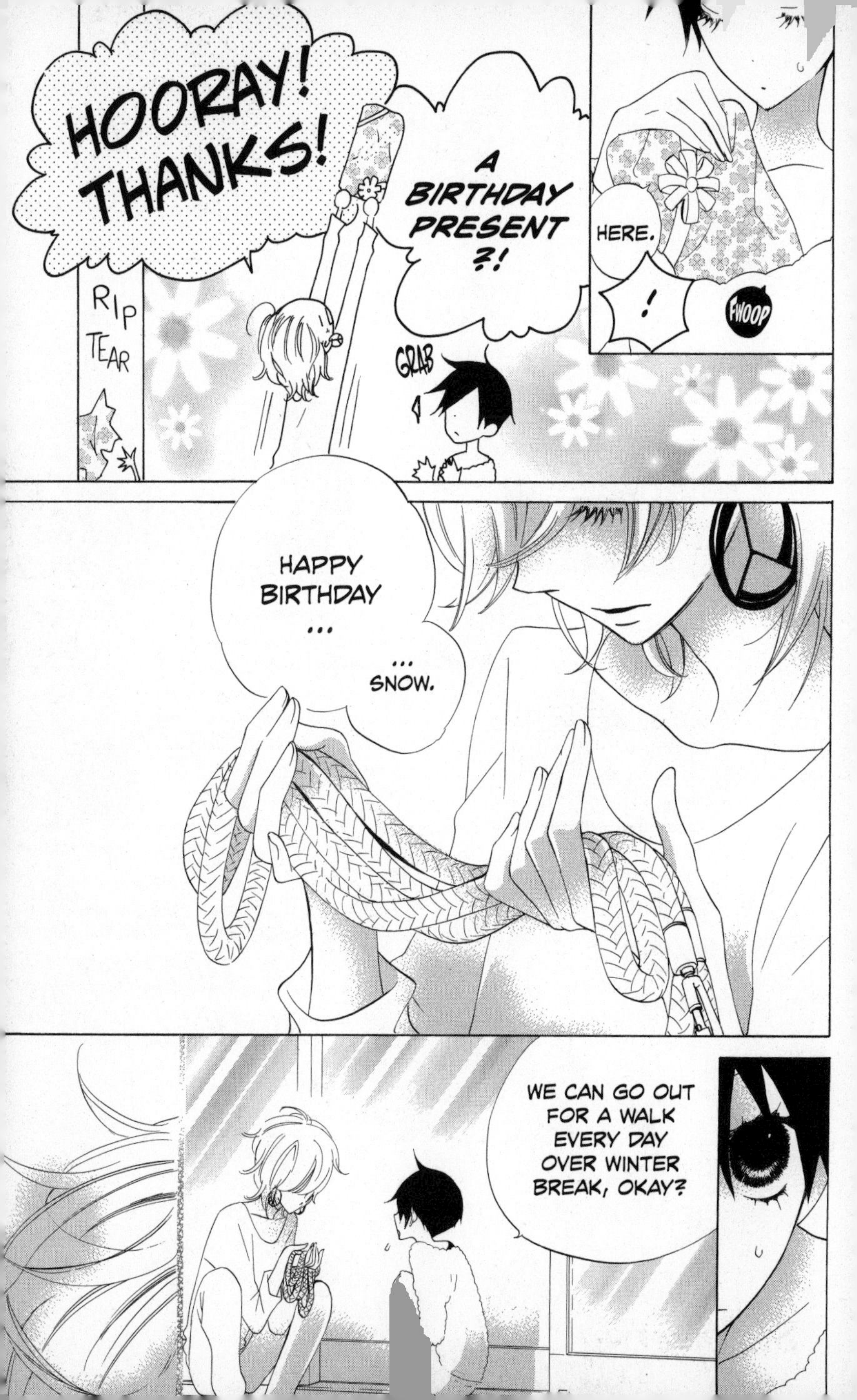
HERE.
!
FWOOP
A BIRTHDAY PRESENT ?!
HOORAY! THANKS!
GRAB
RIP TEAR
HAPPY BIRTHDAY ...
... SNOW.
WE CAN GO OUT FOR A WALK EVERY DAY OVER WINTER BREAK, OKAY?

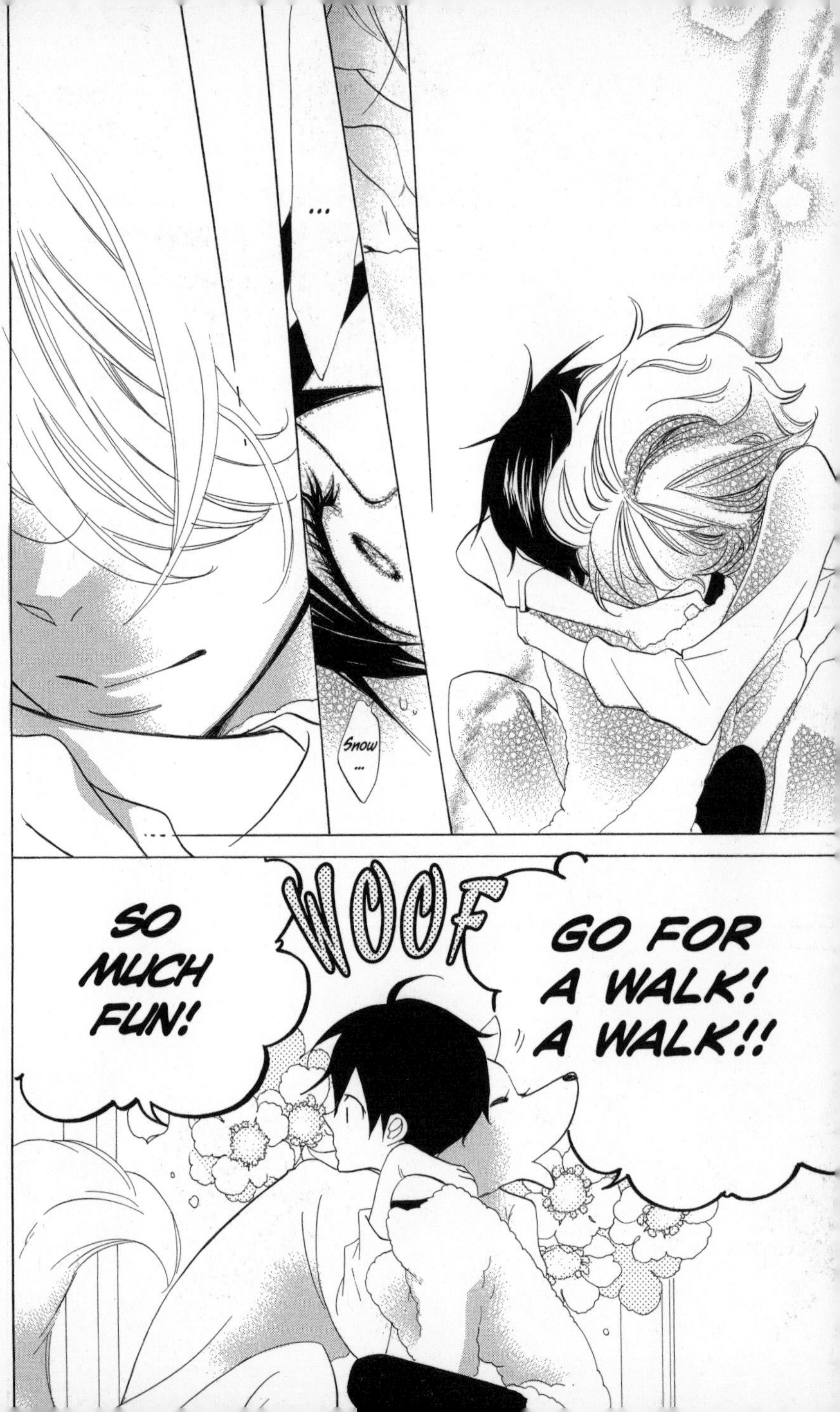
...
Snow ...
GO FOR A WALK! A WALK!!
WOOF
SO MUCH FUN!

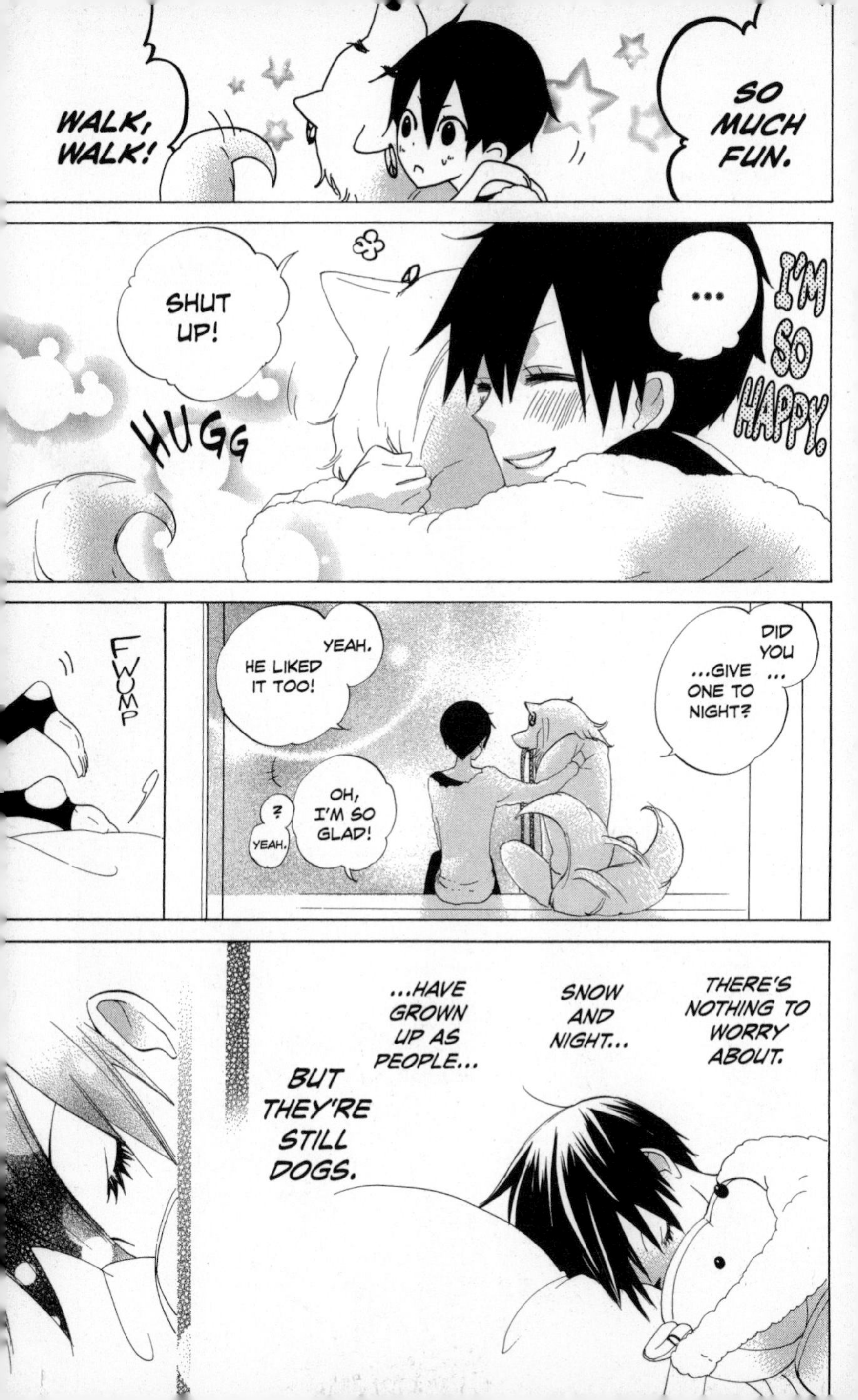
SO MUCH FUN.
WALK, WALK!
I'M SO HAPPY.
...
SHUT UP!
HUGG
DID YOU ...
...GIVE ONE TO NIGHT?
YEAH.
HE LIKED IT TOO!
OH, I'M SO GLAD!
?
YEAH.
FWUMP
THERE'S NOTHING TO WORRY ABOUT.
SNOW AND NIGHT...
...HAVE GROWN UP AS PEOPLE...
BUT THEY'RE STILL DOGS.

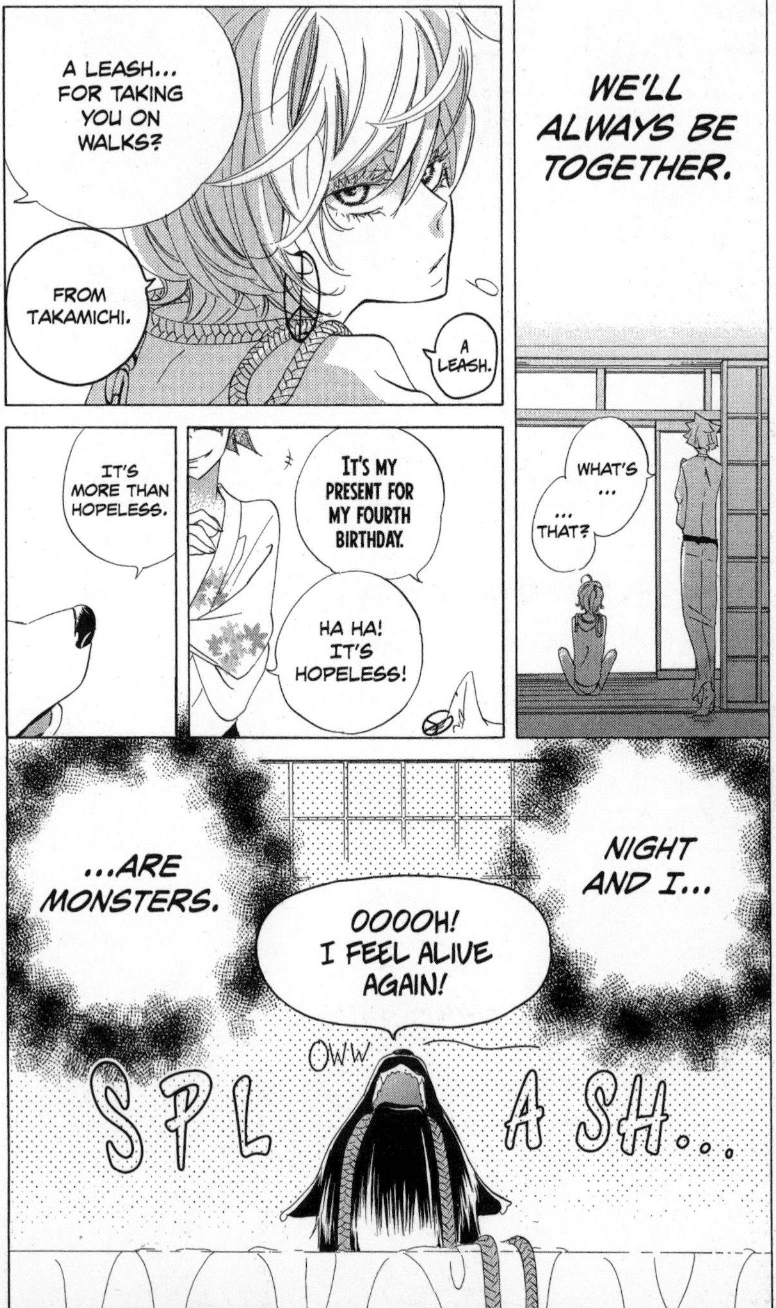
WE'LL ALWAYS BE TOGETHER.
WHAT'S ... ... THAT?
A LEASH.
A LEASH... FOR TAKING YOU ON WALKS?
FROM TAKAMICHI.
IT'S MY PRESENT FOR MY FOURTH BIRTHDAY.
HA HA! IT'S HOPELESS!
IT'S MORE THAN HOPELESS.
NIGHT AND I...
...ARE MONSTERS.
OOOOH! I FEEL ALIVE AGAIN!
OWW
SPLASH...

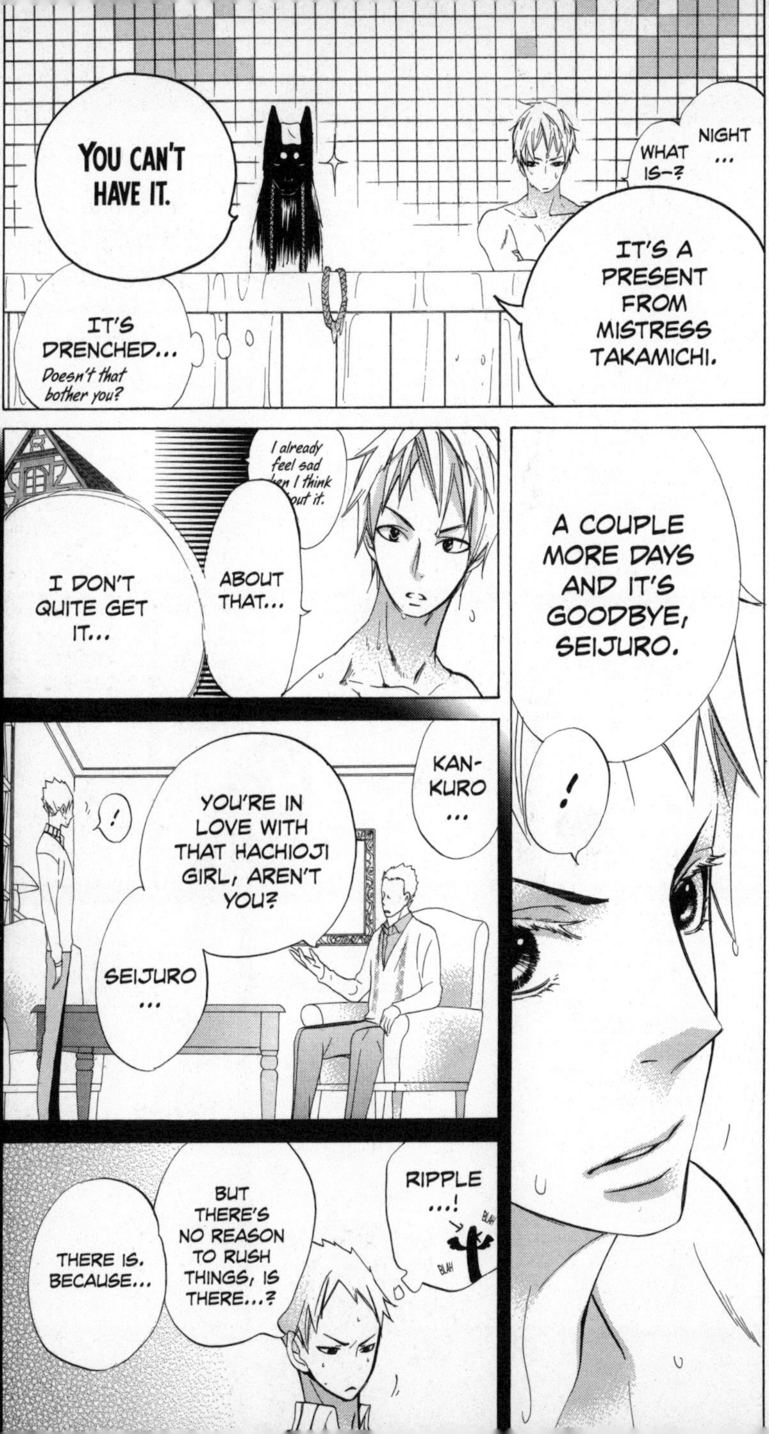
NIGHT... WHAT IS—?
IT'S A PRESENT FROM MISTRESS TAKAMICHI.
YOU CAN'T HAVE IT.
IT'S DRENCHED... Doesn't that bother you?
A COUPLE MORE DAYS AND IT'S GOODBYE, SEIJURO.
!
I already feel sad
ABOUT THAT...
I DON'T QUITE GET IT...
KAN-KURO...
YOU'RE IN LOVE WITH THAT HACHIOJI GIRL, AREN'T YOU?
!
SEIJURO...
RIPPLE ...!
BLAH
BLAH
BUT THERE'S NO REASON TO RUSH THINGS, IS THERE...?
THERE IS. BECAUSE...

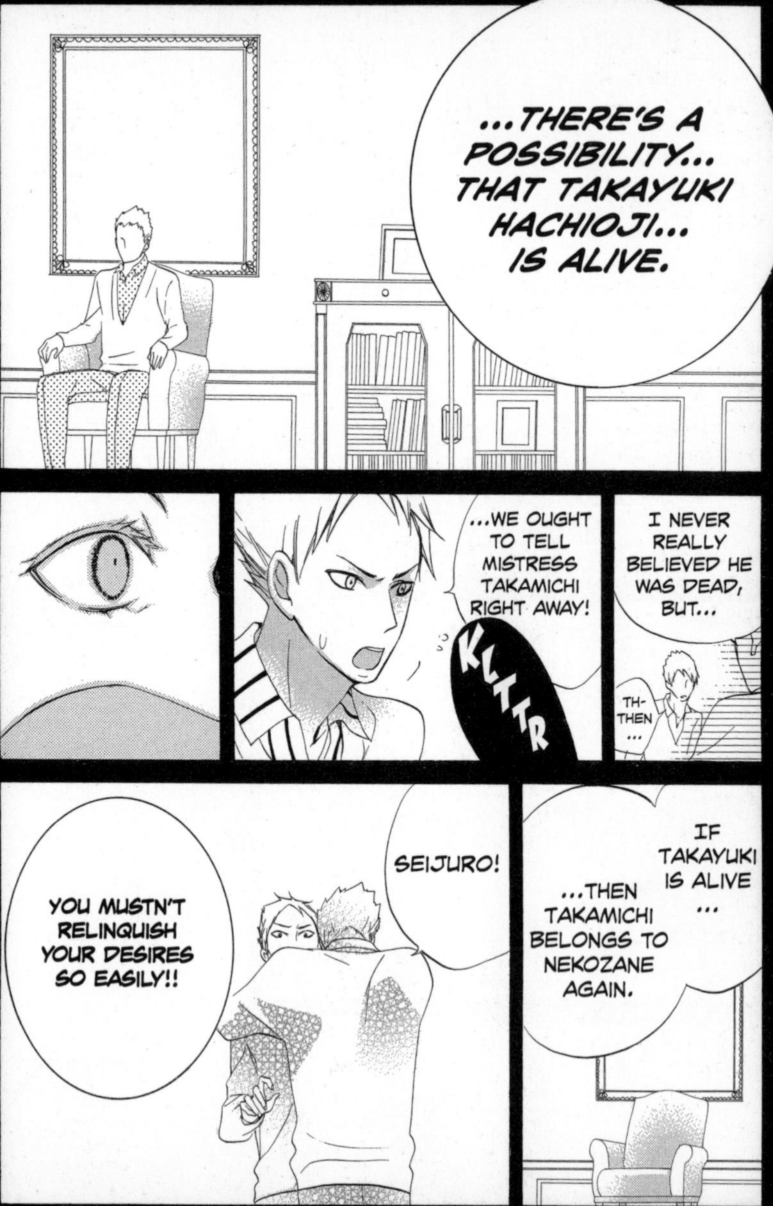
...THERE'S A POSSIBILITY... THAT TAKAYUKI HACHIOJI... IS ALIVE.
I NEVER REALLY BELIEVED HE WAS DEAD, BUT...
TH- THEN ...
...WE OUGHT TO TELL MISTRESS TAKAMICHI RIGHT AWAY!
KLTTR
IF TAKAYUKI IS ALIVE ...
...THEN TAKAMICHI BELONGS TO NEKOZANE AGAIN.
SEIJURO!
YOU MUSTN'T RELINQUISH YOUR DESIRES SO EASILY!!

Which character do you enjoy drawing the most?

Nagasaki Prefecture: Rogetsu

Which character is the hardest to draw?

Kanagawa Prefecture: Yuki

Well, when I feel good, I enjoy drawing all the characters. But when I don't feel good, I have trouble drawing all the characters. Oh, but I think I have trouble drawing Seijuro and Night all the time. And the contours of Mistress Takamichi's body.

What do you pay attention to when drawing?

Aomori Prefecture: Natsumi

There are so many things... I always remember something I've forgotten to do at the very end of working on my final draft. Argh! I'm sure I've forgotten to do something now as well. But the thing I focus on the most is to draw my manga with love.

Who is Fenrir?

Nagasaki Prefecture: Leona

Fenrir is a giant wolf who is probably the most famous monster in Norse mythology.

Moon, Snow and Night are distant descendants.

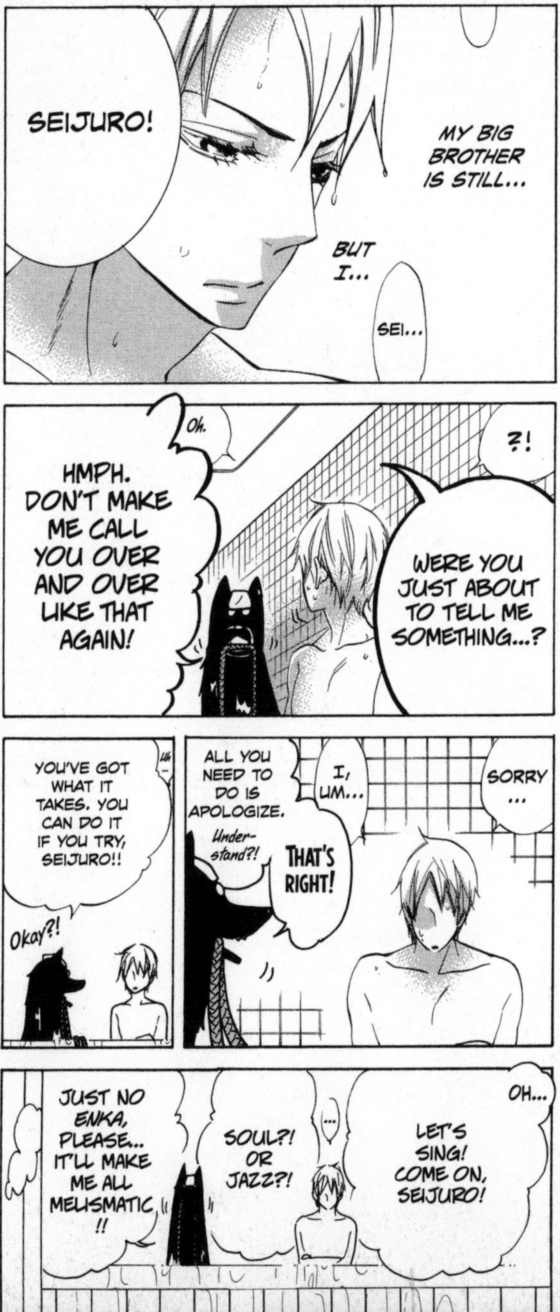
MY BIG BROTHER IS STILL...
BUT I...
SEI...
SEIJURO!
?!
WERE YOU JUST ABOUT TO TELL ME SOMETHING...?
Oh.
HMPH. DON'T MAKE ME CALL YOU OVER AND OVER LIKE THAT AGAIN!
SORRY...
I, UM...
ALL YOU NEED TO DO IS APOLOGIZE.
Understand?!
THAT'S RIGHT!
Uh...
YOU'VE GOT WHAT IT TAKES. YOU CAN DO IT IF YOU TRY, SEIJURO!!
Okay?!
OH...
LET'S SING! COME ON, SEIJURO!
...
SOUL?! OR JAZZ?!
JUST NO ENKA, PLEASE... IT'LL MAKE ME ALL MELISMATIC!!

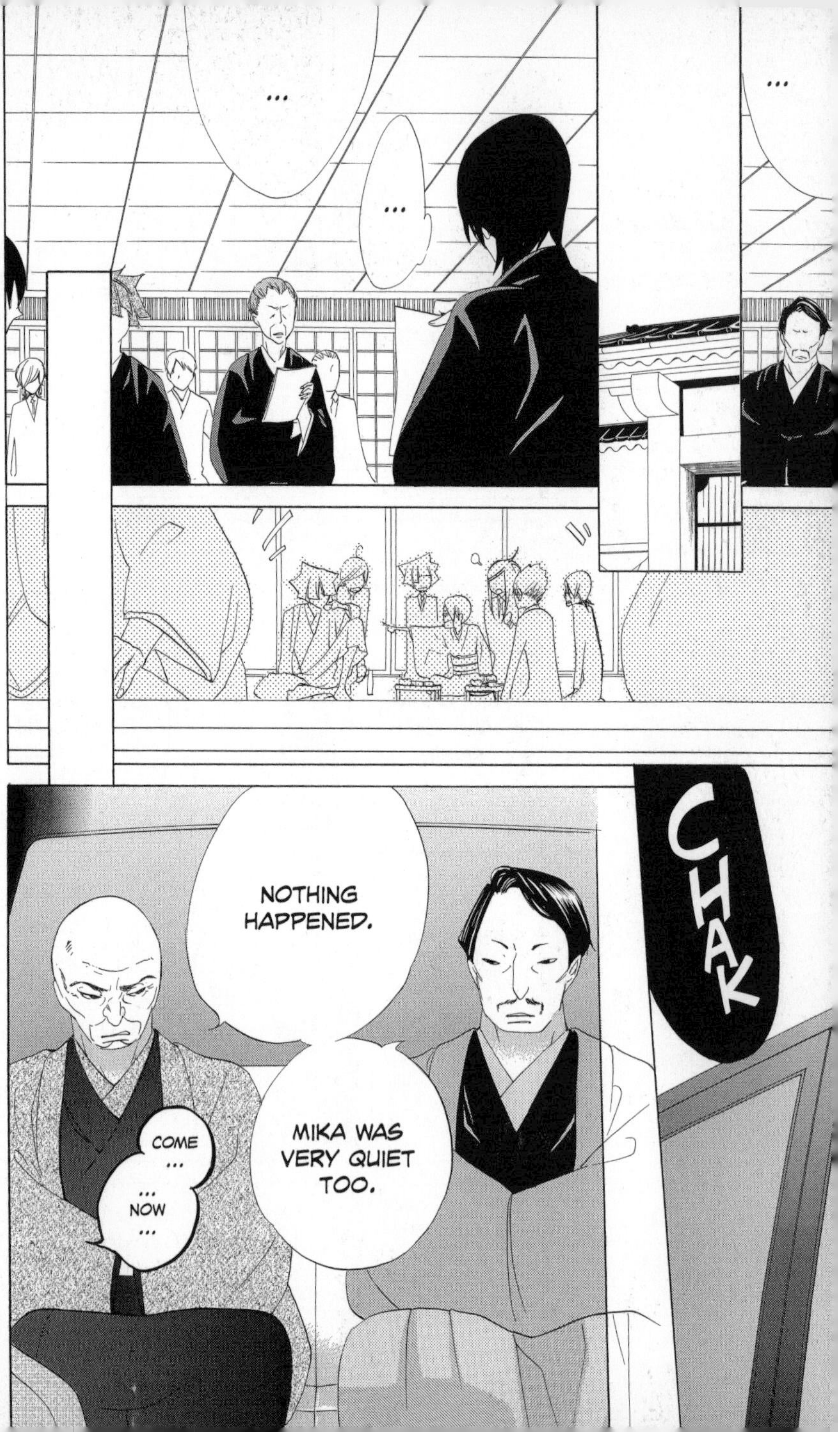
...
...
...
CHAK
NOTHING HAPPENED.
MIKA WAS VERY QUIET TOO.
COME ...
... NOW ...

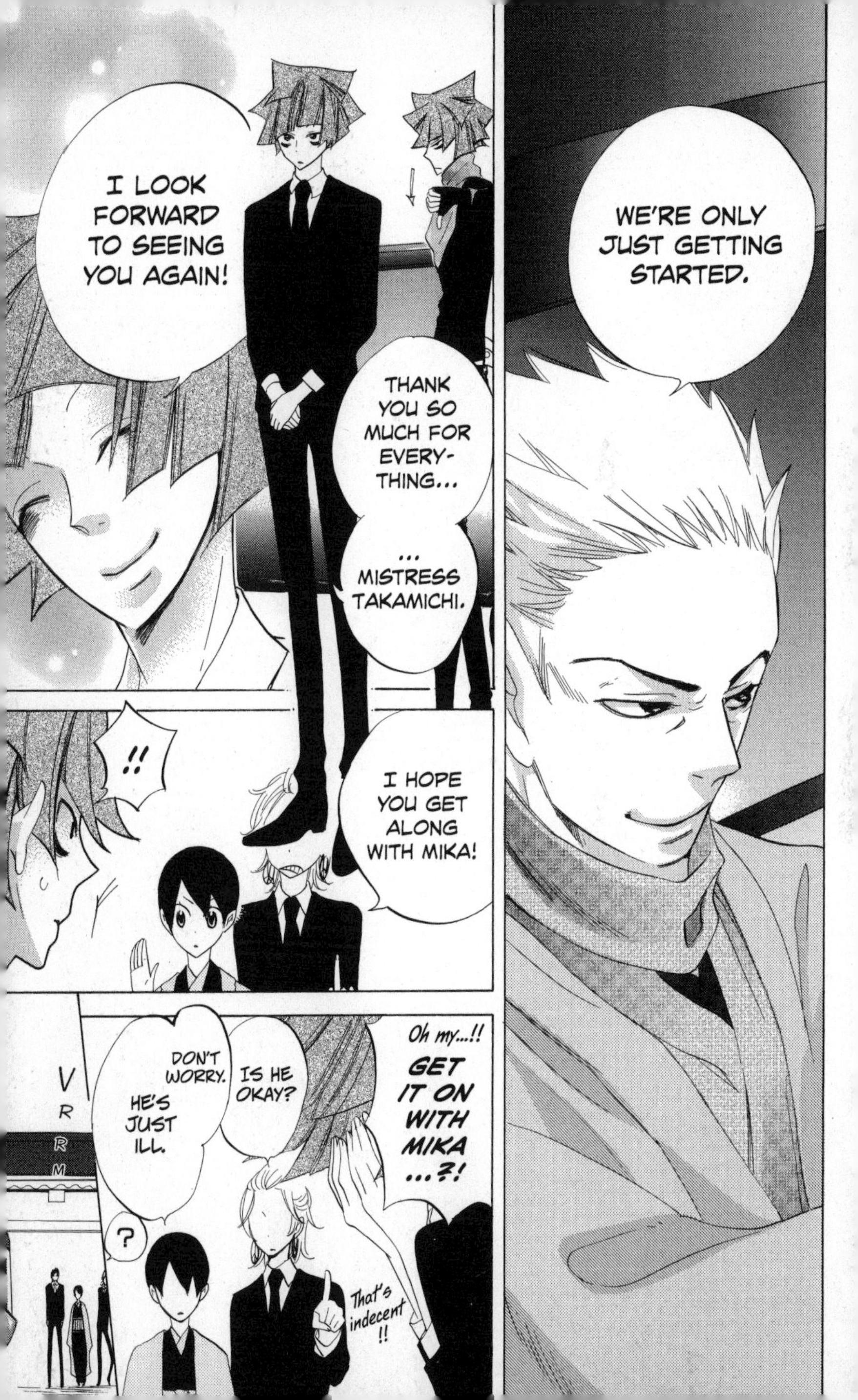
WE'RE ONLY JUST GETTING STARTED.
THANK YOU SO MUCH FOR EVERY-THING...
... MISTRESS TAKAMICHI.
I LOOK FORWARD TO SEEING YOU AGAIN!
I HOPE YOU GET ALONG WITH MIKA!
!!
Oh my...!!
GET IT ON WITH MIKA ...?!
IS HE OKAY?
DON'T WORRY.
HE'S JUST ILL.
?
That's indecent!!
VRRM

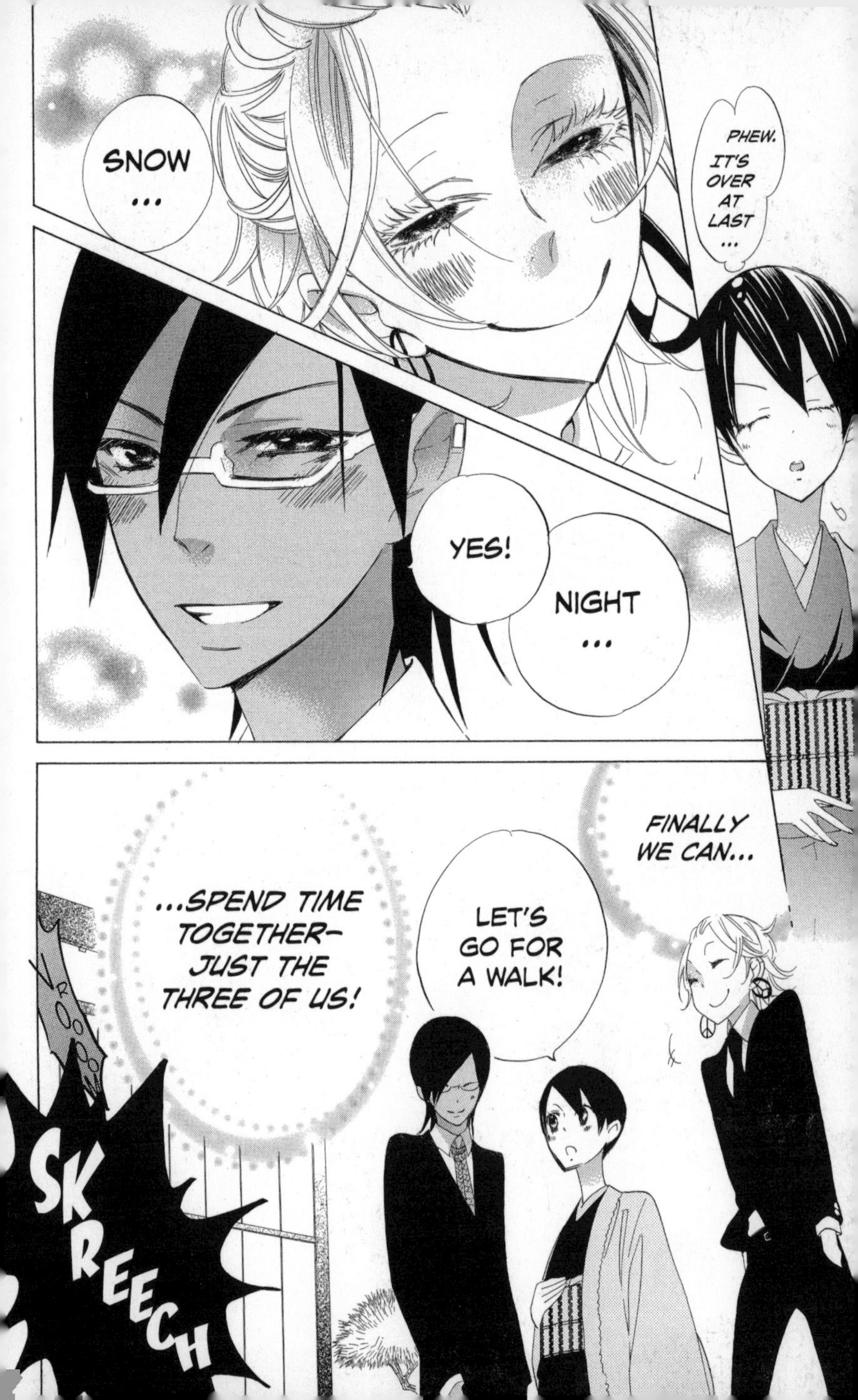
PHEW. IT'S OVER AT LAST...
SNOW...
NIGHT...
YES!
FINALLY WE CAN...
LET'S GO FOR A WALK!
...SPEND TIME TOGETHER— JUST THE THREE OF US!
SKREECH

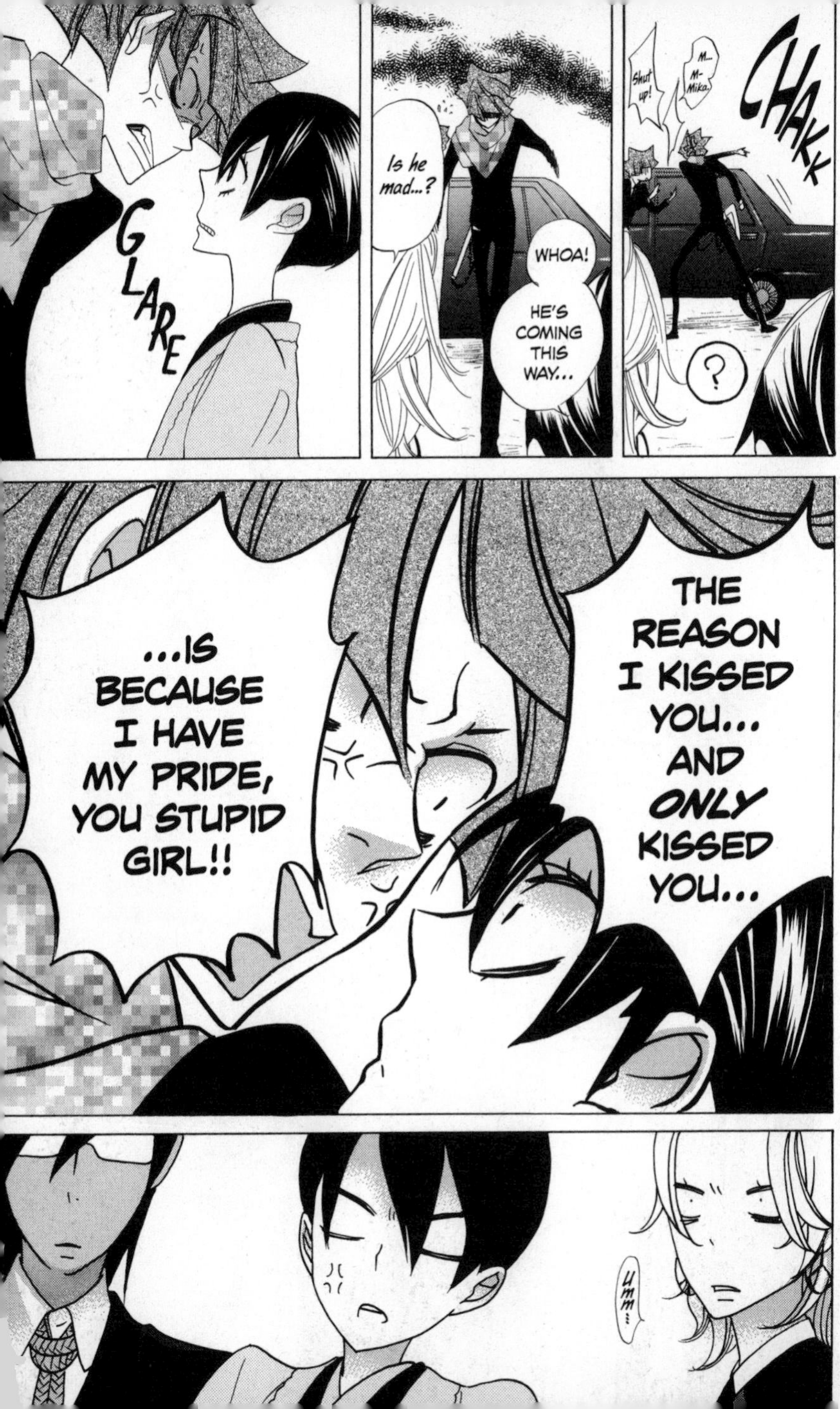
CHAKK
M... M-Mika.
Shut up!
?
Is he mad...?
WHOA!
HE'S COMING THIS WAY...
GLARE
THE REASON I KISSED YOU... AND ONLY KISSED YOU...
...IS BECAUSE I HAVE MY PRIDE, YOU STUPID GIRL!!
Umm...

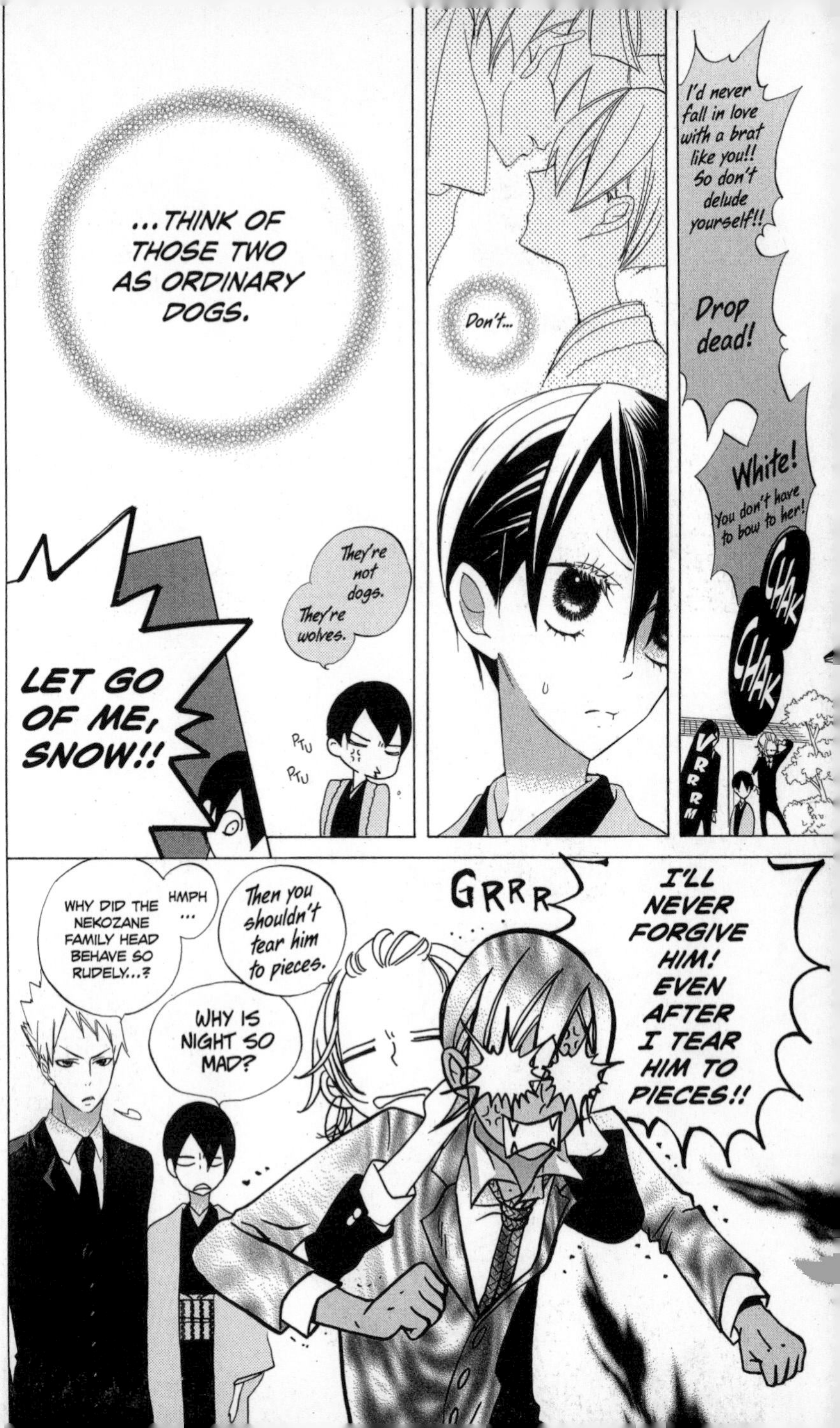

I'd never fall in love with a brat like you!! So don't delude yourself!!
Drop dead!
White!
You don't have to bow to her!
CHAK CHAK CHAK
VRRRM
Don't...
...THINK OF THOSE TWO AS ORDINARY DOGS.
They're not dogs.
They're wolves.
LET GO OF ME, SNOW!!
PTU PTU
I'LL NEVER FORGIVE HIM! EVEN AFTER I TEAR HIM TO PIECES!!
GRRRR
Then you shouldn't tear him to pieces.
HMPH ...
WHY DID THE NEKOZANE FAMILY HEAD BEHAVE SO RUDELY...?
WHY IS NIGHT SO MAD?

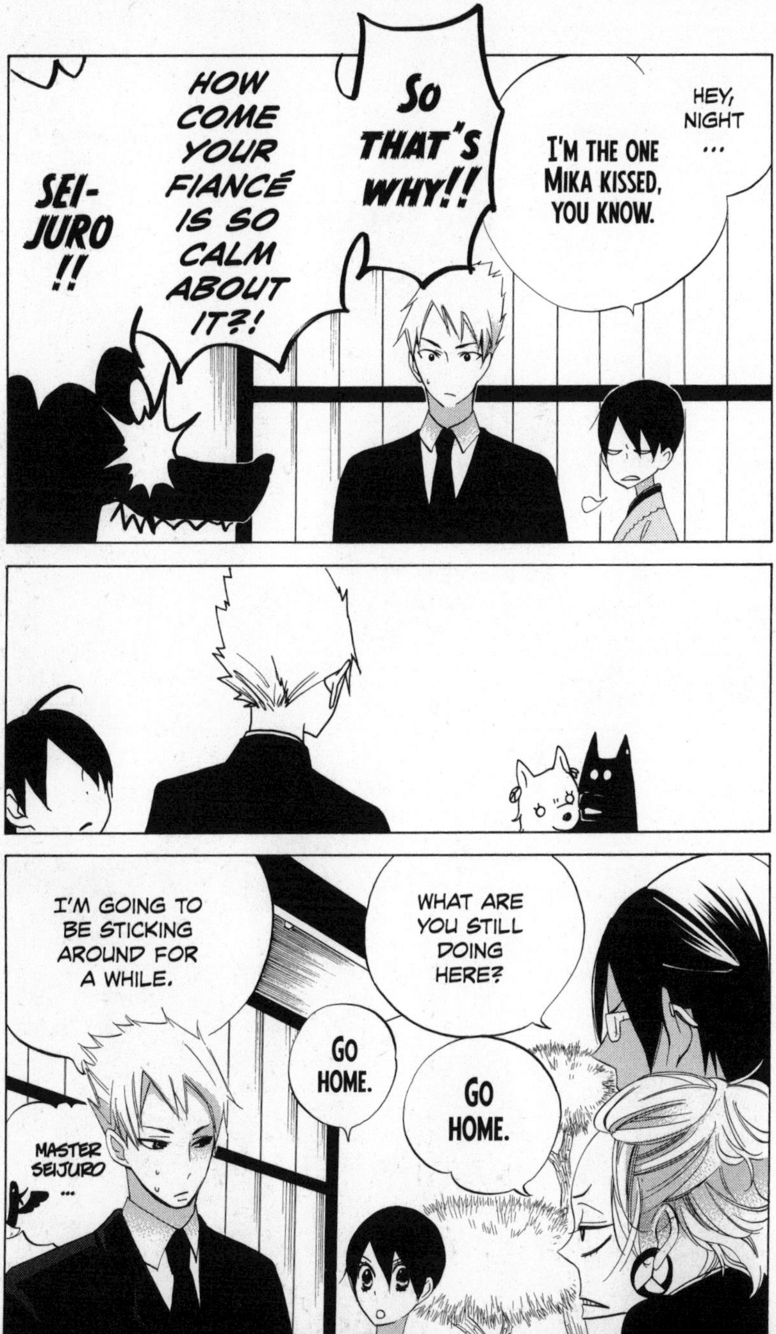
HEY, NIGHT ...
I'M THE ONE MIKA KISSED, YOU KNOW.
SO THAT'S WHY!!
HOW COME YOUR FIANCÉ IS SO CALM ABOUT IT?!
SEI-JURO!!
WHAT ARE YOU STILL DOING HERE?
GO HOME.
GO HOME.
I'M GOING TO BE STICKING AROUND FOR A WHILE.
MASTER SEIJURO ...

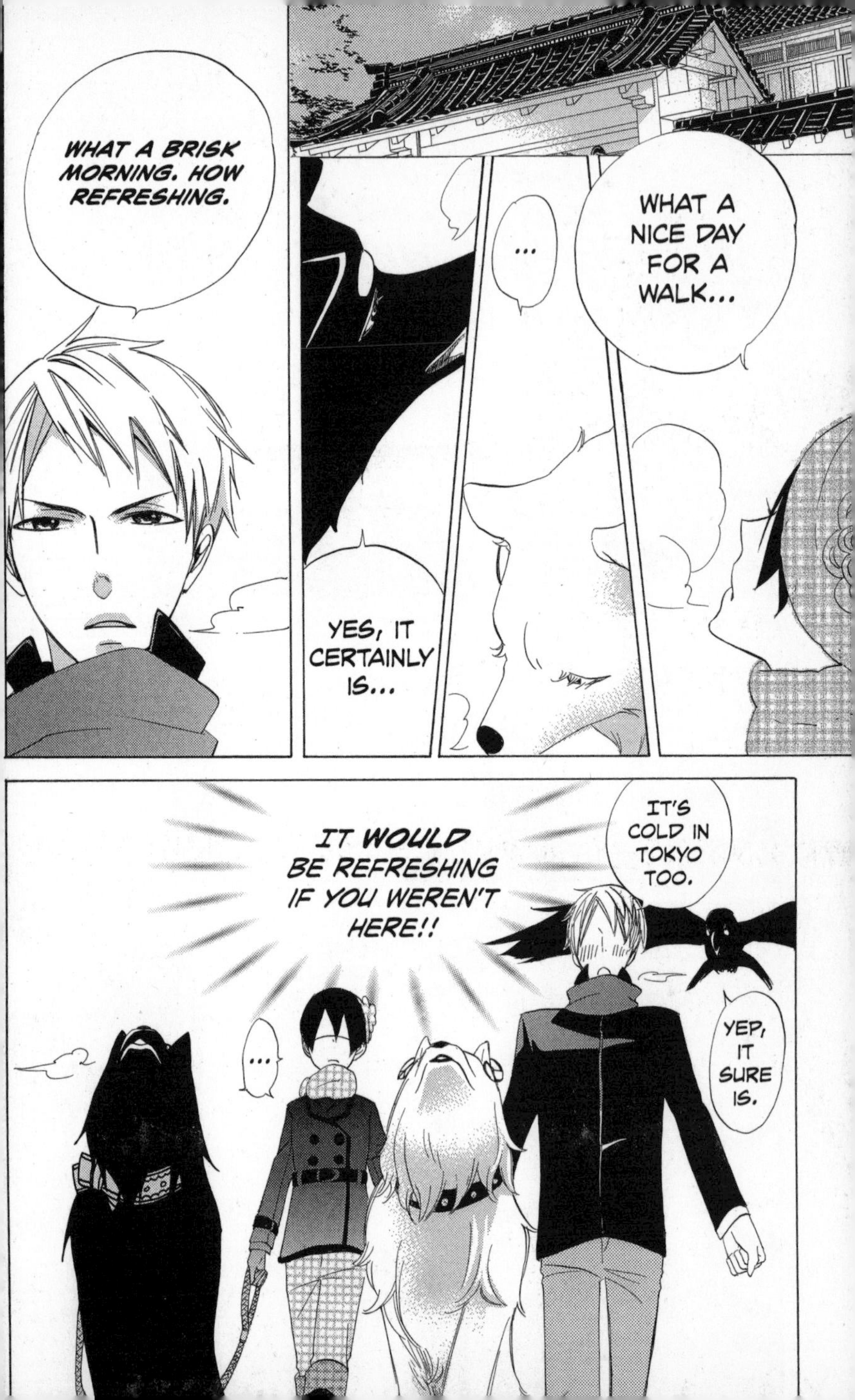
WHAT A NICE DAY FOR A WALK...
...
YES, IT CERTAINLY IS...
WHAT A BRISK MORNING. HOW REFRESHING.
IT'S COLD IN TOKYO TOO.
YEP, IT SURE IS.
IT WOULD BE REFRESHING IF YOU WEREN'T HERE!!
...

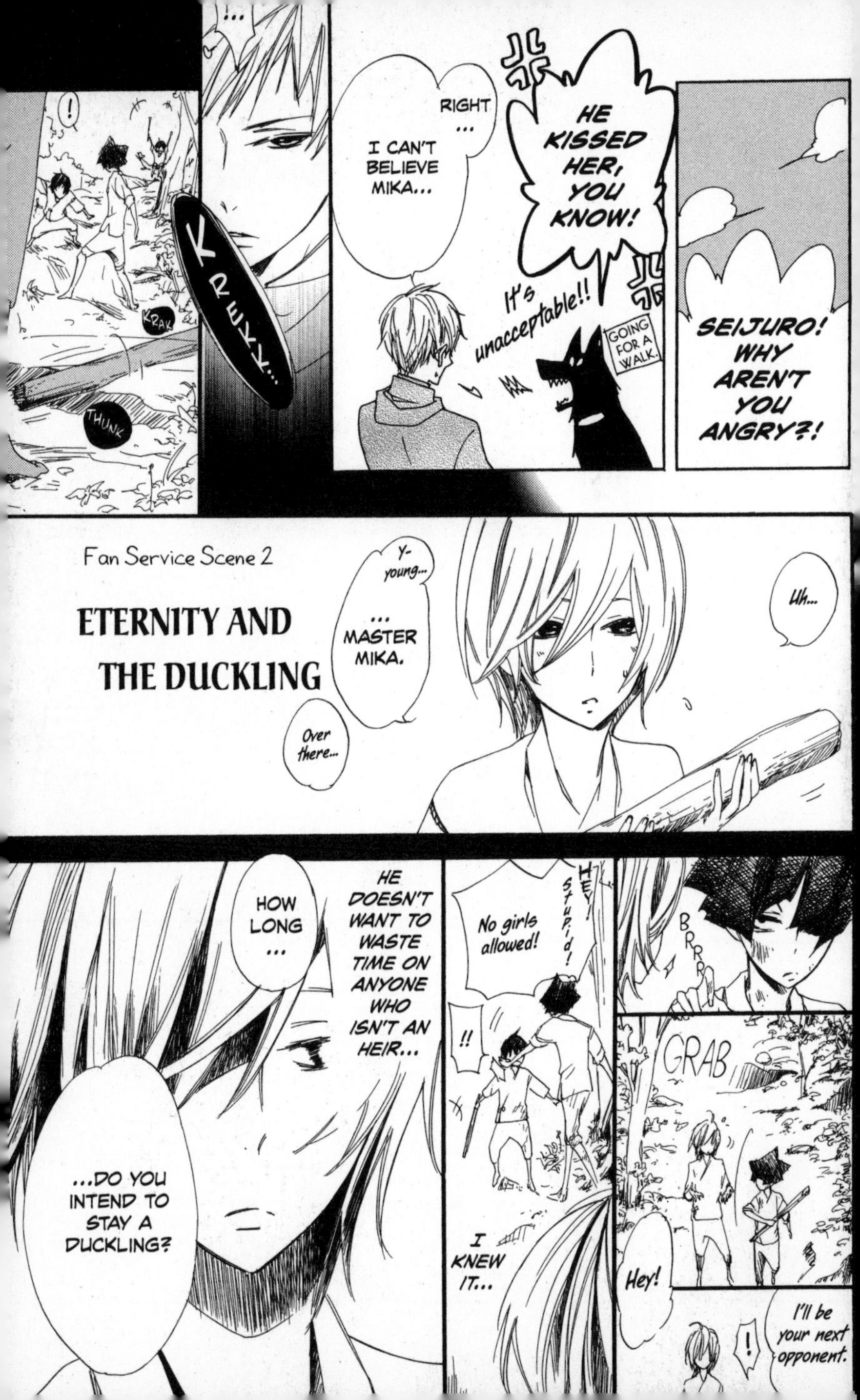
SEIJURO! WHY AREN'T YOU ANGRY?!
HE KISSED HER, YOU KNOW!
It's unacceptable!!
GOING FOR A WALK.
RIGHT...
I CAN'T BELIEVE MIKA...
!...
KREKK...
!
KRAK
THUNK
Uh...
Y-young... ...MASTER MIKA.
Over there...
Fan Service Scene 2
ETERNITY AND THE DUCKLING
BRRR
GRAB
I'll be your next opponent.
!
HEY! Stupid!
No girls allowed!
!!
Hey!
I KNEW IT...
HE DOESN'T WANT TO WASTE TIME ON ANYONE WHO ISN'T AN HEIR...
HOW LONG...
...DO YOU INTEND TO STAY A DUCKLING?

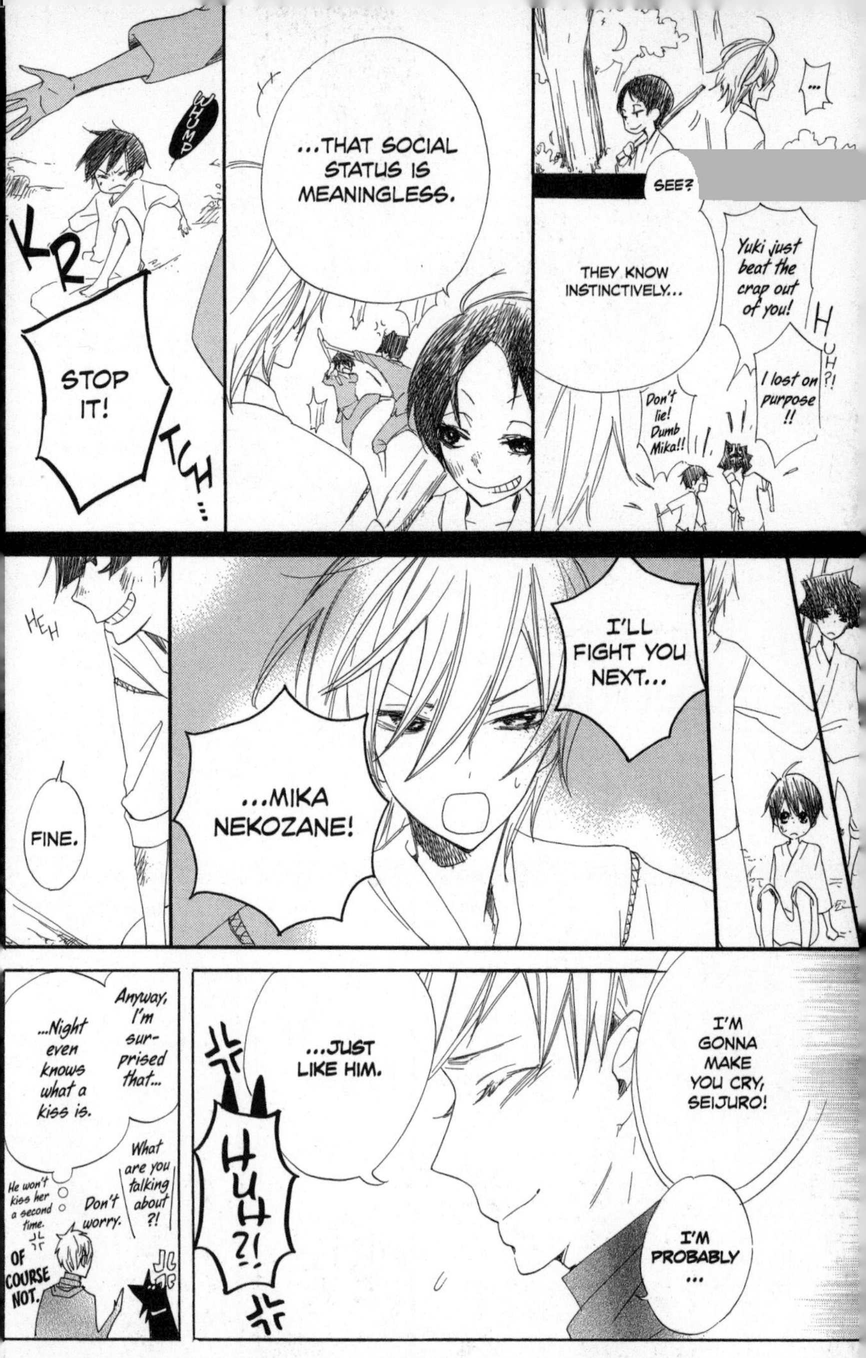
...
SEE?
THEY KNOW INSTINCTIVELY...
Yuki just beat the crap out of you!
HUH?!
I lost on purpose!!
Don't lie! Dumb Mika!!
...THAT SOCIAL STATUS IS MEANINGLESS.
WHUMP
KR
STOP IT!
TCH...
I'LL FIGHT YOU NEXT...
...MIKA NEKOZANE!
HEH
FINE.
I'M GONNA MAKE YOU CRY, SEIJURO!
I'M PROBABLY ...
...JUST LIKE HIM.
HUH?!
Anyway, I'm surprised that...
...Night even knows what a kiss is.
What are you talking about?!
Don't worry.
He won't kiss her a second time.
OF COURSE NOT.

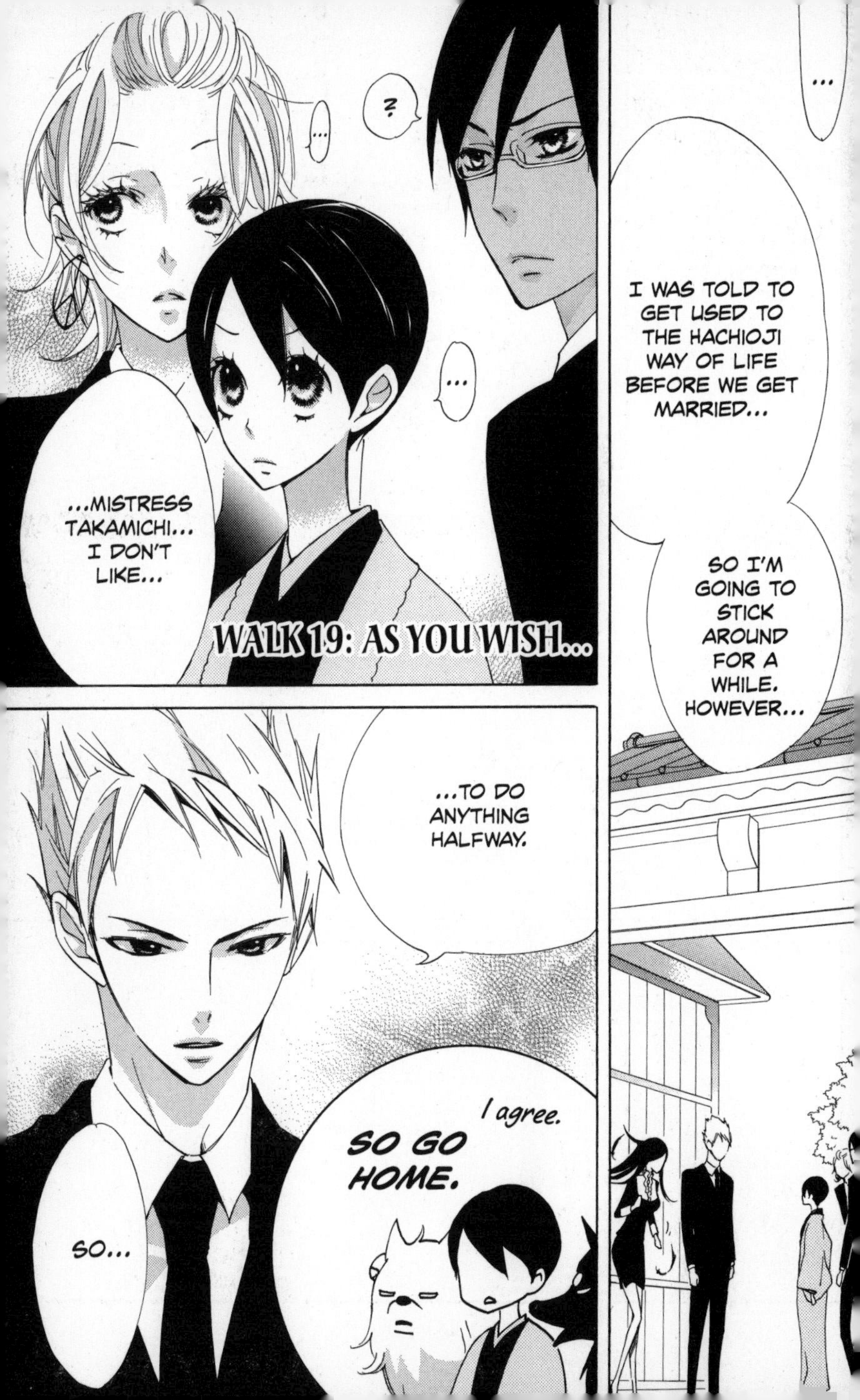
...
I WAS TOLD TO GET USED TO THE HACHIOJI WAY OF LIFE BEFORE WE GET MARRIED...
SO I'M GOING TO STICK AROUND FOR A WHILE. HOWEVER...
?
...
...
...MISTRESS TAKAMICHI... I DON'T LIKE...
WALK 19: AS YOU WISH...
...TO DO ANYTHING HALFWAY.
I agree.
SO GO HOME.
SO...

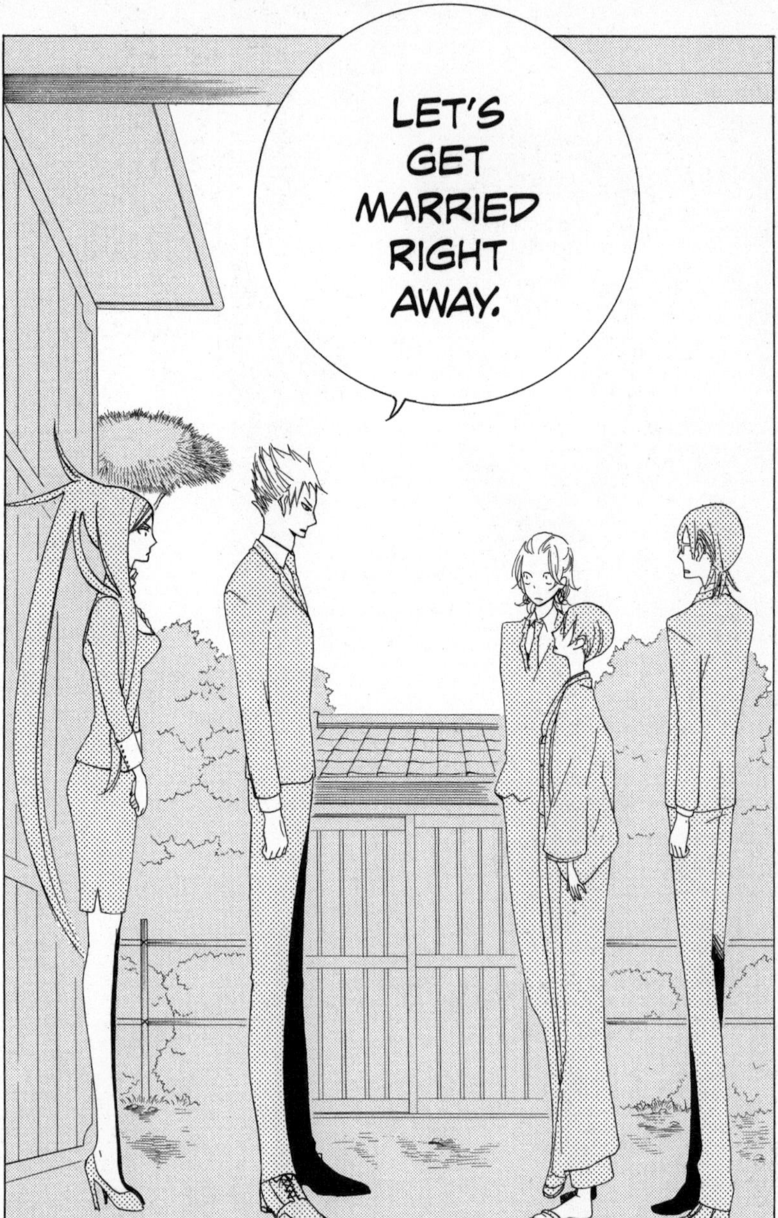
LET'S GET MARRIED RIGHT AWAY.

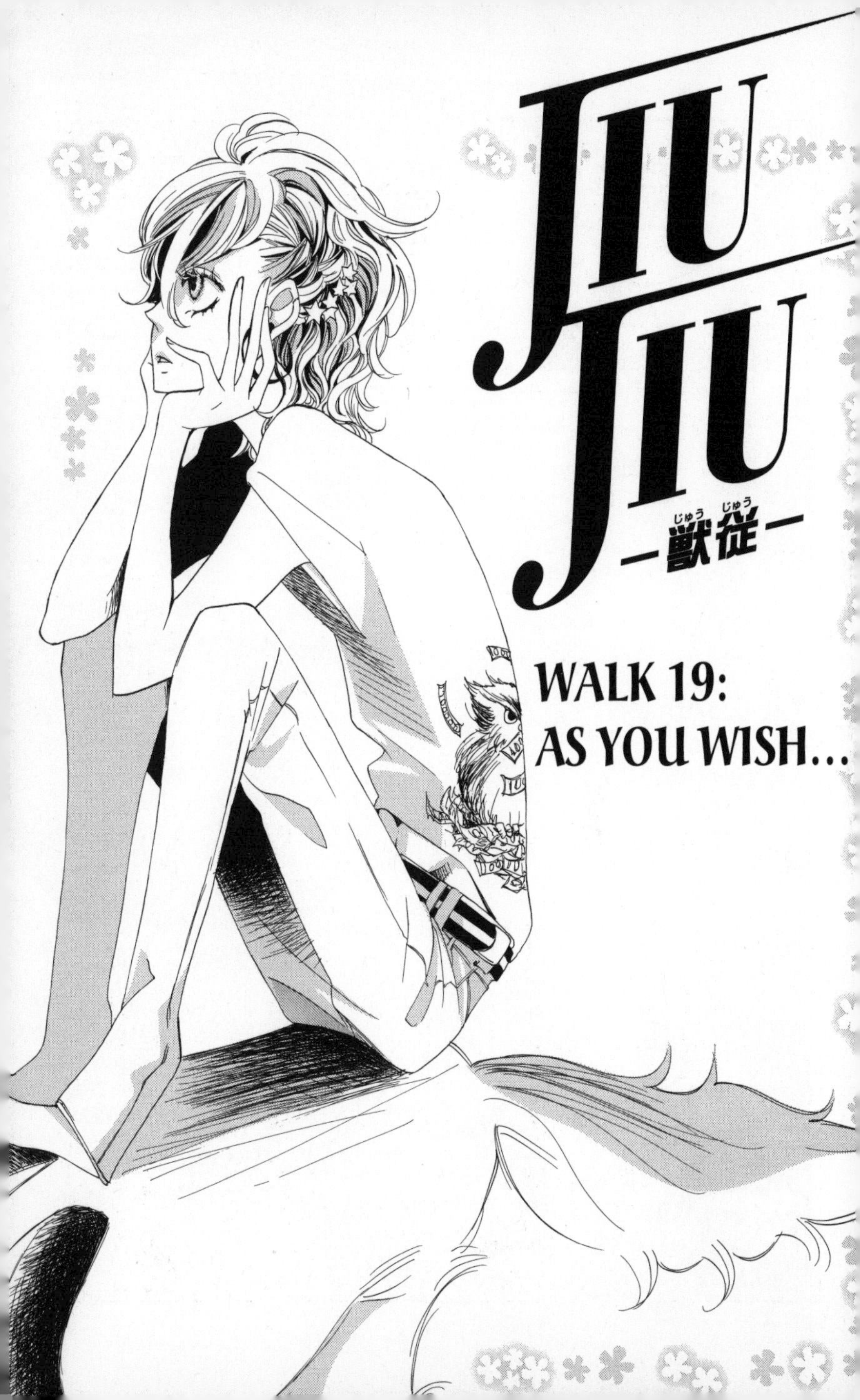
JIU JIU
じゅう じゅう
—獣従—
WALK 19:
AS YOU WISH...

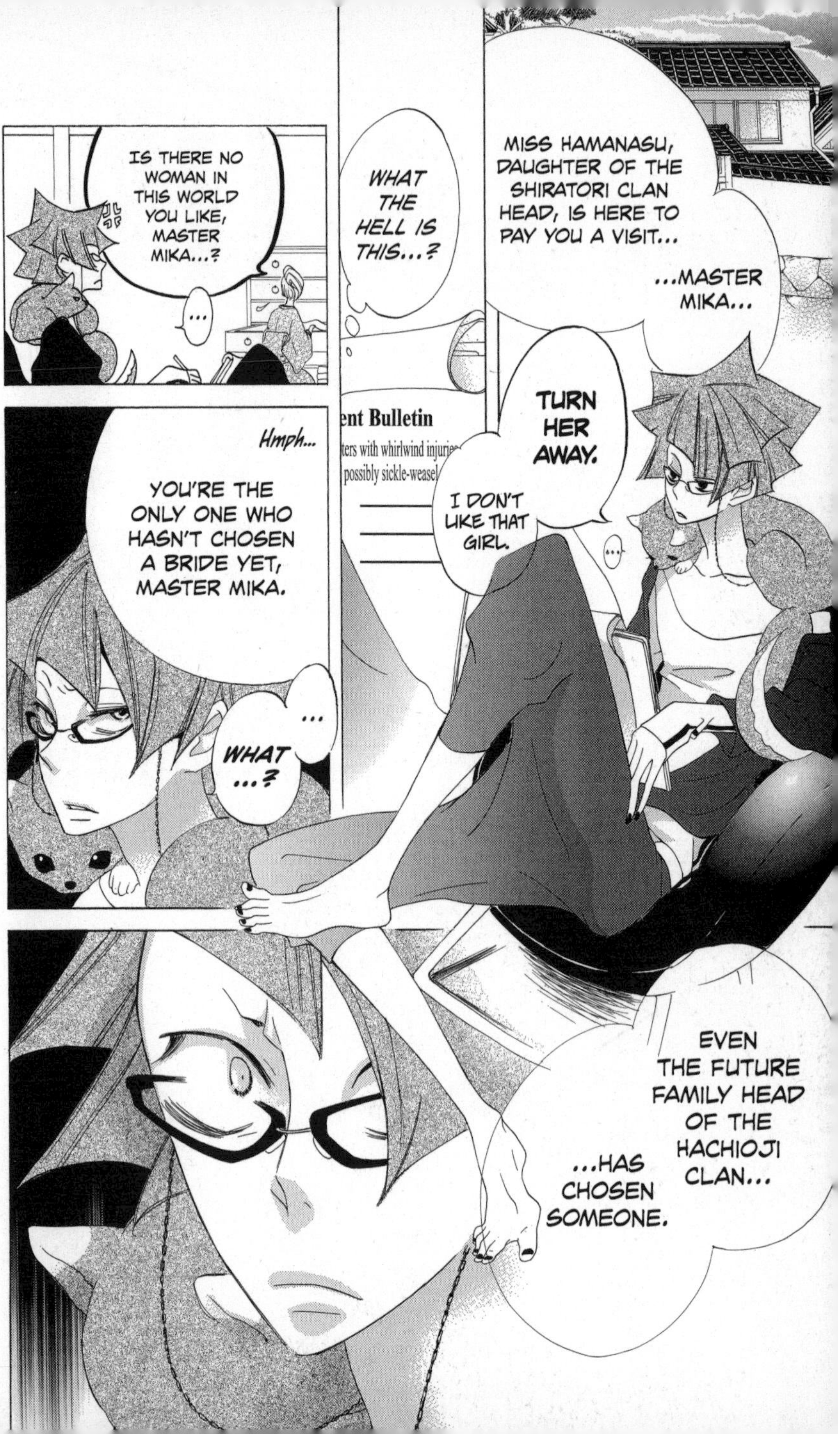
MISS HAMANASU, DAUGHTER OF THE SHIRATORI CLAN HEAD, IS HERE TO PAY YOU A VISIT...
...MASTER MIKA...
TURN HER AWAY.
I DON'T LIKE THAT GIRL.
...
WHAT THE HELL IS THIS...?
ent Bulletin
ters with whirlwind injuries
possibly sickle-weasel
IS THERE NO WOMAN IN THIS WORLD YOU LIKE, MASTER MIKA...?
...
Hmph...
YOU'RE THE ONLY ONE WHO HASN'T CHOSEN A BRIDE YET, MASTER MIKA.
... WHAT ...?
EVEN THE FUTURE FAMILY HEAD OF THE HACHIOJI CLAN...
...HAS CHOSEN SOMEONE.

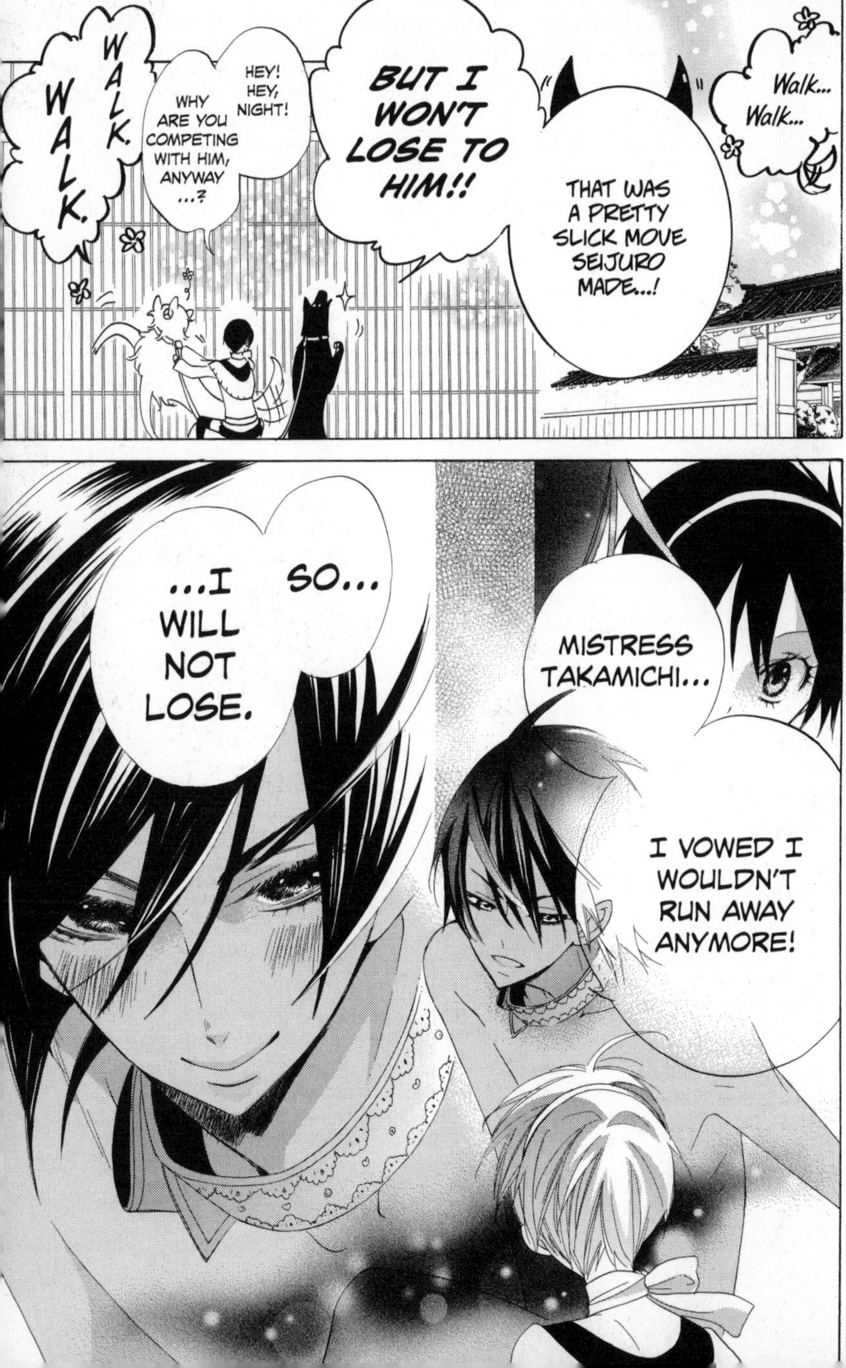
Walk... Walk...
THAT WAS A PRETTY SLICK MOVE SEIJURO MADE...!
BUT I WON'T LOSE TO HIM!!
HEY! HEY, NIGHT!
WHY ARE YOU COMPETING WITH HIM, ANYWAY ...?
WALK. WALK.
MISTRESS TAKAMICHI...
I VOWED I WOULDN'T RUN AWAY ANYMORE!
SO...
...I WILL NOT LOSE.

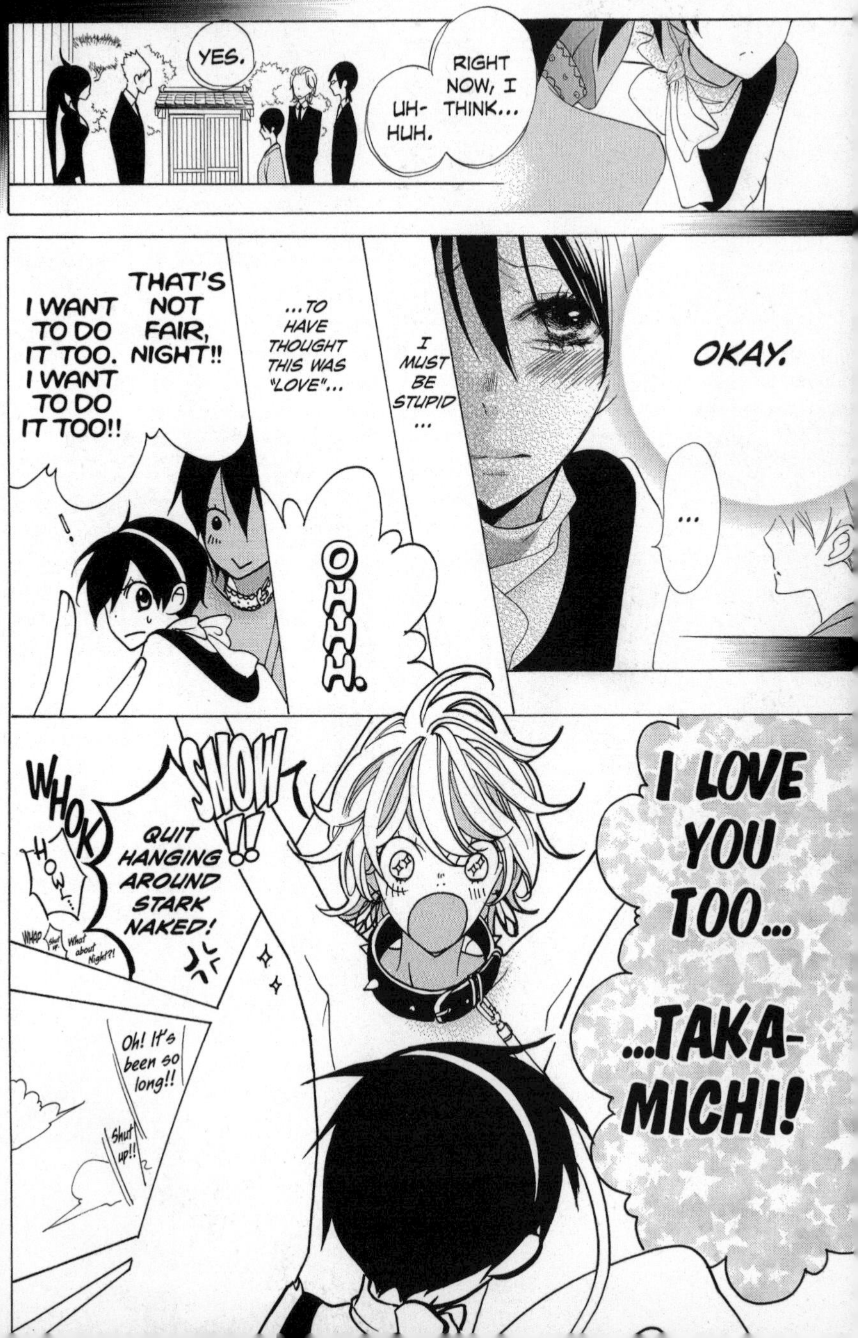
RIGHT NOW, I THINK...
UH-HUH.
YES.
OKAY.
...
I MUST BE STUPID...
...TO HAVE THOUGHT THIS WAS "LOVE"...
OHHHH.
THAT'S NOT FAIR, NIGHT!!
I WANT TO DO IT TOO. I WANT TO DO IT TOO!!
!
I LOVE YOU TOO...
...TAKA-MICHI!
SNOW!!
QUIT HANGING AROUND STARK NAKED!
WHOK
HOWL...
WHAP
Shut up.
What about Night?!
Oh! It's been so long!!
Shut up!!

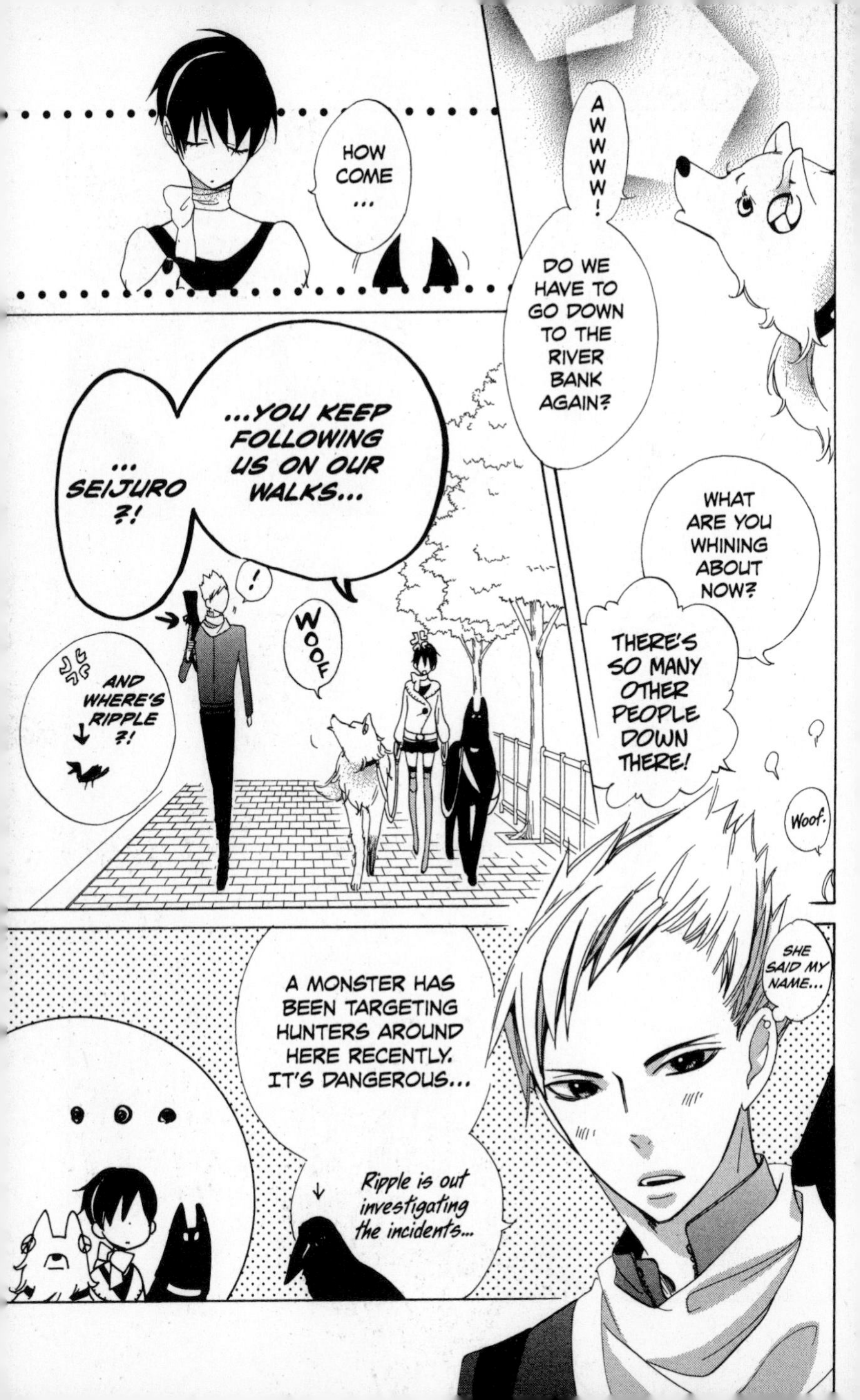
AWWWWW!
DO WE HAVE TO GO DOWN TO THE RIVER BANK AGAIN?
WHAT ARE YOU WHINING ABOUT NOW?
THERE'S SO MANY OTHER PEOPLE DOWN THERE!
Woof.
HOW COME...
...YOU KEEP FOLLOWING US ON OUR WALKS...
...SEIJURO?!
!
WOOF
AND WHERE'S RIPPLE?!
SHE SAID MY NAME...
A MONSTER HAS BEEN TARGETING HUNTERS AROUND HERE RECENTLY. IT'S DANGEROUS...
...
Ripple is out investigating the incidents...

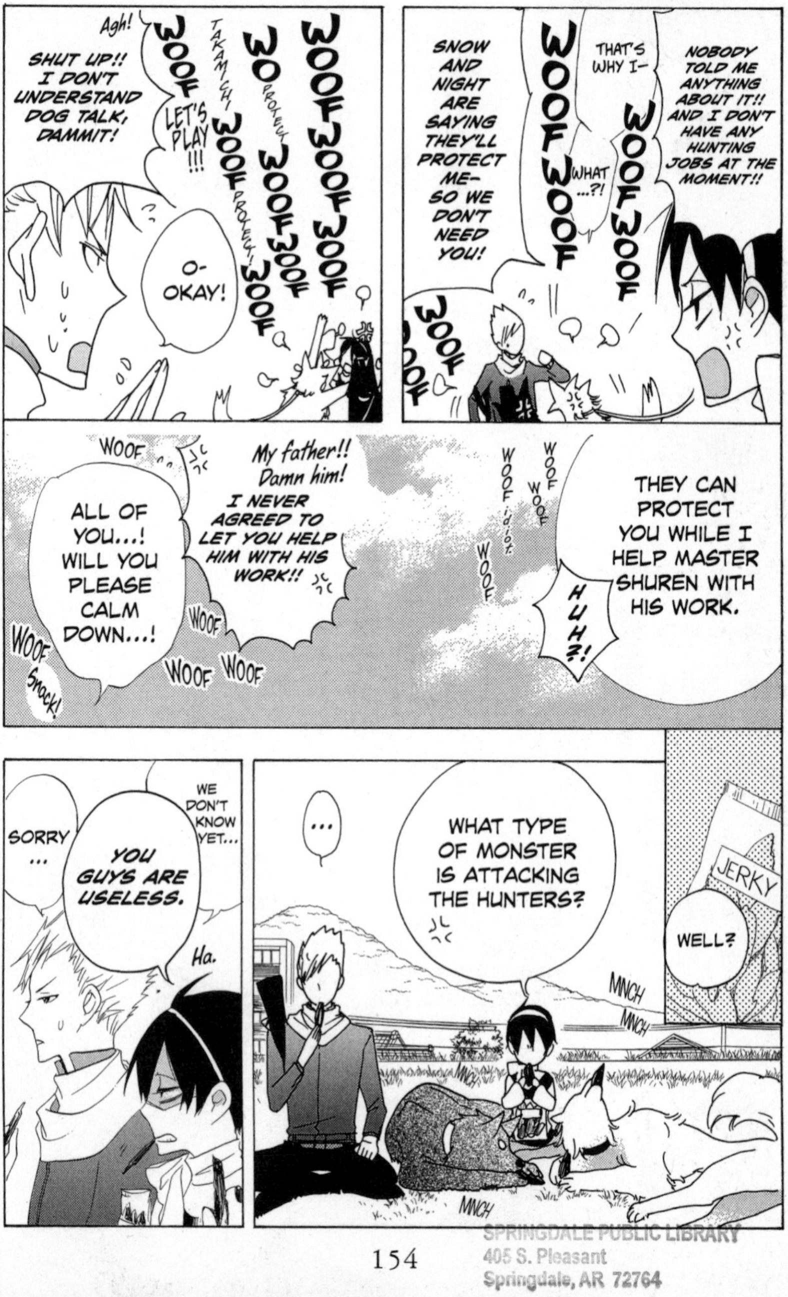
NOBODY TOLD ME ANYTHING ABOUT IT!! AND I DON'T HAVE ANY HUNTING JOBS AT THE MOMENT!!
WOOF WOOF WOOF
THAT'S WHY I-
WHAT ...?!
WOOF WOOF WOOF
SNOW AND NIGHT ARE SAYING THEY'LL PROTECT ME- SO WE DON'T NEED YOU!
WOOF
WOOF WOOF WOOF
WO PROTECT WOOF WOOF
TAKAMICHI WOOF PROTECT! WOOF
WOOF LET'S PLAY!!!
Agh!
SHUT UP!! I DON'T UNDERSTAND DOG TALK, DAMMIT!
O-OKAY!
THEY CAN PROTECT YOU WHILE I HELP MASTER SHUREN WITH HIS WORK.
HUH?!
WOOF WOOF
WOOF idiot
WOOF
My father!! Damn him!
I NEVER AGREED TO LET YOU HELP HIM WITH HIS WORK!!
WOOF
ALL OF YOU...! WILL YOU PLEASE CALM DOWN...!
WOOF
WOOF WOOF
WOOF Snack!
JERKY
WELL?
MNCH MNCH
WHAT TYPE OF MONSTER IS ATTACKING THE HUNTERS?
...
MNCH
MNCH
WE DON'T KNOW YET...
YOU GUYS ARE USELESS.
SORRY ...
Ha.

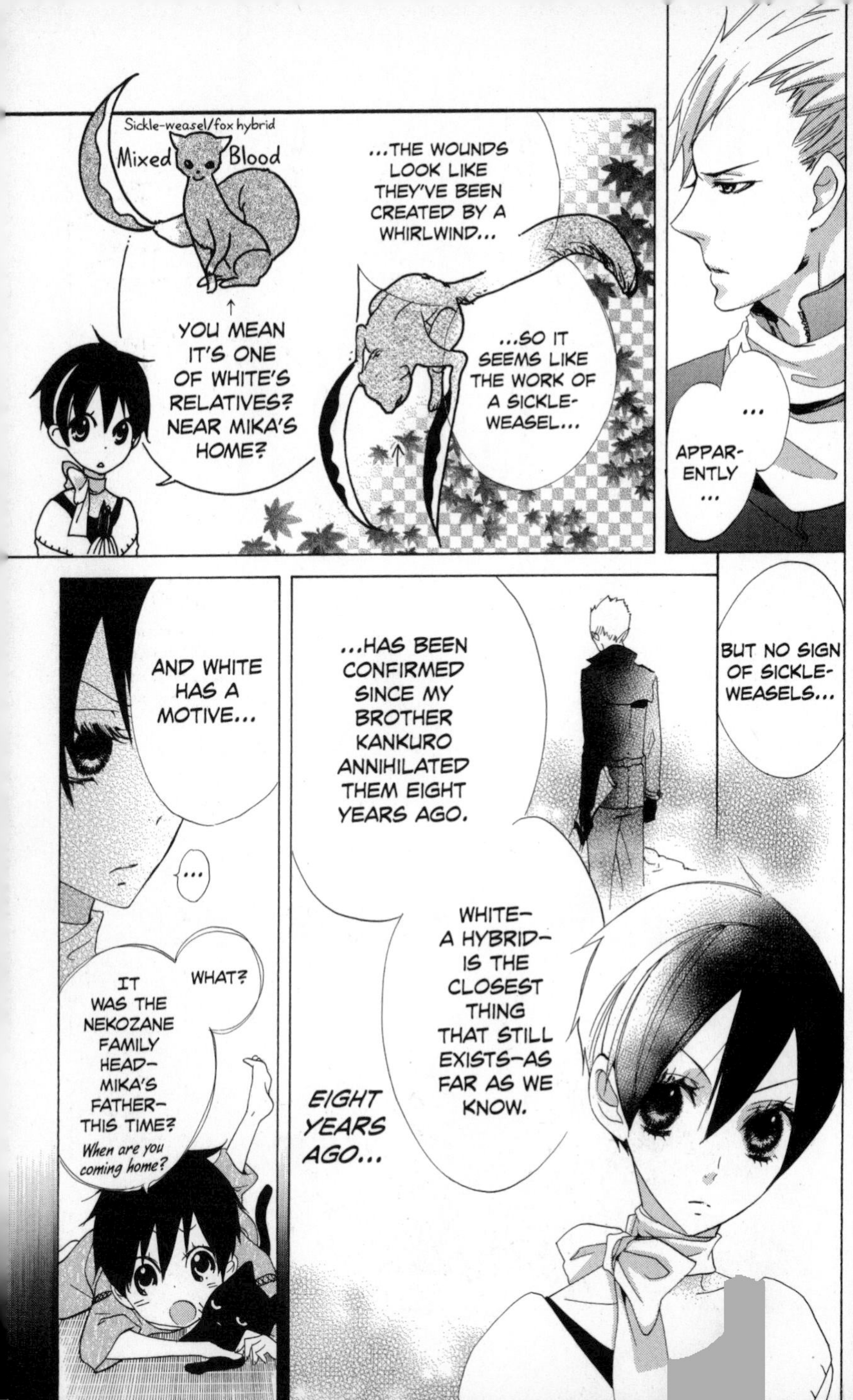
...
APPARENTLY...
...THE WOUNDS LOOK LIKE THEY'VE BEEN CREATED BY A WHIRLWIND...
...SO IT SEEMS LIKE THE WORK OF A SICKLE-WEASEL...
Sickle-weasel/fox hybrid
Mixed Blood
YOU MEAN IT'S ONE OF WHITE'S RELATIVES? NEAR MIKA'S HOME?
BUT NO SIGN OF SICKLE-WEASELS...
...HAS BEEN CONFIRMED SINCE MY BROTHER KANKURO ANNIHILATED THEM EIGHT YEARS AGO.
WHITE—A HYBRID—IS THE CLOSEST THING THAT STILL EXISTS—AS FAR AS WE KNOW.
EIGHT YEARS AGO...
AND WHITE HAS A MOTIVE...
...
WHAT?
IT WAS THE NEKOZANE FAMILY HEAD—MIKA'S FATHER—THIS TIME?
When are you coming home?

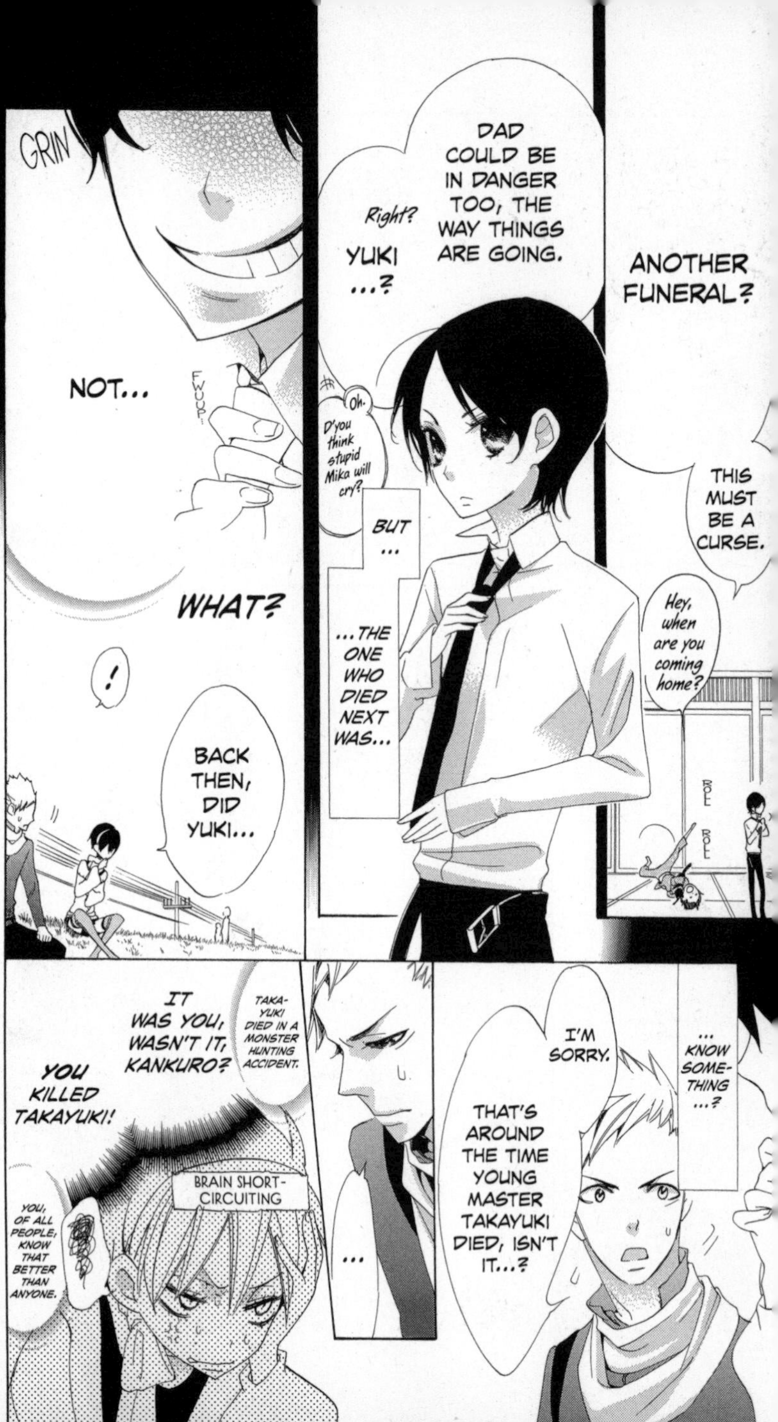

ANOTHER FUNERAL?
THIS MUST BE A CURSE.
Hey, when are you coming home?
ROL ROL
DAD COULD BE IN DANGER TOO, THE WAY THINGS ARE GOING.
Right?
YUKI ...?
Oh.
D'you think stupid Mika will cry?
BUT ...
...THE ONE WHO DIED NEXT WAS...
GRIN
NOT...
FWUUP
WHAT?
!
BACK THEN, DID YUKI...
... KNOW SOMETHING ...?
I'M SORRY.
THAT'S AROUND THE TIME YOUNG MASTER TAKAYUKI DIED, ISN'T IT...?
TAKAYUKI DIED IN A MONSTER HUNTING ACCIDENT.
...
IT WAS YOU, WASN'T IT, KANKURO?
YOU KILLED TAKAYUKI!
BRAIN SHORT-CIRCUITING
YOU, OF ALL PEOPLE, KNOW THAT BETTER THAN ANYONE.

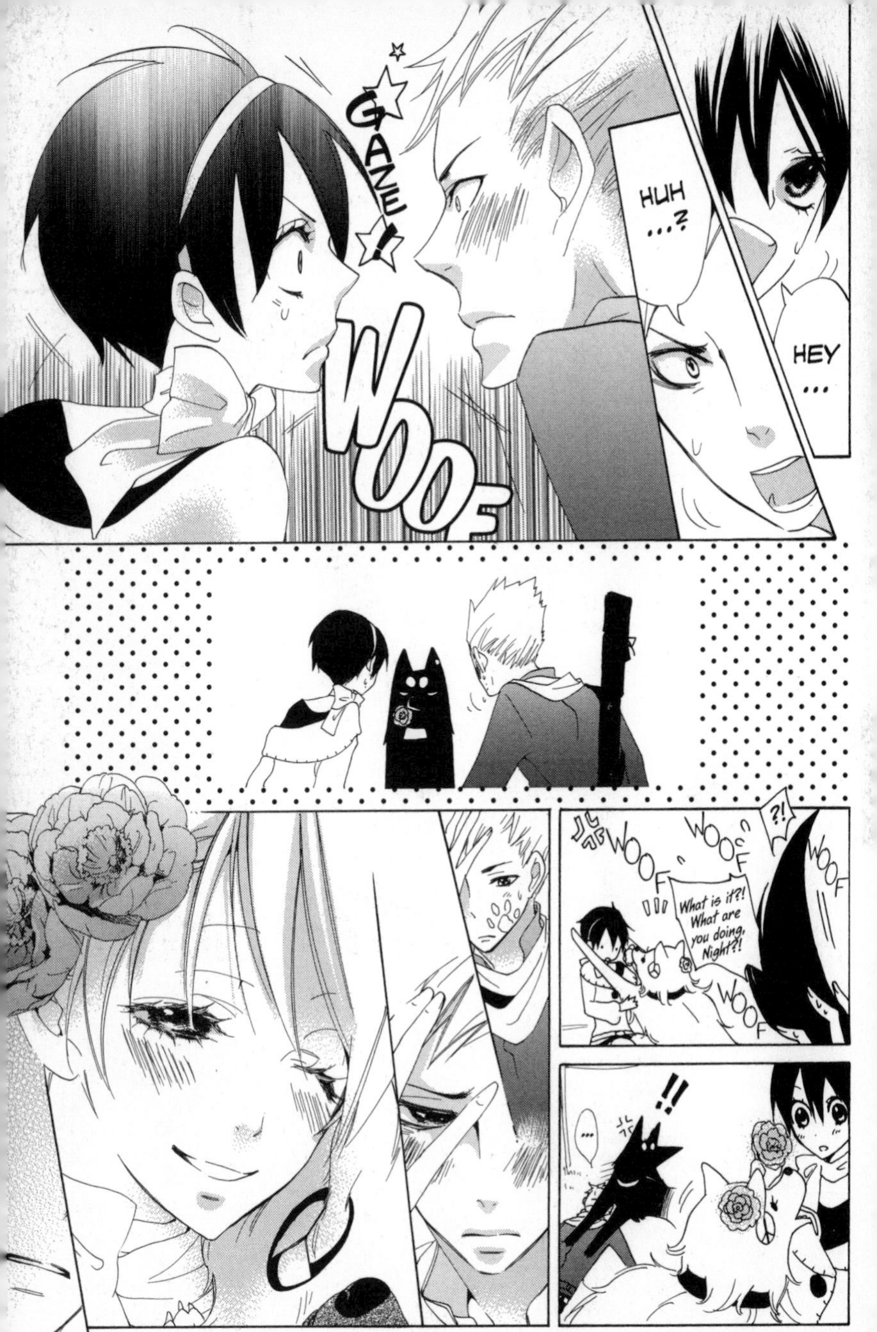
HUH ...?
HEY ...
GAZE!
WOOF
?!
WOOF
WOOF
WOOF
What is it?! What are you doing, Night?!
WOOF
!!
...

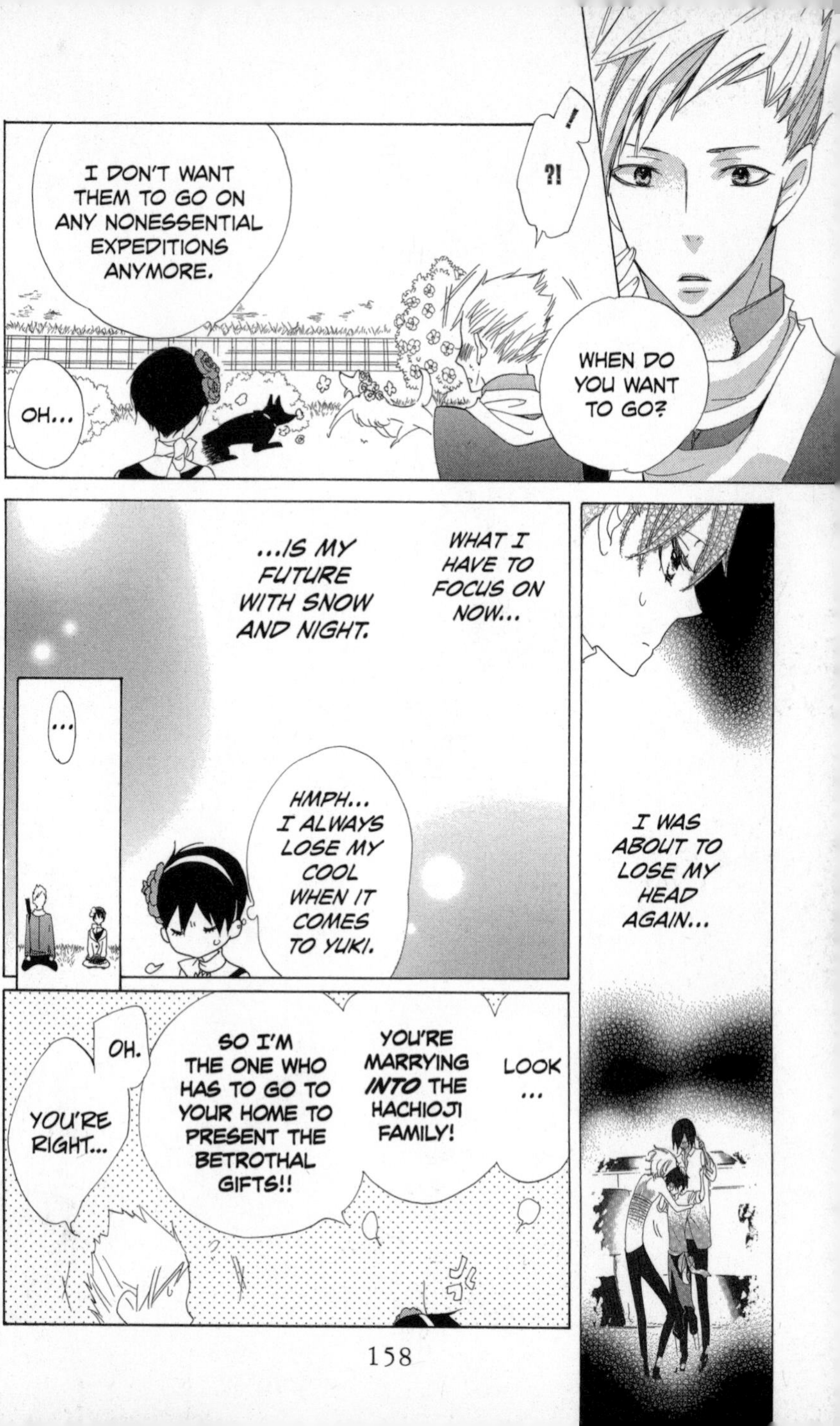
!
?!
I DON'T WANT THEM TO GO ON ANY NONESSENTIAL EXPEDITIONS ANYMORE.
WHEN DO YOU WANT TO GO?
OH...
I WAS ABOUT TO LOSE MY HEAD AGAIN...
WHAT I HAVE TO FOCUS ON NOW...
...IS MY FUTURE WITH SNOW AND NIGHT.
...
HMPH... I ALWAYS LOSE MY COOL WHEN IT COMES TO YUKI.
LOOK...
YOU'RE MARRYING INTO THE HACHIOJI FAMILY!
SO I'M THE ONE WHO HAS TO GO TO YOUR HOME TO PRESENT THE BETROTHAL GIFTS!!
OH.
YOU'RE RIGHT...

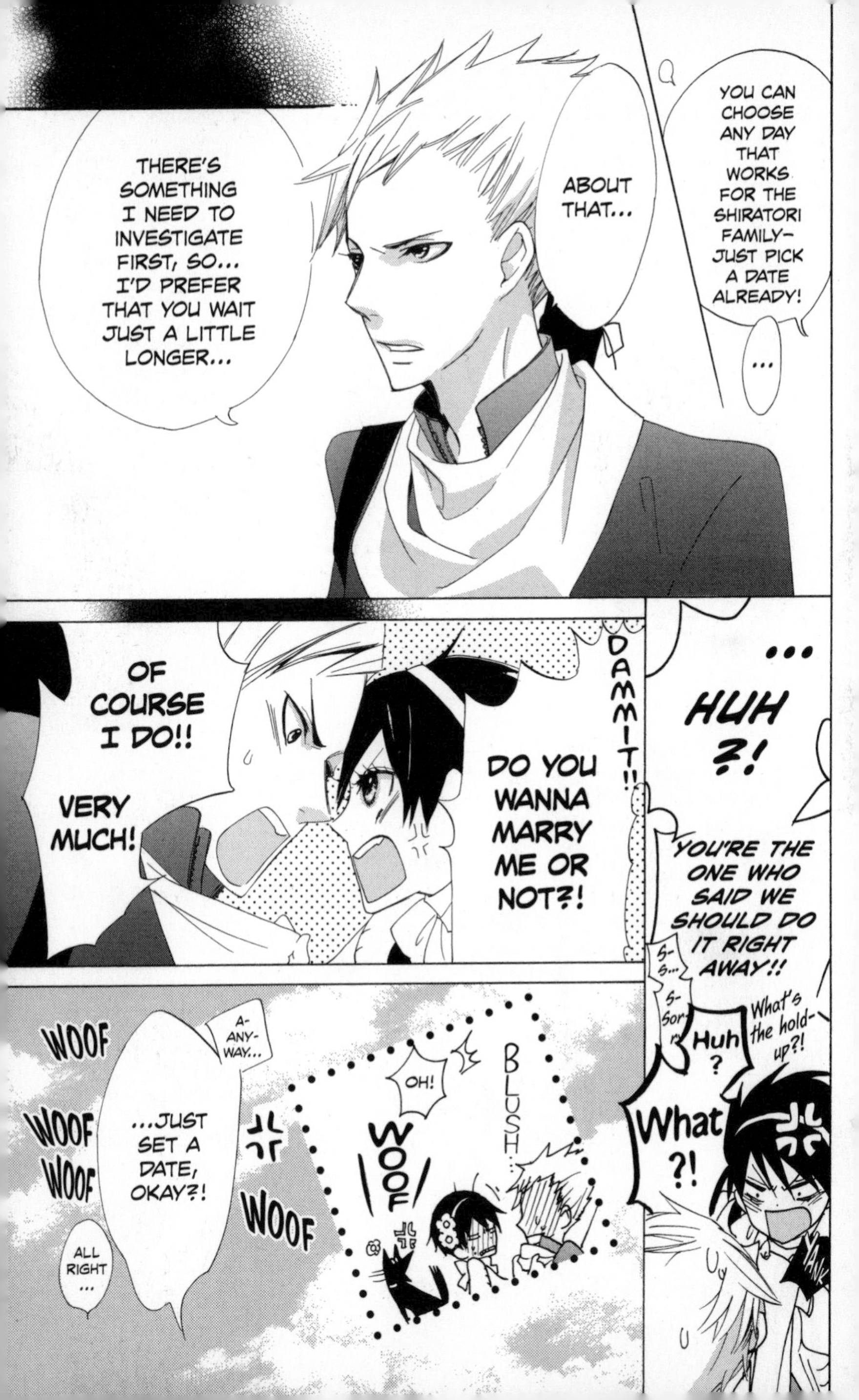
YOU CAN CHOOSE ANY DAY THAT WORKS FOR THE SHIRATORI FAMILY—JUST PICK A DATE ALREADY!
...
ABOUT THAT...
THERE'S SOMETHING I NEED TO INVESTIGATE FIRST, SO... I'D PREFER THAT YOU WAIT JUST A LITTLE LONGER...
...
HUH?!
YOU'RE THE ONE WHO SAID WE SHOULD DO IT RIGHT AWAY!!
What's the hold-up?!
Huh?
S-S...
S-Sorry
What?!
DAMMIT!!
DO YOU WANNA MARRY ME OR NOT?!
OF COURSE I DO!!
VERY MUCH!
OH!
BLUSH
WOOF
A-ANYWAY...
...JUST SET A DATE, OKAY?!
WOOF
WOOF
WOOF
WOOF
ALL RIGHT...

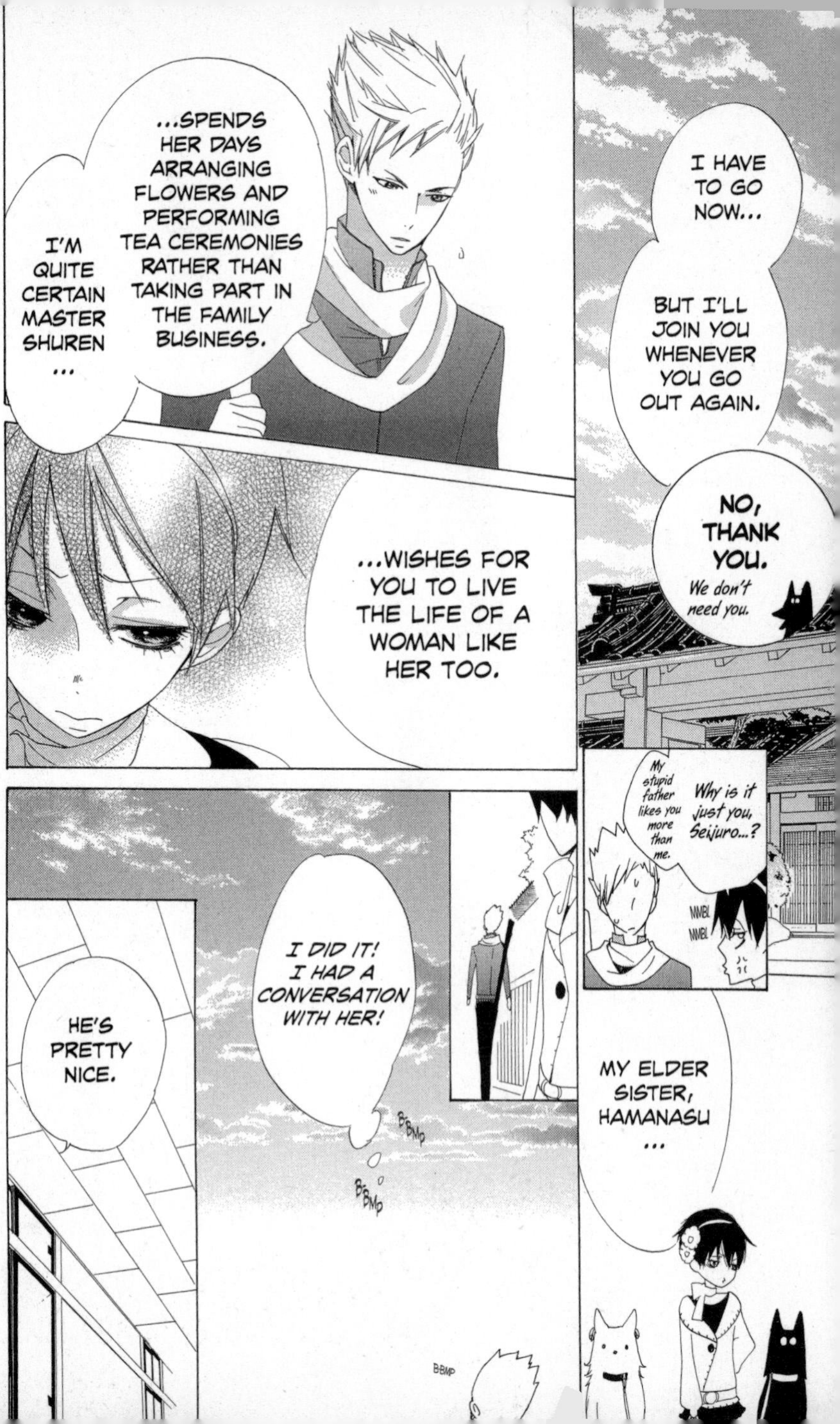
I HAVE TO GO NOW...
BUT I'LL JOIN YOU WHENEVER YOU GO OUT AGAIN.
NO, THANK YOU.
We don't need you.
I'M QUITE CERTAIN MASTER SHUREN ...
...SPENDS HER DAYS ARRANGING FLOWERS AND PERFORMING TEA CEREMONIES RATHER THAN TAKING PART IN THE FAMILY BUSINESS.
...WISHES FOR YOU TO LIVE THE LIFE OF A WOMAN LIKE HER TOO.
Why is it just you, Seijuro...?
My stupid father likes you more than me.
MMBL MMBL
MY ELDER SISTER, HAMANASU ...
I DID IT! I HAD A CONVERSATION WITH HER!
BA-BMP
BA-BMP
HE'S PRETTY NICE.
BBMP

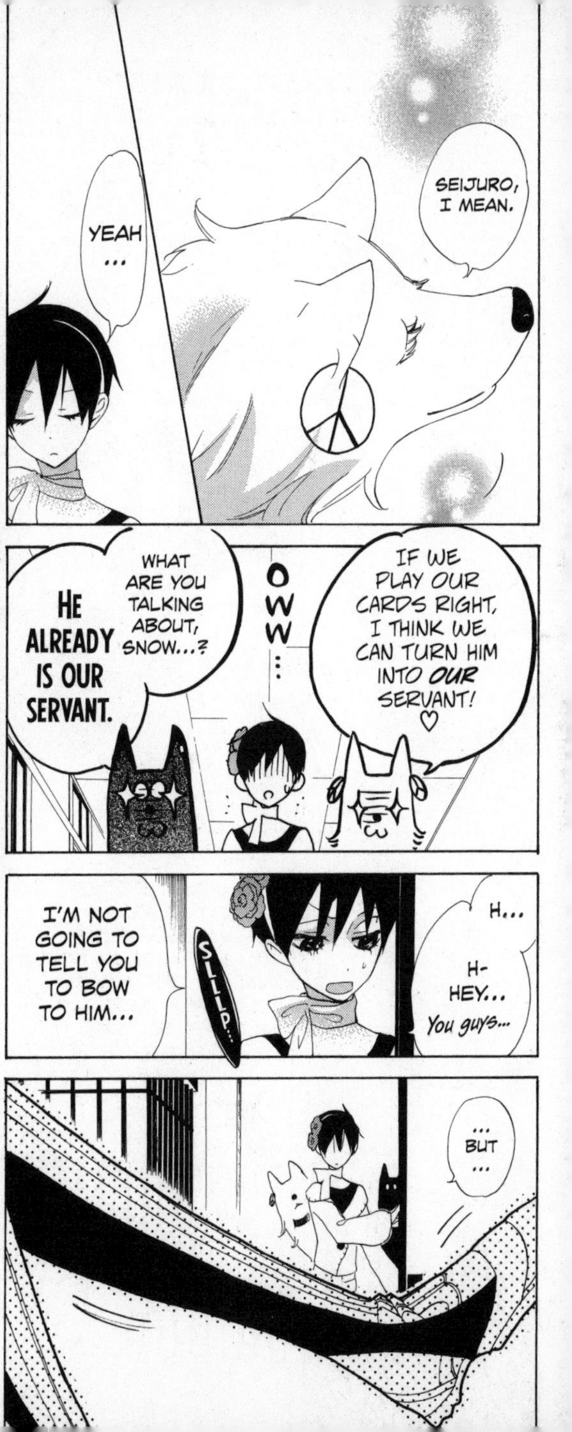
SEIJURO, I MEAN.
YEAH...
IF WE PLAY OUR CARDS RIGHT, I THINK WE CAN TURN HIM INTO OUR SERVANT! ♡
OWW...
WHAT ARE YOU TALKING ABOUT, SNOW...?
HE ALREADY IS OUR SERVANT.
H... H- HEY... You guys...
SLLLP...
I'M NOT GOING TO TELL YOU TO BOW TO HIM...
...BUT...

What do the characters of *Jiu Jiu* fear most and who do they hate?

Saitama Prefecture: Yui

That question sounds kind of mean now that I boiled it down to one line...
Anyway, here are the answers. ↓↓

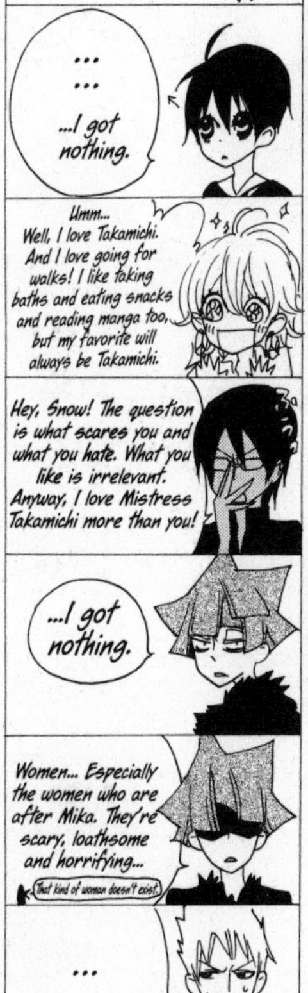
...
...
...I got nothing.
Umm... Well, I love Takamichi. And I love going for walks! I like taking baths and eating snacks and reading manga too, but my favorite will always be Takamichi.
Hey, Snow! The question is what scares you and what you hate. What you like is irrelevant. Anyway, I love Mistress Takamichi more than you!
...I got nothing.
Women... Especially the women who are after Mika. They're scary, loathsome and horrifying...
That kind of woman doesn't exist.
...
TIME OUT.
Uh...men? After all, all men are wolves right?
I'm so scared!
Ooh!
That sounds funny coming from a crow.

Come to think of it, they all hate so many things and are scared of so many things I couldn't come up with a clear answer...

By the way, Hodaka calls Mika "Kitty Cat." I like that because it sounds cute. ✿

Oh, I forgot to answer what I don't like.

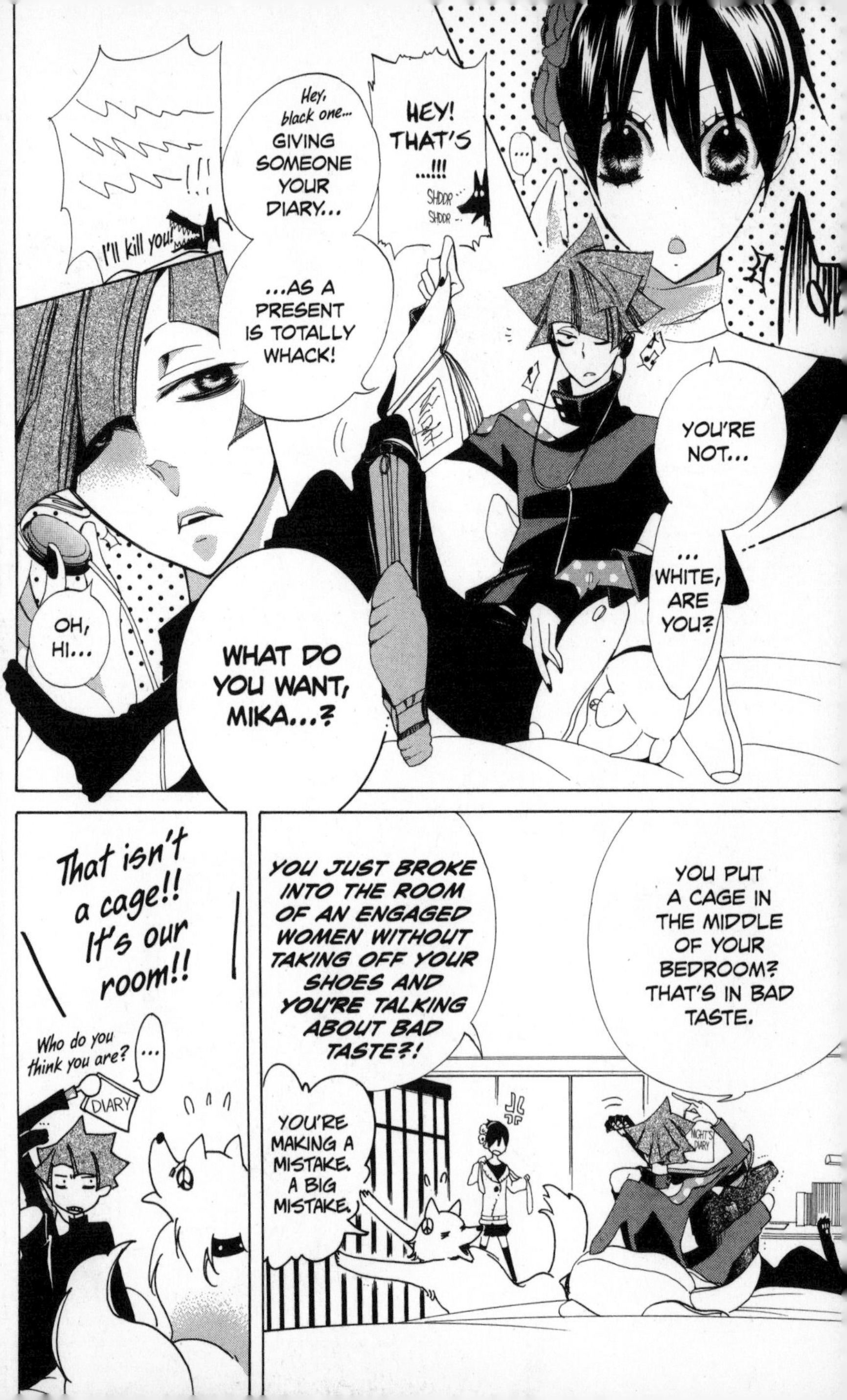
...
HEY! THAT'S ...!!!
SHDDR SHDDR
Hey, black one... GIVING SOMEONE YOUR DIARY...
...AS A PRESENT IS TOTALLY WHACK!
!!!
I'll kill you!
YOU'RE NOT...
...WHITE, ARE YOU?
WHAT DO YOU WANT, MIKA...?
OH, HI...
YOU PUT A CAGE IN THE MIDDLE OF YOUR BEDROOM? THAT'S IN BAD TASTE.
NIGHT'S DIARY
YOU JUST BROKE INTO THE ROOM OF AN ENGAGED WOMEN WITHOUT TAKING OFF YOUR SHOES AND YOU'RE TALKING ABOUT BAD TASTE?!
YOU'RE MAKING A MISTAKE. A BIG MISTAKE.
That isn't a cage!! It's our room!!
...
Who do you think you are?
DIARY

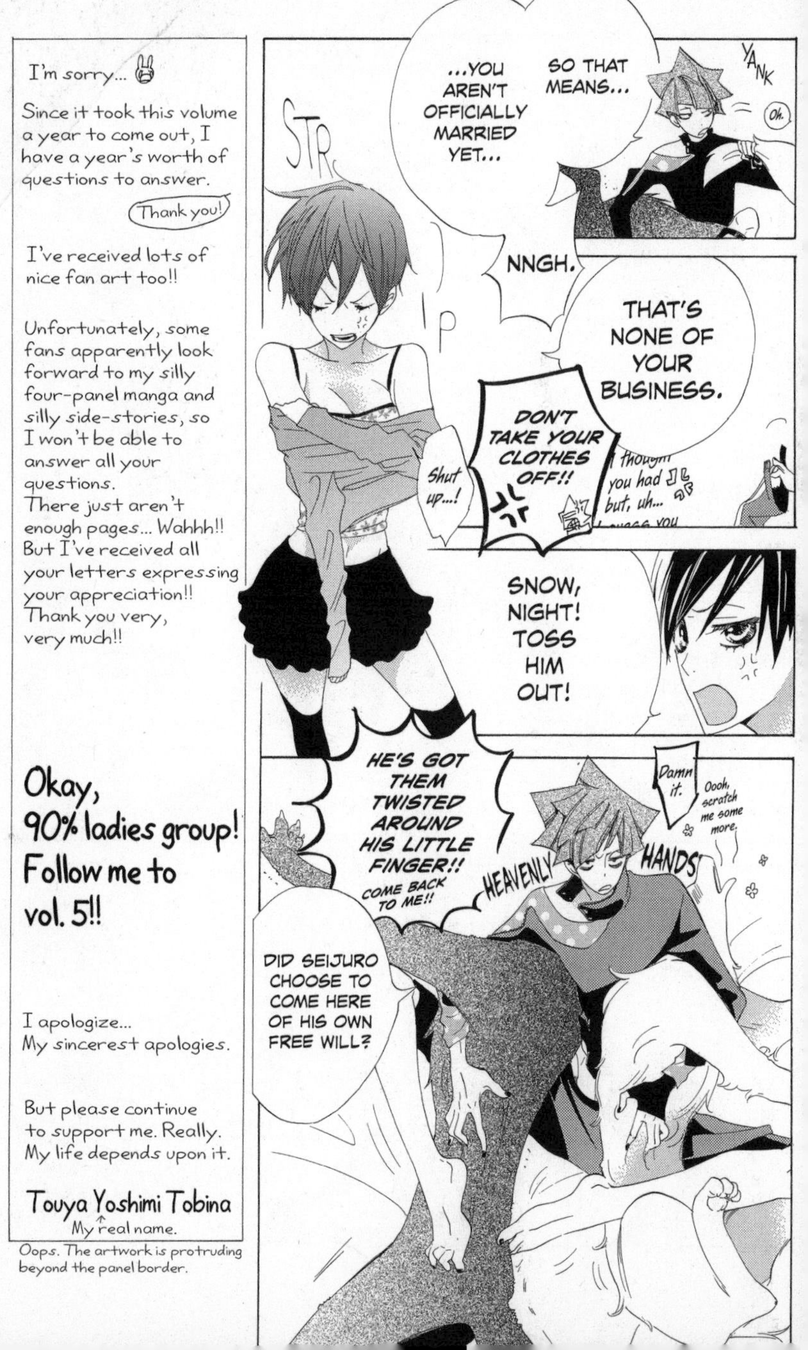
YANK
Oh.
SO THAT MEANS...
...YOU AREN'T OFFICIALLY MARRIED YET...
NNGH.
THAT'S NONE OF YOUR BUSINESS.
DON'T TAKE YOUR CLOTHES OFF!!
you had
but, uh...
SNOW, NIGHT! TOSS HIM OUT!
STRIP
Shut up...!
Damn it.
Oooh, scratch me some more.
HEAVENLY HANDS
HE'S GOT THEM TWISTED AROUND HIS LITTLE FINGER!!
COME BACK TO ME!!
DID SEIJURO CHOOSE TO COME HERE OF HIS OWN FREE WILL?

I'm sorry...

Since it took this volume a year to come out, I have a year's worth of questions to answer.

(Thank you!)

I've received lots of nice fan art too!!

Unfortunately, some fans apparently look forward to my silly four-panel manga and silly side-stories, so I won't be able to answer all your questions.
There just aren't enough pages... Wahhh!!
But I've received all your letters expressing your appreciation!!
Thank you very, very much!!

Okay, 90% ladies group! Follow me to vol. 5!!

I apologize...
My sincerest apologies.

But please continue to support me. Really. My life depends upon it.

Touya Yoshimi Tobina
↑ My real name.

Oops. The artwork is protruding beyond the panel border.

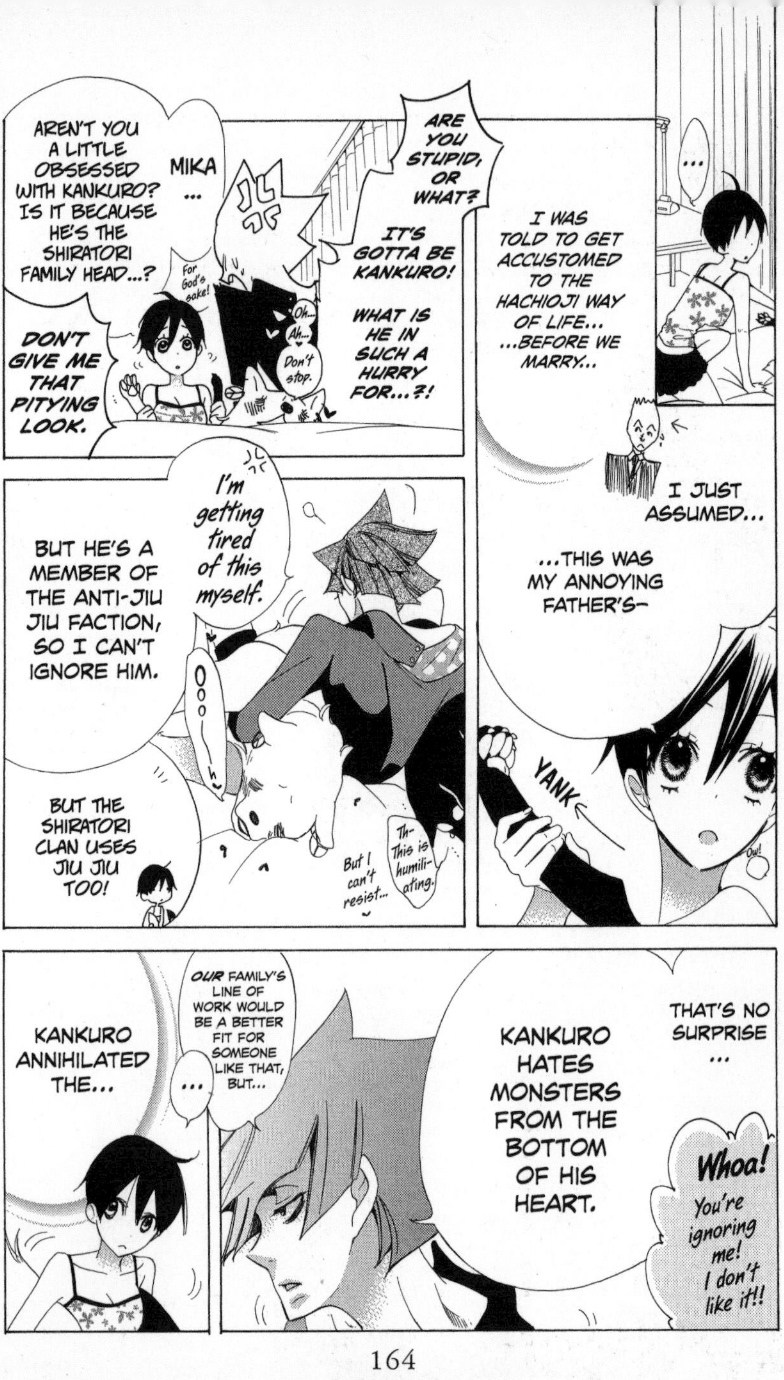
...
I WAS TOLD TO GET ACCUSTOMED TO THE HACHIOJI WAY OF LIFE... ...BEFORE WE MARRY...
I JUST ASSUMED...
...THIS WAS MY ANNOYING FATHER'S—
YANK
Ow!
ARE YOU STUPID, OR WHAT?
IT'S GOTTA BE KANKURO!
WHAT IS HE IN SUCH A HURRY FOR...?!
Oh... Ah... Don't stop.
For God's sake!
MIKA ...
AREN'T YOU A LITTLE OBSESSED WITH KANKURO? IS IT BECAUSE HE'S THE SHIRATORI FAMILY HEAD...?
DON'T GIVE ME THAT PITYING LOOK.
I'm getting tired of this myself.
Th- This is humiliating.
But I can't resist...
Ooo...h
BUT HE'S A MEMBER OF THE ANTI-JIU JIU FACTION, SO I CAN'T IGNORE HIM.
BUT THE SHIRATORI CLAN USES JIU JIU TOO!
THAT'S NO SURPRISE ...
KANKURO HATES MONSTERS FROM THE BOTTOM OF HIS HEART.
Whoa! You're ignoring me! I don't like it!!
OUR FAMILY'S LINE OF WORK WOULD BE A BETTER FIT FOR SOMEONE LIKE THAT, BUT...
...
KANKURO ANNIHILATED THE...

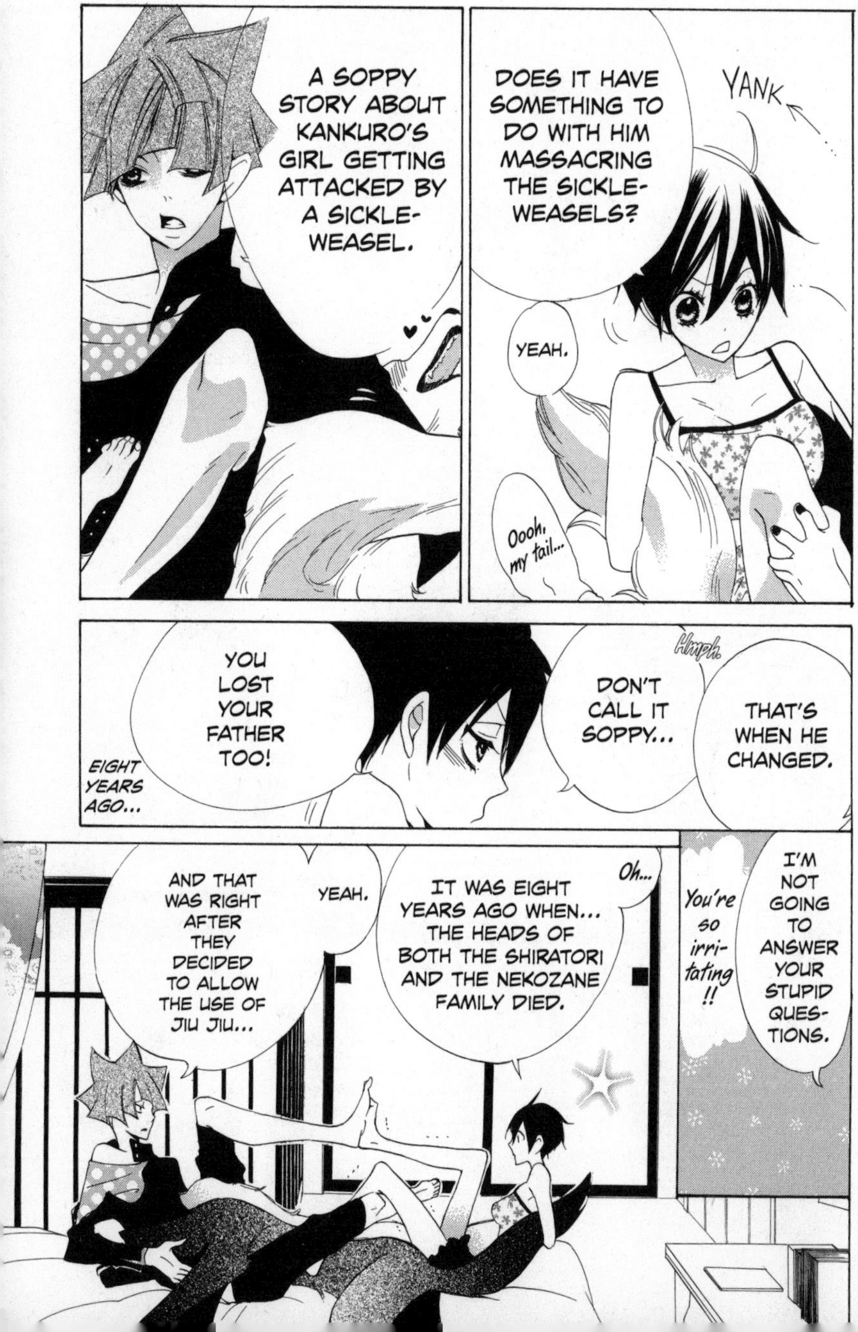
YANK
DOES IT HAVE SOMETHING TO DO WITH HIM MASSACRING THE SICKLE-WEASELS?
YEAH.
Oooh, my tail...
A SOPPY STORY ABOUT KANKURO'S GIRL GETTING ATTACKED BY A SICKLE-WEASEL.
THAT'S WHEN HE CHANGED.
Hmph.
DON'T CALL IT SOPPY...
YOU LOST YOUR FATHER TOO!
EIGHT YEARS AGO...
I'M NOT GOING TO ANSWER YOUR STUPID QUES-TIONS.
You're so irri-tating!!
Oh...
IT WAS EIGHT YEARS AGO WHEN... THE HEADS OF BOTH THE SHIRATORI AND THE NEKOZANE FAMILY DIED.
YEAH.
AND THAT WAS RIGHT AFTER THEY DECIDED TO ALLOW THE USE OF JIU JIU...

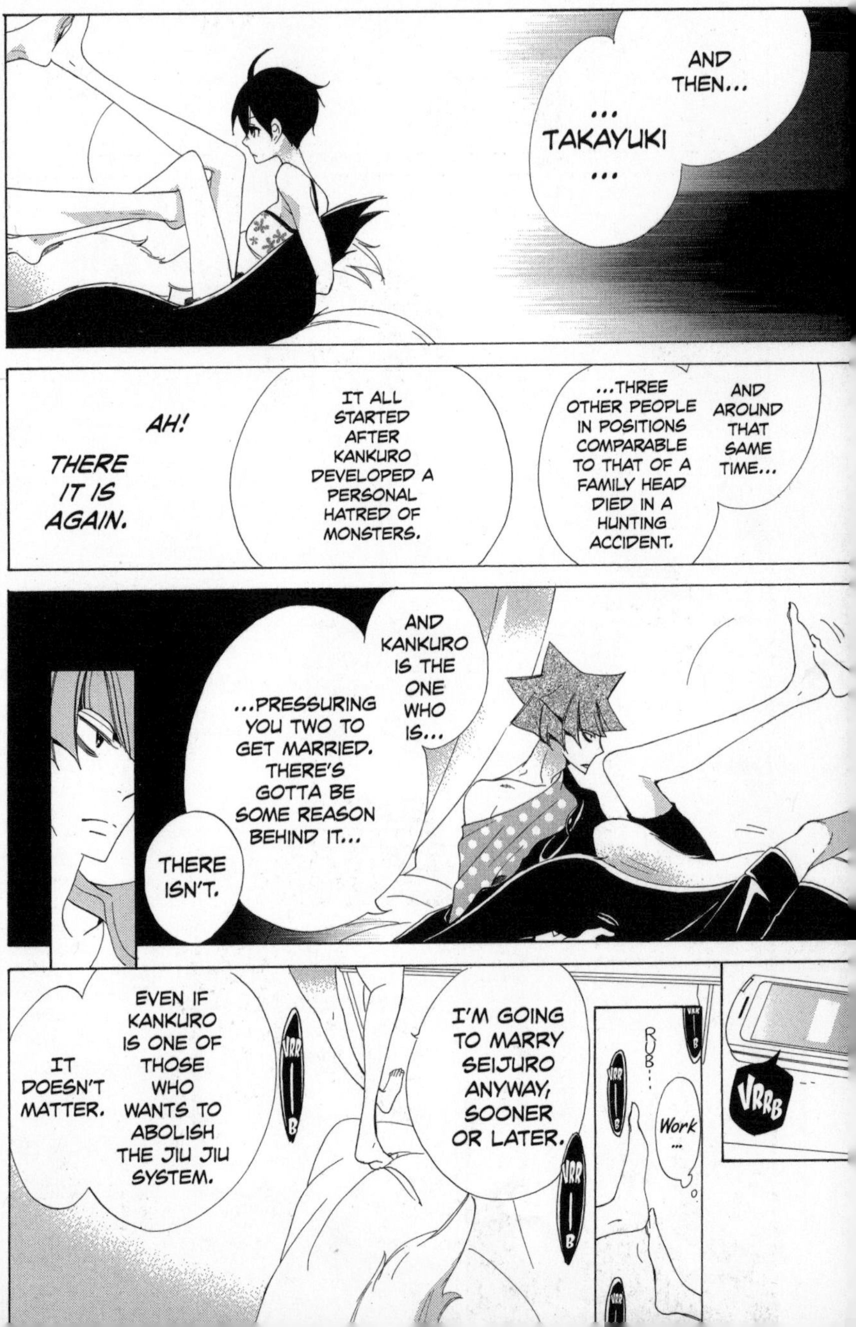
AND THEN... ...TAKAYUKI...
AND AROUND THAT SAME TIME...
...THREE OTHER PEOPLE IN POSITIONS COMPARABLE TO THAT OF A FAMILY HEAD DIED IN A HUNTING ACCIDENT.
IT ALL STARTED AFTER KANKURO DEVELOPED A PERSONAL HATRED OF MONSTERS.
AH! THERE IT IS AGAIN.
AND KANKURO IS THE ONE WHO IS...
...PRESSURING YOU TWO TO GET MARRIED. THERE'S GOTTA BE SOME REASON BEHIND IT...
THERE ISN'T.
VRRB
RUB...
Work...
VRRB
VRRB
I'M GOING TO MARRY SEIJURO ANYWAY, SOONER OR LATER.
VRRB
EVEN IF KANKURO IS ONE OF THOSE WHO WANTS TO ABOLISH THE JIU JIU SYSTEM.
IT DOESN'T MATTER.

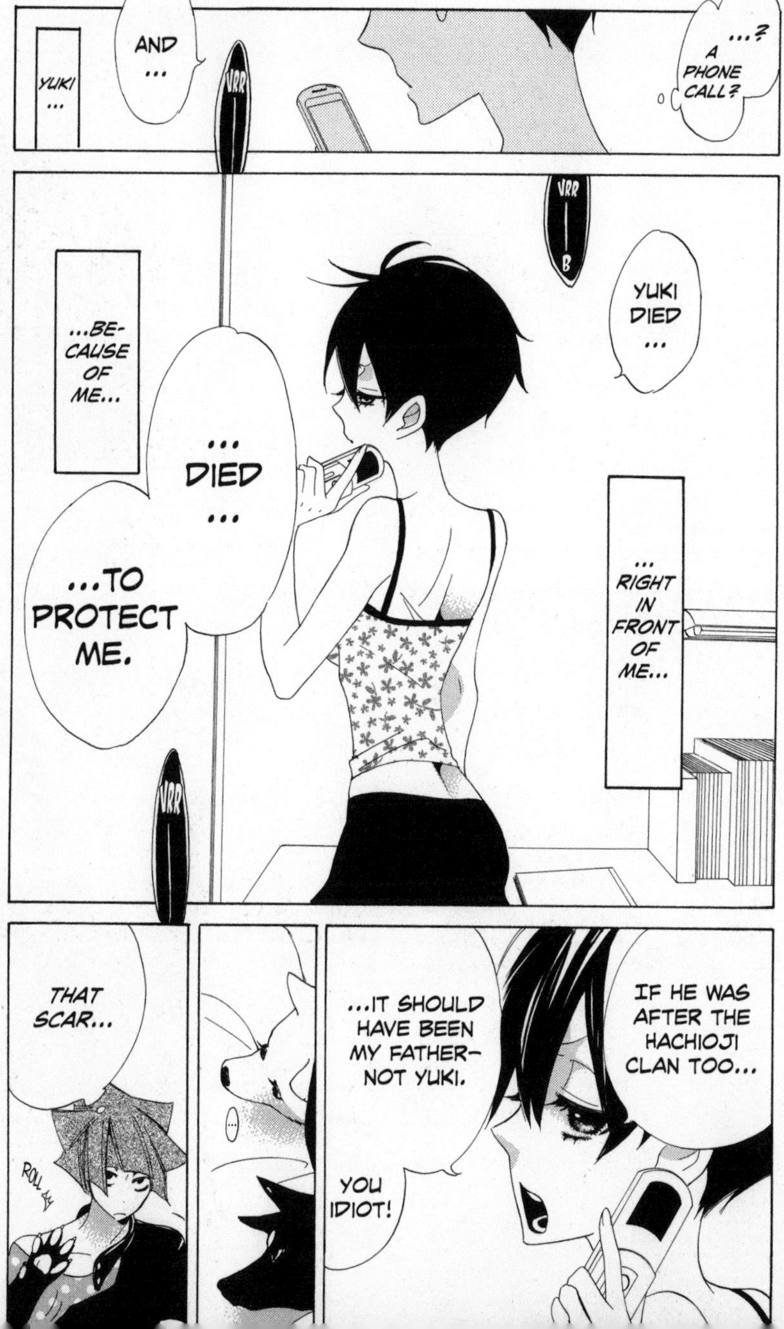
...? A PHONE CALL?
VRR
AND ...
YUKI ...
VRR—B
YUKI DIED ...
... RIGHT IN FRONT OF ME...
...BE-CAUSE OF ME...
... DIED ...
...TO PROTECT ME.
VRR
IF HE WAS AFTER THE HACHIOJI CLAN TOO...
...IT SHOULD HAVE BEEN MY FATHER— NOT YUKI.
YOU IDIOT!
...
THAT SCAR...
ROLL

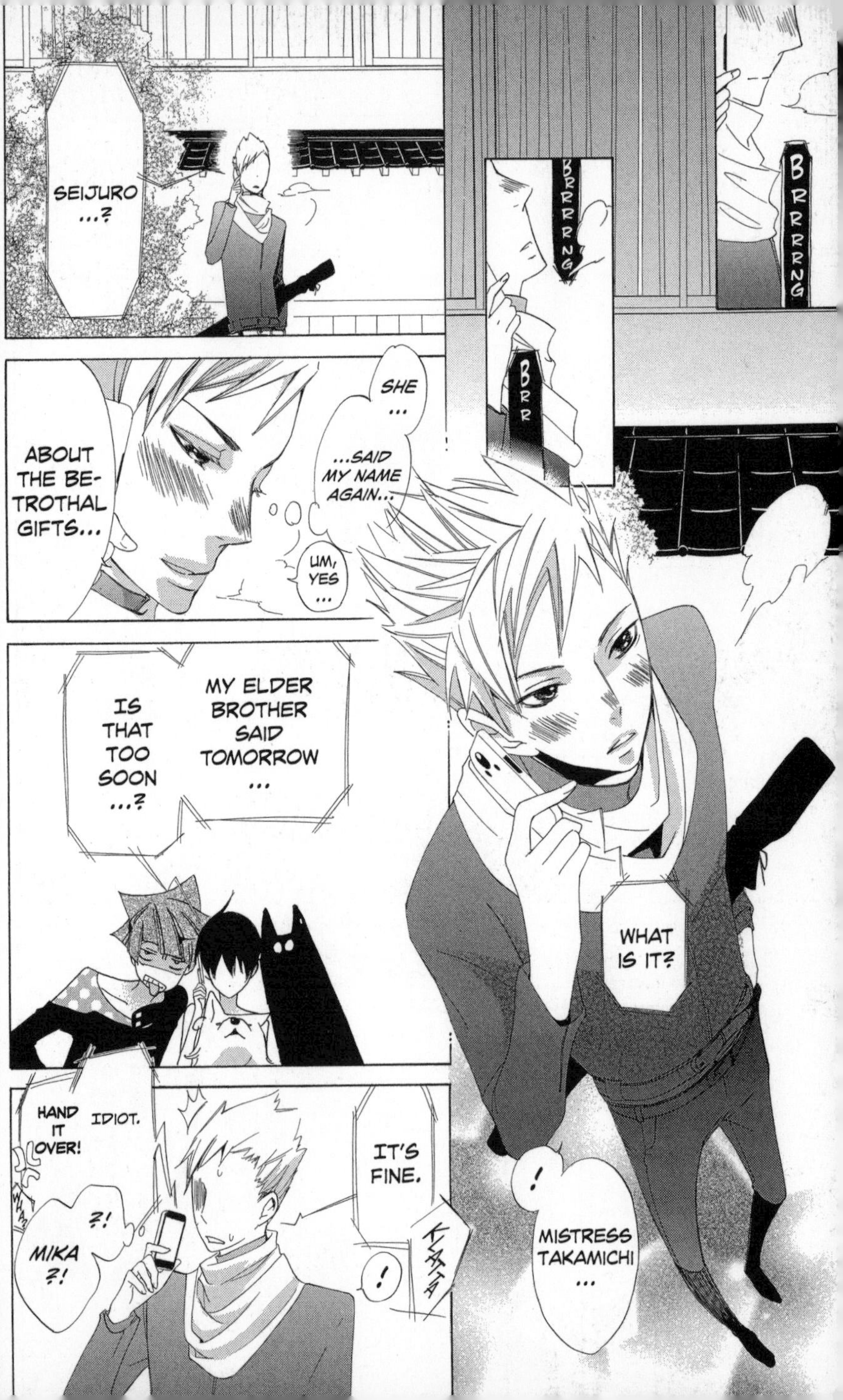
BRRRRNG
BRRRRNG
BRR
SEIJURO ...?
WHAT IS IT?
!
MISTRESS TAKAMICHI ...
ABOUT THE BE-TROTHAL GIFTS...
SHE ...
...SAID MY NAME AGAIN...
UM, YES ...
MY ELDER BROTHER SAID TOMORROW ...
IS THAT TOO SOON ...?
IT'S FINE.
KLATTA
!
HAND IT OVER!
IDIOT.
?! MIKA ?!

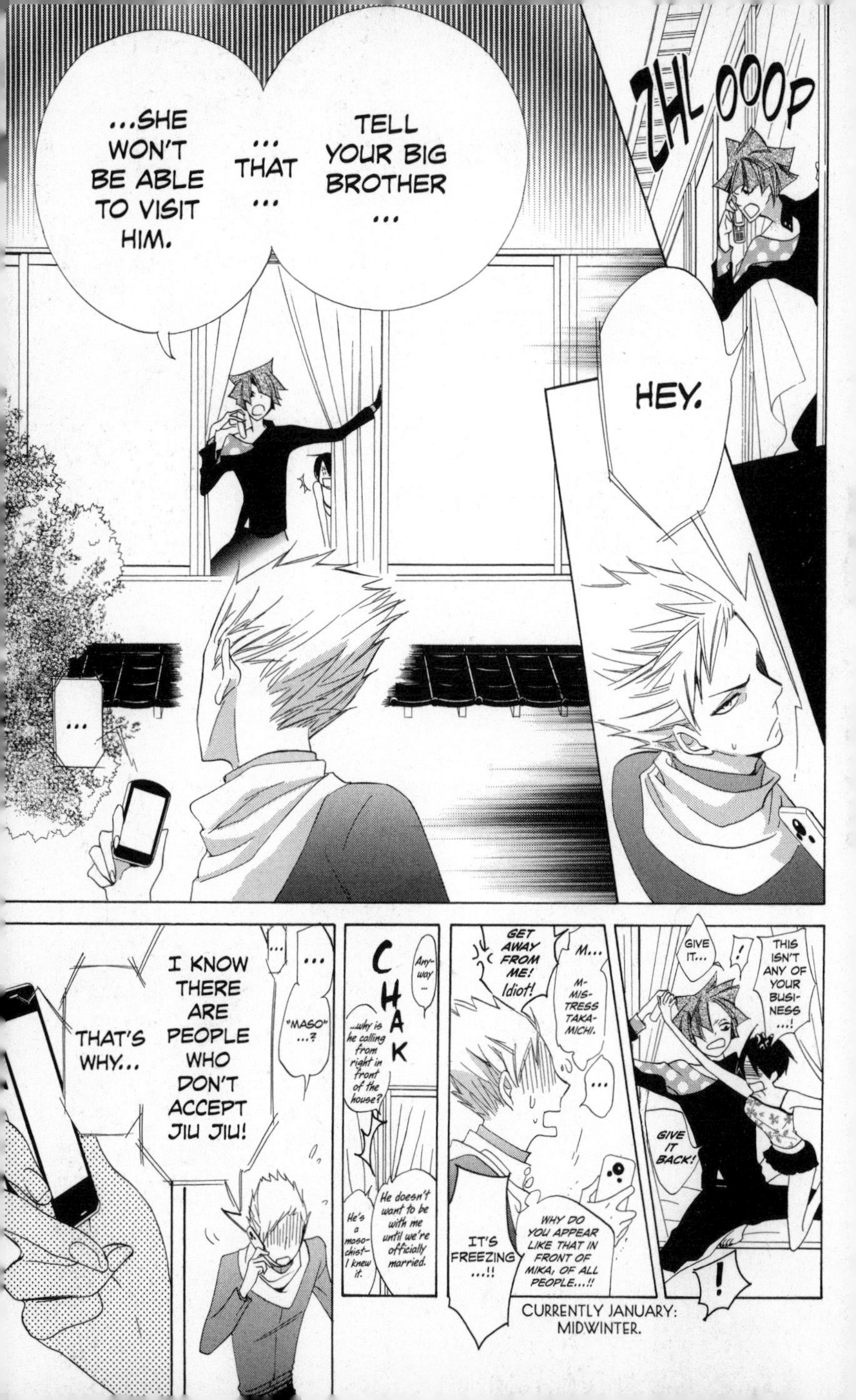
ZHL OOOP
HEY.
TELL YOUR BIG BROTHER...
...THAT...
...SHE WON'T BE ABLE TO VISIT HIM.
...
GIVE IT...
!
THIS ISN'T ANY OF YOUR BUSINESS...!
GIVE IT BACK!
!
CURRENTLY JANUARY: MIDWINTER.
GET AWAY FROM ME! Idiot!
M...
M-MISTRESS TAKAMICHI.
...
WHY DO YOU APPEAR LIKE THAT IN FRONT OF MIKA, OF ALL PEOPLE...!!
IT'S FREEZING...!!
CHAK
Anyway...
...why is he calling from right in front of the house?
He doesn't want to be with me until we're officially married.
He's a masochist- I knew it.
...
...
"MASO"...?
I KNOW THERE ARE PEOPLE WHO DON'T ACCEPT JIU JIU!
THAT'S WHY...

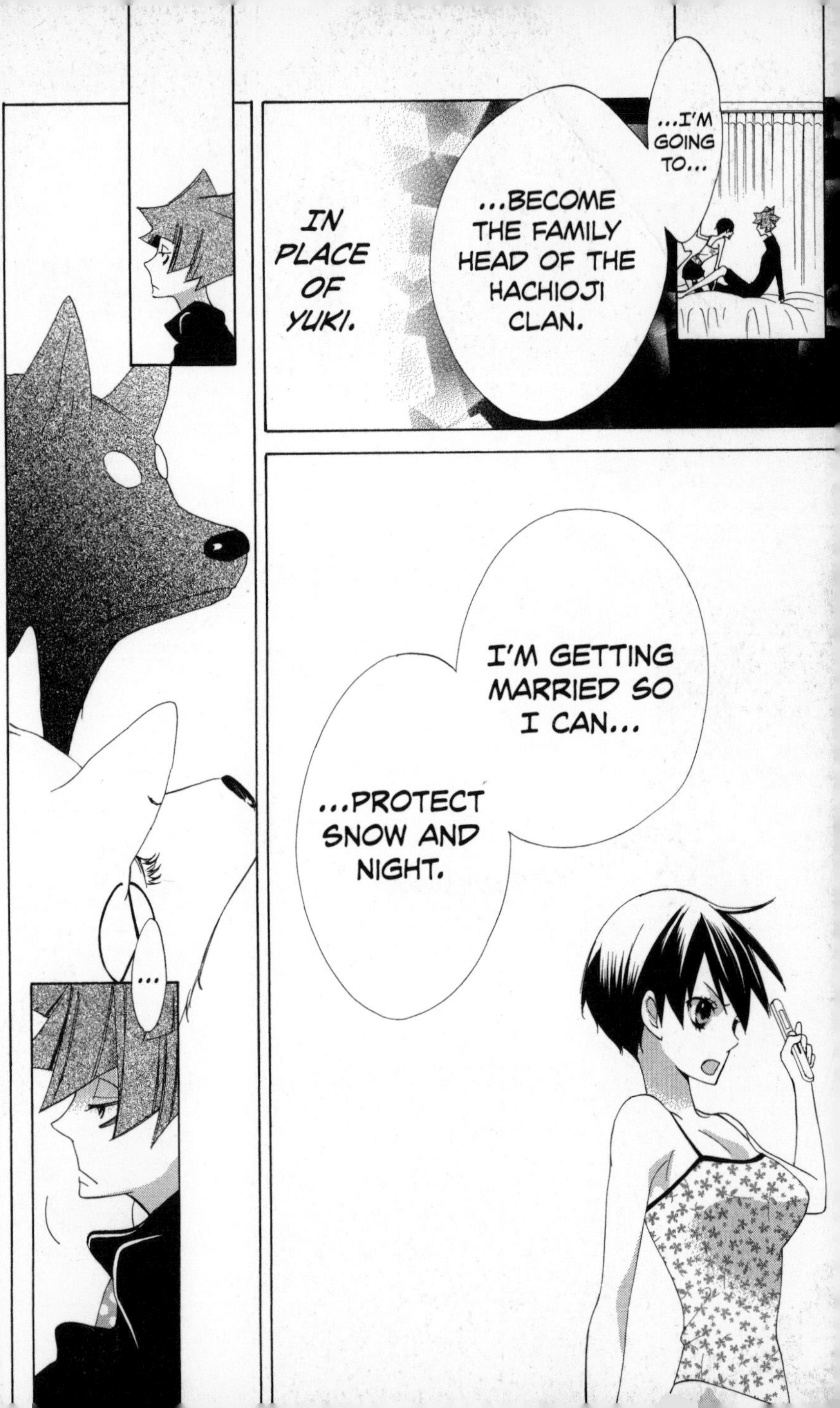
...I'M GOING TO...
...BECOME THE FAMILY HEAD OF THE HACHIOJI CLAN.
IN PLACE OF YUKI.
I'M GETTING MARRIED SO I CAN...
...PROTECT SNOW AND NIGHT.
...

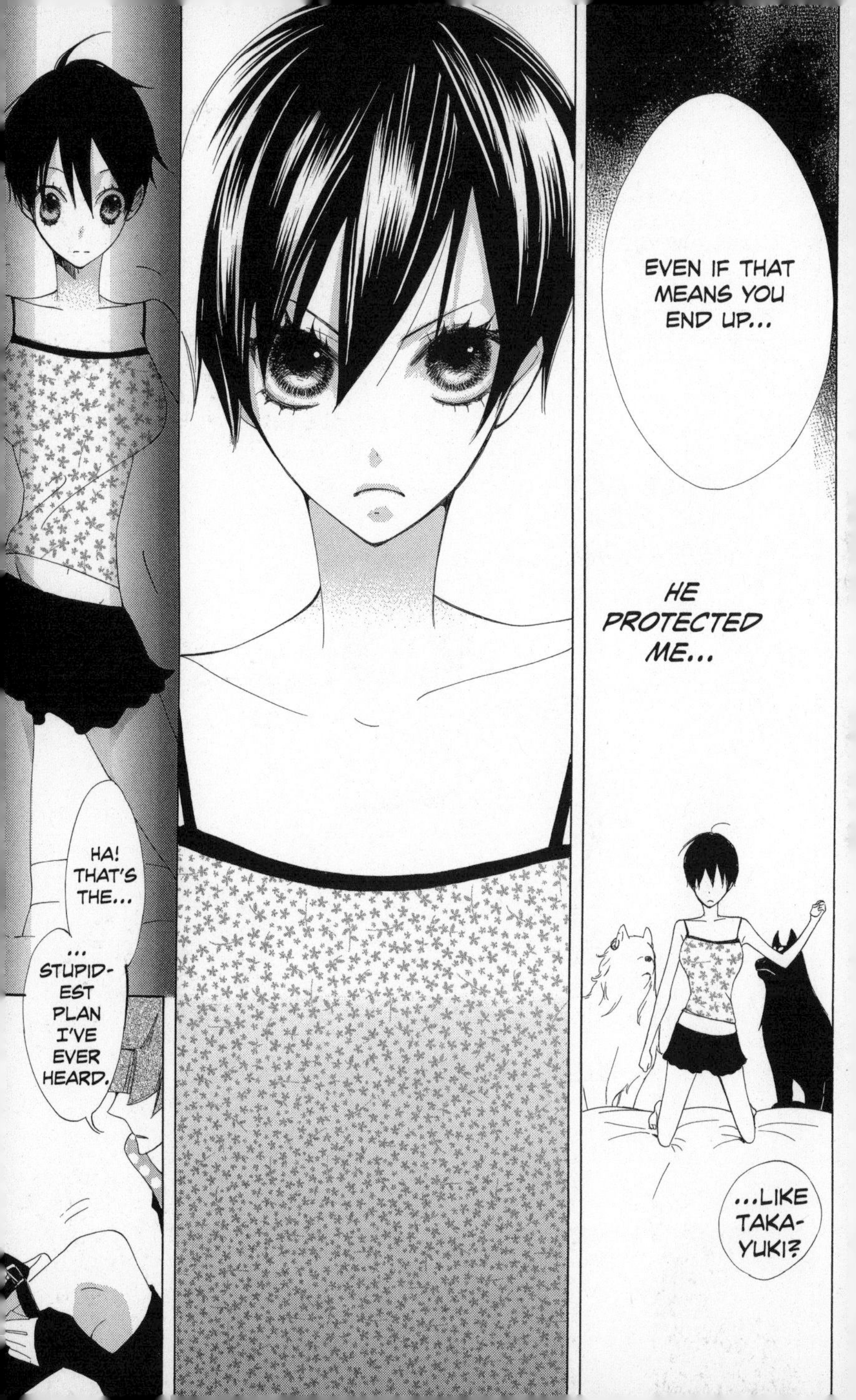
EVEN IF THAT MEANS YOU END UP...
HE PROTECTED ME...
...LIKE TAKA-YUKI?
HA! THAT'S THE...
...STUPID-EST PLAN I'VE EVER HEARD.

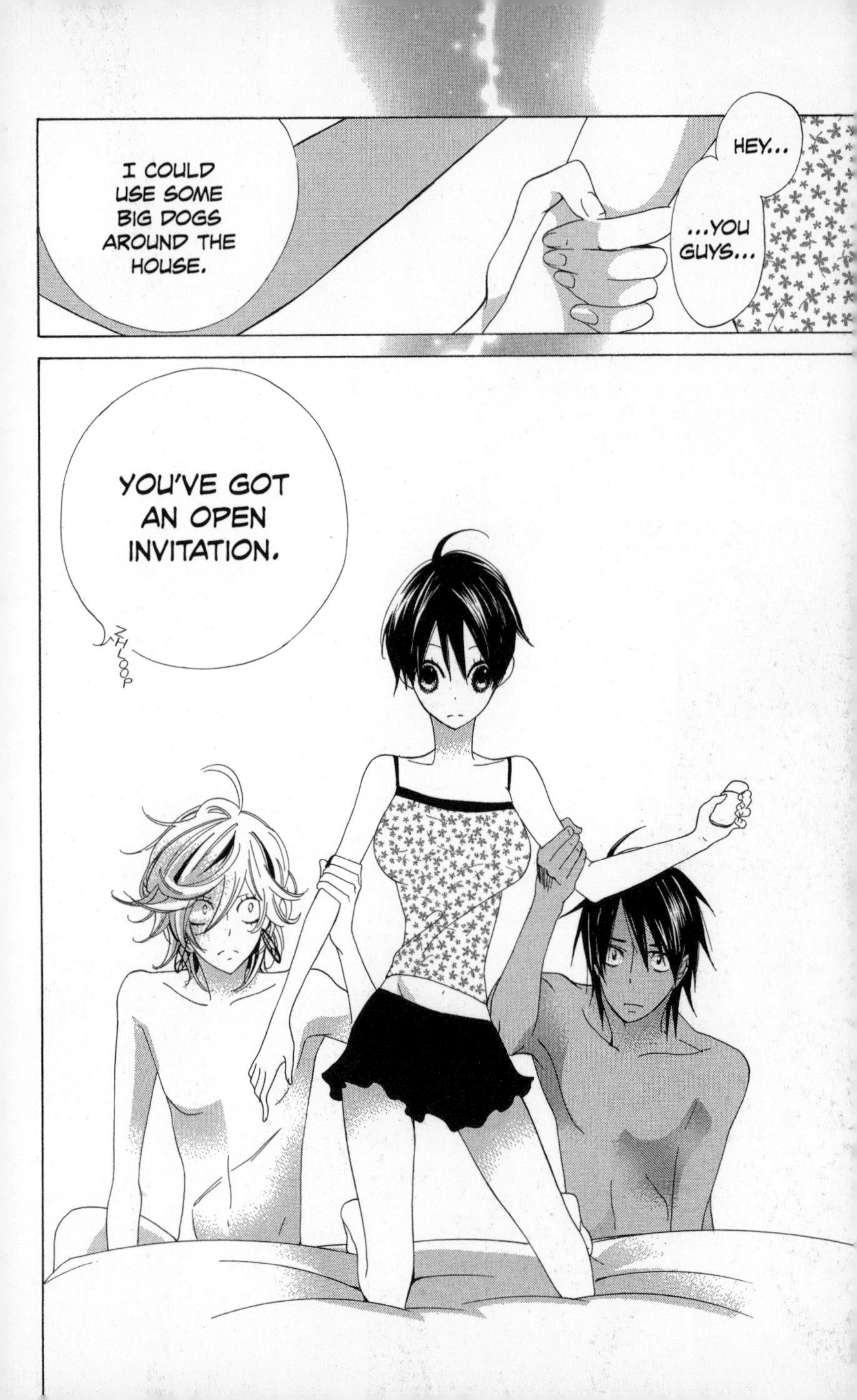
HEY...
...YOU GUYS...
I COULD USE SOME BIG DOGS AROUND THE HOUSE.
YOU'VE GOT AN OPEN INVITATION.
ZHLOOP

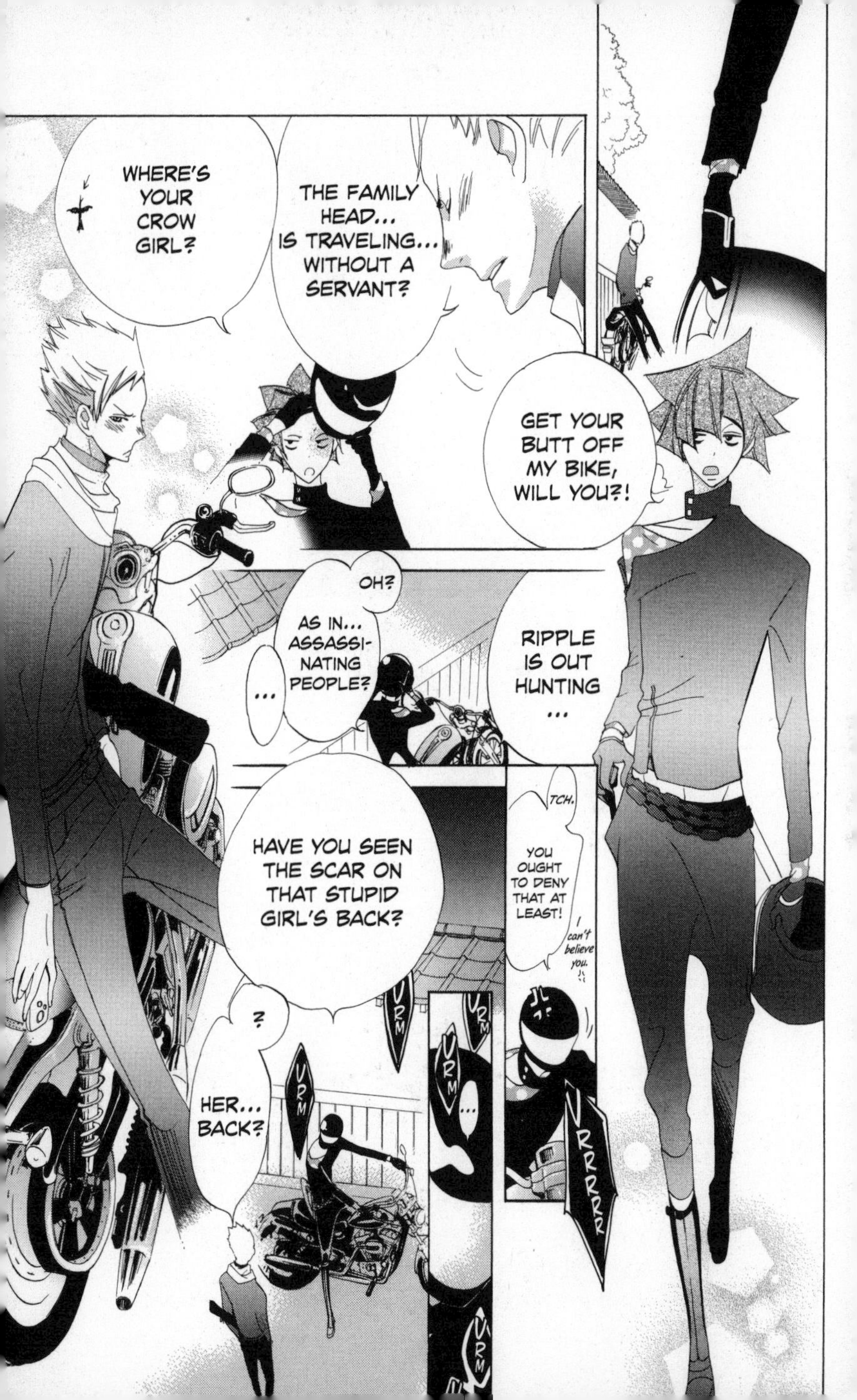
THE FAMILY HEAD... IS TRAVELING... WITHOUT A SERVANT?
WHERE'S YOUR CROW GIRL?
GET YOUR BUTT OFF MY BIKE, WILL YOU?!
RIPPLE IS OUT HUNTING ...
OH?
AS IN... ASSASSINATING PEOPLE?
...
TCH.
YOU OUGHT TO DENY THAT AT LEAST!
I can't believe you.
HAVE YOU SEEN THE SCAR ON THAT STUPID GIRL'S BACK?
URRRRR
URM
URM
...
URM
URM
?
HER... BACK?
URM

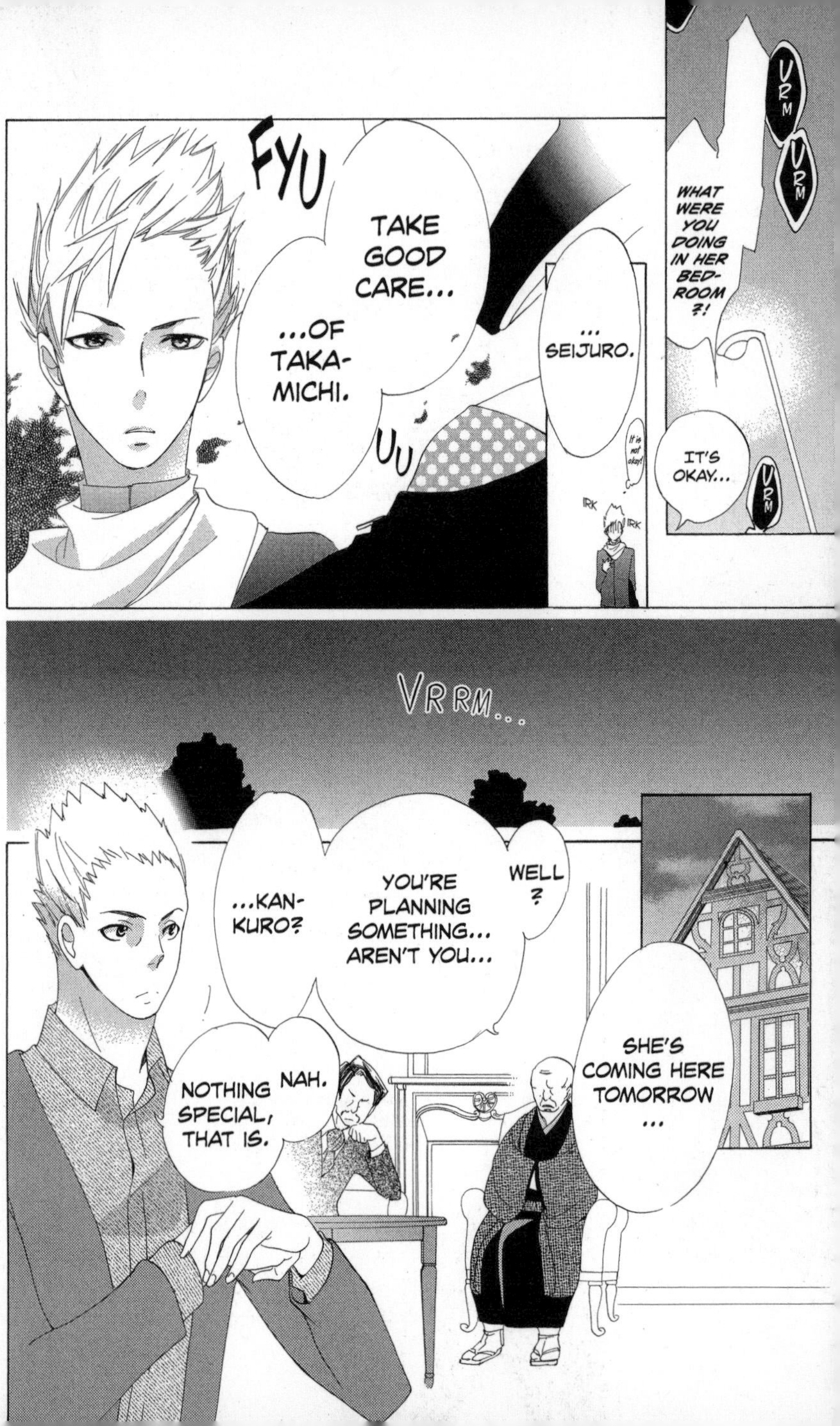
VRM
VRM
WHAT WERE YOU DOING IN HER BED-ROOM?!
IT'S OKAY...
VRM
...SEIJURO.
It is not okay!
IRK
IRK
FYU
TAKE GOOD CARE...
...OF TAKA-MICHI.
UU
VRRM...
SHE'S COMING HERE TOMORROW...
WELL?
YOU'RE PLANNING SOMETHING... AREN'T YOU...
...KAN-KURO?
NAH.
NOTHING SPECIAL, THAT IS.

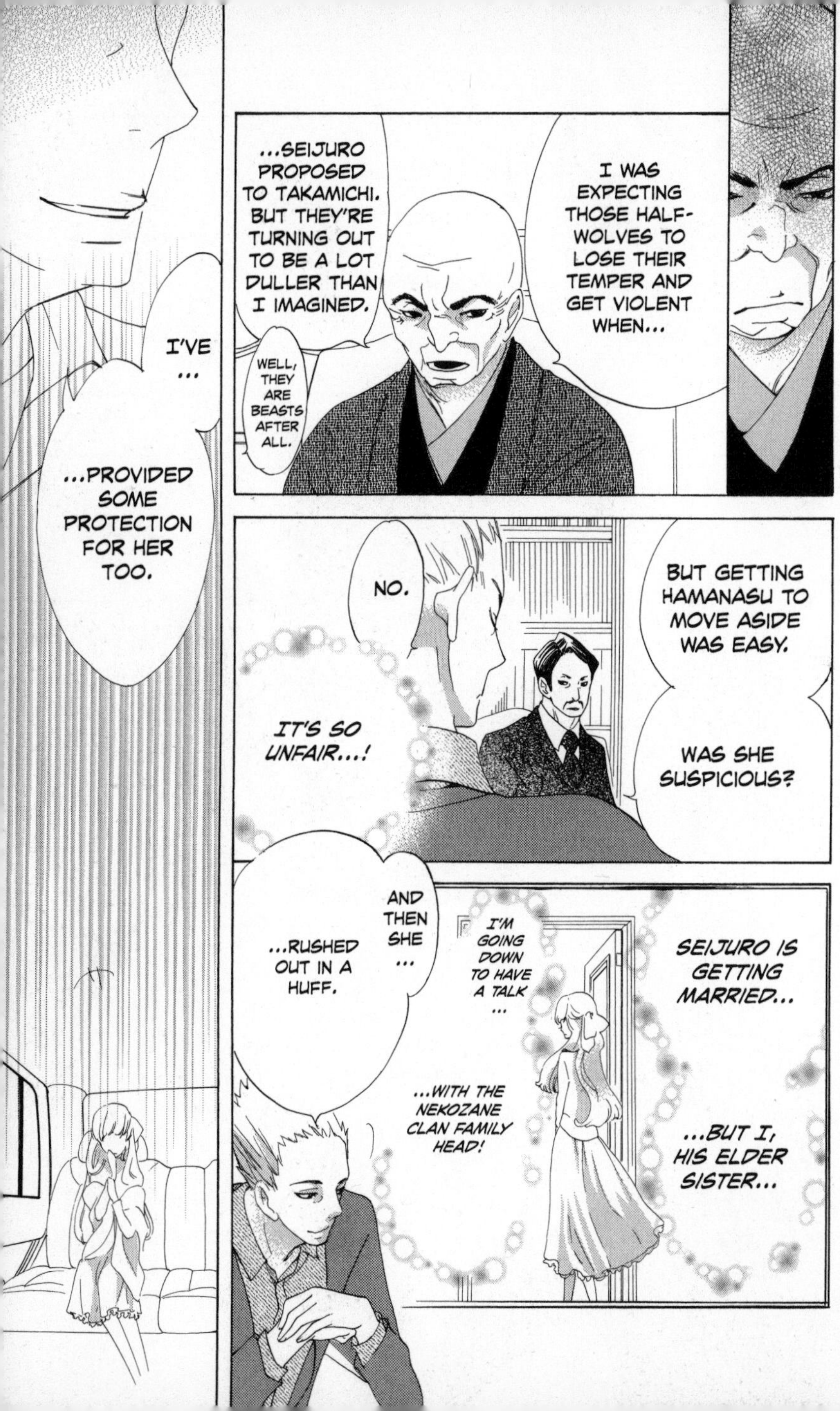
I WAS EXPECTING THOSE HALF-WOLVES TO LOSE THEIR TEMPER AND GET VIOLENT WHEN...
...SEIJURO PROPOSED TO TAKAMICHI. BUT THEY'RE TURNING OUT TO BE A LOT DULLER THAN I IMAGINED.
WELL, THEY ARE BEASTS AFTER ALL.
BUT GETTING HAMANASU TO MOVE ASIDE WAS EASY.
WAS SHE SUSPICIOUS?
NO.
IT'S SO UNFAIR...!
SEIJURO IS GETTING MARRIED...
...BUT I, HIS ELDER SISTER...
I'M GOING DOWN TO HAVE A TALK...
...WITH THE NEKOZANE CLAN FAMILY HEAD!
AND THEN SHE...
...RUSHED OUT IN A HUFF.
I'VE...
...PROVIDED SOME PROTECTION FOR HER TOO.

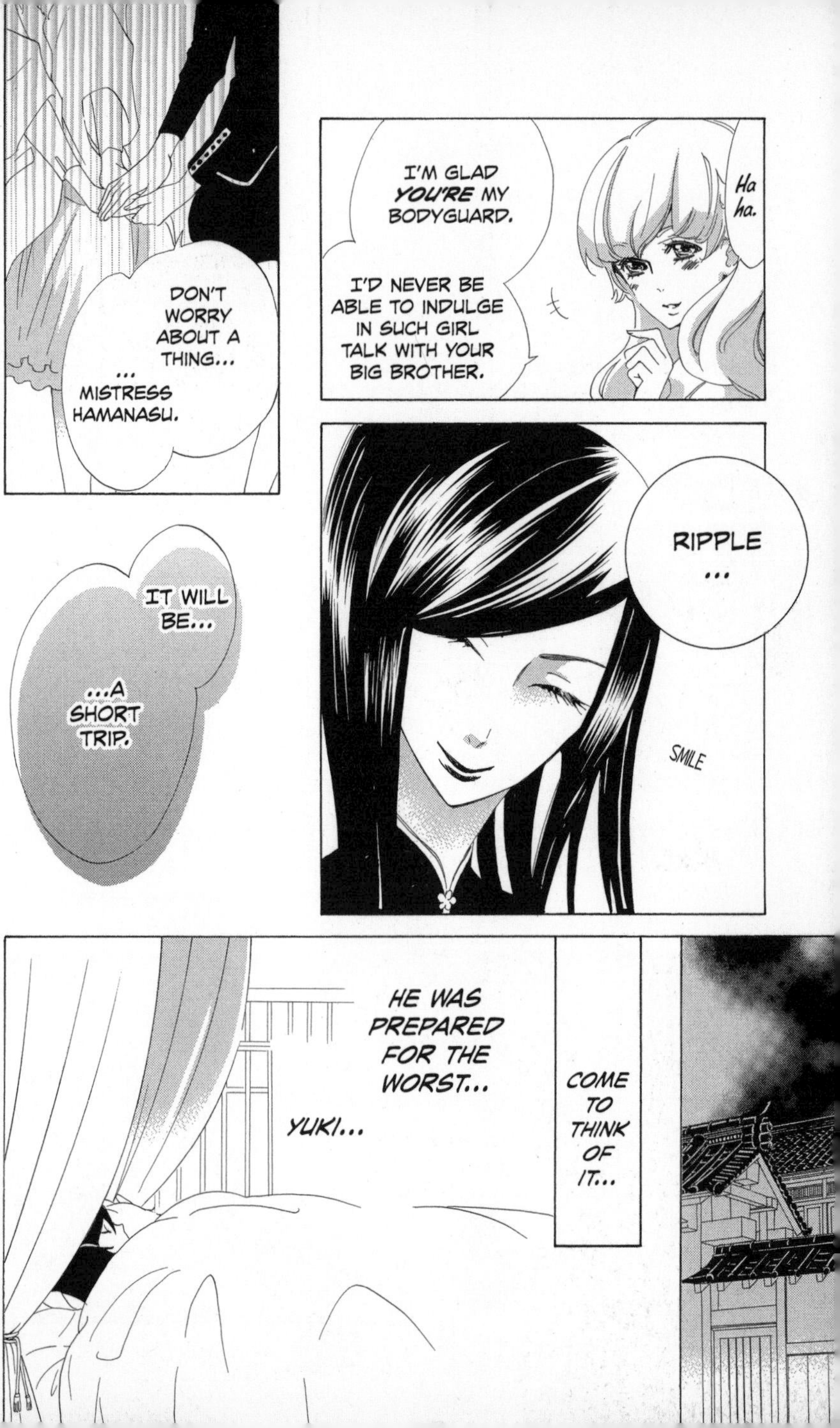
Ha ha.
I'M GLAD YOU'RE MY BODYGUARD.
I'D NEVER BE ABLE TO INDULGE IN SUCH GIRL TALK WITH YOUR BIG BROTHER.
RIPPLE ...
SMILE
DON'T WORRY ABOUT A THING...
... MISTRESS HAMANASU.
IT WILL BE...
...A SHORT TRIP.
COME TO THINK OF IT...
HE WAS PREPARED FOR THE WORST...
YUKI...

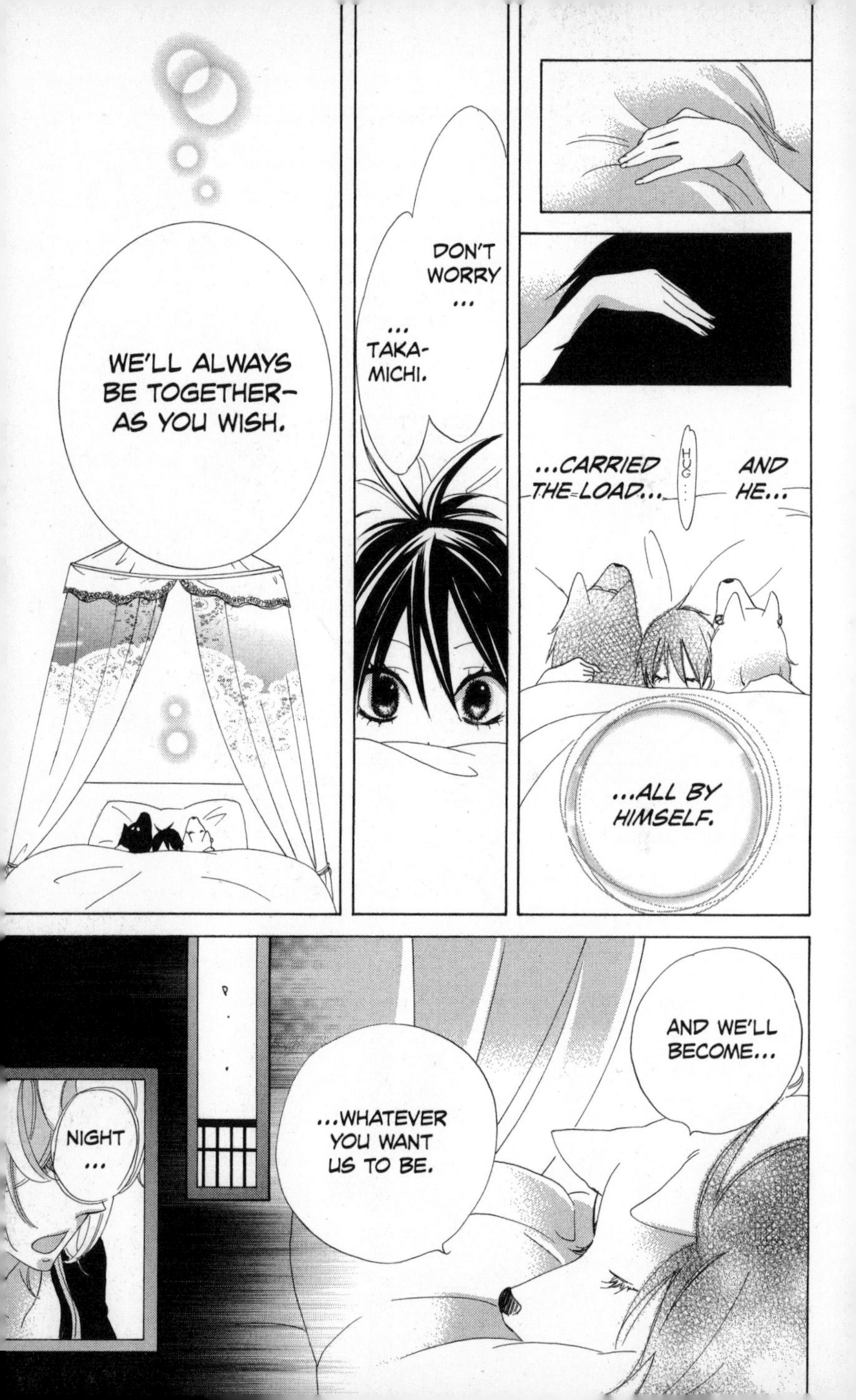
AND HE...
HUG...
...CARRIED THE LOAD...
...ALL BY HIMSELF.
DON'T WORRY...
...TAKAMICHI.
WE'LL ALWAYS BE TOGETHER—AS YOU WISH.
AND WE'LL BECOME...
...WHATEVER YOU WANT US TO BE.
NIGHT...

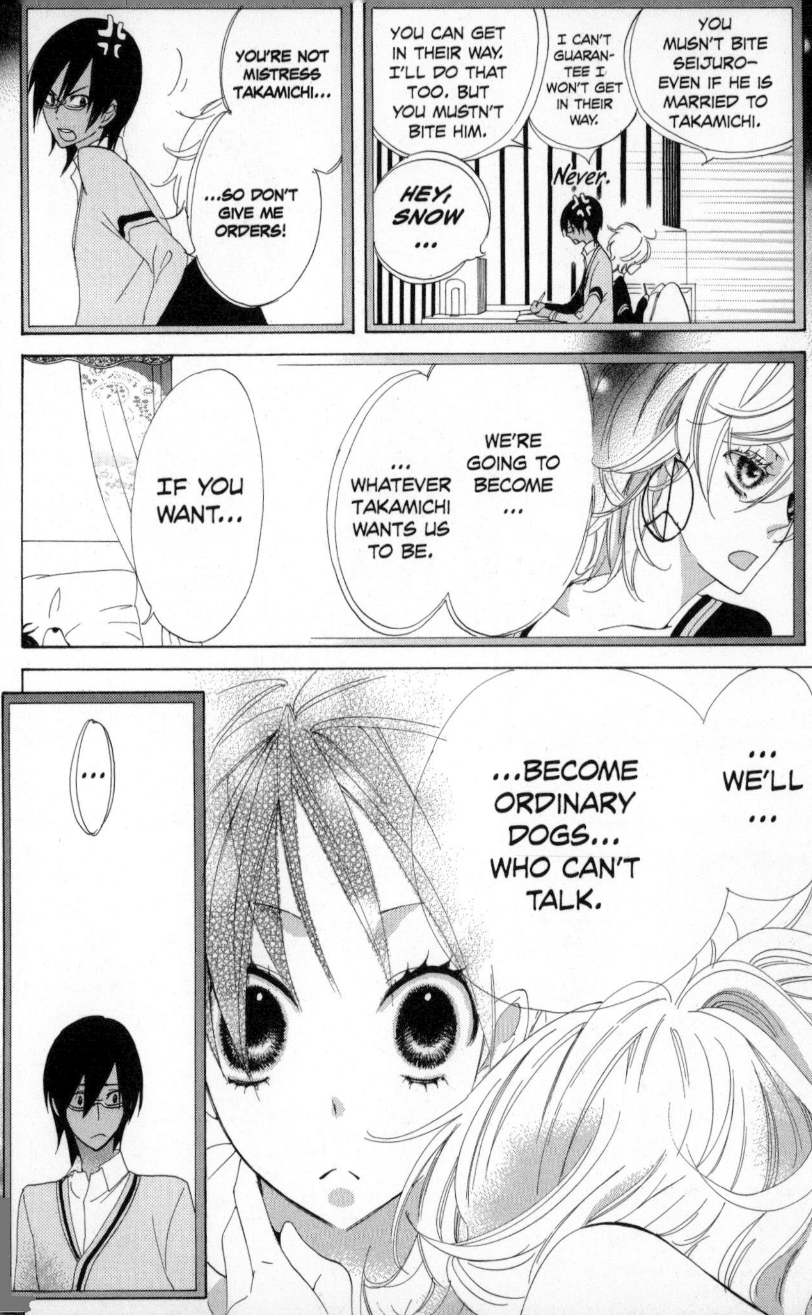
YOU MUSN'T BITE SEIJURO— EVEN IF HE IS MARRIED TO TAKAMICHI.
I CAN'T GUARAN-TEE I WON'T GET IN THEIR WAY.
YOU CAN GET IN THEIR WAY. I'LL DO THAT TOO. BUT YOU MUSTN'T BITE HIM.
Never.
HEY, SNOW ...
YOU'RE NOT MISTRESS TAKAMICHI...
...SO DON'T GIVE ME ORDERS!
WE'RE GOING TO BECOME ...
... WHATEVER TAKAMICHI WANTS US TO BE.
IF YOU WANT...
... WE'LL ...
...BECOME ORDINARY DOGS... WHO CAN'T TALK.
...

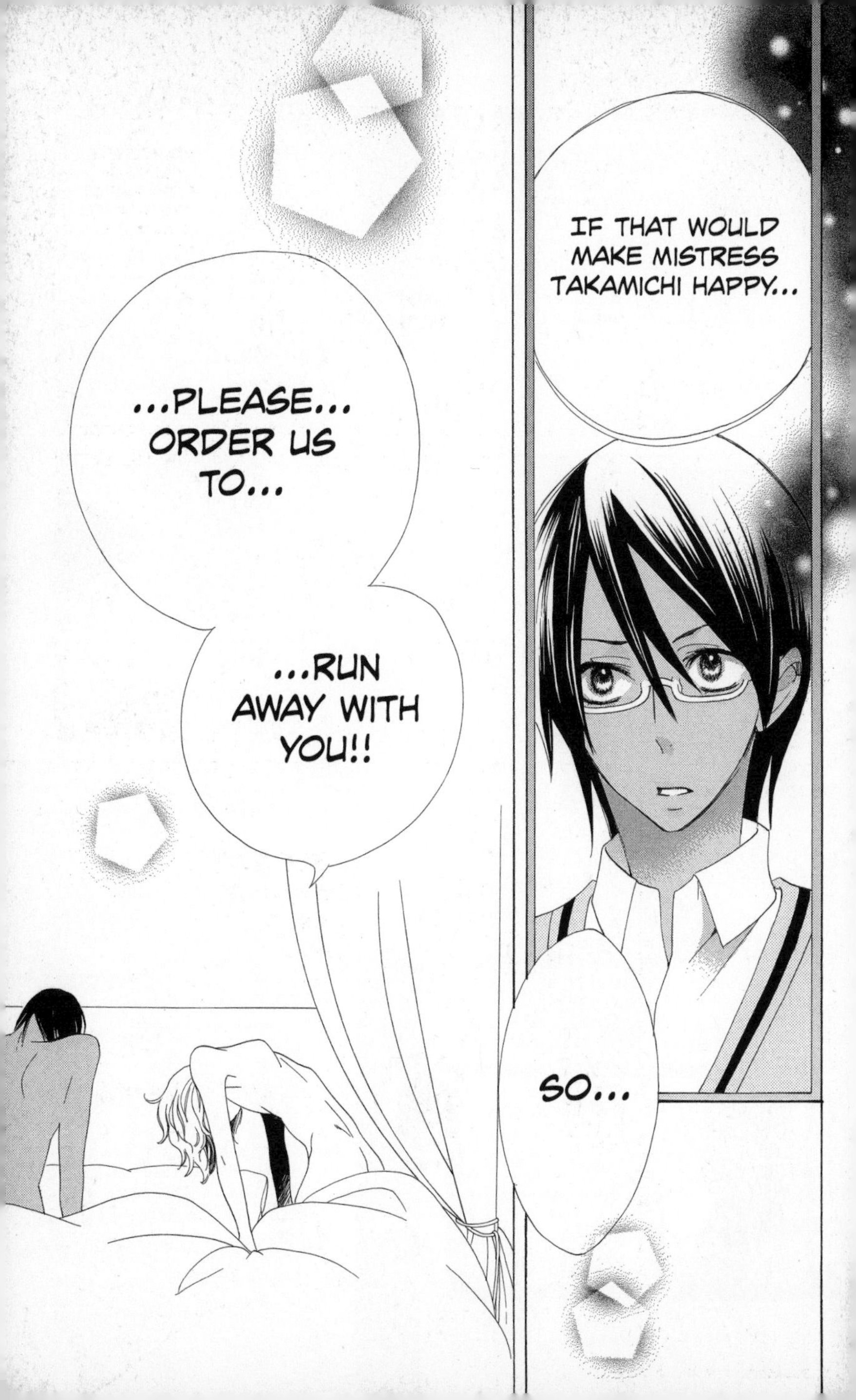
IF THAT WOULD MAKE MISTRESS TAKAMICHI HAPPY...
SO...
...PLEASE... ORDER US TO...
...RUN AWAY WITH YOU!!

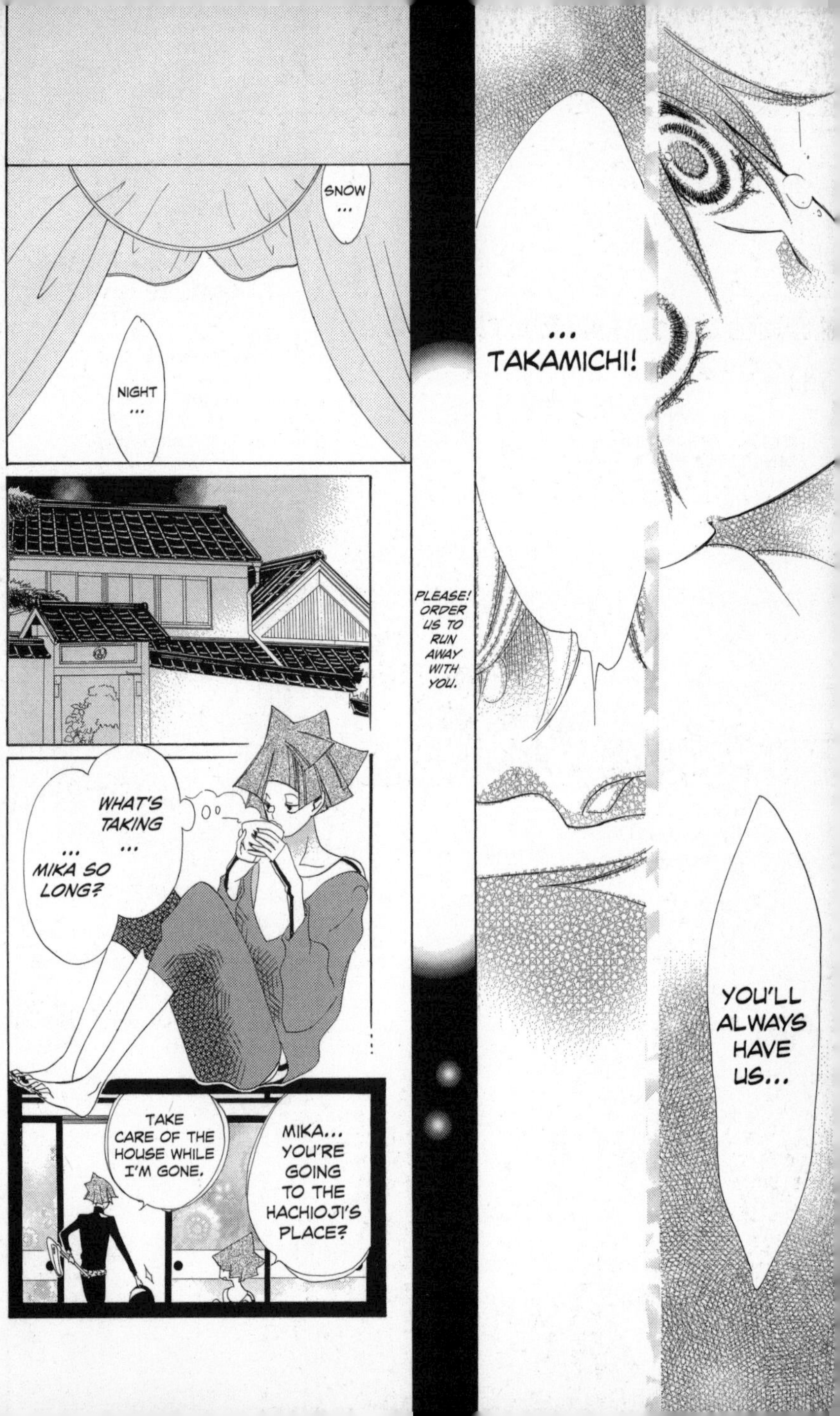
... TAKAMICHI!
YOU'LL ALWAYS HAVE US...
PLEASE! ORDER US TO RUN AWAY WITH YOU.
SNOW ...
NIGHT ...
WHAT'S TAKING ... ... MIKA SO LONG?
MIKA... YOU'RE GOING TO THE HACHIOJI'S PLACE?
TAKE CARE OF THE HOUSE WHILE I'M GONE.

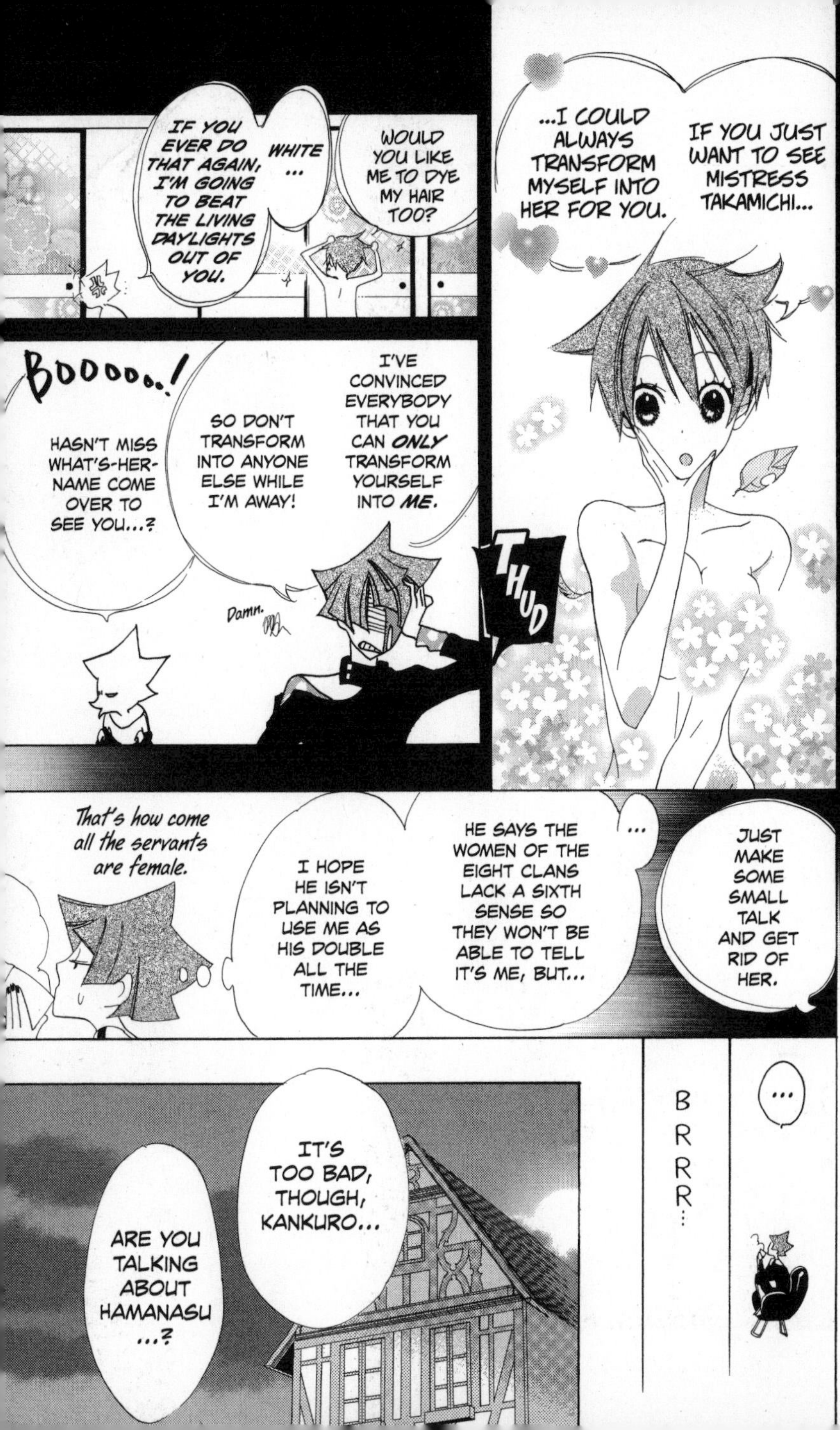

IF YOU JUST WANT TO SEE MISTRESS TAKAMICHI...
...I COULD ALWAYS TRANSFORM MYSELF INTO HER FOR YOU.
WOULD YOU LIKE ME TO DYE MY HAIR TOO?
WHITE...
IF YOU EVER DO THAT AGAIN, I'M GOING TO BEAT THE LIVING DAYLIGHTS OUT OF YOU.
THUD
I'VE CONVINCED EVERYBODY THAT YOU CAN ONLY TRANSFORM YOURSELF INTO ME.
SO DON'T TRANSFORM INTO ANYONE ELSE WHILE I'M AWAY!
Damn.
HASN'T MISS WHAT'S-HER-NAME COME OVER TO SEE YOU...?
BOOOOO..!
JUST MAKE SOME SMALL TALK AND GET RID OF HER.
...
HE SAYS THE WOMEN OF THE EIGHT CLANS LACK A SIXTH SENSE SO THEY WON'T BE ABLE TO TELL IT'S ME, BUT...
I HOPE HE ISN'T PLANNING TO USE ME AS HIS DOUBLE ALL THE TIME...
That's how come all the servants are female.
...
BRRR...
IT'S TOO BAD, THOUGH, KANKURO...
ARE YOU TALKING ABOUT HAMANASU...?

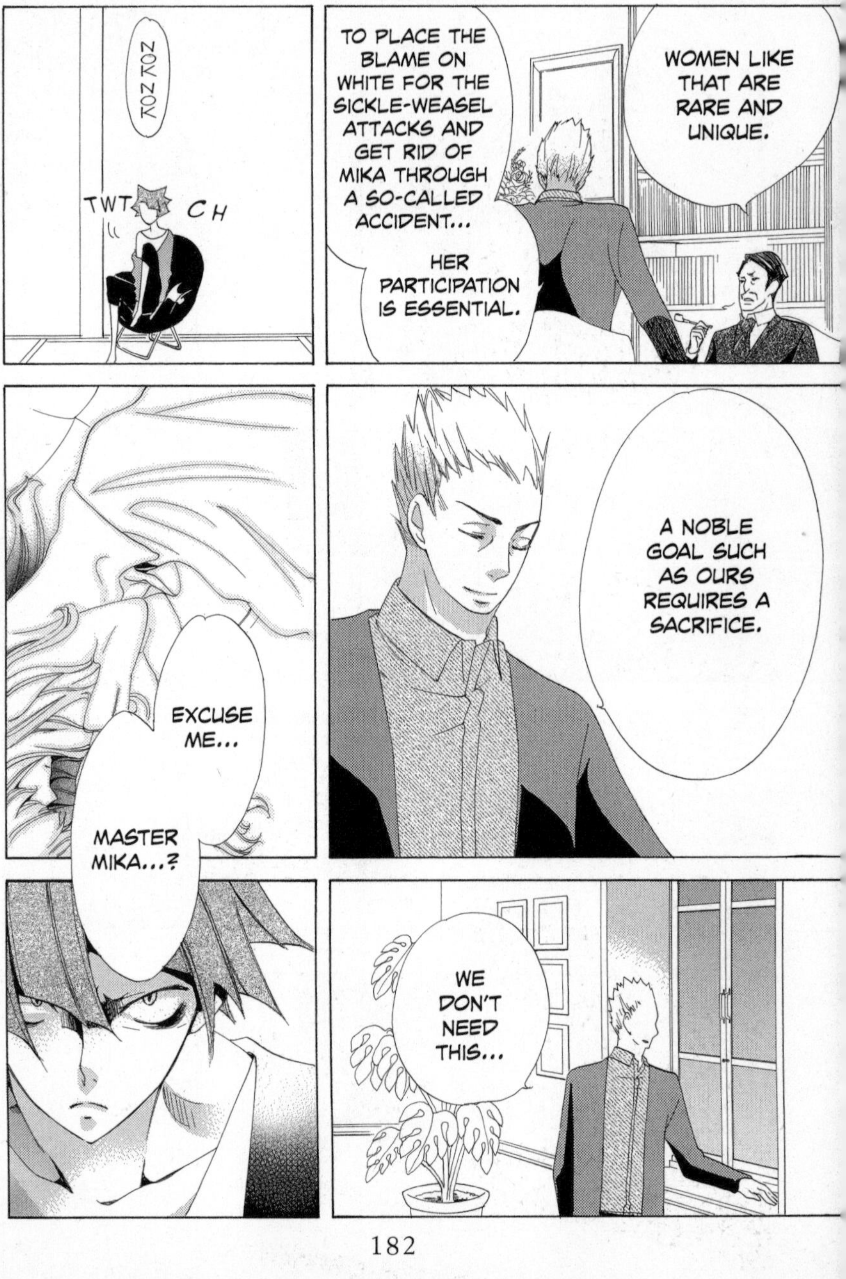
WOMEN LIKE THAT ARE RARE AND UNIQUE.
TO PLACE THE BLAME ON WHITE FOR THE SICKLE-WEASEL ATTACKS AND GET RID OF MIKA THROUGH A SO-CALLED ACCIDENT...
HER PARTICIPATION IS ESSENTIAL.
NOK NOK
TWTCH
A NOBLE GOAL SUCH AS OURS REQUIRES A SACRIFICE.
EXCUSE ME...
MASTER MIKA...?
WE DON'T NEED THIS...

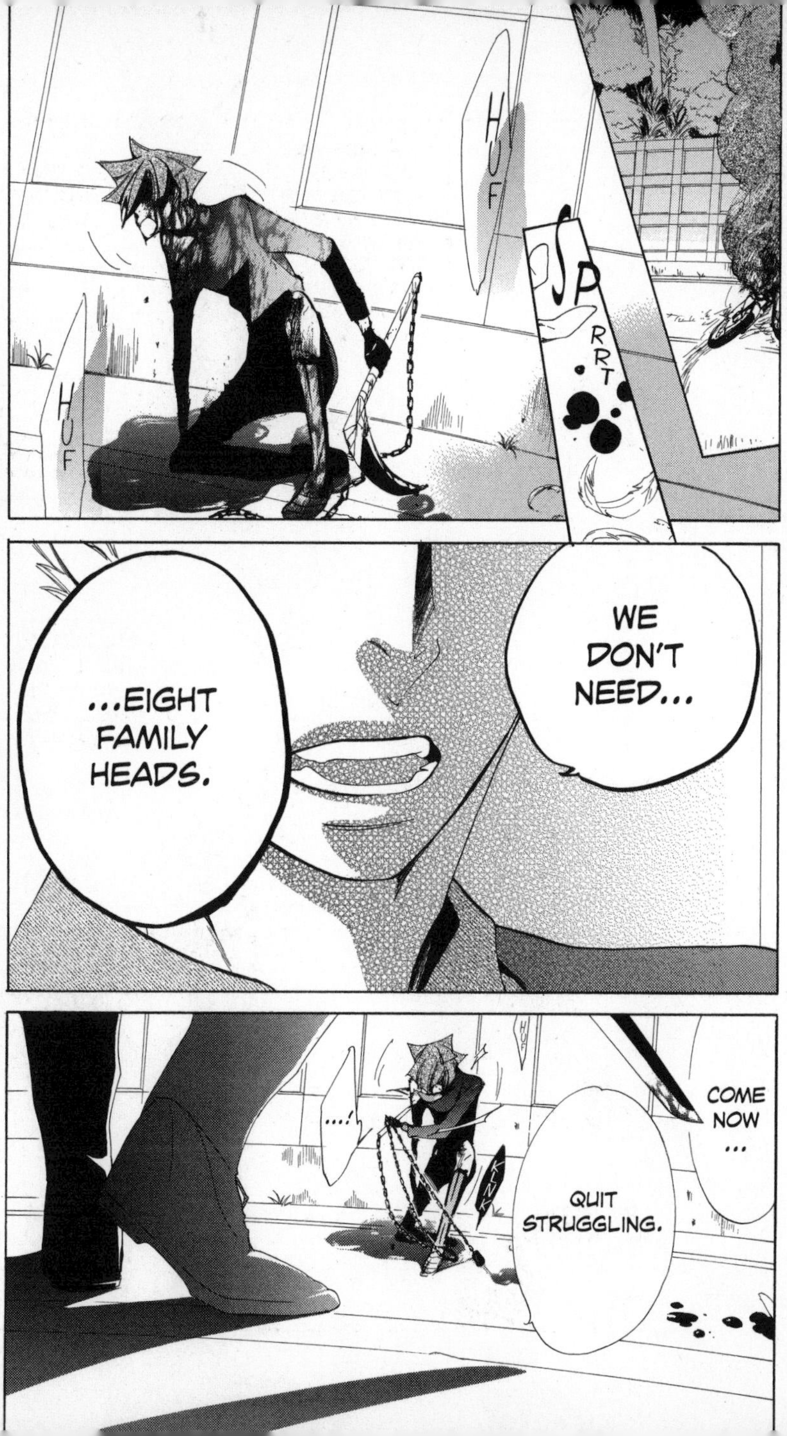
SPRRT
HUF
HUF
WE DON'T NEED...
...EIGHT FAMILY HEADS.
COME NOW...
QUIT STRUGGLING.
KLNK
HUF
...!

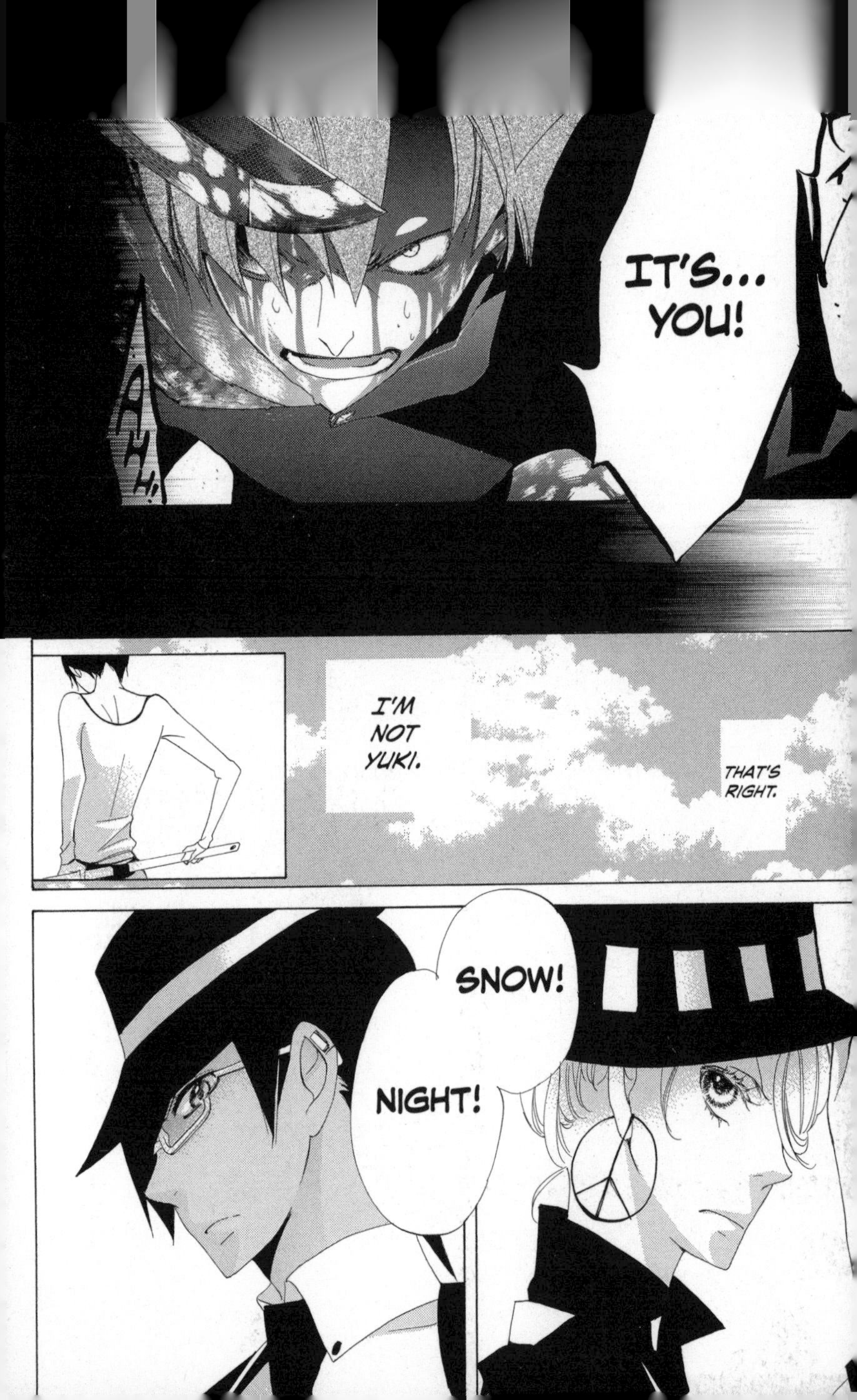
IT'S... YOU!
AHH!
THAT'S RIGHT.
I'M NOT YUKI.
SNOW!
NIGHT!

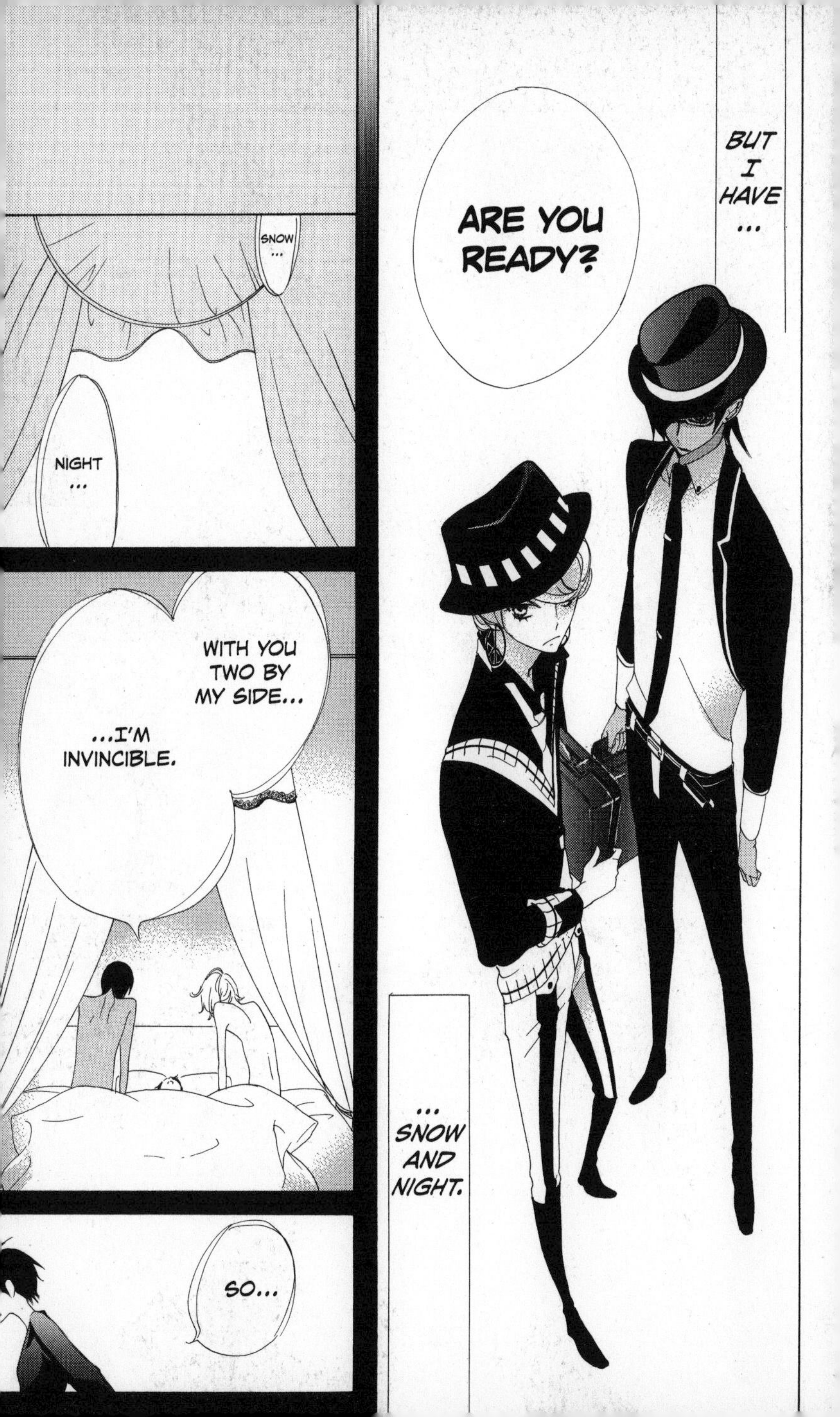
BUT I HAVE...
ARE YOU READY?
...SNOW AND NIGHT.
SNOW...
NIGHT...
WITH YOU TWO BY MY SIDE...
...I'M INVINCIBLE.
SO...

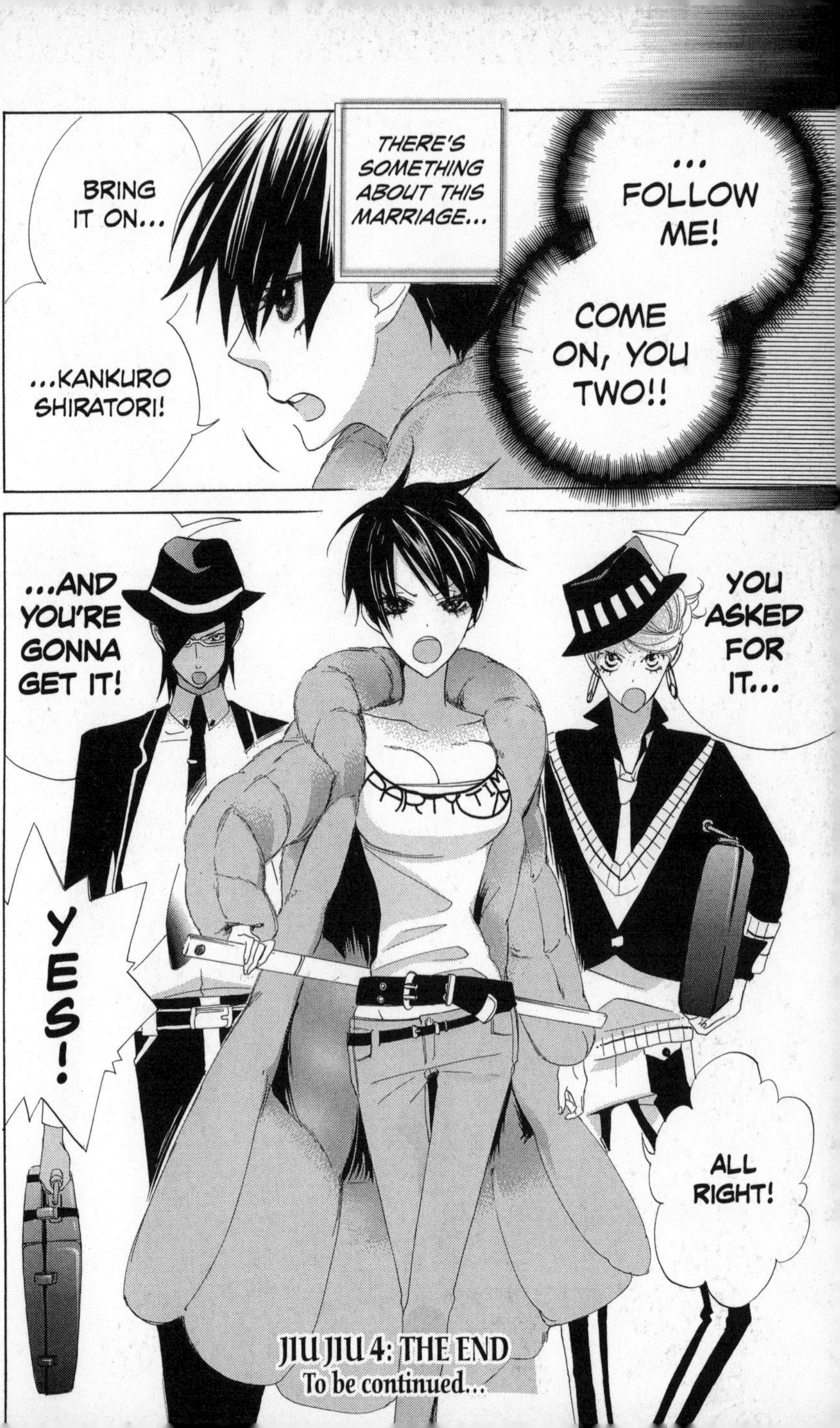
... FOLLOW ME!
COME ON, YOU TWO!!
THERE'S SOMETHING ABOUT THIS MARRIAGE...
BRING IT ON...
...KANKURO SHIRATORI!
YOU ASKED FOR IT...
...AND YOU'RE GONNA GET IT!
YES!
ALL RIGHT!
JIU JIU 4: THE END
To be continued...

Thanks

Naoko Takeda-sama

Hakusensha

Gendai Shoin

Kenju Noro-sama

Haruka Hodaka-sama

Nakamura Family

Ryo Kikitsu-sama

Mizuho Komata-sama

Nana Ginna-sama

Friends

To everybody involved.

And to you for reading this.

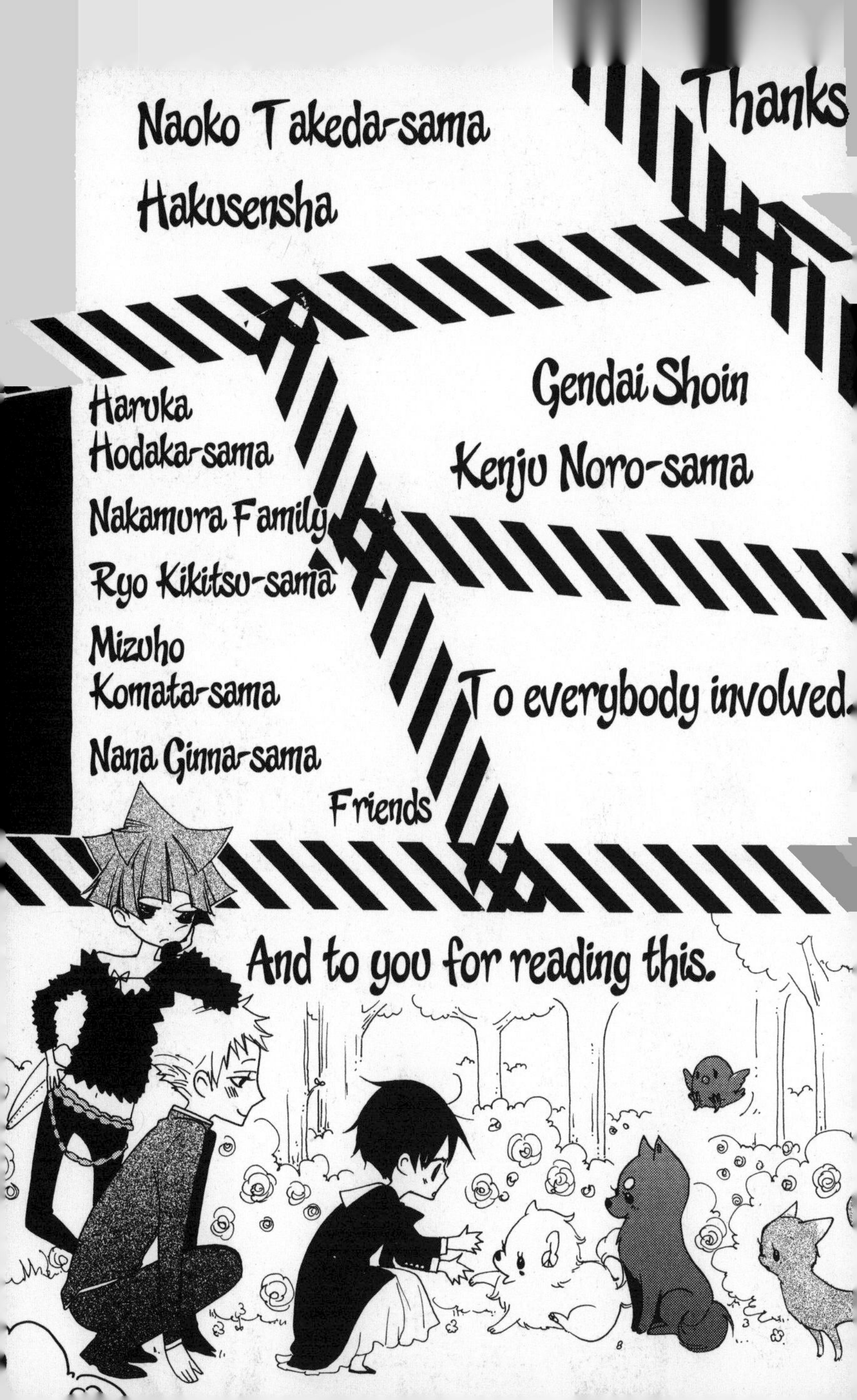

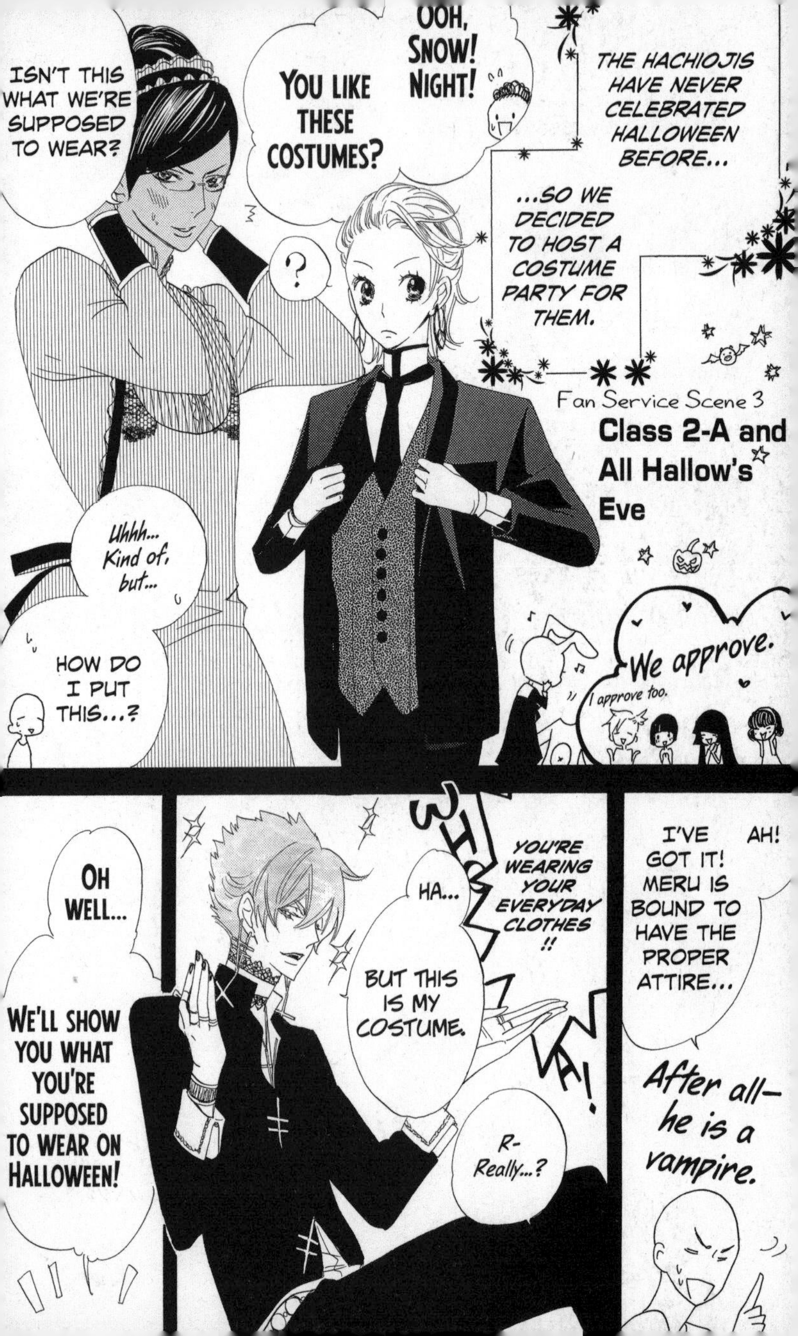
THE HACHIOJIS HAVE NEVER CELEBRATED HALLOWEEN BEFORE...
...SO WE DECIDED TO HOST A COSTUME PARTY FOR THEM.
Fan Service Scene 3
Class 2-A and All Hallow's Eve
OOH, SNOW! NIGHT!
YOU LIKE THESE COSTUMES?
ISN'T THIS WHAT WE'RE SUPPOSED TO WEAR?
?
We approve.
I approve too.
Uhhh... Kind of, but...
HOW DO I PUT THIS...?
AH! I'VE GOT IT! MERU IS BOUND TO HAVE THE PROPER ATTIRE...
After all— he is a vampire.
YOU'RE WEARING YOUR EVERYDAY CLOTHES!!
HA...
BUT THIS IS MY COSTUME.
R- Really...?
OH WELL...
WE'LL SHOW YOU WHAT YOU'RE SUPPOSED TO WEAR ON HALLOWEEN!

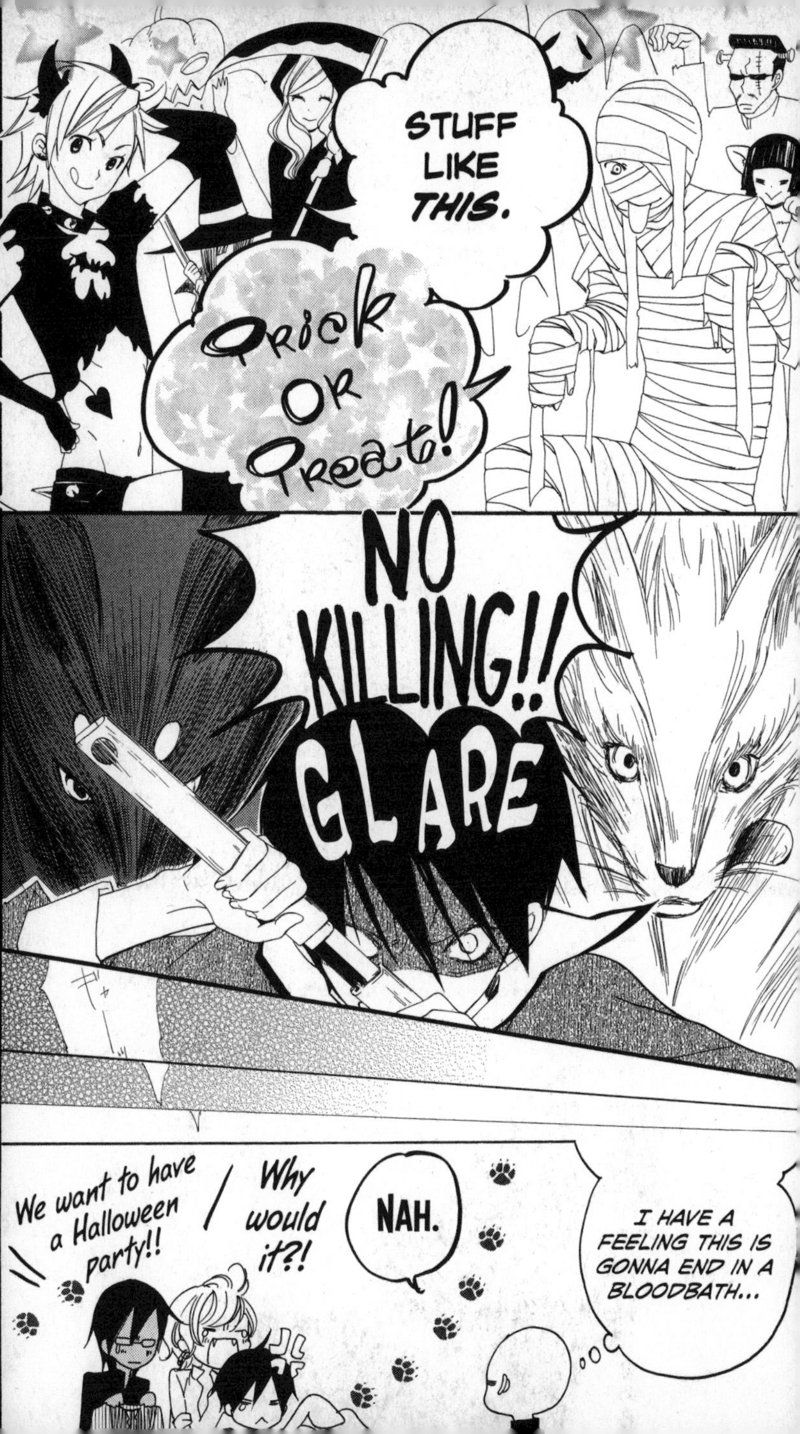
STUFF LIKE THIS.
Trick or Treat!
NO KILLING!!
GLARE
I HAVE A FEELING THIS IS GONNA END IN A BLOODBATH...
NAH.
Why would it?!
We want to have a Halloween party!!

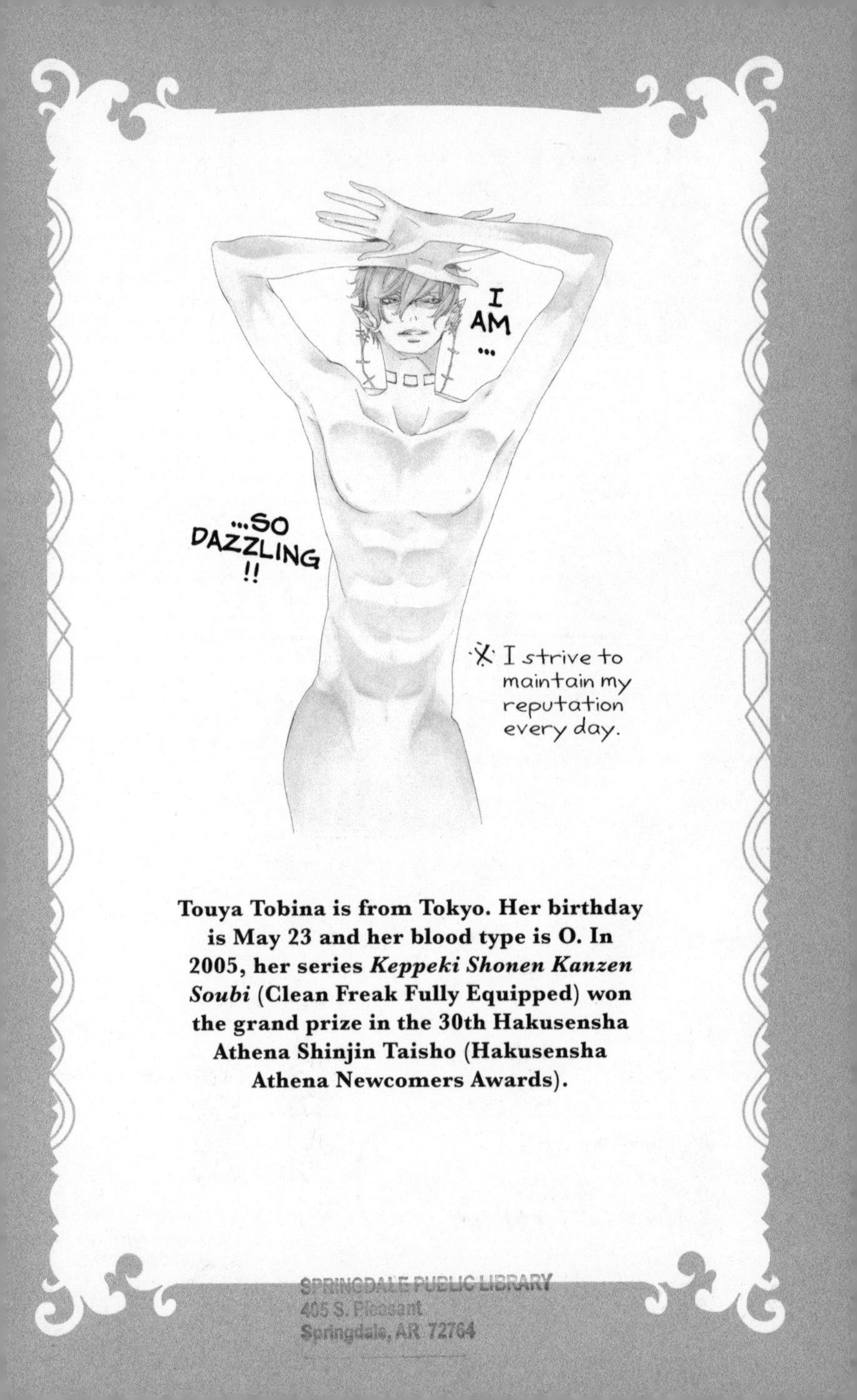
I AM ...
...SO DAZZLING !!
※ I strive to maintain my reputation every day.

Touya Tobina is from Tokyo. Her birthday is May 23 and her blood type is O. In 2005, her series *Keppeki Shonen Kanzen Soubi* (Clean Freak Fully Equipped) won the grand prize in the 30th Hakusensha Athena Shinjin Taisho (Hakusensha Athena Newcomers Awards).

JIU JIU
VOL. 4
Shojo Beat Edition

STORY AND ART BY
Touya Tobina

English Translation/Tetsuichiro Miyaki
English Adaptation/Annette Roman
Touch-up Art & Lettering/James Gaubatz
Design/Yukiko Whitley, Shawn Carrico
Editor/Annette Roman

JIUJIU by Touya Tobina
© Touya Tobina 2011
All rights reserved.
First published in Japan in 2011 by HAKUSENSHA, Inc., Tokyo.
English language translation rights arranged with HAKUSENSHA, Inc., Tokyo.

The rights of the author(s) of the work(s) in this publication to be so identified
have been asserted in accordance with the Copyright, Designs and Patents Act
1988. A CIP catalogue record for this book is available from the British Library.

Printed in the U.S.A.

Published by VIZ Media, LLC
P.O. Box 77010
San Francisco, CA 94107

10 9 8 7 6 5 4 3 2 1
First printing, April 2013

www.viz.com   www.shojobeat.com

THIS STINKS, HUH?

SHIRO

SAZANAMI

This is the last page.

In keeping with the original Japanese comic format, this book reads from right to left—so action, sound effects, and word balloons are completely reversed. This preserves the orientation of the original artwork—plus, it's fun! Check out the diagram shown here to get the hang of things, and then turn to the other side of the book to get started!

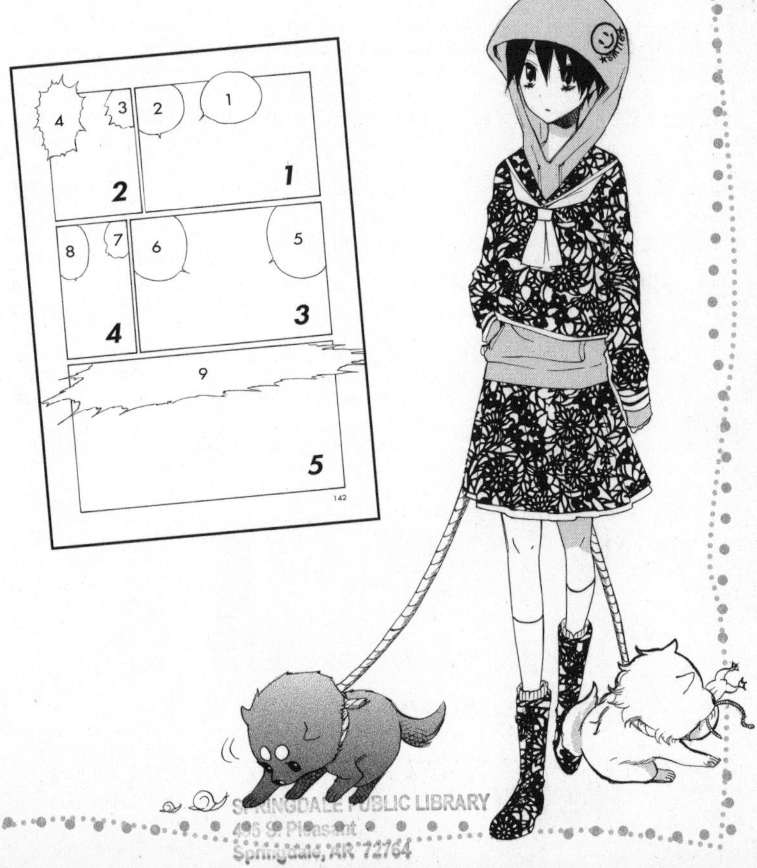
1
2
3
4
1
2
5
6
7
8
3
4
9
5
142